COMMUNICATIONS LAW AND POLICY

CASES AND MATERIALS

SEVENTH EDITION

JERRY KANG
Distinguished Professor of Law
Distinguished Professor of Asian American Studies
Hankook-Ilbo Endowed Chair
Founding Vice Chancellor – Equity, Diversity and Inclusion (2015-20)
University of California, Los Angeles

ALAN BUTLER
Interim Executive Director and General Counsel
Electronic Privacy Information Center

Direct Injection Press
2020

This book is intended to be used for academic and reference purposes only. The publisher and authors are not rendering legal or professional advice and this book is not a substitute for such advice. Any opinions expressed in this book are the authors' alone and should not be imputed to their employers or affiliated organizations.

from Jerry Kang
~ for Sung Hui and Taera ~

from Alan Butler
~ for Rory ~

PREFACE TO SEVENTH EDITION

This text has gone through many editions. The first edition appeared in 2001, published by ASPEN LAW & BUSINESS. The next three editions were published by FOUNDATION PRESS, up to 2012. The fifth edition broke with past models and the traditional legal casebook industry. In 2016, Jerry Kang added a co-author, Alan Butler, and we decided to self-publish. Why? Well, in our view, the costs of legal casebooks had gotten out-of-hand, and legal publishers increasingly did little more than bind pages into a physical item. We've decided we can mostly cut out the intermediary, with remarkable cost savings for the student.

Throughout the editions, the book has retained one fundamental pedagogical principle: Organize the learning via concepts instead of industry. These concepts are currently: power, entry, pricing, access, classification, (indecent) content, privacy, and intermediary. This list has changed only a little in the past two decades, even as we have updated, simplified, and pruned.

In the end, we hope to have created a comprehensive, challenging, yet accessible text that will pay long-lasting educational dividends. And we don't mind disrupting a textbook industry that needs to adapt and change. Supplemental materials helpful to students and professors will continue to be maintained at: http://jerrykang.net/commlaw.

Comments are always welcome.

JERRY KANG
July 2020
Los Angeles, CA

ALAN BUTLER
July 2020
Washington, DC

Acknowledgements

We are grateful for the permissions granted to reproduce excerpts from the following materials:

- Kevin Werbach, *Digital Tornado: The Internet and Telecommunications Policy,* FCC Office of Plans & Policy, Working Paper Series 29 (March 1997). No copyright permission necessary but permission received from author.
- MILTON MUELLER & JOHN MATHIASON, INTERNET GOVERNANCE: THE STATE OF PLAY (Internet Governance Project Sept. 9, 2004). Reprinted by permission of the authors.
- Tim Wu, *Why Have A Telecommunications Law? Anti-Discrimination Norms in Communications,* 5. J. ON TELECOMM. & HIGH TECH L. 15 (2006). Reprinted by permission of the author.

SUMMARY OF CONTENTS

TABLE OF CONTENTS

CHAPTER 1

POWER

Human ingenuity has created extraordinary tools that enable cheap, ubiquitous global communications. These tools allow us to send audio, images, video, and data across great distances almost instantaneously. Consider, for example, how easy it is to make an international telephone call or to send and receive messages almost anywhere on earth. By punching a few numbers on a keypad, we can talk with people on different continents as if they were next door. If telephony no longer amazes you, consider what the internet has enabled. Twenty-five years ago, no average American could publish a message accessible worldwide. Now, doing so is as easy as posting on Facebook.

The *technological power* of modern communications allows us to receive breaking news, coordinate activities across distance, engage in electronic commerce, enjoy entertainment, and share culture. Obviously, this communicative power can be used for good. In 1989, Chinese student dissidents used fax machines to show what happened at Tiananmen Square. In 2011, Arab Spring protesters used social media, such as Facebook and Twitter, to help organize demonstrations. Yet any potent tool can also be used for ill: in 2016 we witnessed coordinated attacks to disrupt the democratic process in the United States, the United Kingdom, and elsewhere. And individuals are even more vulnerable: consider how easily one student can anonymously threaten another student online or how quickly an intimate photograph can be shared and go viral. As communication technologies improve, all of our communicative powers increase, for better and for worse.

How does society distribute these wonderfully powerful communication products and services? In the United States, we leave that generally to the marketplace. Ideally, the push and pull among myriad suppliers and customers set a market price for communication services at just the right level. At this market price, consumers neither under- nor over-consume, which means that society is allocating its resources sensibly. But in practice, markets do not function perfectly. For example, certain entities may gain sufficient *economic power* so that they can set prices higher than they should be. This deprives consumers of valuable communication services even though they are willing and able to pay a fair price. In addition, through economic dominance, a few

1

conglomerates or platforms may gain the power to frame the news, entertainment, and information that shape our culture and politics. Some platforms have become so central to our daily lives that they can shape our basic understanding of reality.

Too much is at stake—economically, socially, and politically—for society not to respond to these rapidly changing technological and market environments. Often, society responds by enacting laws—for example, to regulate the firms that provide communications services or to regulate the content they carry. Government regulation thus implicates power in yet another sense. This *legal power* is exercised horizontally across the various branches of government—legislative, executive, judicial, and regulatory. At the federal level, which is our focus, legal power is wielded principally by Congress (e.g., by enacting statutes such as the Communications Act of 1934), the Federal Communications Commission (FCC) (e.g., by issuing regulations), and the courts (e.g., by reviewing agency action). This power is also shared vertically between the federal government and state and local governments.

The fundamental concept of *power* thus lies at the foundation of our study of communications law and policy. First, technological power creates new forms of information exchange and social interaction, which generate new possibilities (such as electronic commerce) as well as new problems (such as easy access to pornography by minors). Second, in the competitive arena of the marketplace, certain communications firms may come to achieve substantial economic power with which they can set prices, policies, or conditions that are not only economically inefficient but also politically worrisome. Third, legal power (ideally) encourages beneficial development and deployment of communications technologies while attempting to constrain their harms. This chapter examines power in all three senses, as well as their complex interrelations.

A. TECHNOLOGICAL POWER

Starting a legal casebook with a technological discussion is unusual. But, a better understanding of technological power is crucial to understanding the principles and policies that drive modern communications law. It enables judges and policymakers to exercise legal power more intelligently; it also enables lawyers to invoke legal power more persuasively. Just as a medical malpractice lawyer must understand medical science and health care practice to advocate effectively, a communications lawyer or policymaker must understand the fundamental technological building blocks of her subject matter.

At its foundation, communication involves transmitting a message between a source and a destination. This process can be modeled by the following simple steps:

(1) the *source* has some *message* to convey;

(2) a *transmitter* converts that message into a *signal*;

(3) the signal is transmitted along a *channel*, which inevitably adds some noise;

(4) the *received signal* is converted back into the message by a *receiver*;

(5) which is (hopefully) comprehended by the *destination*.

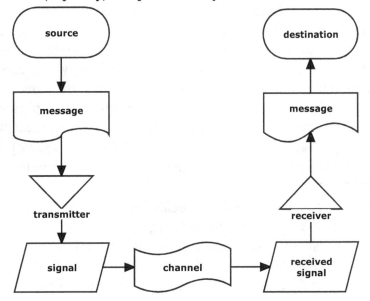

Figure 1.1: Basic Communication Model

This basic model can be applied to any sort of communication. Consider, for example, what your professor might say in class. She (source) wants to convey an order "No surfing the Web during class!" (message). Her vocal cords convert that message into atmospheric vibrations (signal). Those vibrations move through the air (channel) competing against the clickety-clacks of laptop keyboards. Those vibrations (received signal) are then converted by your ear drum (receiver) back into the message, which prompts you (destination) to minimize your browser window.

1. SIGNALS

a. SIGNALS EXPLAINED

A signal is a physical characteristic of the world to which we can attach meaning. It can be any physical characteristic, such as puffs of smoke, lit lanterns, or changes in atmospheric pressure such as the sound of your professor's voice. As long as both source and destination can associate the same meanings to these physical characteristics, a message can be communicated.

Certain physical characteristics function better than others as signals. For instance, smoke signals cannot travel long distances before being scattered by the winds. Whether there are one or two lit lanterns might be hard to see a half-mile away. Your professor's voice, as blaring as it may be, cannot be heard past a few hundred feet. For modern computing-communications, which require rapid transmission of huge amounts of data across continents, the signal of choice is electro-magnetic (e-m) energy. E-m energy is a fundamental phenomenon of nature possessing miraculous properties. Most important, in a vacuum, changes in e-m energy propagate at the speed of light (3×10^8 meters/second). Because it is critical to understanding modern communications, we explore the concept of the e-m wave more deeply.

An *e-m wave* is a self-sustaining oscillation of perpendicular electric and magnetic fields, which propagate through empty space at the speed of light. We are already familiar with e-m waves even if we don't call them as such: They bring us television over the air (broadcast waves), cook our food (microwaves), allow us to see (visible light), and diagnose our fractures (X-rays). Simple e-m waves can be described mathematically as a sine function with three basic variables: amplitude, frequency,[*] and phase. For simplicity, we discuss only amplitude and frequency. In Figure 1.2, the horizontal X axis represents time, and the vertical Y axis represents the strength of the oscillating electric field.

---

[*] In communications law, e-m waves are discussed in terms of their frequency. However, one can equivalently describe them in terms of their wavelength, which is simply the inverse of the e-m frequency. That means the higher the frequency, the lower the wavelength; the lower the frequency, the higher the wavelength. To understand this inverse relationship, note that the speed of any wave can be computed by multiplying the frequency by its wavelength. For instance, suppose that a wave completes two full cycles in one second (frequency = 2 Hz). If this wave moves 10 meters per cycle (wavelength = 10 m), then in one second the wave will have moved a total of 20 meters (speed = 20 m/s). Interestingly, the speed of all e-m waves in a vacuum is identical—the speed of light. Because the speed is a constant, frequency and wavelength have an inverse relationship: When multiplied together they must always equal this constant. Accordingly, high-frequency e-m waves have low wavelength, whereas low-frequency e-m waves have high wavelength. Because of this simple inverse relationship, any e-m wave can be described in terms of either frequency or wavelength.

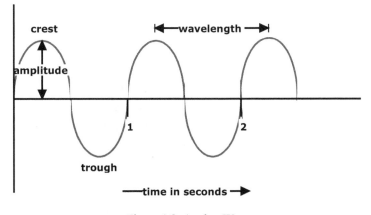

Figure 1.2. Analog Wave

The *amplitude* is the strength of the electric field measured from zero to the highest point reached by the wave, which is the crest (or equivalently, to the lowest point, the trough).

The *frequency* is the number of full cycles—from zero up to the crest, down to the trough, and back to zero—that the electric field makes per second. If the wave goes through one full cycle in one second, as in the above figure, its frequency is one hertz (1 Hz). A standard FM radio signal is 100 MHz, which means that it oscillates 100 million times per second.

The *wavelength*, which is inversely related to the frequency, measures the physical distance the e-m wave travels in the course of completing one full cycle. Thus, if the wave moves one meter in one cycle, then its wavelength is 1 m. That same 100 MHz FM radio signal will travel 3 meters per cycle.

b. SIGNAL TYPES: ANALOG OR DIGITAL

To convert a message into a signal, some physical aspect of that signal must be changed in accordance with the message. Different modes of communication vary different aspects of the e-m wave. Let's suppose that we are interested in varying the amplitude of the e-m wave in accordance with the message. In deciding how to vary the amplitude, we have two basic choices: We can send either an analog or a digital signal.

An *analog signal*, like the one above in Figure 1.2, changes smoothly and continuously between a range of values, in accordance with the message. More important, an analog signal is a *direct representation of the message* itself: As the message changes (e.g., a person's voice grows louder), the analog signal changes accordingly (e.g., the amplitude of the e-m wave grows taller).

By contrast, a *digital signal*, such as the one in Figure 1.3, is always in only one of two discrete states—either zero or maximum amplitude—and changes (almost) instantaneously from one state to the other. A digital signal is not a direct representation of the message; instead, it represents *a string of ones and zeros, which in turn mathematically describe the message.* Put another way, with digital communications, the message is first translated into a pattern of binary digits (ones or zeros). Only then is each number converted into discrete signal states (such as high or low voltage).

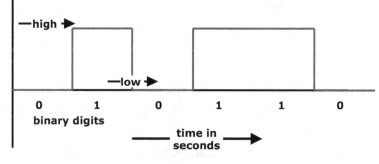

Figure 1.3. Digital Wave

We live in and experience an analog world. Most natural physical processes, such as your voice, are analog phenomena, which can be transduced by a transmitter directly into an analog signal. But any analog signal can be converted into a digital signal. By selecting the appropriate sampling rate and sampling precision, one can generate a string of binary digits that describe the original analog signal as accurately as desired.

Ponder that for a moment. Beethoven's Fifth Symphony can be translated mathematically into a string of ones and zeros. Your baby pictures, again, can be translated into ones and zeros. The movies you're streaming on Netflix—again, just ones and zeros.

But if most natural phenomena are analog, why bother representing them digitally? First, analog signals are much more vulnerable to electrical noise in the environment. Recall that the information within an analog signal is maintained in some physical characteristic of that signal—in our example, its amplitude. Accordingly, slight differences in amplitude are supposed to signify slight differences in the message. Thus, it matters whether the analog signal's amplitude is at 0.3 units or 0.4 units because that difference is supposed to reflect a difference in the original message. Unfortunately, electrical noise in the environment can randomly alter a signal's amplitude. What was originally sent as a 0.3 amplitude signal can be received as a 0.25 or 0.35 amplitude signal, with a correlative distortion of information transmitted.

Digital signals avoid this problem because they are not intended to convey fine gradations in amplitude so as to distinguish between 0.3 and 0.4 units. Instead, they only need to convey whether they are 0 or 1, off or on, zero or maximum amplitude. Even if noise slightly disturbs a digital signal—for example, changing a 0.0 amplitude signal to a 0.2 amplitude signal—the receiver still knows to treat the 0.2 signal as a "zero", not a "one". After enough zeros and ones are collected at the destination, that information can then be mathematically reconstituted into the original message. Therefore, digital signals can transmit a message more accurately, with less distortion than an analog signal.

Second, digital signals represent a string of binary numbers, which is the language of computers. The basic unit of information in any computing system is a bit. A bit has one of only two values—either a "0" or a "1." All the information manipulated by a computer is used in this binary form. Any mathematical procedure that can be accomplished on a computer can thus be easily applied to a digital signal. This produces multiple advantages. It allows computer electronics to use error-checking and correction algorithms to guarantee data integrity—that the message received was in fact the message sent, without intentional or accidental alteration. In addition, digital information can be compressed so that the message takes up less time or channel bandwidth to transmit. Finally, digital data can be easily and powerfully encrypted to ensure confidentiality of a message.

2. CHANNELS

Once a transmitter has converted the message into a signal, it must be sent to the receiver across a *channel.* That channel can be some physical wire or tube, in which case we call the communications system *wireline.* Or that channel can be the general e-m spectrum, without any physical medium, in which case we call the system *wireless.* (Whether a channel is wireline or wireless can have huge First Amendment consequences.) In either case, the central task of the channel is to transmit faithfully the signal across the distance between transmitter and receiver.

a. WIRELESS SYSTEMS

To repeat, e-m waves do not need any physical medium to propagate. (How else would sunlight reach the earth?) Accordingly, a broadcast station can use its antenna tower to transmit e-m waves encoded with your favorite sitcoms without the help of any wires. The channel is some portion of the e-m spectrum itself.

A useful way to divide up the entire e-m spectrum is by frequency of the e-m wave, from the highest frequency gamma rays to the lowest frequency radio waves.

Table 1.1: E-M Frequency Bands

Name	Frequency Range
Gamma rays	$10^{19} - 10^{21}$ Hz
X-Rays	$10^{17} - 10^{19}$ Hz
Ultraviolet	$10^{15} - 10^{16}$ Hz
Visible	10^{14} Hz
Infrared	300 GHz $- 10^{14}$ Hz
Radio	3 Hz $-$ 300 GHz (1GHz $= 10^{9}$ Hz)

Wireless communication systems generally use the portion of the e-m spectrum labeled "radio" frequencies, which run from 3 Hz to 300 GHz. By international convention, this range is subdivided into various bands.

Table 1.2: Radio Frequency Bands

Band #	Symbols	Frequency Range
4	VLF (Very Low Freq.)	3 — 30 kHz
5	LF (Low Freq.)	30 — 300 kHz
6	MF (Medium Freq.)	300 — 3,000 kHz
7	HF (High Freq.)	3 — 30 MHz
8	VHF (Very High Freq.)	30 — 300 MHz
9	UHF (Ultra High Freq.)	300 — 3,000 MHz
10	SHF (Super High Freq.)	3 — 30 GHz
11	EHF (Extremely High Freq.)	30 — 300 GHz

Within this span, the federal government has allocated different frequency ranges to be used for different communications services. Think of this as a sort of *spectrum zoning*. For example, broadcast AM Radio has been allocated the range of 535-1705 kHz (part of the MF range); FM radio operates between 88-108 MHz (part of the VHF range); digital broadcast TV operates between 470-608 and 614-698 MHz (part of the UHF range), and so on.

Does it matter what frequency a communication service actually uses? Sometimes it does because e-m waves propagate differently as a function of their frequency. For example, higher frequency waves are more likely to be absorbed or reflected when they hit buildings. This matters for mobile wireless networks that need to be used indoors in downtown offices. The UHF band is often called "beachfront property" because of its attractive propagation characteristics, especially for mobile communication services.

b. WIRELINE SYSTEMS

In contrast to wireless systems, *wireline* systems send e-m waves through a physical medium that bounds and directs the e-m wave's propagation. The medium may act as a conductor, such as copper wire, or it may act as a tunnel of glass, such as optical fiber. Familiar examples of wireline systems include much of the "public switched telephone network" (PSTN)[*] and cable television systems. In discussing wireless systems, we noted how e-m waves with different frequencies had different propagation properties. Analogously, in wireline systems, different wires have different propagation properties. Most important, each wire type has a different maximum bandwidth, and the greater the bandwidth, the greater the capacity to send information. Table 1.3 compares the different types of wires, their basic uses, and their advantages and disadvantages.

Table 1.3: Wireline Media

Medium	Description & Common Uses	Pros	Cons
Unshielded Twisted Pair (UTP)	A pair of copper wires twisted around each other; commonly used in telephone and computer networks.	Cheap; easy to splice and connect; material used in original telephone system.	Limited bandwidth; interference from nearby wires.
Coaxial Cable	A center of copper wire surrounded by shielding; used in cable television systems and computer networks.	High bandwidth; resistant to interference; relatively easy to splice and connect.	Relatively expensive.
Fiber-optic Cable	A strand of glass surrounded by reflective shielding; used in high speed computer, telephone, and cable television networks.	Very high bandwidth; low signal loss; highly resistant to interference.	Expensive; relatively difficult to splice and connect.

---

[*] Think of the PSTN as the standard, wireline telephone system that was operating in the 1970s, in the United States. This term usually does not include the mobile phone system or telephone service provided over the Internet (known as "VoIP," for Voice over Internet Protocol).

B. ECONOMIC POWER

The next type of power we consider is economic. By *economic power*, we often mean market power in the antitrust sense: the power to set prices higher than we would see in a competitive environment. We explore this idea through two stylized stories. The first is a story of how competition in the "free market" sets prices of goods and services in a way that serves society's interests. The second story explains why the first tale might be thwarted by monopoly, and what society might do in response. The goal here is not to work through economic formulas. Instead, our purpose is to be able both to tell and to understand some basic stories about economic efficiency that constantly circulate in modern policy circles.

Finally, sometimes the term "economic power" is used in a broader and looser sense, to refer to the substantial resources, wealth, and influence that certain communication and media conglomerates grow to have. To explore these nuances, we offer a third story about consolidation, in which firms get bigger and bigger, for better and worse.

1. THE STORY OF COMPETITION

If resources were infinite, we could satisfy everyone's desire without worrying about charging anyone for anything. But in the real world, resources are scarce, and society must find some sensible way to allocate them. In the United States, we rely on the "free market"—that is, on individual producers and consumers, whose behavior is governed by general contract and property law. Why turn over this responsibility to the decentralized processes of the market? The standard answer is that doing so will generate a socially optimal allocation of resources.

A perfectly competitive market. First, suppose we have a perfectly competitive market in which there are many buyers and sellers such that no single consumer or producer can individually influence the market price. In other words, each actor is a price taker. This means that an individual producer cannot set a higher market price for a widget because consumers will simply switch to a competing firm that charges a lower price. Similarly, an individual consumer cannot negotiate a lower price by threatening not to purchase widgets because producers will simply sell their widgets to the next consumer.

Another characteristic of a perfectly competitive market is the availability of perfect and complete information to all consumers and producers regarding all aspects of the market. For example, in making consumption decisions, consumers possess information regarding all available products, their prices, and their quality.

Finally, a perfectly competitive market has no barriers to entry. Any firm wishing to enter the widget market may do so without confronting regulatory or economic restrictions.

Given that all actors in a competitive market are price takers, how is the competitive market price set? The market price is the result of the behavior of two classes of actors—producers of the product, and consumers of that product. Economists assume that all actors are rational maximizers of self-interest: As such, producers seek to maximize profit while consumers try to maximize utility. Under these assumptions, producers will supply that quantity of a good that generates the most total profit, and consumers will demand that quantity of a good that generates the most total utility. The interaction of supply and demand will set the market price.

Setting the market price through supply and demand. Consumer utility is a measure of the satisfaction each consumer derives from consuming a given good. For practical reasons, this is expressed in terms of the number of dollars that the consumer is willing and able to pay for a particular good. For any given price of a good, consumers aim to purchase the quantity that generates the maximum total utility when combined with consumption of other goods. Economists do not assume that consumers have identical preferences. Each consumer values goods differently and would therefore be willing to pay different amounts.

Consider the following consumers, Alice through George, who derive varying levels of utility from USB flash drives (those little thumb-sized devices that allow you to move files from computer to computer):

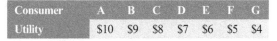

Consumer	A	B	C	D	E	F	G
Utility	$10	$9	$8	$7	$6	$5	$4

If the price of flash drives is $7, how many consumers will buy flash drives—that is, what is the demand for flash drives? Four flash drives will be sold to consumers Alice through Dan. Consumers Elle through George do not derive sufficient utility from flash drives to warrant purchasing one at $7. They will spend their money elsewhere. This is, however, only part of the picture because we do not know how many flash drives will be supplied at any given price. This is determined by the profit-maximizing level of production for each producer.

A producer in a competitive market maximizes profits at the point that the cost of producing the next unit of a good (marginal cost) equals the revenue derived from selling that unit (marginal revenue). The reason is simple: If the revenue from selling the next flash drive exceeds its cost of production, the firm will produce it because that flash drive improves the firm's bottom line. Conversely, if marginal cost exceeds the marginal revenue derived from selling the next flash drive, the firm has no incentive to produce that flash drive. It follows, then, that the firm will continue producing additional flash drives up to the point where the marginal revenue derived from the last flash drive equals its marginal cost.

But what prevents a producer from charging an exorbitant price? Competition. To see why this is so, consult again the previous list of consumers. Assume that consumers Alice through George represent the entire market for flash drives. The utility for all consumers in the market is as shown. Assume further that the marginal cost of producing one flash drive, which by definition includes a reasonable rate-of-return on investment, is $5.*

In the beginning, imagine that Firm 1 is the only producer in the flash drive market. Firm 1 decides to sell its flash drives for $8 each, the price at which the firm believes it will maximize its profits. The firm therefore makes $3 "economic profit" per flash drive (i.e., $3 above the reasonable rate-of-return on investment for each flash drive sold).† As the only firm in the market, Firm 1 is not a "price taker" and can set the market price without fear of consumers defecting to alternative producers of flash drives.‡

Seeing that Firm 1 is making $3 per flash drive more than the reasonable rate-of-return on investment, Firm 2 jumps into the market. After all, in a perfectly competitive market, there are no barriers to entry. Assume that Firm 2 also has a marginal cost of production of $5.§ Firm 2 realizes that if it charges a few dollars less, such as $6 per flash drive, several positive things will happen:

- It can attract consumers Alice through Charlie away from Firm 1, because as rational people, they prefer paying less for the same product;

---

* The marginal cost includes a reasonable (or "normal") rate-of-return on the firm's investment—the profits that investors normally make in ventures involving this level of risk. If a normal rate-of-return were not recovered in the product's price, then firms would have no incentive to make the product and would invest in alternative, more lucrative, ventures. For this reason, firms view a normal rate-of-return as a necessary cost of doing business that must be recovered in the price of the product.

† Be sure to keep the notion of "economic profit" clear and distinct from the reasonable rate-of-return on investment. Economic profit is revenue over and above the reasonable rate-of-return.

‡ Being the only firm does not, however, give Firm 1 the option to charge, say, $30 or $40 per flash drive because consumers will turn to a substitute good. Thus the availability of substitute goods can constrain even a monopolist's prices.

§ This is a big assumption to make. Often, new entrants in the market will have higher costs of production because they have not yet experienced the efficiency gains that come from being established in the market. As we shall see in the next section, differences in costs of production can lead to monopoly power for one firm, which can defeat competition.

- It will induce consumers Dan and Elle, who did not think the flash drive was worth buying at $8, to purchase the flash drive at $6; and
- Firm 2 will still make $1 economic profit per flash drive.

In response to this competition, Firm 1 must reduce its price to $6 to stay in business and to share the market with Firm 2. Otherwise, Firm 1 would lose all of its customers.

Observing that there is still money to be made, Firm 3 enters the market and (assuming the same $5 marginal cost) charges $5 per flash drive. Consumers Alice through Elle will flock to Firm 3 unless Firms 1 and 2 match the lower price. If Firms 1 and 2 do not respond, the demand for their flash drives will fall to zero. Also, demand is again increased at the lower price because Consumer Frank will now purchase a flash drive. At this point, the price of the flash drive is equal to its marginal cost. The price will not fall below $5 because at any lower price, firms wouldn't be able to make a reasonable return on their investment.

The market is now in equilibrium: The market price cannot rest above marginal cost because a new competitor will enter the market and provide the product at marginal cost. This forces other suppliers to match the lower price if they want to keep their customers. Also, the price cannot rest below marginal cost because producers must earn a reasonable rate-of-return to stay in business.

Efficiency. When the price of flash drives is set at marginal cost, society commits just the right amount of scarce resources to producing the flash drives—no more and no less. In other words, we arguably have a socially optimal allocation of resources. To see why this is so, think about what the "marginal cost" of a flash drive signifies. This is the true cost to society—in terms of materials, labor, and capital—to produce that last flash drive. If the price is set below the marginal cost, then consumers who are not willing to pay the true cost of the flash drive will nonetheless be buying one. This creates a problem of over-consumption, in which too many of society's scarce resources are being allocated to flash drive production.

By contrast, if the price is set above marginal cost, consumers who are willing to pay the true cost of the flash drive will forgo purchasing one. Instead, they will endure some more cumbersome alternative, such as burning a CD-ROM. This creates a problem of under-consumption, in which not enough of society's resources are being allocated to flash drive production. However, when a price is set at marginal cost, we have just the right amount of consumption and production of flash drives. Economists often call this state of affairs "allocatively efficient."

NOTES & QUESTIONS

1. *How free is "free"?* The notion of the "free market" as an unregulated forum for exchange between producers and consumers must be qualified by the fact that even the most laissez-faire markets depend on the law for their very existence. Legal rules establish rights and obligations among buyers and sellers (through property and contract law); set the basic rules of exchange (e.g., by punishing fraudulent behavior); and create types of buyers and sellers that would not exist absent regulation (corporations, for example, are entities created and authorized by operation of law). Consider, for example, why corporations enjoy the remarkable benefit of limited liability: It is not because of some natural economic reality; it is because the law says so. Thus, when "free market" enthusiasts demand that government get out of the way, make sure you understand what part of government they want out of the way.

2. *Equivocating efficiency.* The word *efficiency* can mean many different things, depending on the context—for example:

- Pareto efficiency (an outcome is more Pareto efficient if it makes at least one person better off without making anyone else worse off);
  - productive efficiency (sometimes understood as Pareto efficiency among producers, or just that there is no waste in production);
  - distributional efficiency (sometimes understood as Pareto efficiency among consumers);
  - allocative efficiency (sometimes defined as a combination of productive and distributional efficiencies);
- Kaldor-Hicks efficiency (an outcome is Kaldor-Hicks efficient if the benefits to winners outweigh costs to losers such that *in theory* the winners could hypothetically compensate the losers and produce a Pareto efficient outcome);
- Wealth maximization (something like Kaldor-Hicks efficiency, but benefits and costs are measured strictly through dollars that people currently have and are willing and able to pay).

Lawyers, judges, policymakers, politicians, and sometimes even economists throw around the word "efficiency" without definition. Throughout this book, keep a sharp lookout for how courts and agencies employ the term "efficiency," and make sure you understand what they mean. Because you are a future lawyer, not a future economist, the burden is on anyone who uses this language to explain the concept clearly to you, not vice versa.

3. *Imperfection in the real world.* The perfectly competitive market described above rarely, if ever, exists in the real world. Simplifying assumptions

such as the availability of perfect information do not hold true, causing most markets to be less than perfectly competitive. Can you see how imperfect information for consumers (e.g., not knowing that another store is selling flash drives at a lower price) can lead to inefficiency? Can you also see how improved communication technologies can make markets function better?

4. *"Public good" characteristics.* Information has odd properties, quite different from tangible goods, that can make markets misfire. For example, information may have aspects of a "public good": nonrivalrous consumption and nonexcludability.

a. *Nonrivalrous consumption.* If you watch the television program "American Idol," can your friend also watch that very same show? Absolutely. By contrast, if you eat an apple, can your friend eat that very same apple? No. In this sense, the consumption of information by one individual does not preclude the consumption of that same information by another individual.

b. *Nonexcludability.* Depending on how information is treated, it may be hard to exclude those who do not "pay" to access that information. This is especially true in a digitalized environment, where copies—easily made and as good as the original—can be shared quickly and cheaply. Of course, the degree of excludability depends on the underlying intellectual property and contract regime as well as the technologies of data security (e.g., Digital Rights Management, which prevents copying).

c. *The problem of public goods.* The standard concern with public goods, such as clean air or national defense, is that the market will under-produce them because free riders (those who do not pay) cannot be excluded from consuming them. This is the economic rationale for much of intellectual property law, which creates legal rights to exclude people from consuming information.

5. *Law and economics critiques.* The law and economics approach to evaluating markets and crafting regulation embraces efficiency as the normative ideal. Criticisms of the law and economics approach are of two general types. First, critics question the validity of the assumptions underlying its approach (and, by extension, the validity of the assumptions underlying the economic efficiency model). For instance, do individuals in the real world behave as rational utility maximizers all or most of the time? Does the assumption of utility or profit maximization overlook other values, psychological mind-sets, or cognitive biases that motivate and limit consumer choice?

Second, critics question whether the law and economics approach is consistent with equity and justice. For example, traditional economic analysis takes as a given the initial allocation of resources among consumers and producers in society. It simply asks, assuming that consumer A has $1,000,000 and Consumer B has $1, how should A and B spend their money to maximize their utilities? This analysis does not ask why Alice has more than Benjamin. Should society (and regulators) care that Benjamin lacks not only a flash drive but a computer to put one in? Should criteria other than efficiency motivate a regulator's choice of legal rule?

2. THE STORY OF MONOPOLY

Definition of monopoly. At the other extreme from perfect competition is monopoly. A monopoly exists where there is only one producer operating in the entire market for a particular good. The monopolist is able to maintain its position as the sole producer because other firms confront some barrier to entering the market.

These barriers to entry are created (1) by law (a *legal monopoly*); (2) "naturally" by the characteristics of the service and/or market (a *natural monopoly*); and/or (3) as a result of unfair practices, such as predatory pricing, whereby the firm prices its widgets below cost in order to drive competitors out of the market (an *illegal monopoly*).

Legal monopolies are created by operation of law—for example, AT&T's patents back in the 19th century gave it a monopoly in the equipment and service market. The conditions under which natural monopolies emerge, as discussed in the following chapter, are more complex. As we shall soon see, local telephony has been characterized as a natural monopoly, which partially justifies government regulation of entry. The same is often said of cable TV. Finally, illegal monopolies are created by abuse of economic power, which should be checked by antitrust laws. An example is AT&T's early 20th century policies of refusing to interconnect competing local exchanges to its long distance network. Notice that one kind of monopoly can morph into another. For example, a legal monopoly granted through patents can develop into an illegal monopoly based on predatory pricing when the patents expire.

Impact of monopolies on efficiency. In one regard, a firm with monopoly power is no different from a firm operating in a competitive market: Each firm seeks to maximize total profits. Unlike a competitive firm, however, the monopolist will be able to set the price above marginal cost. Consider the following example:

1. Consumer	2. Utility	3. Price	4. Total Revenue	5. Marginal Revenue	6. Marginal Cost	7. Total Cost
A	10	10	(1 × 10) = 10	+ 10	5	(1 x 5) = 5
B	9	9	(2 × 9) = 18	+ 8	5	(2 x 5) = 10
C	8	8	(3 × 8) = 24	+ 6	5	(3 x 5) = 15
D	7	7	(4 × 7) = 28	+ 4	5	(4 x 5) = 20
E	6	6	(5 × 6) = 30	+ 2	5	(5 x 5) = 25
F	5	5	(6 × 5) = 30	0	5	(6 x 5) = 30
G	4	4	(7 × 4) = 28	− 2	5	(7 x 5) = 35

Column 1 identifies the consumer. Column 2 provides the utility each consumer receives from a flash drive, measured in dollars. Column 3 is the price that each consumer is willing to pay for the flash drive: Because consumers are rational, the price each is willing to pay is identical to the utility that each consumer receives from the flash drive. Column 4 is the monopolist's total revenue, which is the product of the number of units sold and the price. So if the price is set at $7, four flash drives will be sold (to consumers Alice through Dan), and the total revenue will be $28 (4 flash drives × $7). Note that as price decreases, demand for flash drives increases. Column 5 is marginal revenue, the additional dollars received from selling the next flash drive. Thus, if the total revenue from selling one flash drive is $10 and the total revenue from selling two flash drives is $18, then the marginal revenue of selling that second flash drive is $8 (= $18 − $10). Column 6 is the marginal cost of producing one more flash drive. For simplicity, assume that the marginal cost of producing a flash drive is $5 across the board. Note, however, that in many real-world applications marginal costs decrease as production increases due to economies of scale. The final column is the total cost of production: the number of flash drives produced multiplied by the cost of producing each drive.

Suppose that Firm 1 is the monopolist. If Firm 1 wanted to sell only one flash drive, it could charge consumer Alice $10 for it. If it wanted to sell two flash drives (say, to Alice and Benjamin), Firm 1 must reduce its price (to $9);

otherwise, Benjamin will not buy that flash drive. In addition, Firm 1 cannot generally lower the price only for Benjamin and keep the price for Alice at $10. This sort of price discrimination is hard to implement. For example, Firm 1 will not know whether a particular consumer, Xena, values the flash drive at $10 or $9. Also, nothing prevents Benjamin from buying the flash drive and then re-selling it immediately to Alice for some price between $9.01 and $9.99.

If you were Firm 1, how many flash drives would you produce to maximize profit? Exactly three. The marginal revenue for the fourth flash drive ($4) is less than the marginal cost ($5); in other words, if it produced that fourth flash drive, the Firm would lose money—an irrational thing to do. Nor will Firm 1 limit itself to selling just two flash drives. So long as marginal revenue exceeds marginal cost, more flash drives will be produced. Firm 1 will therefore charge $8 for the flash drives, the price at which three consumers (consumers Alice through Charlie) are willing to buy flash drives. (Another way to see this is to pick the price that maximizes the Net Revenue, which is the difference between Total Revenue and Total Cost.)

Notice that the monopolist is making an economic profit of $3 per flash drive (price of $8 minus marginal cost of $5). The firm need not worry about competitors driving prices down to marginal cost because Firm 1 has a monopoly: There is no competition. Further, demand will not fall to zero because there will be some consumers who derive utility from flash drives even at a price higher than the marginal cost of production—say, wealthier people who can afford to pay more or consumers that place a higher value on conveniently storing large amounts of data in a pocketable device. As such, the market price for flash drives settles into equilibrium at $8.

By contrast, in a competitive market, we've seen how prices would be pushed down to marginal cost, $5. Thus, in a competitive environment, Consumers Dan, Elle, and Frank would also have purchased flash drives because they are willing and able to pay society's true cost for producing the next flash drive. Because in a monopoly environment these consumers will not purchase flash drives, we have under-consumption. (In more technical terms, this is "dead weight loss"—foregone consumer surplus.) Relatedly, production facilities that should have been employed to produce three additional flash drives are being used for some other purpose. Finally, consumers Alice through Charlie are over-paying because it costs society only $5 to make the flash drives but the consumers must pay $8 to buy them. (Again, in more technical terms, this means that consumer surplus has been replaced by monopoly profits.) The extra $3 of economic profit that goes to Firm 1 is diverted from another product that these consumers would have purchased. As such, the monopoly market results in an inefficient allocation of resources as compared to a competitive market—producer profits rest at supra-competitive levels while consumer demand goes unsatisfied.

In addition to allocative inefficiency, monopoly power may create bad incentives on the part of the monopolist. First, monopoly can reduce the incentive to innovate. The discipline of competitive markets induces firms to search continually for innovative procedures to reduce their costs of production. Firms that innovate are rewarded with economic profits (at least until other firms catch up). A monopolist, on the other hand, may have fewer incentives to innovate because, by definition, it has no competition. Second, a monopoly may increase the incentive to make a shabby product. Instead of cutting costs through innovation, a monopolist may choose the opposite route—it may use cheaper materials to produce a lower-cost, lower-quality product without giving consumers a corresponding price reduction.

3. THE STORY OF CONSOLIDATION

Definition of consolidation. Media firms are getting bigger and bigger. Firms are buying up their competitors in the same city and across the nation. Indeed, they are *consolidating* across industry lines, with cable companies buying Internet companies buying broadcast companies, and so on. Such consolidation must make business sense; otherwise, why would the firms merge in the first place? But is self-interested business sense what's best for society?

In a market economy, the answer is presumably yes: it's the self-interested (i.e. economically rational) behavior of suppliers and consumers acting in a free market that leads to efficient distribution of products and services. But we aren't talking about just any old product—some fungible widget like a toaster. Instead, we are talking about media and communications, which produce and distribute the content that "programs" our polity, configures our culture, and provides the information necessary for democratic self-governance. Should these differences alter the way we think about consolidation? Or is this just an intellectual veneer for an irrational aversion to "bigness"?

In studying consolidation, make sure to distinguish three different "directions" in which firms might get bigger: vertical integration, horizontal consolidation, and cross-ownership. Let's run through some examples in traditional over-the-air broadcast TV. The life cycle of producing, distributing (nationally), and broadcasting (locally) modern broadcast TV is enormously complicated. Not surprisingly, this life cycle has historically required the coordination of many players acting in many stages of a production-distribution-exhibition process.

First, the video programming must be produced—for example, by a Hollywood studio, such as Disney. Next, it must be distributed nationally—for example, by a major television network, such as ABC. Finally, it must be broadcast locally for viewer consumption by a local television station, such as the ABC-owned-and-operated station in Los Angeles, KABC-TV. In this description, the life cycle of the broadcast TV service is broken down into three stages: (1) program production, (2) national distribution, and (3) local exhibition to an audience through local broadcast.

Consolidation between any of these stages is called "vertical." Notice how the output of stage 1 is an input in stage 2, and so on. If a firm that has historically engaged only in national distribution (stage 2) suddenly enters the market of video programming production (stage 1), then that firm has changed its structure by vertically integrating.

By contrast, consolidation entirely within the same stage is called "horizontal." For example, a firm that owns one local television broadcast outlet (stage 3) in Los Angeles may seek to buy another television station (also stage 3) in Los Angeles, which is a direct competitor. This involves *horizontal* consolidation in the same stage of production-distribution-consumption.

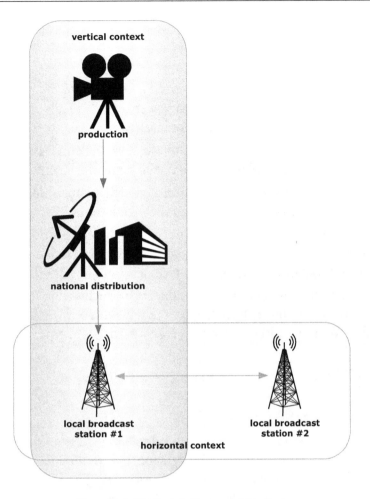

Figure 1.4: Vertical & Horizontal Contexts

Finally, sometimes firms merge across industry lines. For example, consider a television station deciding to buy the local daily newspaper. In these transactions, there is no obvious vertical or horizontal relationship. This sort of consolidation is called "cross-ownership."

So, what's wrong with more horizontal consolidation and cross-ownership? Is it just the fear of monopolies, higher prices and lower innovation? And if so, wouldn't ordinary antitrust law take care of the problem? Or is there something more to worry about? These are some of the hard questions that will be explored throughout the book, especially in Chapter 4: Access.

C. LEGAL POWER

Modern communication technologies, delivered by mega-corporations as well as internet startups, have revolutionized how we exchange information and interact socially. But the exercise of this power by individuals and corporations can create new conflict and problems. For instance:

- What if I want to operate a radio station that uses an e-m wave at a particular frequency, but my neighbor wants to do the same causing interference?

- What if sexually explicit or graphically violent pictures inappropriate for children are made widely available through the internet?

- What if a huge telephone company wants to merge with a huge cable company, and you are worried about a single corporation controlling the pricing and content of the main data channels into the home?

Society responds to the potential excesses of technological and economic power through legal power. Focusing on the federal level, we first discuss how such legal power is exercised across the various branches of government.

1. CONGRESS

a. COMMUNICATIONS ACT

Congress has historically played a central role in regulating communications. As early as 1910, Congress placed interstate telecommunications under the control of the Interstate Commerce Commission (ICC), which was originally created in 1887 to regulate railroads. In 1927, Congress passed the Radio Act, which created the Federal Radio Commission (FRC). Seven years later, prompted by increasing problems with radio interference, Congress passed the seminal Communications Act of 1934. This Act incorporated much of the previous Radio Act and created the Federal Communications Commission (FCC). To this new agency were given all the powers of the dissolved FRC as well as the ICC's power over interstate telephony and telegraph. Over 60 years later, Congress passed the Telecommunications Act of 1996, which substantially reconfigured telecommunications.

The Communications Act of 1934, as amended by the 1996 Telecommunications Act, is extraordinarily complicated. At this point of your study, your goal should be to see the big picture—to get a sense of the forest, not obsess about individual trees, twigs, and leaves.

Title I. General Provisions. Title I creates the Federal Communications Commission and gives the agency its central mission, 47 U.S.C. § 151, provides essential definitions, and makes clear that federal power extends, at least to a first approximation, only to interstate communications, § 152. Section 154(i) acts as a sort of "necessary and proper" clause for the Commission. This provision is crucial to the "ancillary jurisdiction" doctrine we study in CHAPTER 5: CLASSIFICATION.

> 47 U.S.C. § 151. Purposes of chapter; FCC created
>
> For the purpose of regulating interstate and foreign commerce in communication by wire and radio so as to make available, so far as possible, to all the people of the United States, without discrimination on the basis of race, color, religion, national origin, or sex, a rapid, efficient, nationwide, and world-wide wire and radio communication service with adequate facilities at reasonable charges . . . there is hereby created a commission to be known as the "Federal Communications Commission" . . . .
>
> 47 U.S.C. § 152. Application of Act
>
> (a) The provisions of this Act shall apply to all interstate and foreign communication by wire or radio and all interstate and foreign transmission of energy by radio, which originates and/or is received within the United States, and to all persons engaged within the United States in such communication or such transmission of energy by radio, and to the licensing and regulating of all radio stations as hereinafter provided . . . . The provisions of this Act shall apply with respect to cable service, to all persons engaged within the United States in providing such service, and to the facilities of cable operators which relate to such service, as provided in title VI [47 USC §§ 521 et seq.].
>
> 47 U.S.C. § 154(i). Duties and powers
>
> The Commission may perform any and all acts, make such rules and regulations, and issue such orders, not inconsistent with this Act, as may be necessary in the execution of its functions.

Title II. Common Carriers. This Title, which governs our telephone network, has three parts. The most important is Part I, in which Congress sets out the standard obligations of common carriers—essentially, to serve all customers without unreasonable discrimination. Significantly, a common carrier cannot "build, acquire, or discontinue lines" without FCC approval. § 214. Part II, added by the 1996 Telecommunications Act, focuses on developing competitive markets in local telephone service. Specifically, all state and local barriers to entry to provide local phone service are preempted. § 253. In addition, local exchange carriers (those companies that provide local phone service) are required to interconnect with competitors. §§ 251, 252. Finally, Part III (also added by the 1996 Act) addresses what should become of the Bell Operating Companies, which were created by breaking up AT&T back in 1984. Until the 1996 Telecommunications Act, the Bell Operating Companies had been governed by a consent decree. This Part, among other things, outlines the conditions in which Bell Operating Companies, which provide local phone service, can enter the long distance business. §§ 271, 272.

47 U.S.C. § 201. Service and Charges

(a) It shall be the duty of every common carrier . . . to furnish such communication service upon reasonable request therefor . . . .

(b) All charges, practices, classifications, and regulations for and in connection with such communication service, shall be just and reasonable, and any such charge, practice, classification, or regulation that is unjust or unreasonable is hereby declared to be unlawful. . . .

47 U.S.C. § 202. Discriminations and Preferences

(a) Charges, services, etc. It shall be unlawful for any common carrier to make any unjust or unreasonable discrimination in charges, practices, classifications, regulations, facilities, or services for or in connection with like communication service, directly or indirectly, by any means or device . . . .

Title III. Special Provisions Relating to Radio. Most of this Title governs broadcast radio and television. The most important provisions can be found in Part I. Specifically, anyone who wants to become a broadcaster must have a license issued by the FCC. In no way is this license to be construed as ownership. § 301. As the public interest requires, the FCC is empowered to regulate the spectrum in various ways. § 303. In addition to broadcast radio and television, portions of this Title govern wireless telephony. *See, e.g.,* § 332.

47 U.S.C. § 301. License for radio communication or transmission of energy

No person shall use or operate any apparatus for the transmission of energy or communications or signals by radio . . . except under and in accordance with this Act and with a license . . . .

47 U.S.C. § 303. Powers and duties of Commission

[T]the Commission from time to time, as public convenience, interest, or necessity requires, shall—

(c) Assign bands of frequencies to the various classes of stations, and assign frequencies for each individual station . . . .

(f) Make such regulations not inconsistent with law as it may deem necessary to prevent interference between stations . . . .

Title VI. Cable Communications. Cable television did not exist back in 1934. This Title was instead created through legislation in 1984 (Cable Communications Policy Act). Part II of this Title addresses the use of cable channels and the ownership of cable systems. In particular, it specifies that some channel capacity must be made accessible for local broadcast, §§ 534, 535; leased access, § 532; and public interest, educational, and government (PEG) channels, § 531. Part III discusses cable franchising and prohibits local franchising authorities from issuing exclusive franchises (i.e. legal monopolies). § 541.

47 U.S.C. § 541. General franchise requirements

(b) No cable service without franchise; exception under prior law.

(1) [A] cable operator may not provide cable service without a franchise...

Missing Titles. Title IV of the Communications Act establishes the FCC's administrative procedures, whereas Title V sets penalties and enforcement procedures. There is no Title governing the internet, which was in its infancy when the 1996 Telecommunications Act was drafted. That means that new internet services have been challenging to classify, as we study carefully in CHAPTER 5: CLASSIFICATION.

b. ANTITRUST LAW

Antitrust law directly addresses problems of market power and structure. Although antitrust law (called "competition" law in other nations) is a subject you should study carefully in a separate course, a brief summary will be useful here. At the federal level, two antitrust statutes are most relevant to communications: The Sherman Act (passed in 1890) and the Clayton Act (passed in 1914 and amended substantially in 1950).[*]

Section 1 of the Sherman Act prohibits contracts, combinations, and conspiracies between two or more entities that unreasonably restrain interstate trade. *See* 15 U.S.C. § 1. Examples of such conduct include price-fixing and geographically dividing markets among competitors.

Section 2 of the Sherman Act outlaws a monopoly that has been acquired or is maintained through anticompetitive practices. *See* 15 U.S.C. § 2. Monopoly power is "the power to control market prices or exclude competition."[†] The firm must have monopoly power and have intentionally acquired or maintained it—not through honest business acumen or a superior product, but through anticompetitive means. To repeat, having a monopoly in and of itself is not illegal. But getting that monopoly or preserving it through deliberate anticompetitive conduct is. Examples of such illegal conduct include predatory pricing, price squeeze, refusal to deal with competitors while controlling an essential facility (bottleneck), leveraging, and restrictive vertical agreements.

Section 7 of the Clayton Act prohibits mergers or acquisitions that substantially lessen competition or tend to create a monopoly. *See* 15 U.S.C. § 18. Under the Hart-Scott-Rodino Antitrust Improvements Act of 1976, any merger or acquisition above a certain size must be reported to the antitrust division of the Department of Justice and the Federal Trade Commission. Either agency may file for a preliminary injunction to enjoin the transaction.

Violations of the Sherman Act can prompt criminal enforcement actions (leading to fines and prison terms) by the Department of Justice (DOJ).

---

[*] States generally have similar antitrust laws for intrastate trade and commerce.

[†] United States v. DuPont du Nemours and Co., 351 U.S. 377, 391 (1956).

Violations of the Sherman Act and the Clayton Act can also prompt civil enforcement actions brought by the Department of Justice, the Federal Trade Commission (FTC), state attorneys general, and private parties who have standing to sue.

Relationship with telecommunications law. The Supreme Court has clarified the relationship between antitrust law and the regulatory framework established in the Communications Act of 1934, as amended by the Telecommunications Act of 1996. A private plaintiff argued that Verizon's failure to adhere to interconnection requirements with competitive local exchange carriers (CLECs) as required by 47 U.S.C. § 251(c) stated a legal claim under § 2 of the Sherman Act. The Court explained that the 1996 Act had no impact on traditional antitrust principles and pointed specifically to the Act's saving clause—which provides that "nothing in this Act . . . shall be construed to modify, impair, or supersede the applicability of any of the antitrust laws."[*]

This would mean that the plaintiff's claim would have to succeed or fail as a straight antitrust claim, regardless of any communications statutory provision. Conversely, Verizon would not be shielded from any "implied immunity" simply because the field was heavily regulated. As the Court put it, "just as the 1996 Act preserves claims that satisfy existing antitrust standards, it does not create new claims that go beyond existing antitrust standards."[†]

2. AGENCIES

At the federal level, government power is wielded not only by Congress but also by administrative agencies. Independent agencies, such as the FCC and FTC, are created by an act of Congress, which delegates to the agencies some regulatory power over a particular domain. By contrast, Executive Branch agencies, such as the National Telecommunications and Information Administration (NTIA), which resides within the Department of Commerce, are extensions of the Executive Branch.

Before discussing the details of each agency, one might ask a threshold question: Why do we need agencies in the first place? A standard answer is that no other branch of government has the institutional capacity to manage a complicated, dynamic field such as communications. For example, although Congress may be able to pass general laws about communication technologies, it lacks the resources, flexibility, and expertise for daily governance. Some also contend that administrative agencies are better insulated from political pressures

---

[*] 47 U.S.C. § 152, n. 3.

[†] Verizon Communications v. Law Offices of Curtis V. Trinko, 540 U.S. 398, 407 (2004).

than directly elected legislatures. Skeptics retort that regulatory agencies can easily be captured by the industries that they supposedly regulate.

What about the judiciary? Again, the standard response emphasizes that the judiciary lacks the resources and expertise. Moreover, judges make decisions in the context of concrete cases or controversies, which arise in unpredictable, idiosyncratic litigation. This constraint on decision-making makes it hard to generate consistent, proactive regulatory policy through the courts—something agencies can better implement through prospective rulemakings.

a. THE FCC

The single most important agency in understanding modern communications is the Federal Communications Commission (FCC), which is an independent agency charged by Congress in the Communications Act of 1934 to regulate "interstate and foreign commerce in communication by wire and radio."[*] The FCC is directed by five Commissioners appointed by the President and confirmed by the Senate for 5-year terms. The President selects the Chairperson, and only three Commissioners may belong to the same political party. The mission of the FCC is to ensure that the American people have available at reasonable costs and without discrimination rapid, efficient, nation- and world-wide communication services. The Commission is organized into various Bureaus and Offices that periodically change depending on the FCC's agenda and framing.

The FCC has the power to promulgate rules and make adjudications.[†] Adjudications resolve a specific dispute or controversy involving specific parties; by contrast, rulemakings are legislative-like processes that generate prospective rules generally applicable to all parties.

In the past, formal adjudications played a more important role in the Commission's work.[‡] For example, when television and radio license renewals were more easily contestable under the substantive law, trial-like procedures known as comparative hearings were held to determine the challenged license's fate. But now, as explained *infra* in CHAPTER 2: ENTRY, license renewal is almost guaranteed, and comparative hearings don't occur often. This does not mean, however, that adjudications have gone extinct. For example, at the FCC's

---

[*] 47 U.S.C. § 151.

[†] The technical procedures by which rules and adjudications are produced are codified in 47 C.F.R. Part 1 (Practice and Procedure).

[‡] The basic procedures for adjudications are outlined in the Administrative Procedure Act. *See, e.g.*, 5 U.S.C. § 554, and 47 C.F.R. Part 1.B (Hearing Proceedings).

discretion, it may hold a full hearing to adjudicate the merits of a forfeiture penalty for willful violations of Commission regulations.[*]

Like most agencies, the FCC does most of its important work through informal rulemaking following what is called the "notice and comment" procedures outlined in the Administrative Procedure Act (APA).[†]

1. Triggers for Action

The FCC's rulemaking process can be triggered in three different ways, depicted in Figure 1.5.

Mandatory triggers. Through legislation, Congress may require the FCC to promulgate new rules to implement new measures. For example, the Telecommunications Act of 1996 forced the FCC to issue myriad new regulations under tight deadlines. Also, the judiciary may vacate and remand, or reverse FCC rules that have been legally challenged. This will trigger a rulemaking process that will amend, delete, or clarify the litigated rules.

Optional triggers. Through its oversight powers, Congress can informally suggest regulatory action. Recall that all the Commissioners were confirmed by the Senate, that Congress enjoys the power of the purse (i.e. the funding of the agency), and that Congress created the Commission and gave it its principal powers and obligations. Also, although the FCC is an independent agency, Executive Branch officials, advisory committees, departments, or agencies may informally suggest that the Commission make new rules or change existing ones. Remember that the Commissioners are appointed by the President. Finally, the FCC itself may initiate changes on its own accord (*sua sponte*).

---

[*] *See* 47 C.F.R. § 1.80(g) (notice of opportunity for hearing, which triggers "full evidentiary hearing before an administrative law judge").

[†] The basic procedures for such rulemaking are outlined in the Administrative Procedure Act, *see, e.g.*, 5 U.S.C. § 553, and 47 C.F.R. Part 1.C (Rulemaking Proceedings). The FCC's internal procedural rules are contained in Part I of the FCC's rules and regulations. *See generally* 47 C.F.R. § 1.1 *et seq.* For rulemaking proceedings, see specifically 47 C.F.R. §§ 1.399-1.430.

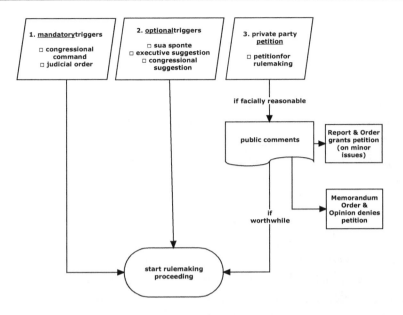

Figure 1.5. Rulemaking Trigger

Petition for rulemaking. Finally, any "interested person" may file a formal petition for rulemaking to the FCC.[*] When a formal petition is filed by private parties, it is forwarded to the relevant FCC bureau or office that has jurisdiction. If the petition is deemed facially reasonable by the bureau or office,[†] the petition is then publicly noticed on the FCC's web site and the FEDERAL REGISTER.[‡]

The bureau or office responsible will next analyze any received comments. If no further study or comment is necessary, the FCC will dispose of the petition, either by denying it in a "Memorandum Opinion & Order" (MO&O),[§] or by

---

[*] *See* 47 C.F.R. § 1.401(a) ("Any interested person may petition for the issuance, amendment or repeal of a rule or regulation.").

[†] *See* 47 C.F.R. § 1.401(e) ("Petitions which are moot, premature, repetitive, frivolous, or which plainly do not warrant consideration by the Commission may be denied or dismissed without prejudice to the petitioner.").

[‡] Enacted in 1935, the Federal Register Act, 44 U.S.C. § 1501 et seq., designated the FEDERAL REGISTER as the single official publication of proposed rules and final rules, which would provide the public notice for federal regulatory decisionmaking. The FEDERAL REGISTER publishes proposed rules, rules, notices, and presidential documents.

[§] In addition to being used to deny a petition for rulemaking, a MO&O is used to "modify a decision, grant or deny a petition for reconsideration, or grant or deny an application for review of a decision. A second or third Memorandum Opinion and Order may be issued (2nd MO&O, 3rd MO&O). Other appropriate titles may also be used, e.g., Order on Reconsideration or Order on Review." *See* http://wireless.fcc.gov/csinfo/ruleterms.html#moo. The last part is important. Even though a petition for rehearing may be denied on an "Order on Reconsideration," it is equivalent to a MO&O.

issuing some final "Report & Order" (R&O) amending the rules in minor ways. Alternatively, it may decide that the petition warrants a full rulemaking.

2. Rulemaking proceeding

Collecting comments. Generally, the FCC starts by releasing a "Notice of Proposed Rule Making" (NPRM), stating proposed additions or changes to current rules. Sometimes, the Commission is more tentative—as a matter of either policy or politics—and wants to collect more information and perspectives before even floating any concrete proposal. In that case, it will start by issuing a "Notice of Inquiry" (NOI), which describes the problem and asks for general reactions. A summary of the full NOI and NPRM text is published in the FEDERAL REGISTER.

The FCC gives the public a specified period of time to submit comments following the initial publication. After the comments are received, another period is provided for reply comments. In extraordinary cases, the FCC can require oral argument or some other hearing-like process.[*]

Making decisions. Once the FCC receives sufficient comments and reply comments on a NOI, it may issue a follow-up NPRM to continue the matter or issue a MO&O to conclude the inquiry. To conclude an NPRM, the Commission must issue a "Report & Order" (R&O), which states what the new or amended rule is and provides the Commission's reasoning. It is not unusual for the FCC to issue many R&Os within any given rulemaking with each R&O addressing some subset of the entire proceeding and the remaining unresolved issues rolled over to a "Further Notice of Proposed Rulemaking" (FNPRM). Since R&Os provide the explanation for rule changes, they become critical to analyzing whether the Commission has been "arbitrary or capricious" under an Administrative Procedure Act challenge.

---

[*] *See* 47 C.F.R. § 1.423 (Oral argument and other proceedings).

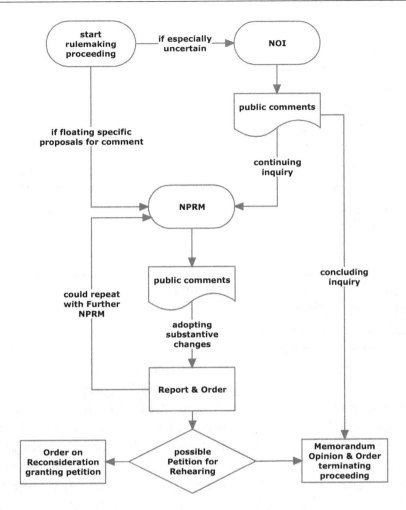

Figure 1.6. Rulemaking Process

Within 30 days of the Order's publication in the FEDERAL REGISTER, a dissatisfied party may file a written "Petition for Reconsideration" (PFR).* Interested parties may file "Oppositions," which may trigger "Replies to Oppositions." The FCC reviews the petition and issues a MO&O denying the petition or issues an "Order on Reconsideration" that modifies the R&O.

---

* *See generally* 47 U.S.C. § 405. In certain cases, filing a petition for rehearing with the Commission may be a pre-requisite for challenging the agency's action in court. *See* 47 C.F.R. § 1.429(j) (identifying cases in which the person seeking review "was not a party to the proceeding . . . or relies on questions of fact or law upon which the Commission has been afforded no opportunity to pass").

3. Agency oversight

Many different types of oversight, ranging from informal to formal, exist over the Commission's work. For example, since the President appoints Commissioners, with Senate approval, the Executive Branch may be able to collect political debts and influence Commission decisionmaking. More formally, Congress can hold hearings and request answers, information, and testimony from the Commission and its staff.

Congress can also exercise the power of the purse, and condition agency funding on specific action. It can also pass direct legislation requiring the FCC to act (or not act) in a particular way. How the judiciary supervises the Commission is discussed below.

b. OTHER AGENCIES

Other federal agencies play an important role in law and policy concerning modern communications.

National Telecommunications & Information Administration (NTIA). A part of the U.S. Department of Commerce, the NTIA claims to be "the agency that is principally responsible by law for advising the President on telecommunications and information policy issues."[*] Query whether the NTIA is truly the principal voice; however, it does play an important role in representing the Administration's position before various fora, including the FCC. Operating partly as a think tank, NTIA also undertakes research and generates public policy reports used by policymakers, academics, and community advocates. Finally, this agency also manages the government's (including the military's) use of the e-m spectrum, which is becoming an increasingly significant issue as policymakers debate the proper allocation of spectrum between public and private sectors.

The Federal Trade Commission (FTC). An independent agency comprising a bipartisan group of five presidentially-appointed Commissioners, the FTC is charged with enforcing federal antitrust and consumer protection laws. The FTC's three Bureaus focus on: Consumer Protection, Competition, and Economics. The FTC's antitrust enforcement power is shared with the Department of Justice, Antitrust Division. The FTC's consumer protection mission is focused primarily on preventing and responding to "unfair or deceptive acts or practices."[†] The agency's Bureau of Consumer Protection is further subdivided into divisions focused on marketing practices, advertising

---

[*] https://www.ntia.doc.gov/about (last visited June 10, 2020).
[†] 15 U.S.C. § 45(a)(1).

practices, and financial practices, as well as the Division on Privacy and Identity Protection (DPIP). The FTC's DPIP has become increasingly important over the last two decades as the risk of identity theft and privacy violations have increased in the internet ecosystem.

Department of Justice, Antitrust Division: The Department of Justice (DOJ) enforces general antitrust laws that prohibit restraints on trade, price-fixing conspiracies, corporate mergers that undermine competition, and predatory acts designed to achieve or maintain monopoly power. The DOJ can bring both criminal and civil actions for violation of antitrust laws. DOJ antitrust enforcement led to the breakup of AT&T in 1984. Greater details about the enforcement of the nation's antitrust laws appear in CHAPTER 4: ACCESS.

3. COURTS

Obviously, federal courts play an important role in enforcing the substantive rights created by federal statute and the U.S. Constitution (such as the First Amendment). They also play an important role in reviewing the work of administrative agencies. Judicial review of agency action is necessary for many reasons, including the fact that agencies can exceed the powers delegated to them by Congress. In addition, agency actions may be irrational or violate the Constitution.

Let's focus specifically on FCC action, which can be directly reviewed by federal courts of appeals under the mutually exclusive provisions of 47 U.S.C. § 402(a) or (b). Under § 402(b), a "notice of appeal" can be filed to challenge a very narrow set of FCC decisions—specifically, FCC licensing and construction permit decisions. Venue lies exclusively with the U.S. Court of Appeals for the D.C. Circuit.

More generally, under § 402(a), a "petition for review" can be filed "to enjoin, set aside, annul, or suspend any order of the Commission under this Act." This includes rulemaking actions, policy statements, and declaratory rulings. This is the default procedural path for most judicial challenges to FCC action. Such proceedings are processed according to generic review procedures of agency action, as outlined in 28 U.S.C. ch. 158 (Orders of Federal Agencies; Review).

Venue lies in the judicial circuit in which the petitioner resides or has its principal office, or in the D.C. Circuit.[*] If the FCC is sued in multiple courts of appeal by multiple parties, the Commission must notify the Judicial Panel on

---

[*] *See* 28 U.S.C. § 2343.

Multidistrict Litigation, which randomly assigns the consolidated cases to one of the courts of appeal.* This random assignment procedure makes pointless any race to file petitions with specific courts.

That said, after random assignment, it is not unusual for parties to try to move the case to a preferred circuit via transfer†—often to the D.C. Circuit, which has historically shown skepticism of FCC regulation and has also developed significant expertise in communications cases. Besides considering the standard transfer factors, which are "the interest of justice" and "convenience of the parties," courts also consider whether the transferee court has had the same or interrelated proceeding previously. A mere similarity in topic is insufficient. As the U.S. Court of Appeals for the Sixth Circuit wrote, "the D.C. Circuit is not to function as a specialized tribunal with expertise in agency matters, and a general familiarity with the legal questions presented by case is decidedly different from acquaintance with the proceedings that gave rise to the order in suit."‡

To be clear, the judicial challenge does not go first to the district courts.§ Instead, per the "Hobbs Act," subject matter jurisdiction for direct review of FCC action lies with the federal court of appeals.

> 28 U.S.C. § 2342. Jurisdiction of court of appeals
>
> The court of appeals (other than the United States Court of Appeals for the Federal Circuit) has exclusive jurisdiction to enjoin, set aside, suspend (in whole or in part), or to determine the validity of—
>
> > (1) all final orders of the Federal Communications Commission made reviewable by section 402(a) of title 47

Upon review, an FCC action may be invalidated on three principal grounds. First, it may be contrary to the statutory command of Congress. For instance, if Congress explicitly told the FCC to issue a particular type of regulation and the

---

* *See* 28 U.S.C. § 2112(a)(3).

† *See* 28 USC §2112(a)(5) ("For the convenience of the parties in the interest of justice, the court in which the record is filed may thereafter transfer all the proceedings with respect to that order to any other court of appeals.").

‡ Order, United Church of Christ Office of Communications, Inc. v. FCC, Nos. 08-3245, 3369, 3370, 3450, 34522-3 (6th Cir. May 22, 2008) (internal quotation and citation omitted).

§ While the issue of proper venue to challenge FCC interpretations and rules is not often raised or debated, it was the subject of a U.S. Supreme Court case in 2019: PDR Network, LLC v. Carlton & Harris Chiropractic, LLC, 588 U.S. _____ , 139 S. Ct. 2051 (2019). Specifically, the Court considered whether district courts reviewing a private enforcement action claim (under the Telephone Consumer Protection Act of 1991) were bound to follow an applicable FCC Order because of the Hobbs Act. Without providing definitive answers, the Court explained that two prior questions would have to be answered. First, was the FCC Order merely "interpretive" (and not "legislative"), in which case the Order would not be binding. Second, did the party disputing the FCC Order have an adequate, prior opportunity to challenge the Order when it was originally issued, as required by the Administrative Procedure Act, 5 U.S.C. § 703.

FCC did just the opposite, then that regulation would be invalid. In reviewing the Commission's interpretation of a federal statute that the FCC administers, the courts apply what is known in administrative law as the *Chevron* doctrine. If Congress has spoken clearly on the particular issue, no deference is given to the agency interpretation. However, if the statute is "silent or ambiguous," then the court should only ask whether the agency interpretation "is based on a permissible construction of the statute."[*]

Second, the FCC action may be inconsistent with general rationality norms required of agency actions by the Administrative Procedure Act, 5 U.S.C. § 706, *et seq.* Most important, its action may be "arbitrary and capricious."[†]

Finally, the FCC action may be invalidated if it is unconstitutional. Since we are addressing communications, the First Amendment's protection of freedom of expression looms large in FCC litigation.

4. FEDERALISM

In the previous sections, we focused on how legal power was exercised horizontally by different branches of the federal government. What makes communications law more convoluted, however, is that government power is also shared vertically between the federal government and state and local government. This power-sharing arrangement is unusual and, by some accounts, unique to the United States. What follows is the briefest of summaries; federalism issues will be examined in greater detail throughout the text.

a. FEDERAL / STATE DIVIDE

Which branch of government, federal or state, can exercise power over a particular matter is fundamentally a question of federal constitutional law. The federal government is a government of limited powers. Accordingly, it must be able to point to some constitutional grant of affirmative power for each of its regulatory actions. Generally, the source of Congress's power to regulate telecommunications has been the Interstate Commerce Clause, U.S. CONST.,

---

[*] *See* Chevron v. NRDC, 467 U.S. 837, 843 (1984). This deference is only for statutes that the agency is charged to administer or interpret. *See, e.g.*, Garcia-Lopez v. Ashcroft, 334 F.3d 840, 843 (9th Cir. 2003) (declining to give *Chevron* deference to the Board of Immigration Appeal's interpretation of a California state statute). The Supreme Court recently added that *Chevron* deference also applies to an agency's interpretation of a statutory ambiguity regarding its own jurisdiction. *See* City of Arlington, TX v. FCC, 133 S. Ct. 1863 (2013).

[†] The exact phrase is "arbitrary, capricious, an abuse of discretion, or otherwise not in accordance with law." 5 U.S.C. § 706(2). Accordingly, some call this standard "arbitrary *or* capricious" although courts regularly call it "arbitrary *and* capricious." Nothing turns on this distinction.

ART. I, § 8, which has been read broadly. However, for telecommunication matters that are genuinely outside of the reach of the commerce clause, the federal government has no power to regulate.

More relevant are statutory constraints on FCC power, which draw an interstate-intrastate distinction. Since the 1934 Communications Act, the FCC has enjoyed jurisdiction over "*interstate and foreign* commerce in communication by wire and radio." 47 U.S.C. § 151 (emphasis added). However, the states retained their authority to regulate intrastate communication service. *See* § 152(b).

> 47 U.S.C. § 152. Application of chapter
>
> (b) Except as provided in [various sections] nothing in this chapter shall be construed to apply or to give the Commission jurisdiction with respect to (1) charges, classifications, practices, services, facilities, or regulations for or in connection with intrastate communication service by wire or radio of any carrier . . . .

We have subsequently moved away from the traditional boundaries between federal (interstate) and state governments (intrastate). For example, in 1993, Congress preempted state regulation of mobile telephony, much of which is obviously intrastate.[*] Similarly, the 1996 Telecommunications Act preempted crucial aspects of local telephone service that had previously been in the purview of state regulators.[†] In their place, we see what some call "cooperative federalism," in which states help implement federal policies set by the FCC.

However, in recent years this relationship has become strained as both states and municipalities have sought to play a more active role in both the development and regulation of their communications infrastructure. For example, many cities and municipalities have begun deploying their own broadband internet systems and some states have, in response, passed laws prohibiting such systems. The FCC attempted to preempt these state laws, but has been unsuccessful.[‡] Other states are now considering enacting legislation to impose "net neutrality" rules similar to those described in CHAPTER 4: ACCESS that the FCC recently repealed.

---

[*] *See* 47 U.S.C. § 332(c)(3) (preempting state and local governments from regulating entry or rates of commercial mobile radio services).

[†] *See, e.g.,* 47 U.S.C. § 253 (providing that no state or local law or regulation "may prohibit or have the effect of prohibiting the ability of any entity to provide any interstate or intrastate telecommunications service").

[‡] *See* Tennessee v. FCC, 832 F.3d 597 (6th Cir. 2016).

b. STATE PUBLIC UTILITIES COMMISSIONS

Each state has an independent regulatory commission, typically called a public utilities commission (PUC) or a public service commission (PSC). Created by state constitution or statute, these commissions have varying degrees of regulatory power over firms that fall under the rubric "public utilities."[*] State commissioners are typically appointed by governors with state senate approval, but some are directly elected.

Especially relevant to this course is the PUC's authority over wireline telephony. Although their powers differ as a function of state law, these commissions typically regulate the entry, pricing, and service quality of intrastate telephony. State commissions cooperate through the National Association of Regulatory Utility Commissioners (NARUC), especially on matters concerning the distribution of power between federal and state regulators.

State PUCs are also increasingly becoming the local franchising authorities that license cable television services on a state-wide basis. Historically, state law tended to designate a sub-state unit such as the county, municipality, or city as the franchising authority.

c. GLOBAL STRUCTURES

Just as communications cross state borders, they cross national borders. Not surprisingly, many of the issues that arise out of international communications are addressed by bilateral treaties between nations. For example, the United States and Mexico have numerous agreements to avoid broadcast interference along their shared border.[†] That said, many communications issues are fundamentally global and are addressed through international organizations.

European Union (EU) institutions. The EU comprises several of the world's most important international institutions, which date back to the formation of the European Economic Community (EC) in the Treaties of Rome in 1958. The EU was formed under the Maastricht Treaty in 1993 and was further integrated with EC institutions under the Treaty of Lisbon in 2009. The European Council is a summit of heads of state that provides general policy directions. The Council

---

[*] In California, for example, CAL. CONST. ART. XII, § 3 specifies the PUC's jurisdiction to include: "Private corporations and persons that own, operate, control, or manage a line, plant, or system for the transportation of people or property, the transmission of telephone and telegraph messages, or the production, generation, transmission, or furnishing of heat, light, water, power, storage, or wharfage directly or indirectly to or for the public, and common carriers..."

[†] The Department of State, with coordination of the FCC, the NTIA, and other federal agencies, negotiates such bilateral agreements.

of the European Union, which is responsible for concluding international agreements, acts together with the European Parliament as a legislative body. The Parliament also exerts democratic control over the European Commission, which is the executive branch responsible for implementing policies, administering the budget, and negotiating international agreements. The Court of Justice of the European Union (CJEU) acts as the judicial branch and ensures the uniform application and interpretation of European law. The EU also has a central bank and auditors responsible for the budget.

Because the EU represents a significant economic block, its laws and regulations have a major impact on international trade and economic policy. Since its modern inception, the EU has been actively engaged in implementing communications regulations, including those focused on privacy and data protection on the internet. More recently, the European Parliament and Council enacted a General Data Protection Regulation (GDPR), a comprehensive regime that governs how companies collect, handle, and protect EU citizens' personal data. This law will have a significant impact on data practices worldwide.

International Telecommunications Union (ITU). The ITU is the most important institution in international communications. Its origins can be traced back to agreements made in the 1860s by European nations regarding the telegraph. The ITU has since evolved to become a specialized agency of the United Nations (1947), expanding its scope far beyond the telegraph to telecommunications, radio broadcast, and satellites. The ITU's foundational documents are two multilateral treaties known as the ITU Constitution and the ITU Convention. Additional provisions for structure, procedure, and regulation are embodied in supplementary documents, such as the International Telecommunications Regulations and Radio Regulations.

The ITU plays a central role in e-m spectrum allocations. For example, four separate ITU multilateral agreements affect the use of AM broadcasting within the United States. (The transmission frequencies allocated to AM broadcasting can travel long distances at night, in the form of sky waves, bouncing off the ionosphere, and thus create international interference. In contrast, frequencies allocated to television broadcast are not the subject of ITU agreements because e-m waves at these frequencies do not travel as far.)

The ITU also manages satellite orbits. Historically, orbital assignments have been granted first-come, first-served. However, out of concern for developing nations, the ITU has reserved some orbits for every member of the ITU. Finally, the ITU conducts studies and makes recommendations with a view toward standardizing and assisting the development of telecommunications worldwide.

Some countries have called for more active ITU involvement in internet governance, to the consternation of some U.S. officials.

Internet Corporation for Assigned Names & Numbers (ICANN). The internet's design and reach requires an addressing scheme, called the domain name system, that ensures that each computer has a globally unique address. This naming system is controlled by ICANN, a private nonprofit California corporation created in 1998 to take over the administration of the internet's domain name system from the United States government and its agents. In addition to government representation, ICANN advisory committees include representation of commercial, civil society, technical, and other private interests. However, the ICANN Board of Directors has final decision-making authority. To increase legitimacy, ICANN's bylaws require some aspect of global representation in various leadership positions.

ICANN manages the "top level domains" on the internet (*e.g.,* .com, .uk, .biz) and accredits other companies to register domains within each top level domain. Through this accreditation mechanism, ICANN can set certain internet policies. For instance, ICANN requires registrars to follow the uniform dispute resolution policy (UDRP) to resolve disputes on domain name ownership. Also, ICANN is responsible for the stable operation of the "root" servers, which are ultimately responsible for what domains and other internet resources are available to all internet users.

In this chapter, we have examined the first concept essential to understanding communications law and policy: *power.* By power, we mean technological, economic, and legal power. The interplay of these three different types of power—wielded by individuals, corporations, and the state—generates the possibilities, problems, and the solutions featured in the rest of this text. Although this chapter required study of technology and economics, you now have a solid interdisciplinary foundation, with which to tackle the difficult communications issues to come.

CHAPTER 2

ENTRY

Consider the profession that you are training to *enter*. After graduating from law school, could you simply put out a shingle and provide legal services? The answer (perhaps regrettably) is no. To practice as an attorney, you must first receive permission from the state in the form of a license. This is not true of all professions. For instance, if you wanted to be a portrait painter, you would not need to get prior permission from the government before you started your business. Why the difference?

Imagine now that you are an entrepreneur ready to exploit some new communications technology. This could be radio broadcasting in the 1910s or the internet in the 1990s. Your technology allows people to communicate in novel and amazing ways. Your decision to enter this field will, of course, be a function of basic business and technological calculations, such as: Does the technology work? Also, will the public buy it at a price that allows an adequate return on investment?

But in addition to answering these questions, you need to determine if entry is also regulated by law—if you have to first obtain government permission. Entry into many communication services is regulated by the government. In this chapter, we focus on the broadcast, telephony, cable TV, and Internet as case studies. In our examination, a few basic questions repeatedly arise. Why should the government regulate entry? Is entry regulation consistent with the First Amendment, which protects the freedom of speech? Finally, how should the government regulate entry?

A. BROADCAST

1. TECHNOLOGY

The term "broadcast" refers to both over-the-air radio (audio) and over-the-air television (video). From a technological perspective, radio and television broadcasting operate similarly. Some message, whether audio or video, is converted into an e-m signal, then encoded onto a carrier wave that is radiated out from a transmitting antenna. These e-m waves propagate (wirelessly), at a particular frequency, using the spectrum as the channel. When those e-m signals arrive at a receiving antenna such as the "rabbit ears" on an old television set, they are decoded back into the audio or video message.

Since communications law is filled with both technological and legal terms-of-art, it's always helpful to look for concrete definitions. One place to start is 47 U.S.C. § 153, which is in Title I of the Communications Act. It lists some 50 definitions, including:

> 47 U.S.C. § 153. Definitions
>
> (5) Broadcast station. The term "broadcast station", "broadcasting station", or "radio broadcast station" means a radio station equipped to engage in broadcasting. . . .
>
> (6) Broadcasting. The term "broadcasting" means the dissemination of radio communications intended to be received by the public, directly or by . . . relay stations.
>
> (35) Radio station. The term "radio station" or "station" means a station equipped to engage in radio communication or radio transmission of energy.

You know that there are two bands of radio stations, AM (amplitude modulation) and FM (frequency modulation), which have historically been analog services. This is an appropriate point to study *modulation*, a basic concept relevant to all forms of e-m signal processing. Modulation simply means that some e-m carrier wave is being changed (i.e., modulated) in accordance with the message to be transmitted.

Amplitude modulation. In amplitude modulation (AM), the amplitude of some carrier wave is altered in accordance with the amplitude of the message signal. Recall that amplitude is one of the three basic properties of an e-m wave (the "height" in the typical diagram). The process looks like this.

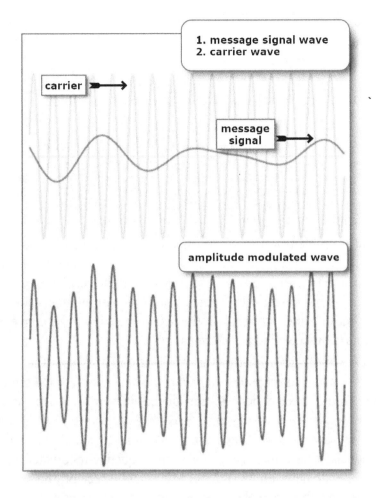

Figure 2.1: Amplitude Modulation

The carrier wave's frequency (i.e., the number of times per second the wave starts at zero, runs up to the crest, down to the trough, and back to zero) never changes. However, the wave's amplitude changes as a function of the message signal. If the message signal's height is high at one point, the carrier signal's amplitude increases; conversely, if the message signal's height is low at one point, the carrier signal's amplitude decreases. Once this modulated e-m signal is received, the modulation process can be reversed—the carrier signal is removed from the modulated signal—to reproduce the original message signal.

The FCC has allocated the AM radio service to carrier waves that operate between 535 and 1705 kHz. Each station is licensed by the FCC a bandwidth of 10 kHz, which is why your AM radio tunes in 10 kHz steps. Each step represents a potential carrier wave for a broadcast station.

If you were curious to find legal definitions and looked in volume 47 of the United States Code (where federal statutes regarding communications are codified), you wouldn't find anything as specific as "AM station." But another place to look is volume 47 of the Code of Federal Regulations, where the regulations that the FCC has enacted are compiled. For example:

> 47 C.F.R. § 73.14. AM broadcast definitions.
>
> *AM broadcast band.* The band of frequencies extending from 535 to 1705 kHz.
>
> *AM broadcast channel.* The band of frequencies occupied by the carrier and the upper and lower sidebands of an AM broadcast signal with the carrier frequency at the center. Channels are designated by their assigned carrier frequencies. The 117 carrier frequencies assigned to AM broadcast stations begin at 540 kHz and progress in 10 kHz steps to 1700 kHz. (See § 73.21 for the classification of AM broadcast channels).

One major problem with AM transmissions is noise. As the e-m waves travel through the spectrum channel, ambient e-m waves in the environment alter the amplitude of the transmitted waves, thus affecting the received signal. Because broadcast radio has historically been analog, any difference in amplitude is decoded to mean some difference in the actual message to be conveyed. Noise thus corrupts the received signal and message.

Frequency modulation. Frequency modulation (FM) uses the amplitude of the message signal to change the *frequency* of some carrier wave rather than its amplitude. Audio information is transduced into a message signal whose frequency ranges from 0 to 150 kHz. Each FM station is granted 200 kHz of bandwidth by law, which affords some padding to avoid interference with adjacent signals. These message signals are frequency-modulated onto carrier waves that operate between 88 and 108 MHz. Upon receipt, the carrier wave is removed, leaving the original message signal, which is transduced back into audio.

As noted above, ambient noise tends to alter amplitude but not frequency. FM transmissions therefore resist noise better than AM signals, which is one reason why FM radio sounds better than AM radio. Another reason is that FM stations are granted far more bandwidth: an FM message signal carries frequency ranges up to 150 kHz, whereas AM message signals are clipped at a maximum of 10 kHz. Because music often uses frequencies higher than 10 kHz, FM message signals have greater audio fidelity. It makes sense that talk radio formats appear mostly on AM stations since the lower fidelity matters less to their audience. Of course, FM's greater fidelity comes at a cost in bandwidth: A single AM station requires only 10 kHz; by contrast, a single FM station requires 200 kHz. In other words, one could squeeze 20 AM stations into the bandwidth taken up by one FM station.

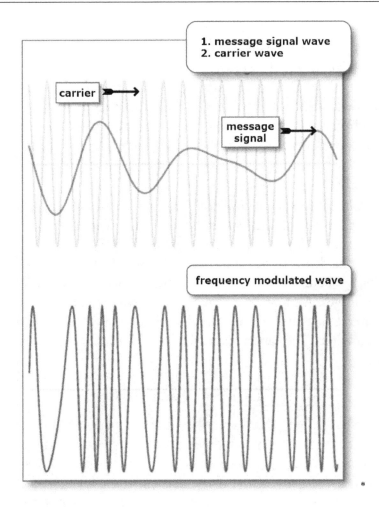

Figure 2.2: Frequency Modulation

The carrier wave frequencies allocated to FM radio propagate differently than the carrier wave frequencies allocated to AM radio. For example, the higher frequencies used by FM do not bounce off the ionosphere at night (something AM frequencies do), which means that the signals can travel only as far as the line-of-sight from the transmitting antenna.

Broadcast television. As with broadcast radio, the information contained in a television program is transduced into e-m waves that emanate from the transmitting antenna. Upon reception, these e-m waves produce an electric current pattern in the receiving antenna. Broadcast TV in the United States was originally an analog service. When it operated in analog mode, audio information

---

* Figures 2.1 and 2.2 were derived from images by Stephan Walter, available at http://commons.wiki media.org/wiki (CC Attribution ShareAlike 2.0).

was conveyed by frequency modulation (FM) while video information was conveyed by amplitude modulation (AM).

As you might expect, broadcast television shares many of the characteristics of broadcast radio. Differences are attributable to the video component of television broadcasts, which requires more bandwidth—6 MHz for analog television channels. (In other words, we could fit 30 FM radio stations or 600 AM radio stations into the bandwidth taken up by a single television station.) These message signals are modulated onto carrier waves, which for analog TV ranged from 54 to 806 MHz.

In the United States, full powered broadcast TV transitioned from analog to digital in June 2009. This means that the audio and video are now converted into a string of binary digits, which are then modulated onto the carrier signal (through a modulation scheme called 8VSB—8 level vestigial sideband modulation). There are substantial benefits to digital TV, including higher resolution images. Also, because digital signals can be more easily compressed, stations can actually carry multiple video streams in the 6 MHz of spectrum they have been granted. The carrier waves for digital broadcast TV range from 54 to 698 MHz.

NOTES & QUESTIONS

1. *Allocation.* The three different broadcast services—AM radio, FM radio, and TV—all use carrier waves in different frequency bands. These bands were *allocated* (a legal term of art) to these services by the FCC, as part of its management of the e-m spectrum. Legal regulation and history, much more than physics, explains why AM carrier waves are at one frequency range (535 and 1705 kHz) and FM (88 and 108 MHz) at another and so on. The legal allocation does have physical consequences, however. For example, carrier waves allocated to the AM band bounce off the ionosphere at night (called "skywaves") but the frequencies allocated to the FM band do not. The carrier waves allocated to TV are considered to be beachfront property, especially attractive for mobile telephony and data.

> 47 C.F.R. § 2.1. Allocation (of a frequency band)
>
> Entry in the Table of Frequency Allocations of a given frequency band for the purpose of its use by one or more terrestrial or space radiocommunication services or the radio astronomy service under specified conditions. This term shall also be applied to the frequency band concerned.

2. *Interference.* Suppose two adjacent radio stations broadcast interviews simultaneously. At each station, microphones convert the interview into analog e-m waves that vary in accordance with the human voices of the interviewer and

the person interviewed. Both stations then transmit the signals from their antennae, which radiate out spherical e-m waves to nearby residents. Both signals are products of human speech, which range across shared vocal frequencies; therefore, the signals could interfere with each other in the spectrum channel. To avoid interference, station operators need some way to send Station 1's message at one carrier frequency and Station 2's message at a different carrier frequency. Then the audience could tune their radios to one or the other frequency and receive either station without interference. Should the stations negotiate with each other privately and sign a contract to come to some mutually non-interfering arrangement?

3. *Assignment.* Instead of private negotiations, what if the government *assigned* (also a term of art) Station 1 to transmit its message on one carrier frequency (e.g., 88.1 MHz) and Station 2 to transmit on another carrier frequency (107.9 MHz). Because each station now uses a different part of the spectrum, there is no interference, and we can choose which signal to receive simply by tuning our radios to the appropriate carrier frequency.

> 47 C.F.R. § 2.1. Assignment (of a radio frequency or radio frequency channel)
> Authorization given by an administration for a radio station to use a radio frequency or radio frequency channel under specified conditions.

4. *A zoning analogy.* "Allocation" is like urban planning—setting permissible uses for various areas in the city; of course, instead of physical space, we are "zoning" the spectrum demarcated by frequency. Just as factories are built on one side of the town whereas single family homes are built on the other side, AM radio is allocated at one place on the radio frequency dial and TV is allocated to another. By contrast, "assignment" takes place only after allocation is finished. To continue the analogy, focus on the area zoned for single family homes. In this area, building permits must be given out to individual owners before any construction starts. Similarly, in the TV band, a station operator must be specifically assigned a license at a specific transmission frequency, geographical location, and power level.

5. *Mixing metaphors: trucks.* Think of the carrier signal as a truck that is designed to move on a particular "lane" (frequency) and can carry a message payload. As already explained, for AM radio, the message payload is placed on the carrier truck through amplitude modulation. As for the lanes, consider the total band *allocated* to AM radio services (535-1705 KHz) to be a strip of unmarked pavement (i.e. the AM highway). Without lines to create lanes, perhaps only one truck at a time could safely use the pavement. After all, if there were no lanes, trucks would be weaving in and out and crashing constantly.

However, by allotting 10 KHz-wide lanes per truck, and *assigning* each truck to a specific lane, dozens of trucks can use the highway safely at the same time.

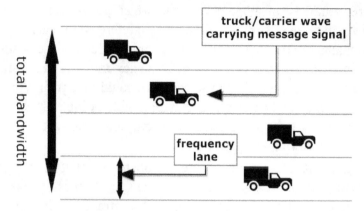

Figure 2.3: Frequency Division Multiplexing

Thus, at any given moment, dozens of trucks—each in its own frequency lane—are delivering their payloads to our radio receivers. By turning the dial, we tune the receiver to a particular lane. All of the channels are coming into the home (over the air), but only one modulated wave at a time gets stripped of information and converted back into the music we hear on the radio.

6. *Legal relevance.* This technical material explains what AM and FM stand for on your radio dial—something you may not have well understood before this course. More important, this discussion introduces you to the concept of interference in broadcasting, and how assigning specific carrier waves to specific stations can solve the problem.

2. CONTEXT

By the late 1830s, the telegraph had been invented and patented. This invention allowed communication over great distances, via e-m signals (i.e., the dots and dashes of Morse code), carried along long stretches of copper wire strung up on wooden poles. But it was not until the 1870s and 1880s that physicists began to understand better the connection between electricity and magnetism, through the work of physicists James Maxwell and Heinrich Hertz. This research allowed Guglielmo Marconi in the latter half of the 1890s to invent, patent, and bring to market what he called the "wireless telegraph"—a way to transmit signals without the wire.

It did not take long for the wireless telegraph (one-to-one communication service, transmitting Morse code) to be converted into broadcast (one-to-many, transmitting audio). On Christmas Eve 1906, Reginald Aubrey Fessenden made the first musical and vocal AM radio broadcast from a station he built at Brant Rock, Massachusetts. He played "O, Holy Night" on the violin to ships in the Atlantic. By 1910 music from the Metropolitan Opera House was broadcast to a New York audience.

As more individuals started to experiment with the new wireless technology, interference became a major problem: To use our truck analogy, no one was required to drive on any specific lane, so folks tried to occupy the same lane at the same time. There was special concern about interference with emergency distress signals and Navy communications. For example, when the ship Titanic sank in 1912, interference hindered rescue operations and produced faulty news reports. Accordingly, with little debate, Congress passed the Radio Act of 1912, which for the first time required all radio broadcasters to obtain a federal license.

> Radio Act of 1912, 37 Stat. 302 (Aug. 13, 1912)
>
> [A] person, company, or corporation within the jurisdiction of the United States shall not use or operate any apparatus for radio communication as a means of commercial intercourse among the several States, or with foreign nations, or upon any vessel of the United States engaged in interstate or foreign commerce, or for the transmission of radiograms or signals the effect of which extends beyond the jurisdiction of the State or Territory in which the same are made, or where interference would be caused thereby with the receipt of messages or signals from beyond the jurisdiction of the said State or Territory, except under and in accordance with a license, revocable for cause, in that behalf granted by the Secretary of Commerce . . . .

After World War I—during which time the Navy took practical control of the airwaves by taking over important ship-to-shore transmitters—broadcasting began to expand as a commercial industry. In 1920, Westinghouse's KDKA in Pittsburgh, Pennsylvania, became the first commercial radio station in the United States. By 1924 more than 1,000 radio stations were in operation in the United States. Not surprisingly, the problem of interference intensified.

From 1922 to 1927, Herbert Hoover, then Secretary of Commerce (and later President), attempted to manage the interference problem by moving broadcasters from frequency to frequency or requiring time-sharing at the same frequency, on a case-by-case basis. However, Hoover was managing the situation without express legal authority to do so. Eventually, the judiciary recognized as much.[*] The ensuing chaos forced Congress to act.

Act it did, by passing the Radio Act of 1927,[†] the first attempt to create a comprehensive scheme for regulating broadcasting. The Radio Act made clear that the electromagnetic spectrum is not private property; it is owned by the

---

[*] *See* Hoover v. Intercity Radio Co., 286 F. 1003 (D.C. Cir. 1923); United States v. Zenith Radio, 12 F.2d 614 (N.D. Ill. 1926).

[†] 44 STAT. 1162 (1927).

government and held in public trust. The government licenses the spectrum to private parties in order to further the "public interest, convenience or necessity." The 1927 Act also created the Federal Radio Commission, the precursor to the FCC. Seven years later, Congress passed the Communications Act of 1934, which created the FCC. This Act was passed to bring the regulatory powers held by the Federal Radio Commission and the power to regulate common carriage (telephones) then exercised by the Interstate Commerce Commission (ICC) under a single new agency.

As for television, in the 1920s and 1930s much of the basic technology necessary for television broadcasting was developed, but television did not take off until 1939, when the first commercial set was made available for purchase and regular TV broadcasts began. In the 1940s, color television was introduced. Indeed, only hours after the bombing of Pearl Harbor on December 7, 1941, CBS station WCBW in New York presented a special news show that included pictures, maps, charts, and montage effects all illustrating television's extraordinary power.

The following case, *NBC v. United States* (1943), was seminal in establishing the legal power to regulate broadcast. Here is some useful context. Created in 1926, the National Broadcasting Corporation (NBC) was the first radio "network." A subsidiary of the powerful Radio Corporation of America (RCA), NBC owned a few radio stations. More important was its creation of high quality radio content and its national distribution to affiliated stations. The only other competitor network was Columbia Broadcasting System (CBS), which was created two years later in 1928.

Concerned that affiliate stations were increasingly becoming mere puppets of these radio networks, the FCC promulgated regulations against "chain broadcasting," which was defined as "simultaneous broadcasting of an identical program by two or more connected stations."[*] The goal was to decrease the power of national radio networks, such as NBC, and to fortify the affiliate station's independence. NBC challenged these regulations in court.

---

[*] 47 U.S.C. § 153(9) (defining "chain broadcasting").

3. SPECTRUM SCARCITY

NBC v. UNITED STATES
319 U.S. 190 (1943)

Mr. Justice FRANKFURTER delivered the opinion of the Court.

These suits were brought . . . to enjoin the enforcement of the Chain Broadcasting Regulations promulgated by the Federal Communications Commission . . . .

The Commission found that at the end of 1938 there were 660 commercial stations in the United States, and that 341 of these were affiliated with national networks. 135 stations were affiliated exclusively with the National Broadcasting Company, Inc., known in the industry as NBC, which operated two national networks, the 'Red' and the 'Blue'. NBC was also the licensee of 10 stations, including 7 which operated on so-called clear channels with the maximum power available, 50 kilowatts . . . . 102 stations were affiliated exclusively with the Columbia Broadcasting System, Inc., which was also the licensee of 8 stations, 7 of which were clear-channel stations operating with power of 50 kilowatts. . . . In addition, 25 stations were affiliated with both NBC and Mutual, and 5 with both CBS and Mutual. . . . [The Commission] pointed out that the stations affiliated with the national networks utilized more than 97% of the total night-time broadcasting power of all the stations in the country. NBC and CBS together controlled more than 85% of the total night-time wattage, and the broadcast business of the three national network companies amounted to almost half of the total business of all stations in the United States.

The Commission found that eight network abuses were amenable to correction within the powers granted it by Congress . . . . [The Court next summarized these abuses, and the regulations designed to stop them.]

The appellants attack the validity of these Regulations along many fronts. They contend that the Commission went beyond the regulatory powers conferred upon it by the Communications Act of 1934; . . . and that, in any event, the Regulations abridge the appellants' right of free speech in violation of the First Amendment. We are thus called upon to determine whether Congress has authorized the Commission to exercise the power asserted by the Chain Broadcasting Regulations, and if it has, whether the Constitution forbids the exercise of such authority.

Federal regulation of radio begins with the Wireless Ship Act of June 24, 1910, which forbade any steamer carrying or licensed to carry fifty or more persons to leave any American port unless equipped with efficient apparatus for radio communication, in charge of a skilled operator.... But it was not until 1912, when the United States ratified the first international radio treaty, that the need for general regulation of radio communication became urgent. In order to fulfill our obligations under the treaty, Congress enacted the Radio-Communications Act of August 13, 1912. This statute forbade the operation of radio apparatus without a license from the Secretary of Commerce and Labor. ...

The enforcement of the Radio Act of 1912 presented no serious problems prior to the World War. Questions of interference arose only rarely because there were more than enough frequencies for all the stations then in existence. The war accelerated the development of the art, however, and in 1921 the first standard broadcast stations were established. They grew rapidly in number, and by 1923 there were several hundred such stations throughout the country. The Act of 1912 had not set aside any particular frequencies for the use of private broadcast stations; consequently, the Secretary of Commerce selected two frequencies, 750 and 833 kilocycles, and licensed all stations to operate upon one or the other of these channels. The number of stations increased so rapidly, however, and the situation became so chaotic, that the Secretary, upon the recommendation of the National Radio Conferences which met in Washington in 1923 and 1924, established a policy of assigning specified frequencies to particular stations. The entire radio spectrum was divided into numerous bands, each allocated to a particular kind of service. The frequencies ranging from 550 to 1500 kilocycles (96 channels in all, since the channels were separated from each other by 10 kilocycles) were assigned to the standard broadcast stations. But the problems created by the enormously rapid development of radio were far from solved. The increase in the number of channels was not enough to take care of the constantly growing number of stations. Since there were more stations than available frequencies, the Secretary of Commerce attempted to find room for everybody by limiting the power and hours of operation of stations in order that several stations might use the same channel. The number of stations multiplied so rapidly, however, that by November, 1925, there were almost 600 stations in the country, and there were 175 applications for new stations. Every channel in the standard broadcast band was, by that time, already occupied by at least one station, and many by several.... The National Radio Conference which met in November, 1925 ... called upon Congress to remedy the situation through legislation.

The Secretary of Commerce was powerless to deal with the situation. It had been held that he could not deny a license to an otherwise legally qualified applicant on the ground that the proposed station would interfere with existing private or Government stations. *Hoover v. Intercity Radio Co....* [A]n Illinois district court held that the Secretary had no power to impose restrictions as to frequency, power, and hours of operation, and that a station's use of a frequency not assigned to it was not a violation of the Radio Act of 1912. *United States v. Zenith Radio Corp.* This was followed ... by an opinion of Acting Attorney General Donovan that the Secretary of Commerce had no power, under the Radio Act of 1912, to regulate the power, frequency or hours of operation of stations. The next day the Secretary of Commerce issued a statement abandoning all his efforts to regulate radio and urging that the stations undertake self-regulation.

But the plea of the Secretary went unheeded. From July, 1926, to February 23, 1927, when Congress enacted the Radio Act of 1927, almost 200 new stations went on the air. These new stations used any frequencies they desired, regardless of the interference.... Existing stations changed to other frequencies and increased their power and hours of operation at will. The result was confusion and chaos. With everybody on the air, nobody could be heard.

The plight ... was attributable to certain basic facts about radio as a means of communication—its facilities are limited; they are not available to all who may wish to use them; the radio spectrum simply is not large enough to accommodate everybody. There is a fixed natural limitation upon the number of stations that can operate without interfering with one another. Regulation of radio was therefore as vital to its development as traffic control was to the development of the automobile. In enacting the Radio Act of 1927, the first comprehensive scheme of control over radio communication, Congress acted upon the knowledge that if the potentialities of radio were not to be wasted, regulation was essential.

The Radio Act of 1927 created the Federal Radio Commission, composed of five members, and endowed the Commission with wide licensing and regulatory powers. We do not pause here to enumerate the scope of the Radio Act of 1927 and of the authority entrusted to the Radio Commission, for the basic provisions of that Act are incorporated in the Communications Act of 1934, the legislation immediately before us.

Section 1 of the Communications Act states its 'purpose of regulating interstate and foreign commerce in communication by wire and radio so as to make available, so far as possible, to all the people of the United States a rapid, efficient, Nationwide, and world-wide wire and radio communication service with adequate facilities at reasonable charges'. Section 301 particularizes this general purpose with respect to radio: 'It is the purpose of this Act, among other things, to maintain the control of the United States over all the channels of interstate and foreign radio transmission; and to provide for the use of such channels, but not the ownership thereof, by persons for limited periods of time, under licenses granted by Federal authority, and no such license shall be construed to create any right, beyond the terms, conditions, and periods of the license.' To that end a Commission composed of seven members was created, with broad licensing and regulatory powers.

The Act itself establishes that the Commission's powers are not limited to the engineering and technical aspects of regulation of radio communication. Yet we are asked to regard the Commission as a kind of traffic officer, policing the wave lengths to prevent stations from interfering with each other. But the Act does not restrict the Commission merely to supervision of the traffic. It puts upon the Commission the burden of determining the composition of that traffic. The facilities of radio are not large enough to accommodate all who wish to use them. Methods must be devised for choosing from among the many who apply. And since Congress itself could not do this, it committed the task to the Commission.

The Commission was, however, not left at large in performing this duty. The touchstone provided by Congress was the 'public interest, convenience, or necessity', a criterion which 'is as concrete as the complicated factors for judgment in such a field of delegated authority permit'. *Federal Communications Comm. v. Pottsville Broadcasting Co.* 'This criterion is not to be interpreted as setting up a standard so indefinite as to confer an unlimited power. The requirement is to be interpreted by its context, by the nature of radio transmission and reception, by the scope, character, and quality of services. . . .' *Federal Radio Communications v. Nelson Bros. Bond & Mortgage Co.*

The 'public interest' to be served under the Communications Act is thus the interest of the listening public in 'the larger and more effective use of radio'. § 303(g). The facilities of radio are limited and therefore precious; they cannot be left to wasteful use without detriment to the public interest. 'An important element of public interest and convenience affecting the issue of a license is the ability of the licensee to render the best practicable service to the community reached by his broadcasts.' *Federal Communications Comm. v. Sanders Bros. Radio Station.* The Commission's licensing function cannot be discharged, therefore, merely by finding that there are no technological objections to the granting of a license. If the criterion of 'public interest' were limited to such matters, how could the Commission choose between two applicants for the same facilities, each of whom is financially and technically qualified to operate a station? Since the very inception of federal regulation by radio, comparative considerations as to the services to be rendered have governed the application of the standard of 'public interest, convenience, or necessity'.

The avowed aim of the Communications Act of 1934 was to secure the maximum benefits of radio to all the people of the United States. To that end Congress endowed the Communications Commission with comprehensive powers to promote and realize the vast potentialities of radio. Section 303(g) provides that the Commission shall 'generally encourage the larger and more effective use of radio in the public interest'; subsection (i) gives the Commission specific 'authority to make special regulations applicable to radio stations engaged in chain broadcasting'; and subsection (r) empowers it to adopt 'such rules and regulations and prescribe such restrictions and conditions, not inconsistent with law, as may be necessary to carry out the provisions of this Act'.

These provisions, individually and in the aggregate, preclude the notion that the Commission is empowered to deal only with technical and engineering impediments to the 'larger and more effective use of radio in the public interest'. We cannot find in the Act any such restriction of the Commission's authority. Suppose, for example, that a community can, because of physical limitations, be assigned only two stations. That community might be deprived of effective service in any one of several ways. More powerful stations in nearby cities might blanket out the signals of the local stations so that they could not be heard at all. The stations might interfere with each other so that neither could be clearly heard. One station might dominate the other with the power of its signal. But the community could be deprived of good radio service in ways less crude. One man, financially and technically qualified, might apply for and obtain the licenses of both stations and present a single service over the two stations, thus wasting a frequency otherwise available to the area. The language of the Act does not withdraw such a situation from the licensing and regulatory powers of the Commission, and there is no evidence that Congress did not mean its broad language to carry the authority it expresses.

In essence, the Chain Broadcasting Regulations represent a particularization of the Commission's conception of the 'public interest' sought to be safeguarded by Congress in enacting the Communications Act of 1934. The basic consideration of policy underlying the Regulations is succinctly stated in its Report: 'With the number of radio channels limited by natural factors, the public interest demands that those who are entrusted with the available channels shall make the fullest and most effective use of them. If a licensee enters into a contract with a network organization which limits his ability to make the best use of the radio facility assigned him, he is not serving the public interest....

We come, finally, to an appeal to the First Amendment. The Regulations, even if valid in all other respects, must fall because they abridge, say the appellants, their right of free speech. If that be so, it would follow that every person whose application for a license to operate a station is denied by the Commission is thereby denied his constitutional right of free speech. Freedom of utterance is abridged to many who wish to use the limited facilities of radio. Unlike other modes of expression, radio inherently is not available to all. That is its unique characteristic, and that is why, unlike other modes of expression, it is subject to governmental regulation. Because it cannot be used by all, some who wish to use it must be denied. But Congress did not authorize the Commission to choose among applicants upon the basis of their political, economic or social views, or upon any other capricious basis. If it did, or if the Commission by these Regulations proposed a choice among applicants upon some such basis, the issue before us would be wholly different. The question here is simply whether the Commission, by announcing that it will refuse licenses to persons who engage in specified network practices (a basis for choice which we hold is comprehended within the statutory criterion of 'public interest'), is thereby denying such persons the constitutional right of free speech. The right of free speech does not include, however, the right to use the facilities of radio without a license. The licensing system established by Congress in the Communications Act of 1934 was a proper exercise of its power over commerce. The standard it provided for the licensing of stations was the 'public interest, convenience, or necessity.' Denial of a station license on that ground, if valid under the Act, is not a denial of free speech. *Affirmed.*[*]

NOTES & QUESTIONS

1. *Licensing requirement.* To understand the mechanics of how the FCC controls entry into broadcasting, start with Title III of the Communications Act of 1934, which regulates broadcast. Title III begins with 47 U.S.C. § 301, which makes clear that spectrum is owned by the United States; that no one may broadcast without a license from the federal government; and that a license does not create any fee simple property rights. Instead, a license is simply that— permission to use the spectrum at a particular frequency, geographical area, and power level. As made explicit in § 307(c)(1), that permission is limited in time— currently, eight years. (Back when *NBC v. FCC* was being litigated, the license duration for broadcast was only 2 years). *See also* § 309(h) (making clear the limited license rights that are given to applicants). In § 303, the FCC is

---

[*] Justice Murphy's dissent, which was joined by Justice Roberts, has been deleted.—ED.

empowered to manage e-m frequency allocation to further the "public convenience, interest, or necessity" (the "public interest" standard). In particular, the FCC is given the power to assign frequencies to individual stations. § 303(c). The general standard for granting licenses is whether the public interest would thereby be served. § 309.

    2. *Policy justification.*

        a. *Interference or scarcity?* Make sure you understand the policy justification for requiring federal regulation of entry into broadcasting. At times, the court speaks of what might be called *interference*: "confusion and chaos." At other times, the court emphasizes *scarcity*: "the radio spectrum simply is not large enough to accommodate everybody." Are interference and scarcity identical concepts? If not, in what ways are they related?

> 47 C.F.R. § 2.1. Interference
>
> The effect of unwanted energy due to one or a combination of emissions, radiations, or inductions upon reception in a radiocommunication system, manifested by any performance degradation, misinterpretation, or loss of information which could be extracted in the absence of such unwanted energy.

        b. *Other justifications.* Are these justifications (interference and scarcity) common to all entry regulations? Compare, for example, state laws that require attorneys to be licensed to practice. Do such regulations exist because lawyers might interfere with each other and because the number of practicing lawyers is capped by technology and nature?

    3. *Technological versus legal power.* In CHAPTER 1: POWER, we studied three different types of power: technological, economic, and legal. In one sense, *NBC v. United States* represents a tension between technological and legal power. The technological power is the ability to transmit one's message from a distance in ways that interfere with others doing the same. What was the legal power response?

    4. *Legal authority: affirmative delegation of power.* Just because something sounds like a good idea does not mean that the FCC has the power to do it. Remember that an independent agency such as the FCC is a creature of limited powers created by Congress. Congress, however, did grant to the FCC full authority to issue licenses in the 1927 Radio Act as well as in the 1934 Communications Act. *See* 47 U.S.C. § 301. Other relevant powers are listed below.

> 47 U.S.C. § 303. Powers and duties of Commission
>
> (i) Have authority to make special regulations applicable to radio stations engaged in chain broadcasting;
>
> (r) Make such rules and regulations and prescribe such restrictions and conditions, not inconsistent with law, as may be necessary to carry out the provisions of this Act, or any

| | international radio or wire communications treaty or convention, or regulations annexed | |
| | thereto, including any treaty or convention insofar as it relates to the use of radio . . . | |

5. *First Amendment: negative limitation on power.*

a. *Books.* Suppose that before one could publish a book, magazine, or newspaper article, a federal license was necessary. After all, such publications can do tremendous harm, such as defame innocent private figures. Under current First Amendment doctrine, such a policy would constitute an impermissible prior restraint on speech. This is standard First Amendment wisdom, but it is not so easy to cite a case as clean authority.[*]

b. *Broadcast.* But isn't a broadcast license requirement the same thing? If so, do you have the same gut reaction? Should you? According to the courts, no. For instance, in a celebrated 1932 case concerning the Reverend Doctor Schuler, the FCC refused to renew his station's license on grounds of repeated defamation. The D.C. Circuit made clear that although prior restraints are frowned upon, this licensing decision was constitutional.

> "It is enough now to say that the universal trend of decisions has recognized the guaranty of the amendment to prevent previous restraints upon publications, as well as immunity of censorship, leading to correction by subsequent punishment those utterances or publications contrary to the public welfare. . . . But this does not mean that the government, through agencies establish by Congress, may not refuse a renewal of license to one who has abused it to broadcast defamatory and untrue matter. In that case there is not a denial of the freedom of speech, but merely the application of the regulatory power of Congress in a field within the scope of its legislative authority." [†]

6. *Scarcity ascendant.* In the next two cases, we continue our exploration of the scarcity rationale. A conceptual note: These cases do not directly concern entry, the subject of this chapter. Rather, they both involve a "right of reply," which organizationally could appear later in CHAPTER 4: ACCESS. That said, they relate centrally to the principal rationale for regulating broadcast *entry* and are too important to delay.

---

[*] *See, e.g.,* Matthew L. Spitzer, *The Constitutionality of Licensing Broadcasters,* 64 N.Y.U. L. REV. 990, 993 (1989) ("Although it is virtually impossible to find a case that directly so holds, it is fairly clear that any attempt to license a newspaper or magazine would violate the Constitution.").

[†] Trinity Methodist Church v. FRC, 62 F.2d 850 (D.C. Cir. 1932). *See also* KFKB Broad. Ass'n v. Fed. Radio Comm'n, 47 F.2d 670 (D.C. Cir. 1931) (the case of the "goat-gland doctor").

RED LION BROADCASTING CO. V. FCC

395 U.S. 367 (1969)

Mr. Justice WHITE delivered the opinion of the Court.

The Federal Communications Commission has for many years imposed on radio and television broadcasters the requirement that discussion of public issues be presented on broadcast stations, and that each side of those issues must be given fair coverage. This is known as the fairness doctrine. . . .

The Red Lion Broadcasting Company is licensed to operate a Pennsylvania radio station, WGCB. On November 27, 1964, WGCB carried a 15-minute broadcast by the Reverend Billy James Hargis as part of a 'Christian Crusade' series. A book by Fred J. Cook entitled 'Goldwater—Extremist on the Right' was discussed by Hargis, who said that Cook had been fired by a newspaper for making false charges against city officials; that Cook had then worked for a Communist-affiliated publication; that he had defended Alger Hiss and attacked J. Edgar Hoover and the Central Intelligence Agency; and that he had now written a 'book to smear and destroy Barry Goldwater.' When Cook heard of the broadcast he concluded that he had been personally attacked and demanded free reply time, which the station refused. . . . [T]he FCC declared that the Hargis broadcast constituted a personal attack on Cook [and that] the station must provide reply time. . . . On review in the Court of Appeals for the District of Columbia Circuit, the FCC's position was upheld. . . .

The broadcasters challenge the fairness doctrine and its specific manifestations in the personal attack and political editorial rules on conventional First Amendment grounds. . . .

A.

Although broadcasting is clearly a medium affected by a First Amendment interest, differences in the characteristics of new media justify differences in the First Amendment standards applied to them. *Joseph Burstyn, Inc. v. Wilson* (1952). For example, the ability of new technology to produce sounds more raucous than those of the human voice justifies restrictions on the sound level, and on the hours and places of use, of sound trucks so long as the restrictions are reasonable and applied without discrimination. *Kovacs v. Cooper* (1949).

Just as the Government may limit the use of sound-amplifying equipment potentially so noisy that it drowns out civilized private speech, so may the Government limit the use of broadcast equipment. The right of free speech of a broadcaster, the user of a sound truck, or any other individual does not embrace a right to snuff out the free speech of others. *Associated Press v. United States* (1945).

When two people converse face to face, both should not speak at once if either is to be clearly understood. But the range of the human voice is so limited that there could be meaningful communications if half the people in the United States were talking and the other half listening. Just as clearly, half the people might publish and the other half read. But the reach of radio signals is incomparably greater than the range of the human voice and the problem of interference is a massive reality. The lack of know-how and equipment may keep many from the air, but only a tiny fraction of those with resources and intelligence can hope to communicate by radio at the same time if intelligible communication is to be had, even if the entire radio spectrum is utilized in the present state of commercially acceptable technology.

It was this fact, and the chaos which ensued from permitting anyone to use any frequency at whatever power level he wished, which made necessary the enactment of the Radio Act of 1927 and the Communications Act of 1934, as the Court has noted at length before.

Where there are substantially more individuals who want to broadcast than there are frequencies to allocate, it is idle to posit an unabridgeable First Amendment right to broadcast comparable to the right of every individual to speak, write, or publish. If 100 persons want broadcast licenses but there are only 10 frequencies to allocate, all of them may have the same 'right' to a license; but if there is to be any effective communication by radio, only a few can be licensed and the rest must be barred from the airwaves. It would be strange if the First Amendment, aimed at protecting and furthering communications, prevented the Government from making radio communication possible by requiring licenses to broadcast and by limiting the number of licenses so as not to overcrowd the spectrum.

This has been the consistent view of the Court. Congress unquestionably has the power to grant and deny licenses and to eliminate existing stations. *FRC v. Nelson Bros. Bond & Mortgage Co.* (1933). No one has a First Amendment right to a license or to monopolize a radio frequency; to deny a station license because 'the public interest' requires it 'is not a denial of free speech.' *National Broadcasting Co. v. United States* (1943).

By the same token, as far as the First Amendment is concerned those who are licensed stand no better than those to whom licenses are refused. A license permits broadcasting, but the licensee has no constitutional right to be the one who holds the license or to monopolize a radio frequency to the exclusion of his fellow citizens. There is nothing in the First Amendment which prevents the

Government from requiring a licensee to share his frequency with others and to conduct himself as a proxy or fiduciary with obligations to present those views and voices which are representative of his community and which would otherwise, by necessity, be barred from the airwaves.

This is not to say that the First Amendment is irrelevant to public broadcasting. On the contrary, it has a major role to play as the Congress itself recognized in § 326, which forbids FCC interference with 'the right of free speech by means of radio communication.' Because of the scarcity of radio frequencies, the Government is permitted to put restraints on licensees in favor of others whose views should be expressed on this unique medium. But the people as a whole retain their interest in free speech by radio and their collective right to have the medium function consistently with the ends and purposes of the First Amendment. It is the right of the viewers and listeners, not the right of the broadcasters, which is paramount. *See FCC v. Sanders Bros. Radio Station* (1940); *FCC v. Allentown Broadcasting Corp.* (1955). It is the purpose of the First Amendment to preserve an uninhibited marketplace of ideas in which truth will ultimately prevail, rather than to countenance monopolization of that market, whether it be by the Government itself or a private licensee. *Associated Press v. United States* (1945); *New York Times Co. v. Sullivan* (1964); *Abrams v. United States* (1919) (Holmes, J., dissenting). '(S)peech concerning public affairs is more than self-expression; it is the essence of self-government.' *Garrison v. Louisiana* (1964). It is the right of the public to receive suitable access to social, political, esthetic, moral, and other ideas and experiences which is crucial here. That right may not constitutionally be abridged either by Congress or by the FCC.

B.

Rather than confer frequency monopolies on a relatively small number of licensees, in a Nation of 200,000,000, the Government could surely have decreed that each frequency should be shared among all or some of those who wish to use it, each being assigned a portion of the broadcast day or the broadcast week. The ruling and regulations at issue here do not go quite so far. They assert that under specified circumstances, a licensee must offer to make available a reasonable amount of broadcast time to those who have a view different from that which has already been expressed on his station. The expression of a political endorsement, or of a personal attack while dealing with a controversial public issue, simply triggers this time sharing. As we have said, the First Amendment confers no right on licensees to prevent others from broadcasting on 'their' frequencies and no right to an unconditional monopoly of a scarce resource which the Government has denied others the right to use.

In terms of constitutional principle, and as enforced sharing of a scarce resource, the personal attack and political editorial rules are indistinguishable from the equal-time provision of § 315, a specific enactment of Congress requiring stations to set aside reply time under specified circumstances and to which the fairness doctrine and these constituent regulations are important complements. That provision, which has been part of the law since [the] Radio Act of 1927, has been held valid by this Court.... The constitutionality of the statute under the First Amendment was unquestioned. *Farmers Educ. & Coop. Union v. WDAY* (1959).

Nor can we say that it is inconsistent with the First Amendment goal of producing an informed public capable of conducting its own affairs to require a broadcaster to permit answers to personal attacks occurring in the course of discussing controversial issues, or to require that the political opponents of those endorsed by the station be given a chance to communicate with the public. Otherwise, station owners and a few networks would have unfettered power to make time available only to the highest bidders, to communicate only their own views on public issues, people and candidates, and to permit on the air only those with whom they agreed. There is no sanctuary in the First Amendment for unlimited private censorship operating in a medium not open to all. 'Freedom of the press from governmental interference under the First Amendment does not sanction repression of that freedom by private interests.' *Associated Press v. United States* (1945).

C.

It is strenuously argued, however, that if political editorials or personal attacks will trigger an obligation in broadcasters ... then broadcasters will be irresistibly forced to self-censorship and their coverage of controversial public issues will be eliminated or at least rendered wholly ineffective.

At this point, however, as the Federal Communications Commission has indicated, that possibility is at best speculative. The communications industry, and in particular the networks, have taken pains to present controversial issues in the past, and even now they do not assert that they intend to abandon their efforts in this regard.... [I]f experience with the administration of those doctrines indicates that they have the net effect of reducing rather than enhancing the volume and quality of coverage, there will be time enough to reconsider the constitutional implications. The fairness doctrine in the past has had no such overall effect.

[Also,] the Commission is not powerless to insist that they give adequate and fair attention to public issues. It does not violate the First Amendment to treat licensees given the privilege of using scarce radio frequencies as proxies for the entire community, obligated to give suitable time and attention to matters of great public concern. To condition the granting or renewal of licenses on a willingness to present representative community views on controversial issues is consistent with the ends and purposes of those constitutional provisions forbidding the abridgment of freedom of speech and freedom of the press. Congress need not stand idly by and permit those with licenses to ignore the problems which beset the people or to exclude from the airways anything but their own views of fundamental questions.

D.

We need not and do not now ratify every past and future decision by the FCC with regard to programming. There is no question here of the Commission's refusal to permit the broadcaster to carry a particular program or to publish his own views; of a discriminatory refusal to require the licensee to broadcast certain views which have been denied access to the airwaves; of government censorship of a particular program contrary to § 326; or of the official government view dominating public broadcasting. Such questions would raise more serious First Amendment issues.

E.

It is argued that even if at one time [there was a] lack of available frequencies . . . this condition no longer prevails so that continuing [government] control is not justified. To this there are several answers.

Scarcity is not entirely a thing of the past. Advances in technology, such as microwave transmission, have led to more efficient utilization of the frequency spectrum, but uses for that spectrum have also grown apace. Portions of the spectrum must be reserved for vital uses unconnected with human communication, such as radio-navigational aids used by aircraft and vessels. . . . 'Land mobile services' such as police, ambulance, fire department, public utility, and other communications systems have been occupying an increasingly crowded portion of the frequency spectrum and there are, apart from licensed amateur radio operators' equipment, 5,000,000 transmitters operated on the 'citizens' band' which is also increasingly congested. Among the various uses for radio frequency space, including marine, aviation, amateur, military, and common carrier users, there are easily enough claimants to permit use of the whole with an even smaller allocation to broadcast radio and television uses than now exists.

The rapidity with which technological advances succeed one another to create more efficient use of spectrum space on the one hand, and to create new uses for that space by ever growing numbers of people on the other, makes it unwise to speculate on the future allocation of that space.... Nothing in this record, or in our own researches, convinces us that the resource is no longer one for which there are more immediate and potential uses than can be accommodated, and for which wise planning is essential.

Even where there are gaps in spectrum utilization, the fact remains that existing broadcasters have often attained their present position because of their initial government selection in competition with others before new technological advances opened new opportunities for further uses. Long experience in broadcasting, confirmed habits of listeners and viewers, network affiliation, and other advantages in program procurement give existing broadcasters a substantial advantage over new entrants, even where new entry is technologically possible. These advantages are the fruit of a preferred position conferred by the Government. Some present possibility for new entry by competing stations is not enough, in itself, to render unconstitutional the Government's effort to assure that a broadcaster's programming ranges widely enough to serve the public interest.

[W]e hold the regulations and ruling at issue here are both authorized by statute and constitutional.[28]

NOTES & QUESTIONS

1. *The fairness doctrine.* The fairness doctrine, which is no longer in effect, had two components. First, there was a minimum threshold requirement: Broadcasters were required to cover public issues of importance to the local community. Second, there was a responsive programming requirement: In certain circumstances, broadcasters were required to provide rights of reply. This general doctrine was articulated in more specific FCC regulations, such as the personal attack and political editorial rules mentioned in *Red Lion.* (We discuss the fate of the fairness doctrine in CHAPTER 4: ACCESS.)

2. *Entry and content.* In *NBC v. United States,* we were introduced to the scarcity/interference rationale for regulating entry into broadcast. Does the

---

[28] We need not deal with the argument that even if there is no longer a technological scarcity of frequencies limiting the number of broadcasters, there nevertheless is an economic scarcity in the sense that the Commission could or does limit entry to the broadcasting market on economic grounds and license no more stations than the market will support. Hence, it is said, the fairness doctrine or its equivalent is essential to satisfy the claims of those excluded and of the public generally. A related argument, which we also put aside, is that quite apart from scarcity of frequencies, technological or economic, Congress does not abridge freedom of speech or press by legislation directly or indirectly multiplying the voices and views presented to the public through time sharing, fairness doctrines, or other devices which limit or dissipate the power of those who sit astride the channels of communication with the general public. *Cf. Citizen Publishing Co. v. United States* (1969).

scarcity/interference justification for regulating entry suffice to regulate content, as in *Red Lion*? Put another way, if we have good reason to require broadcasters to get a federal license before broadcasting, do we necessarily have good reason to force broadcasters to transmit certain content against their will?

3. *Clash of free speech interests.* In analyzing First Amendment issues, we must remember that multiple parties have expressive interests at stake. First, and most obviously, we have the First Amendment interest of the broadcasters, who act as speakers. Second, however, we have the First Amendment interests of the audience, the listeners. Even if one is a First Amendment absolutist, one must recognize that there are interests on both sides, and sometimes these interests do not align. Can you articulate why limiting the free expression liberties of broadcasters may promote the First Amendment rights of the audience? What does the *Red Lion* Court say about this type of argument?

4. *Quid pro quo.* The Court wrote, "the First Amendment confers no right on licensees to prevent others from broadcasting on 'their' frequencies and no right to an unconditional monopoly of a scarce resource which the Government has denied others the right to use." Based on this text, consider the following argument:

> A broadcast license is government property held in the public trust. No single individual has a constitutional right to an exclusive piece of this property. If the government decides to lease it to an individual, the government can do so with reasonable "strings" attached. One of those strings may be to serve the public interest, in part by adhering to the fairness doctrine.

Descriptively, is this in fact what the Court is saying? Do you buy the argument normatively?

5. *Technological advances.* What happens if communication technologies improve such that scarcity and interference problems practically disappear? When the underlying technologies change, must the doctrine follow? In *Red Lion*, the Supreme Court specifically rejected the claim that scarcity was no longer a concern. Has technology changed enough today such that, even if the scarcity justification made sense in 1969, it no longer makes sense in the 21st century?

6. *The difference the medium makes.* Consider the next case, which casebooks always pair with *Red Lion*. The "right of reply" regulation seems functionally identical; however, the constitutional result is radically different. Why?

MIAMI HERALD PUBLISHING CO. V. TORNILLO
418 U.S. 241 (1974)

Mr. Chief Justice BURGER delivered the opinion of the Court.

The issue in this case is whether a state statute granting a political candidate a right to equal space to reply to criticism and attacks on his record by a newspaper violates the guarantees of a free press.

I

[A]ppellee, Executive Director of the Classroom Teachers Association, . . . was a candidate for the Florida House of Representatives. . . . [A]ppellant printed editorials critical of appellee's candidacy. In response to these editorials appellee demanded that appellant print verbatim his replies. . . . Appellant declined to print the appellee's replies and appellee brought suit. . . . The action was premised on Florida Statute § 104.38 (1973), a 'right of reply' statute which provides that if a candidate for nomination or election is assailed regarding his personal character or official record by any newspaper, the candidate has the right to demand that the newspaper print, free of cost to the candidate, any reply the candidate may make to the newspaper's charges.

III

B

It is urged that at the time the First Amendment to the Constitution was ratified in 1791 as part of our Bill of Rights the press was broadly representative of the people it was serving. . . . Entry into publishing was inexpensive; pamphlets and books provided meaningful alternatives to the organized press for the expression of unpopular ideas and often treated events and expressed views not covered by conventional newspapers. A true marketplace of ideas existed in which there was relatively easy access to the channels of communication.

Access advocates submit that . . . the press of today is in reality very different from that known in the early years of our national existence. In the past half century a communications revolution has seen the introduction of radio and television into our lives, the promise of a global community through the use of communications satellites, and the spectre of a 'wired' nation by means of an expanding cable television network with two-way capabilities. The printed press, it is said, has not escaped the effects of this revolution. Newspapers have become big business and there are far fewer of them to serve a larger literate population. Chains of newspapers, national newspapers, national wire and news services, and one-newspaper towns are the dominant features of a press that has become noncompetitive and enormously powerful and influential in its capacity to manipulate popular opinion and change the course of events.

The elimination of competing newspapers in most of our large cities, and the concentration of control of media that results from the only newspaper's being owned by the same interests which own a television station and a radio station, are important components of this trend toward concentration of control of outlets to inform the public.

The result of these vast changes has been to place in a few hands the power to inform the American people and shape public opinion. Much of the editorial opinion and commentary that is printed is that of syndicated columnists distributed nationwide and, as a result, we are told, on national and world issues there tends to be a homogeneity of editorial opinion, commentary, and interpretive analysis. The abuses of bias and manipulative reportage are, likewise, said to be the result of the vast accumulations of unreviewable power in the modern media empires. In effect, it is claimed, the public has lost any ability to respond or to contribute in a meaningful way to the debate on issues. The monopoly of the means of communication allows for little or no critical analysis of the media except in professional journals of very limited readership.

The obvious solution, which was available to dissidents at an earlier time when entry into publishing was relatively inexpensive, today would be to have additional newspapers. But the same economic factors which have caused the disappearance of vast numbers of metropolitan newspapers, have made entry into the marketplace of ideas served by the print media almost impossible. It is urged that the claim of newspapers to be 'surrogates for the public' carries with it a concomitant fiduciary obligation to account for that stewardship. From this premise it is reasoned that the only effective way to insure fairness and accuracy and to provide for some accountability is for government to take affirmative action. The First Amendment interest of the public in being informed is said to be in peril because the 'marketplace of ideas' is today a monopoly controlled by the owners of the market.

Proponents of enforced access to the press take comfort from language in several of this Court's decisions which suggests that the First Amendment acts as a sword as well as a shield, that it imposes obligations on the owners of the press in addition to protecting the press from government regulation. In *Associated Press v. United States* (1945), the Court, in rejecting the argument that the press is immune from the antitrust laws by virtue of the First Amendment, stated:

'The First Amendment, far from providing an argument against application of the Sherman Act, here provides powerful reasons to the contrary. That

Amendment rests on the assumption that the widest possible dissemination of information from diverse and antagonistic sources is essential to the welfare of the public, that a free press is a condition of a free society. Surely a command that the government itself shall not impede the free flow of ideas does not afford non-governmental combinations a refuge if they impose restraints upon that constitutionally guaranteed freedom. Freedom to publish means freedom for all and not for some. Freedom to publish is guaranteed by the Constitution, but freedom to combine to keep others from publishing is not. Freedom of the press from governmental interference under the First Amendment does not sanction repression of that freedom by private interests.'

IV

However much validity may be found in these arguments . . . governmental coercion . . . brings about a confrontation with the express provisions of the First Amendment. . . .

[T]he Court has expressed sensitivity as to whether a restriction or requirement constituted the compulsion exerted by government on a newspaper to print that which it would not otherwise print. The clear implication has been that any such compulsion to publish that which "'reason' tells them should not be published" is unconstitutional. A responsible press is an undoubtedly desirable goal, but press responsibility is not mandated by the Constitution and like many other virtues it cannot be legislated.

Appellee's argument that the Florida statute does not amount to a restriction of appellant's right to speak because 'the statute in question here has not prevented the Miami Herald from saying anything it wished' begs the core question. . . . The Florida statute exacts a penalty on the basis of the content of a newspaper. The first phase of the penalty . . . is exacted in terms of the cost in printing and composing time and materials and in taking up space that could be devoted to other material the newspaper may have preferred to print. It is correct . . . that a newspaper is not subject to the finite technological limitations of time that confront a broadcaster but it is not correct to say that, as an economic reality, a newspaper can proceed to infinite expansion of its column space. . . .

Faced with the penalties . . . editors might well conclude that the safe course is to avoid controversy. Therefore, under the operation of the Florida statute, political and electoral coverage would be blunted or reduced.

Even if a newspaper would face no additional costs to comply with a compulsory access law . . . the Florida statute fails to clear the barriers of the First Amendment because of its intrusion into the function of editors. A newspaper is more than a passive receptacle or conduit for news, comment, and advertising. The choice of material to go into a newspaper, and the decisions made as to limitations on the size and content of the paper, and treatment of public issues and public officials—whether fair or unfair—constitute the exercise of editorial control and judgment.

It has yet to be demonstrated how governmental regulation of this crucial process can be exercised consistent with First Amendment guarantees of a free press as they have evolved to this time. Accordingly, the judgment of the Supreme Court of Florida is reversed.[*]

NOTES & QUESTIONS

1. *Applying* Red Lion. Put aside for the moment the actual analysis that the Supreme Court applied in *Miami Herald*. Instead, apply mechanically the reasoning of *Red Lion*. In *Red Lion*, the Court emphasized scarcity of broadcast frequencies: Far more people wanted to broadcast than was possible. In *Miami Herald*, the Court concedes the scarcity of newspapers: Economically, it has become impossible to maintain multiple newspapers in many cities. Thus far more people want to publish newspapers than is possible. In *Red Lion*, because of the scarcity, the fairness doctrine was deemed constitutional. After all, the rights of listeners—the "little people"—were paramount. In the same vein, in *Miami Herald*, a right-of-reply statute should similarly be deemed constitutional. Right? But, as you know, the Florida right-of-reply statute was struck down. Why? Can these two cases be reconciled?

2. *Distinguishing cases.* The obvious way to try to reconcile these two cases is to differentiate the media. Somehow broadcasting, which uses e-m waves in a wireless channel, differs from newsprint, which uses the written alphabet as signals on a paper channel. Should this technological distinction make a constitutional difference?

3. *Embracing both cases.* Prof. Lee Bollinger has argued that the First Amendment itself justifies these two different regulatory regimes because they promote two separate First Amendment values–"access in a highly concentrated press and minimal governmental intervention."[†] Bollinger explains that theoretically we could have applied the opposite regimes to broadcast and print, but that history explains why we adopted one for print and the other for broadcast. What's important is that there is one industry that is largely

---

[*] The concurring opinions of Justices Brennan and White have been omitted.—ED.

[†] *See* Lee Bollinger, *Freedom of the Press and Public Access: Toward a Theory of Partial Regulation of the Mass Media*, 75 MICH. L. REV. 1 (1976).

unregulated and another industry that provides some right of access. What's your reaction?

4. *Scarcity critiqued: economics.* The scarcity rationale has come under blistering criticism, not only from commentators[*] but from the courts. First, e-m spectrum is scarce in the same way that all resources are "scarce." Before auctions started in the late 1990s, we gave e-m spectrum out to licensees for free. (We study auctions soon.) Most products or services if given out for free will generate more demand than supply. Society normally responds by letting market prices determine who ends up owning the resource.

Second, interference is not unique to e-m spectrum; arguably, interference destroys the value of any resource. For example, if you and I scribble on the same piece of paper, my writing will interfere with yours, thus making both messages hard to decode. You and I cannot sit on a single chair simultaneously—our bodies interfere with each other. Normally, we solve such interference problems through property rights. If it is my piece of paper, I can prevent you from scribbling on it. Similarly, if it is my chair, I can prevent you from sitting on it. So what makes spectrum so different? Consider what Nobel Laureate economist Ronald Coase wrote back in 1959:

> Land, labor, and capital are all scarce, but this, of itself, does not call for government regulation. It is true that some mechanism has to be employed to decide who, out of the many claimants, should be allowed to use the scarce resource. But the way this is usually done in the American economic system is to employ the price mechanism, and this allocates resources to users without the need for government regulation.[†]

5. *The judicial response.* Some judges have shown contempt for the scarcity justification. Judge Robert Bork once wrote:

> [T]he line drawn between the print media and the broadcast media, resting as it does on the physical scarcity of the latter, is a distinction without a difference. . . . It is certainly true that broadcast frequencies are scarce but it is unclear why that fact justifies content regulation of broadcasting in a way that would be intolerable if applied to the editorial process of the print media. All economic goods are scarce, not least the newsprint, ink, delivery trucks, computers, and other resources that go into the production and dissemination of print journalism. . . . Since scarcity is a universal fact, it can hardly explain regulation in one context and not another. The attempt to use a universal fact as a distinguishing principle necessarily leads to analytical confusion.[‡]

---

[*] *See, e.g.,* Christopher S. Yoo, *The Rise and Demise of the Technology-Specific Approach to the First Amendment,* 91 GEO. L.J. 245 (2003).

[†] R. H. Coase, *The Federal Communications Commission,* 2 J.L. & ECON. 1, 14 (1959).

[‡] Telecommunication Research & Action Ctr. v. FCC, 801 F.2d 501, 508 (D.C. Cir. 1986).

Still, the Supreme Court has expressly declined to reject the scarcity rationale in the broadcast context:

> The prevailing rationale for broadcast regulation based on spectrum scarcity has come under increasing criticism in recent years. Critics, including the incumbent Chairman of the FCC, charge that with the advent of cable and satellite television technology, communities now have access to such a wide variety of stations that the scarcity doctrine is obsolete. . . . We are not prepared, however, to reconsider our longstanding approach without some signal from Congress or the FCC that technological developments have advanced so far that some revision of the system of broadcast regulation may be required.[*]

B. TELEPHONY

Having studied the justifications for regulating entry in broadcast (a wireless, one-to-many medium), we now examine entry regulation of wireline telephony (a wireline, principally one-to-one medium). By wireline telephony, we're talking about the traditional telephone system your parents' generation used in the United States. Will physical scarcity and the First Amendment play the same roles here? Any role whatsoever?

1. TECHNOLOGY

The traditional public switched telephone network (PSTN) is based on the simple idea of an electrical circuit that provides a wireline path for electric current between source (calling party) and destination (called party). The simplest telephone system has only two telephones connected by a twisted pair of copper wires, which provides the electrical circuit between telephones. When the caller speaks into the telephone, the message carried by the human voice (in the form of pressure waves in the atmosphere) is encoded by a microphone onto the electrical current flowing through the circuit. These changes in the electrical current, detected almost immediately on the receiver's end, are decoded by a speaker back into the human voice.

Network topographies. If we add a third telephone, then that new telephone must have a wireline connection to each of the other two phones. A fourth person will need three more connections, and so on, as each new phone must be

---

[*] FCC v. League of Women Voters, 468 U.S. 364, 376 n.11 (1984). *See also* Turner Broadcasting System v. FCC, 512 U.S. 622, 638 (1994) ("We have declined to question its continuing validity as support for our broadcast jurisprudence . . . and see no reason to do so here.").

connected to all existing phones. These connections form a mesh network, the original telephone network topography. The mesh network becomes impractical as more and more users join the network because each new telephone must be connected by a separate line to every other telephone in existence. A mesh network in use today would require every household to have hundreds of millions of copper wires running to its backyard.

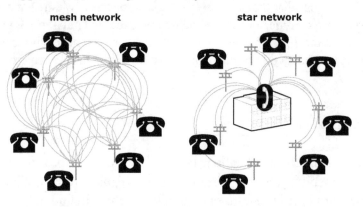

Figure 2.4: Comparison of Mesh and Star Networks

Avoiding this problem requires changing the network topography. Rather than connecting each subscriber to every other subscriber, each telephone is connected to a local switch via the local loop.* This topography drastically reduces the total number of connections required among the telephones in the network. Subscribers now have a single connection to the local switch, with no direct connections to other subscribers. This is often called a star network.

Switches. In the early days of telephony, the local switch was maintained by human operators who manually created a circuit between any two subscribers through a plug board. Originally, operators connected parties by name, but this soon gave way to telephone numbers. The circuit between caller and receiver remained in place for the duration of the conversation, after which the plug connections were manually removed, freeing up resources for use by other callers.

Although the switched star network is a tremendous improvement over the mesh network, the manual plug board switch was labor-intensive. Switching machines soon replaced human operators. These switches evolved from electro-mechanical to completely electronic devices, which increased both speed and capacity.

---

* This twisted pair of wires that connect the consumer to the local switch is called the "local loop," the "subscriber loop," or sometimes just the "loop."

To summarize, the basic components in the PSTN include (i) telephones, (ii) switches (which allow us to create efficient network topographies), and (iii) lines such as the local loop (the wires that connect telephones to the local switch).[*]

2. CONTEXT

In studying broadcast technology, we discussed how the first modern telecommunications device, the telegraph, developed in the late 1830s. The telegraph industry grew for many years largely unregulated. In 1866 Congress passed the Post Roads Act,[†] which granted rights-of-way over public lands to help construct telegraph lines. However, in return, the various telegraph companies had to interconnect with each other even though they were competitors. In the 1870s, the telegraph industry consolidated such that by the 1880s, one company—Western Union—was effectively a monopolist. But technology would not stand still.

Basic telegraph technology was pushed along different research tracks. As explained, one track pursued by inventors such as Marconi sought a *wireless* version of the telegraph, which soon evolved to radio broadcast. Another track sought to transmit more than Morse code (dots and dashes) along the telegraph wires. Could we, instead, transmit the human voice?

The question was answered "yes" by Alexander Graham Bell, who patented the telephone in March 1876, a few hours before his competitor, Elisha Gray. This technology was quickly commercialized and in a few years posed stiff competition for the decades-older telegraph industry. By the early 1890s, the Bell Telephone Company was flourishing, whereas Western Union was shrinking. Bell had become the dominant force in the telephony market (due to its patents), leasing telephones and providing local phone service.

But by 1894, Bell's patents had expired, and competition increased in both telephone manufacturing and telephone service, with competitors wiring up communities that Bell had ignored. Soon after the turn of the century, there was substantial head-to-head competition among rival telephone service providers in

[*] Each of these elements could be made more complicated. First, telephones are a subset of a larger class of customer premises equipment (CPE), which includes, for example, a private branch exchange (PBX)—a sort of private, in-house switchboard—at the sites of large businesses with large call volumes. Second, switches can be "small" ones that connect one local caller to a nearby neighbor or they could be "big" tandem switches (a switch for switches) that connect switches to other switches. Finally, lines could mean "thin" local loops that carry traffic from the customer to the local switch, or they could be "thick" transport links that carry traffic from switch to switch, nearby or across the country.

[†] 14 STAT. 221 (1866).

many cities.[*] But Bell then acquired new patents that gave his company a competitive edge in long distance communications. Because Bell refused to interconnect local exchanges that were not Bell affiliates through its long distance network,[†] the Bell System grew again in power and influence, raising the eyebrows of antitrust regulators. The antitrust history is discussed further in CHAPTER 4: ACCESS.

3. COMMON CARRIAGE

From its inception, entry into local telephony has been governed extensively by state and local governments. This should not be surprising. To install a wireline telephone system, one had to string up copper wires on poles or place them underground. This required digging up public property and accessing public "rights of way" (easements) on private property. It would be bizarre if any private individual could start jackhammering major thoroughfares and climbing trees in private backyards without state and local government permission. Here is a representative case from the early part of the 20th century.

NW TEL. EXCHANGE CO. v. CITY OF ST. CHARLES
154 F. 386 (C. C. D. Minn. 1907)

LOCHREN, District Judge.

The case ... all depends upon one question, and that is, whether the complainant company has the right, without the consent of the city authorities of the city of St. Charles, to establish a telephone exchange in that city at the present time. . . .

It appears that the complainant company was established under chapter 34 of the General Statutes of the state of Minnesota, in the month of December, 1878, and that on the 7th day of March in the year 1881 an act was passed by the Legislature of the state of Minnesota . . .

> "Any telegraph or telephone corporation organized under this title has power and right to use the public roads and highways in this state, on the line of their route, for the purpose of erecting posts or poles on or over the same to

---

[*] *See* Bornholz & Evans, *The Early History of Competition in the Telephone Industry, in* BREAKING UP BELL 7, 17-18 (D. EVANS ED. 1983).

[†] Although interconnection was a legal requirement for telegraphs under the Post Roads Act of 1866, no such statutory requirement was imposed on telephones. Further, the Supreme Court held that a common carrier's duty to serve all comers did not extend to serving competitors. *See* Express Packages Cases, 117 U.S. 1 (1886).

sustain the wires or fixtures; provided that the same shall be so located as in no way to interfere with the safety or convenience of ordinary travel on or over the said roads or highways."

Then on April 19, 1893, an act was passed, amending the same title, providing that:

"No corporation formed under this title shall have the right to construct, maintain or operate upon or within any street, alley or other highway of any city or village, any improvement of whatsoever nature or kind, without first obtaining a franchise therefor from such city or village according to the terms of its charter, and without first making just compensation therefor, as herein provided."

And on the 13th day of April, 1901, there was an act passed by the Legislature of the state of Minnesota, which provided that:

"Nothing herein shall be construed to grant to any person, persons, associations or corporation, any rights for the maintenance of a telephone system within the corporate limits of any city or village in this state, until such person, persons, associations or corporation shall have obtained the right to maintain such system in such village or city, nor for a period beyond that for which the right to operate such system is granted by such city or village."

Now it is unquestioned that the Legislature of the state has the power, as a governmental function, to control the highways of the state, which include streets in cities and villages, as well as alleys; and that has always been the law. Under this amendment of March 7, 1881, there was granted to telegraph and telephone companies the right and privilege of placing their poles bearing wires upon the public highways of the state. . . . This, in my opinion, constituted a license to telegraph or telephone companies . . . equivalent to a contract on the part of the state that such corporation should have the right to continue to use the poles and wires so constructed and erected, and, of course, to make the necessary repairs from time to time to keep the line in efficient condition.

But I cannot assent to the idea that the offer of this privilege or license took away from the state in any manner the continuing power of absolute control over the use of the highways and streets in the state. . . . It had the right, so far as companies had not taken advantage of the license that was offered, at any time to change the terms upon which it would assent to the use of the streets for telegraph or telephone purposes, or to abolish those privileges altogether. There would be nothing in the shape of a contract between any such company and the state, except so far as the companies had used that license and expended money upon it. . . .

Now the evidence shows that the complainant company made no attempt to use the streets and alleys of the city of St. Charles until the year 1896, when it applied to the city council for authority to erect its poles and wires upon certain streets, and by resolution of the council it was granted permission to erect poles and wires for a telephone line upon [certain specific] streets. . . .

[B]ut it never has obtained such permission with respect to any other streets; and at the present time it has no right or authority to build its lines upon any other streets than those so named. It seems that on the 22d day of August, 1905, the city council of St. Charles passed an ordinance which provided that:

> "No person or persons or corporation shall erect or set any telephone, telegraph, electric light, or power poles of any sort for the support of wires in any public street, road, or alley, or in any public ground, in the city of St. Charles, unless authorized by ordinance or resolution duly passed and adopted by the city council of said city; nor shall any person or corporation, unless so authorized, string, place, or fasten upon any pole, tree, building, or otherwise any telephone, telegraph, or electric light or power wire in or upon any such public places or grounds, or fasten any cross-arms, brackets, or other support in or upon the same."

Then the ordinance denounces severe penalties for any violation of its provisions. It is to restrain the city council from enforcing this ordinance that this suit is brought. As the city council has, under the charter of the city, the control, supervision, and management of the streets and alleys of the city, it seems to me that it is proper, and within the power of the city council, to pass an ordinance of this kind and to enforce it in the manner provided in the ordinance. It seems to me that it does not affect any rights of the complainant company, because it does not apply to any case where the occupation of the streets or alleys has been authorized by ordinance or resolution duly passed or adopted by the city council. . . .

My opinion, therefore, is that the bill should be dismissed.

NOTES & QUESTIONS

1. *Franchising* intrastate *telephony.* We have already learned that in order to broadcast, one needs a license granted exclusively by the federal government. *See* 47 U.S.C. § 301 ("No person shall use or operate any apparatus for the transmission of energy or communications or signals by radio . . . except under and in accordance with this Act and with a license in that behalf granted under the provisions of this Act"). What about entering telephony? As the above case clarifies, a franchise is required under state and local law to provide *intrastate* telephony. Accordingly, a state public utilities commission (PUC) would have to first issue the appropriate certificate of public convenience and necessity, unless some specific exemption applied. As an example, consider California law:

> Cal. Pub. Util. Code § 1001. Certificate required prior to commencement of construction
>
> No railroad corporation whose railroad is operated primarily by electric energy, street railroad corporation, gas corporation, electrical corporation, telegraph corporation, telephone corporation, water corporation, or sewer system corporation shall begin the construction of a street railroad, or of a line, plant, or system, or of any extension thereof, without having first obtained from the commission a certificate that the present or future public convenience and necessity require or will require such construction.

2. *No scarcity.* Now, turn to the justifications for entry regulation. Notice that there is no mention of spectrum scarcity or interference. What is the technological reason why?

3. *Government property.* According to the court, what role does the idea of government or public property play in justifying entry regulation for telephony? Was a similar argument made in broadcast?

4. *Common carrier model.* The above opinion focused on the state and city's inherent power over its public ways. Connected to this idea was the notion that telegraphy and telephony were common carriers (or functionally similar to them as a sort of public service corporation).

The category "common carrier" originally applied to transportation companies, such as railroads and ferries, which used public ways to deliver people and tangible goods. A thorough history of common carriers is beyond the scope of this book. Suffice it to say that common carriers were viewed as a subset of businesses "affected with a public interest," which was an accepted justification for regulating various other industries such as grain elevators, grist mills, and cotton gins.[*] It matters that they were viewed as somehow providing a public service. Otherwise, they would not have gained permission to use public rights-of-way or to exercise the power of eminent domain. In fact, courts specifically denied private individuals and non-telephone corporations the right to string up lines for their private benefit.[†]

---

[*] *See, e.g.,* Munn v. Illinois, 94 U.S. 113 (1876) (grain elevators) (when one "devotes his property to a use in which the public has an interest, he, in effect grants to the public and interest in such use, and must . . . submit to be controlled by the public for the common good, to the extent of the interest is thus created."). For an industry that was later determined not to be affected with the "public interest", see New State Ice Co. v. Liebmann, 285 U.S. 262 (1932). In this case, the Court held that the ice making business was not affected with the "public interest."

[†] *See, e.g.,* Acme Cement Plaster Co. v. American Cement Plaster Co., 167 S.W. 183, 184 (Tex. Civ. App. Amarillo 1914) ("[A]ppellees are not corporations organized and chartered for the purpose of constructing and maintaining a magnetic telegraph line, and had no right as such to construct over the public roads of which appellant has the fee [simple]."); Benton v. Yarborough, 123 S.E. 204 (S.C. 1924) (holding that a private individual has no right to construct a telephone line across a public highway over property owner's protest).

A "common carrier" designation entailed specific burdens and benefits. Here is a representative burden: Common carriers had to serve the entire public nondiscriminately and guarantee a certain level of care in service. Here is a representative benefit: In addition to being granted access to public rights-of-way, common carriers were not held liable for the contents they carried; after all, as common carriers, they had little choice about what to carry. After telephony was classified as a common carrier (like telegraphy had been before), it was natural for state governments to regulate local telephony like it regulated other common carriers.

5. *Quid pro quo.* The government property and common carriage justifications both have a sort of "quid pro quo" argument embedded in them. If you want to use public rights of way, you must get permission and play by certain rules. Were similar arguments made with broadcast?

6. *Countervailing interests.*

a. *First Amendment?* While studying broadcasting, we labored over whether entry regulations conflicted with the First Amendment. Why doesn't telephony present the same tough issues?

b. *Reliance?* The lack of First Amendment objections does not mean that anything goes. Consider, for instance, how the Minnesota court discusses business reliance interests. Were they protected adequately?

7. *Franchising* interstate *telephony.* So far, we have discussed how state (and local) law regulates entry into intrastate telephony. But the federal government also plays an important role. The rough division has historically been between intra- and interstate telephony.

a. *Mann-Elkins Act (1910).* Federal statutory regulation of telephony started when Congress passed the Mann-Elkins Act. In this Act Congress granted to the Interstate Commerce Commission (ICC) authority over interstate telephone and telegraph. (Before then, the ICC had regulated only the railroads, another industry designated as "common carriage.") Interstate telephony was to be regulated explicitly as a "common carrier," similar to the telegraph and railroad industries. The ICC, however, did not much exercise the power it had been granted, and in only four cases did it review the reasonableness of rates set by telephone companies.

b. *Communications Act (1934).* In the 1934 Communications Act, Congress moved the ICC's regulatory power over telephony into the newly created FCC and codified a common carriage model into Title II. The Act provides, unfortunately, a tautological definition of "common carrier."

> 47 U.S.C. § 153(10). Common carrier
>
> The term "common carrier" or "carrier" means any person engaged as a common carrier for hire, in interstate or foreign communication by wire or radio or interstate or foreign radio transmission of energy, except where reference is made to common carriers not subject to this chapter; but a person engaged in radio broadcasting shall not, insofar as such person is so engaged, be deemed a common carrier.

Common carriers are required to serve all customers upon reasonable request and interconnect with another carrier upon FCC command, § 201(a). Various pricing regulations appear in § 201(b) (just and reasonable rates), § 202 (no discrimination), and § 203 (tariffing). We study rate regulation in CHAPTER 3: PRICING.

A related term is "telecommunications carrier," which was added in the 1996 Telecommunications Act:

> 47 U.S.C. § 153(51). Telecommunications carrier
>
> The term "telecommunications carrier" means any provider of telecommunications services, except that such term does not include aggregators of telecommunications services (as defined in section 226 [47 USC § 226]). A telecommunications carrier shall be treated as a common carrier under this Act only to the extent that it is engaged in providing telecommunications services, except that the Commission shall determine whether the provision of fixed and mobile satellite service shall be treated as common carriage.

To properly understand this term would require us to look up the definition of "telecommunications services," etc., and in CHAPTER 5: CLASSIFICATION, we will see how important it is to classify a newly created communication service as either a telecommunications service or something else. But for now, just know that a "telecommunications carrier" is essentially a "common carrier" as the definition suggests.[*]

   c. *Section 214.* Directly relevant to this chapter's focus on entry is § 214(a). This section suggests that the FCC regulates entry of all *interstate* lines on an individualized basis.

> 47 U.S.C. § 214. Extension of lines or discontinuance of service; certificate of public convenience and necessity
>
> No carrier shall undertake the construction of a new line or of an extension of any line, or shall acquire or operate any line . . .unless and until there shall first have been obtained from the Commission a certificate that the present or future public convenience and necessity require or will require the construction, or operation, or construction and operation, of such additional or extended line: Provided, That no such certificate shall be required under this section for the construction, acquisition, or operation of (1) a line within a single State . . . . No carrier shall discontinue, reduce, or impair service to a community, or part of a community, unless and until there shall first have been obtained

---

[*] *See, e.g.,* Virgin Islands Tel. Corp. v. FCC, 198 F.3d 921, 926 (D.C. Cir. 1999) (accepting the FCC's interpretation that telecommunications carrier "means essentially the same as common carrier" under *Chevron* standard).

> from the Commission a certificate that neither the present nor future public convenience and necessity will be adversely affected thereby

From this you might infer that right now, firms that want to provide interstate telephone service must get specific, individual permission from the FCC before building out any such line. That is not, however, how things currently work. The FCC has historically had some flexibility to forbear from enforcing its regulations. In the Telecommunications Act of 1996, Congress explicitly granted this forbearance authority to the FCC as regards to § 214.[*] Invoking this authority, various telephone firms individually petitioned for forbearance from entry regulations. Instead of granting individual forbearance petitions, the FCC granted in 1999 "blanket entry certification" to all domestic carriers.

> 47 C.F.R. § 63.01. Authority for all domestic common carriers
>
> (a) Any party that would be a domestic interstate communications common carrier is authorized to provide domestic, interstate services to any domestic point and to construct or operate any domestic transmission line as long as it obtains all necessary authorizations from the Commission for use of radio frequencies.[†]

The exit procedures were also streamlined. The basic rationale for this blanket permission was that competition made stricter regulations unnecessary.

8. *Federalism.*

a. *The state line divide.* Historically, the single most important geographical boundary for legal power was the state line. The 1934 Communications Act conferred upon the FCC the power to regulate "all *interstate* and *foreign* communication by wire or radio" 47 U.S.C. § 152(a) (emphasis added), while expressly denying it power with respect to "charges, classifications, practices, services, facilities, or regulations for or in connection with *intrastate* communication service by wire or radio of any carrier," § 152(b) (emphasis added). Accordingly—at least to a first approximation—the FCC has jurisdiction over interstate communications whereas each state's PUC has jurisdiction over intrastate services.

b. *Modern complications: increasing federal power.* The Telecommunications Act of 1996 substantially altered this balance of power. As we study in greater detail in CHAPTER 4: ACCESS, a central goal of the 1996 Act was to promote competition in local telephony. To do so, Congress federalized

---

[*] *See* Telecommunications Act of 1996, PUB. L. NO. 104-104, § 402(b)(2), 110 STAT. 129 (1996) (codified as a "note" in 47 U.S.C. § 214). In the same Act, Congress adopted a more general forbearance provision concerning telecommunications carriers and telecommunications services. *See* 47 U.S.C. § 160(a).

[†] *See also In the Matter of Implementation of Section 402(b)(2)(A) of the Telecommunications Act of 1996,* R&O, 14 FCC Rcd. 11364 (1999).

the rules by which competition in local telephone markets might start.[*] In particular, Congress preempted all state barriers to entry. What this means is that although a state franchise is still necessary to enter intrastate telephony, a state PUC must provide one unless there is some good reason.[†] Under federal law, maintaining a legal state monopoly is not a good reason.

> 47 U.S.C. § 253. Removal of barriers to entry
>
> (a) In general. No State or local statute or regulation, or other State or local legal requirement, may prohibit or have the effect of prohibiting the ability of any entity to provide any interstate or intrastate telecommunications service.
>
> (b) State regulatory authority: Nothing in this section shall affect the ability of a State to impose, on a competitively neutral basis and consistent with section 254 of this section, requirements necessary to preserve and advance universal service, protect the public safety and welfare, ensure the continued quality of telecommunications services, and safeguard the rights of consumers.
>
> (c) State and local government authority: Nothing in this section affects the authority of a State or local government to manage the public rights-of-way or to require fair and reasonable compensation from telecommunications providers, on a competitively neutral and nondiscriminatory basis, for use of public rights-of-way on a nondiscriminatory basis, if the compensation required is publicly disclosed by such government.
>
> (d) Preemption: If, after notice and an opportunity for public comment, the Commission determines that a State or local government has permitted or imposed any statute, regulation, or legal requirement that violates subsection (a) or (b) of this section, the Commission shall preempt the enforcement of such statute, regulation, or legal requirement to the extent necessary to correct such violation or inconsistency.

Notice that subsections (b) and (c) make clear that states and local governments continue to retain some authority to promulgate regulations, such as competitively neutral rules that further universal service, promote consumer safety, and allow management of public ways and the like.[‡] But, at bottom, they cannot be obstructionist. When states and localities have adopted cumbersome requirements, telephone companies have successfully sued under § 253 to have such requirements federally pre-empted.

9. *Deeper justifications: natural monopoly.* So far, we have seen use of public property and classification as a common carrier as two sets of related justifications for regulating telephone entry. (Since there is no First Amendment problem with such entry regulation, no especially powerful reason is necessary.) But these justifications do not explain why regulators have historically limited entry to a *single* monopolist provider. To understand the choice to have only one provider in any given territory, we must study the concept of natural monopoly.

---

[*] *See, e.g.* §§ 251, 252 (imposing duties, inter alia, to interconnect with competitors and establishing procedures to resolve differences through state agency arbitration).

[†] *See* AT&T v. Iowa Util. Bd., 525 U.S. 366 (1999) (affirming federal power to implement the local competition provisions of the 1996 Act).

[‡] *See, e.g.* §§ 253(b), (c).

NOTE: NATURAL MONOPOLY

By the time of the passage of the 1934 Communications Act, federal and state regulators generally believed that telephony was a natural monopoly. In other words, the technology of the telephone made monopoly the natural state of affairs. Even robust competition would eventually lead to a single firm prevailing over all others. Because competition was seen as pointless, it made economic sense to designate a single company as monopolist and to bar the entry of any foolhardy competitors. Regulators in telephony generally accepted that the Bell system (a.k.a. AT&T) would be that monopolist. Instead of permitting futile competition, government officials would instead supervise service quality and prices, as well as promote broad telephone penetration throughout the United States.

A natural monopoly can exist "in a particular market if and only if a single firm can produce the desired output at lower cost than any combination of two or more firms."[*] In other words, the average cost per unit must decrease across the entire demand curve. This productive efficiency and resulting market dominance can arise from some combination of the following three characteristics.

Economies of scale. The term *"economies of scale"* describes a production situation where a firm's average cost declines as it increases output. Average cost is simply a firm's total cost divided by the number of units produced. (It differs from marginal cost, which refers to the cost of producing the next unit of a good.) For example, in the local telephone market, a large portion of the cost of wiring a row of homes lies in extending the telephone network to the street on which the homes are built. Once the network is extended to that street, subscribers along the street can be added at little additional cost. Thus, once the initial investment is made, the average cost declines rapidly as additional subscribers are added at a small incremental cost.

Economies of scale exist in most industries, but at some level of output, costs per unit typically start to rise because the size of the company gets unwieldy or substantial additional capital investments become necessary. Such markets can accommodate more than one firm. In some industries, however, scale economies operate so much that a single firm can most efficiently (in terms of cost per unit) serve the entire market before its average cost of production begins to rise. Given the superior efficiency of one large firm over two smaller firms, the total cost of producing the total industry output is less if only one firm is operating.

---

[*] *See* WILLIAM SHARKEY, THE THEORY OF NATURAL MONOPOLY 55 (1972).

High up-front, fixed costs. High initial investments characterize local telephone and cable industries. Laying down cable or phone lines and building infrastructure are expensive prerequisites to entering the industry. These costs are "fixed" because they are "insensitive to variations in output."[*] In other words, if it costs $10 million to lay down the basic telephone infrastructure in a local market, this cost will not vary whether one or 1,000 customers are served. To serve even one customer in this market, a competitor must make the same large initial investment in the telephone infrastructure as the incumbent has already made. With each additional subscriber, this high upfront fixed cost can be spread more broadly; accordingly each additional subscriber pays a smaller portion of that fixed cost.

New firms may be reluctant to enter such markets for two reasons. First, once made, the investment is "sunk," meaning it is not recoverable on exit from the industry (observing a new firm's failed attempt to compete with the incumbent will deter potential competitors from entering the market and buying that firm's infrastructure when it goes out of business). Second, because of the economies of scale already attained by the incumbent, the new, smaller firm by definition will have a higher average cost until its output is the same as the incumbent's. Moreover, the new firm most likely cannot survive to the point where its output matches the incumbent's because, to attract customers, it must match the incumbent's price. This will require the new firm to price below its own cost of production and therefore operate at a loss.

Network externality. Some products become more valuable when more people consume them. This effect is known as a network externality. An example is telephony: A telephone network consisting of only one phone is useless because the subscriber cannot communicate with anyone; adding another phone increases the network's value to the subscriber because she can speak to another person. Adding still more subscribers increases still further the value of the telephone network. In fact, the value of the network to each subscriber increases as additional subscribers are added.

If two firms are competing in the local telephone market with incompatible systems, customers of the firm with the smaller subscriber base have an incentive to switch to the other company, which allows them to call more people, thereby making the telephone service more valuable to them. The smaller firm will lose revenue as customers start to defect and will have trouble attracting new ones. This creates a domino effect, whereby the departure of each subscriber induces other subscribers to follow, until eventually the smaller firm

---

[*] *Id.* at 37.

loses all of the subscribers it originally attracted. For fledgling competitors challenging entrenched incumbents, this is particularly problematic because, as noted above, the upstart is trying to grow in order to achieve the scale economies necessary to bring its average costs down to the same level as the incumbent's.

Due to some combination of the above three market attributes, a monopoly may be the natural long-term equilibrium. In that case, competition is "wasteful." Because only one firm will prevail in such a natural monopoly market, other firms should simply devote their resources to alternative uses. Private investment by potential competitors will result in wasteful duplication of infrastructure because competition will be short-lived. Put another way, the nature of the industry inevitably gives supervening *economic power* to a single firm: There can be only one.

NOTES & QUESTIONS

1. *What's the problem?* If economies of scale operate to make a natural monopoly the most efficient producer of a good, then what is the problem? Won't we have efficiently produced goods?

2. *Identifying natural monopolies.* Are the three characteristics—economies of scale, large initial fixed cost, and network externalities—necessary and/or sufficient to produce a "natural monopoly"? Consider telephony, cable television, or FedEx as potential examples of natural monopoly.

3. *The regulatory response.* If a particular market gives rise to a natural monopoly, what should regulators do?

a. *Codify the natural monopoly into a legal monopoly?* One option is to bless the natural monopoly—indeed, enshrine it in law—but also regulate prices and quality of service. Historically, this was the approach toward telephone service. This would mean legally preventing any competitor from (foolishly) trying to enter the market. This is one way to read the entry regulations embedded in 47 U.S.C. § 214(a), which according to some legislative history was "designed to prevent useless duplication of facilities, with consequent higher charges upon the users of services."[*]

b. *Dismantle the monopoly through interconnection?* Another option is to try to destroy the natural monopoly by dismantling the entry barriers—for instance, by requiring interconnection between the incumbent monopolist and the upstart competitor. At the least, this would erase the incumbent's network externality advantage. The 1996 Telecommunications Act adopted this policy for local telephone service. In particular, state regulators can no longer provide

---

[*] 78 CONG. REC. 10314 (1934) (Remarks of Rep. Rayburn).

exclusive franchises to a single local telephone company, § 253(a), and telecommunications carriers must interconnect with each other, § 251(a)(1) (all carriers), § 251(c)(2) (special requirements for incumbent local exchange carriers).

c. *Do nothing?* What about the response of no response? Just as markets may fail, so may regulators. Are there cases in which the costs of regulation will outweigh the potential benefits of regulating a natural monopoly? Might this be especially true in times of rapidly changing technologies, which make even monopoly markets contestable? In the age of the internet, does any high-tech or communication company really sit on its laurels?

4. *Deep but not too deep of a justification.* We are studying the concept of natural monopoly because it fits tightly with the traditional set of justifications for regulating common carriers. But there is a danger here of over-reading. Even though viewing telephony as a natural monopoly is consistent with its categorization as a common carrier, monopoly power has never been strictly necessary. Nineteenth century common law did not require monopoly power to exist before a particular line of business or service would be called common carriage. Similarly, 19th century statutory frameworks, such as the Interstate Commerce Act of 1887, did not assume that competition would somehow make common carriage obligations unnecessary for railroads. Finally, the 1934 Communications Act's definition of "common carrier" in no way turns on a specific finding of monopoly power.

NOTE: MOBILE TELEPHONY

Having discussed entry in wireline telephony, what about "cell phones" or mobile telephony? A terminological note: What this book calls "mobile telephony" is known technically in FCC parlance as *commercial mobile radio services* (CMRS), a communications category created by Congress in 1993.[*] It applies to any mobile service provided for profit that interconnects with the public switched telephone network (PSTN) and is made available to a substantial portion of the public.

> 47 U.S.C. § 332. Mobile services
>
> (d) Definitions. For purposes of this section—
>
> > (1) the term "commercial mobile service" means any mobile service (as defined in [47 U.S.C. § 153]) that is provided for profit and makes interconnected service

---

[*] The Omnibus Budget Reconciliation Act of 1993, Pub. L. No. 103-66, Title VI, § 6002(b), amending the Communications Act of 1934 and codified at 47 U.S.C. § 332(c). In the statute, it's called "commercial mobile services" but it's come to be called "commercial mobile *radio* services."

> available (A) to the public or (B) to such classes of eligible users as to be
> effectively available to a substantial portion of the public, as specified by
> regulation by the Commission;
>
> (2) the term "interconnected service" means service that is interconnected with the
> public switched network (as such terms are defined by regulation by the
> Commission) or service for which a request for interconnection is pending
> pursuant to subsection (c)(1)(B);
>
> 47 U.S.C. § 153. Definitions
>
> (27) Mobile service. The term "mobile service" means a radio communication service
> carried on between mobile stations or receivers and land stations, and by mobile
> stations communicating among themselves . . . .

Technology. Think of mobile telephony as a wireless network that plugs
seamlessly into the wireline public switched telephone network (PSTN). When
a mobile user initiates a telephone call, the telephone broadcasts a request
message modulated onto e-m waves at designated frequencies, which propagate
outward spherically—just like a mini-radio station. A nearby "cell tower"
antenna tuned to these frequencies receives this request (like your radio receives
the signal broadcast by a nearby radio station) and establishes a communications
circuit with the telephone. Acting as a bridge, the antenna then sends a signal to
its associated mobile telephone switching office (MTSO),* either by microwave
links (point-to-point, wireless) or by wireline copper or fiber-optic cable. Finally,
the MTSO is connected to the local central office of the PSTN. It is this final
interconnection that allows wireless users to communicate as if they were using a
standard wireline phone.

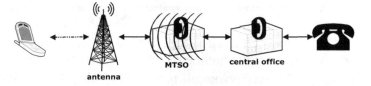

Figure 2.5: Wireless to Wireline

At this point, if the intended recipient is on a wireline telephone, the final legs of
the circuit are handled exactly the same way as any other call made on the
PSTN. Once the recipient answers, the circuit is completed from the wireless
telephone to the PSTN telephone. The "channel" for this communication will
be part wireless, part wireline.

---

* The mobile telephone switching office (MTSO) is similar to the central office of the public switched
telephone network (PSTN). Each MTSO serves a specified geographical area, just like a PSTN central
office. Each commercial mobile radio service (CMRS) provider runs its own MTSO.

Entry. From the above description, it should be obvious that entry into mobile telephony is regulated by the federal government, at least in the sense that CMRS spectrum bands have been allocated and specific licenses must be assigned. The obvious justification for entry regulation is the same as we saw in broadcast—spectrum scarcity and interference. Section 301, which institutes the Title III licensing requirement, is not limited to broadcasting: Instead, it covers "any apparatus for the transmission of energy or communications or signals by radio," which includes mobile telephony. We should not be entirely surprised, then, that the mobile telephony section, § 332 (Mobile Services), is codified in Title III, which concerns Broadcast.

Notwithstanding the title where CMRS is codified, Congress also made clear that CMRS would be treated as a "common carrier" governed under Title II of the Communications Act. After all, mobile telephony is telephony—just without the wires.

> 47 U.S.C. § 332. Mobile Services
>
> (c) Regulatory treatment of mobile services
>
> (1) Common carrier treatment of commercial mobile services
>
> (A) A person engaged in the provision of a service that is a commercial mobile service shall, insofar as such person is so engaged, be treated as a common carrier for purposes of this chapter, *except for* such provisions of subchapter II of this chapter as the Commission may specify by regulation as inapplicable to that service or person. In prescribing or amending any such regulation, the Commission may not specify any provision of section 201, 202, or 208 of this title, and may specify any other provision only if the Commission determines that—
>
> (i) enforcement of such provision is not necessary in order to ensure that the charges, practices, classifications, or regulations for or in connection with that service are just and reasonable and are not unjustly or unreasonably discriminatory;
>
> (ii) enforcement of such provision is not necessary for the protection of consumers; and
>
> (iii) specifying such provision is consistent with the public interest.

However, in the very same section (starting with the text "except for" italicized above), Congress granted substantial forbearance authority to the FCC, which the FCC has exercised. Significantly, the FCC has decided not to enforce the § 214 entry/exit regulations for the entire industry. In other words, the FCC does not require CMRS providers to "[s]ubmit applications for new facilities or discontinuance of existing facilities."[*] Once they have acquired the spectrum from the FCC, they are good to go.

---

[*] *See, e.g.,* 47 C.F.R. § 20.15(b)(3).

But what about the states? With wireline telephony, federal and state governments shared power roughly along inter/intrastate lines. Does wireless follow a similar scheme? The answer to this question was once quite complicated and uncertain; however, Congress simplified matters substantially in 1993. As part of the Omnibus Reconciliation Act of 1993 (1993 ORA), Congress made several changes to the Communications Act of 1934 to promote the growth of mobile telephony. Significantly, Congress put CMRS entry (and rates) strictly under the control of the FCC.

> 47 U.S.C. § 332(c)(3). State Preemption
>
> (A) [N]o State or local government shall have any authority to regulate the entry of or the rates charged by any commercial mobile service ... except that this paragraph shall not prohibit a State from regulating the other terms and conditions of commercial mobile services.

So, if states are preempted from entry regulation, and the FCC is forbearing from any § 214 examinations, is there no litigation about mobile telephony entry? Not exactly. Although Congress preempted state entry regulations, it specifically preserved local zoning authority to state and local governments.

> 47 U.S.C. § 332(c)(7). Preservation of local zoning authority
>
> (A) General authority. Except as provided in this paragraph, nothing in this Act shall limit or affect the authority of a State or local government or instrumentality thereof over decisions regarding the placement, construction, and modification of personal wireless service facilities.

At the same time, in the very next subsection, Congress imposed limitations on the zoning power.

> 47 U.S.C. § 332(c)(7)(B). Limitations
>
> (i) The regulation of the placement, construction, and modification of personal wireless service facilities by any State or local government or instrumentality thereof—
>
> > (I) shall not unreasonably discriminate among providers of functionally equivalent services; and
> >
> > (II) shall not prohibit or have the effect of prohibiting the provision of personal wireless services.
>
> (ii) A State or local government or instrumentality thereof shall act on any request for authorization to place, construct, or modify personal wireless service facilities within a reasonable period of time after the request is duly filed with such government or instrumentality, taking into account the nature and scope of such request.
>
> (iii) Any decision by a State or local government or instrumentality thereof to deny a request to place, construct, or modify personal wireless service facilities shall be in writing and supported by substantial evidence contained in a written record.
>
> (iv) No State or local government or instrumentality thereof may regulate the placement, construction, and modification of personal wireless service facilities on the basis of the environmental effects of radio frequency emissions to the extent that such facilities comply with the Commission's regulations concerning such emissions.
>
> (v) Any person adversely affected by any final action or failure to act by a State or local government or any instrumentality thereof that is inconsistent with this subparagraph may,

within 30 days after such action or failure to act, commence an action in any court of competent jurisdiction. The court shall hear and decide such action on an expedited basis. Any person adversely affected by an act or failure to act by a State or local government or any instrumentality thereof that is inconsistent with clause (iv) may petition the Commission for relief.

These statutory zoning limitations have, not surprisingly, been repeatedly litigated. Generally speaking, local authorities have tried to limit the number of towers, and federal authorities (both FCC and federal courts) have been skeptical of such attempts.

C. CABLE TELEVISION

Now we press on to cable television. It's just TV with wires, right? Do you imagine that entry will be regulated more like broadcast because it's TV? Or will it be regulated more like telephony because it uses wires? Some combination of both? Neither?

1. TECHNOLOGY

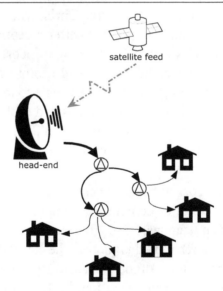

Figure 2.6: Typical Cable Plant

In technology, cable television differs from broadcast television mainly in the channel used for the video message. Instead of *wireless* communications from the broadcast station antenna all the way to the television, cable television—as the name suggests—uses *wireline* communications. Cable signals originate at the cable operator's head end, which receives video programming content from multiple sources (often via satellite or directional antenna). From the head end, the e-m signals propagate down to subscribers' homes through a root-like hybrid network built out of (newer) fiber and (older) coaxial cable.

A fundamental similarity between broadcast television and cable television is the unidirectional method of communication. Television signals are sent from the broadcast station or the cable head end in one direction, to the consumer's television set. Messages are not generally sent back from the individual consumer to the broadcast station or cable head end. There are, however, minor exceptions, which allow for some subscriber interaction. For instance, how do you take advantage of pay-per-view? Is it by telephoning your cable company, or is there some mechanism to send information back up the cable system using your cable set-top box? Of course, as cable networks are upgraded to provide broadband internet access, bi-directional communication is becoming far more common in cable systems.

2. CONTEXT

Cable television has grown from humble origins to become a fundamental part of our communications infrastructure. During the late 1940s and 1950s, cable television was used simply to provide better reception in locations where over-the-air broadcast television reception was poor. Large antennae in advantageous locations, such as hilltops, would capture over-the-air broadcast signals, then transport those signals via coaxial cable to individual homes. As of 1950, only 70 communities in the United States had cable systems, which were referred to as community antenna television (CATV). These systems served 14,000 homes. Indeed, from 1949–1962, cable television was not regulated at all by the federal government.

Soon, however, the goal of better reception changed to the goal of better content. One way to get better content is to import distant broadcast signals from faraway television stations, through microwave relay (point-to-point, focused, wireless transport). But this piqued the interest of the FCC, which controls the nation's spectrum. Although back in 1959[*] the FCC claimed that it had no authority to regulate cable television, by 1962, in the *Carter Mountain* decision,[†] the FCC asserted authority indirectly by denying common carrier microwave authorization to a cable operator who sought to import distant

---

[*] *CATV and TV Repeater Services*, 26 F.C.C. 403 (1959).

[†] *In re Application of Carter Mountain Transmission Corp.*, 32 F.C.C. 459 (1962), *aff'd*, Carter Mountain Transmission Corp. v. FCC, 321 F.2d 359 (D.C. Cir. 1963).

broadcast station signals to a local cable system. The FCC expressed concern that local television stations would be harmed if cable television could provide better content imported from far away.

By 1966 the FCC had concluded that cable television would substantially affect broadcast television in large markets. It thus asserted jurisdiction over cable television generally (without regard to the common-carrier microwave link justification). This "ancillary jurisdiction", asserted under general provisions of Title I of the Communications Act of 1934, was affirmed by the Supreme Court in *United States v. Southwestern Cable Co.*

> [T]he authority which we recognize today under § 152(a) is restricted to that reasonably ancillary to the effective performance of the Commission's various responsibilities for the regulation of television broadcasting. The Commission may, for these purposes, issue 'such rules and regulations and prescribe such restrictions and conditions, not inconsistent with law,' as 'public convenience, interest, or necessity requires.' 47 U.S.C. § 303(r). We express no views as to the Commission's authority, if any, to regulate CATV under any other circumstances or for any other purposes.[*]

The complexities of ancillary jurisdiction over cable TV have become moot because Congress granted specific statutory authority to the FCC to regulate cable TV in the 1984 Cable Communications Policy Act[†] and the 1992 Cable Television Consumer Protection and Competition Act.[‡] These statutes created what is now Title VI of the Communications Act. (That said, the general problem of how to regulate a burgeoning communications service when no specific legislation exists is an ongoing problem, as we will study in CHAPTER 5: CLASSIFICATION.) In this chapter, our focus remains on cable entry.

3. MEDIUM SCARCITY

COMMUNITY COMMUNICATIONS CO. V.
BOULDER
660 F.2d 1370 (10th Cir. 1981)

SEYMOUR, Circuit Judge.

In 1964, the City Council of Boulder granted a nonexclusive, revocable permit to ... CCC [Community Communications Co.], authorizing but not requiring the company to provide cable broadcasting services to all of Boulder.

---

[*] U.S. v. Southwestern Cable Co., 392 U.S. 157, 178 (1968).

[†] PUB. L. 98-549, 98 STAT. 2779.

[‡] PUB. L. 102-385, 106 STAT. 1460.

The permit was issued in the form of an ordinance allowing use of the public ways to string cable for a period of twenty years, with the reservation that the City Council could revoke the permit at its pleasure at any time.

Under the permit, CCC chose for roughly 15 years to provide cable television service only to the University Hill area of Boulder, an area comprising of approximately 20% of Boulder's residential units and blocked off from normal reception of Denver television stations. In 1979, CCC informed the City of its plans to expand the area it served and the programming it carried. Shortly thereafter, the City received a request from Boulder Communications Company (BCC) for a cable television permit. BCC indicated that regardless of the action the City took in regard to CCC, it planned to begin building a new system as soon as possible after it received a permit.

In response to these developments, the City undertook a study of cable broadcasting technology and concluded that cable systems are natural monopolies. Consequently, the City became concerned that CCC, because of its headstart, would always be the only cable operator in Boulder if allowed to expand, even though it might not be the best operator Boulder could otherwise obtain. The City decided to place a moratorium on CCC's expansion . . . .

The City concluded that direct competition in Boulder between cable companies within the same geographic area will not be possible in the foreseeable future. It settled on districting as the best practicable alternative. Under the City's plan, CCC will be restricted to servicing a single district comprising approximately one-third of the City's population. One or more cable companies will be granted permits to service other districts within Boulder. The City believes that although it cannot have direct competition, the districting plan will at least provide comparison. That is, by having more than one cable company operating in Boulder, the City will have a comparative basis for evaluating permit renewal applications.

As an initial matter, we note that the cable broadcasting industry has a prior history of federal, state, and local regulation. Generally, regulation has been premised upon cable companies' need to use public streets and rights of way to lay or string their cable. Local regulation has commonly taken the form of licensing or franchising cable companies. The question in the present case is whether the City has gone too far under . . . the First Amendment in its efforts to regulate CCC's cable operations.

CCC contends that the districting ordinance violates the First Amendment . . . . [T]he ordinance is alleged to be an unconstitutional content-based restraint on expression, because it bans CCC's communications from most of Boulder so that a "better" speaker, i.e., one who will offer special services such as two-way communications, may service that area. [Also], CCC . . . essentially argues that the City's ordinance must be summarily declared unconstitutional because analogous prohibitions on a newspaper's right to reach even a small portion of its audience would be struck down as First Amendment violations. CCC contends that cases involving regulation of wireless broadcasters are wholly inapposite.

The City responds that (1) cable companies should not be analogized in every respect to newspapers for First Amendment purposes; (2) cable systems are natural monopolies, so that subjecting them to some reasonable regulation designed to achieve optimal use of the cable broadcasting medium does not offend the First Amendment; and (3) the districting ordinance, contemplating as it does the ultimate interconnection of all cable systems operating in Boulder, is a content-neutral regulation that promotes citizenry First Amendment interests in diverse and state-of-the-art communications services and programming, without impeding any cable operator's ability to reach audiences, since all audiences in the City will ultimately be reachable through interconnection.

These contentions reach us in the context of requests by both CCC and the City for preliminary injunctive relief. The touchstone for obtaining such relief is a showing of irreparable harm coupled with a substantial likelihood of success on the merits.

Cable operators, like publishers and wireless broadcasters, are entitled to First Amendment protection. We also agree with the district court that "[t]o the extent that First Amendment rights are infringed, irreparable injury is presumed." Elrod v. Burns (1976). But we believe that in comparing "the competing claims of irreparable injury," the district court failed to consider that the citizens of Boulder also have significant First Amendment interests at stake. The City claims that its districting plan will advance its citizens' First Amendment interests in high quality and diverse cable communications services and programming, including two-way cable services that will enable its citizens to be disseminators of information as well as recipients.

The Supreme Court has relied on the uniqueness of the wireless broadcasting medium coupled with the recognition that "[i]t is the purpose of the First Amendment to preserve an uninhibited marketplace of ideas . . . rather than to countenance monopolization of that market," and that "[i]t is the right of the viewers and listeners, not the right of the broadcasters, which is paramount," to uphold affirmative regulation by the Government to enhance the diversity of information in broadcasting. *Red Lion Broadcasting Co. v. FCC* (1969). . . . We raise these points here to show that the First Amendment interests of cable viewers cannot be left out of the equation for permissible regulation of cable companies.

With respect to the likelihood of success on the merits . . . [a]t this juncture, facing as we do challenges to preliminary injunctive relief and an incomplete factual record, we cannot dispose of all the points raised by CCC and the City. We do, however, agree with the City's contention that it was inappropriate for the district court to summarily apply to cable operators the First Amendment principles governing newspapers. The nature and degree of protection afforded to First Amendment expressions in any given medium depends upon the medium's particular characteristics. For example, the degree to which the First Amendment shields the editorial discretion of wireless broadcasters differs substantially from the degree to which newspaper publishers are shielded from governmental interference. *Compare Red Lion* with *Miami Herald Publishing Co. v. Tornillo* (1974). The Supreme Court has repeatedly emphasized that "[e]ach medium of expression, of course, must be assessed for First Amendment purposes by standards suited to it," Southeastern Promotions, Ltd. v. Conrad (1975), for "differences in the characteristics of news media justify differences in the First Amendment standards applied to them." *Red Lion.*

To disseminate information, a newspaper need not use public property in the same way that a cable operator does. A newspaper may reach its audience simply through the public streets or mails, with no more disruption to the public domain than would be caused by the typical pedestrian, motorist, or user of the mails. But a cable operator must lay the means of his medium underground or string it across poles in order to deliver his message. Obviously, this manner of using the public domain entails significant disruption, especially to streets, alleys, and other public ways. Some form of permission from the government must, by necessity, precede such disruptive use of the public domain. We do not see how it could be otherwise. A city needs control over the number of times its citizens must bear the inconvenience of having its streets dug up and the best times for it to occur. Thus, government and cable operators are tied in a way that government and newspapers are not.

A second basis for government regulation of cable . . . is "medium scarcity." More specifically, the City asserts that there are physical and economic limitations on the number of cable systems that can practicably operate in a given geographic area. In physical terms, the City alleges a sheer limit on the number of cables that can be strung on existing telephone poles. Economically, the City argues that cable broadcasting is a monopolistic industry because it is not economically viable for more than one cable company to operate in any given geographic area. Together, the City contends, these limitations give cable companies the character of a natural monopoly and thus make the cable broadcasting medium "scarce" in much the same way that the finiteness of the electromagnetic spectrum makes wireless broadcasting a medium of essentially limited access.

Inherent limitations on the number of speakers who can use a medium to communicate has been given as a primary reason why extensive regulation of wireless broadcasting is constitutionally permissible. *See Columbia Broadcasting System, Inc. v. Democratic National Committee* (1973); *Red Lion*; *National Broadcasting Co. v. United States* (1943). When such limitations exist, and the medium requires use of a limited and valuable part of the public domain, the government must step in to allocate entry into that medium. In such circumstances, it confuses analysis to say that denying a potential disseminator the right to reach an audience is a prior restraint. No individual disseminator has the constitutional right to be the particular person who obtains the privilege to use the medium. *See Red Lion.*

[R]elying on *Miami Herald*, the district court rejected economic monopoly as justifying any degree of regulation whatsoever. In *Miami Herald*, notwithstanding contentions that the nation is dominated by one-newspaper cities and that economic conditions have made new entry into the newspaper industry virtually impossible, the Supreme Court held that a state imposed public right of access to the pages of a newspaper violates the First Amendment.

Miami Herald, however, must be read in context. The Court was writing about newspapers, a communication medium protected by a long-standing and powerful tradition that keeping government's hands off is the best way to achieve the "profound national commitment to the principle that debate on public issues should be uninhibited, robust, and wide-open...." *New York Times Co. v. Sullivan* (1964). Moreover, *Miami Herald* involved an effort by state government to compel public access to a medium that is not tied to government in the way cable companies necessarily are. There, the characteristic of economic scarcity was unrelated to a disruptive use of the public domain requiring a government license.

The cable broadcasting medium presents very different circumstances. As already noted, this industry has always been regulated in many respects. There is no tradition of nearly absolute freedom from government control. Most importantly, a cable company must significantly impact the public domain in order to operate. . . .

If when faced with a request for a license from a cable operator, government reasonably anticipates the kind of "medium scarcity" we have discussed, it must be permitted to deal with the effects of the scarcity that may attend the use of the license it is about to issue. That is, government must have some authority in such a context to see to it that optimum use is made of the cable medium in the public interest. In view of the lengthy franchises that cable operators seem to require, the City's districting ordinance might be justifiable as a means to avoid locking into an outmoded or less than state-of-the-art cable communications system.

The conclusion that natural monopoly is a constitutionally permissible justification for some degree of regulation of cable operators does not mean that the full panoply of principles governing the regulation of wireless broadcasters necessarily applies to cable operators.... For example, differences in (1) the degree of natural monopoly or "scarcity" characterizing the medium, (2) the pace and potential for technological change, or (3) the uses and possible uses of the medium such as two-way cable communications or even interconnection, might make kinds of regulations constitutionally permissible in one medium that would be forbidden in another. But we caution: the power to regulate is not one whit broader than the need that evokes it. Whether that power has been permissibly exercised by the City in this case calls for a particularized inquiry into the unique attributes of the cable broadcasting medium. The district court is best suited for such inquiry in the first instance upon a fully developed factual record.

In sum, the significant First Amendment issues create a presumption of irreparable harm on both sides in this case and present a fair ground for litigation for both parties. Each side has moved for preliminary relief. Balancing the hardships, we cannot agree with the district court's essentially one-sided grant of preliminary injunctive relief to CCC. Rather, we believe that relief... must be tailored so as to minimize irreparable harm to both sides and at the same time to permit a meaningful grant of whatever permanent relief may be warranted. This is best accomplished by freezing the parties in their present circumstances until trial on the merits.

NOTES & QUESTIONS

1. *Franchising requirement.*

   a. *Federal law.* If you want to enter the cable business, you must get a franchise. Why? Because federal law says so.

> 47 U.S.C. § 541. General franchise requirements
>
> (b) No cable service without franchise; exception under prior law.
>
>   (1) [A] cable operator may not provide cable service without a franchise.

By the way, what precisely is a "cable operator"?

> 47 U.S.C. § 522. Definitions
>
> (5) the term "cable operator" means any person or group of persons (A) who provides cable service over a cable system and directly or through one or more affiliates owns a significant interest in such cable system, or (B) who otherwise controls or is responsible for, through any arrangement, the management and operation of such a cable system;

Notice that this definition now requires us to understand what counts as a "cable service" and "cable system"?

> 47 U.S.C. § 522. Definitions
>
> (6) the term "cable service" means—
>
>> (A) the one-way transmission to subscribers of (i) video programming, or (ii)   other programming service, and
>> (B) subscriber interaction, if any, which is required for the selection or use of such video programming or other programming service;

Yet more ambiguous terms. What's "video programming"?

> 47 U.S.C. § 522. Definitions
>
> (20) the term "video programming" means programming provided by, or generally considered comparable to programming provided by, a television broadcast station.

Finally, what's a "cable system"?

> 47 U.S.C. § 522. Definitions
>
> (7) the term "cable system" means a facility, consisting of a set of closed transmission paths and associated signal generation, reception, and control equipment that is designed to provide cable service which includes video programming and which is provided to multiple subscribers within a community, but such term does not include (A) a facility that serves only to retransmit the television signals of 1 or more television broadcast stations; (B) a facility that serves subscribers without using any public right-of-way; (C) a facility of a common carrier which is subject, in whole or in part, to the provisions of title II of this Act, except that such facility shall be considered a cable system (other than for purposes of section 621(c)) [47 USC § 541(c)] to the extent such facility is used in the transmission of video programming directly to subscribers, unless the extent of such use is solely to provide interactive on-demand services; (D) an open video system that complies with section 653 of this title [47 USC § 573] or (E) any facilities of any electric utility used solely for operating its electric utility systems;

The point of navigating this definitional maze is two-fold. First, it provides you the legal definitions of who must receive a franchise for what type of service. This will help you answer questions such as whether Netflix needs a cable franchise for its instant streaming service. Second, it vividly demonstrates how communications law often requires you to chase a line of statutes and regulations just to define basic terms. You can't perform legal analysis without definitions.

b. *State law mixture.* In addition, cable franchising mixes in state law. In contrast to broadcast and more similar to telephony, entry into cable television is regulated by the federal government in conjunction with state and local authorities. State law determines which government body acts as the franchisor:

the state, county, municipality, or city. For example, before 2007, the State of California granted to cities and counties the power to franchise cable operators. Consistent with national trends, after 2007, the franchising power moved to a state-level agency, the California Public Utilities Commission.*

Historically, when a franchising authority wanted to grant an initial cable TV franchise, it issued a request for proposals and selected the best submission through local government decision-making procedures. A franchise contract would govern the relationship between the franchising authority and the selected cable operator. That said, most of the most important terms in that contract were and still are constrained by federal law. Examples include the requirement to provide public, education, and government (PEG) channels, 47 U.S.C. § 531, and maximum franchise fees (5% of gross revenues), § 542. As for franchise renewals, the Cable Communications Policy Act of 1984[†] (1984 Cable Act) ensured robust renewal expectations. § 546. Typically, cable franchises run approximately 15 years. By the way, why do you think they run longer than the 8 year duration for broadcast licenses?

2. *Distinguishing broadcast television.* Why does the "e-m spectrum scarcity" rationale not work with cable television? Is this the same reason why scarcity was irrelevant to wireline telephony?

3. *Distinguishing telephony.* Entry into telephony was regulated on multiple grounds: use of government property, classifying telephony as a common carrier, and natural monopoly. Do these justifications apply also to cable television? One element clearly does not: by federal law, a cable system providing cable television service is not a common carrier.

> 47 U.S.C. § 541. General franchise requirements
>
> (c) Status of cable system as common carrier or utility. Any cable system shall not be subject to regulation as a common carrier or utility by reason of providing any cable service.

4. *Medium scarcity.* What precisely is "medium scarcity"? The court suggests that this type of scarcity has both physical and economic components. What are these components? How do these justifications compare to the justifications given for regulating entry into broadcast or telephony?

5. *Distinguishing print.* If medium scarcity is a justification for regulating entry, why did that justification not work equally well for newspapers and

---

* *See* Digital Infrastructure and Video Competition Act of 2006 (DIVCA), Public Utilities Code § 5800 et seq.

[†] PUB. L. NO. 98-549, 98 STAT. 2780.

magazines in *Miami Herald v. Tornillo.* If the answer is that different media may be treated differently, the next question is why?

PREFERRED COMMUNICATIONS V. LOS ANGELES
13 F.3d 1327 (9th Cir. 1994)

KOZINSKI, SILER, and KLEINFELD, Circuit Judges, per curiam:

BACKGROUND

Los Angeles, like most large cities, requires permits for those seeking to provide cable television.... Under its Charter, the city may grant any "franchise, permit or privilege to erect, construct, lay, maintain and operate, poles, pipes, conduits, wires or cable upon, over, under, in, across or along any street... road or other place... for the purpose of... communication by telephone, telegraph or signal systems." Los Angeles, Cal., Ordinance No. 58,200, § 2(4). The ordinance specifies that franchises are to be awarded through a process known as a notice of sale ("NOS").

Under [the Cable Communications in Los Angeles Master Plan], the city is divided into fourteen cable franchise areas; each area is served by one cable operator. Once the city decides to issue an NOS for an area, it receives bids; if it decides to award a franchise, it must award it to the highest "responsible" bidder, which means that considerations other than the dollar amount of the bid are taken into account.

In 1980, the city issued an NOS for cable service in South Central Los Angeles. It received three applications, but no franchise was awarded. In 1982 the city issued another South Central NOS. Only one application was received, and the city granted the applicant the South Central franchise.

Preferred Communications, Inc., was formed in 1983 to provide cable service to South Central Los Angeles. Since it didn't exist at the time of either the 1980 or 1982 NOS, it participated in neither. In 1983 Preferred requested pole attachment service—permission to lease space on utility poles to string the necessary cable wires—from Pacific Telephone and Telegraph Company and the Los Angeles Department of Water and Power. Each utility informed Preferred that it would first have to obtain a franchise from the city. Preferred then asked the city for a franchise. It was informed that the city would issue only one franchise to each area, and that the franchise in South Central had already been awarded.

Preferred then sued the city.... The district court dismissed Preferred's complaint for failure to state a claim. We reversed, holding that the activity Preferred sought to engage in—providing cable service—was entitled to First

Amendment protection. Taking as true the allegations in Preferred's complaint, we held that the city could not limit the award of franchises to a single operator in each area of the city, if the city's infrastructure was capable of accommodating additional providers. *Preferred I.*

The Supreme Court affirmed our decision, but did so "on a narrower ground." *Preferred II* (1986). The Court . . . remanded to the district court for the development of a record on "the present uses of the public utility poles and rights-of-way and how respondent proposes to install and maintain its facilities on them."

On remand the district court decided the case on cross motions for summary judgment. Most notably, the court invalidated the city's one operator/one area policy, through which the city awarded only one franchise per cable service area. Both sides appeal.

DISCUSSION

It is now well established that regulation of cable operators implicates both the Free Speech and Free Press Clauses of the First Amendment. *See, e.g., Leathers v. Medlock* (1991).

The city first argues it has a substantial interest in preventing the disruption and visual blight caused by additional cable wiring. It claims that further cable systems would force the rearrangement and replacement of existing utility poles and that the installation of another system would pose safety hazards to the public who use the streets and to the DWP employees who must work on the poles. The city's proof doesn't alter the analysis in *Preferred I,* which assumed these were substantial interests. *Preferred I* held that limiting the market to a single cable operator was not narrowly tailored to advance the government's interests. There is nothing in this record to change that conclusion, and we adhere to it.

The same concerns that underlay Judge Sneed's excellent opinion in *Preferred I* trouble us as well: "[A]llowing only the single company selected through the franchise auction process to erect and operate a cable system in each region" exacts too heavy a toll on the First Amendment interests at stake here. Competition in the marketplace of ideas—as in every other market—leads to a far greater diversity of viewpoints (and better service) than if a single vendor is granted a crown monopoly. The risk that a single operator will be captured by city hall (or in turn will capture regulators) is far greater than where two or more operators face off against each other and must contend with the harsh realities of competition.

This is not to say that the city must grant access to its utility infrastructure to "all cable-television comers, regardless of size, shape, quality, qualifications or threat to the ultimate capacity of the system." *Pacific West Cable Co. v. City of Sacramento* (9th Cir. 1986). Once the city awards a second franchise, the First Amendment calculus may shift. The marginal benefits of another operator will be considerably less when the monopoly is broken and competition is introduced; at the same time, the burden on the city will increase as more cable systems are added. There will thus surely come a point where the city may refuse to grant an additional cable franchise because the added benefit of another franchise is low while the cost in terms of the city's utility-carrying capacity is high. We hold today only that limiting speech to a single operator is "substantially broader than necessary to achieve the government's interest," and therefore invalid. *Ward v. Rock Against Racism* (1989).

The city also argues, as it did in *Preferred I,* that the physical scarcity of its utility infrastructure justifies the one area/one operator requirement. The city has conceded, however, that its infrastructure could accommodate at least one further cable system. The essence of the city's argument, therefore, is not that there is no space whatsoever for another cable system but that permitting additional cable systems will bring South Central's utility infrastructure closer to exhaustion. The city claims it may need additional space to expand existing uses or to provide novel, undiscovered services. At bottom, then, the city would rather reserve the space for some other uses than give it to Preferred.

This, too, we considered and rejected in *Preferred I.* "We cannot accept the City's contention that, because the available space on such facilities is to an undetermined extent physically limited, the First Amendment ... permit[s] it to restrict access and allow only a single cable provider to install and operate a cable television system."[5] Given the city's concession that at least one more cable system can be added, the reasoning of *Preferred I* controls.

Admittedly, this alternative is not without costs. Even if the cable operator pays to reconfigure the wires and erect new poles, the city will still suffer significant disruption. We have already recognized that these are substantial interests, yet for the same reasons already given the monopoly policy is not narrowly tailored to further those interests.

---

[5] We note also that the city already has an alternative way of ensuring the availability of space for future uses if and when it becomes necessary. The California Public Utility Code provides that, in the event additional space is needed, the cable company must either surrender its occupation of the poles or bear the expense of creating additional capacity. *See* CAL. PUB. UTIL. CODE § 767.5(d). Given that state law already provides a mechanism by which the city may obtain additional space, a monopoly policy is not narrowly tailored to further the city's interest.

The city does advance one interest that was left open in *Preferred I.* That only one cable system can profitably operate in South Central and the city therefore has an interest in creating a regulated monopoly to operate a franchise. This is the so-called "natural monopoly" argument which has been rejected as a justification for regulation of print media. *See Miami Herald Pub. Co. v. Tornillo* (1974).

There are important differences between print and cable media, however. Most significant is that cable systems place a strain on public resources: They disrupt traffic and take up public easements and rights of way. Unlike newspapers, a "cable company must significantly impact the public domain in order to operate." Community Communications Co., Inc. v. City of Boulder (10th Cir. 1981). The economic oddities of cable, coupled with the burden on public resources caused by the entry—and exit—of additional operators, may arguably justify some limitations on the number of operators. *Id.*; *see also Omega Satellite Products Co. v. City of Indianapolis* (7th Cir. 1982) (Posner, J.). But this is just another way of expressing the city's interest in avoiding traffic disruption and visual blight, which we have already disposed of. Repackaging these interests under the rubric of natural monopoly makes them no more compelling. For the reasons discussed above, the one operator/one area limitation is not narrowly tailored to advance this interest. We emphasize again: The city may restrict the number of entrants into the cable market, but it may not restrict the number to only one.[6]

NOTES & QUESTIONS

1. *The First Amendment applies.* The Ninth Circuit cites to the Supreme Court's opinion in *Leathers v. Medlock* (1991) for the proposition that cable operators are protected by the First Amendment:

> Cable television provides to its subscribers news, information, and entertainment. It is engaged in "speech" under the First Amendment, and is, in much of its operation, part of the "press." *See Los Angeles v. Preferred Communications, Inc.*, 476 U.S. 488 (1986).[*]

In *Leathers*, the Supreme Court cited as authority its prior opinion in *Preferred I*:

> [T]hrough original programming or by exercising editorial discretion over which stations or programs to include in its repertoire, respondent [cable

---

[6] Though we are aware of the 1992 Cable Television Consumer Protection and Competition Act, 47 U.S.C. § 541, our ruling today does not implicate it since the parties agreed it was not relevant.

[*] Leathers v. Medlock, 499 U.S. 439, 444 (1991).

operator] seeks to communicate messages on a wide variety of topics and in a wide variety of formats. We recently noted that cable operators exercise "a significant amount of editorial discretion regarding what their programming will include." *FCC v. Midwest Video Corp.*, 440 U.S. 689 (1979). Cable television partakes of some of the aspects of speech and the communication of ideas as do the traditional enterprises of newspaper and book publishers, public speakers, and pamphleteers. Respondent's proposed activities would seem to implicate First Amendment interests as do the activities of wireless broadcasters, which were found to fall within the ambit of the First Amendment in *Red Lion Broadcasting Co. v. FCC*, even though the free speech aspects of the wireless broadcasters' claim were found to be outweighed by the Government interests in regulating by reason of the scarcity of available frequencies.*

2. *State interests.* According to the court, the City of Los Angeles presented three different state interests to justify its monopoly franchise policy: physical disruption of streets and roads; physical scarcity (space on utility poles); and natural monopoly. Are these interests the same or different from those presented in *CCC?*

3. *Medium analogies.* We know already that the First Amendment standard of review applied to broadcast differs from that applied to print. Did the *CCC* court think that cable should be treated just like broadcast? Did the *Preferred Communications* court think that cable should be treated just like print? If the answer to both questions is no, then what hybrid standard is being applied to cable?

4. *Miami Herald.* Both *CCC* and the *Preferred Communications* court cite *Miami Herald.* Do the two courts interpret this case similarly as applied to cable television?

5. *Natural monopoly.* In both cases, we see courts referring to the economic concept of natural monopoly, which we have already studied with wireline telephony. Consider what Judge Richard Posner, a prominent practitioner of law and economics, has said on the subject:

> The cost of the cable grid appears to be the biggest cost of a cable television system and to be largely invariant to the number of subscribers the system has. We said earlier that once the grid is in place—once every major street has a cable running above or below it that can be hooked up to the individual residences along the street—the cost of adding another subscriber probably is small. If so, the average cost of cable television would be minimized by having a single company in any given geographical area; for if there is more than one company and therefore more than one grid, the cost of each grid will be spread

---

* Los Angeles v. Preferred Comm'ns, Inc., 476 U.S. 488, 494-95 (1986).

over a smaller number of subscribers, and the average cost per subscriber, and hence price, will be higher.

If the foregoing accurately describes conditions in Indianapolis... it describes what economists call a "natural monopoly," wherein the benefits, and indeed the very possibility, of competition are limited. You can start with a competitive free-for-all—different cable television systems frantically building out their grids and signing up subscribers in an effort to bring down their average costs faster than their rivals—but eventually there will be only a single company, because until a company serves the whole market it will have an incentive to keep expanding in order to lower its average costs. In the interim there may be wasteful duplication of facilities. This duplication may lead not only to higher prices to cable television subscribers, at least in the short run, but also to higher costs to other users of the public ways, who must compete with the cable television companies for access to them. An alternative procedure is to pick the most efficient competitor at the outset, give him a monopoly, and extract from him in exchange a commitment to provide reasonable service at reasonable rates.*

What regulatory consequences should flow from such a conclusion—that cable is a natural monopoly?

6. *No more exclusive franchises.* In the 1950s and '60s, when the first cable franchises were being granted, there was little competition. In the 1970s, as the value of a cable franchise increased, competition for franchises also increased. In the Cable Television Consumer Protection and Competition Act of 1992 (1992 Cable Act),[†] Congress expressly forbade exclusive franchises. This means that although cable entry is still regulated—in that a franchise is still necessary— exclusive franchises are prohibited. Franchising authorities must act reasonably in deciding to award additional competitive franchises and also act promptly. *See* 47 U.S.C. § 541(a)(1). An applicant whose franchise application has been denied can appeal this decision in both federal and state courts. *See* 47 U.S.C. § 555.

§ 541. General franchise requirements

(a) Authority to award franchises; public rights-of-way and easements; equal access to service; time for provision of service; assurances.

(1) A franchising authority may award, in accordance with the provisions of this title, 1 or more franchises within its jurisdiction; except that a franchising authority may not grant an exclusive franchise and may not unreasonably refuse to award an additional competitive franchise. Any applicant whose application for a second franchise has been denied by a final decision of the franchising authority may appeal such final decision pursuant to the provisions of section 635 [47 USC § 555] for failure to comply with this subsection.

---

* Omega Satellite Products Co. v. City of Indianapolis, 694 F.2d 119 (7th Cir. 1982).

† PUB. L. NO. 102-385, 106 STAT. 1460.

7. *Video franchising for cable-like companies.* In later chapters, we will study more about the increase in competition in cable TV. But for now, you should simply know that there's been little build-out of cable TV networks by competitors in regions already served by some incumbent cable operator. Instead, competition has come from direct broadcast satellite (DBS) and entry by historically telephone companies, which have refurbished their networks and built out fiber-optic lines toward customer neighborhoods and premises. More recently, competition has come in the form of "over-the-top" (OTT) video streaming services (e.g. Slingbox, Youtube, Disney+, etc.). From the consumer's perspective, services provided by Verizon and AT&T are indistinguishable from digital cable television service, with high definition video and easy recording options. And increasingly the OTT offerings provide substantially similar service as well. How should these services be regulated? In particular, which entry regulations should apply?

D. INTERNET

We have so far discussed every major communications service *except* the one that we now use most: the internet. Before discussing how entry regulations impact the internet, we start with a brief technological introduction.

1. TECHNOLOGY

KEVIN WERBACH, DIGITAL TORNADO:
THE INTERNET AND
TELECOMMUNICATIONS POLICY
FCC, Office of Policy & Planning, Working Paper Series 29 (March 1997)

A. General Description

The Internet is an interconnected global computer network of tens of thousands of packet-switched networks using the Internet protocol (IP).[12]

The Internet is a network of networks. For purposes of understanding how the Internet works, three basic types of entities can be identified: end users, Internet service providers, and backbone providers. *End users* access and send

---

[12] IP defines the structure of data, or "packets," transmitted over the Internet. The higher-level "transmission control protocol" (TCP) and "user-defined protocol" (UDP) control the routing and transmission of these packets across the network. Most Internet services use TCP, and thus the Internet is often referred to as a "TCP/IP" network.

information either through individual connections or through organizations such as universities and businesses. End users in this context include both those who use the Internet primarily to receive information, and content creators who use the Internet to distribute information to other end users. *Internet service providers* (ISPs), such as Netcom, PSI, and America Online, connect those end users to Internet backbone networks.[14] *Backbone providers*, such as MCI, UUNet, and Sprint, route traffic between ISPs, and interconnect with other backbone providers.

This tripartite division highlights the different functionalities involved in providing Internet connectivity. The actual architecture of the Internet is far more complex. Backbone providers typically also serve as ISPs; for example, MCI offers dial-up and dedicated Internet access to end users, but also connects other ISPs to its nationwide backbone. End users such as large businesses may connect directly to backbone networks, or to access points where backbone networks exchange traffic. ISPs and backbone providers typically have multiple points of interconnection, and the inter-relationships between these providers are changing over time. It is important to remember that the Internet has no "center" and that individual transmissions may be routed through multiple different providers due to a number of factors.

End users may access the Internet though several different types of connections, and unlike the voice network, divisions between "local service" providers and "long-distance" providers are not always clear. Most residential and small business users have dial-up connections,* which use analog modems to send data over the plain old telephone service (POTS) lines of local exchange carriers (LECs) to ISPs. Larger users often have dedicated connections using high-speed ISDN, frame relay or T-1 lines, between a local area network at the customer's premises and the Internet. Although the vast majority of Internet access today originates over telephone lines, other types of communications companies, such as cable companies, terrestrial wireless, and satellite providers, are also beginning to enter the Internet access market.

* * *

---

[14] Dedicated Internet service providers, which offer a connection to the Internet but no proprietary content, are distinguished from online service providers (such as America Online) that provide access to proprietary content and also allow their users to access the Internet. Such distinctions are blurring, however, as online service providers such as the Microsoft Network move their content to the Internet, and as dedicated Internet service providers begin to offer some local content. For purposes of this paper, all of these providers are labeled as "ISPs," because all of them, as a component of their service, connect end users to the Internet.

* This was true back in 1997. —ED.

C. How the Internet Works

1. *Basic Characteristics*

Just as hundreds of millions of people who make telephone calls every day have little conception of how their voice travels almost instantaneously to a distant location, most Internet users have only a vague understanding of how the Internet operates. The fundamental operational characteristics of the Internet are that it is a distributed, interoperable, packet-switched network.

A *distributed* network has no one central repository of information or control, but is comprised of an interconnected web of "host" computers, each of which can be accessed from virtually any point on the network. Thus, an Internet user can obtain information from a host computer in another state or another country just as easily as obtaining information from across the street, and there is hierarchy through which the information must flow or be monitored. Instead, routers throughout the network regulate the flow of data at each connection point. By contrast, in a centralized network, all users connect to a single location. The distributed nature of the Internet gives it robust survivability characteristics, because there is no one point of failure for the network, but it makes measurement and governance difficult.

An *interoperable* network uses open protocols so that many different types of networks and facilities can be transparently linked together, and allows multiple services to be provided to different users over the same network. The Internet can run over virtually any type of facility that can transmit data, including copper and fiber optic circuits of telephone companies, coaxial cable of cable companies, and various types of wireless connections. The Internet also interconnects users of thousands of different local and regional networks, using many different types of computers. The interoperability of the Internet is made possible by the TCP/IP protocol, which defines a common structure for Internet data and for the routing of that data through the network.

A *packet-switched* network means that data transmitted over the network is split up into small chunks, or "packets." Unlike "circuit-switched" networks such as the public switched telephone network (PSTN), a packet-switched network is "connectionless." In other words, a dedicated end-to-end transmission path (or circuit) does not need to be opened for each transmission.[28] Rather, each router calculates the best routing for a packet at a particular

---

[28] In actuality, much of the PSTN, especially for long-distance traffic, uses digital multiplexing to increase transmission capacity. Thus, beyond the truly dedicated connection along the subscriber loop to the local switch, the "circuit" tied up for a voice call is a set of time slices or frequency assignments in multiplexing systems that send multiple calls over the same wires and fiber optic circuits.

moment in time, given current traffic patterns, and sends the packet to the next router. Thus, even two packets from the same message may not travel the same physical path through the network. This mechanism is referred to as "dynamic routing." When packets arrive at the destination point, they must be reassembled, and packets that do not arrive for whatever reason must generally be re-sent. This system allows network resources to be used more efficiently, as many different communications can be routed simultaneously over the same transmission facilities. On the other hand, the inability of the sending computer under such a "best effort" routing system to ensure that sufficient bandwidth will be available between the two points creates difficulties for services that require constant transmission rates, such as streaming video and voice applications.

2. Addressing

When an end user sends information over the Internet, the data is first broken up into packets. Each of these packets includes a header which indicates the point from which the data originates and the point to which it is being sent, as well as other information. TCP/IP defines locations on the Internet through the use of "IP numbers." IP numbers include four address blocks consisting of numbers between 0 and 256, separated by periods (e.g., 165.135.0.254). Internet users generally do not need to specify the IP number of the destination site, because IP numbers can be represented by alphanumeric "domain names" such as "fcc.gov" or "ibm.com." "Domain name servers" throughout the network contain tables that cross reference these domain names with their underlying IP numbers. Thus, for example, when an Internet user sends e-mail to someone at "microsoft.com," the network will convert the destination into its corresponding IP number and use that for routing purposes.

3. Services Provided Over the Internet

The actual services provided to end users through the Internet are defined not through the routing mechanisms of TCP/IP, but depend instead on higher-level application protocols, such as hypertext transport protocol (HTTP); file transfer protocol (FTP); network news transport protocol (NNTP), and simple mail transfer protocol (SMTP). Because these protocols are not embedded in the Internet itself, a new application-layer protocol can be operated over the Internet through as little as one server computer that transmits the data in the proper format, and one client computer that can receive and interpret the data. The utility of a service to users, however, increases as the number of servers that provide that service increases.

By the late 1980s, the primary Internet services included electronic mail or "e-mail," Telnet, FTP, and Usenet news. E-mail, which is probably the most widely-used Internet service, allows users to send text-based messages to each other using a common addressing system. Telnet allows Internet users to "log into" other proprietary networks, such as library card catalogs, through the Internet, and to retrieve data as though they were directly accessing those networks. FTP allows users to "download" files from a remote host computer onto their own system. Usenet "newsgroups" enable users to post and review messages on specific topics.

Despite the continued popularity of some of these services, in particular news and e-mail, the service that has catalyzed the recent explosion in Internet usage is the World Wide Web.

NOTES & QUESTIONS

1. *Internet as English.* In a popular essay, science fiction writer Bruce Sterling writes:

> The Internet's "anarchy" may seem strange or even unnatural, but it makes a certain deep and basic sense. It's rather like the "anarchy" of the English language. Nobody rents English, and nobody owns English. As an English-speaking person, it's up to you to learn how to speak English properly and make whatever use you please of it (though the government provides certain subsidies to help you learn to read and write a bit). Otherwise, everybody just sort of pitches in, and somehow the thing evolves on its own, and somehow turns out workable. And interesting. Fascinating, even. Though a lot of people earn their living from using and exploiting and teaching English, "English" as an institution is public property, a public good. Much the same goes for the Internet. Would English be improved if the "The English Language, Inc." had a board of directors and a chief executive officer, or a President and a Congress? There'd probably be a lot fewer new words in English, and a lot fewer new ideas.[*]

2. *The internet's grammar: TCP/IP.* If we stick with the language analogy, what then are the grammar rules? It's TCP/IP. Here's a little more on how TCP/IP works. The best way to understand how these protocols operate is to imagine the data you want to send as a long document, with TCP and IP acting as special internal and external envelopes.

First, the "transmission control protocol" (TCP) breaks down data (the document) into "packets" (individual pages) of information and puts each packet into an internal envelope that is numbered on the outside for later

---

[*] Bruce Sterling, *Science: Internet,* MAGAZINE OF FANTASY & SCI. FICTION, Feb. 1993, at 99.

reassembly (e.g., 1 of 7). On this internal envelope is also bookkeeping information that helps ensure that each packet (page) arrives intact and that all the packets of data (the entire document) arrive *in toto.*

Second, the "internet protocol" (IP) places each internal envelope into an external envelope labeled with the destination IP address. As you recall, each computer on the internet has a unique IP address, just as telephones each have a unique telephone number.[*]

Third, the physical and protocol layers operate together to send this double-enveloped packet of information to the nearest router, which reads the external envelope's IP address and forwards it along to whatever router seems geographically closer to the destination. A router is a computer that functions as a switch (conceptually similar to the local switch within the PSTN). A router forwards packets through the network based on the current network topology, current network traffic, and the destination address of the packet. When a packet is received by a router, it calculates the best path for that packet, and forwards the packet on to the next router. This process repeats until the packet finally arrives at the destination computer.

Upon receipt, the process is reversed. The external envelope is discarded. From the internal envelope, the destination computer acquires the critical information necessary to reassemble the document. For example, it might discover that this particular envelope contains the contents that represent page 2 of a seven-page document. The computer therefore dutifully waits for all the pages to arrive. Also, from the bookkeeping information on the internal envelope, the computer can examine if the contents were somehow damaged during transport. After all the pages arrive in good condition, the document is reassembled and provided to the application layer.

3. *Defining internet.* Now that you have read about the internet, how would you define it? Put yourself in the shoes of a legislative staffer who has to write a draft bill regulating some aspect of the internet. Try to draft the subsection defining the internet.

---

[*] Of course, multiple telephones within the same household tend to have the same number (unless the household has more than one telephone line). In that case, the telephone number uniquely identifies the household. Telephone numbers for cellular telephones uniquely identify the particular cellular telephone. Similarly, multiple computers sharing the same Internet connection may share the same *public* IP address, but are also assigned *private* IP addresses to identify them on the local network.

2. CONTEXT

KEVIN WERBACH, DIGITAL TORNADO
(CONTINUED):
FCC, Office of Policy & Planning, Working Paper Series 29 (March 1997)

B. An Extremely Brief History of the Net

The roots of the current Internet can be traced to ARPANET, a network developed in the late 1960s with funding from the Advanced Research Projects Administration (ARPA) of the United States Department of Defense. ARPANET linked together computers at major universities and defense contractors, allowing researchers at those institutions to exchange data. As ARPANET grew during the 1970s and early 1980s, several similar networks were established, primarily between universities. The TCP/IP protocol was adopted as a standard to allow these networks, comprised of many different types of computers, to interconnect.

In the mid-1980s, the National Science Foundation (NSF) funded the establishment of NSFNET, a TCP/IP network that initially connected six NSF-funded national supercomputing centers at a data rate of 56 kilobits per second (kbps). NSF subsequently awarded a contract to a partnership of Merit (one of the existing research networks), IBM, MCI, and the State of Michigan to upgrade NSFNET to T-1 speed (1.544 megabits per second (Mbps)), and to interconnect several additional research networks. The new NSFNET "backbone," completed in 1988, initially connected thirteen regional networks. [I]ndividual sites such as universities could connect to one of these regional networks, which then connected to NSFNET, so that the entire network was linked together in a hierarchical structure. Connections to the federally-subsidized NSFNET were generally free for the regional networks, but the regional networks generally charged smaller networks a flat monthly fee for their connections.

The military portion of ARPANET was integrated into the Defense Data Network in the early 1980s, and the civilian ARPANET was taken out of service in 1990, but by that time NSFNET had supplanted ARPANET as a national backbone for an "Internet" of worldwide interconnected networks. In the late 1980s and early 1990s, NSFNET usage grew dramatically, jumping from 85 million packets in January 1988 to 37 billion packets in September 1993. The capacity of the NSFNET backbone was upgraded to handle this additional demand, eventually reaching T-3 (45 Mbps) speed.

In 1992, the NSF announced its intention to phase out federal support for the Internet backbone, and encouraged commercial entities to set up private backbones. Alternative backbones had already begun to develop because NSFNET's "acceptable use" policy, rooted in its academic and military background, ostensibly did not allow for the transport of commercial data. In the 1990s, the Internet has expanded decisively beyond universities and scientific sites to include businesses and individual users connecting through commercial ISPs and consumer online services.

Federal support for the NSFNET backbone ended on April 30, 1995. The NSF has, however, continued to provide funding to facilitate the transition of the Internet to a privately-operated network. The NSF supported the development of three priority Network Access Points (NAPs), in Northern California, Chicago, and New York, at which backbone providers could exchange traffic with each other, as well as a "routing arbiter" to facilitate traffic routing at these NAPs.

Since the termination of federal funding for the NSFNET backbone, the Internet has continued to evolve. Many of the largest private backbone providers have negotiated bilateral "peering" arrangements to exchange traffic with each other, in addition to multilateral exchange points such as the NAPs. Several new companies have built nationwide backbones. Despite this increase in capacity, usage has increased even faster, leading to concerns about congestion.

MILTON MUELLER & JOHN MATHIASON, INTERNET GOVERNANCE: THE STATE OF PLAY
(Internet Governance Project Sept. 9, 2004).

What is meant by "governance?" . . . . [T]hree distinct types of governance functions have been identified . . . . They are: 1) technical standardization, 2) resource allocation and assignment, and 3) policy formulation, policy enforcement, and dispute resolution.

TECHNICAL STANDARDIZATION

The first function is technical standardization. This has to do with how decisions are made regarding the basic networking protocols, software applications, and data format standards that make the Internet work. Organizations that perform these functions define, develop and reach consensus on technical specifications. The specifications are then published and have value as a means of coordinating equipment manufacturing, software design and service provision in ways that ensure technical compatibility and interoperation. The technical standardization functions of the Internet have been performed mainly by non-State actors . . . .

RESOURCE ALLOCATION AND ASSIGNMENT

The second function is resource allocation and assignment. When usage of a global resource, such as the IP address space, radio spectrum or telephone country number codes, must be exclusive, usage must be coordinated or administered by an organization or some other mechanism. The assignment authority allocates or partitions the resource space and assigns parts of it to specific users. They also develop policies, procedures or rules to guide the allocation and assignment decisions. This function was the original source of controversy in Internet governance, where disputes concerning the assignment of top-level domain names led to the creation of the Internet Corporation for Assigned Names and Numbers (ICANN).

Resource assignment is not the same thing as technical standardization. Technical standards may create a virtual resource that requires exclusive assignment when put into operation (e.g., the technical standards defining the IP protocol creates an address space, and the DNS protocol defines the domain name space). But defining and reaching consensus on the standard is a completely different function from the subsequent allocation and assignment of the resources. . . . The issue of the authority behind the organizations or mechanisms is important in resource allocation. Who is ultimately responsible for the decisions made, in legal and political terms, becomes important and often the entity that has legitimate authority can affect how resources are assigned. When resources are scarce, control of the institutions becomes important to the concerned actors.

POLICY FORMULATION, ENFORCEMENT AND DISPUTE RESOLUTION

The third function is policy making. This refers to the formulation of policy, enforcement and monitoring, and dispute resolution. It involves the development of norms, rules and procedures that govern the conduct of people and organizations, as opposed to the structure and operation of the technology. While the Internet itself is merely a channel for communication and, in that sense, is policy-neutral, many public policy issues arise either as a consequence of its use by a growing number of people in an international context, or because States and non-State actors want to respond to national and international problems by regulating the technological system itself.

* * *

The Internet protocols create two critical resource spaces: the IP address space and the domain name space.

Four key organizations perform the resource assignment functions for the Internet: 1) the Internet Corporation for Assigned Names and Numbers (ICANN), 2) the regional Internet address registries (RIRs), 3) the Internet Software Consortium, and 4) International Telecommunication Union (ITU). In addition to these four identifiable entities, there is also a diverse set of root server operators in the U.S., Europe and Japan associated with different organizations but not formally integrated into a corporate entity nor formally bound to any governance regime.

ICANN (Nonstate/Formal)

ICANN is a California nonprofit public benefit corporation, the creation of which was invoked by the U.S. Department of Commerce following a public proceeding in 1997-98 that invited international participation. ICANN took over the resource assignment functions associated with the Internet Assigned Numbers Authority (IANA), an informal IETF-associated entity run by University-based computer scientist and Internet pioneer Jon Postel. IANA had been funded via grants from U.S. government agencies. In 1998 it was detached from the IETF complex of organizations, and bundled with a new, policy formulation body (ICANN). ICANN was deliberately set up as a private sector, multistakeholder governance organization, although it included some governmental input through its Governmental Advisory Committee (GAC) and its contractual relations with the U.S. government.

RIRs (NonState/Formal)

The Regional Internet Registries (RIRs) are responsible for distribution of Internet Number resources, including Autonomous System Numbers and IPv4 and IPv6 addresses. IP addresses are the most important identifiers for the Internet's operation. IP packets cannot work without unique address assignment and scalable routing techniques that permit packets to find their destination. There are now four RIRs: ARIN (encompassing North America, parts of the Caribbean and parts of Africa); RIPE-NCC (Western and Eastern Europe, parts of Africa, parts of the Middle East); APNIC (Asia, Far East); and LACNIC (Latin America). Efforts are underway to create an African RIR (AfriNIC). All existing registries are private sector nonprofits with roots in the Internet technical community and a membership composed primarily of Internet Service Providers, telephone companies and Internet hosting services.

Root Server Operators (Mostly Non-state/Informal)

Root servers are a critical part of the resource assignment regime of the Internet. They provide authoritative data about the top level of the domain name hierarchy. Most of the Internet domain name system's 13 root server operators are not formally tied into a governance regime of any kind. Those operated by ICANN itself, and a special root server operated by VeriSign under contract with the U.S. Department of commerce, (and perhaps also those operated by the US military) are contractually or legally bound to the ICANN regime or accountable to the US government. The others, however, are operated by heterogeneous actors in different nations. An informal "Root Server Technical Operations Association" at www.rootservers.org now gives them something of a common voice. They describe themselves as "different professional engineering groups" and stress that they are not involved in policy making or data modification – they just publish (and do not edit) the root zone file and answer queries. Their presentations emphasize the value of diversity and coordination over hierarchy and coercion in coordinating the resource.

ccTLD Associations (nonState/Formal)

Country code domain name registries by themselves might be thought of as exclusively a national issue. However, the refusal of many ccTLD managers to join the ICANN regime fully and their self-organization into associations makes them an alternate source of global domain name governance to some degree. The ccTLDs control a considerable part of the name space. Two organizations of note are CENTR, the Council of European National TLD Registries, and APTLD, the Asia-Pacific Top Level Domain Association.

3. BANDWIDTH SCARCITY?

With this introduction to the internet, ask yourself whether you need any sort of government license, franchise, or permission to become an internet service provider (ISP). To perform as an ISP, you need to be able to speak TCP/IP, but that's an open standard for which you need no prior permission.

What about addresses? As an ISP, you do need to be able to allocate IP addresses to your end-users either dynamically or statically. It turns out that any scarcity in the IP address space is a (somewhat) solvable technological problem, with various solutions including recycling local IP addresses and upgrading the systemwide protocols (e.g. IPv6 which radically increases the number of IP addresses available). The bottom line is that any scarcity in addresses has not prompted states or the federal government to control ISP entry.

Does this mean that there are no entry regulations whatsoever for ISPs? To a first approximation, the answer is yes. But there is second-order complexity, generated by the need for high bandwidth channels that can only be provided if ISPs own or have access to high bandwidth wires or spectrum. If new wires have to be laid down across public streets and easements, any such build out will trigger entry questions similar to those we've already studied with wireline telephony and cable TV. If, instead, large swatches of spectrum are to be used, the ISP must get a license for that spectrum, which raises the sort of entry questions we've already seen with broadcast and mobile telephony.

E. THE "HOW" QUESTION

Up to now, this Chapter has addressed different *justifications* for the government to regulate entry in broadcast, wireline telephony, cable TV, and internet. In other words, it has examined the "Why" question. Why regulate entry? Now suppose that the justification has been made and society agrees that there is good reason to regulate entry. Another question then arises: How? How precisely should these scarce licenses and franchises be allocated to specific applicants? Conceptually, there are three methods: merit, luck, or money. We explore these concepts, in the industry context of broadcast.

1. MERIT

A merit system grants a license or franchise to the applicant who has the most "merit." Let's unpack how a merit system might work using the example of broadcast. Historically, broadcast licenses have been allocated on the basis of merit defined as serving the "public interest." And when multiple applicants have applied for the same license, often a comparative hearing was conducted to decide who was worthy in terms of the "public interest." But what does the "public interest" mean? Ever since the 1940s, the FCC has struggled with this question.

In an important 1965 *Policy Statement*, the FCC attempted to specify, with greater texture, its conception of "merit" and identified "best practicable service to the public" and "maximum diffusion of control of the media of mass communications" as desiderata. In turn, these goals would be measured by more specific factors, including: (1) diversification of control of mass media communications; (2) proposed programming service; (3) past broadcast record; (4) efficient use of the frequency; (5) character; and, (6) owners' full-time participation in station operations (the integration criterion).[*] The largest weight would be given to the diversification and integration factors. In 1993, however,

---

[*] *See FCC Policy Statement on Comparative Broadcast Hearings*, 1 F.C.C.2d 393 (1965).

this articulation of merit was voided by the D.C. Circuit as "arbitrary and capricious" in violation of the Administrative Procedure Act.[*]

Subsequent legislation made a precise definition of "public interest" for purposes of license assignment less necessary by making comparative hearings largely extinct. First, in 1996, Congress made license renewals trivially easy. At renewal, the FCC is no longer permitted to engage in comparative hearings simply because a competitor applies for the same license. The incumbent broadcaster must be renewed as long as it has not committed serious violations of the Communications Act or the FCC's rules.

> 47 U.S.C. § 309(k). Broadcast station renewal procedures
>
> (1) Standards for renewal. If the licensee of a broadcast station submits an application to the Commission for renewal of such license, the Commission shall grant the application if it finds, with respect to that station, during the preceding term of its license—
>
> > (A) the station has served the public interest, convenience, and necessity;
> >
> > (B) there have been no serious violations by the licensee of this Act or the rules and regulations of the Commission; and
> >
> > (C) there have been no other violations by the licensee of this Act or the rules and regulations of the Commission which, taken together, would constitute a pattern of abuse.

If and only if the incumbent flunks this easy test can the agency consider any other license applicants. Second, in 1997, Congress required new licenses to be distributed through auctions (money).[†]

2. LUCK

Instead of focusing on contentious definitions of *merit*, society could distribute scarce entry licenses randomly, through luck. Lotteries were used most prominently by the FCC in doling out cellular licenses,[‡] in the rollout of the first generation of mobile telephony. Back in the 1980s, Congress granted the FCC the authority to conduct lotteries to distribute certain cellular telephony licenses because "merit" determinations were taking too long.

---

[*] 10 F.3d 875, 886 (D.C. Cir. 1993).

[†] *See* 47 U.S.C. § 309(j)(1). This command has been interpreted by the FCC broadly to cover not only primary broadcast licenses (the standard television signals you receive), but also secondary licenses (e.g., low-power television, FM, and television translators). FM and television translator stations rebroadcast existing stations to small areas that cannot be reached by the original broadcast signal. There are a few exceptions for safety radio, digital television, and noncommercial television broadcast licenses.

[‡] In addition to cellular licenses, low-power television licenses have also been lotteried. *See, e.g.,* 2nd R&O, *Amendment of the Commission's Rules to Allow the Selection from Among Certain Applications Using Random Selection of Lotteries Instead of Comparative Hearings*, 93 F.C.C.2d 952 (1983).

> 47 U.S.C. § 309. Application for license
>
> (i) Certain initial licenses and permits; random selection procedure; significant preferences; rules.
>
> > (1) General authority. [I]f there is more than one application for any initial license or construction permit, then the Commission shall have the authority to grant such license or permit to a qualified applicant through the use of a system of random selection.

Unfortunately, lotteries took much longer than expected, partly because so many applicants decided to enter the lottery. After all, "buying a ticket" to enter the lottery was relatively cheap. And initially, nothing prevented the winner from immediately flipping the license to a third party for the fair market value of cellular telephony spectrum, which could be millions of dollars. By 1997, in the same legislation empowering the FCC to use auctions (described below), Congress terminated the FCC's authority to issue licenses via lottery.[*]

3. MONEY

A third method of regulating entry is to provide the resource to whoever will pay the most money in an auction. Auctions have been used by the Department of the Interior to distribute tracts in the outer continental shelf, federal coal leases, treasury bills, and seized or unclaimed property. Why not, then, use auctions to distribute communications licenses and franchises?

One could claim that auctions by definition provide the most optimal allocations by giving licenses to those who value them most—as measured by willingness and ability to pay. As compared to a comparative merit hearing between two applicants for a license, an auction should also be easier to administer and less burdensome to the parties because an auction avoids controversial determinations about merit. Instead of focusing on who might serve the public interest most, which cannot be objectively measured, one can objectively determine who makes the highest bid. Also, there should not be the same problem as with lotteries—too many applicants—because applicants will have to put up real money in their bids.

In the Omnibus Reconciliation Act (ORA) of 1993,[†] Congress authorized the FCC to auction off spectrum licenses used to receive direct payments from subscribers for receiving or transmitting information (in other words, mobile telephony-like services). Using sophisticated computer software to allow for efficient remote auctioning over the internet, the process has generally worked

---

[*] *See* § 309(i)(5) (terminating authority after July 1, 1997). Again, here, there are minor exceptions involving noncommercial broadcast stations.

[†] Pub. L. No. 103-66, 107 Stat. at 312. 47 U.S.C. § 309(j).

well, leading to rapid distribution of licenses that have earned billions of dollars for the U.S. government. In 1997 Congress instructed the FCC to use auctions in cases of mutually exclusive applications for any initial license (which includes broadcast).[*] As of summer 2011, the FCC has concluded over 90 auctions, producing net winning bids of over $78 billion, which is viewed as a significant revenue success.

NOTES & QUESTIONS

1. *Law school admissions.* Another way to think about the different forms of entry regulation is to think about how law school admissions. The number of spots in your law school are "scarce"—more people would like admission than there are seats. (By the way, is this physical or economic scarcity? Is there any meaningful difference?) Your law school has decided that it must regulate entry and that it is lawful to do so. What precise method has the administration adopted? Is it merit, luck, or money?

a. *Merit?* No doubt most law schools would like to emphasize merit, but does money have nothing to do with it? For instance, do the children of large donors have increased chances of entry? What about legacies? Also, how does one define merit in this context? Is it your LSAT and undergraduate GPA? Is it the likelihood that you will pass the bar exam? Is it some "public interest" standard, or is the institutional goal of your law school not primarily the public interest?

b. *Renewal expectations.* Continuing with the above analogy, would it be reasonable to undertake a full-fledged merit evaluation for each student after each year of law school? Or are there reasonable reliance interests that should allow a student to return each year except in extraordinary circumstances? In attending law school, several of your costs are sunk: opportunity cost of a year spent studying, moving expenses, and so on. Would you be willing to incur these costs without a strong expectation that you will be permitted to finish law school and receive your degree?

c. *Paying for admissions.* Many commentators have forcefully argued in favor of auctions in allocating scarce resources. They argue that it is economically efficient—thus the socially optimal way to distribute broadcast licenses. If this sounds right to you intuitively, why not do the same thing for law school spots? Indeed, why not do it for grades in this class? Would it not be more efficient?

---

[*] There are a few exceptions. *See* § 309(j)(2) (listing exemptions, such as public safety radio and non-commercial and public broadcast stations).

2. *Points of comparison.* On what variables might we compare and contrast the three forms of regulating entry—merit, luck, and money? First, consider social optimality: Who ends up with the license or franchise? Put another way, is the final distribution of scarce resources socially optimal? Of course, this begs the question of what we mean by "socially optimal." For instance, does the touchstone of "public interest, necessity, and convenience" mean the same thing as "economic efficiency"? Second, consider administrability: Is the process administrable? What are the transaction costs involved in getting the license to the applicant? On these two points of comparison, how do the merit-, luck-, and money-based processes compare and contrast?

3. *Merit versus money.* According to economic thinking, the auction produces the most optimal allocation. It gives the license to the person who values it most. But many complain that this system provides licenses to the most wealthy, not to the most worthy. A rejoinder is that even with merit-based licensing, nothing prevents the initial applicant from selling the license to a third party, soon after receiving the license.[*] Thus auction advocates argue that the end result does not depend on how the government initially distributes licenses, either through auctions or comparative hearings. However, by adopting auctions, society avoids subsequent transaction costs, and instead of providing windfalls to private individuals who win the initial license, the windfall goes to the public fisc.

4. *Incentive auctions.* The use of "money" can also facilitate transitions of critical resources that would otherwise block entry. Consider what happens when scarce resources (e.g. spectrum) that were previously licensed for one use (e.g., broadcast TV) become more valuable in some other sector, like the mobile broadband internet market? Economically, it would be more efficient for the spectrum to be used for internet. But effecting that transition is challenging when current broadcast licensees resist any such transition. The FCC has spent the last decade struggling with this challenge. Its solution is the "incentive auction."[†]

---

[*] There is very little constraint on how quickly one may "flip" a broadcast station. Since 1962, a licensee had to hold the license for at least three years. But in 1982 this anti-trafficking "three-year rule" was eliminated by the FCC. A one-year holding requirement was preserved for licenses obtained through comparative hearing. *See In the Matter of Amendment of Section 73.3597 of the Commission's Rules,* 52 Rad. Reg. 2d (P & F) 1081 (1982). In 1985, the FCC added to the one-year requirement licenses obtained through the FCC's Minority Ownership Policy. *See* 99 F.C.C.2d 971 (1985).

[†] FCC, *How It Works: The Incentive Auction Explained* (2018), https://www.fcc.gov/about-fcc/fcc-initiatives/incentive-auctions/how-it-works.

FCC, *HOW IT WORKS:*
THE INCENTIVE AUCTION EXPLAINED

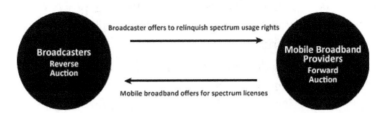

A NOVEL DESIGN FOR A NOVEL PROCESS

The broadcast incentive auction itself will comprise two separate but interdependent auctions—a reverse auction, which will determine the price at which broadcasters will voluntarily relinquish their spectrum usage rights; and a forward auction, which will determine the price companies are willing to pay for flexible use wireless licenses.

The lynchpin joining the reverse and the forward auctions is the "repacking" process. Repacking involves reorganizing and assigning channels to the remaining broadcast television stations in order to create contiguous blocks of cleared spectrum suitable for flexible use. The vast majority of stations that remain on the air after the auction will be assigned channels in the TV band; in a few markets where the post-auction TV band is not large enough to accommodate every station, stations may be assigned a channel in the wireless band.

In order to be successful, each of the components must work together. Ultimately, the reverse auction requires information about how much bidders are willing to pay for spectrum licenses in the forward auction; and the forward auction requires information regarding what spectrum rights were tendered in the reverse auction, and at what price; and each of these depend on efficiently repacking the remaining broadcasters.

INTEGRATION OF THE REVERSE AND FORWARD AUCTIONS

The reverse and forward auctions will be integrated in a series of stages. Each stage will consist of a reverse auction and a forward auction. Prior to the first stage, the initial spectrum clearing target will be determined. Broadcasters will indicate through the pre-auction application process their willingness to relinquish spectrum usage rights at the opening prices.

Based on broadcasters' collective willingness, the initial spectrum clearing target will be set at the highest level possible (up to 126 megahertz of spectrum) without exceeding a pre-determined national aggregate cap on the interference between wireless providers and TV stations ("impairments") created when TV stations must be assigned to the wireless band. Under this approach, the auction system will establish a band of wireless spectrum that is generally uniform in size across all markets. Then the reverse auction bidding process will be run to determine the total amount of incentive payments to broadcasters required to clear that amount of spectrum.

The forward auction bidding process will follow the reverse auction bidding process. If the "final stage rule" is satisfied, the forward auction bidding will continue until there is no excess demand, and then the incentive auction will close. If the final stage rule is not satisfied, additional stages will be run, with progressively lower spectrum targets in the reverse auction and less spectrum available in the forward auction.

FINAL STAGE RULE

The final stage rule is a set of conditions that must be met in order to close the auction at the current clearing target; failure to satisfy the rule would result in running a new phase at the next lowest clearing target.

The final stage rule is a reserve price with two components, both of which must be satisfied. The first component requires that the average price for low impairment licenses in the forward auction meets or exceeds $1.25 per MHz-pop at a 70 MHz cleared benchmark. Alternatively, if the spectrum clearing target at a particular stage is greater than 70 MHz, then the first component will be met if the total proceeds of the forward auction exceed the product of $1.25 per MHZ/pop x 70 MHz x the total number of pops for the high-demand Partial Economic Areas (PEAs) with at least one Category 1 block in this stage. This alternative formulation will allow the auction to close if the incentive auction repurposes a relatively large amount of spectrum for wireless uses, even if the price per-MHz-pop is less than the benchmark price.

The second component of the final stage rule requires that the proceeds of the forward auction be sufficient to meet mandatory expenses set forth in the Spectrum Act. If the requirements of both components of the reserve price are met, then the final stage rule is satisfied.

On January 18, 2017, the auction satisfied both of the conditions of the final stage rule, assuring that the auction will close in Stage 4.

NOTES & QUESTIONS

1. *Wait, what just happened?* After bidding closed on March 30, 2017, the FCC announced that it had successfully repurposed 84 MHz of spectrum, which

will be divided into licensed (70 MHz) and unlicensed (14 MHz) uses. The auction yielded $19.8 billion in revenue, including $10.05 billion for broadcast "bidders" and $7 billion for the U.S Treasury. Can you explain who was paid and what they were paid for?

2. *So what happens next?* The FCC provided for a "post-auction transition period" through July 13, 2020, to allow broadcasters and others to modify their systems and shift over to new their new frequency allocations. But what will happen after that? The bulk of licenses in the 600 MHz band (sold in the "forward" auction) are going to be used for wireless data connections. Providers are already starting to offer fifth generation (5G) connectivity and promise higher speeds and lower latency for data transfers (10 Gbps and <1 ms latency). Early 5G adopters rely on mobile "hotspot" devices because most smart phones currently lack compatible hardware for high speed 5G transfers, but providers expect that future generations of both fixed and mobile connected devices will have the capability built in (think "smart" devices and other embedded systems).

3. *Where did my stories go?* As with any major transition, the changes are sure to cause confusion and consternation. The "bidders" in the incentive auction used to broadcast TV signals on a particular frequency; now they sold that right. So where will they go? Some will close, others will "repack" and move to license or share different spectrum. But TV consumers might be surprised when they wake up one day and "Channel 5" doesn't work the way it used to. This is why the FCC has required prior notification by channels that are planning to move to a new frequency.

4. *Going all the way—privatizing the spectrum.* All this talk about buying and selling licenses begs a question: Why not totally privatize the spectrum? Instead of giving out licenses (with strong renewal expectancies that have to be bought out), why not give out "fee simple absolutes" to the spectrum and let the owner use the spectrum for whatever purposes it desires? By creating sharply defined property rights over spectrum, one could avoid the interference chaos we saw at the beginning of the 20th century. Consider what Ronald Coase wrote back in 1959:

> [T]he real cause of trouble was that no property rights were created in these scarce frequencies. A private-enterprise system cannot function properly unless property rights are created in resources, and, when this is done, someone wishing to use a resource has to pay the owner to obtain it. Chaos disappears; and so does the government except that a legal system to define property rights and to arbitrate disputes is, of course, necessary. But there is certainly no need for the kind of regulation which we now find in the American radio and television industry.[*]

Rules of general applicability, such as property, tort, and contract law, could determine the final distribution and use of the resources. And if some mobile internet provider needs a huge swatch of spectrum, how is that different than a real estate developer needing a huge swatch of land? What might the advantages of this privatization approach be?

5. *Commons.* Instead of converting a public resource into private property, why not turn it loose into the commons, freely usable by all? If this sounds too fanciful, realize that leaving spectrum in some form of commons is not entirely new. For example, under Part 95 of the FCC's rules, CB (citizens band) radio is "licensed by rule" to an entire class, for collective use.[*] This sort of licensing is specifically authorized in 47 U.S.C. § 307(e).

> 47 U.S.C. § 307(e) Operation of certain radio stations without individual licenses
>
> (1) Notwithstanding any license requirement established in this chapter, if the Commission determines that such authorization serves the public interest, convenience, and necessity, the Commission may by rule authorize the operation of radio stations without individual licenses in the following radio services: (A) the citizens band radio service . . .
>
> (3) For purposes of this subsection, the terms "citizens band radio service", "radio control service" . . . shall have the meanings given them by the Commission by rule.

Finally, some uses of spectrum do not require a license at all. Consider, for example, the ubiquitous 802.11 "Wi-Fi" networks, as well as cordless phones, garage door openers, and remote controls. Instead of obtaining a license, the individual devices need only comply with 47 C.F.R. Part 15, which allows use of particular frequencies at low power so as to minimize interference. (Recall that after the incentive auctions, 14 MHz of spectrum was set aside for unlicensed uses.)

6. *Medium scarcity and crowded skies.* Being the winner of an auction or purchaser of a piece of spectrum real estate isn't a guarantee of success. Just ask Ligado Networks (formerly LightSquared), a satellite communications company that has been trying for nearly twenty years to enter the mobile (terrestrial) communications market.[†] Through mergers and acquisitions, the company currently owns 40 MHz of spectrum licenses in the 1500 to 1700 MHz block. The FCC recently ended a 17-year proceeding and granted Ligado permission to operate a 5G network that will be used for Internet of Things (IoT) devices.

---

[*] Ronald H. Coase, *The Federal Communications Commission*, 2 J. L. & ECON. 14 (1959).

[*] *See* 47 C.F.R. Part 95 ("Personal Radio Service"); § 95.404 ("You do not need an individual license to operate a CB station. You are authorized by this rule to operate your CB station in accordance with the rules in this subpart.").

[†] *See Lightsquared Tech. Working Grp. Rep. Lightsquared License Modification Application*, No. FCC 20-48 (2020), 2020 WL 1963885.

Why was this authorization so complicated and controversial? Interference. The Global Positioning Service (GPS) satellites that operate in the United States to provide position, navigation, and timing (PNT) services run in the 1559-1610 MHz band using several different standards. Ligado was originally authorized to operate earth-to-satellite communications using the 1525-1599 MHz and 1626.5-1660.6 MHz bands, but requested authorization to supplement that network with terrestrial towers. They faced opposition from the GPS industry and others who felt that the terrestrial operations would interfere with their signals. The potential negative impact of this interference with the GPS system was a direct barrier to Ligado's entry, and it has taken them almost two decades to come to a resolution (and even that could be challenged). Managing spectrum is a tricky business.

In this chapter, we have examined the second concept essential to understanding communications law and policy: *entry*. We have examined the most common justifications for regulating entry, which include spectrum scarcity, government property, common carriage, natural monopoly, and medium scarcity. For these reasons, we tolerate government regulation of entry notwithstanding the First Amendment's protection of freedom of expression. In addition, we discussed examples of how we might allocate licenses or franchise, via merit, luck, and money.

CHAPTER 3

PRICING

O nce a firm has been allowed to enter the market, it must set some price for its communication service. Should the state get involved in setting that price? To answer this question intelligently, we must apply some of the economic theory introduced in CHAPTER 1: POWER. In a market economy, prices are generally set by the marketplace and, under ideal circumstances, the market price will be "efficient." However, in the real world, a firm may exercise sufficient economic power—even total monopoly power—such that we cannot rely on the market to price a service. This is the principal justification for government ratemaking. Assuming that the justification for regulating prices has been made, numerous legal and policy issues arise about how the government should set prices correctly. Ratemaking also creates questions about how firms might challenge prices if they disagree on the pricing formula. In some cases, the government may even need to subsidize prices to ensure that everyone has access to essential communications tools.

A. TELEPHONY

We start by studying the pricing of wireline telephony services. This section is extremely technical—both as a matter of technology and regulation. You may wonder whether the payoff is worth the effort, especially as wireline telephony has become less important. But the fundamentals you learn here will apply to pricing in other industries. This will also help you understand the legal treatment of common carriers, which has become increasingly relevant to understanding the legal regulation of the internet.

1. SETTING PRICES

a. MAPPING THE PLAYERS

As introduced in CHAPTER 2: ENTRY, the three basic elements of the public switched telephone network (PSTN) are phone, line, and switch. The simplest phone call takes place when the caller and receiver connect to the same local switch. The basic connectivity to the local switch provided to customers like you and me is called *exchange service*, and the twisted-pair copper wire connecting the end-user to the switch is called the "local loop."

> 47 U.S.C. § 153(47). Telephone exchange service
>
> The term 'telephone exchange service' means (A) service within a telephone exchange, or within a connected system of telephone exchanges within the same exchange area operated to furnish to subscribers intercommunicating service of the character ordinarily furnished by a single exchange, and which is covered by the exchange service charge, or (B) comparable service provided through a system of switches, transmission equipment, or other facilities (or combination thereof) by which a subscriber can originate and terminate a telecommunications service.

If the caller and receiver are far apart and not served by the same local switch, the call must be transported from the switch servicing the caller to the switch servicing the receiver. The hauling of communications from one switch to another is called *transport service*, and the line connecting the two switches is called a "trunk." (See Figure 3.1, which depicts exchange services in vertical boxes, and transport service in a horizontal box.)

Until the 1980s, a single monopoly firm, AT&T, essentially provided all of telephony—including exchange service (customer to local switch, except in some rural areas) and transport service (switch to switch)—in an integrated package. But competition was slowly permitted to grow in the transport sector. As competitors (e.g., "MCI") branched out to try to provide a complete alternative long distance service, they ran into a thorny problem: they needed cooperation from their archrival, AT&T. Although MCI could provide transport service between switches, the caller and receiver were themselves still connected to the PSTN through AT&T's exchange service. MCI thus needed access to the local exchange (*exchange access*) from AT&T in order to originate and terminate the long distance calls transported by MCI.

> 47 U.S.C. § 153(16). Exchange access
>
> The term "exchange access" means the offering of access to telephone exchange services or facilities for the purpose of the origination or termination of telephone toll services.

From the Department of Justice's perspective, AT&T refused to play nice with its competitors, in violation of federal antitrust laws. So the federal government sued and reached a settlement that broke up AT&T and severed exchange service from transport service.[*] Henceforth, a *local exchange carrier* (LEC) would provide the former, but an *interexchange carrier* (IXC) would provide the latter.

---

[*] We study the breakup of AT&T carefully in CHAPTER 4: ACCESS.

47 U.S.C. § 153(26). Local exchange carrier.

The term 'local exchange carrier' means any person that is engaged in the provision of telephone exchange service or exchange access. Such term does not include a person insofar as such person is engaged in the provision of a commercial mobile service under section 332(c) of this title, except to the extent that the Commission finds that such service should be included in the definition of such term.

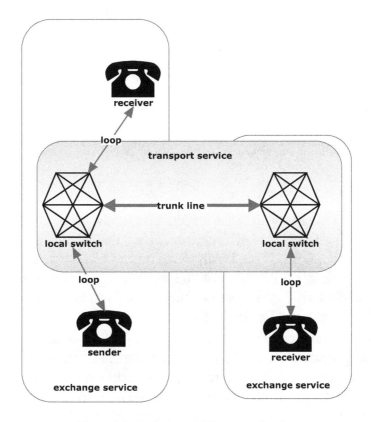

Figure 3.1: Exchange and Transport Services

It was, however, impractical to prevent a LEC from performing any and all transport—if "transport" is defined strictly as connecting any switch to another switch. After all, at the time, there were approximately 19,000 local switches in use, and many were geographically close to each other.* It made no sense to force multiple firms to coordinate the completion of a call traveling just a few miles simply because it involved two switches. Instead, nearby local switches were clumped together into a wholly new regulatory territory called the *local access and transport area* (LATA).

---

* *See* RAY HORAK, COMMUNICATIONS SYSTEMS & NETWORKS: VOICE, DATA, AND BROADBAND TECHNOLOGIES (1997) (reporting the number of Class 5 Central Offices as of 1997).

The Modified Final Judgment, which is the consent decree that broke up AT&T, defined the LATA as "one or more contiguous local exchange areas serving common social, economic, and other purposes, even where such configuration transcends municipal or other local government boundaries."[*] In the end, the United States was divided into 163 LATAs, with an average population of 500,000 per LATA.[†]

The Telecommunications Act of 1996 continued using the LATA territory and codified the following definition:

> 47 U.S.C. § 153(25). Local access and transport area
>
> The term "local access and transport area" or "LATA" means a contiguous geographic area—
>
>   (A) established before the date of enactment of the Telecommunications Act of 1996 [enacted Feb. 8, 1996] by a Bell operating company such that no exchange area includes points within more than 1 metropolitan statistical area, consolidated metropolitan statistical area, or State, except as expressly permitted under the AT&T Consent Decree; or
>
>   (B) established or modified by a Bell operating company after such date of enactment and approved by the Commission.

The local switches within a LATA are typically interconnected through larger tandem switches[‡] although sometimes they are directly interconnected in a mesh network. A LEC was legally permitted to transport communications anywhere *within* a LATA. Even if the caller and receiver were served by different switches, as long as those switches resided within the same LATA, the LEC—all by itself—could make the connection.

By contrast, any communications *across* a LATA boundary required the services of a separate IXC, which provided the transport between the local switches servicing the caller and receiver, located in separate LATAs. These IXCs would have points-of-presence (POP) typically connected to a LEC's tandem switch. To complete the long distance call, the IXC would need the cooperation of both the originating LEC (providing exchange service to the caller) and the terminating LEC (providing exchange service to the receiver). In other words, the IXC would have to purchase *exchange access* from both LECs. (See Figure 3.2 on the next page.)

---

[*] 552 F. Supp. 131, 229 (D.D.C. 1982).

[†] For instance, California has 11 LATAs. San Francisco is in LATA 1; Los Angeles is in LATA 5.

[‡] Tandem switches are switches that connect other switches.

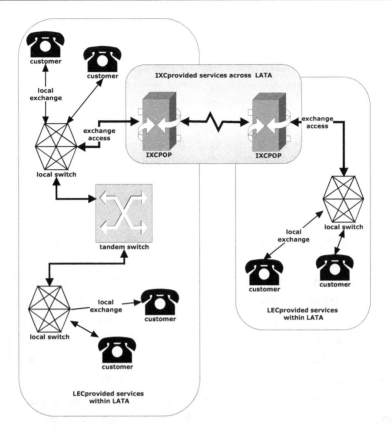

Figure 3.2: LEC and IXC services

In sum, the 1984 breakup of AT&T created a new salient regulatory boundary besides state lines: the LATA. AT&T was split up into seven Regional Bell Operating Companies (RBOCs) and AT&T.[*] Each RBOC was given one region of the country to serve, in which the RBOC could act as a LEC and provide only intra-LATA "local" service.[†] By contrast, AT&T would become an IXC and provide inter-LATA "long distance" service in competition with

---

[*] The original seven RBOCs were: Ameritech Operating Companies (Ameritech), Bell Atlantic Telephone Companies (Bell Atlantic), BellSouth Corporation (BellSouth), New York Telephone Company and New England Telephone and Telegraph Company (NYNEX), Pacific Bell and Nevada Bell (Pactel), Southwestern Bell Telephone Company (SWB), and Mountain States Telephone and Telegraph Company, Northwestern Bell Telephone Company and Pacific Northwest Bell Telephone Company (US West).

[†] In addition to the 7 RBOCs, a few other independent LECs of substantial size existed at the time. GTE was comparably sized to an RBOC, but was never part of the Bell System. In addition, Southern New England Telephone and Cincinnati Bell were smaller, independent LECs. Still smaller companies operated in rural communities. Of course, since the breakup of AT&T, many of these firms have merged together again. For example, GTE merged with Bell Atlantic and MCI and is now part of Verizon.

other long distance providers, such as MCI. With this admittedly complex background, let's run through some examples.

1. *The most "local" call: same switch.* The call is between subscribers within the same local switch service area (e.g., your neighbor down the block). The call is handled exclusively through the shared local switch. Because this is an *intra*-LATA call, the only player involved is the LEC. Also, applying basic federalism principles, because this is an intrastate call, power to regulate the price of this call is in the state's Public Utilities Commission (PUC). Generally, PUCs have established uniform rates for such "local" calls statewide. Typically the customer is charged a flat monthly rate, regardless of the quantity and duration of such calls.

2. *Crossing the switch boundary: different switches, but same LATA.* This call is outside the local switch area but within the same LATA. Once the caller's local switch determines that a call is destined for a different local switch area, the switch seizes a trunk line and creates a circuit to a tandem switch, which then connects to the receiver's local switch. The destination switch then completes the circuit to the receiver's telephone. Because this is an *intra*-LATA call, the only player involved remains the LEC. Because this is an intrastate call,[*] power to regulate the price of this call again remains with the state's PUC.

PUCs decide whether such a call will be charged as a plain *local call* (included in the flat-rate monthly service fee) or under *local toll rates* (per minute). The farther the distance between caller and sender (e.g., over 12 miles), the more likely that the PUC will permit the charging of toll rates. Remember that a single LATA can cover huge ground. For example, in all of California, there are only 11 LATAs. Do not confuse a LATA with a local calling area.

> 47 U.S.C. § 153(48). Telephone toll service
>
> The term "telephone toll service" means telephone service between stations in different exchange areas for which there is made a separate charge not included in contracts with subscribers for exchange service.

3. *Crossing the LATA boundary: different LATAs, same state.* This call is outside the caller's LATA but within the caller's state. A call destined for a different LATA is sent by the local switch in the originating LATA to the IXC's point of presence (POP). At the POP, responsibility for handling the phone call transfers from the LEC to the IXC. The IXC's own switches then direct the call across its own network to the destination LATA, at which point it hands off the call to the receiver's LEC, which completes the call. For assistance on both ends of completing a long distance phone call (exchange access), IXCs pay LECs

---

[*] Almost all LATAs are contained within a state's boundaries, although there are a few exceptions.

"access charges." IXCs maintain a network of switches connected to the LATAs throughout the United States.

Because this is an *inter*-LATA call, both LECs and IXC must participate, as just described. Because this is an intrastate call, power to regulate the price of this call is *still* entirely in the state's PUC. Note that there are multiple legs of this phone call that must be priced: the charge to the caller by the IXC for the intrastate long distance transport, and the intrastate access charge to the IXC by the LECs for helping at each end of the connection.

4. *Crossing the state boundary: different states.* The call is outside the caller's LATA and outside the caller's state. Because this is an *inter*-LATA call, again both LECs and IXC must participate in a series of hand-offs. Because this is an interstate call, power to regulate the price of this call is wielded by the Federal Communications Commission (FCC). Federal pricing regulation centers on this fourth category of calls (interstate, inter-LATA). Again, multiple legs of this phone call need to be priced: (i) the charge to the caller by the IXC for the interstate long distance transport, and (ii) the interstate access charge to the IXC by the LECs for helping at both ends of the connection.

Figure 3.3 summarizes who receives what service from whom: the dashed lines show services provided, whereas the double lines show the monies paid. (The arrowheads reveal the direction in which either services or monies are being provided.)

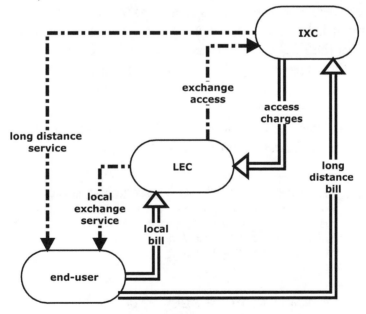

Figure 3.3: Services and Charges in Long Distance Call

b. REVIEWING THE METHODS

So, what does federal law have to say about pricing? We start with Title II of the Communications Act, which regulates the behavior of common carriers.[*] A distinctive attribute of common carriers is that they must serve everyone who reasonably requests carriage.[†] More relevant to this chapter are the federal pricing requirements. Under federal law, all rates charged by interstate common carriers must be "just and reasonable."[‡] In implementing this mandate, the FCC is required to ensure that rates fall within a vaguely defined "zone of reasonableness."[§] Also, a telephone company may not unreasonably discriminate in rates between consumers.[**] Finally, the FCC can hold hearings on the reasonableness of rates, and after the hearing, specify new rates.[††] (Most states have similar regulatory regimes to set intrastate pricing through their PUCs.)

We are now ready to discuss how governments might set prices of telephony services. Recall the central problem: telephony has historically been a legal monopoly. As the only firm in the market, a monopolist lacks the discipline that competitive markets provide in setting prices. Thus it can get away with setting prices above marginal cost, which produces inefficiency. Moreover, it has weaker incentives to provide high-quality service because there is no competition. Regulators can respond by trying to break up the monopoly, which may not make economic sense if monopoly is the "natural" state of affairs. Alternatively, regulators can anoint a single legal monopolist, then set its prices to what would have been charged under competitive circumstances. This is precisely what the FCC has historically attempted to do, at least in theory. We now examine how successful the FCC has been in practice.

1. Continuing Surveillance

From 1934 (when the Communications Act was passed) until the mid-1960s, AT&T (a.k.a. the Bell System) operated what was in effect a national monopoly.

---

[*] Common carriers share the characteristic "of holding [themselves] out to serve indiscriminately" the clientele they are "suited to serve." Nat'l Ass'n of Reg. Util. Comm'rs v. FCC, 525 F.2d 630 (D.C. Cir. 1976). By contrast, cable operators and broadcasters are not treated as common carriers. The FCC recently issued an order "reclassifying" Broadband Internet Access Service (BIAS) providers as common carriers. We will study this order closely in CHAPTER 4: ACCESS.

[†] See 47 U.S.C. § 201(a).

[‡] 47 U.S.C. § 201(b).

[§] See Nader v. FCC, 520 F.2d 182, 192 (D.C. Cir. 1975); Washington Gas Light Co. v. Baker, 188 F.2d 11, 15 (D.C. Cir. 1950).

[**] 47 U.S.C. § 202(a).

[††] 47 U.S.C. §§ 204-205.

It provided all long distance, and most local service.* During this era of undisputed monopoly, the FCC tried to ensure that Bell charged "just and reasonable" prices for interstate communications through the method of *continuing surveillance.*

This was not any systematic or formal procedure; instead, it was essentially eyeballing the prices that AT&T charged for reasonability. According to the FCC,

> only once during this period did this Commission initiate a comprehensive investigation of such matters. This inquiry in the late 1930s cost millions of dollars and occupied approximately 300 researchers for several years. The staff's efforts culminated in the preparation of a voluminous report on Bell System costs and operations, but allegations of inflated costs and rates—and substantial cost shifting between unregulated Western Electric and regulated telephone company operations—were never documented to the Commission's satisfaction. Ultimately, no action was taken on the report's major recommendations, and the investigation produced no significant changes in Commission or Bell System procedures.†

2. Rate-of-Return Regulation

In the late 1960s, competition began in various business fields that AT&T had thus far dominated. As upstart long distance companies, such as Microwave Communications, Inc. (MCI), leveraged new technologies, including microwave transmissions, to compete against AT&T in long distance transport, AT&T responded with aggressive price cuts. Regulators grew concerned that these price cuts in increasingly competitive markets were cross-subsidized by charging supra-competitive prices in monopoly markets, where AT&T faced no competition. Confused about whether AT&T's new prices were properly set, in 1967 federal regulators adopted a more formal method of setting prices—rate-of-return regulation.‡

The rate-of-return. The rate-of-return is what a firm earns, expressed as a percentage of the firm's dollar investment in capital. For example, if AT&T earns (total revenues minus total expenses) $100 this year, and it has invested $1,000 in plant equipment and telephone poles, the firm's rate-of-return on investment will be 10 percent. The concept of rate-of-return is significant because AT&T must earn that level of return that entices its investors to provide

---

* Many rural areas were served by small independent local exchange companies to which the Bell System connected.

† *Policy and Rules Concerning Rates for Dominant Carriers,* R&O and Further NPRM, 4 FCC Rcd. 2873, ¶ 20 (1989).

‡ *See In the Matter of AT&T,* 9 F.C.C.2d 30 (1967).

the future capital (in the form of debt and equity) needed to run the company. If the rate-of-return is set too low by regulators, the firm will not be able to attract the necessary capital. On the other hand, if the rate-of-return is set too high, then AT&T is inappropriately enriched.

Revenue requirement. In theory at least, rate-of-return regulation works because it prevents dominant common carriers from charging prices that yield return on investment that is higher than the competitive level, thereby preventing the carrier from abusing its market power. It is thus the regulator's job to decide the amount of revenue that the firm will be permitted to earn. As the D.C. Circuit has explained, the "revenue requirement" comprises (1) operating expenses and (2) a reasonable return on investment:

> The FCC determines the permissible revenue requirements of BOCs [Bell Operating Companies] by first estimating operating costs including taxes. To this figure the agency adds an estimate of the cost of financing necessary investment in plant and equipment, i.e., the cost of capital. The FCC estimates this figure by calculating a rate base and multiplying the rate base by a rate of return. The mathematical representation is $I \times r + C = R$, where I is the rate base, r is the rate of return, C is operating costs, and R is the total revenue requirement.... The FCC derives I from the cost to acquire "used and useful" equipment and other assets, less any depreciation the company has recognized.[*]

Imagine that you were czar of the telecommunications universe, and you could set the revenue requirement in any way that you thought best. How would you set these numbers (represented above): I, r, and C? If you had a team of research assistants, what questions would you ask them? Is this a purely technical exercise that simply requires accurate financial information? Or does this require some moral or policy judgment about what is "fair"? Finally, does this system of rate regulation create any odd incentives for the firm?

X-inefficiency. In the revenue requirement formula, $R = I \times r + C$, focus on operating expenses, C. If you are reimbursed dollar for dollar for your costs, do you have strong incentive to be on the lookout for savings? No. This is called an X-inefficiency.[†] By contrast, in competitive markets, where firms have little control over market prices, the only way a firm can increase its profitability is by decreasing its costs. This provides competitive firms with the incentive to generate cost-cutting innovations that is absent in an rate-of-return regulated market.

Averch-Johnson effect. Now focus on the return on investment, $I \times r$. Recall that "r" is supposed to be set at the rate necessary to attract the capital required

---

[*] Illinois Bell Tel. Co. v. FCC, 988 F.2d 1254, 1258 (D.C. Cir. 1993).

[†] *See* Leibenstein, *Allocative Efficiency vs. X-Efficiency*, 56 AM. ECON. REV. 392, 392–415 (1966).

to keep the telephone service operating—not any higher or lower. But regulators are not perfect, so suppose that r is set higher than the true cost of capital. To simplify, imagine a situation in which the only capital sought is debt at a lending rate of 5 percent; however, r is set at 10 percent, which creates a 5 percent arbitrage. For every dollar borrowed from the bank, the telephone company potentially earns a 5 percent premium since r was set too high. In these circumstances, regulators would borrow as much as possible for some plausible capital investment. This is called the *Averch-Johnson effect*, sometimes also referred to as *gold-plating.*[*]

There were other complexities in implementing rate-of-return regulation. And notwithstanding extensive investigations in the 1970s, the FCC made no significant changes to the Bell System's pricing choices.

3. Price-Cap Regulation

In 1984, the Bell System was broken apart into seven regional Bell Operating Companies (RBOCs), which would provide intra-LATA services (local exchange service provided to end-consumers who needed a dial tone, and exchange access provided to long-distance companies) and AT&T, which would provide inter-LATA transport. Before divestiture (the break-up), the FCC had regulated the rates of AT&T's long distance services because AT&T was dominant in the long distance market. After divestiture, the FCC treated the seven newly formed RBOCs also as dominant common carriers in their respective local exchange markets. The FCC now had to regulate not only the rates that AT&T charged to its end-user customers (like you and me) for interstate long distance but also the rates RBOCs[†] would charge IXCs for originating and terminating interstate long distance calls (what we earlier identified as exchange access). During this period, the FCC began to turn away from rate-of-return regulation and adopted a more advanced methodology called *price-cap* regulation— for AT&T in 1990, and for the RBOCs in 1991.[‡]

Set cap. The gist of price-cap regulation is to set a maximum price for providing services, often the market price at some given date. Since prices are capped, the firm is driven to minimize costs in order to increase profits.

---

[*] *See* Averch & Johnson, *Behavior of the Firm Under Regulatory Constraints*, 52 AM. ECON. REV. 1052 (1962).

[†] In addition to the newly created RBOCs, GTE was also regulated as a dominant LEC. GTE was not a part of the Bell System. It merged into what is now Verizon.

[‡] *See Policy and Rules Concerning Rates for Dominant Carriers*, 2nd R&O, 5 FCC Rcd. 6786, 6818-20 (1990) (LEC Price Cap Order). This change also applied to GTE. Smaller ILECs could voluntarily opt into price cap regulation if they so desired.

Annual increases. Of course, this price cap can't stay fixed permanently. For instance, the cap should increase to keep up with the pace of inflation. Also, if there are increased costs due to matters entirely outside the firm's control (exogenous costs)—such as increased taxes—the price cap should increase accordingly.

Annual decreases. Also, there may be reasons why the price cap should decrease over time. For example, some industries get more productive over time than the rest of the economy. Think about what a $1,000 laptop could do back in 2000 as compared to a $1,000 laptop now. This productivity factor, also known as the X-factor, could justify forcing prices down annually in certain industries, so that firms don't earn some windfall that's not warranted.

The benefits of the price-cap system is that it avoids many of the defects of rate-of-return regulation. For instance, since there is no dollar-for-dollar reimbursement, there can be no X-inefficiency. Also, since regulators do not set a rate-of-return "r," there is no chance that regulators might set that value too high, thereby encouraging inefficient capital investments. For other reasons, the price cap system may also be easier to administer. Of course, no system is perfect, and price caps may also have some costs. For instance, if quality is hard to measure, the strong incentives to decrease costs to increase profits may produce lower quality service.

* * *

Let's review what we've learned so far about wireline telephony and ratemaking. First, we learned that the breakup of AT&T brought into existence different kinds of firms (e.g., LECs and IXCs) that provided different kinds of services, sensitive to new political geographies (e.g., LATAs). Second, we learned about various pricing methodologies, with the recognition that price cap methodology has generally won the day. What remains of all this today?

First, the breakup of AT&T has now receded in importance over the past three decades. Most important, in the 1996 Telecommunications Act, Congress removed the strict firewall that previously separated LECs and IXCs. Right now (as opposed to back in 1984) a single firm such as Verizon can and does act as *both* your LEC and IXC. You should also know that since 1984, the seven original RBOCs have been merged into three firms: AT&T, Verizon, and CenturyLink.[*]

---

[*] The current AT&T includes the previous (1) Southwestern Bell, (2) Pacific Telesis, (3) Ameritech, (4) Bell South RBOCs (and the AT&T long distance services). The current Verizon includes the previous (5) Nynex, (6) Bell Atlantic, and the independent GTE (and the IXC known as MCI). The RBOC (7) US West was merged into Qwest, which has been renamed CenturyLink.

Second, due to increased competition in various services, rate regulation has receded in importance. For example, the FCC no longer regulates the rates that phone companies charge to *end-users* (customers like you and me) for interstate calls. However, the FCC continues to regulate the *interstate* component of access charges that LECs charge to IXCs for originating and terminating calls (exchange access). This is done mostly under a price-cap method although smaller, often rural LECs have stayed under rate-of-return regulation.

2. CHALLENGING PRICES: ADMINISTRATIVE RATIONALITY

So far, you have played the role of a ratemaker, exploring the different methods of setting prices. Now, put on the hat of a litigator, whose client is unhappy with the formula for setting prices that some bureaucrat has adopted. How might you challenge that formula in a court of law?

First, if the current Communications Act gave no authority to the FCC to regulate rates, you as a lawyer would surely make that argument.

Second, you could argue that the agency acted contrary to what Congress directed. For example, if Congress explicitly instructed the FCC to use rate-of-return regulation and the FCC adopted price-caps instead, you would again have a good argument.

Third, under the Administrative Procedure Act (APA), which establishes general norms and procedures for federal agencies, you could argue that the agency acted irrationally. The APA authorizes federal courts to set aside federal agency action that is "arbitrary, capricious, an abuse of discretion, or otherwise not in accordance with law."[*] This is the famous "arbitrary and capricious" standard of administrative law. But what does this verbiage *really* mean?

To get any thorough idea, you need to study Administrative Law and read dozens of sample cases. In the meantime, here are some prominent articulations by the Supreme Court. In *Citizens to Preserve Overton Park, Inc. v. Volpe* (1971), the Court explained:

> To make this finding [on arbitrary and capricious] the court must consider whether the decision was based on a consideration of the relevant factors and whether there has been a clear error of judgment. Although this inquiry into the facts is to be searching and careful, the ultimate standard of review is a narrow one. The court is not empowered to substitute its judgment for that of the agency.[†]

---

[*] 5 U.S.C. § 706(2)(A).

In *Motor Vehicle Manufacturers of the United States, Inc. v. State Farm Mutual Automobile Insurance Company* (State Farm) (1983), the Supreme Court wrote:

> The scope of review under the 'arbitrary and capricious' standard is narrow and a court is not to substitute its judgment for that of the agency. Nevertheless, the agency must examine the relevant data and articulate a satisfactory explanation for its action including a 'rational connection between the facts found and the choice made.' In reviewing that explanation, we must 'consider whether the decision was based on a consideration of the relevant factors and whether there has been a clear error of judgment. Normally, an agency rule would be arbitrary and capricious if the agency has relied on factors which Congress has not intended it to consider, entirely failed to consider an important aspect of the problem, offered an explanation for its decision that runs counter to the evidence before the agency, or is so implausible that it could not be ascribed to a difference in view or the product of agency expertise. The reviewing court should not attempt itself to make up for such deficiencies; we may not supply a reasoned basis for the agency's action that the agency itself has not given. We will, however, "uphold a decision of less than ideal clarity if the agency's path may reasonably be discerned."[*]

These excerpts suggest that the arbitrary and capricious standard should be deferential to the administrative agency, especially if it is working on extremely technical material such as ratemaking. That said, intellectually sharp judges have often shown their regulatory chops and asked stringent questions that evidence a much more exacting standard of scrutiny.

USTA V. FCC *ERROR! BOOKMARK NOT DEFINED.*
188 F.3d 521 (D.C. Cir. 1999)

WILLIAMS, Circuit Judge:

Long-distance telephone traffic is ordinarily transmitted by a local exchange carrier ("LEC") from its origin to a long-distance carrier (or interexchange carrier or "IXC"). The IXC carries the traffic to its region of destination and hands it off to the LEC there. The IXC charges the customer for the call and pays "access charges" to the LECs at either end. In a 1997 rulemaking the Federal Communications Commission amended its methodology for limiting these charges, as applied to the largest LECs.

In regulating access charges the FCC currently uses a "price-cap" method. . . . The price caps were initially set at the levels of each carrier's rates on July 1, 1990. From the outset they have been subject to various annual

---

[†] 401 U.S. 402, 416 (1971) (internal citations omitted).
[*] 429 U.S. 29, 43 (internal citations omitted).

adjustments, including reduction by a "productivity offset," or "X-Factor." See 47 CFR § 61.45. In the order under review, the agency revised the method for determining the X-Factor. . . . In the Matter of Price Cap Performance Review for Local Exchange Carriers, Fourth Report & Order, 12 FCC Rcd. 16,642 (1997) ("1997 Order"). Because the access charges are in the aggregate so enormous, even small changes in the X-Factor have a large monetary value; the LECs claim (without dispute) that each 0.1% change in the factor represents a $23 million change in the industry-wide access charge.

I. THE HISTORIC PRODUCTIVITY COMPONENT OF THE X-FACTOR

The X-Factor is aimed at capturing a portion of expected increases in carrier productivity, so that these improvements, as under competition, will result in lower prices for consumers. Apart from a "consumer productivity dividend" ("CPD") described below, i[I]t is based on an assumption that historic productivity increases will be matched in the future. The agency resolved in the 1997 Order that the X-Factor (apart from the CPD) . . . should be calculated as the sum of the difference in productivity growth and the difference in input price growth between the LECs and the economy as a whole. It can thus be expressed as follows: X = (Δ% LEC TFP − Δ% TFP) + (Δ% U.S. input prices − Δ% LEC input prices), where TFP = total factor productivity.[1] The formula may be more readily conceptualized as X = (Δ% LEC TFP − Δ% LEC input prices) − (Δ% U.S. TFP − Δ% U.S. input prices).

---

[1] This equation is apparently derived as follows from the FCC's general rule that the X-Factor is to "provide a reliable measure of the extent to which changes in the LECs' unit costs have been less than the change in level of inflation," see 1997 Order, 12 FCC Rcd. at 16,647, ¶ 5: The general rule yields X = U − L, where U is the "change in level of inflation," and L is the change in the LECs' unit costs. The FCC then observes that "changes in a firm's unit costs come from two sources: (1) changes in productivity, and (2) changes in input prices," id. at n. 16. Thus, L = Δ% LEC input price − Δ% LEC productivity. Reading "change in level of inflation" as "change in unit costs in the economy as a whole," we get the similar expression: U = Δ% U.S. input price − Δ% U.S. productivity. Substituting these values into the equation X = U − L, using "TFP" for productivity, and performing a little algebraic manipulation yields the equation in the text.

As the Commission also increases the cap by general price inflation, the net effect of these adjustments is (roughly, subject to effects of the use of different indices) to increase the cap by the LECs' estimated change in unit costs. It is somewhat as if the overall adjustment ("A") were (using the terms of the prior paragraph) A = U − X = U − (U − L) = L.

Several parties submitted estimates of historical X-Factors. In a determination unchallenged here, the FCC accorded the greatest weight to its own estimates, although it also gave "some weight" to AT&T's estimates. . . . The estimates the FCC considered, and the averages of those estimates over specified periods, are the following:

Year	FCC	AT&T	Year	Specified periods (averaged)	
1986	−0.5%	0.2%	1986–95	5.2	6.2
1987	5.0	4.1	1987–95	5.9	6.9
1988	5.0	6.4	1988–95	6.0	7.2
1989	7.9	8.8	1989–95	6.1	7.3
1990	8.8	11.0	1990–95	5.8	7.1
1991	5.8	6.0	1991–95	5.2	6.3
1992	3.4	4.1	Range of Averages		
1993	4.7	6.0		5.2–6.1	6.2–7.3
1994	5.4	5.9			
1995	6.8	9.4			

1997 Order, 12 FCC Rcd. at 16,696, ¶ 137.

The FCC consulted the moving averages to establish a range of reasonableness from 5.2% to 6.3% and then selected 6.0% as the historical (i.e., non-CPD) component of the X-Factor. The LECs argue that the FCC did not give a rational explanation of that choice, and we agree. None of the reasons given for choosing 6.0% holds water.

A. Devaluation of 1986–95 and 1991–95 averages

First, in choosing a point within the range of reasonableness, the FCC determined that it was "reasonable to place less weight" on two lowest averages, the ones for 1986–95 and 1991–95. It said that the first, 1986–95, "is heavily influenced by the improbably low 1986 estimate of −0.5 percent." But the Commission gave no reason for condemning the 1986 estimate as "improbable," and mere divergence from the other numbers does not justify such a conclusion. The FCC invokes our cases upholding the elimination of outlying data points, but in them the agency explained why the outliers were unreliable or their use inappropriate. See Bell Atlantic Tel. Cos. v. FCC, 79 F.3d 1195, 1202 (D.C. Cir. 1996) (study indicated outlier erroneous); Association of Oil Pipe Lines v. FERC, 83 F.3d 1424, 1434 (D.C. Cir. 1996) (skewed data distribution required outlier elimination to avoid windfall profits to many oil pipelines).

As to the 1991–95 average, the Commission said it was the one "most affected by the low 1992 estimate," which it in turn diagnosed as "an artifact of a one-year jump in the measured productivity of the national economy as economic activity increased, rather than a change in the growth rate of LEC productivity or input prices." This is mystifying. If the productivity component of the X-Factor is to reflect the difference between LEC and overall productivity growth, a proposition that is built into the Commission's formula, there seems no reason to slight a datum because its anomalous character stems from the unusual magnitude of the second term rather than of the first.

B. Alleged upward trend

In justification of its choice of 6.0% the FCC also cites an upward trend in the X-Factor during the last years it surveyed. The FCC's reliance on the upward trend necessarily reflects the (unexplained) assumption that the trend will continue, at least in the immediate future. Explanation might be reasonably omitted if there were no obvious reason to doubt continuation of an observed trend. But two such reasons exist.

First, the trend appears to be part of a cyclical pattern. Although the X-Factor did increase steadily in the 1992–95 period, it also decreased from 1990 to 1992, after rising from 1986 to 1990. Perhaps there was reason to believe that there would be no cyclical downturn during the expected life of this X-Factor determination, which was to be reviewed about two years after being made. But the FCC offered no such reason.

Second, the X-Factor is calculated as the sum of two components, neither of which followed a trend during the period in question. In fact, their year-to-year fluctuations swamped the trend increments:

Year	Difference between LEC & U.S. changes in total factor productivity	Difference between LEC and US changes in input prices
1992	0.21	3.21
1993	1.44	3.26
1994	3.69	1.71
1995	1.78	5.04

Where's the trend? As the underlying variables appear to be thrashing about wildly, the FCC's conclusion that the trend in the difference between the two had some predictive value requires explanation.

C. Partial reliance on AT&T estimates

Finally, the LECs argue that in its treatment of AT&T's X-Factor estimates the FCC "implicitly endorsed methodologies that it had earlier discredited." The FCC incorporated the aspects of AT&T's method that it deemed reasonable into its own method, and then gave independent weight to AT&T's X-Factor estimates in deciding to extend the range of reasonableness upward, and to select a value near the top of the range. We agree that both these uses of AT&T's estimates appear irrational; any differences between the FCC's and

AT&T's estimates presumably resulted from elements of AT&T's analysis that the FCC specifically rejected. The FCC's argument that AT&T's estimates were "helpful" because AT&T's methodology was "similar," fails to overcome that logic. If there is an explanation—for example, conceivably the Commission gave some weight to AT&T's conclusions out of concern for the risk that it had erred in rejecting specific elements of AT&T's analysis—the FCC has failed to mention it.

The Commission having failed to state a coherent theory supporting its choice of 6.0%, we remand for further explanation.

NOTES & QUESTIONS

1. *What is being regulated?* Apply your understanding of political geography and telephone structure to identify which prices are being regulated: the price that IXCs charge end-consumers like you and me or what LECs charge IXCs for "exchange access"?

2. *Threshold questions.*

    a. *Statutory power.* Did the FCC act within the scope of its delegated powers? Relatedly, did the FCC act contrary to Congress's direct instructions by using this specific price-cap formula? No. Congress has not been that explicit in the pricing methods that the FCC should use.[*]

    b. *Constitutional limitation.* Is there some constitutional argument available, such as the First Amendment? No. Why not? What if we were regulating the prices of cable TV?

    c. *What's left?* Only the Administrative Procedure Act (challenging agency rationality and decision-making procedures) is left, which is exactly what is at issue in this case. Can you articulate the legal standard that the FCC supposedly violated?

3. *Rationality.* At bottom, the court is saying that the FCC has been arbitrary and capricious in setting the X-factor. Do you agree? For instance, did the FCC pick these numbers randomly out of a hat?

    a. *1986 estimate.* The FCC underweighted the 1986 datum, noting that "-0.5" was improbable. The court said "mere divergence from other numbers does not justify such a conclusion." Here's what the FCC said in the Report & Order:

---

[*] *See Rates for Dominant Carriers,* 4 FCC Rcd. 2873, ¶ 17 (1989) ("With regard to the ratemaking process, the courts have determined that there is *no single method* or formula that agencies must use to satisfy the requirements in Title II of the Act . . . that rates be just and reasonable. . . .") (emphasis added).

The first average is heavily influenced by the improbably low 1986 estimate of -0.5 percent. The estimate for 1986, the first period for which we have data, is improbably low in comparison to all the other estimates: the next lowest estimate is +3.4 percent and seven of the ten estimates are +5 percent or higher.[*]

What about the fact that this was the first year of data collection? If the number were -10.0%, would it be enough just to note that that was a ridiculous number that was many, many standard deviations away from the average?

b. *1992 estimate.* The court called it "mystifying" to underweight the 1992 estimate simply because that year the national economy was unusually productive. Again, here's the full FCC explanation:

> The decline in the measured X-Factor in 1992 appears to be an artifact of a one-year jump in the measured productivity of the national economy as economic activity increased, rather than a change in the growth rate of LEC productivity or input prices. The measured TFP of the U.S. economy appears to be more sensitive to the business cycles than the measured TFP of LECs.[†]

The point about business cycles is nowhere discussed by the court. Are you surprised that it wasn't? Given that ratemaking is hardly an exact science, is the D.C. Circuit asking too much from the FCC? Put another way, if this is deferential review, what would strict scrutiny look like?

4. *Competency in the face of complexity.* As you were reading this opinion, you may have felt overwhelmed by the complexity. This complexity arises not only from algebra, which is rarely seen in judicial opinions, but also the source of data that a government agency must rely on. If setting prices involves such complexity, what is the proper role of the judiciary? Should it defer to the expertise of the agency given the court's lack of institutional capacity to analyze such issues? Or is the judiciary perfectly able to conduct an independent examination? If the answer is yes, to what extent is this an attribute of specific judges, such as Judge Stephen Williams, a former law professor?

5. *Prisoner price caps.* One type of telephone service provider, in particular, is notorious for charging high rates—inmate calling service (ICS) providers. To avoid confusion, these are not rates charged by LECs to IXCs as in the *USTA* case above. Instead, these are rates charged to end-users (prisoners) who are held captive, in a literal sense. In response to concern about the rising cost of inmate phone calls, the FCC issued an Order and Notice of Proposed Rulemaking in November 2015. Among other things, the Commission adopted rate caps for both interstate and intrastate calls through ICS providers.[‡] In the

---

[*] 12 FCC Rcd. 16642 at ¶ 139.

[†] *Id.*

[‡] *In re Rates for Interstate Inmate Calling Services,* 30 FCC Rcd. 12763 (2015). Previously, the FCC had

order, the FCC noted that some inmates face rates up to $14 per minute. The new order would cap rates at 11 cents per minute. But a number of ICS providers challenged the new intrastate price caps, and the D.C. Circuit granted their petition for review, in part, in 2017.[*] The court blocked the FCC's attempt to regulate the prices for intrastate inmate calls, and also took issue with the Commission's method of setting rate caps "using a weighted average per minute cost," and the Commission's decision to exclude "site commissions" (a portion of profits paid to the correctional facilities) as costs in the calculus.[†]

3. SUBSIDIZING PRICES

So far, we have been analyzing the problem of ratemaking as a response to monopoly power. The goal has been to set prices via regulation that mimic the prices that a competitive market would have produced. But in some situations, even a competitive market price may be higher than what people can afford to pay. What then? On the one hand, government can respond with "that's life" in a market economy. On the other hand, government can choose to subsidize prices to make services more affordable, in which case complex questions arise:

- Which communication services should be subsidized in a world of rapid technological advancement?
- Who should pay into the subsidy fund and how much?
- Who should benefit from the subsidy fund and how much?
- How should the subsidy be collected and distributed?

Lurking behind these questions is a fundamental question: Why should those who cannot afford the service nonetheless receive it? We barely do this for medical care. Why do it for communications? It is in telephony where the history and practice of subsidizing prices have been longest and most convoluted. At the core is the goal of "universal service"—that all Americans should have access to local telephone service.

a. BEFORE 1996: IMPLICIT SUBSIDIES

The policy of universal service was promoted by state and federal regulators working together to keep basic telephony pricing low—mostly through implicit subsidies. "Implicit" subsidies are created when a telephone company is allowed to price certain services above their actual cost in order to price other services

---

issued an order providing for price caps only on interstate calling rates.

[*] Global Tel*Link v. FCC, 866 F.3d 397 (D.C. Cir. 2017).

[†] *Id.* at 401–02.

below cost. The most significant subsidies were controlled by state public utilities commissions (PUCs). As you recall, state regulators have the power to set all intrastate (wireline) telephony prices. A simple way to ensure "universal service" is for PUCs to set the price for local residential telephone service at an affordable rate—if necessary, below the true cost of providing such service.

To make up for losses, the local exchange carrier must be allowed to charge above cost for other services, such as "vertical" services (e.g., call waiting, call return); local toll calls (calls that are outside the area defined as "local" by state regulators and charged per-minute but are still intra-LATA); and access given to interexchange carriers (IXCs) for intrastate calls. In addition, the PUC can allow the local exchange carrier to price discriminate and charge businesses more than the true cost of providing them service. All of these "above cost" charges offset the "below cost" charges for local residential telephone service.

State regulators also generally require local residential telephone service to be priced identically across the entire state, regardless of differences in the actual cost of servicing different areas. So even if a particular location has a low population density and a difficult terrain that makes it costly to run telephone wires, basic local residential telephone service will cost the same there as everywhere else in the state.

The federal government also provided subsidies. Some of these were "explicit," in the sense that specific funding programs targeted financial relief to local exchange carriers that had high costs[*] and to low-income end-users.[†] Much more important, however, was the federal government's setting of implicit subsidies via artificial inflation of the interstate access charge. The subject of access charges is grotesquely complicated, so we just skim the surface.

Jurisdictional separations and the federal base. The local telephone plant (the local loop and the local switch) is essential for both intrastate and interstate communications. Accordingly, it would not make sense to recoup all of the costs associated with the local telephone plant in intrastate rates exclusively. Instead, some portion of those costs should be attributed to interstate rates.[‡] This requires a jurisdictional *separation* that allocates the "correct" proportion of the

---

[*] Examples included the Universal Service Fund (to address high local loop costs); Dial Equipment Minutes Weighting (to address high switching costs); Long-Term Support (to allow high cost local exchange carriers (LECs) to charge a national average access charge.

[†] The programs included Link Up (to facilitate initial sign-up of telephone service) and Lifeline Assistance (to decrease monthly payments).

[‡] *See* Smith v. Illinois Bell Telephone Co., 282 U.S. 133 (1930) (invalidating a state's telephone rates because they did not distinguish between the intrastate and interstate property).

joint and common costs to the intrastate (state-controlled) and interstate (federally controlled) rate bases.

Federal regulators, with cooperation from the states, have historically attributed a disproportionately high percentage of the local telephone plant to the interstate rate base. This meant that interstate (long distance) communications would be priced higher; conversely, intrastate (including local residential) communications would be priced lower. The technical details[*] here are not as important as the general idea of inflating the federal rate base.

Rise of access charges. The local exchange carrier, which owns, operates, and maintains the local telephone plant, has to be compensated for allowing its plant to be used in completing long distance calls. When AT&T was a monopoly, this usually meant that AT&T (Long Lines department) settled internal accounts with its own local exchange units. However, as competition increased and AT&T was broken up, such internal agreements had to be replaced with more formal charges. By 1984, the FCC adopted a system of uniform "access charges" for interstate long distance.[†] Thus, all IXCs were required to pay all LECs access charges for originating and terminating interexchange telephone calls.[‡]

Focus now on interstate access charges. These access charges were set so that local exchange carriers could recover what was due them according to the

---

[*] Here's how the FCC explains rate setting for incumbent LECs (ILECs) and where jurisdictional separations fits in:

> Jurisdictional separations is the third step in a four-step regulatory process that begins with an incumbent local exchange carrier's accounting system and ends with the establishment of tariffed rates for the [incumbent local exchange carrier's] ILEC's interstate and intrastate regulated services. First, carriers record their costs into various accounts in accordance with the Uniform System of Accounts ("USOA") prescribed by Part 32 of our rules. Second, carriers divide the costs in these accounts between regulated and nonregulated activities in accordance with Part 64 of our rules. We require this division to ensure that the costs of nonregulated activities will not be recovered in regulated interstate service rates. Third, carriers separate the regulated costs between the intrastate and interstate jurisdictions in accordance with our Part 36 separations rules. Finally, carriers apportion the interstate regulated costs among the interexchange services and rate elements that form the cost basis for their exchange access tariffs. For carriers subject to rate-of-return regulation, this apportionment is performed in accordance with Part 69 of our rules.

Jurisdictional Separations Reform and Referral to the Federal-State Joint Board, NPRM, 12 FCC Rcd. 22120 (1997).

[†] *MTS and WATS Market Structure*, 3d R&O, 93 F.C.C.2d 241, *recon.*, M&O, 97 F.C.C.2d 682 (1983), *second recon.*, M&O, 97 F.C.C.2d 834 (1984).

[‡] In fact, there were two different types of access charges that employed different rate structures. One type of access charge, the subscriber line charge (SLC) was billed as a flat rate directly to the local residential service subscriber. Another type of access charge, the carrier common line charge (CCL), was billed per minute to the IXC. This charge was then passed on to IXC customers.

jurisdictional separations process. But, as discussed above, that process artificially inflated the federal rate base. Thus, interstate access charges would also be inflated. These higher prices would be passed on to the caller.

Status report and the future. The upshot is that federal regulators have historically subsidized local residential service by raising the price of interstate service. In very crude terms, the FCC kept long distance artificially expensive in order to keep local service artificially cheap. But it's important to keep relative perspective: More significant than any of these federal subsidies are the state-controlled subsidies, which have set the price for local residential service below cost.

b. AFTER 1996: EXPLICIT SUBSIDIES

In the 1996 Telecommunications Act, Congress made substantial changes to the universal service regime. For the first time, Congress actually codified the term "universal service" as an "evolving level of telecommunications services that the [FCC] shall establish taking into account advances in telecommunications and information technologies and services." § 254(c)(1). On the recommendation of a special Universal Service Federal-State Joint Board, created by the Act, the FCC initially defined this level of service essentially to be standard wireline touch-tone telephony.

In addition to defining what services should be universally available (and therefore worthy of subsidization), the 1996 Act began the process of converting federal implicit subsidies into explicit ones. First, interstate access charges would no longer be inflated to help subsidize local telephone service.* Second, the Universal Service Fund (USF), administered by a newly created Universal Service Administering Company (USAC),† would be used as the sole source of subsidization, with clearly identified contributors and beneficiaries.

Who pays into the USF? Before the 1996 Act, almost all of the contributions into the universal service fund (USF) were made by long distance companies, or more formally speaking, interexchange carriers (IXCs). After the 1996 Act, "[e]very telecommunications carrier that provides interstate telecommunications services shall contribute, on an equitable and

---

* *See Universal Service Order*, R&O, 12 FCC Rcd. 8776, ¶ 15 (1997) ("[T]hrough this Order and the Access Charge Reform Order, interstate implicit support for universal service will be identified and removed from interstate access charges, and will be provided through explicit interstate universal service support mechanisms.").

† The Universal Service Administering Company (USAC) is a private, non-profit corporation, which is a subsidiary of the National Exchange Carriers Association (NECA). It was created in 1997 to administer the Universal Service Fund (USF). Its CEO and Board of Directors are appointed by the FCC.

nondiscriminatory basis, to the specific, predictable, and sufficient mechanisms established by the Commission to preserve and advance universal service." § 254(d). That means in addition to IXCs, now LECs (local exchange carriers), CMRS (commercial mobile radio services, or mobile phone companies), paging, and payphone providers contribute to the USF. By contrast, in the 1996 Act, Internet Service Providers were not made to contribute.

How much? The amount that interstate telecommunications carriers contribute into the USF equals the product of the contribution factor and their interstate end-user revenues. The USAC sets this contribution factor quarterly. For example, in the 3rd Quarter of 2016, the factor was 17.9%. It is customary for carriers who pay into the USF to pass that cost through to their end-users. The FCC, however, does not require this, and was peeved that many carriers listed USF itemizations on end-user billing statements that were higher than what the carriers in fact paid. In April 2003, the FCC has made clear that the "line-item charge may not exceed the interstate telecommunications portion of that customer's bill times the relevant contribution factor."[*]

Who benefits from the USF? "Eligible telecommunications carriers"[†] (ETCs) can receive monies from the universal service fund (USF) through one of four programs administered by the USAC: High Cost; Low Income (or Lifeline); Rural Health Care; Schools and Libraries (or E-rate). To be clear, end-users (like you and me) do not draw directly from the USF. Instead, ETCs draw from the USF to offset their high cost or to reimburse them for the discounts they have given to certain end-users (the poor, rural health care providers, or schools and libraries). The precise details are not important here.[‡] But note that the 1996 Act designated rural nonprofit health care providers and schools/libraries as new beneficiaries.

Universal service is a massive subsidy program. In 2013, the USAC disbursed over $8.33 billion through its four programs: High Cost ($4.17B); Low Income ($1.8B); Rural Health Care ($159M); Schools & Libraries ($2.2B).[§] It doesn't take much imagination to see that almost every decision made by the FCC in setting up such a program could be challenged. Let's focus on the Commission's attempt to reform access charges.

---

[*] 47 C.F.R. § 54.712.

[†] *See* §§ 254(e) ("[O]nly an eligible telecommunications carrier designated under section 214(e) shall be eligible to receive specific Federal universal service support.").

[‡] The details can be found in 47 C.F.R. Part 54.

[§] http://www.usac.org/about/about/universal-service/faqs.aspx .

NOTE: BROADBAND DEPLOYMENT AND THE CONNECT AMERICA FUND

Since the enactment of Section 706 in the Telecommunications Act of 1996, the FCC has sought to promote the deployment of broadband infrastructure in the United States and to increase access to broadband for all Americans. The urgency of this issue has increased as access to high speed internet has become a necessary part of professional, educational, and personal life. But there has been significant disagreement within the Commission in recent years over the extent of the problem and how best to fix it.

So what are the facts? The FCC reported in 2016 that tens of millions of Americans lack access to both fixed broadband (25 Mbps/3 Mbps) and mobile broadband (10 Mbps/1 Mbps) services, including:

- 10 percent of all Americans (34 million)
- 39 percent of rural Americans (23 million)
- 41 percent of those living on tribal lands (1.6 million)
- 66 percent of those living in U.S. territories (2.6 million).

The report also concluded that approximately 41 percent of schools cannot meet the Commission's goal of 100 Mbps per 1,000 students/staff.[*] The report concluded that more work was necessary to comply with the advanced telecommunications obligations in § 706.

But then in 2018 the Commission issued a new report where it concluded that (1) fewer than 15 million Americans lack access to both fixed and mobile broadband, and (2) advanced telecommunications capability "is being deployed to all Americans in a reasonable and timely fashion."[†] So what changed in two years? Mostly methodology. The FCC in its 2018 report determined that satellite services, which had previously been excluded from the measurement due to high latency, should be included. The Commission also concluded that its efforts to "remove barriers to infrastructure investment" (reversing the net neutrality rules) were sufficient to support a "positive" finding of meeting the Section 706 obligations.

---

[*] *In the Matter of Inquiry Concerning the Deployment of Advanced Telecommunications Capability to All Americans in a Reasonable and Timely Fashion, and Possible Steps to Accelerate Such Deployment Pursuant to Section 706 of the Telecommunications Act of 1996, as Amended by the Broadband Data Improvement Act,* 31 FCC Rcd. 699 (2016).

[††] *In the Matter of Inquiry Concerning the Deployment of Advanced Telecommunications Capability to All Americans in a Reasonable and Timely Fashion,* 33 FCC Rcd. 1660 (2018).

Congress responded by passing the "Broadband Deployment Accuracy and Technological Availability Act" in 2020.[*] The law requires that the Commission draw more accurate and granular broadband maps, collect and verify coverage data, and adopt rules to make the data more uniform and useable. The FCC has not yet unveiled the new rules and methods, but the law requires that they do so before issuing their report in 2021.

Despite this recent disagreement over broadband deployment, the FCC continues to pursue its effort to expand advanced mobile telecommunications coverage. One obvious way would be to target universal service funds toward the rollout of broadband in those areas. Unfortunately, the USF that was created after the 1996 Telecommunications Act was limited to voice telephone service.

In the BROADBAND PLAN, the FCC changed course and recommended replacing the current high-cost program component of the USF (targeted to rural and high-cost areas) and the implicit subsidies still embedded in interstate access charges (as well as other forms of intercarrier compensation) with a new Connect America Fund (CAF) that would help address the broadband availability gap. In November 2011, the FCC released a significant Order that did just that.[†]

First, the FCC adopted a new universal service principle, which adoption is specifically authorized under 47 U.S.C. § 254(b)(7): support for modern, broadband-capable networks.

Second, it created a new Connect America Fund (CAF) to replace the High Cost Fund. The goals of CAF include not only universal service of voice telephony but also universal availability of modern networks that can provide broadband internet service as well as advanced mobile services (both voice and data). It's worth highlighting that the FCC is paying explicit attention to mobile services. Indeed, the Commission created a targeted CAF Mobility Fund, "the first universal service mechanism dedicated to ensuring availability of mobile broadband networks in areas where a private-sector business case is lacking."[‡] Finally, the FCC adopted a goal of keeping prices reasonably comparable in all regions of the nation.

Third, the FCC adopted a specific budget for CAF, with annual funding capped at $4.5 billion over the next six years. In the past, there had been many complaints and anxieties about fraud and waste within various components of the USF, and the FCC made clear its desire to increase financial accountability.

---

[*] Pub. L. 116-130 (codified at 47 U.S.C. §§ 641 et seq.).

[†] *See In the Matter of Connect Am. Fund*, 26 FCC Rcd. 17663 (2011).

[‡] *Id.* at ¶ 28.

Fourth, eligible telecommunications carriers (ETCs) who receive USF monies must not only provide voice telephony services but also broadband services to their customers.

Fifth, the FCC adopted various phase-in timetables depending on whether the territory is served by LECs rate regulated under "price caps" (large carriers) or "rate-of-return" (smaller carriers, operating in more difficult and expensive areas to serve). The phase-in details are beyond the scope of the text.

The FCC's decision was upheld by the U.S. Court of Appeals for the Tenth Circuit on a petition to review filed by a number of service providers.[*] The current program is called Mobility Fund Phase II and involves an allocated $4.53 billion over the next ten years to advance deployment of 4G LTE service to underserved areas.[†] No doubt the details will take a lot of time and litigation to work through. The bigger picture to keep in mind, however, is the FCC's decision to add broadband internet as well as mobile voice and data to the list of services deemed worthy of universal service.

NOTES & QUESTION

1. *Moving forward with USF and broadband subsidies.* The FCC has moved forward with the USF modernization process, which involves several billions of dollars in support for rural providers to build out broadband infrastructure. Thinking back to what we have already learned about pricing, can you explain the difference between a "price cap" carrier and a "rate of return" carrier? Why might the FCC use different funding methods for price cap carriers vs. rate of return carriers? For price cap carriers, the FCC's new plan calls for a "competitive bidding process" for the carriers to obtain support from the Connect America Fund. Describe how you think that bidding process might work. Who is bidding for what?

2. *Transitioning the lower-income lifeline program.* In 1985 the FCC established the Lifeline program to provide subsidies for qualifying low-income consumers who could not afford phone service. Congress further required in the Telecommunications Act of 1996 that both affordable telephone service and advanced telecommunications service be made available to lower income consumers. In 2016, the FCC issued a Report and Order on the modernization of the Lifeline program.[‡] The Commission order allows individuals to receive lifeline support for "standalone fixed and mobile broadband" while continuing

---

[*] *In re FCC 11-161*, 753 F.3d 1015 (10th Cir. 2014).

[†] *In re Connect America Fund Universal Service Reform – Mobility Fund*, 32 FCC Rcd. 2152 (2017).

[‡] *In re Lifeline and Link Up Reform and Modernization*, 31 FCC Rcd. 3962 (Apr. 27, 2016).

to provide support for "bundled voice and broadband services." The Commission also established "minimum service standards" for broadband and mobile voice. This issue has subsequently garnered a lot of attention from congressional oversight committees and the more conservative commissioners within the FCC, who are concerned about waste, fraud, and abuse in subsidization programs.

B. CABLE TELEVISION

1. SETTING PRICES

Now we move on to another industry, cable TV. Setting prices in this medium is conceptually similar to setting prices in telephony and is, thankfully, technically simpler.

Overview: Rates and Tiers. Prior to 1984, the federal government played no role in regulating the rates of cable television service; that work was left to the local franchising authorities, who negotiated these rates when they issued the franchise contract. However, in 1984 Congress passed the Cable Communications Policy Act, which created a comprehensive federal statutory regime for cable TV (Title VI of the Communications Act). In the Act, Congress deregulated pricing for premium channels and permitted franchising authorities to regulate "basic tier" pricing only if there was no "effective competition."

> FCC, General Cable Television Industry and Regulation Information, Fact Sheet (Aug. 1999).
>
> "A tier is a category of cable service or services provided by a cable operator for which a separate rate is charged by the cable operator. There are three types of cable service: basic service, cable programming service, and per-channel or per-program (sometimes called pay-per-view) service.
>
> * *Basic service* is the lowest level of cable service a subscriber can buy. It includes, at a minimum, all over-the-air television broadcast signals carried pursuant to the must-carry requirements of the Communications Act, and any public, educational, or government access channels required by the system's franchise agreement. It may include additional signals chosen by the operator. . . .
>
> * *Cable programming service* includes all program channels on the cable system that are not included in basic service, but are not separately offered as per-channel or per-program service. . . . There may be one or more tiers of cable programming service.
>
> * *Per-channel or per-program service* includes those cable services that are provided as single-channel tiers by the cable operator, and individual programs for which a separate rate is charged by the cable operator."

The critical statutory term "effective competition" was left to the FCC to define, which it did incredibly broadly. If a household could receive three different broadcast television channels, there was effective competition. That's right: Receiving a mere three over-the-air TV stations was competitive enough. This meant that as of December 29, 1986, 97 percent of all cable systems were deregulated in pricing. Cable rates increased dramatically after deregulation—far faster than the rate of inflation.

Congress reacted to these price increases by passing the 1992 Cable Television Consumer Protection and Competition Act, which re-regulated pricing.[*] Local franchising authorities were empowered to regulate the rates for basic service according to formulas established by the FCC.[†] As for upper tiers, the FCC would regulate prices directly.

Finally, in the Telecommunications Act of 1996, Congress repealed rate regulation of all cable programs in upper tiers effective in 1999.[‡] Currently, only basic tier cable service is rate regulated, mostly by local franchising authorities who have been certified by the FCC to do so and who apply FCC-approved formulas.[§]

Certification process. In order for a franchising authority to regulate the rates of the basic tier, it must register with and be certified by the FCC. The certification process is simple. The franchising authority must attest to the fact that: (a) the franchising authority will act consistently with FCC regulations; (b) under state law, the franchising authority has the legal power to franchise cable systems; (c) the franchising authority has adopted fair procedures for resolving disputes; and (d) the cable system is not yet subject to effective competition, which the franchising authority can presume unless it knows otherwise.

In some sense, then, the FCC acts as a regulator of regulators. In other words, a local franchising authority may act as a regulator by setting prices on the basic tier, but only after it receives permission from the super-regulator, the FCC. The super-regulator's job includes making sure that cable operators get a fair shake from franchising authorities.

---

[*] *See* 47 U.S.C. § 543(a)(2)(A) ("the rates . . . of basic cable service shall be subject to regulation by a franchising authority").

[†] *See* § 543(b)(2) (requiring FCC to issue rate regulations). In the Telecommunications Act of 1996, Congress set rate regulation of the *cable programming* tier to expire in 1999, which it has. *See* § 543(c)(4).

[‡] It also added a new way in which "effective competition" could come into existence—competition by open video systems (essentially, video programming services that regulators thought might be provided by the telephone company).

[§] As you might have guessed, most subscribers sign up for something more than basic service. As of January 1, 2009, only 13% subscribed to basic service only. *See* FCC, REPORT ON CABLE INDUSTRY PRICES ¶ 11 (2011).

Price-Cap Regulation. Congress in 1992 required the FCC to "ensure that the rates for the basic service tier are reasonable." 47 U.S.C. § 542(b)(1). Specifically, the Commission was tasked with setting prices that would have been in effect if there were "effective competition." This required the FCC to devise a formula by which certified local franchising authorities could set the rates for the basic tier of cable television service. The Commission decided to go with price-caps.* What differed, however, from our study of price-caps in telephony was a need to roll back rates to what they would have been had there been effective competition. (Remember that because of the FCC's prior lax definition of effective competition, cable operators had been able to jack up prices way above competitive levels.) Here's how the FCC went about calculating that rollback.

First, the FCC collected data on the rates charged by cable operators who were subject to competition and those who weren't. Second, it computed a competitive differential in pricing between competitive and noncompetitive systems. Third, it rolled back rates by the competitive differential. After this one-time rollback, the FCC would permit the annual adjustments typical to any price-cap scheme.† Originally, the Commission calculated a competitive differential of only 10%. In a subsequent 1994 action, the FCC recalculated the competitive differential to be much higher—17%.‡ Not surprisingly, this action ended up in court.

We skip the "arbitrary and capricious" APA arguments, which were conceptually analogous to those we have already studied in telephony. Instead, we focus on what's new: the First Amendment.

---

* *See Implementation of Sections of the Cable Television Consumer Protection and Competition Act of 1992*, R&O and FNPRM, 8 FCC Rcd. 5631 (1993).

† The full, complicated methodology is stated in 47 C.F.R. § 76.922 (Rates for the basic service tier and cable programming services tiers).

‡ *See Implementation of Sections of the Cable Television Consumer Protection and Competition Act of 1992: Rate Regulation*, Second Order on Reconsideration, Fourth R&O, and Fifth NPRM, 9 F.C.C.R. 4119, 4155-59 (1994).

2. CHALLENGING PRICES: FIRST AMENDMENT

TIME WARNER ENTERTAINMENT CO., L.P. v. FCC
56 F.3d 151 (D.C. Cir. 1995)

RANDOLPH, Circuit Judge:

II

The First Amendment forbids some but not all economic regulations affecting speech. Some laws survive so long as they have a rational basis. Other laws will fall unless they rest on some extraordinary justification. Still other laws need to satisfy a standard somewhere between these two extremes. As to the Commission's cable rate regulations, we know from Turner Broadcasting v. FCC (1994), that rational basis cannot be the test. *Turner Broadcasting* holds that cable operators are entitled to [First Amendment] protection . . . and that laws of less than general application aimed at the press or elements of it are "always subject to at least some degree of heightened First Amendment scrutiny." *Turner.* The question is what "degree"? The cable petitioners say the scrutiny must be "strict," which means, among other things, that the government's interest must be "compelling" and that the law is presumptively invalid. The Commission and the United States . . . say that an "intermediate" standard is warranted, requiring only an "important or substantial governmental interest" and restrictions no greater than "essential" to further the interest. See United States v. O'Brien (1968).

The Supreme Court's decision in *Turner Broadcasting*, applying the less rigorous of the two "heightened" standards to the "must-carry" provision of the 1992 Cable Act, stands rather firmly against the cable petitioners on this point. One frequently-mentioned reason for imposing the more demanding First Amendment standard petitioners advocate is that the law is content-based, that it differentiates "favored speech from disfavored speech on the basis of the ideas or views expressed." *Turner Broadcasting.* No serious claim can be made that the cable rate regulations are of this sort. All cable systems not facing effective competition are covered, and they are covered regardless of the content of the programs they transmit. Neither the 1992 Cable Act nor the Commission's rate regulations have a content-based purpose. Congress became concerned about rising cable rates after it deregulated rates in 1984. The 1992 Cable Act sought to promote competition and lower monopolistic cable rates. In compliance with the Act, the Commission focused its cable rate regulation on the method of transporting the speech rather than the speech itself, comparing the rates of competitive cable operators—that is, cable systems lacking bottleneck control over transport service—with those of noncompetitive ones—systems with bottleneck control over transport service.

But if regulating cable rates is not done according to the nature of the programming, it nevertheless may affect the content of programs transmitted, so the cable petitioners tell us. This impact on content, they say, triggers strict scrutiny under Riley v. National Federation of the Blind of North Carolina, Inc. (1988). *Riley* is doubtless petitioners' strongest precedent. The state law in that case regulated professional fundraisers in the interest of preventing fraud, capping the percentage of donations fundraisers could retain as their fees for soliciting contributions to charitable organizations. If their fees exceeded 35 percent of the amount collected, the fees were presumed unreasonable, a presumption the fundraisers could rebut by showing that the charge was necessary because they were disseminating information at the charity's behest or because otherwise the charity's ability to raise funds would be significantly impaired. This violated the fundraisers' First Amendment rights. Soliciting charitable contributions is protected speech. The burden the cap imposed was, the Court said, "hardly incidental to speech"—"the desired and intended effect of the statute [was] to encourage some forms of solicitation and discourage others." *Id.* Since the state law constituted "a direct restriction on the amount of money a charity can spend on fundraising activity" and hence "a direct restriction on protected First Amendment activity," the Court subjected the law to "exacting First Amendment scrutiny" and struck it down. *Id.*

The analogy of this case to *Riley* fails at several critical junctures. Neither the "desired" nor the "intended effect" of the cable rate regulations is to encourage some types of speech while discouraging others. The premise of the cable petitioners' argument from *Riley* is that the rate regulations will have a deleterious impact on the content of the programming transmitted. Yet the Commission's study revealed that the content of programming was not one of the three key system characteristics that largely explained the variance in rates charged by cable systems nationwide. Pressure exerted on cable operators to drop expensive programming or to add only inexpensive programming in response to a lowering of their rates is relieved by the Commission's "going forward" rules. A cable operator who adds a channel may "fully recover . . . the actual level of programming expense incurred," along with an overhead charge and "a 7.5 percent markup." *Second Reconsideration.* An operator who drops a channel must make a corresponding adjustment. Cable operators thus have no reason to prefer low-quality versus high-quality channels, which is why at least some cable programmers favored the Commission's approach. Whatever impact rate regulation might have on the content of cable programming is, moreover, considerably less significant than the effect on content of the must-carry rules considered in *Turner Broadcasting*. The must-carry rules required cable operators to devote about one-third of their channels to broadcasters and to transmit the programming the broadcasters selected, yet *Turner Broadcasting* held that intermediate, rather than strict, scrutiny applied. The cable rate regulations, on the other hand, merely require cable operators to charge reasonable rates.

We accept, *arguendo*, the cable petitioners' contention that the government could not, consistently with the First Amendment, cap the price of a newspaper at 25 cents in order to limit monopoly profits and make the paper more affordable. But it does not follow that cable rate regulations must also be strictly judged. Cable systems are not functionally equivalent to newspapers.

The monopolies most cable operators now enjoy resulted from exclusive franchises granted by local authorities. Exclusive franchising ended in 1992, but the effects linger on. While newspapers in some localities also may lack effective competition, this is not due to actions of the government. Furthermore... a newspaper, no matter how secure its monopoly, is incapable of blocking its readers' access to competing publications. A cable operator, by contrast, has "bottleneck, or gatekeeper control over most (if not all) of the television programming that is channeled into the subscriber's home" because the operator owns and controls the transmission facility. *Turner Broadcasting*. Cable service thus involves more than programming; it includes as well a transportation element. When a cable operator has a monopoly in a franchise area, that operator has exclusive control over the transportation element. This is why the Commission set its benchmark by examining the rates cable operators charged in competitive markets, that is, those markets where this exclusive control over the transportation element did not exist. Neither the benchmark/competitive differential nor the price cap depended on the content of speech and the administration of the benchmark/competitive differential and the price cap requires no reference to the content of speech.

The fact that the regulations apply only to cable systems does not make them especially suspect. As economic measures that may incidentally affect speech, the rate regulations must be analyzed by the same "intermediate" standard the Supreme Court applied in *Turner Broadcasting*.

III

The government's interest in regulating cable rates is evident—protecting consumers from monopoly prices charged by cable operators who do not face effective competition. One need look no further than *Turner Broadcasting* to determine that this interest is to be treated as "important or substantial": "the Government's interest in eliminating restraints on fair competition is always substantial, even when the individuals or entities subject to particular regulations are engaged in expressive activity protected by the First Amendment."

Since the government's interest is substantial, the remaining question deals with the manner in which the rate regulations seek to promote that interest. Do the regulations "burden substantially more speech than is necessary"? Ward v. Rock Against Racism (1989). We shall assume that rules requiring cable operators to charge reasonable rates burden speech, although it is by no means clear how they do so. Still, the rate regulations are narrow enough: rate regulation is triggered by the absence of effective competition and ceases when effective competition emerges.... If any operator believes that it would be justified in charging higher rates, there is a safety valve: the operator may invoke the cost-of-service option. This ensures that every cable operator will be able to recover its reasonable costs and earn an 11.25 percent rate of return on investment....

The cable rate regulations are subject to intermediate scrutiny under the First Amendment and are not unconstitutional. The government has demonstrated a substantial interest in reducing cable rates and the Commission's regulations issued ... are narrowly tailored to meet that interest.

NOTES & QUESTIONS

1. *Whose speaking rights?* On a cable system, there are multiple players who arguably have speech interests: the cable operator itself (e.g., Time Warner); the video programming source, such as a national cable network (e.g., MTV) or over-the-air broadcast television station (e.g., KCAL-9, a TV station in Los Angeles); and the cable television subscribers. Whose speech rights are burdened by price regulation?

2. *First Amendment: standard of review.* As a matter of formal First Amendment doctrine, the standard of review is critical. If strict scrutiny is required, the government regulation must satisfy a "compelling interest" and the means adopted must be "narrowly tailored" to furthering that compelling interest. Accordingly, it is likely that the government infringement on speech will be struck down as unconstitutional. By contrast, if intermediate scrutiny is appropriate, the government regulation must satisfy only an "important" or "substantial" interest, and the means adopted must not "burden speech more substantially than necessary." Accordingly, it is much more likely that the regulation will be upheld. Given these stark differences, much First Amendment

dueling involves persuading the court to adopt a particular standard of review. Notice the significant role that the *Turner* case (1994) plays in the court's analysis.

3. *Content neutrality.* The critical variable in setting the standard of review is content neutrality. If the regulation is deemed "content-based," then strict scrutiny is appropriate. By contrast, if the regulation is considered "content-neutral," then intermediate scrutiny is appropriate. (As any student of the First Amendment quickly realizes, it is not always easy to determine whether a burden on speech is content-neutral or content-based.) Does this doctrine make sense to you?

4. *Medium warp.* When dealing with communications law and policy, another critical variable enters the picture. The communications medium seems to affect the constitutional protection of the message. For example, as we have studied in CHAPTER 2: ENTRY, what is constitutionally impermissible in print is perfectly okay in broadcasting. Compare how rights-of-reply were handled in *Miami Herald* versus *Red Lion.*

5. *Pulling the analysis together.* In this case, according to Judge Randolph, what is the appropriate standard of review? Is the pricing regulation content-based or content-neutral? Is cable television more like print or broadcast television? How should the answers to the separate questions be merged together to set the appropriate standard of review? Compare your answer to the standard-of-review analysis we have already seen regarding cable television franchising in CHAPTER 2: ENTRY. (The constitutional status of cable television will arise many more times throughout this book.)

6. *Means-ends analysis.* After establishing the appropriate standard of review, how does the court apply that standard to the facts at hand? In other words, how do we know whether the ends sought are "compelling" or "important"? How do we know whether the means adopted achieve the ends in a "narrowly tailored" way or does not "burden speech more substantially than necessary"?

7. *Telephony comparison.* With cable television pricing, cable operators raise both agency rationality and First Amendment arguments. Why were no First Amendment arguments raised regarding telephony pricing?

8. *Deregulation because of effective competition.*

a. *Defining effective competition.* Under current law, basic tier rate regulation is only permitted if there is no effective competition.

> 47 U.S.C. § 543(a). Regulation of rates
>
> (2) Preference for competition. If the Commission finds that a cable system is subject to effective competition, the rates for the provision of cable service by such system shall not

> be subject to regulation by the Commission or by a State or franchising authority under this section.

Accordingly, what counts as "effective competition" is very important. Here's a summary from the FCC:

> Under the Cable Act, a cable operator may obtain a finding of "effective competition" for a community that meets one of four tests:
>
> (1) fewer than 30 percent of households subscribe to the cable operator's service (low penetration test);
>
> (2) at least two multichannel video programming distribution ("MVPD") providers each offer a comparable service to at least 50 percent of households and at least 15 percent of all households subscribe to service other than from the largest MVPD (50/15 test);
>
> (3) a municipality offers MVPD service to at least 50 percent of households (municipal test); or
>
> (4) a local exchange carrier (LEC) or its affiliate, or an MVPD using the facilities of such carrier or its affiliate, offers MVPD service by means other than direct broadcast satellite in an area that is also served by an unaffiliated cable operator (LEC test). *See* 47 C.F.R. § 76.905(b).

      b. *Defining Multichannel Video Programming Distributor* (MVPD). Throughout the book, we will see this term "MVPD" frequently. Here are statutory and regulatory definitions.

> 47 U.S.C. §522(13)
>
> the term "multichannel video programming distributor" means a person such as, but not limited to, a cable operator, a multichannel multipoint distribution service, a direct broadcast satellite service, or a television receive-only satellite program distributor, who makes available for purchase, by subscribers or customers, multiple channels of video programming

> 47 C.F.R. § 76.905(d)
>
> A multichannel video program distributor, for purposes of this section, is an entity such as, but not limited to, a cable operator, a BRS/EBS provider, a direct broadcast satellite service, a television receive-only satellite program distributor, a video dialtone service provider, or a satellite master antenna television service provider that makes available for purchase, by subscribers or customers, multiple channels of video programming.

The principal MVPDs are cable operators, DBS, and video services provided by (historically) telephone companies such as Verizon and AT&T.[*]

      c. *Recent competition figures.* According to the most recent FCC data available, as of 2016, a total of 10,569 communities out of 33,600 total have been officially relieved of rate regulation due to effective competition.[†] (A cable

---

[*] Verizon and AT&T rolled out their video services in 2005 and 2006 respectively. We study their regulatory classification in CHAPTER 5: CLASSIFICATION.

[†] *Report on Cable Industry Prices* ¶ 28 (2018).

community or community unit[*] can be smaller than a franchise area.) More interesting than percentage of communities is percentage of subscribers: 47% of subscribers resided in effective competition communities whereas the rest (53% of subscribers) lived in noncompetitive communities.

    d. *Direct Broadcast Satellite.* Most of the "effective competition" findings were driven by the availability of Direct Broadcast Satellite (DBS) television. Under the 50/15 test (option #2 described above), two conditions must be satisfied. First, there must be at least two unaffiliated MVPDs, each of which offers comparable video programming to at least 50% of the households in the franchise area.[†] Given the national footprint of DBS signals, this requirement is satisfied as long as there is evidence of advertising that alerts potential subscribers of DBS availability. Second, the percentage of households in the franchise area subscribing to some other MPVD besides the largest one (generally speaking, the incumbent cable operator) must exceed 15%.[‡]

    Back when the *Time Warner* case was litigated, DBS did not have that kind of market share; accordingly, overbuild markets involved multiple cable operators. But now, "overbuild" competition is arising mostly through DBS penetration. When the 15% penetration can be demonstrated in any specific franchising area, the FCC will revoke the local franchising authority's certification to regulate basic tier rates.[§] And in 2015, the Commission decided that the "ubiquitous nature" of DBS service "made it appropriate to presume that the 50/15 test of effective competition is met in all cases, unless a showing is made to the contrary to rebut this presumption."[**]

    In this chapter, we have examined the third concept essential to understanding communications law and policy: *pricing.* The specific methods of ratemaking are technically complex, but as competition increases the need for such ratemaking has decreased. And in challenging government prices, we've

---

[*] 47 C.F.R. § 76.5(dd) ("System community unit: Community unit. A cable television system, or portion of a cable television system, that operates or will operate within a separate and distinct community or municipal entity (including unincorporated communities within unincorporated areas and including single, discrete unincorporated areas"). Before a cable operator begins operation, it must file Form 322 in accordance with 47 C.F.R. § 76.1801, which identifies the communities it serves.

[†] *See* 47 U.S.C. § 543(l)(1)(B)(i).

[‡] *See* 47 U.S.C. § 543(l)(1)(B)(ii).

[§] *See, e.g., Cablevision of Paterson*, MO&O, 17 FCC Rcd. 17239 (2002) (revoking certifications of New Jersey Board of Public Utilities' Office of Cable Television to regulate basic cable service rates).

[**] *Report of Cable Industry Practices* ¶16 (2018).

seen two central lines of argument—administrative rationality and freedom of speech—which will reappear throughout our study of communications law.

CHAPTER 4

ACCESS

Recall the basic model of communication introduced in CHAPTER 1: POWER. A sender encodes a message onto a signal, which is transmitted across a channel and then decoded back into the message by the receiver. All communication technologies enable this process. What happens, however, when a player essential to some communicative process who has control over a "choke point" refuses to participate? Is it just tough luck? Or could it be that certain players in certain circumstances must participate whether they like it or not? In other words, might the law force them to provide *access* to their system? Under what circumstances should such access be mandated? And is it lawful to do so? Should the rules governing access be different based on the communications medium or platform used?

A. BROADCAST TV

To locate the choke points in any communications service, it is important to understand the structural relationships among multiple firms who cooperate to provide the service. In the case of broadcast, these firms can be usefully categorized into three stylized layers: production, large-scale distribution, and last-leg connection.

Let's run through a concrete example of the television show *Scandal*. First, someone has to create the content—a television production company such as ShondaLand. Next, someone has to distribute the program nationally—a broadcast network such as Disney–ABC Domestic Television. Finally, someone has to broadcast the program locally for viewer consumption—a local broadcast station such as KABC-TV, the ABC-owned-and-operated station in Los Angeles.* Access could be denied at each layer.

---

* It is now commonplace for ABC and other production networks to distribute shows like *Scandal* directly to viewers over one or more streaming platforms. So the "last-leg" connection for many TV programs could also read "broadband internet streaming platform." More on this later.

Layer	Industry Player
1. Production	Studio
2. Large-scale Distribution	Broadcast Network
3. Last-leg Connection	Local Station

1. ACCESS TO THE STATION:
FAIRNESS DOCTRINE

Let's focus on the choke point on *layer 3: last-leg connection.* Suppose that you are the leader of a small libertarian reading group called "Books for Freedom." One day, while you are watching broadcast television, you hear a news commentator mock "Books for Freedom," calling you a bunch of right wing lunatics. You are deeply insulted, and you think that your group and its maverick mission have been badly mischaracterized. You call up the broadcast station and complain vigorously. You ask for time to tell the audience what the real truth is. Oozing elitist contempt, the broadcast station manager says "Buzz off!"

You think to yourself that the broadcast spectrum is a public resource. Why should this one station be able to monopolize that resource and broadcast nasty opinions about your organization with no chance for rebuttal? Isn't it only fair that you be given access to the local TV station, in some reasonable and limited manner, to reply?

The doctrine. We were briefly introduced to the fairness doctrine back in CHAPTER 2: ENTRY, when we examined the justifications for regulating broadcast entry and studied *Red Lion.*[*] Originally adopted in 1949, the doctrine comprised two separate requirements. First, broadcasters were required to cover important and controversial issues, especially if they were relevant to the community they served. Second, broadcasters were required to provide reasonable opportunities for contrasting and dissenting views on the controversial topics covered.[†] The first requirement was hardly an issue: Covering controversy was something broadcasters naturally did, and the FCC rarely complained. By contrast, the second requirement led to specific access (or right of reply) claims that generated complex litigation, as in *Red Lion.*

In 1967, partly codifying and partly extending the fairness doctrine, the FCC adopted specific regulations pertaining to personal attacks and political editorials. The *personal attack rules* required that during the airing of

---

[*] *See* Red Lion Broadcasting Co. v. FCC, 395 U.S. 367 (1969).
[†] *See Editorializing by Broadcast Licensees,* 13 F.C.C. 1246, 1249 (1949).

controversial issues of public significance, if an "attack is made upon the honesty, character, integrity or like personal qualities of an identified person or group," the station must give timely notice to the attacked person or group and a reasonable opportunity to respond.[*] The *political editorial rules* required that if a licensee endorses or opposes a legally qualified candidate in a televised editorial, then that candidate must receive timely notice and be given a reasonable opportunity to respond.[†]

In addition to these FCC policies and regulations, specific federal statutory provisions forced equal access requirements on broadcasters for qualifying political candidates. As a threshold matter, broadcasters must provide a *reasonable opportunity* for federal political candidates to purchase access.[‡] In addition, Congress passed *equal access* provisions, codified at 47 U.S.C. § 315, which basically require a licensee to provide equal broadcast opportunities to all candidates for a political office if any one candidate has been allowed to use the station.[§] Finally, political candidates are given some price protections and must be charged the "*lowest unit charge*" for a comparable broadcast spot within a recent time period.[**] These three statutory provisions are sometimes called the political broadcasting requirements.

In *Red Lion*, the Supreme Court—emphasizing spectrum scarcity and the public ownership of the airwaves—upheld the constitutionality of the fairness doctrine, as well as the personal attack and political editorial rules. In its analysis, the court also spoke approvingly of the statutory equal access provisions, whose constitutionality was upheld a decade earlier.[††]

Its demise. In 1985, a deregulatory FCC renounced the fairness doctrine.[‡‡] As a matter of policy, the FCC argued that the fairness doctrine was no longer necessary to further the public interest. The marketplace alone would generate sufficient viewpoint diversity, and intrusion by the government unnecessarily restricted the journalistic freedom of broadcasters. The FCC also questioned the continuing validity of the spectrum scarcity justification, which undergirded the

---

[*] *See* 47 C.F.R. § 73.1920 (repealed).

[†] *See* 47 C.F.R. § 73.1930 (repealed).

[‡] *See* 47 U.S.C. § 312(a)(7). This section authorizes the FCC to revoke the license of any station "for willful or repeated failure to allow reasonable access to or to permit purchase of reasonable amounts of time for the use of a broadcasting station by a legally qualified candidate for Federal elective office on behalf of his candidacy." *See also* 47 C.F.R. § 73.1944 ("reasonable access" implementing regulations).

[§] *See* § 315(a). *See also* 47 C.F.R. § 73.1941 ("equal opportunities" implementing regulations).

[**] *See* § 315(b). *See also* 47 C.F.R. § 73.1942 ("candidate rates" implementing regulations).

[††] *See* Farmers Educ. & Coop. Union v. WDAY, 360 U.S. 525 (1959).

[‡‡] *See In re Inquiry into Section 73.1910 of the Commission's Rules and Regulations Concerning the General Fairness Doctrine Obligations of Broadcast Licensees*, 102 F.C.C.2d 143 (1985).

Red Lion opinion. If scarcity no longer existed, then the fairness doctrine could not be justified under the First Amendment. The Commission concluded, "were the balance ours alone to strike, the fairness doctrine would thus fall short of promoting those interests necessary to uphold its constitutionality."[*]

The FCC did not, however, repeal the fairness doctrine in its 1985 Report. One reason was confusion as to whether the doctrine was *statutorily* required after a 1959 congressional amendment to § 315.[†]   Another reason was that substantial legislative debate was taking place on the future of the fairness doctrine and the FCC. Accordingly, the FCC stated that it would continue enforcing the doctrine notwithstanding its conclusions that the fairness doctrine disserved the public interest and had likely become unconstitutional.

This conflicted stance could not be sustained for long. In 1986, the D.C. Circuit made clear that the fairness doctrine was not statutorily required. Rather, it was simply an administrative construction crafted by the FCC pursuant to its power to regulate broadcast in the "public interest."[‡] When Congress subsequently passed a bill doing what the D.C. Circuit said Congress had not been done, the bill was vetoed by President Ronald Reagan. At this point, in 1987, the FCC buried the fairness doctrine.[§] In its view, the fairness doctrine was unconstitutional and thus against the public interest.

NOTES & QUESTIONS

1. *Constitutional requirement or policy judgment?* In its explanation, the FCC concluded that the fairness doctrine was unconstitutional on First Amendment grounds. However, the D.C. Circuit affirmed the Commission's actions on "public interest" grounds, not constitutional grounds.[**] In the rest of this chapter, we will see different sorts of "access" regulations being applied to different types of communications service providers. In certain contexts, the

---

[*]   *Id.* at 156.

[†]   The amendment made clear that "bona fide newscasts, bona fide news interviews, bona fide news documentaries, and on-the-spot coverage of bona fide news events" would not trigger an equal access requirement. In making the changes, however, Congress added the following language to § 315(a): "Nothing in the foregoing sentence shall be construed as relieving broadcasters, in connection with the presentation of newscasts, news interviews, news documentaries, and on-the-spot coverage of news events, from the obligation imposed upon them under this chapter to operate in the public interest and to afford reasonable opportunity for the discussion of conflicting views on issues of public importance." Arguably, this new text codified the fairness doctrine.

[‡]   *See* Telecommunications Research and Action Center v. FCC, 801 F.2d 501 (D.C. Cir. 1986).

[§]   *See* Syracuse Peace Council, MO&O 2 FCC Rcd. 5043 (1987).

[**]   *See* Syracuse Peace Council v. FCC, 867 F.2d 654 (D.C. Cir. 1989) (affirming on "public interest," not constitutional grounds).

First Amendment will be crucial. In other contexts, the analysis will sound much more like an economic and policy judgment-call (not a constitutional mandate). As you read this chapter, ask yourself whether these different approaches are warranted.

2. *Fairness on cable?* What about the fairness doctrine and the related political broadcast provisions as applied to cable television? The FCC did impose elements of the fairness doctrine on cable TV. But as noted above, the general doctrine as well as its related political attack and editorial rules have been repealed for both broadcast and cable TV.[*] What about the political broadcasting provisions, which still remain in effect in broadcast? In 1972,[†] Congress made clear that § 315 applied to cable operators.[‡] Thus, equal access[§] and lowest unit pricing[**] requirements exist for origination cablecasting.[††] As for § 312(a)(7), it could have no direct effect on cable operators since that provision enforces a reasonable access requirement by threatening revocation of broadcast license—which cable operators neither have nor need.

3. *What survives?* In repealing the fairness doctrine, the FCC did not specifically abolish the related personal attack or political editorial rules. This decision, or lack of decision, generated its own convoluted story. Although various parties petitioned the FCC to invalidate these rules as early as 1987, the FCC did not take any action. In 1997 the FCC announced publicly that it could not reach consensus on this issue. One year later, even after four new commissioners joined the FCC, the Commission was still at loggerheads. After more complicated procedural moves, the D.C. Circuit finally issued a writ of mandamus ordering the FCC to repeal these rules.[‡‡] In 2000, the FCC heeded the court's command.[§§] To conclude, the only laws still on the books associated with the fairness doctrine in broadcast are the political broadcasting provisions,

---

[*] The only regulation that remains is 47 C.F.R. § 76.209, which reads: "A cable television system operator engaging in origination cablecasting shall afford reasonable opportunity for the discussion of conflicting views on issues of public importance."

[†] PUB L. NO. 92-225, 86 STAT. 3 (1972).

[‡] *See* §§ 315(c)(1), (c)(2).

[§] *See* 47 C.F.R. §76.205 (Origination cablecasts by legally qualified candidates for public office; equal opportunities).

[**] *See* 47 CFR §76.206 (Candidate rates).

[††] *See* 47 C.F.R. §76.5(p) (Definition of origination cablecasting).

[‡‡] *See* Radio-Television News Dirs. Ass'n v. FCC, 2000 U.S. App. LEXIS 25269 (Oct. 11, 2000). The Court did, however, make clear that the FCC could institute a new rulemaking proceeding to determine whether the personal attack and political editorial rules should be readopted.

[§§] *See In re Repeal or Modification of the Personal Attack and Political Editorial Rules,* 15 FCC Rcd. 20697 (2000) (repealing personal attack and political editorial rules for broadcast as well as cable television).

codified at § 312(a)(7) (reasonable access) and § 315 (equal access, lowest unit pricing), and their implementing regulations.

4. *Fairness on the internet?* In the last few years, the debate over content moderation online has grown heated, and part of that debate has focused on allegations of "bias" in the promotion, blocking, or presentation of material on social media platforms. Central to this debate is Section 230 of the Communications Decency Act, which we will discuss in detail in CHAPTER 8: INTERMEDIARY LIABILITY. But even though Section 230 has nothing to do with the Fairness Doctrine or with allegations of political bias, prominent Members of Congress have put forth proposals to mimic components of the Fairness Doctrine on the internet. For example, Senator Josh Howley introduced the Ending Support for Internet Censorship Act,[*] which would limit the intermediary liability immunity (under Section 230) to those online service providers that obtain an "immunity certification" from the Federal Trade Commission. The certification is meant to establish that the company "does not moderate information provided by other information content providers in a manner that is biased against a political party, political candidate, or political viewpoint."[†] Would this law survive a First Amendment challenge if it was enacted? How might a service provider challenge a denial of their certification request by the Federal Trade Commission on the grounds that they are biased against a "political viewpoint"?

2. ACCESS TO THE BROADCAST NETWORK

For the fairness doctrine, we focused on the choke point at *layer 3: last-leg connection*, which was the local broadcast TV station. But choke points also exist on other layers. Consider, for example, *layer 2: large-scale distribution*, which is the broadcast network. What choke points does the network potentially control? What if you're an independent producer who has created a wonderful pilot for a TV series but can't get it picked up for national distribution by a network? Or what if you're a local independent TV station that wants access to high-quality network programming but the broadcast network only feeds it to its network affiliates?

Networks. At the core of this discussion stands the television broadcast network. In simple terms, a network is a vertically integrated firm that owns in-

---

[*]   S. 1914, 116th Cong. (2019).

[†] S. 1914, § 2(a).

house production facilities (to produce its own television video programming), owns and operates television stations in important markets (such as New York and Los Angeles), affiliates itself with independently owned television stations throughout the entire nation, and maintains telecommunications links among all these stations to distribute (e.g., via satellite) video programming.

Historically, there were three television networks: ABC, NBC, and CBS. In 1986, a fourth major network, FOX, appeared. These four networks are recognized as the Big 4, with clear national reach and influence. Since 1995, smaller broadcast networks have come online. In 1995, the Warner Brothers (WB) network and the United Paramount Network (UPN) were launched, and in 2006 merged to form The CW (so named because it is a joint venture between CBS and Warner Brothers).

Producers. Upstream from the network are video programming producers (*layer 1: production*), who generate the content seen on broadcast television. (Many of these studios are the same ones that produce major motion pictures, released in theaters.) As just explained, some of this video programming is created by the networks themselves through in-house studios (or studios owned by the same media conglomerate). The rest of the video programming is created by studios that are independent from the networks and sell their material to various customers including broadcast TV networks, syndicators, and broadcast TV stations.

Stations. Downstream from the network are local television stations (*layer 3: last-leg connection*), which broadcast the content to viewers. Again, some of the stations are owned and operated by networks themselves. Most others are contractually affiliated with networks. Still other stations are completely independent, without any network affiliation.

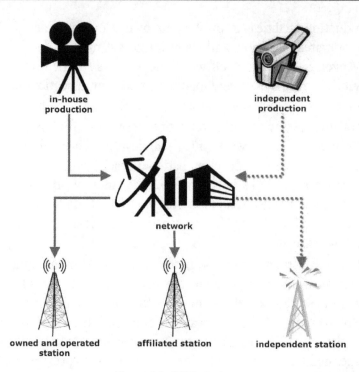

Figure 4.1: TV Industry

The following excerpts from the FCC flesh out the relationships among producers, networks, and stations. The excerpts are dated, so focus on the general definitions and relationships instead of specific numbers.

4. Television stations obtain programming for delivery to their viewers in a variety of ways. First, stations that affiliate with a television network obtain an entire package or schedule of programming directly from their network (the network "feed"). . . . For clearing their airtime for network programming, the affiliates are compensated according to the time of the day they clear time for network programming and the size of their potential audience.

5. The networking of programs intended for the early evening hours that are the "prime time" for adult television viewing gives advertisers access to a substantial number of American households simultaneously. This, in turn, enables the networks to charge high prices for advertising time that are necessary to defray the cost of obtaining the programming most desired by television viewers. Networks encourage their affiliates to carry the entire network "feed" so as to maximize the national audience they can sell to advertisers.

6. Network affiliates also program part of the broadcast day independently of their network. They air locally originated programming, primarily local news and sports programming. They also obtain programming from suppliers called "syndicators," entities that sell programming to television stations on an

individual basis. "Wheel of Fortune" is an example of a program supplied by a syndicator, in this case King World. Having no fixed set of affiliated stations, syndicators traditionally distributed their programming by sending film or tapes of their programs to each television station, a relatively expensive form of program distribution. The advent of satellite technology, however, has made it possible for them to distribute their programming simultaneously to their television station customers, just as the networks provide programming to their affiliates.

7. Stations that do not affiliate with a network are called "independent" stations. There are over 450 independent stations nationwide. The owner of an independent station is responsible for obtaining programming for the entire broadcast day on a program-by-program basis from a number of sources (including, in some cases, a network). While independent stations air some locally originated programming, most of their programming is obtained from program producers or syndicators. Programs such as movies that have been previously shown in theaters, television series that were previously aired on network affiliates (i.e., off-network programs like "The Cosby Show"), and series that have been produced originally for the independent stations (i.e., first-run syndication like "Star Trek: The Next Generation") make up the bulk of an independent station's program schedule.

8. Programs aired on broadcast television are produced by program production companies. The major broadcast television networks historically have produced a small number of programs through their in-house production companies.[5] Unlike those networks, however, Fox Broadcasting Company ("Fox") produces a large amount of programming; it is affiliated with a major movie studio, 20th Century Fox. Most television programs that are produced for the networks or independent stations are produced by either the major movie studios (e.g., Fox, Time Warner, Sony, Disney), other independent program producers who often affiliate with a movie studio in order to produce the program, or syndicators (e.g., King World). Programs intended for network distribution are supplied directly to the networks for airing on their affiliated stations. Programs intended for viewing on a non-network or syndicated basis are sold through the syndication "arm" of a production company, or the production company will sell the "syndication" rights to an independent syndicator who is then responsible for negotiating with the individual stations.[*]

Finally, here's a little more background on how television shows are produced and the relationship between the various financial interests.

---

[5] Under a consent decree, ABC, CBS and NBC were until 1990 prohibited from producing, through a wholly owned program production company, more than a very limited number of prime time programs. That prohibition lapsed in 1991, and since 1993, when corresponding limitations in the FCC rules were repealed, the networks have been free to produce an unlimited amount of programs themselves.

[*] *Prime Time Access Rule,* NPRM, 9 FCC Rcd. 6328 (1994).

3. The process of developing an entertainment series varies among the networks, although there are some common elements. In general, program ideas come from network development departments or producers. A producer can either present an idea directly to a network or to the network through an agent or major studio. A program passes through four stages of development: 1) the treatment; 2) a pilot script; 3) a pilot; and 4) series production. The network development departments finance the first three stages and may terminate the process at any point. The financial terms negotiated between networks and producers at the developmental stages vary greatly, but may include fees, delivery dates, options and possibly the license fee if the program should become a series. Since pilots are expensive, relatively few are made in proportion to the number of treatments and scripts ordered by the networks, and only a fraction of the pilots that are made become series. For example, CBS had pilots made for 32 shows out of the 155 scripts it had ordered for the 1982–83 TV season. From these 32 pilots, 13 new prime time series were created.

4. The producer of a TV series is paid a license fee by the network for each episode produced. The license fee entitles the network to exclusive rights to air the program for a period of time. Typical license fees are about $300,000 for a half hour show and approximately $600,000 for an hour series. License fees can be renegotiated during the run of a series.

5. Successful network programs have value beyond their network run. They can be sold to individual stations through the syndication market. Syndicators may be studios, multiple station groups, advertisers or companies set up specifically to act as syndicators. Under individual contract terms, off-network syndication may begin following the expiration of the licensing network's exclusivity protection for each episode. The most important characteristic common to all off-network syndicated programs is that they have achieved successful network runs in prime time. For a program to be syndicatable, it must have run long enough on the network to have approximately 80–100 episodes. The large number of episodes is required because the off-network syndicated series is usually broadcast daily, in the same time period, a practice known as stripping.

6. The rights to syndicate a program are often negotiated early in the production process. An established producer may even be able to obtain a cash advance from a syndicator based on prospective syndication of a series. The negotiations between producers and syndicators focus on the basic arrangements for dividing syndication revenues, the duration of the syndication rights, the territory where the program may be sold, and any cash advances. A syndicator operates by contacting stations individually and, if enough stations are willing to buy a particular program, then the off-network show feasibly can go into syndication. The price a station pays for a syndicated show is largely dependent on the station's market size. In recent years, local stations in New York and Los Angeles have paid as much as $90,000 per episode for a syndicated program. Typically, syndicators keep 30% to 40% of the syndication revenues as their fee.

Out of this, they pay their operating expenses, which normally include only the costs of distributing the program and the residuals fees that must be paid to actors.[*]

NOTES & QUESTIONS

1. *Why networks?*

    a. *Physics.* Television networks facilitate the national distribution of video programming. Recall broadcast physics. From a terrestrial station, an antenna sends out spherical e-m carrier waves modulated with the video message, which is received by our television sets, then decoded back into the video. However, that signal (depending on the power of the transmitter) goes no farther than approximately 50 miles. This is why you cannot receive in Los Angeles a signal from a San Francisco (much less New York City) television station. In this sense, all terrestrial broadcast is local. However, information is easily replicated, and nothing prevents the same show from being seen by different communities at the same time (what economists call non-rivalrous consumption). Accordingly, a television network can use satellites to distribute the same content (the network feed) nationally to all of its stations (owned-and-operated, as well as affiliated), which then broadcast that content at regularly scheduled times to their local communities.

    b. *Economics.* Networks decrease transaction costs. For example, if an advertiser wants to address a national audience, instead of negotiating individually with each station in hundreds of communities, the advertiser can negotiate with a single network. In addition, networks exploit economies of scale to produce or purchase more expensive video programming. To see why, compare local and national news broadcasts. A local news show generally has little audience outside of its community. Accordingly, its audience is limited. Assuming hypothetically that a news program producer can afford to invest $1 per viewer, then in a market of 1 million viewers, only $1 million can be invested. By contrast, a national news show has a national audience. Thus, if the national audience is 100 million viewers, then $100 million can be invested. This $100 million show can then be copied perfectly and distributed nationally at a trivial cost through the telecommunications links maintained by the network. Of course, money does not necessarily guarantee quality. Still, a show that has $1 million to spend will have difficulty competing against a show that has $100 million in its coffers. This explains why programming designed for a national

---

[*] *Syndication and Financial Interest Rules, Tentative Decision and Request for Further Comments,* 94 F.C.C.2d 1019 (1983).

audience (e.g., through networks) often seems superior, at least in production value, to programming designed for a local community.

2. *Network dominance.* Can the not-quite-monopoly network power be "abused"? If networks are too powerful, they may abuse independent video programming producers upstream in the vertical chain. Or they may abuse network affiliates and independent stations downstream, who may depend on the network for access to video programming. Abuses of market power raise questions of antitrust law. And, indeed, antitrust consent decrees (from 1977-1990) have played important roles in regulating the vertical structure of broadcast television. But in addition to antitrust laws, the FCC has enacted various rules to regulate the relationships between networks and parties both upstream and downstream. Prominent examples include the Financial Syndication Rules (FinSyn) and Prime Time Access Rules (PTAR), both adopted in 1970, which are now long defunct. There remain specific rules that govern a network and its affiliates, codified in 47 C.F.R. § 73.658. Among the matters covered by these rules are an affiliate station's right to broadcast programming delivered by other networks; an affiliate station's right to reject programming (recall how preemption of network feeds was used to measure "localism"); an affiliate station's right not to have its advertising rates set by the network on non-network programming.

B. CABLE TELEVISION

In our study of broadcast TV, we identified three stylized layers that helped categorize the various players necessary to provide a communications service. Let's continue using that three layer model to analyze access issues in cable television.

Layer	Broadcast TV Players	Cable TV Players
1. Production	Studio	*Cable Network*
2. Large-scale Distribution	Broadcast Network	*Multiple System Operators*
3. Last-leg Connection	Local Station	*Cable Operator*

Let's start with *layer 1: production.* In cable TV, a cable "network" produces the video content. To avoid confusion, notice that a cable "network" (e.g. Comedy Central) isn't quite the same thing as a broadcast TV "network" (e.g. NBC). In broadcast TV, networks fit best into *layer 2: large-scale distribution* because they acquire programming from producers, bundle it together (for a prime time feed), then distribute it nationally to owned or affiliated stations for exhibition. By contrast, it's best to think of cable networks as slotting into the *layer 1: production*. In other words, a cable network is really a cable *programming* network, a channel of similarly themed content, such as Discovery, CNN, ESPN, or Comedy Central. These networks acquire content or produce it themselves, then bundle it together into a linear 24x7 stream.

In cable TV, who then occupies the other two layers? *Layer 3: last-leg connection* is occupied by the local cable operator, who owns the cable system that connects the head-end to each subscriber's home through physical coaxial and fiber wires. The clear analogue in broadcast TV would be the local broadcast station.

What about *layer 2: large-scale distribution*? If a cable programming network is to be viable, it must spread the costs of producing high quality programming over a large number of subscribers, perhaps as many as 15 million. That means that the cable network has to be carried on a large number of cable systems throughout the country. A handful of firms, called Multiple System Operators (MSOs), own huge numbers of those cable systems around different regions of the country. They include, for example, Comcast, Charter, and Cox. The analogue in broadcast TV would be the broadcast network.

We start by examining choke points on *layer 3: last-leg connection*, the local cable operator's cable system.

1. ACCESS TO THE CABLE SYSTEM

a. MUST-CARRY

Suppose you had high quality video content that you wanted carried by your local cable operator on its cable system. But that cable operator took a look and said "not interested." Could you nevertheless force access onto the cable system despite the cable operator's wishes? If your intuition is "no," might it matter that you're a local television station serving the same geographical area as that cable operator? This raises the issue known as "must-carry."

TURNER BROADCASTING V. FCC
512 U.S. 622 (1994)

Justice KENNEDY announced the judgment of the Court and delivered the opinion of the Court, except as to Part III-B.

I

B

At issue in this case is the constitutionality of the so-called must-carry provisions, contained in §§ 4 and 5 of the [1992 Cable] Act, which require cable operators to carry the signals of a specified number of local broadcast television stations.

Section 4 requires carriage of "local commercial television stations" . . . that operate within the same television market as the cable system. Cable systems with more than 12 active channels, and more than 300 subscribers, are required to set aside up to one-third of their channels for commercial broadcast stations that request carriage. Cable systems with more than 300 subscribers, but only 12 or fewer active channels, must carry the signals of three commercial broadcast stations.

Section 5 of the Act imposes similar requirements regarding the carriage of local public broadcast television stations . . .

C

Congress enacted the 1992 Cable Act after conducting three years of hearings. . . . In brief, Congress found that the physical characteristics of cable transmission, compounded by the increasing concentration of economic power in the cable industry, are endangering the ability of over-the-air broadcast television stations to compete for a viewing audience and thus for necessary operating revenues.

In particular, Congress found that over 60 percent of the households with television sets subscribe to cable, and for these households cable has replaced over-the-air broadcast television as the primary provider of video programming. In addition, Congress concluded that due to "local franchising requirements and the extraordinary expense of constructing more than one cable television system to serve a particular geographic area," the overwhelming majority of cable operators exercise a monopoly over cable service. § 2(a)(2).

According to Congress, this market position gives cable operators the power and the incentive to harm broadcast competitors. The power derives from the cable operator's ability, as owner of the transmission facility, to "terminate the retransmission of the broadcast signal, refuse to carry new signals, or reposition a broadcast signal to a disadvantageous channel position." § 2(a)(15). The incentive derives from the economic reality that "cable television systems and broadcast television stations increasingly compete for television advertising revenues." § 2(a)(14). By refusing carriage of broadcasters' signals, cable operators, as a practical matter, can reduce the number of households that have access to the broadcasters' programming, and thereby capture advertising dollars that would otherwise go to broadcast stations.

Congress found, in addition, that increased vertical integration in the cable industry is making it even harder for broadcasters to secure carriage on cable systems, because cable operators have a financial incentive to favor their affiliated programmers. Congress also determined that the cable industry is characterized by horizontal concentration, with many cable operators sharing common ownership. This has resulted in greater "barriers to entry for new programmers and a reduction in the number of media voices available to consumers." § 2(a)(4).

In light of these technological and economic conditions, Congress concluded that unless cable operators are required to carry local broadcast stations ... "the economic viability of free local broadcast television and its ability to originate quality local programming will be seriously jeopardized." § 2(a)(16).

II

By requiring cable systems to set aside a portion of their channels for local broadcasters, the must-carry rules regulate cable speech in two respects: The rules reduce the number of channels over which cable operators exercise unfettered control, and they render it more difficult for cable programmers to compete for carriage on the limited channels remaining.

A

We address first the Government's contention that regulation of cable television should be analyzed under the same First Amendment standard that applies to regulation of broadcast television. It is true that our cases have permitted more intrusive regulation of broadcast speakers than of speakers in other media. *Compare Red Lion Broadcasting Co. v. FCC* (1969) (television), and *National Broadcasting Co. v. United States* (1943) (radio), *with Miami Herald Publishing Co. v. Tornillo* (print). But the rationale for applying a less rigorous standard of First Amendment scrutiny to broadcast regulation, whatever its validity in the cases elaborating it, does not apply in the context of cable regulation.

Although courts and commentators have criticized the scarcity rationale since its inception, we have declined to question its continuing validity as support for our broadcast jurisprudence, and see no reason to do so here. The broadcast cases are inapposite in the present context because cable television does not suffer from the inherent limitations that characterize the broadcast medium. Indeed, given the rapid advances in fiber optics and digital compression technology, soon there may be no practical limitation on the number of speakers who may use the cable medium. Nor is there any danger of physical interference between two cable speakers attempting to share the same channel. In light of these fundamental technological differences between broadcast and cable transmission, application of the more relaxed standard of scrutiny adopted in *Red Lion* and the other broadcast cases is inapt when determining the First Amendment validity of cable regulation.

This is not to say that the unique physical characteristics of cable transmission should be ignored.... But whatever relevance these physical characteristics may have in the evaluation of particular cable regulations, they do not require the alteration of settled principles of our First Amendment jurisprudence.

[The government] advances a second argument for application of the *Red Lion* framework to cable regulation. It asserts that the foundation of our broadcast jurisprudence is not the physical limitations of the electromagnetic spectrum, but rather the "market dysfunction" that characterizes the broadcast market. Because the cable market is beset by a similar dysfunction, the Government maintains, the *Red Lion* standard of review should also apply to cable.

While we agree that the cable market suffers certain structural impediments, the Government's argument is flawed in two respects. First, as discussed above, the special physical characteristics of broadcast transmission, not the economic characteristics of the broadcast market, are what underlies our broadcast jurisprudence. Second, the mere assertion of dysfunction or failure in a speech market, without more, is not sufficient to shield a speech regulation from the First Amendment standards applicable to nonbroadcast media.

By a related course of reasoning, the Government and some appellees maintain that the must-carry provisions are nothing more than industry-specific antitrust legislation, and thus warrant rational basis scrutiny.... [W]hile the enforcement of a generally applicable law may or may not be subject to heightened scrutiny under the First Amendment, laws that single out the press, or certain elements thereof, for special treatment "pose a particular danger of abuse by the State," *Arkansas Writers' Project, Inc. v. Ragland* (1987), and so are always subject to at least some degree of heightened First Amendment scrutiny. Because the must-carry provisions impose special obligations upon cable operators and special burdens upon cable programmers, some measure of heightened First Amendment scrutiny is demanded.

B

Deciding whether a particular regulation is content-based or content-neutral is not always a simple task. We have said that the "principal inquiry in determining content-neutrality . . . is whether the government has adopted a regulation of speech because of [agreement or] disagreement with the message it conveys." *Ward v. Rock Against Racism* (1989). The purpose, or justification, of a regulation will often be evident on its face. But while a content-based purpose may be sufficient in certain circumstances to show that a regulation is content-based, it is not necessary to such a showing in all cases. Nor will the mere assertion of a content-neutral purpose be enough to save a law which, on its face, discriminates based on content.

As a general rule, laws that by their terms distinguish favored speech from disfavored speech on the basis of the ideas or views expressed are content-based. By contrast, laws that confer benefits or impose burdens on speech without reference to the ideas or views expressed are in most instances content-neutral.

C

Insofar as they pertain to the carriage of full power broadcasters, the must-carry rules, on their face, impose burdens and confer benefits without reference to the content of speech.[6] . . . [T]he extent of the interference [with cable operators' editorial discretion] does not depend upon the content of the cable operators' programming. The rules impose obligations upon all operators . . . regardless of the programs or stations they now offer or have offered in the past.

---

[6] The must-carry rules also require carriage, under certain limited circumstances, of low power broadcast stations. Under the Act, a low power station may become eligible for carriage only if, among other things, the FCC determines that the station's programming "would address local news and informational needs which are not being adequately served by full power television broadcast stations because of the geographic distance of such full power stations from the low power station's community of license." § 534(h)(2)(B). We recognize that this aspect of § 4 appears to single out certain low-power broadcasters for special benefits on the basis of content. Because the District Court did not address whether these particular provisions are content-based, and because the parties make only the most glancing reference to the operation of, and justifications for, the low-power broadcast provisions, we think it prudent to allow the District Court to consider the content-neutral or content-based character of this provision in the first instance on remand.

In a similar vein, although a broadcast station's eligibility for must-carry is based upon its geographic proximity to a qualifying cable system, the Act permits the FCC to grant must-carry privileges upon request to otherwise ineligible broadcast stations. In acting upon these requests, the FCC is directed to give "attention to the value of localism" and, in particular, to whether the requesting station "provides news coverage of issues of concern to such community . . . or coverage of sporting and other events of interest to the community." § 534(h)(1)(C)(ii). Again, the District Court did not address this provision, but may do so on remand.

Nothing in the Act imposes a restriction, penalty, or burden by reason of the views, programs, or stations the cable operator has selected or will select. The number of channels a cable operator must set aside depends only on the operator's channel capacity; hence, an operator cannot avoid or mitigate its obligations under the Act by altering the programming it offers to subscribers.

The must-carry provisions also burden cable programmers by reducing the number of channels for which they can compete. But, again, this burden is unrelated to content . . . . And finally, the privileges conferred by the must-carry provisions are also unrelated to content. The rules benefit all full power broadcasters who request carriage—be they commercial or noncommercial, independent or network-affiliated, English or Spanish language, religious or secular.

It is true that the must-carry provisions distinguish between speakers in the television programming market. But they do so based only upon the manner in which speakers transmit their messages to viewers, and not upon the messages they carry: Broadcasters, which transmit over the airwaves, are favored, while cable programmers, which do not, are disfavored. Cable operators, too, are burdened by the carriage obligations, but only because they control access to the cable conduit. So long as they are not a subtle means of exercising a content preference, speaker distinctions of this nature are not presumed invalid under the First Amendment.

That the must-carry provisions, on their face, do not burden or benefit speech of a particular content does not end the inquiry. Our cases have recognized that even a regulation neutral on its face may be content-based if its manifest purpose is to regulate speech because of the message it conveys.

Congress' overriding objective in enacting must-carry was not to favor programming of a particular subject matter, viewpoint, or format, but rather to preserve access to free television programming for the 40 percent of Americans without cable.

Appellants and the dissent make much of the fact that, in the course of describing the purposes behind the Act, Congress referred to the value of broadcast programming. In particular, Congress noted that broadcast television is "an important source of local news[,] public affairs programming and other local broadcast services critical to an informed electorate," and that noncommercial television "provides educational and informational programming to the Nation's citizens." We do not think, however, that such references cast any material doubt on the content-neutral character of must-carry. That Congress acknowledged the local orientation of broadcast programming and the role that noncommercial stations have played in educating the public does not indicate that Congress regarded broadcast programming as more valuable than cable programming. Rather, it reflects nothing more than the recognition that the services provided by broadcast television have some intrinsic value and, thus, are worth preserving against the threats posed by cable.

The operation of the Act further undermines the suggestion that Congress' purpose in enacting must-carry was to force programming of a "local" or "educational" content on cable subscribers. The provisions, as we have stated, benefit all full power broadcasters irrespective of the nature of their programming. In fact, if a cable system were required to bump a cable programmer to make room for a broadcast station, nothing would stop a cable operator from displacing a cable station that provides all local or education-oriented programming with a broadcaster that provides very little. Appellants do not even contend, moreover, that broadcast programming is any more "local" or "educational" than cable programming.

We likewise reject the suggestion ... that the must-carry rules are content-based because the preference for broadcast stations "automatically entails content requirements." It is true that broadcast programming, unlike cable programming, is subject to certain limited content restraints imposed by statute and FCC regulation.[7] But it does not follow that Congress mandated cable carriage of broadcast television stations as a means of ensuring that particular programs will be shown, or not shown, on cable systems.

As an initial matter, the argument exaggerates the extent to which the FCC is permitted to intrude into matters affecting the content of broadcast programming. The FCC is forbidden by statute from engaging in "censorship".... 47 U.S.C. § 326....

Stations licensed to broadcast over the special frequencies reserved for "noncommercial educational" stations are subject to no more intrusive content regulation than their commercial counterparts. Noncommercial licensees must operate on a nonprofit basis, may not accept financial consideration in exchange for particular programming, and may not broadcast promotional announcements or advertisements on behalf of for-profit entities. What is important for present purposes, however, is that noncommercial licensees are not required by statute

---

[7] See, e.g., 47 U.S.C. § 303b (directing FCC to consider extent to which license renewal applicant has "served the educational and informational needs of children"); note following 47 U.S.C. § 303 (restrictions on indecent programming); 47 U.S.C. § 312(a)(7) (allowing FCC to revoke broadcast license for willful or repeated failure to allow reasonable access to broadcast airtime for candidates seeking federal elective office); 47 CFR § 73.1920 (1993) (requiring broadcaster to notify victims of on-air personal attacks and to provide victims with opportunity to respond over the air); En Banc Programming Inquiry, 44 F.C.C.2d 2303, 2312 (1960) (requiring broadcasters to air programming that serves "the public interest, convenience or necessity").

or regulation to carry any specific quantity of "educational" programming or any particular "educational" programs. Noncommercial licensees, like their commercial counterparts, need only adhere to the general requirement that their programming serve "the public interest, convenience or necessity." *En Banc Programming Inquiry*, 44 F.C.C.2d 2303, 2312 (1960).

In addition, although federal funding provided through the Corporation for Public Broadcasting (CPB) supports programming on noncommercial stations, the Government is foreclosed from using its financial support to gain leverage over any programming decisions.

In short, the must-carry provisions are not designed to favor or disadvantage speech of any particular content. Rather, they are meant to protect broadcast television from what Congress determined to be unfair competition by cable systems. . . .

D

Appellants advance . . . additional arguments to support their view that the must-carry provisions warrant strict scrutiny.

1

Appellants maintain that the must-carry provisions trigger strict scrutiny because they compel cable operators to transmit speech not of their choosing. Relying principally on *Miami Herald Publishing Co. v. Tornillo* (1974), appellants say this intrusion on the editorial control of cable operators amounts to forced speech. . . . interest. *Tornillo* affirmed an essential proposition: The First Amendment protects the editorial independence of the press. . . .

The same principles led us to invalidate a similar content-based access regulation in *Pacific Gas & Electric*. At issue was a rule requiring a privately-owned utility . . . to include with its monthly bills an editorial newsletter published by a consumer group critical of the utility's ratemaking practices. . . . [T]he plurality held that the same strict First Amendment scrutiny [as in *Tornillo*] applied. Like the statute in *Tornillo*, the regulation conferred benefits to speakers based on viewpoint, giving access only to a consumer group opposing the utility's practices.

Tornillo and *Pacific Gas & Electric* do not control this case for the following reasons. First, unlike the access rules struck down in those cases, the must-carry rules are content-neutral in application.

Second, appellants do not suggest, nor do we think it the case, that must-carry will force cable operators to alter their own messages to respond to the broadcast programming they are required to carry. Given cable's long history of serving as a conduit for broadcast signals, there appears little risk that cable viewers would assume that the broadcast stations carried on a cable system convey ideas or messages endorsed by the cable operator.... Moreover, in contrast to the statute at issue in *Tornillo*, no aspect of the must-carry provisions would cause a cable operator or cable programmer to conclude that "the safe course is to avoid controversy," *Tornillo*, and by so doing diminish the free flow of information and ideas.

Finally, the asserted analogy to *Tornillo* ignores an important technological difference between newspapers and cable television. Although a daily newspaper and a cable operator both may enjoy monopoly status in a given locale, the cable operator exercises far greater control over access to the relevant medium. A daily newspaper, no matter how secure its local monopoly, does not possess the power to obstruct readers' access to other competing publications. ...

The same is not true of cable. When an individual subscribes to cable, the physical connection between the television set and the cable network gives the cable operator bottleneck, or gatekeeper, control over most (if not all) of the television programming that is channeled into the subscriber's home. Hence, simply by virtue of its ownership of the essential pathway for cable speech, a cable operator can prevent its subscribers from obtaining access to programming it chooses to exclude. A cable operator, unlike speakers in other media, can thus silence the voice of competing speakers with a mere flick of the switch.

The potential for abuse of this private power over a central avenue of communication cannot be overlooked. The First Amendment's command that government not impede the freedom of speech does not disable the government from taking steps to ensure that private interests not restrict, through physical control of a critical pathway of communication, the free flow of information and ideas.

3

Finally, appellants maintain that strict scrutiny applies because the must-carry provisions single out certain members of the press—here, cable operators—for disfavored treatment.

Regulations that discriminate among media, or among different speakers within a single medium, often present serious First Amendment concerns.

It would be error to conclude, however, that the First Amendment mandates strict scrutiny for any speech regulation that applies to one medium (or a subset thereof) but not others.

The must-carry provisions, as we have explained above, are justified by special characteristics of the cable medium: the bottleneck monopoly power exercised by cable operators and the dangers this power poses to the viability of broadcast television. Appellants do not argue, nor does it appear, that other media . . . are subject to bottleneck monopoly control, or pose a demonstrable threat to the survival of broadcast television. It should come as no surprise, then, that Congress decided to impose the must-carry obligations upon cable operators only.

III

A

[T]he appropriate standard by which to evaluate the constitutionality of must-carry is the intermediate level of scrutiny applicable to content-neutral restrictions that impose an incidental burden on speech. *See Ward v. Rock Against Racism* (1989); *United States v. O'Brien* (1968). Under *O'Brien*, a content-neutral regulation will be sustained if

> "it furthers an important or substantial governmental interest; if the governmental interest is unrelated to the suppression of free expression; and if the incidental restriction on alleged First Amendment freedoms is no greater than is essential to the furtherance of that interest."

To satisfy this standard, a regulation need not be the least speech-restrictive means of advancing the Government's interests. "Rather, the requirement of narrow tailoring is satisfied 'so long as the . . . regulation promotes a substantial government interest that would be achieved less effectively absent the regulation.'" *Ward.* Narrow tailoring in this context requires, in other words, that the means chosen do not "burden substantially more speech than is necessary to further the government's legitimate interests." *Ward.* Congress declared that the must-carry provisions serve three interrelated interests: (1) preserving the benefits of free, over-the-air local broadcast television, (2) promoting the widespread dissemination of information from a multiplicity of sources, and (3) promoting fair competition in the market for television programming. [V]iewed in the abstract, we have no difficulty concluding that each of them is an important governmental interest.

As we recognized in [*United States v.] Southwestern Cable* [(1968)], the importance of local broadcasting outlets "can scarcely be exaggerated, for broadcasting is demonstrably a principal source of information and entertainment for a great part of the Nation's population." The interest in maintaining the local broadcasting structure does not evaporate simply because cable has come upon the scene. . . . Likewise, assuring that the public has access to a multiplicity of information sources is a governmental purpose of the highest order, for it promotes values central to the First Amendment. Indeed, "it has long been a basic tenet of national communications policy that "the widest possible dissemination of information from diverse and antagonistic sources is essential to the welfare of the public." *United States v. Midwest Video Corp.* (plurality opinion) (quoting *Associated Press v. United States*). Finally, the Government's interest in eliminating restraints on fair competition is always substantial, even when the individuals or entities subject to particular regulations are engaged in expressive activity protected by the First Amendment.

B

That the Government's asserted interests are important in the abstract does not mean, however, that the must-carry rules will in fact advance those interests. When the Government defends a regulation on speech as a means to redress past harms or prevent anticipated harms, it must do more than simply "posit the existence of the disease sought to be cured." *Quincy Cable TV, Inc. v. FCC* (CADC 1985). It must demonstrate that the recited harms are real, not merely conjectural, and that the regulation will in fact alleviate these harms in a direct and material way.

Thus, in applying *O'Brien* scrutiny we must ask first whether the Government has adequately shown that the economic health of local broadcasting is in genuine jeopardy and in need of the protections afforded by must-carry. Assuming an affirmative answer to the foregoing question, the Government still bears the burden of showing that the remedy it has adopted does not "burden substantially more speech than is necessary to further the government's legitimate interests." *Ward.* On the state of the record developed thus far, and in the absence of findings of fact from the District Court, we are unable to conclude that the Government has satisfied either inquiry.

[The court summarized the ways in which the record was factually inadequate.—ED.]

[B]ecause there are genuine issues of material fact still to be resolved on this record, we hold that the District Court erred in granting summary judgment in favor of the Government.

The judgment below is vacated, and the case is remanded for further proceedings consistent with this opinion.

It is so ordered.

Justice O'CONNOR, with whom Justice SCALIA and Justice GINSBURG join, and with whom Justice THOMAS joins as to Parts I and III, concurring in part and dissenting in part.

I

A

I cannot avoid the conclusion that [Congress's] preference for broadcasters over cable programmers is justified with reference to content. The findings, enacted by Congress ... make this clear. "There is a substantial governmental and First Amendment interest in promoting a diversity of views provided through multiple technology media." § 2(a)(6). "Public television provides educational and informational programming to the Nation's citizens, thereby advancing the Government's compelling interest in educating its citizens." § 2(a)(8)(A). "A primary objective and benefit of our Nation's system of regulation of television broadcasting is the local origination of programming. There is a substantial governmental interest in ensuring its continuation." § 2(a)(10). "Broadcast television stations continue to be an important source of local news and public affairs programming and other local broadcast services critical to an informed electorate." § 2(a)(11).

Similar justifications are reflected in the operative provisions of the Act. In determining whether a broadcast station should be eligible for must-carry in a particular market, the FCC must "afford particular attention to the value of localism by taking into account such factors as ... whether any other [eligible station] provides news coverage of issues of concern to such community or provides carriage or coverage of sporting and other events of interest to the community." 47 U.S.C. § 534(h)(1)(C)(ii). In determining whether a low-power station is eligible for must-carry, the FCC must ask whether the station "would address local news and informational needs which are not being adequately served by full power television broadcast stations." 47 U.S.C. § 534(h)(2)(B). Moreover, the Act distinguishes between commercial television stations and noncommercial educational television stations, giving special benefits to the latter.

Preferences for diversity of viewpoints, for localism, for educational programming, and for news and public affairs all make reference to content. They may not reflect hostility to particular points of view, or a desire to suppress certain subjects because they are controversial or offensive. They may be quite benignly motivated. But benign motivation, we have consistently held, is not enough to avoid the need for strict scrutiny of content-based justifications. The First Amendment does more than just bar government from intentionally suppressing speech of which it disapproves. It also generally prohibits the government from excepting certain kinds of speech from regulation because it thinks the speech is especially valuable.

This is why the Court is mistaken in concluding that the interest in diversity—in "access to a multiplicity" of "diverse and antagonistic sources"— is content neutral. . . . The interest in ensuring access to a multiplicity of diverse and antagonistic sources of information, no matter how praiseworthy, is directly tied to the content of what the speakers will likely say.

C

Content-based speech restrictions are generally unconstitutional unless they are narrowly tailored to a compelling state interest.

The interest in localism, either in the dissemination of opinions held by the listeners' neighbors or in the reporting of events that have to do with the local community, cannot be described as "compelling". . . . [T]he same is true of the interest in diversity of viewpoints: While the government may subsidize speakers that it thinks provide novel points of view, it may not restrict other speakers on the theory that what they say is more conventional. *Cf.* Metro Broadcasting, Inc. v. FCC (1990) (O'CONNOR, J., dissenting).

The interests in public affairs programming and educational programming seem somewhat weightier, though it is a difficult question whether they are compelling. . . . We have never held that the Government could impose educational content requirements on, say, newsstands, bookstores, or movie theaters; and it is not clear that such requirements would in any event appreciably further the goals of public education.

But even assuming arguendo that the Government could set some channels aside for educational or news programming, the Act is insufficiently tailored to this goal. To benefit the educational broadcasters, the Act burdens more than just the cable entertainment programmers. It equally burdens CNN, C-SPAN, the Discovery Channel, the New Inspirational Network, and other channels with as much claim as PBS to being educational or related to public affairs.

II

Even if I am mistaken about the must-carry provisions being content based, however, in my view they fail content-neutral scrutiny as well.

The must-carry provisions are fatally overbroad, even under a content-neutral analysis: They disadvantage cable programmers even if the operator has no anticompetitive motives, and even if the broadcaster that would have to be dropped to make room for the cable programmer would survive without cable access. None of the factfinding that the District Court is asked to do on remand will change this. . . .

III

Having said all this, it is important to acknowledge one basic fact: The question is not whether there will be control over who gets to speak over cable—the question is who will have this control. Under the FCC's view, the answer is Congress, acting within relatively broad limits. Under my view, the answer is the cable operator.

I have no doubt that there is danger in having a single cable operator decide what millions of subscribers can or cannot watch. And I have no doubt that Congress can act to relieve this danger. In other provisions of the Act, Congress has already taken steps to foster competition among cable systems. Congress can encourage the creation of new media, such as inexpensive satellite broadcasting, or fiber-optic networks with virtually unlimited channels, or even simple devices that would let people easily switch from cable to over-the-air broadcasting. And of course Congress can subsidize broadcasters that it thinks provide especially valuable programming.

Congress may also be able to act in more mandatory ways. If Congress finds that cable operators are leaving some channels empty—perhaps for ease of future expansion—it can compel the operators to make the free channels available to programmers who otherwise would not get carriage. *See PruneYard Shopping Center v. Robins* (1980) (upholding a compelled access scheme because it did not burden others' speech). Congress might also conceivably obligate cable operators to act as common carriers for some of their channels, with those channels being open to all through some sort of lottery system or timesharing arrangement. Setting aside any possible Takings Clause issues, it stands to reason that if Congress may demand that telephone companies operate as common carriers, it can ask the same of cable companies; such an approach would not suffer from the defect of preferring one speaker to another.

But the First Amendment as we understand it today rests on the premise that it is government power, rather than private power, that is the main threat to free expression; and as a consequence, the Amendment imposes substantial limitations on the Government even when it is trying to serve concededly praiseworthy goals. . . . Accordingly, I would reverse the judgment below.[*]

---

[*] The opinions of Justices Blackmun, Stevens, and Ginsburg were omitted. —ED.

NOTES & QUESTIONS

1. *The problem.* Somehow, Congress believed that the rise of cable TV threatened the viability of free over-the-air broadcast TV. How and why would cable's popularity threaten broadcast?

2. *Choke point.* The problem that cable causes for broadcast TV is not merely competition for scarce advertising dollars. After all, cable TV acquires most of its revenues from subscription payments, not advertising dollars. The other problem is that a cable operator enjoys control over a choke point, the cable system, through which increasing numbers of people watch television. If you believed that cable operators were abusing their power over the cable system infrastructure, what policy options would you have?

3. *Content neutrality.* The central dispute between the plurality opinion and Justice O'Connor's opinion revolves around the concept of content neutrality. Justice Kennedy, writing for the plurality, believes that the must-carry rules are content-neutral. By contrast, Justice O'Connor believes that they are content-based. Who has the better argument? On the basis of this case, how does one decide whether any particular speech restriction is content-based? Stepping back from the formal doctrine for a moment, does it make sense that so much of the constitutional analysis should turn on this question, which requires a binary answer: yes or no? In truth, isn't the answer much more a continuous gradient, more like an analog signal?

4. *Means-ends analysis.* In the end, the Court decides that the factual record is not developed sufficiently to conduct an adequate means-ends analysis. However, it does consider the "ends" of the must-carry rules. Do you think that the ends are "compelling"? Do you think that they are "important"? What do the various justices think?

5. *Turner II.* On remand, the District Court made very detailed findings of fact and again granted summary judgment to the government. On direct appeal to the Supreme Court, a majority applied intermediate scrutiny (based on its previous judgment of content neutrality) and affirmed.[*] Specifically, the Court concluded that the must-carry rules further important government interests of preserving free over-the-air broadcast television, promoting widespread information dissemination through a multiplicity of sources, and encouraging fair competition in the market for television programming. The Court also concluded that the must-carry rules were sufficiently well-tailored to achieving these objectives.

---

[*] *See* Turner Broadcasting System v. FCC, 520 U.S. 180 (1997) (*Turner II*).

6. *Takings.* Any time the federal government forces channels of speech on another's private property, there may be a constitutionally cognizable taking for which just compensation must be paid.[*] Indeed, Justice O'Connor, in her opinion, specifically mentions this possibility in the context of forcing cable operators to open up some channels for "common carrier" usage. Current Fifth Amendment takings jurisprudence is complicated. Here's a simplified story.

The paradigm takings clause case is permanent, physical occupation of real property by the government. No matter how small the space taken, there is a per se taking.[†] Accordingly, the government must arrange for just compensation. In addition, ever since Justice Oliver Wendell Holmes' pronouncement that "while property may be regulated to a certain extent, if regulation goes too far it will be recognized as a taking,"[‡] courts have struggled with the contours of a *regulatory* taking.

What precisely is regulation that has gone "too far"? Answering this question requires an ad hoc calculus that considers the following factors: the regulation's economic impact on the claimant; the regulation's disruption of investment-backed expectations; the character of the government action.[§] Given the vagueness of these factors, it should not be surprising that takings jurisprudence has been difficult to systematize or to predict.

That said, federal courts have grown increasingly receptive to the idea of regulatory takings. For example, in 1992, the Supreme Court made clear that regulation that "denies all economically beneficial or productive use of land" is a taking.[**] Lower courts have also suggested that even if all benefit is not regulated away, there may be a partial regulatory takings claim.[††] To be clear, takings claims are not limited to real or other especially physical forms of property.[‡‡] Accordingly, we should not be surprised to see communications service

---

[*] *See* U.S. CONST. amend. V ("nor shall private property be taken for public use without just compensation").

[†] *See* Loretto v. Teleprompter Manhattan CATV Corp., 458 U.S. 419 (1982) (government's permitting cable company to install cables and boxes on landlord's property is a taking); Gulf Power Co. v. United States, 187 F.3d 1324 (11th Cir. 1999) (holding that the Pole Attachments Act, as amended by the Telecommunications Act of 1996, which requires utilities to provide cable companies access to its utility poles, effects a taking); Bell Atl. Telephone Cos. v. FCC, 24 F.3d 1441, 1445–1446 (D.C. Cir. 1994) (holding that physical collocation of competitive access provider's (CAP's) equipment on ILEC premises constitutes a taking).

[‡] Pennsylvania Coal Co. v. Mahon, 260 U.S. 393, 415 (1922).

[§] *See* Penn Central Transportation Co. v. City of New York, 438 U.S. 104 (1978).

[**] *See* Lucas v. South Carolina Coastal Council, 505 U.S. 1003, 1015 (1992).

[††] *See, e.g.,* Florida Rock Industries, Inc., v. United States, 45 Fed. Cl. 21 (1999).

[‡‡] *See, e.g.,* Ruckelshaus v. Monsanto Co., 467 U.S. 986, 1003–1004 (1984) (holding that data recognized as trade secret under state law counts as property under Fifth Amendment takings clause).

providers raise a takings claim in addition to their standard First Amendment arguments.*

NOTE: RISE OF RETRANSMISSION CONSENT

Our study of "must carry" regulation might lead you to believe that broadcasters are still trying desperately to force themselves onto unwilling cable operators. Actually, the tables have now largely turned, and broadcasters are instead demanding payment for "retransmission consent." Start by reading this statutory provision:

> 47 U.S.C. § 325. False, fraudulent, or unauthorized transmissions
>
> (a). False distress signals; rebroadcasting programs
>
> No person within the jurisdiction of the United States shall knowingly utter or transmit, or cause to be uttered or transmitted, any false or fraudulent signal of distress, or communication relating thereto, nor shall any broadcasting station rebroadcast the program or any part thereof of another broadcasting station without the express authority of the originating station.
>
> (b) Consent to retransmission of broadcasting station signals
>
> (1) No cable system or other multichannel video programming distributor shall retransmit the signal of a broadcasting station, or any part thereof, except
>
> (A) with the express authority of the originating station;

Here's more background as explained by the FCC:

Signal Carriage Requirements

The 1992 Cable Act established new standards for television broadcast station signal carriage on cable systems. Under these rules, each local commercial television broadcast station was given the option of selecting mandatory carriage (must-carry) or retransmission consent (may carry) for each cable system serving the same market as the commercial television station.

Must-Carry/Retransmission Consent Election

Every three years, every local commercial television station has the right to elect either must-carry or retransmission consent.

---

* In Lingle v. Chevron, 544 U.S. 528 (2005), the Supreme Court held that the "substantially advances" formula from Agins v. City of Tiburon, 447 U.S. 255 (1980), did not state an independent test for a Fifth Amendment taking. *See* 544 U.S. at 542. *Agins* had suggested that there would be a taking if a regulation does "not substantially advance legitimate state interests" *or* "denies an owner economically viable use of the land." In *Lingle*, the Court admitted that its language was "regrettably imprecise" and rejected the "substantially advances" basis for a taking.

Election of Must-Carry Status

Generally, if a local commercial television station elects must-carry status, it is entitled to insist on cable carriage in its local market. Each cable system with more than 12 channels must set aside up to one-third of its channel capacity for must-carry stations. For example, if a cable system has 60 channels, it must set aside 20 of those channels for must-carry stations. If there are 25 stations in the market which elected must-carry, the cable operator may choose 20 to carry. On the other hand, if only 15 stations elected must-carry in the market, the cable system would have to carry all 15 of these stations. A must-carry station has a statutory right to a channel position, usually its over-the-air channel number, or another channel number on which it has historically been carried.

Retransmission Consent Election

A cable system is not permitted to carry a commercial station without the station's consent. Therefore, if the local commercial television station elects retransmission consent, the cable system must obtain that station's consent prior to carrying or transmitting its signal. Except for "superstations," a cable system may not carry the signal of any television broadcast station that is not located in the same market as the cable system without that broadcaster's consent. Superstations are transmitted via satellite, usually nationwide, and the cable system may carry such stations outside their local market without their consent. The negotiations between a television station and a cable system are private agreements which may, but need not, include some form of compensation to the television station such as money, advertising time or additional channel access.[*]

In sum, every three years, broadcasters can insist on retransmission consent from cable operators (or other MVPDs, such as satellite TV providers) instead of must-carry. In the past, a cable operator often acquired retransmission consent rights in exchange for in-kind benefits, such as advertising time or carriage of other channels affiliated with the broadcaster on the cable system. However, broadcasters are now insisting on direct financial payments. Bickering between the local cable operator and local broadcast station over the financial terms of retransmission consent have produced customer confusion and ire. Since these are contractual negotiations between sophisticated parties, the FCC can do little more than encourage "good faith" negotiation.

NOTE: CABLE AND BROADCAST TV RELATIONS

The must-carry / retransmission consent rules constitute only one facet of the labyrinthine relationship between broadcast and cable television. As you

---

[*] FCC, Cable Television Information Bulletin, Fact Sheet, August 1999.

recall from CHAPTER 2: ENTRY, cable television had very humble origins. As community antenna television, it provided improved reception of broadcast television by connecting households with coaxial cable to well-situated over-the-air antennas. Under this business model, cable television posed little threat to broadcast television. Indeed, it expanded broadcast television's viewership.

However, cable television started to provide content different from local broadcast stations. It did so first by importing broadcast television signals from other cities through microwave links. Suddenly, cable television became competition to broadcast television. Individuals could be now forced to choose between watching the message provided over the coaxial cable (featuring the video programming of a distant broadcast station) or the message provided over the air (featuring the video programming of the local broadcast television station). Such a choice would split the local station's viewership, decrease its audience, and thereby threaten its advertising base.

Put yourself in the shoes of a regulator concerned about broadcast television's viability. How might you control or limit the threat posed by cable television especially if you think free broadcast TV is "good content"? First, as seen in *Turner*, you might mandate "must-carry." Cable television-subscribing households would then not have to make an either-or choice between cable or local broadcast content because the local broadcast content would also be carried over the cable connection.

Second, you might limit the number of distant television signals that cable television may import without the prior consent of the distant television stations ("distant signal import" / "retransmission consent"). Fewer signals would mean fewer programs to draw away viewers from the local broadcast station.*

Third, you might adopt rules that would protect any exclusive exhibition rights enjoyed by the local broadcast station. For example, imagine that the broadcast station is an NBC affiliate. Normally, the only way for households in the area covered by the affiliate to see NBC programming is to view that NBC affiliate. But what if the local cable television operator imports a distant

---

* You may be wondering why intellectual property laws did not require permission from the distant broadcast station in the first place. In 1968 and 1974, the Supreme Court held that a cable television system's retransmission of broadcast television signals did not violate the then-applicable 1909 Copyright Act. *See* Teleprompter Corp. v. CBS, Inc., 415 U.S. 394 (1974); Fortnightly Corp. v. United Artists Television, Inc., 392 U.S. 390 (1968). This was subsequently changed in the 1976 modifications to the Copyright Act, which created a compulsory license regime, with royalty payments paid to the copyright office for redistribution to copyright holders. No royalty would have to be paid for the retransmission of local broadcast stations or of network programming. In these cases, Congress felt that the copyright holder was not being harmed. However, payments would be necessary for retransmission of non-network programming imported outside of its local broadcast area.

television signal of another NBC affiliate? The local affiliate's network programming loses its exclusivity. "Network nonduplication" rules attempt to address this problem. Analogously, the local broadcast station may have negotiated exclusive exhibition rights from a syndicator. What happens if that same video programming is available, however, on an imported distant television signal? Once again, the local affiliate's supposedly "exclusive" programming loses its uniqueness. "Syndicated exclusivity" rules attempt to address this problem.

As you know, cable television expanded far beyond the importation of distant broadcast signals in its goal to provide different and better content. For example, it started to bid for exhibition rights to motion pictures, taking them away from broadcast television. Putting yourself again in the position of a regulator concerned about broadcast television, how might you respond? One way might be to adopt "anti-siphoning" rules, which constrained how certain types of high-quality content could be bid away from broadcast television onto cable television.

For the past four decades, the FCC, Congress, and the courts have adopted, modified, and removed myriad combinations of these sorts of rules. The technical and historical details are beyond the scope of this book.

b. PUBLIC, EDUCATIONAL, GOVERNMENT CHANNELS

Above, we learned that Congress gave special rights to local broadcast stations to force access onto the local cable system via "must-carry" if they so choose. The 1984 Cable Act also stated that local franchising authorities "may ... require as part of a [cable] franchise ... [or] franchise renewal ... that channel capacity be designated for public, educational, or governmental [PEG] use."[*] Franchise agreements generally require some capacity for PEG channels, which appear on the basic tier of service to all cable subscribers. Not surprisingly, this statute was challenged on First Amendment grounds.

In *Time Warner Entertainment Co. v. FCC*,[†] the D.C. Circuit upheld the set-aside of PEG channels against a facial constitutional challenge, on the authority of *Turner*:

> We can, of course, imagine PEG franchise conditions that would raise serious constitutional issues. For example, were a local authority to require as a franchise condition that a cable operator designate three-quarters of its channels for "educational" programming, defined in detail by the city council, such a

---

[*] 47 U.S.C. § 531(b).

[†] 93 F.3d 957 (D.C. Cir. 1996).

requirement would certainly implicate First Amendment concerns. At the same time, we can just as easily imagine a franchise authority exercising its power without violating the First Amendment. For example, a local franchise authority might seek to ensure public "access to a multiplicity of information sources," *Turner*, by conditioning its grant of a franchise on the cable operator's willingness to provide access to a single channel for "public" use, defining "public" broadly enough to permit access to everyone on a nondiscriminatory, first-come, first-serve basis. Under *Turner*, such a scheme would be content-neutral, would serve an "important purpose unrelated to the suppression of free expression," id., and would be narrowly tailored to its goal. Time Warner's facial challenge therefore fails.[*]

c. LEASED ACCESS

So far, we've learned that if you're a local broadcast station, you can force access onto the local cable system, courtesy of federal statute. Also, if you're a PEG channel, the franchise contract may also provide for access. But what if you're just a private citizen? If the cable operator doesn't want to give you access, can you nevertheless force it? The answer is potentially yes, through "commercial leased access." Federal statute requires cable operators to reserve 10–15 percent of capacity for such leased access.[†] Is that constitutional too?

TIME WARNER ENTERTAINMENT CO. v. FCC
93 F.3d 957 (DC Cir. 1996)

[T]he 1984 Act compelled cable operators of systems with more than thirty-six channels to set aside between 10 and 15 percent of their channels for commercial use by persons unaffiliated with the operator. 47 U.S.C. § 532(b)(1). . . . "Leased access" was originally aimed at bringing about "the widest possible diversity of information sources" for cable subscribers. *Id.* § 532(a). Congress thought cable operators might deny access to programmers if the operators disapproved the programmer's social or political viewpoint, or if the programmers' offerings competed with those the operators were providing. "Diversity," as the 1984 Act used the term, referred not to the substantive content of the program on a leased access channel, but to the entities—the "sources"-responsible for making it available.

The 1984 Act gave cable operators the authority to establish the price, terms, and conditions of the service on their leased access channels. With respect to those channels, then, the operator stood in the position of a common carrier. If

---

[*] *Id.* at 973.
[†] *See* 47 U.S.C. § 532.

an operator refused to provide service, persons aggrieved had the right either to bring an action in district court or to petition the Commission for relief. The operator's rates, terms, and conditions were presumed reasonable, a presumption that could be overcome "by clear and convincing evidence to the contrary." 47 U.S.C. § 532(f). The operator was free to use any of the channels set aside for leased access until someone signed up.

The 1984 legislation did not accomplish much. Unaffiliated programming on leased access channels rarely appeared. Exactly why is uncertain. Cable operators said the reasons were high production costs and low demand in the face of the already wide array of programming operators were already providing. Others laid the blame at the feet of the operators, claiming they had set unreasonable terms for leased access.

Amendments enacted in 1992 authorized the FCC to establish a maximum price for leased access, to regulate terms and conditions, and to establish procedures for the expedited resolution of disputes. 47 U.S.C. § 532(c)(4)(A). At the same time, Congress added a second rationale for leased access: "to promote competition in the delivery of diverse sources of video programming." *Id.* § 532(a), as amended.

Time Warner's initial point regarding the leased access provisions is that they should be subject to the most stringent of the standards used to evaluate restrictions on speech. As the company sees it, the provisions are content-based; the government therefore must demonstrate a compelling interest to overcome their presumptive invalidity. There is nothing to this. The provisions are not content-based. They do not favor or disfavor speech on the basis of the ideas contained in the speech or the views expressed. *Turner.* Whether, and how many, channels a cable operator must designate for public leasing depends entirely on the operator's channel capacity. What programs appear on the operator's other channels—that is, what speech the operator is promoting— matters not in the least. So too with respect to the speech of those who use the leased access channels.... The statutory objective, as well as the provisions carrying it forth, are framed in terms of the sources of information rather than the substance of the information. This is consistent with the First Amendment's "assumption that the widest possible dissemination of information from diverse and antagonistic sources" promotes a free society. *Associated Press v. United States* (1945). The Supreme Court has determined that regulations along these lines are content-neutral. *Turner.*

Hence the standard must be intermediate scrutiny .... Time Warner thinks the leased access provisions fail even this test. The company's attack is not on the sufficiency of the governmental interest. After *Turner,* "promoting the widespread dissemination of information from a multiplicity of sources" and "promoting fair competition in the market for television programming" must be treated as important governmental objectives unrelated to the suppression of speech. The problems Time Warner sees are elsewhere: there is first the lack of any demonstration that the leased access provisions address a real, non-conjectural harm; and there is second the loose fit between the remedy of setting aside a percentage of channel capacity and the supposed harm.

As to the alleged lack of any real harm . . . [u]nder section 532(b)(4), a "cable operator may use any unused channel capacity" set aside for leased access "until the use of such channel capacity is obtained, pursuant to a written agreement, by a person unaffiliated with the operator." That is, if unaffiliated programmers have not and, as Time Warner predicts, will not exploit the leased access provisions, then the provisions will have no effect on the speech of the cable operators. None of their programming would have to be dropped.

The same analysis applies to Time Warner's argument that the leased access provisions are not narrowly tailored to achieve their ends. One of the alleged defects stems from the statutory requirement that the larger the number of channels in the system, the greater the number of channels the operator must set aside. 47 U.S.C. § 532(b)(1). The company states that "because a cable system has more channels does not mean there are any more unaffiliated programmers" being excluded, and that "the more channels a cable operator has, the fewer unaffiliated programmers would be excluded from carriage...." Yet if this is accurate, operators of large cable systems would scarcely have any customers asking to lease the access channels; and the operators would thus be free to fill the unused capacity as they saw fit.

NOTES & QUESTIONS

1. *Content-based?* Whether some regulation is content-based or content-neutral is a legal conclusion. The truth is that most regulations fall within a spectrum between these poles. One way, then, to determine content neutrality to perform low-level analogical comparison. For example, as between "must-carry" of broadcast stations and "leased access" by random commercial entities, which is more content-based? If "must-carry" is deemed content-neutral, then what should "leased access" be?

2. *Result without escape valve?* What if § 532(b)(4)—which allows the cable operator to use any and all capacity not asked for by third parties—didn't exist. Then, would the access channels be somehow unconstitutional?

3. *Leased Commercial Access Order.* In 2008, the FCC released a Report & Order that addressed various issues with leased access channels.[*]

a. *Failure to attract.* According to the FCC, cable systems carried only 0.7 leased access channels on average.[*]

b. *Better information.* The FCC passed various regulations that tried to perfect the market, for instance, by requiring cable operators to make more information about leased access available and to force them to respond faster to inquiries and negotiations, with potential fines as inducements. The Order also tried to promote transparency by requiring annual reporting of information regarding leased access channels.

c. *Ratemaking.* The most important matter, however, was reducing prices that cable operators were charging. Before this order, the FCC had permitted a formula called the "average implicit fee, " which calculated the monetary value of the average channel. This formula was replaced by the "marginal implicit fee," which instead focused on the monetary value of the weakest voluntarily-carried channel.[†] The FCC also put a maximum price cap of $0.10 per subscriber per month.[‡]

d. *Infomercials cannot benefit.* The FCC was concerned that these lower prices would be taken advantage of by "programmers that predominantly transmit sales presentations or program length commercials."[§] Apparently these programmers currently "pay" cable operators directly or enter into some revenue-sharing agreement to carry their infomercials. Commissioner Robert McDowell wrote in dissent:

> Moreover, the Commission developed the current "average implicit fee" methodology in 1997 after extensive review of the economic studies and policy discussions submitted at that time. The record in this proceeding, and our consideration of it, do not come close to reaching that level of careful analysis. The least we could have done was to seek comment on any changes to the current rate formula. This Order even fails to do that. The result of this radical change in rates, as many independent programmers have stated in the record, will be the opposite of what is intended. The result will be a loss in the diversity of programming as cable operators are forced to drop lesser-rated channels in favor of a flood of leased access requests seeking distribution distorted below cost and market rates.

> Perhaps to ameliorate this result, the majority concludes that the new rate methodology will not apply to programmers that predominantly transmit sales presentations, or program-length commercials, and seeks additional public

---

[*] *Leased Commercial Access*, R&O, 23 FCC Rcd. 2909 (2008).

[*] *See id.* at ¶ 39.

[†] *See id.* at ¶¶ 44-45.

[‡] *See id.* at ¶ 36.

[§] *Id.* at ¶ 37.

comment on related issues. This too is extremely problematic. I cannot fathom how distinguishing programmers based on the content they deliver can be constitutional. Perhaps the courts will guide us.

e. *Judicial stay.* The National Cable Television Association moved for an emergency stay of the FCC's orders, pending judicial review. That motion was granted by the Sixth Circuit.* So far, as of 2016, these new rules have not gone into effect.

4. *Quaint?* Does the idea of commercial leased access seem entirely quaint to you? Given the existence of social media and free access to YouTube and other streaming services, is it still important or relevant to be able to purchase time with a local cable operator to air videos?

2. ACCESS TO THE MULTIPLE SYSTEM OPERATOR

Now we move from *layer 3: last-leg connection* at the local cable operator's cable system up one level to *layer 2: large-scale distribution*, which is controlled by the Multiple System Operator. Similar to broadcast TV networks, MSOs enjoy a great deal of power because they own so many cable systems and thus have so many subscribers. Might they use that power against unaffiliated cable programming channels (upstream, in layer 1) or against competitor cable or video distribution systems (downstream, in layer 3)? The upstream problems have been addressed through "program carriage" rules; the downstream problems have been addressed through "program access" rules.

Program carriage rules. In the 1992 Cable Act, Congress passed 47 U.S.C. § 536, which instructed the FCC to "establish regulations governing program carriage agreements and related practices between cable operators or other multichannel video programming distributors and video programming vendors." The FCC implemented such rules:

> § 76.1301 Prohibited practices.
>
> (a) Financial interest. No cable operator or other multichannel video programming distributor shall require a financial interest in any program service as a condition for carriage on one or more of such operator's/provider's systems.
>
> (b) Exclusive rights. No cable operator or other multichannel video programming distributor shall coerce any video programming vendor to provide, or retaliate against such a vendor for failing to provide, exclusive rights against any other multichannel video programming distributor as a condition for carriage on a system.

---

* Order, United Church of Christ Office of Commc'n, Inc. v. FCC, No. 08-3245 (6th Cir. May 22, 2008). *See also Leased Commercial Access*, MB Docket No. 07-42, R&O and Further NPRM, 23 FCC Rcd. 2909 (2008). The Office of Management and Budget (OMB) also disapproved under the Paperwork Reduction Act.

> (c) Discrimination. No multichannel video programming distributor shall engage in conduct the effect of which is to unreasonably restrain the ability of an unaffiliated video programming vendor to compete fairly by discriminating in video programming distribution on the basis of affiliation or non-affiliation of vendors in the selection, terms, or conditions for carriage of video programming provided by such vendors.

Notice how the (a) "financial interest" and (b) "exclusive rights" provisions protect against MSOs attempting to buy intellectual property rights from an independent video programming vendor who would rather not sell them. Have you seen anything like this before?

The (c) "discrimination" provision requires MSOs not to treat unaffiliated programming vendors worse than affiliated ones. In other words, this is a behavioral regulation that requires equal treatment of affiliated and unaffiliated programmers. It's very difficult, however, for unaffiliated programmers to show that they've been discriminated against. (Think how hard it is generally to make a showing that any person has been treated worse on some prohibited grounds). After all, there are always myriad reasons to prefer one channel over another, and MSOs will argue that the preferred channel was more meritorious and that its affiliation with the MSO was irrelevant.[*]

Given that behavioral regulations entail difficult, case-specific, factual questions about the existence of "discrimination," lawmakers sometimes enact structural regulations that operate more like quotas. In the 1992 Cable Act, Congress also instructed the FCC to "prescribe rules and regulations establishing reasonable limits on the number of channels on a cable system that can be occupied by a video programmer in which a cable operator has an attributable interest."[†] The FCC enacted the following *channel occupancy* regulations:

> § 76.504 Limits on carriage of vertically integrated programming.
>
> (a) Except as otherwise provided in this section no cable operator shall devote more than 40 percent of its activated channels to the carriage of national video programming services owned by the cable operator or in which the cable operator has an attributable interest.
>
> (b) The channel occupancy limits set forth in paragraph (a) of this section shall apply only to channel capacity up to 75 channels.
>
> (c) A cable operator may devote two additional channels or up to 45 percent of its channel capacity, whichever is greater, to the carriage of video programming services owned by the

---

[*] *See, e.g., Herring Broad., Inc. d/b/a Wealth TV,* 26 FCC Rcd. 8971 (2001) (affirming administrative law judge's recommended decision that there was no discrimination against Wealth TV in favor of the MOJO channel). Even in the rare case that the FCC finds discrimination, the reviewing court may reverse. *See, e.g.,* Comcast Cable Comm., LLC v. FCC, 2013 WL 2302737 (D.C. Cir. 2013) (Williams, J.) (finding lack of "substantial evidence"). The FCC has recently adopted additional rules that altered the procedures by which programming carriage complaints would be adjudicated. *See In the Matter of Revision of the Commission's Program Carriage Rules,* 2nd R&O, MB Docket No. 11-131, FCC 11-119 (August 1, 2011).

[†] 47 U.S.C. § 533(f)(1)(B).

cable operator or in which the cable operator has an attributable interest provided such video programming services are minority-controlled.

(d) Cable operators carrying video programming services owned by the cable operator or in which the cable operator holds an attributable interest in excess of limits set forth in paragraph (a) of this section as of December 4, 1992, shall not be precluded by the restrictions in this section.

(e) Minority-controlled means more than 50 percent owned by one or more members of a minority group.

(f) Minority means Black, Hispanic, American Indian, Alaska Native, Asian and Pacific Islander.

By capping channel occupancy, the FCC ensured that channels would be left open for unaffiliated programmers. Of course, these regulations were also challenged. In 2001, the D.C. Circuit (per Judge Stephen Williams) invalidated these rules as violating the First Amendment. Applying intermediate scrutiny with a bite, the court was skeptical about how the FCC picked 40%. Moreover, it did not understand why cable operators who were subject to "effective competition" and thus no longer rate regulated should still be subject to channel occupancy rules. In the end, the court found that the 40% occupancy rules burdened substantially more speech than necessary and was thus unconstitutional. On remand, the Commission issued a new version of the subscriber limit rules in 2008, which were again challenged in the D.C. Circuit.[*] The court ruled against the FCC again, this time on arbitrary and capriciousness grounds, finding that the rules did not take into account competition from non-cable video programming distributors. Currently, there are no channel occupancy rules in force.

Program access rules. Access rules are concerned about how MSOs might exercise power downstream, against competing cable operators or other multichannel video programming distributors ("MVPDs"). We were first introduced to this term back in CHAPTER 3: PRICING, when we studied how "effective competition" released cable operators from rate regulation. An MVPD offers "multiple channels of video programming"[†] and includes, at least, cable operators and Digital Broadcast Satellite (DBS) distributors. If a MSO has an ownership interest in a popular cable programming network, the MSO may prevent other MVPDs from carrying that network.[‡] Accordingly, one of these program access rules used to prohibit "exclusive contracts" (in areas served by the cable operator) between the cable operator and satellite-delivered programming vendors[§] in which that cable operator has an ownership interest.[**]

---

[*] Comcast Corp. v. FCC, 579 F.3d 1 (D.C. Cir. 2009).

[†] 47 U.S.C. § 522(13); see also 47 C.F.R. §§ 76.64(d), 76.71(a), 76.905(d), 76.1000(e), 76.1200(b), 76.1300(d).

[‡] *See* 47 U.S.C. § 538; 47 C.F.R. § 76.1002.

The goal was to ensure that content from these vendors could be purchased by other MVPDs who are competing with the cable operator in the same geographical market. Recently, the FCC allowed this categorical ban to expire because it was deemed no longer necessary in the public interest. The Commission agreed to hear complaints instead on a case-by-case basis.[*]

The FCC has initiated a rulemaking to "modernize" its definition of the definition of a MVPD in order to account for new next generation video services, which we will discuss further in the next chapter.[†] For now, we examine DBS systems, which can be likened to the large cable MSOs.

C. DIRECT BROADCAST SATELLITE

1. TECHNOLOGY

Generally the term "direct broadcast satellite" (DBS) refers to satellite delivery of video programming, whereas "satellite radio" (also called DARS for "digital audio radio service") refers to the delivery of audio programming. The underlying technologies of both services, however, are quite similar: think of the satellite as a floating mirror in the sky that bounces back signals received from Earth. Our focus here is on DBS, which has three major components.

Transmission station. The first component is a terrestrial transmission station that provides an "uplink" to the satellite. After acquiring the programming content (e.g., through satellite relay, fiber optics, or digital tape), the video is compressed, encrypted, modulated onto the correct transmission frequency, then sent up to the satellite.[‡]

Satellite. DBS uses satellites in geostationary orbit 22,300 miles above the equator. Because these satellites remain in the same location in the sky relative to any position on Earth, the receiving antenna does not have to physically

---

[§] The statute only applied to programming transmitted or retransmitted by satellite for reception by cable operators. Back in 1992, this was nearly the exclusive way that cable operators received their programming.

[**] 47 U.S.C. § 548(c)(2)(D); 47 C.F.R. § 76.1002(c)(2).

[*] *See* R&O, *In the matter of Revision of the Commission's Program Access rules,* 27 FCC Rcd. 12605 (2012).

[†] *In re Promoting Innovation and Competition in the Provision of Multichannel Video Programming Distribution Services,* 29 FCC Rcd. 15995 (2014).

[‡] DBS systems use frequencies in the Ku-band. The Ku Band extends from 10.7 – 18.1 GHz. Satellite radio transmits in the S Band at 2.3 GHz.

"track" or find the satellites. By international treaty, the United States has been allocated eight satellite orbits for DBS service.* Each orbit can be occupied by a single satellite. On each satellite, there can be a maximum of 32 transponders, each communicating at a specific frequency, with a specific bandwidth. Once the signal is received from the transmission station by the transponder (uplinks at 17.3 – 17.8 GHz), the information is amplified, then bounced back to Earth on a paired "downlink" frequency (downlinks at 12.2 – 12.7 GHz). The geographical area that can receive the signal from the satellite is called the "footprint." Typically, the footprint is huge; three of the eight orbits produce a footprint of the entire contiguous United States (known as a "full-CONUS" signal).† Recently, certain satellites have started to use "spot beams," which enable narrower targeting of the downlink to specific metropolitan areas.

Receiving dish. The receiving dish is a parabolic antenna that can receive the satellite's downlink transmission. Satellite-transmitted video programming has gotten much more popular recently because of the miniaturization of this dish (now, approximately 2 feet in diameter). In the past, receiving dishes were expensive and huge (approximately 4-8 feet in diameter) because the satellites in space transmitted at lower power.‡ But current DBS systems operate at much higher power, which allows users to install more convenient-sized dishes on rooftops and balconies.

Given the frequencies used for its communication, DBS requires a direct line of sight between the satellite and the receiving dish. In urban environments, large buildings can obstruct this view. Satellite radio services solve this problem by installing antennae on top of buildings, which then repeat the satellite signals just like a terrestrial broadcast station.

After the signal is received, a set-top box or receiver decrypts the transmission, uncompresses the video, and converts it into a format compatible with your television. All DBS systems use digital signals.

2. CONTEXT

Satellites have been in use for communications for quite some time. For example, starting in the late seventies, television networks started using satellites

---

* This is in accordance with the International Telecommunication Union (ITU) "Region 2 Plan adopted at the 1983 Regional Administrative Radio Conference ("RARC-83")." *In the Matter of Revision of Rules and Policies for the Direct Broadcast Satellite Service*, NPRM, 11 FCC Rcd. 1297, ¶ 5 (1995).

† CONUS means contiguous United States. "Half-CONUS" signals cover approximately half the continental United States.

‡ These older services operated in the C-band, but with the rise of DBS, C-band users are quickly dwindling.

to distribute programming to local stations. Because these transmissions were not generally encrypted, the first-generation of large satellite dishes were installed by individuals who were eager to tap into these transmissions. Soon, however, the networks started encrypting the signals, which frustrated any attempt at reception without subscription.

In 1980, the FCC began to form its DBS policies by releasing a *Notice of Inquiry* based on two FCC staff reports, which explored both the technical and regulatory foundations for direct broadcast satellite.[*] (Satellite radio was allocated spectrum in 1992 by the FCC.) The Commission gave out its first license to start first phase construction of a DBS system in 1982.[†] Until 1995, the FCC distributed the scarce orbits/channels on a pro-rata basis among credible potential DBS operators. In 1995, the FCC decided that auction would be the best way forward.[‡]

There are two DBS service providers: DirecTV (launched in 1994) and EchoStar Dish Network (launched in 1996).[§] From our study of "effective competition" in cable pricing, recall that these services have quickly gained in popularity. As of 2011, DBS had 33 million subscribers (in comparison to cable TV, which had 60 million subscribers).[**] Given the bandwidth available as well as state-of-the-art compression, each transponder can relay approximately 5-10 video signals. In practice, this means that each of the DBS system can provide anywhere form 450-500 channels of video programming. (As technologies and frequency assignments change, this capacity will also change.)

Finally, recall the three layer model we used to diagnose the choke points in cable TV. Where do DBS providers fall in this conceptual scheme? In many ways, they are just like the large cable MSOs Comcast, Charter, and Cox. But given DBS's national footprint (from orbiting satellite directly to your rooftop

---

[*] *See* 45 Fed. Reg. 72719 (November 3, 1980). *See also* Bruno Pattan, Technical Aspects Related to Direct Broadcast Satellite Systems (Federal Communications Commission, Office of Science and Technology, September 1980); Florence O. Setzer, Bruce A. Franca, and Nina W. Cornell, Policies for Regulation of Direct Broadcast Satellites (Federal Communications Commission, Office of Plans and Policy, October 1980).

[†] *In re Application of Satellite Television Corporation*, MO&O, 91 F.C.C.2d 953 (1982) (giving permission to Satellite Television Corp., a subsidiary of COMCAST).

[‡] *See Revision of Rules and Policies for the Direct Broadcast Satellite Service*, NPRM, 11 FCC Rcd. 1297 (1995).

[§] The two players in satellite radio are XM Radio and Sirius Satellite Radio. They won licenses in an auction held in 1997. In August 2008, the FCC approved their merger. *See Applications for Consent to the Transfer of Control of Licenses, XM Satellite Radio Holdings Inc., Transferor, to Sirius Satellite Radio Inc., Transferee*, MB Docket No. 07-57, MO&O and R&O, FCC 08-178 (rel. August 5, 2008).

[**] *See* Further NOI, *Annual Assessment of the Status of Competition in the Market for the Delivery of Video Programming*, 2011 WL 1509704 ¶ 2 (April 21, 2011).

antenna), there's no distinction between *layer 2: large-scale* distribution and *layer 3: last-leg connection.*

Layer	Cable TV Players	DBS Players
1. Production	Cable Network	*Cable Network*
2. Large-scale Distribution	Multiple System Operators	*DBS*
3. Last-leg Connection	Cable Operator	

With this introduction, you should naturally be curious about how the must-carry, PEG, and leased access rules apply to DBS. Do the same rules that apply to cable TV also apply to DBS? At least similar ones?

3. ACCESS TO THE DBS SYSTEM

a. MUST-CARRY?

When we studied cable, we studied how local broadcast TV stations could insist on access to the cable operator operating in its geographical area of service. Is there an analog for DBS? (One immediate complication is that the geographical area of service for DBS is the entire nation. Would that mean each and every broadcast station in the nation could insist on carriage?) Actually, there is no must-carry statute that applies to DBS. That said, there is a related rule worth discussion, which should remind you of must-carry and retransmission consent.

One key competitive weakness of DBS as compared to cable television has been the lack of local broadcast stations. In 1999, Congress passed the Satellite Home Viewer Improvement Act of 1999 (the "SHVIA"),[*] in order to establish rough parity between DBS and cable television vis-à-vis local broadcast stations.

First, SHVIA gives DBS providers a free compulsory license to retransmit copyrighted *content* originally transmitted by local television stations to subscribers within the stations' local market.[†] This is called "local-into-local" retransmission. Second, SHVIA makes clear that DBS providers must obtain consent from the broadcast station to retransmit its *signal.* Note: this retransmission consent for the signal is separate from the compulsory license for the underlying content embedded within the signal. Third, there's a must-carry-like string attached. If a DBS provider takes advantage of the compulsory license

---

[*] Pub. L. 106-113, 113 Stat. 1501, 1501A-526 to 1501A-545 (Nov. 29, 1999). Readers should distinguish this from a prior statute called the Satellite Home Viewer Act of 1988 (SHVA), Pub. L. No. 100-667, 102 Stat. 3949.

[†] *See* 17 U.S.C. § 122.

to carry even one station, then the DBS operator must also carry any other station within that market that requests carriage ("carry-one, carry all").* In other words, a DBS operator cannot cherry-pick local broadcast stations if it is taking advantage of the compulsory license.

The DBS operator is under no obligation to "must-carry" local TV stations (a key difference from cable).† Also, the DBS operator does not have to use the compulsory copyright license and could instead negotiate privately with all parties who own copyright to the content shown on any given broadcast station. In such cases, the "carry one, carry all" requirement would not be triggered. The "carry one, carry all" provision has been held constitutional.‡

b. PEG CHANNELS OR LEASED ACCESS?

There's no direct analog to the PEG channel requirement for DBS either. Nor is there a direct analog to the leased access provision we have studied. But there is a statute that is a hybrid of both. In the 1992 Cable Act (the same Act that required must-carry), Congress required 4–7% of DBS channel capacity be reserved for educational or informational noncommercial programming.§ There was no requirement that it had to be access provided for free, as in must-carry. So, in some sense, this requirement operated more like leased access but exclusively for noncommercial programming.

Back in 1992, there were no commercially successful DBS systems in operation. But as these providers came on-line, the FCC selected the 4% end of the range, which translated to roughly 20 to 40 channels set-aside. Not surprisingly, DBS providers challenged this set-aside on First Amendment grounds. A D.C. Circuit panel upheld the constitutionality of this provision in a *per curiam* opinion, with no dissent on this specific issue. After the opinion was released, there was a suggestion to rehear the case *en banc*. However, a bare majority of the judges in active service declined. We read the *per curiam* panel opinion, then a dissent from the refusal to hear the case en banc.

---

* *See* 47 U.S.C. § 338(a)(1).

† There is an exception for Alaska and Hawaii, in which must-carry requirements do exist for DBS. *See* 47 U.S.C. § 338(a)(4).

‡ *See* Satellite Broadcasting and Communications Ass'n v. FCC, 275 F.3d 337 (4th Cir. 2001).

§ *See* 47 U.S.C. § 335.

TIME WARNER ENTERTAINMENT CO. V. FCC
93 F.3d 957 (D.C. Cir. 1996)

Before BUCKLEY, RANDOLPH, and TATEL, Circuit Judges.
Per curiam: [*]

VI. THE DBS PROVISIONS

Section 25 of the 1992 [Cable] Act provides:

> The Commission shall require, as a condition of any provision, initial authorization, or authorization renewal for a provider of direct broadcast satellite service providing video programming, that the provider of such service reserve a portion of its channel capacity, equal to not less than 4 percent nor more than 7 percent, exclusively for noncommercial programming of an educational or informational nature.

47 U.S.C. § 335(b)(1). DBS providers have no editorial control over the educational or informational programming they are required to carry under this provision. § 335(b)(3). The district court held that section 25 is invalid because the government provided no evidence that regulation of DBS providers is necessary to serve any significant interest.

B. MERITS

Time Warner insists, for a variety of reasons, that the DBS set-aside provisions must be subjected to strict scrutiny . . . .

The Supreme Court recognized, in 1969, that because of the limited availability of the radio spectrum for broadcast purposes, "only a tiny fraction of those with resources and intelligence can hope to communicate by radio at the same time...." *Red Lion Broadcasting Co., Inc. v. FCC* (1969). The same is true for DBS today. Because the United States has only a finite number of satellite positions available for DBS use, the opportunity to provide such services will necessarily be limited. Even before the first DBS communications satellite was launched in 1994, the FCC found that "the demand for channel/orbit allocations far exceeds the available supply." *Continental Satellite Corp.,* 4 F.C.C.R. 6292, 6293 (1989). Recently, the last DBS license was auctioned off for $682.5 million, the largest sum ever received by the FCC for any single license to use the airwaves. As the Supreme Court observed,

> [w]here there are substantially more individuals who want to broadcast than there are frequencies to allocate, it is idle to posit an unabridgeable First Amendment right to broadcast comparable to the right of every individual to speak, write, or publish.

---

[*] Judge Tatel's dissent in part did not apply to the DBS provisions. The opinion has been omitted.—ED.

Red Lion.

In such cases, the Court applies a "less rigorous standard of First Amendment scrutiny," based on a recognition that

> the inherent physical limitation on the number of speakers who may use the ... medium has been thought to require some adjustment in traditional First Amendment analysis to permit the Government to place limited content restraints, and impose certain affirmative obligations, on broadcast licensees.

Turner. Because the new DBS technology is subject to similar limitations, we conclude that section 25 should be analyzed under the same relaxed standard of scrutiny that the court has applied to the traditional broadcast media.

Both broadcasters and the public have First Amendment rights that must be balanced when the government seeks to regulate access to the radio spectrum. Nonetheless, the Supreme Court has held that "[i]t is the right of the viewers and listeners, not the right of the broadcasters, which is paramount.... It is the right of the public to receive suitable access to social, political, esthetic, moral and other ideas and experiences which is crucial here." *Red Lion.* An essential goal of the First Amendment is to achieve "the widest possible dissemination of information from diverse and antagonistic sources." *FCC v. National Citizens Comm. for Broadcasting* (1978) (*"NCCB"*) (quoting *Associated Press*). Broadcasting regulations that affect speech have been upheld when they further this First Amendment goal. For example, in *NCCB,* the Supreme Court recognized that "efforts to enhance the volume and quality of coverage of public issues through regulation of broadcasting may be permissible where similar efforts to regulate the print media would not be." *Id.*

The government asserts an interest in assuring public access to diverse sources of information by requiring DBS operators to reserve four to seven percent of their channel capacity for noncommercial educational and informational programming. Indeed, a stated policy of the 1992 Act is to "promote the availability to the public of a diversity of views and information through cable television and other video distribution media." 1992 Act, § 2(b)(1). This interest lies at the core of the First Amendment: "Assuring that the public has access to a multiplicity of informational sources is a governmental purpose of the highest order, for it promotes values central to the First Amendment." *Turner.*

While Time Warner does not dispute the validity of these interests, it asserts that the government made no findings regarding the need for channel set-asides on DBS. . . . [W]hile it is true that Congress made no specific findings in support of section 25, "Congress is not obligated, when enacting its statutes, to make a record of the type that an administrative agency or court does to accommodate judicial review." *Turner* (plurality opinion). Indeed,

> [s]ound policymaking often requires legislators to forecast future events and to anticipate the likely impact of these events based on deductions and inferences for which complete empirical support may be unavailable.

Turner (plurality opinion).

In this instance, Congress could not have made DBS-specific findings for the simple reason that no DBS system was in operation at the time the 1992 Act was enacted. Congress had to base its decision to require set-asides on its long experience with the broadcast media. In 1967, when it enacted the Public Broadcasting Act, Congress recognized that "the economic realities of commercial broadcasting do not permit widespread commercial production and distribution of educational and cultural programs which do not have a mass audience appeal." Congress noted the same problem in 1989, when it established the National Endowment for Children's Educational Television. As the Supreme Court has observed, since 1939, the government has "recogniz[ed] the potential effect of ... commercial pressures on educational stations" by reserving radio frequencies and television channels for educational use. *League of Women Voters.*

Section 25, then, represents nothing more than a new application of a well-settled government policy of ensuring public access to noncommercial programming. The section achieves this purpose by requiring DBS providers to reserve a small portion of their channel capacity for such programs as a condition of their being allowed to use a scarce public commodity. The set-aside requirement of from four to seven percent of a provider's channel capacity is hardly onerous, especially in light of the instruction, in the Senate Report, that the FCC "consider the total channel capacity of DBS systems operators" so that it may "subject DBS systems with relatively large total channel capacity to a greater reservation requirement than systems with relatively less total capacity." Furthermore, a DBS provider "may utilize for any purpose any unused channel capacity required to be reserved under this subsection pending the actual use of such channel capacity for noncommercial programming of an educational or informational nature." 47 U.S.C. § 335(b)(2).

We note, further, that the government does not dictate the specific content of the programming that DBS operators are required to carry. What the Court in *Turner* found to be true with regard to the must-carry rules is just as true for DBS:

> The design and operation of the challenged provisions confirm that the purposes underlying [their] enactment ... are unrelated to the content of speech.

The rules ... do not require or prohibit the carriage of particular ideas or points of view. They do not penalize [DBS] operators or programmers because of the content of their programming. They do not compel [DBS] operators to affirm points of view with which they disagree. They do not produce any net decrease in the amount of available speech. And they leave [DBS] operators free to carry whatever programming they wish on all channels not subject to [the set-aside] requirements.

The Supreme Court found that Congress's "overriding objective in enacting must-carry was not to favor programming of a particular subject matter, viewpoint, or format, but rather to preserve access to free television programming for . . . Americans without cable." Section 25 serves a similar objective; its purpose and effect is to promote speech, not to restrict it. Because section 25 is "a reasonable means of promoting the public interest in diversified mass communications," it does not violate the First Amendment rights of DBS providers.

| TIME WARNER ENTERTAINMENT CO. v. FCC |
| 105 F.3d 723 (D.C. Cir. 1997) |

WILLIAMS, Circuit Judge, dissenting from the denial of rehearing in banc:*

[Judge Williams argued that *Red Lion* should not be extended to DBS and that § 25's preference for non-commercial programming was not content-neutral.—ED.]

3. *Rust v. Sullivan, et al.*

The government may subsidize some activities and not others. In *Rust v. Sullivan,* the Court held that Congress could prohibit grantees of federal funds for certain family planning services from using those funds for the "counseling, referral, and the provision of information regarding abortion...." Rejecting arguments that the requirement was unconstitutionally viewpoint-based, the Court stated that the government was "simply insisting that public funds be spent for the purposes for which they are authorized." In its response to the petition for rehearing, the government makes an oblique allusion to this analysis, suggesting that it was within the government's power to retain control over the "public domain" to have reserved 4-to-7% of channel capacity for itself.

Echoes of this idea can be found in the various opinions in the recent case of *Denver Area Educational Telecommunications Consortium v. FCC* (1996).[†] And in *Red Lion* itself, the Court used the language of conditioned grants:

---

* The dissent was joined by Chief Judge EDWARDS, Judge SILBERMAN, Judge GINSBURG and Judge SENTELLE.

To condition the granting or renewal of licenses on a willingness to present representative community views on controversial issues is consistent with the ends and purposes of those constitutional provisions forbidding the abridgment of freedom of speech and freedom of the press.

On the other hand, the Court has not clearly committed itself to treating spectrum licenses as conditioned grants. For example, when in *FCC v. League of Women Voters* (1984), it struck down Congress's ban on editorializing by stations receiving monetary grants from the Corporation for Public Broadcasting, it considered only those grants and found them inadequate to justify the restriction. It did not consider the stations' positions as holders of broadcast licenses.

There is, perhaps, good reason for the Court to have hesitated to give great weight to the government's property interest in the spectrum. First, unallocated spectrum is government property only in the special sense that it simply has not been allocated to any real "owner" in any way. Thus it is more like unappropriated water in the western states, which belongs, effectively, to no one.

Further, the way in which the government came to assert a property interest in spectrum has obscured the problems raised by government monopoly ownership of an entire medium of communication. We would see rather serious First Amendment problems if the government used its power of eminent domain to become the only lawful supplier of newsprint and then sold the newsprint only to licensed persons, issuing the licenses only to persons that promised to use the newsprint for papers satisfying government-defined rules of content. *See* Matthew L. Spitzer, "The Constitutionality of Licensing Broadcasters," 64 N.Y.U. L. Rev. 990, 1041-66 (1989).

If the subsidy model is suitable for spectrum, the DBS licenses are properly viewed as subsidies, even though there is no cash transfer to the DBS providers for the support of educational programming. The character varies depending on whether the license was granted free, or in an auction occurring after the enactment of the 1992 Act. (There appear to be no licenses auctioned *before* the

---

† Speaking of the rule allowing cable operators to veto indecency on "leased" channels, Justice Breyer (joined in this aspect by Justices Stevens, O'Connor & Souter) stressed that the section merely gave operators permission to "regulate programming that, but for a previous Act of Congress, would have had no path of access to cable channels free of an operator's control." Part of Justice Breyer's reasoning seems to be that Congress may, in its redistribution away from the cable operators, attach content-based strings to its grant to the lessees. The opinion of Justice Thomas, for himself as well as Chief Justice Rehnquist and Justice Scalia, takes a similar tack, observing that the rights of the petitioners to access cable have been "governmentally created at the expense of cable operators' editorial discretion." Compare (Kennedy, J., concurring in part and dissenting in part, with whom Ginsburg, J., joined) (analyzing the provision under the public forum doctrine). [This text has been moved from the body text to a footnote.—ED.]

1992 Act.) As for DBS providers that received their licenses gratis, the subsidy is clear, although it is troubling that all the DBS providers that did so received them before the condition was attached.

There is also a subsidy in the auction setting. Those bidding for the DBS channels necessarily discounted their bids in light of the known prospect that a portion of the channels would be allocated for educational programming (and that the DBS provider would bear at least some of the operating costs and overhead). This differential—money that the government could have received had it not imposed the programming requirement—constitutes a subsidy exactly matching the pecuniary burden imposed by the provision. Thus the government may be said to have given the educational channels to the DBS providers.

Analogizing from *Rust v. Sullivan,* then, the government may argue that it has not required "the [licensee] to give up [non-educational] speech . . . ." but simply to use those channels granted by the government for educational and informational programming for that "specific and limited purpose."

Because I can see no principled basis for upholding the requirements imposed on DBS operators without resolving these questions, I dissent from the denial of the petition for rehearing *en banc.*

NOTES & QUESTIONS

1. *Medium warp.* These opinions should have reminded you of the many cases we have read trying to ascertain the appropriate First Amendment standard of review for cable television.

a. *Scarcity found.* The *per curiam* panel concluded that the scarcity in broadcast television applied also to DBS. Explain how and why. In particular, scarcity of what? Frequencies in the Ku band, frequencies generally, satellite orbits? Or is this about interference, not scarcity?

b. *Scarcity challenged.* In the dissent from rehearing *en banc,* Judge Williams forcefully challenged any notion of scarcity. He wrote:

DBS is more than an order of magnitude less scarce than traditional broadcasting. Over 50% of the conventional broadcast markets receive fewer than five commercial broadcast channels (including UHF channels), and only 20% receive seven or more. While this number of channels is greater than those available in 1969 when *Red Lion* was decided, it pales in comparison to cable or DBS. Cable operators currently offer about fifty channels, but compression techniques and new technology may eventually lead to 500 channels or more.

DBS has even greater channel capacity. The three orbital slots that permit broadcast throughout the continental United States can accommodate at least 120 video channels each, using existing compression technology, for a total of

360 channels. This does not include the other five orbital slots (4 usable for west coast broadcasting and 1 for east coast broadcasting), which raise the number of channels available to *480* (4 X 120) for the east coast, and *840* (7 X 120) for the west coast. DBS compression is expected to increase the number of channels fivefold by the year 2000.

Who has the better argument?

2. *Content-neutrality.*

a. *Neutrality found.* In addition to finding the scarcity rationale applicable, the *per curiam* seems to suggest that this set-aside is "content neutral" or at least as content neutral as the must-carry rules at issue in the *Turner* litigation.

b. *Neutrality challenged.* In Judge Williams' dissent, he distinguishes *Turner* from the DBS case:

> [W]hereas the must-carry provisions reviewed in *Turner* mandate access for particular *stations* regardless of their programming content, the DBS provision speaks directly to content, creating an obligation framed in terms of "noncommercial programming of an educational or informational nature." 47 U.S.C. § 335(b)(1).

> *Turner* hardly provides support for categorical programming requirements of this type, as the Court there took pains to distinguish the must-carry rules from such requirements.

> The panel opinion states that Congress's purpose is not to favor particular programming, but to promote "diversified mass communications," which would be a content-neutral purpose under *Turner.* I don't see that one can accurately characterize Congress's concern in § 25 as relating merely to *variety* of programming. Rather, § 25 explicitly seeks to advance one particular type of programming—"noncommercial programming of an educational or informational nature." 47 U.S.C. § 335(b)(1); see also H.R. Conf. Rep. 102-862 (1992) ("[t]he purpose of this section is to define the obligation of [DBS] service providers to provide a minimum level of educational programming"; "[t]he pricing structure was devised to enable national educational programming suppliers to utilize this reserved channel capacity").

> [I]f this regulation is acceptable, it is hard to see what content regulation (short of viewpoint-based ones) would be impermissible.

Again, who has the better of the argument? By the way, do you think Judge Williams would have thought even the must-carry rules to be content-neutral? Recall that Justice O'Connor dissented in *Turner* on just this point.

3. *Quid pro quo.* We have examined the quid pro quo notion many times before—the idea that because the government gives the licensee something of value that it did not have to, the licensee can be asked to give back something in

return. Judge Williams explores the legal contours of that argument as applied to the DBS set-aside for noncommercial programming. What did the government give to the licensees (even those who won at auction)? What can the government expect in return for that gift? Does this type of argument prove too much, and allow for too much regulation?

D. INTERNET

Recall that we covered the basics of Internet architecture in CHAPTER 2: ENTRY. Now we will examine the several-decades-long fight over internet chokepoints that we now collectively refer to as "net neutrality."

1. ACCESS TO THE BROADBAND NETWORK

a. THE PROBLEM

To focus on the issue of access to the internet, we can invoke the same strategy of describing internet service in a stylized three-layer model. The internet first grew out of the telephone system, and emails and chats do feel like they serve a similar function to talking on the phone, so perhaps we could borrow the layers from telephony:

Layer	Telephony	Internet
1. Long-distance	IXCs	*Backbone Provider*
2. Local exchange	LECs	*Broadband Provider*
3. Customer hardware	Manufacturers	*Edge Device Manufacturers*

But we also consume a huge amount of video and audio content through the internet, in which case perhaps the model from broadcast and cable TV is more appropriate:

Layer	Broadcast TV Players	Cable TV Players	Internet Players
1. Production	Studio	Cable Network	*Edge Content Provider*
2. Large-scale Distribution	Broadcast Network	MSOs	*Backbone Provider*
3. Last-leg Connection	Local Station	Cable Operator	*Broadband Provider*

Regardless of the model used, for the internet, who controls the most powerful choke point? It is the broadband provider, who can be analogized to the LEC if we apply the telephony model (*layer 2: local exchange*) or, perhaps, the local TV station or local cable operator if we apply the TV model (*layer 3: last leg connection*). Nothing from the internet can reach you without going through that broadband provider's pipe.

What if that broadband provider decides not to deliver information from certain edge content providers, such as web pages from specific foreign sources, or to prohibit specific applications, such as Skype? Should they be able to discriminate in this way? Or should broadband providers remain "neutral" and provide access to all sources of information and to all applications? What if the broadband provider decides to provide faster access to certain websites or video streaming services for a fee? These questions have all come up in the debates over "net neutrality" and the "Open Internet" rules.

In abstract terms, the question is whether the broadband provider may discriminate in favor of or against some informational entity X on the basis of some attribute Y? To elaborate, "X" can be data (e.g., packet or stream), application service, hardware (e.g., consumer premises equipment), or some transport infrastructure. "Y" can be any attribute associated with these entities, such as semantic content, digital rights management status, identities of communicating parties, type of application service, hardware manufacturer, and so on.*

Here are some concrete examples. We start with a banal case. Suppose a broadband provider sells different levels of service to end-users depending on the bandwidth desired. An end-user who bought the lowest tier of service (e.g., 512 Kbps throughput) would not receive the highest tier of bandwidth (e.g., 10 Mbps) because that end-user did not pay for it (X= bandwidth; Y= subscription status). Although this is a departure from strict neutrality, no one objects to this sort of discrimination.

Let's take the other extreme. Suppose a broadband provider, which is owned by a patriotic media mogul, blocks websites that stream videos of American troops killed by Iraqi snipers (X=video content; Y=unpatriotic offensiveness). This sort of discrimination, which raises serious freedom of expression concerns, is not purely hypothetical. In the broadcast industry, Cumulus Media Inc. kicked off the Dixie Chicks when they criticized the sitting President for starting the Iraq war.† In the internet domain, a Pearl Jam performance webcast through

---

* Some of this text comes from Jerry Kang, *Race.net Neutrality* (6 J. Telecom. & High Tech. L. 1-22 (2007))

† *See* Geoff Boucher, *Fans Not Buying Chicks' Apology*, L.A. TIMES, March 19, 2003.

AT&T's Blue Room was (mistakenly?) edited to remove certain lyrics from a song titled "Daughter": "George Bush, leave this world alone", and "George Bush find yourself another home."[*]

There are countless hard cases in between these extremes. What if a broadband service provider: ˙

1. blocks IP packets necessary for Voice-over-IP (VoIP) or streaming video because VoIP competes with its own telephony or cable TV service;

2. speeds up delivery of certain services, such as videoconferencing or gaming, which indirectly slows down all other content, such as e-mail;

3. blocks content on the basis of digital rights management under a cramped reading of "fair use";

4. provides better connections to an affiliated service provider (e.g., Microsoft instead of Google) in exchange for payment from that provider;

Case #1 represents the oft-cited example of Madison River Communications, a rural LEC, which blocked VoIP packets over their DSL networks in order to keep customers from leaving their traditional phone service.[†] Case #2 describes the Quality of Service guarantees that broadband service providers allege that "network neutrality" regulations prevent. Case #3 represents AT&T's announcement that it will scan for and not transport any content deemed to violate intellectual property laws.[‡] Case #4 describes broadband service providers' wish to take advantage of two-sided markets, which would allow AT&T to collect revenues not only from end-users (e.g., customers like you) but also content providers (e.g., YouTube). As AT&T Chairman Ed Whiteacre infamously exclaimed:

> Now what they would like to do is use my pipes free, but I ain't going to let them do that be-cause we have spent this capital and we have to have a return on it. So there's going to have to be some mechanism for these people who use these pipes to pay for the portion they're using. Why should they be allowed to use my pipes? The Internet can't be free in that sense, because we and the cable companies have made an investment and for a Google or Yahoo! or Vonage or anybody to expect to use these pipes [for] free is nuts![§]

---

[*] *See* Conor McKay, Portions Censored from Pearl Jam Webcast, CMJ (Aug. 8, 2007), http://prod1.cmj.com/articles/display_article.php?id=44047312. AT&T said that this editing was a mistake made by a content monitor.

[†] *See Madison River LLC and Affiliated Companies,* File No. EB-05-IH-0110, Order, 20 FCC Rcd. 4295 (Enf. Bur. 2005).

[‡] See James S. Granelli, COPYRIGHT; AT&T to target pirated content; It joins Hollywood in trying to keep bootleg material off its network, June 13, 2007, p. C1.

[§] *See, e.g.,* Patricia O'Connell, *At SBC, It's All About "Scale and Scope,"* BUSINESS WEEK, ONLINE EXTRA (Nov. 7, 2005), http://www.businessweek.com/magazine/content/05_45/b3958092.htm.

In considering these harder cases, how might we decide when "neutrality" should be required and when "discrimination" should be permitted? Perhaps we can simply try to predict the likely costs and benefits of neutrality rules.

TIM WU, WHY HAVE A TELECOMMUNICATIONS LAW? ANTI-DISCRIMINATION NORMS IN COMMUNICATIONS
5 J. Telecomm. & High Tech. L. 15 (2006).

I see the regulators' task as trying, as best as possible, to foster the vibrancy and health of the part of the nation's public infrastructure called its information networks. Information networks make possible a large range of activities - commercial, such as corporate meetings; political, such as news distribution; and purely personal; such as the planning of birthday parties and happy hours. Networks also catalyze innovation, both in the network itself, and in activities that depend on the transport network, from voice communications through online travel agents. A chief goal of telecommunications policy, in this view, is to maximize the value of the information networks as a catalyst for all these activities.

Both network ideology and government policies can affect how valuable the networks are as a catalyst or input into other activities. The more general-purpose the network is, the more generally valuable the network is. That is the essence of the infrastructure theory of networks, and also what motivated the "end-to-end" principle of network design. The essence of the end-to-end principle is that the most valuable network is that which supports the broadest number of uses.

The analogy to urban planning is obvious but worth repeating. A street and a sidewalk have a value that in part derives from their multiplicity of uses. Stores on Fifth Avenue can sell hats, coats, toys and coffee. The urban planner doesn't need to decide the use, and does better by not deciding. A dedicated network is like a street designed from the outset to sell, say, top hats. Surely the dedicated network, in the beginning, is not useless, but less useful than perhaps it could be. It is also a street that could face a serious problem when top hats go out of fashion.

If the goal is to maximize the value of the information networks as a catalyst for commercial, political, and personal activities, it would be useful to speak of the dangers that face the telecommunications regulator. The first is overplanning, both public and private. Government has sometimes had success planning the future, usually by funding scientists who then build what they think the future should be (the story of the internet's origins). But unless they give money to scientists, regulators' and legislative efforts to plan the future, influenced by what today's powers think that future should be, have a storied history of failure. In the 1960s television broadcasters managed to convince the FCC that UHF was the technology of the future, cable a trifle and threat to localism. . . .

Such tales may give rise to libertarian twitching and thoughts of total deregulation, but the flip-side of government inaction is no less serious. The non-hypothetical danger is that private network owners will individually destroy the collective value of the public networks. Of course, the value of activities that depend on a network also make the network valuable, leading to a natural incentive to support a network with varied and valuable uses. However, we also know network owners may have good reason to deviate from what is in the collective interest. Consider two persistent reasons. First, it is no secret or surprise that incumbent firms act first and foremost to preserve their existing investments and to nullify competitive threats. To the extent activities facilitated by the network challenge the incumbent firm's existing investments, firms try to block them. This is particularly a threat to dramatic innovation that threatens to take over vested interests. Stated otherwise, no firm plans on its own death, even if the downfall of the firm is actually in the public interest.

Second, firms cannot internalize or capture all of the public benefits of an infrastructure they own, particularly those benefits that are hard to commodify. As Brett Frischman and Mark Lemley observe, infrastructures are a form of good that tend to create spillovers. Consider urban planning again. How possibly could the owner of a sidewalk capture the value of conversations held walking along, or thoughts that ramble, or the joys of window-shopping? The problem is that incumbent firms may make sad efforts to capture some of the value of what their infrastructure inspires. In the process of trying to capture for themselves more of the public value of what transpires on their network, firms can lessen or destroy the value of the network as a catalyst for other activities. This is the great tragedy of badly executed "value-added" network models. By trying to extract side payments for services usually otherwise available and better provided elsewhere, the risk is diminishing the real value of the network.

NOTES & QUESTIONS

1. *The importance of being dumb.* Wu states that "general purpose" networks are more valuable and refers to "infrastructure theory" and "end to end" design principles. Let's unpack these ideas.

a. *The end-to-end (e2e) principle.* The e2e principle was introduced by Jerome Saltzer, David Reed, and David Clark in an influential paper in the early

1980s.* A network can be modeled as a stack of vertical layers. (Caution: this use of "layer" is different from the way we have been using it to describe the whole industry.) At the very bottom, we have a physical layer (of wires and computers); in the middle, we have various layers, including network and transmission layers (where TCP/IP do their work); at the very top, we have application layers (e.g., Microsoft Word, or Adobe Acrobat reader). The e2e principle espouses a preference for implementing functionality at the highest layers possible (e.g., in the application layer, in software installed on your laptop) instead of lower layers (such as the routers owned by your telephone company, closer to the core of the network).† Even if this preference generates short-term costs by preventing performance optimizations in the network's core, the e2e principle contends that there are greater long-term benefits of network reliability, flexibility, and innovation.

b. *Infrastructure.* Based on the above explanation of the e2e principle, in what way does the internet act as infrastructure, such as roads or highways? In answering this question, consider Wu's description of streets specially designed for top hats.

c. *The appeal of being smart.* The internet was designed according to this e2e principle. In this sense, the internet is a "dumb" network, in which the computers within the network do little beyond reading addresses and tossing packets along. "Dumb" is intended to be a compliment here, and without question, the internet's dumb nature has fostered decentralized innovation. Consider, for instance, user installed applications such as Skype, which among other things enables global computer-to-computer voice communications, without getting permission from a single telephone company or having to change a single piece of hardware or software within the network's core. But, even if dumb networks have been good for society in the past, must this always be so? Can't specialized networks, upgraded to be "smarter" at their core, provide better services?

2. *Who should decide?* Whether dumb networks (with intelligence embedded in the edges, on computers owned by end-users) or smart networks (with intelligence embedded in the core, on computers owned by telephone

---

* *See* J.H. Saltzer et al., *End-to-End Arguments in System Design*, 2 ACM TRANSACTIONS ON COMPUTER SYS. 277 (1984).

† As Barbara Van Schewick has explained, in the original articulation of the e2e principle, this "preference" was not so much a preference as an entailment of technical correctness: certain functions simply cannot be correctly implemented at lower layers. In later versions of the principle, the authors were truly expressing a preference, a policy judgment. *See* BARBARA VAN SCHEWICK, ARCHITECTURE & INNOVATION: THE ROLE OF THE END-TO-END ARGUMENTS IN THE ORIGINAL INTERNET 89-101(2008).

companies, cable operators, and ISPs) are better for society is an open empirical question. If substantive certainty is impossible, maybe we can ask the process question: *who* should decide?

a.   *Trust the market?* Why not let the market decide? If dumb networks are better for society, then the market will drive broadband service providers toward that direction. By contrast, if smart networks are better for society, then the market will drive in that direction. Why might you be skeptical?

b.   *Trust the state?* Why not let the government decide? Again, why might you be skeptical about such state-sponsored industrial policy?

3. *Disincentivizing buildout?* If broadband service providers cannot discriminate between certain content providers or certain applications, they claim that they will not be able to raise the funds necessary to continue their broadband buildout. Do you think the existence of net neutrality rules will make or break the decision to invest? How might we find out?

4. *Raising the stakes: democracy.* The above questions focused on utilitarian calculations based on uncertain empirical predictions about architecture and innovation. But there is something more going on in the net neutrality debate that is not easily captured in economic terms. For example, the "Save the Internet" FAQ states:

> Net Neutrality is the reason why the Internet has driven economic innovation, *democratic participation, and free speech online.* It's why the Internet has become an unrivaled environment for open communications, *civic involvement* and free speech."
>
> On the Internet, *consumers are in ultimate control* — deciding between content, applications and services available anywhere, no matter who owns the network.[*]

Are these concerns relevant to the net neutrality debate, or are they confused distractions?

---

[*] Save the Internet, *Frequently Asked Questions, available at* http://www.savetheinternet.com/=faq.

5. *Lowering the stakes: just making some money.* Broadband service providers might suggest that all this anxiety about free speech and content manipulation is overblown, almost paranoid. Even the yammering about "innovation" is beside the point. All they want to do is make some more money. They want to be able to charge premium customers premium prices. They also want to be able to exploit two-sided markets and charge not only end-user subscribers but also content/application providers. What's the big economic deal?

b. THE NET NEUTRALITY SAGA

For the first decade of the internet's existence, roughly 1995–2005, the FCC took a "deregulatory" approach. Even though the internet was in some sense a data-centric extension of wireline telephony, the Commission specifically declined to classify the internet as telephony or impose common carriage rules on internet providers. The FCC was extremely wary of importing these complex regulations under Title II of the Communications Act, which were historically designed for a very different technology and industry, to a burgeoning communications service. That said, it's important to remember that in the early days of the internet, most services relied on wireline telephone or other common carriage "backbone" providers to reach their customers. That changed with the emergence of high speed broadband providers, and the lack of any common carriage element to the network raised concerns about neutrality and a lack of competition between providers.

Starting in 2005, the FCC began to take incremental steps urging more "neutral" operation of broadband services. The Commission spent the better part of the next decade attempting to adopt different regulatory frameworks aimed at protecting neutrality without "classifying" broadband providers as common carriers. (We study this carefully in the next chapter.) But those attempts were repeated challenged in court, often successfully on the grounds that the FCC lacked power to issue enforcement orders or rules.

For now, we skip over this complex regulatory history. Questions pertaining to what authority the FCC has to regulate the internet, under which title of the Communications Act, are deferred to the next chapter. Here, we instead focus specifically on the substantive question of access.

To repeat, within any communication service, there are potential choke points. With internet service, the most powerful choke point is exercised by the broadband provider. What access rights should other players have to that last-leg connection? As administrations have changed and the battle over net neutrality has waged on, the Commission's answer to this question has shifted somewhat.

But despite the polarized rhetoric used in this debate, there is a substantial amount of agreement on certain core principles. Let's begin by reviewing the Commission's first articulation of these principles under Chairman Powell.

BROADBAND POLICY STATEMENT
20 FCC Rcd 14986 (2005)

4. The Communications Act charges the Commission with "regulating interstate and foreign commerce in communication by wire and radio." The Communications Act regulates telecommunications carriers, as common carriers, under Title II. Information service providers, "by contrast, are not subject to mandatory common-carrier regulation under Title II." The Commission, however, "has jurisdiction to impose additional regulatory obligations under its Title I ancillary jurisdiction to regulate interstate and foreign communications." As a result, the Commission has jurisdiction necessary to ensure that providers of telecommunications for Internet access or Internet Protocol-enabled (IP-enabled) services are operated in a neutral manner. Moreover, to ensure that broadband networks are widely deployed, open, affordable, and accessible to all consumers, the Commission adopts the following principles:

- To encourage broadband deployment and preserve and promote the open and interconnected nature of the public Internet, consumers are entitled to access the lawful Internet content of their choice.

- To encourage broadband deployment and preserve and promote the open and interconnected nature of the public Internet, consumers are entitled to run applications and use services of their choice, subject to the needs of law enforcement.

- To encourage broadband deployment and preserve and promote the open and interconnected nature of the public Internet, consumers are entitled to connect their choice of legal devices that do not harm the network.

- To encourage broadband deployment and preserve and promote the open and interconnected nature of the public Internet, consumers are entitled to competition among network providers, application and service providers, and content providers.

NOTES & QUESTIONS

1. *The "Four Freedoms".* The Policy Statement outlines what is known as the "Four Freedoms," first described by then Chairman Powell.

a. *Legal content.* The first freedom suggests that consumers are entitled to access lawful content of their choice. But, what if the broadband service provider simply does not want to provide offensive (but legal) content? Examples could include virtual child pornography or anti-American "propaganda." Are there First Amendment challenges waiting in the wings? (Hint: think cable operator.)

b. *Legal applications.* The second freedom entitles consumers to run lawful applications. What about applications that eat into the market for the broadband service providers' other lines of business? Applications that provide video might compete against cable television. Applications that provide voice might compete against traditional wireline telephony. Why should broadband service providers have to tolerate such apps? After all, it's *their* network.

c. *Non-harmful devices.* The third freedom entitles consumers to connect devices to the network as long as they are not harmful. But what does it mean to be "harmful"? What about slowing down the network through congestion—is that "harmful"? What about installing wireless access points that gives away Internet access to the entire apartment building? Harmful? (Imagine splitting and amplifying cable television signals throughout your apartment building.)

d. *Competition.* The fourth freedom entitles consumers to competition among network, application, and service providers. What does it mean to be entitled to competition? How much competition do you currently enjoy? If you aren't getting as much as you are entitled to, what can you do about it?

e. *The fifth freedom.* Although there are only *four* freedoms in the Policy Statement, a *fifth* principle of nondiscrimination surfaced in the conditions placed on the AT&T + Bell South merger in 2006. (The FCC must sign off on mergers involving the transfer of spectrum or common carriage licenses.) In that merger, the firms voluntarily agreed not to discriminate based on the identity of the communicating parties or the ownership of any service:

> AT&T/BellSouth also commits that it will maintain a neutral network and neutral routing in its wireline broadband Internet access service. This commitment shall be satisfied by AT&T/BellSouth's agreement not to provide or to sell to Internet content, application, or service providers, including those affiliated with AT&T/BellSouth, any service that privileges, degrades or prioritizes any packet transmitted over AT&T/BellSouth's wireline broadband Internet access service based on its source, ownership or destination.[*]

---

[*] *AT&T Inc. and BellSouth Corporation Application for Transfer of Control,* WC Docket No. 06-74, Memorandum Opinion and Order, FCC 06-189, Appendix F (rel. Mar. 26, 2007)

(Specifically excluded from this agreement was AT&T's business services and IPTV initiative.) Do you think this is a reasonable condition?

2. *The Net Neutrality NOI.* Next, in April 2007, the FCC issued a very brief Notice of Inquiry on net neutrality. The FCC requested information about packet discrimination and the pricing practices of broadband service providers. The Commission also asked whether a new fifth principle of nondiscrimination should be generally adopted.

3. *Getting some teeth.* In 2008 the FCC brought its first enforcement action for violation of the net neutrality principles.[*] The Commission concluded that Comcast's throttling of BitTorrent, a peer-to-peer file transfer service, violated the principles and did not constitute "reasonable network management." The FCC ordered Comcast to disclose its network management practices to both the Commission and the public and to submit a compliance plan describing how it intends to stop the throttling. Comcast challenged the order in court and the D.C. Circuit ruled in 2010 that the Commission did not have the authority to issue the order under its "ancillary jurisdiction."[†]

4. *From four freedoms to three rules.* A few months after the D.C. Circuit vacated the order in *Comcast*, the Commission issued its first net neutrality rules.

PRESERVING THE OPEN INTERNET
R&O, 25 FCC Rcd 17905 (2010)

I. PRESERVING THE FREE AND OPEN INTERNET

1. [W]e adopt three basic rules that are grounded in broadly accepted Internet norms, as well as our own prior decisions:

i. **Transparency.** Fixed and mobile broadband providers must disclose the network management practices, performance characteristics, and terms and conditions of their broadband services;

ii. **No blocking.** Fixed broadband providers may not block lawful content, applications, services, or non-harmful devices; mobile broadband providers may not block lawful websites, or block applications that compete with their voice or video telephony services; and

iii. **No unreasonable discrimination.** Fixed broadband providers may not unreasonably discriminate in transmitting lawful network traffic.

---

[*] MO&O, *Formal Complaint of Free Press and Public Knowledge Against Comcast,* 23 FCC Rcd. 13028 (2008).

[†] Comcast Corp. v. FCC, 600 F.3d 642 (D.C. Cir. 2010).

We believe these rules, applied with the complementary principle of reasonable network management, will empower and protect consumers and innovators while helping ensure that the Internet continues to flourish, with robust private investment and rapid innovation at both the core and the edge of the network. This is consistent with the National Broadband Plan goal of broadband access that is ubiquitous and fast, promoting the global competitiveness of the United States.

NOTES & QUESTIONS

1. *The sequel: 2 Fast 2 Freedoms.* How do these rules relate to the principles outlined in the Commission's four freedoms policy statement? Recall that we discussed earlier how transparency could promote competition among broadband providers. The no blocking rule is almost directly transposed from the policy statement. And the anti-discrimination rule is an expansion of the "fifth freedom" that the FCC had flagged in the AT&T/Bell South merger review.

2. *A new challenger emerges.* As you might expect, broadband providers were not happy with these new rules either and they challenged them again in the D.C. Circuit. The Commission believed that it had "fixed" the jurisdictional problem that the court had flagged in *Comcast* and that it had authority to issue regulations under Section 706(a) of the Communications Act. The D.C. Circuit agreed in part, affirming the Commission's first rule (transparency / openness).[*] But the court rejected the other two rules (anti-blocking and anti-discrimination) because they amounted to common carrier regulation.

3. *Broader than must-carry for cable?* The challengers successfully argued that the anti-discrimination rule was akin to a common carriage mandate. In response, the FCC argued that the anti-discrimination rule was no more onerous than the must-carry rules imposed on Cable TV providers dating back to the 1960s. The Supreme Court upheld such rules in *Southwestern Cable* in 1968 and again in *Turner Broadcasting* in 1994. Recall that we discussed the Court's decision in *Turner* earlier in this chapter. But the D.C. Circuit was not persuaded:

> Such a rule is plainly distinguishable from the Open Internet Order's anti-discrimination rule because the *Southwestern Cable* regulation imposed no obligation on cable operators to hold their facilities open to the public generally, but only to certain specific broadcasters if and when the cable operators acted in ways that might harm those broadcasters. As the Court later explained in

---

[*] Verizon v. FCC, 740 F.3d 623 (D.C. Cir. 2014).

Midwest Video II, the *Southwestern Cable* rule "was limited to remedying a specific perceived evil," and "did not amount to a duty to hold out facilities indifferently for public use." The Open Internet Order's anti-discrimination provision is not so limited, as the compelled carriage obligation applies in all circumstances and with respect to all edge providers.

Do you agree that the anti-discrimination rule is broader than the must-carry rule? Can you think of a way to change the rule so that it would not cross the line into common carriage regulation?

4. *Is there daylight between anti-blocking and anti-discrimination?* The court wasted no time concluding that the anti-discrimination rule was clearly a common carriage regulation, but it found that the anti-blocking rule was a closer call:

> Whether the *Open Internet Order*'s anti-blocking rules, applicable to both fixed and mobile broadband providers, likewise establish per se common carrier obligations is somewhat less clear. According to Verizon, they do because they deny "broadband providers discretion in deciding which traffic from ... edge providers to carry," and deny them "discretion over carriage terms by setting a uniform price of zero." This argument has some appeal. The anti-blocking rules establish a minimum level of service that broadband providers must furnish to all edge providers: edge providers' "content, applications [and] services" must be "effectively [ ]usable." The Order also expressly prohibits broadband providers from charging edge providers any fees for this minimum level of service. In requiring that all edge providers receive this minimum level of access for free, these rules would appear on their face to impose per se common carrier obligations with respect to that minimum level of service.

> At oral argument, however, Commission counsel asserted that "[i]t's not common carriage to simply have a basic level of required service if you can negotiate different levels with different people." This contention rests on the fact that under the anti-blocking rules broadband providers have no obligation to actually provide any edge provider with the minimum service necessary to satisfy the rules. If, for example, all edge providers' "content, applications [and] services" are "effectively usable," at download speeds of, say, three mbps, a broadband provider like Verizon could deliver all edge providers' traffic at speeds of at least four mbps. Viewed this way, the relevant "carriage" broadband providers furnish might be access to end users more generally, not the minimum required service. In delivering this service, so defined, the anti-blocking rules would permit broadband providers to distinguish somewhat among edge providers, just as Commission counsel contended at oral argument. For example, Verizon might, consistent with the anti-blocking rule—and again, absent the anti-discrimination rule—charge an edge provider like Netflix for high-speed, priority access while limiting all other edge providers to a more standard service. In theory, moreover, not only could Verizon negotiate

separate agreements with each individual edge provider regarding the level of service provided, but it could also charge similarly-situated edge providers completely different prices for the same service. Thus, if the relevant service that broadband providers furnish is access to their subscribers generally, as opposed to access to their subscribers at the specific minimum speed necessary to satisfy the anti-blocking rules, then these rules, while perhaps establishing a lower limit on the forms that broadband providers' arrangements with edge providers could take, might nonetheless leave sufficient "room for individualized bargaining and discrimination in terms" so as not to run afoul of the statutory prohibitions on common carrier treatment.

But unfortunately for the Commission, the court found that this potentially persuasive defense of the anti-blocking rule had not been advanced in either the Order itself or in the agency briefs. The court found that the Commission made "no distinction at all between the anti-discrimination and anti-blocking rules, seeking to justify both types of rules with explanations that, as we have explained, are patently insufficient."

5. *If at first you don't succeed...* The D.C. Circuit again vacated the Commission's attempt to impose net neutrality principles, and again the Commission went back to the drawing board. But this time was different because the court had made clear in *Verizon* what the FCC needed to do if it wanted to issue these rules: classify broadband providers as common carriers. More on that in the next CHAPTER 5: CLASSIFICATION. The Commission on remand issued new rules on certain broadband providers that it classified as common carriers.

PROTECTING AND PROMOTING
THE OPEN INTERNET
R&O, 30 FCC Rcd. 5601 (2015)

7. Just over a year ago, the D.C. Circuit in *Verizon v. FCC* struck down the Commission's 2010 conduct rules against blocking and unreasonable discrimination. But the *Verizon* court upheld the Commission's finding that Internet openness drives a "virtuous cycle" in which innovations at the edges of the network enhance consumer demand, leading to expanded investments in broadband infrastructure that, in turn, spark new innovations at the edge. The *Verizon* court further affirmed the Commission's conclusion that "broadband providers represent a threat to Internet openness and could act in ways that would ultimately inhibit the speed and extent of future broadband deployment."

8. Threats to Internet openness remain today . . . Verizon frankly told the court at oral argument, but for the 2010 rules, it would be exploring agreements

to charge certain content providers for priority service. Indeed, the wireless industry had a well-established record of trying to keep applications within a carrier-controlled "walled garden" in the early days of mobile applications. That specific practice ended when Internet Protocol (IP) created the opportunity to leap the wall. But the Commission has continued to hear concerns about other broadband provider practices involving blocking or degrading third-party applications.

9. Emerging Internet trends since 2010 give us more, not less, cause for concern about such threats. First, mobile broadband networks have massively expanded since 2010. They are faster, more broadly deployed, more widely used, and more technologically advanced. At the end of 2010, there were about 70,000 devices in the U.S. that had LTE wireless connections. Today, there are more than 127 million. . . . mobile broadband is becoming an increasingly important pathway to the Internet independent of any fixed broadband connections consumers may have, given that mobile broadband is not a full substitute for fixed broadband connections. And consumers must be protected, for example from mobile commercial practices masquerading as "reasonable network management." Second, and critically, the growth of online streaming video services has spurred further evolution of the Internet. Currently, video is the dominant form of traffic on the Internet. These video services directly confront the video businesses of the very companies that supply them broadband access to their customers.

10.   The Commission, in its May *Notice of Proposed Rulemaking*, asked a fundamental question: "What is the right public policy to ensure that the Internet remains open?"

11.   Three overarching objectives have guided us . . . based on the vast record before the Commission: America needs more broadband, better broadband, and open broadband networks. These goals are mutually reinforcing, not mutually exclusive. Without an open Internet, there would be less broadband investment and deployment. And, as discussed further below, all three are furthered through the open Internet rules and balanced regulatory framework we adopt today.[12]

---

[12] Consistent with the Verizon court's analysis, this Order need not conclude that any specific market power exists in the hands of one or more broadband providers in order to create and enforce these rules. Thus, these rules do not address, and are not designed to deal with, the acquisition or maintenance of market power or its abuse, real or potential. Moreover, it is worth noting that the Commission acts in a manner that is both complementary to the work of the antitrust agencies and supported by their application of antitrust laws. *See generally* 47 U.S.C. § 152(b) ("[N]othing in this Act . . . shall be construed to modify, impair, or supersede the applicability of any of the antitrust laws."). Nothing in this Order in any way precludes the Antitrust Division of the Department of Justice or the Commission itself from fulfilling their respective responsibilities

A. Strong Rules That Protect Consumers from Past and Future Tactics that Threaten the Open Internet

1. Clear, Bright-Line Rules

15.   *No Blocking.* Consumers who subscribe to a retail broadband Internet access service must get what they have paid for—access to all (lawful) destinations on the Internet.... Thus, this Order adopts a straightforward ban:

A person engaged in the provision of broadband Internet access service, insofar as such person is so engaged, shall not block lawful content, applications, services, or non-harmful devices, subject to reasonable network management.

16.   *No Throttling.* The 2010 open Internet rule against blocking contained an ancillary prohibition against the degradation of lawful content, applications, services, and devices, on the ground that such degradation would be tantamount to blocking. This Order creates a separate rule to guard against degradation targeted at specific uses of a customer's broadband connection:

A person engaged in the provision of broadband Internet access service, insofar as such person is so engaged, shall not impair or degrade lawful Internet traffic on the basis of Internet content, application, or service, or use of a non-harmful device, subject to reasonable network management.

17.   The ban on throttling is necessary both to fulfill the reasonable expectations of a customer who signs up for a broadband service that promises access to all of the lawful Internet, and to avoid gamesmanship designed to avoid the no-blocking rule by, for example, rendering an application effectively, but not technically, unusable. It prohibits the degrading of Internet traffic based on source, destination, or content. It also specifically prohibits conduct that singles out content competing with a broadband provider's business model.

18.   *No Paid Prioritization.* Paid prioritization occurs when a broadband provider accepts payment (monetary or otherwise) to manage its network in a way that benefits particular content, applications, services, or devices. To protect against "fast lanes," this Order adopts a rule that establishes that:

A person engaged in the provision of broadband Internet access service, insofar as such person is so engaged, shall not engage in paid prioritization.

"Paid prioritization" refers to the management of a broadband provider's network to directly or indirectly favor some traffic over other traffic, including through use of techniques such as traffic shaping, prioritization, resource reservation, or other forms of preferential traffic management, either (a) in

under Section 7 of the Clayton Act (15 U.S.C. §18), or the Commission's public interest standard as it assesses prospective transactions.

exchange for consideration (monetary or otherwise) from a third party, or (b) to benefit an affiliated entity.[18]

19.   The record demonstrates the need for strong action. . . . Although there are arguments that some forms of paid prioritization could be beneficial, the practical difficulty is this: the threat of harm is overwhelming, case-by-case enforcement can be cumbersome for individual consumers or edge providers, and there is no practical means to measure the extent to which edge innovation and investment would be chilled. And, given the dangers, there is no room for a blanket exception for instances where consumer permission is buried in a service plan—the threats of consumer deception and confusion are simply too great.

2. No Unreasonable Interference or Unreasonable Disadvantage to Consumers or Edge Providers

21.   The bright-line bans on blocking, throttling, and paid prioritization will go a long way to preserve the virtuous cycle. But not all the way. Gatekeeper power can be exercised through a variety of technical and economic means, and without a catch-all standard, it would be that, as Benjamin Franklin said, "a little neglect may breed great mischief." Thus, the Order adopts the following standard:

> *Any person engaged in the provision of broadband Internet access service, insofar as such person is so engaged, shall not unreasonably interfere with or unreasonably disadvantage (i) end users' ability to select, access, and use broadband Internet access service or the lawful Internet content, applications, services, or devices of their choice, or (ii) edge providers' ability to make lawful content, applications, services, or devices available to end users. Reasonable network management shall not be considered a violation of this rule.*

22.   This "no unreasonable interference/disadvantage" standard protects free expression, thus fulfilling the congressional policy that "the Internet offer[s] a forum for a true diversity of political discourse, unique opportunities for cultural development, and myriad avenues for intellectual activity."[25] And the standard will permit considerations of asserted benefits of innovation as well as threatened harm to end users and edge providers.

3. Enhanced Transparency

> *A person engaged in the provision of broadband Internet access service shall publicly disclose accurate information regarding the network management practices, performance, and commercial terms of its broadband Internet access*

---

[18] Unlike the no-blocking and no-throttling rules, there is no "reasonable network management" exception to the paid prioritization rule because paid prioritization is inherently a business practice rather than a network management practice.

[25] 47 U.S.C. § 230(a)(3).

services sufficient for consumers to make informed choices regarding use of such services and for content, application, service, and device providers to develop, market, and maintain Internet offerings.

24.   Today's Order reaffirms the importance of ensuring transparency, so that consumers are fully informed about the Internet access they are purchasing and so that edge providers have the information they need to understand whether their services will work as advertised. To do that, the Order [e]nhances the transparency rule for both end users and edge providers, including by adopting a requirement that broadband providers always must disclose promotional rates, all fees and/or surcharges, and all data caps or data allowances; adding packet loss as a measure of network performance that must be disclosed; and requiring specific notification to consumers that a "network practice" is likely to significantly affect their use of the service.

4. Scope of the Rules

25.   The open Internet rules described above apply to both fixed and mobile broadband Internet access service. Consistent with the 2010 Order, today's Order applies its rules to the consumer-facing service that broadband networks provide, which is known as "broadband Internet access service" (BIAS) and is defined to be:

> *A mass-market retail service by wire or radio that provides the capability to transmit data to and receive data from all or substantially all Internet endpoints, including any capabilities that are incidental to and enable the operation of the communications service, but excluding dial-up Internet access service. This term also encompasses any service that the Commission finds to be providing a functional equivalent of the service described in the previous sentence, or that is used to evade the protections set forth in this Part.*

26.   As in 2010, BIAS does not include enterprise services, virtual private network services, hosting, or data storage services. Further, we decline to apply the open Internet rules to premises operators [e.g., coffee shops, bookstores] to the extent they may be offering broadband Internet access service as we define it today.

27.   In defining this service we make clear that we are responding to the *Verizon* court's conclusion that broadband providers "furnish a service to edge providers" . . . . As discussed further below, we make clear that broadband Internet access service encompasses this service to edge providers. Broadband providers sell retail customers the ability to go anywhere (lawful) on the Internet. Their representation that they will transport and deliver traffic to and from all or substantially all Internet endpoints includes the promise to transmit traffic to and from those Internet endpoints back to the user.

32. *Reasonable Network Management.* As with the 2010 rules, this Order contains an exception for reasonable network management, which applies to all but the paid prioritization rule (which, by definition, is not a means of managing a network):

> *A network management practice is a practice that has a primarily technical network management justification, but does not include other business practices. A network management practice is reasonable if it is primarily used for and tailored to achieving a legitimate network management purpose, taking into account the particular network architecture and technology of the broadband Internet access service.*

33. Recently, significant concern has arisen when mobile providers' have attempted to justify certain practices as reasonable network management practices, such as applying speed reductions to customers using "unlimited data plans" in ways that effectively force them to switch to price plans with less generous data allowances. For example, in the summer of 2014, Verizon announced a change to its "unlimited" data plan for LTE customers, which would have limited the speeds of LTE customers using grandfathered "unlimited" plans once they reached a certain level of usage each month. Verizon briefly described this change as within the scope of "reasonable network management," before changing course and withdrawing the change.

34. With mobile broadband service now subject to the same rules as fixed broadband service, the Order expressly recognizes that evaluation of network management practices will take into account the additional challenges involved in the management of mobile networks, including the dynamic conditions under which they operate. It also recognizes the specific network management needs of other technologies, such as unlicensed Wi-Fi networks.

NOTES & QUESTIONS

1. *The economic case for neutrality.* What does the FCC mean when it mentions the "virtuous cycle" created by the open Internet rules? Who benefits from the virtuous cycle? Can you give examples of similar cycles happening in the past? Would the broadband providers benefit from this cycle? If so, why do they oppose the rules? Might there be a vicious cycle?

2. *Rule: no blocking.* What does "no blocking" mean?

3. *Rule: no throttling.* What is the difference between the no blocking and no throttling provisions? What does the Commission predict would happen if the no throttling provision were not included?

4. *Rule: no paid prioritization.* How do you think this will affect existing services? Will removing "fast lanes" make things run more or less smoothly

from the user's perspective? Will this mean more buffering while you binge-watch Netflix?

5. *Standard: no unreasonable interference/disadvantage.* What is the difference between a "rule" and a "standard"? And given the clear, bright line rules of no blocking, no throttling, and no paid prioritization, why is an additional standard necessary?

6. *Transparency.* What impact, if any, do you think the transparency will have on end-user behavior? On ISP marketing and business practices? Do you think that end-users can "vote with their feet" on these issues?

7. *Treating fixed and mobile the same.* In the 2010 Order, the FCC had carefully distinguished between "fixed" and "mobile" broadband providers, and gave "mobile" providers greater flexibility. In the 2015 version, however, the FCC abandoned this distinction. Here's some of the reasoning:

88. Today, we find that changes in the mobile broadband marketplace warrant a revised [regulatory] approach. We find that the mobile broadband marketplace has evolved, and continues to evolve, but is no longer in a nascent stage. [M]obile broadband networks are faster, more broadly deployed, more widely used, and more technologically advanced than they were in 2010. We conclude that it would benefit the millions of consumers who access the Internet on mobile devices to apply the same set of Internet openness protections to both fixed and mobile networks.

90. As consumers use smartphones and tablets more, they increasingly rely on mobile broadband as a pathway to the Internet. . . . In addition, evidence shows that consumers in certain demographic groups, including low income and rural consumers and communities of color, are more likely to rely on mobile as their only access to the Internet. . . . Additionally, rural consumers and businesses often have access to fewer options for Internet service, meaning that these customers may have limited alternatives when faced with restrictions to Internet openness imposed by their mobile provider. Furthermore, just as consumer reliance on mobile broadband has grown, edge providers increasingly rely on mobile broadband to reach their customers.

96. Although mobile providers generally argue that additional rules are not necessary to deter practices that would limit Internet openness, concerns related to the openness practices of mobile broadband providers have arisen. [I]n 2012, the Commission reached a $1.25 million settlement with Verizon for restricting tethering apps on Verizon smartphones, based on openness requirements attached to Verizon's Upper 700 MHz C Block licenses[, voluntary terms that Verizon had agreed to in the spectrum auction]. Also in 2012, consumers complained when they encountered problems accessing Apple's FaceTime application on AT&T's network. More recently, significant concern has arisen when mobile providers' have attempted to justify certain

practices as reasonable network management practices, such as applying speed reductions to customers using "unlimited data plans" . . . . Other commenters . . . also cite mobile providers' blocking of the Google Wallet e-payment application. Although providers claimed that the blocking was justified based on security concerns, [one group noted] that "this carrier behavior raised anticompetitive concerns when AT&T, Verizon and T-Mobile later unveiled their own mobile payment application, a competitor to Google Wallet . . ." [We] find that the rules we adopt today for mobile network providers will help guard against future incidents that have the potential to affect Internet openness and undermine a mobile broadband consumer's right to access a free and open Internet.

8. *Objections.* Here are some objections that broadband providers might raise, as a matter of policy. Try to articulate the FCC's response.

a. *Curtail broadband deployment.* Rolling out broadband is expensive. By preventing new ways to raise funds, the FCC is making it harder for us to bring broadband to all Americans. That's perverse.

b. *Trickle down.* If we make more money through other sources, we can charge less to our individual subscribers. That means more affordable broadband for all Americans.

c. *Self-regulation.* Competitive forces will make sure that we can't abuse our customers. Trust the market. Get the government out of regulating the internet. That's the American way.

9. *Improvements?* If you don't like the Open Internet rules, what would you have done differently?

10. *Freedom of speech.* With broadcast, cable TV, and DBS, we've encountered First Amendment objections to forcing access. Are broadband providers similar to these video providers? Or are they more like telephone companies, who aren't speaking? The FCC's 2015 Open Internet rules were challenged in court on many grounds, including arbitrary and capriciousness and the First Amendment. Let's see how the court addressed the constitutional question.

USTA v. FCC
825 F.3d 674 (2016)

We finally turn to [the] First Amendment challenge to the open internet rules. . . . [W]e conclude that the First Amendment poses no bar to the rules.

Alamo argues that the open internet rules violate the First Amendment by forcing broadband providers to transmit speech with which they might disagree. We are unpersuaded. We have concluded that the Commission's reclassification of broadband service as common carriage is a permissible exercise of its Title II authority, and Alamo does not challenge that determination. Common carriers have long been subject to nondiscrimination and equal access obligations akin to those imposed by the rules without raising any First Amendment question. Those obligations affect a common carrier's neutral transmission of *others'* speech, not a carrier's communication of its own message.

Because the constitutionality of each of the rules ultimately rests on the same analysis, we consider the rules together. The rules generally bar broadband providers from denying or downgrading end-user access to content and from favoring certain content by speeding access to it. In effect, they require broadband providers to offer a standardized service that transmits data on a nondiscriminatory basis. Such a constraint falls squarely within the bounds of traditional common carriage regulation.

The "basic characteristic" of common carriage is the "requirement [to] hold [ ] oneself out to serve the public indiscriminately." That requirement prevents common carriers from "mak[ing] individualized decisions, in particular cases, whether and on what terms to deal." In the communications context, common carriers "make[ ] a public offering to provide communications facilities whereby all members of the public who choose to employ such facilities may communicate or transmit intelligence of their own design and choosing." That is precisely what the rules obligate broadband providers to do.

Equal access obligations of that kind have long been imposed on telephone companies, railroads, and postal services, without raising any First Amendment issue. The Supreme Court has explained that the First Amendment comes "into play" only where "particular conduct possesses sufficient communicative elements," that is, when an "intent to convey a particularized message [is] present, and in the surrounding circumstances the likelihood [is] great that the message would be understood by those who viewed it." The absence of any First Amendment concern in the context of common carriers rests on the understanding that such entities, insofar as they are subject to equal access mandates, merely facilitate the transmission of the speech of others rather than engage in speech in their own right.

As the Commission found, that understanding fully applies to broadband providers. In the Order, the Commission concluded that broadband providers "exercise little control over the content which users access on the Internet" and "allow Internet end users to access all or substantially all content on the Internet, without alteration, blocking, or editorial intervention," thus "display[ing] no such intent to convey a message in their provision of broadband Internet access services." In turn, the Commission found, end users "expect that they can obtain access to all content available on the Internet, without the editorial intervention of their broadband provider." Because "the accessed speech is not edited or controlled by the broadband provider but is directed by the end user," the Commission concluded that broadband providers act as "mere conduits for the messages of others, not as agents exercising editorial discretion subject to First Amendment protections." Petitioners provide us with no reason to question those findings.

Because the rules impose on broadband providers the kind of nondiscrimination and equal access obligations that courts have never considered to raise a First Amendment concern—i.e., the rules require broadband providers to allow "all members of the public who choose to employ such facilities [to] communicate or transmit intelligence of their own design and choosing"—they are permissible. Of course, insofar as a broadband provider might offer its own *content*—such as a news or weather site—separate from its internet access service, the provider would receive the same protection under the First Amendment as other producers of internet content. But the challenged rules apply only to the provision of internet access as common carriage, as to which equal access and nondiscrimination mandates present no First Amendment problem.

Petitioners and their amici offer various grounds for distinguishing broadband service from other kinds of common carriage, none of which we find persuasive. For instance, the rules do not automatically raise First Amendment concerns on the ground that the material transmitted through broadband happens to be speech instead of physical goods. Telegraph and telephone networks similarly involve the transmission of speech. Yet the communicative intent of the individual speakers who use such transmission networks does not transform the networks themselves into speakers.

Likewise, the fact that internet speech has the capacity to reach a broader audience does not meaningfully differentiate broadband from telephone networks for purposes of the First Amendment claim presented here. Regardless of the scale of potential dissemination, both kinds of providers serve as neutral platforms for speech transmission. And while the extent of First Amendment protection can vary based on the content of the communications—speech on "matters of public concern," such as political speech, lies at the core of the First Amendment—both telephones and the internet can serve as a medium of transmission for all manner of speech, including speech addressing both public and private concerns. The constitutionality of common carriage regulation of a particular transmission medium thus does not vary based on the potential audience size.

To be sure, in certain situations, entities that serve as conduits for speech produced by others receive First Amendment protection. In those circumstances, however, the entities are not engaged in indiscriminate, neutral transmission of any and all users' speech, as is characteristic of common carriage. For instance, both newspapers and "cable television companies use a portion of their available space to reprint (or retransmit) the communications of others, while at the same time providing some original content." Through both types of actions—creating "original programming" and choosing "which stations or programs to include in [their] repertoire"—newspapers and cable companies "seek[ ] to communicate messages on a wide variety of topics and in a wide variety of formats."

In selecting which speech to transmit, newspapers and cable companies engage in editorial discretion. Newspapers have a finite amount of space on their pages and cannot "proceed to infinite expansion of ... column space."* Accordingly, they pick which articles and editorials to print, both with respect to original content and material produced by others. Those decisions "constitute the exercise of editorial control and judgment." Similarly, cable operators necessarily make decisions about which programming to make available to subscribers on a system's channel space. As with newspapers, the "editorial discretion" a cable operator exercises in choosing "which stations or programs to include in its repertoire" means that operators "engage in and transmit speech."† The Supreme Court therefore applied intermediate First Amendment scrutiny to (but ultimately upheld) must-carry rules constraining the discretion of a cable company concerning which programming to carry on its channel menu.

In contrast to newspapers and cable companies, the exercise of editorial discretion is entirely absent with respect to broadband providers subject to the Order. Unlike with the printed page and cable technology, broadband providers face no such constraints limiting the range of potential content they can make available to subscribers. Broadband providers thus are not required to make, nor have they traditionally made, editorial decisions about which speech to transmit. In that regard, the role of broadband providers is analogous to that of telephone companies: they act as neutral, indiscriminate platforms for transmission of speech of any and all users.

Of course, broadband providers, like telephone companies, can face capacity constraints from time to time. Not *every* telephone call will be able to get

* Miami Herald Publishing Co. v. Tornillo, 418 U.S. 241, 257 (1974).
† Turner Broadcasting System, Inc. v. FCC, 512 U.S. 622, 636 (1994) (internal quotation marks omitted).

through instantaneously at every moment, just as service to websites might be slowed at times because of significant network demand. But those kinds of temporary capacity constraints do not resemble the structural limitations confronting newspapers and cable companies. The latter naturally occasion the exercise of editorial discretion; the former do not.

If a broadband provider nonetheless were to *choose* to exercise editorial discretion—for instance, by picking a limited set of websites to carry and offering that service as a curated internet experience—it might then qualify as a First Amendment speaker. But the Order itself excludes such providers from the rules. The Order defines broadband internet access service as a "mass-market retail service"—i.e., a service that is "marketed and sold on a standardized basis"—that "provides the capability to transmit data to and receive data from all or substantially all Internet endpoints." That definition, by its terms, includes only those broadband providers that hold themselves out as neutral, indiscriminate conduits. Providers that may opt to exercise editorial discretion— for instance, by offering access only to a limited segment of websites specifically catered to certain content—would not offer a standardized service that can reach "substantially all" endpoints. The rules therefore would not apply to such providers.

With standard broadband internet access, by contrast, there is no editorial limitation on users' access to lawful internet content. As a result, when a subscriber uses her broadband service to access internet content of her own choosing, she does not understand the accessed content to reflect her broadband provider's editorial judgment or viewpoint. If it were otherwise—if the accessed content were somehow imputed to the broadband provider—the provider would have First Amendment interests more centrally at stake. But nothing about affording indiscriminate access to internet content suggests that the broadband provider *agrees* with the content an end user happens to access. Because a broadband provider does not—and is not understood by users to—"speak" when providing neutral access to internet content as common carriage, the First Amendment poses no bar to the open internet rules.

NOTES & QUESTIONS

1. *The pipes don't have speech rights.* Recall our discussion of the *Miami Herald* case in CHAPTER 2: ENTRY, which concerned a right-of-reply statute (a form of access forced on the newspaper). Why does the court find that broadband providers don't have the same free speech rights as newspapers?

2. *All in the name.* What we've been calling "broadband provider" has a more technical name, with an unfortunate acronym since we are trying to

promote neutrality. The FCC calls them "BIAS" providers—broadband internet access service providers. How does the FCC's definition of BIAS, which includes "the capability to transmit data to and receive data from all or substantially all Internet endpoints," influence the court's analysis?

3. *Not enough editorializing.* How could a broadband provider exercise editorial discretion? What would such a service look like? Do you think it would be popular?

4. *Keeping it kosher.* Consider an example: a company decides to offer a special broadband internet package for strictly kosher customers who are concerned about being exposed to inappropriate material.[*] For a fee, the provider will grant access to certain "whitelisted" sites, block access to "blacklisted" sites, and even filter out certain types of videos and images (e.g., exposed skin). Would this service fit the definition of a BIAS? Would it violate the FCC's "No Blocking" rule?

5. *Where do they draw the line?* Go back to the description of internet services at the beginning of this chapter. Can you identify which services and segments of the network will fall within the FCC's definition of BIAS? Imagine you turn on Netflix and queue up a movie. What (if anything) is your broadband provider prohibited from doing under the new FCC rules? What about Netflix, which is an edge content provider? What about Netflix's own broadband provider, which it presumably has? What about the company that transfers data between Netflix's broadband provider and your broadband provider? Is this what we mean by "backbone provider"?

6. *The FCC giveth and the FCC taketh away.* Elections, as they say, have consequences. And one of the consequences of the 2016 Presidential Election was that control of the FCC passed to Chairman Ajit Pai, a staunch critic of the agency's net neutrality rules and of common carriage regulation of broadband providers. While he does not oppose the principles outlined in the 2005 policy statement, he has stated publicly that he believes only Congress should impose such rules on internet providers. In line with this view, the Commission initiated a rulemaking in 2017 and issued a final rule in 2018 rescinding the FCC's 2015 Order and replacing it instead with transparency rules.

---

[*]   *See* Venish Martem, *TheJnet,* http://venishmartem.com/solutions/network/item/thejnet?category_id=198.

RESTORING INTERNET FREEDOM
DR, R&O, and O, 25 FCC Rcd 17905 (2017)

1. Over twenty years ago, in the Telecommunications Act of 1996, President Clinton and a Republican Congress established the policy of the United States "to preserve the vibrant and competitive free market that presently exists for the Internet . . . unfettered by Federal or State regulation." Today, we honor that bipartisan commitment to a free and open Internet by rejecting government control of the Internet. We reverse the Commission's abrupt shift two years ago to heavy-handed utility-style regulation of broadband Internet access service and return to the light-touch framework under which a free and open Internet underwent rapid and unprecedented growth for almost two decades. We eliminate burdensome regulation that stifles innovation and deters investment, and empower Americans to choose the broadband Internet access service that best fits their needs.

2. We take several actions in this Order to restore Internet freedom. First, we end utility- style regulation of the Internet in favor of the market-based policies necessary to preserve the future of Internet freedom. . . .

3. Next, we require ISPs to be transparent. Disclosure of network management practices, performance, and commercial terms of service is important for Internet freedom because it helps consumers choose what works best for them and enables entrepreneurs and other small businesses to get technical information needed to innovate. Individual consumers, not the government, decide what Internet access service best meets their individualized needs. We return to the transparency rule the Commission adopted in 2010 with certain limited modifications to promote additional transparency, and we eliminate certain reporting requirements adopted in the Title II Order that we find to be unnecessary and unduly burdensome.

4. Finally, we eliminate the Commission's conduct rules. The record evidence, including our cost-benefit analysis, demonstrates that the costs of these rules to innovation and investment outweigh any benefits they may have. In addition, we have not identified any sources of legal authority that could justify the comprehensive conduct rules governing ISPs adopted in the *Title II Order*. Lastly, we find that the conduct rules are unnecessary because the transparency requirement we adopt, together with antitrust and consumer protection laws, ensures that consumers have means to take remedial action if an ISP engages in behavior inconsistent with an open Internet.

*   *   *

87. . . . We find that the gatekeeper theory, the bedrock of the *Title II Order*'s overall argument justifying its approach, is a poor fit for the broadband

Internet access service market. Further, even if there may be potential harms, we find that pre-existing legal remedies, particularly antitrust and consumer protection laws, sufficiently address such harms so that they are outweighed by the well-recognized disadvantages of public utility regulation. As such, we find that public policy considerations support our legal finding that broadband Internet access service is an information service under the Act.

1. Title II Regulation Imposes Substantial Costs on the Internet Ecosystem

88.   The Commission has long recognized that regulatory burdens and uncertainty, such as those inherent in Title II, can deter investment by regulated entities and, until the Title II Order, its regulatory framework for cable, wireline, and wireless broadband Internet access services reflected that reality. . . .

89.   *Investment by ISPs.* As the Commission has noted in the past, increased broadband deployment and subscribership require investment, and the regulatory climate affects investment. The mechanisms by which public utility regulation can depress investment by the regulated entity are well-known in the regulatory economics literature. The owners of network infrastructure make long-term, irreversible investments. In theory, public utility regulation is intended to curb monopoly pricing just enough that the firm earns a rate of return on its investments equivalent to what it would earn in a competitive market. In practice, public utility regulation can depress profits below the competitive rate of return for a variety of reasons. This reduction in the expected return reduces the incentive to invest. Importantly, the risk that regulation might push returns below the competitive level also creates a disincentive for investment.

*   *   *

2. Utility-Style Regulation of Broadband Is a Solution in Search of a Problem

109.   *The Internet was open before Title II, and many economic factors support openness.* The Internet thrived for decades under the light-touch regulatory regime in place before the *Title II Order*, as ISPs built networks and edge services were born. We find that the sparse evidence of harms discussed in the *Title II Order*—evidence repeated by commenters in this proceeding as the basis for adopting a Title II classification—demonstrates that the incremental benefits of Title II over light-touch regulation are inconsequential, and pale in comparison to the significant costs of public-utility regulation.

*   *   *

3.   Pre-Existing Consumer Protection and Competition Laws Protect the Openness of the Internet

140.   In the unlikely event that ISPs engage in conduct that harms Internet openness, despite the paucity of evidence of such incidents, we find that utility-style regulation is unnecessary to address such conduct. Other legal regimes—particularly antitrust law and the FTC's authority under Section 5 of the FTC Act to prohibit unfair and deceptive practices—provide protection for consumers. These long- established and well-understood antitrust and consumer protection laws are well-suited to addressing any openness concerns, because they apply to the whole of the Internet ecosystem, including edge providers, thereby avoiding tilting the playing field against ISPs and causing economic distortions by regulating only one side of business transactions on the Internet.

* * *

IV.   A LIGHT-TOUCH FRAMEWORK TO RESTORE INTERNET FREEDOM

207.   For decades, the lodestar of the Commission's approach to preserving Internet freedom was a light-touch, market-based approach. This approach debuted at the dawn of the commercial Internet during the Clinton Administration, when an overwhelming bipartisan consensus made it national policy to preserve a digital free market "unfettered by Federal or State regulation." It continued during the Bush Administration, as reflected in the "Four Freedoms" articulated by Chairman Powell in 2004 and was then formally adopted by a unanimous Commission in 2005 as well as in a series of classification decisions reviewed above. And it continued for the first six years of the Obama Administration. We reaffirm and honor this longstanding, bipartisan commitment by adopting a light-touch framework that will preserve Internet freedom for all Americans. . . .

A.   Transparency

209.   "Sunlight," Justice Brandeis famously noted, "is . . . the best of disinfectants." This is the case in our domain. Properly tailored transparency disclosures provide valuable information to the Commission to enable it to meet its statutory obligation to observe the communications marketplace to monitor the introduction of new services and technologies, and to identify and eliminate potential marketplace barriers for the provision of information services. Such disclosures also provide valuable information to other Internet ecosystem participants; transparency substantially reduces the possibility that ISPs will engage in harmful practices, and it incentivizes quick corrective measures by providers if problematic conduct is identified. Appropriate disclosures help consumers make informed choices about their purchase and use of broadband

Internet access services. Moreover, clear disclosures improve consumer confidence in ISPs' practices while providing entrepreneurs and other small businesses the information they may need to innovate and improve products. ...

215.   Today, we retain the transparency rule as established in the *[2010] Open Internet Order,* with some modifications, and eliminate the additional reporting obligations of the *Title II Order.* We find many of those additional reporting obligations significantly increased the burdens imposed on ISPs without providing countervailing benefits to consumers or the Commission. As a result, we recalibrate the requirements under the transparency rule. Specifically, we adopt the following rule:

> *Any person providing broadband Internet access service shall publicly disclose accurate information regarding the network management practices, performance, and commercial terms of its broadband Internet access services sufficient to enable consumers to make informed choices regarding the purchase and use of such services and entrepreneurs and other small businesses to develop, market, and maintain Internet offerings. Such disclosure shall be made via a publicly available, easily accessible website or through transmittal to the Commission.*

216.   In doing so, we note that the record overwhelmingly supports retaining at least some transparency requirements. Crucially, the transparency rule will ensure that consumers have the information necessary to make informed choices about the purchase and use of broadband Internet access service, which promotes a competitive marketplace for those services. Disclosure supports innovation, investment, and competition by ensuring that entrepreneurs and other small businesses have the technical information necessary to create and maintain online content, applications, services, and devices, and to assess the risks and benefits of embarking on new projects.

217.   What is more, disclosure increases the likelihood that ISPs will abide by open Internet principles by reducing the incentives and ability to violate those principles, that the Internet community will identify problematic conduct, and that those affected by such conduct will be in a position to make informed competitive choices or seek available remedies for anticompetitive, unfair, or deceptive practices. Transparency thereby "increases the likelihood that harmful practices will not occur in the first place and that, if they do, they will be quickly remedied." We apply our transparency rule to broadband Internet access service, as well as functional equivalents or any service that is used to evade the transparency requirements we adopt today.

a.   Content of Required Disclosures

218. We require ISPs to prominently disclose network management practices, performance, and commercial terms of their broadband Internet access service, and find substantial record support (including from ISPs) for following the course set out by the Open Internet Order. ...

219. *Network Management Practices.* In the Open Internet Order, the Commission required ISPs to disclose their congestion management, application-specific behavior, device attachment rules, and security practices. We adopt those same requirements and further require ISPs to disclose any blocking, throttling, affiliated prioritization, or paid prioritization in which they engage. Although requiring disclosure of network management practices imposes some burden on ISPs, we find the benefits of enabling the public and the Commission to identify any problematic conduct and suggest fixes substantially outweigh those costs. The record generally supports disclosure of ISP network practices.

220. We specifically require all ISPs to disclose:

- *Blocking.* Any practice (other than reasonable network management elsewhere disclosed) that blocks or otherwise prevents end user access to lawful content, applications, service, or non-harmful devices, including a description of what is blocked.

- *Throttling.* Any practice (other than reasonable network management elsewhere disclosed) that degrades or impairs access to lawful Internet traffic on the basis of content, application, service, user, or use of a non-harmful device, including a description of what is throttled.

- *Affiliated Prioritization.* Any practice that directly or indirectly favors some traffic over other traffic, including through use of techniques such as traffic shaping, prioritization, or resource reservation, to benefit an affiliate, including identification of the affiliate.

- *Paid Prioritization.* Any practice that directly or indirectly favors some traffic over other traffic, including through use of techniques such as traffic shaping, prioritization, or resource reservation, in exchange for consideration, monetary or otherwise.

- *Congestion Management.* Descriptions of congestion management practices, if any. These descriptions should include the types of traffic subject to the practices; the purposes served by the practices; the practices' effects on end users' experience; criteria used in practices, such as indicators of congestion that trigger a practice, including any usage limits triggering the practice, and the typical frequency of congestion; usage limits and the consequences of exceeding them; and references to engineering standards, where appropriate.

- *Application-Specific Behavior.* Whether and why the ISP blocks or rate-controls specific protocols or protocol ports, modifies protocol fields in ways not prescribed by the protocol standard, or otherwise inhibits or favors certain applications or classes of applications.

- *Device Attachment Rules.* Any restrictions on the types of devices and any approval procedures for devices to connect to the network.

- *Security.* Any practices used to ensure end-user security or security of the network, including types of triggering conditions that cause a mechanism to be invoked (but excluding information that could reasonably be used to circumvent network security).

NOTES & QUESTIONS

1. *Freedom isn't free?* The Commission has now dialed back the regulations adopted in the *2015 Order*, citing the cost of regulation and burden on network investment. What does the Commission believe will happen now that the yoke of common carriage status has been removed from the backs of the small ISPs doing the yeoman's work in rural America? What good might come from this regulatory reset?

2. *So ... what now?* Assume that this order stays in place. How would you characterize the official position of the FCC on net neutrality? How about the Commission's position on a free and open internet? From a big picture standpoint, perhaps not much has changed. But what about the specific issues previously identified? Is the Commission now pro blocking or anti blocking? What about throttling? Paid prioritization? Is there anything (other than common carrier status) that the Commission disapproved of in 2015 that it approves of now?

3. *Some light bedtime reading.* In addition to the network management practices identified above, the Commission also ordered ISPs to disclose certain "performance characteristics" and "commercial terms." But the Commission eliminated certain additional disclosures and performance metrics that the *2015 Order* and subsequent guidance had required. Now that the Commission and the internet going public have access to these disclosures, what might they do with them? Do you think they will be used by individual consumers? If not, are there others who would review them on behalf of consumers? On behalf of the public? What actions can the Commission take in response to an unreasonable network management practice disclosed by an ISP?

4. *Is the sky falling? Did it fall already?* It took the FCC more than a year after the notice to put this new rule into effect, but the outcome was predictable as early as November 2016. And the policy debates over net neutrality have raged on since the 2015 order was issued. Chairman Pai and some of the industry representatives had argued in no uncertain terms that consumers would suffer as a result of the regulations imposed in 2015. Yet those regulations were in place for more than two years without clear evidence of any harmful effect. Similarly, in the lead up to the *2018 Order*, net neutrality advocates have warning that consumers will suffer as a result of the removal of the net neutrality rules. A common refrain and meme among industry supporters on the day that the rules went into effect (June 11, 2018) was some version of "did the internet end?"

If you were working in the general counsel's office at a broadband service provider, what would you advise your client about the potential for blocking, throttling, or paid prioritization agreements after June 2018? Do you think that it would be wise for a company to start throttling or blocking? If not, why not? What consequences might there be to such behavior, even if it is not currently prohibited by an FCC regulation? How might this dynamic play out in the years ahead?

5. *Into the breach again.* As will all of the earlier neutrality orders, the Commission's new rule was challenged and the case consolidated in the D.C. Circuit. Except this time, the challengers are not service providers, they are states and consumer protection groups. We will discuss the likely track of those cases in more detail in the next chapter.

2. ACCESS TO THE INTERNET BACKBONE

So far we have discussed the FCC's rules concerning *layer 3: broadband providers*. But what about neutrality at *layer 2: backbone providers*? Might they also exercise control over choke points? To answer this question, we need to get a better handle on what backbone providers actually are and do.

NOTE: NEUTRALITY DEEPER IN THE CLOUD

Analogy with telephony. Recall how wireline telephony works. Steve, an end-user, has a phone at his home in Los Angeles. That home is connected via wire to the local switch provided by Verizon. From that local switch, the call is connected through other lines and switches to reach Jane, who lives far away, in New York. We learned that it is infeasible to have any home be directly wired to every other landline telephone in the world (mesh network). That's why we have switches (star network)—indeed networks of switches connected via transport lines. Finally, we learned the difference between local exchange access provided by Local Exchange Carriers (LECs) and long distance transport across Local Access Transport Areas (LATAs) provided by interexchange carriers (IXCs).

Now, let's compare this phone call to sending an email. Steve, an end-user, has a laptop at his Los Angeles home. That home is connected via his broadband provider, Verizon (using DSL). Somehow his email (cut up into packets using the TCP/IP protocol) must now get across the country to Charter, the broadband provider who serves Jane, in New York. How does it do so? Well, broadband providers function a bit like LECs. Similar to how LECs hand off calls to IXCs, broadband providers have to hand off IP packets to *backbone providers.*

Neutrality at the backbones. Not all backbone providers are equal. You can consider "Tier 1" level backbone providers to be at the top of the hierarchy, with mutual settlement-free "peering" arrangements with each other. Through these peering arrangements between each of the Tier 1 providers, every point on the public internet can be reached. By contrast, smaller "Tier 2" level providers have to pay for "transit" to a Tier 1 level provider to reach all of the internet. What this means is that a small broadband provider might have to pay a Tier 2 backbone provider, who then must pay a Tier 1 backbone provider, for "transit."

Now, at any given tier, is it possible that a backbone provider will start discriminating between packets? Sure, it's possible. But the FCC previously decided that it was premature to apply its Open Internet rules to backbone providers directly. We'll explore the reasons in greater detail soon.

Neutrality at other interconnections. Special challenges have been posed by the rapid increase in video content delivery over the internet. Although emails back and forth from Steve and Jane will be low bandwidth, not especially sensitive to delays, and roughly equivalent in the amount of data moving in both directions, watching movies from an edge provider such as Netflix is radically different. Video requires high-bandwidth, has little tolerance for buffering or jitter, and involves deeply asymmetric flows of data from Netflix to the viewer and not vice versa.[*] Moreover, video edge providers often need to transmit a lot of data at the same time to meet peak demand during prime viewing hours.

---

[*] For instance, Netflix recommends a connection speed of at least 5 Mbps to watch its content in HD, while Google has reported that at least 2.5 Mbps is needed to sustain an average YouTube HD video playback at 720p resolution. Netflix, Internet Connection Speed Recommendations, https://support.netflix.com/en/node/306.

Indeed, video streaming services make up for an estimated 57 percent of peak internet download traffic.[*]

For these kinds of dataflows, do you think Netflix would register with an ordinary broadband provider, which will have to hand off traffic to a Tier 2 backbone provider, which will have to hand off the traffic again to a Tier 1 backbone provider, and so on, until the packets arrive at the viewer's screen? This is highly unlikely because sending data up and down this hierarchy of backbone providers would be inefficient and slow. What, then, are the alternatives?

One alternative for Netflix is to create a more direct connection with the broadband providers that serve its customers, such as Verizon, in Steve's case. But when Netflix tries to make that direct connection—either through its own vertically integrated backbone or through a third-party transit service firm (a company like Level 3 Communications)—can Verizon just decline the interconnection? Or would that violate the Open Internet rules? And even if Verizon says yes to the direct connection, who pays whom and how much?

Another alternative for Netflix could be to make use of new intermediaries, such as content delivery networks (CDNs). CDNs cache (temporarily store) popular content on their own servers near end-users. When CDNs try to interconnect directly with the broadband providers of Netflix subscribers, again, must Verizon allow it? And who pays for this? Should broadband providers pay CDNs like they would pay third-party backbone providers for transit service? Or should CDNs pay the broadband providers under something like a sender-pays principle. Or should there just be a settlement-free peering process? And putting aside intercarrier compensation issues, what if a broadband provider cuts a better deal with one CDN that happens to serve Hulu as compared to another CDN that happens to serve Netflix?

We're only scratching the surface of an evolving internet traffic ecosystem, with rapidly changing interconnection patterns. As with backbone providers, the FCC in 2015 decided that the Open Internet rules would not apply to these thorny interconnection questions and explained:

> 200. The record reflects competing narratives. Some edge and transit providers assert that large broadband Internet access service providers are creating artificial congestion by refusing to upgrade interconnection capacity at their network entrance points for settlement-free peers or CDNs, thus forcing edge providers and CDNs to agree to paid peering arrangements. These parties

---

[*] Sandvine, *The Global Internet Phenomenon Report COVID019 Spotlight* (May 2020), https://www.sandvine.com/hubfs/Sandvine_Redesign_2019/Downloads/2020/Phenomena/COVID%20Internet%20Phenomena%20Report%2020200507.pdf .

suggest that paid arrangements resulting from artificially congested interconnection ports at the broadband Internet access service provider network edge could create the same consumer harms as paid arrangements in the last-mile, and lead to paid prioritization, fast lanes, degradation of consumer connections, and ultimately, stifling of innovation by edge providers. Further, edge providers argue that they are covering the costs of carrying this traffic through the network, bringing it to the gateway of the Internet access service, unlike in the past where both parties covered their own costs to reach the Tier 1 backbones where traffic would then be exchanged on a settlement-free basis. Edge and transit providers argue that the costs of adding interconnection capacity or directly connecting with edge providers are *de minimis.* . . . Thus, these edge and transit providers assert that a focus on only the last-mile portion of the Internet traffic path will fail to adequately constrain the potential for anticompetitive behavior on the part of broadband Internet access service providers that serve as gatekeepers to the edge providers, transit providers, and CDNs seeking to deliver Internet traffic to the broadband providers' end users.

201. In contrast, large broadband Internet access service providers assert that edge providers such as Netflix are imposing a cost on broadband Internet access service providers who must constantly upgrade infrastructure to keep up with the demand. Large broadband Internet access service providers explain that when an edge provider sends extremely large volumes of traffic to a broadband Internet access service provider— e.g., through a CDN or a third-party transit service provider—the broadband provider must invest in additional interconnection capacity (e.g., new routers or ports on existing routers) and middle-mile transport capacity in order to accommodate that traffic, exclusive of "last-mile" costs from the broadband Internet access provider's central offices, head ends, or cell sites to end-user locations. Commenters assert that if the broadband Internet access service provider absorbs these interconnection and transport costs, *all* of the broadband provider's subscribers will see their bills rise. They argue that this is unfair to subscribers who do not use the services, like Netflix, that are driving the need for additional capacity. Broadband Internet access service providers explain that settlement-free peering fundamentally is a barter arrangement in which each side receives something of value. These parties contend that if the other party is only sending traffic, it is not contributing something of value to the broadband Internet access service provider.

Gaping hole? Did the FCC's 2015 Order leave the agency powerless by not applying the rules to backbone providers and other intermediaries, such as CDNs? Probably not. The FCC defined broadband internet access service as a telecommunications service. That service "includes the exchange of Internet traffic by an edge provider or an intermediary with the broadband provider's network."[*] That means that the FCC still had its Title II powers, under 47

U.S.C. §§ 201, 202, and 208, which prohibit unjust and unreasonable practices. That all went away when the FCC repealed the Open Internet rules in 2018, but it the FCC may very well decide to bring those rules back in a future administration.

NOTES & QUESTIONS

1. *Scanning the new ecosystem.* Explain how the rise of video streaming services has altered the economics of the internet service ecosystem. How has it impacted providers in each of the three layers of our models? Do you think these changes increase or decrease the neutrality of the network? Make sure you understand all of the new terminology used to describe this ecosystem.

    a. *Interconnection.* What is interconnection and why is it important to edge providers?

    b. *Peering.* What is peering and why is it important for backbone providers? For Tier 2 providers?

2. *Evaluating interconnection disputes.* Would a paid peering agreement between Netflix and Verizon violate the paid prioritization rule? Who might complain about such an agreement? How do you think the FCC would resolve that complaint under the Open Internet rules? What if Netflix instead paid a CDN, with a direct interconnection to Verizon, to store cached copies of its movies nearby? Would it matter if Verizon charged the CDN for the privilege? What if Verizon decided to purchase an edge content provider? Would there even be a need to interconnect if the content provider were housed on the same network?

3. *A new market segment emerges.* How do you think the FCC's decision not to issue rules to resolve traffic exchange disputes would affect the behaviors of edge providers, backbone providers, and broadband providers? What impact would these new services have on end users? On edge providers? On incumbents? Has the FCC adequately accounted for these changes?

E. TELEPHONY

In the various video communications services we've studied in this chapter, we used a three-layer model that distinguished production, large-scale distribution, and last-leg connection to parse the industry players and identify

---

choke points. Unfortunately, the same model doesn't seem to apply to wireline telephony. For example, we don't use the telephone to hear professionally produced content; accordingly, there's no real production layer. Also, we don't need our phone calls to be delivered to a massive listening audience to achieve economies of scale. To the contrary, telephony is essentially one-to-one or few-to-few communications. That said, we do want our calls to have national and international reach, which requires firms to transport calls over long distances (transport service). And, of course, as end-users, we do need a dial-tone, which means that there must be some last-leg connection between the equipment in our homes to the telephone company's nearby switch (exchange service).

With these differences in mind, and the background already provided in CHAPTER 3: PRICING, consider a different three layer model that distinguishes among: long-distance, local exchange, and customer premises equipment (e.g., telephones).

Layer	Players
1. Long-distance	IXCs
2. Local exchange	LECs
3. Customer hardware	Manufacturers

Notice how a firm in *layer 2: local exchange* could deny access to long-distance providers upstream and to independent manufacturers of telephone equipment downstream. This conceptual framing will help you understand the rise and fall of AT&T, which is of historical importance and also provides useful background for understanding the internet.

1. BREAKUP OF AT&T

The breakup of AT&T is an enormously complex story. As it recedes into the past, now by more than three decades, its importance has substantially diminished. But some familiarity with that history is necessary for any student of American telecommunications. In addition, the breakup of AT&T has influenced the internet and its regulation. We tell the story in four simplified Acts.

Act I: AT&T the Monopoly. As you recall from CHAPTER 3: PRICING, the telephone was patented by Alexander Graham Bell back in 1876. Throughout the 1880s, Bell aggressively commercialized his technology, and his company grew to dominance in telephone manufacturing and local telephone service. But in 1894, Bell's patents expired, and competition ensued. Competitors started manufacturing telephones as well as providing local telephone service, first in cities that Bell did not serve and later in head-to-head competition in cities that

Bell already served. However, Bell refused to interconnect its customers with those of its competitors. Accordingly, in cities with head-to-head competition, businesses sometimes had two telephones—one to talk with Bell customers, the other to talk with non-Bell customers.

At the turn of the 20th century, Bell adopted a business strategy that disparaged this dual service as wasteful. Under the catchy slogan of "One System, One Policy, Universal Service," Bell bought out or created exclusive affiliations with once-competitors and thus reduced head-to-head competition. In addition, Bell acquired new patents that made its long distance service superior to all others. Because the company refused to interconnect nonaffiliated local exchanges to its long distance network, Bell grew dominant once again. Although in 1914 the Bell System entered into an antitrust consent decree (the Kingsbury Commitment, named after a Bell vice president) with the Department of Justice, which required it to interconnect nonaffiliated local exchanges to its long distance lines, this concession did not much increase competition.

This complete dominance by the Bell System persisted until the 1970s. To be more precise, the "Bell System" included AT&T, Western Electric, and Bell Telephone Laboratories. At that time, AT&T provided nearly all long distance service and 80 percent of all local service. (The remainder of local service was provided by small firms, especially in rural and remote areas.) Bell also dominated the equipment market, requiring all subscribers to rent customer premises equipment through its completely owned subsidiary, Western Electric, and purchasing all telecommunications equipment from itself. State and federal regulators blessed this monopoly as natural, inevitable, and manageable through processes such as entry, rate, and quality-of-service regulation.

Act II: The Competition. But starting in the 1960s and progressing through the '70s, competition in the equipment and long distance markets emerged. Competition appeared on two layers.

Layer 3: customer premises equipment. Bell had historically provided all customer premises equipment, through Western Electric, which included the telephones in end-user dwellings. Indeed, ever since 1913, AT&T forbade what it called "foreign attachments" from connection to the Public Switched Telephone Network (PSTN). So, if you wanted to plug anything into the phone network, it had to be provided by Bell.

Not surprisingly, technological innovation started to produce competition in the phone peripheral markets. For instance, in the 1960s, a device called the Carterfone was invented, which allowed the connection of a two-way radio system to a standard telephone. Pursuant to its policy, AT&T disallowed attachment of the device, but in 1968, the FCC held that the Carterfone posed no danger to the network.*

In response to the *Carterfone* decision, AT&T began to allow the attachment of substitute telephones and other peripherals created by other independent manufacturers. However, in the name of network safety, AT&T required something called a Protective Connection Arrangement (PCA), which was a physical device engineered by AT&T that would have to sit between the attachment and the network. By 1976, the FCC had decided that these PCAs were largely unnecessary and could be replaced by a simpler certification and registration system for customer premises equipment, including substitute telephones.

Layer 1: Long distance. Before the 1970s, AT&T essentially provided all long distance services. But piecemeal competition started in the early 1970s. Most important, in 1969, the FCC authorized MCI to provide private line service (something like an interoffice microwave radio transport service) from St. Louis to Chicago.[†] The FCC slowly allowed more general competition in private line services. Over time, firms like MCI pushed the envelope on these incremental permissions in order to provide what amounted to a full-blown alternative to long-distance service from AT&T — all with federal court urging.[‡] By 1980, there was open competition in the long distance service market.

Not surprising, AT&T responded to competition by lowering its prices aggressively. From AT&T's perspective, competitors were "cream skimming," selectively picking only those routes that could be serviced at a very low cost due to high volume and ease of connection. By contrast, AT&T had to provide connections everywhere. In turn, competitors responded by complaining to the FCC that AT&T was engaged in predatory pricing, purposefully lowballing rates on competitive routes while keeping rates in monopoly areas high enough to make up the difference.

Act III: The Lawsuit. In 1974, the Department of Justice filed an antitrust lawsuit against the Bell System, for violating section 2 of the Sherman Act. On behalf of customer premises equipment manufacturers, the DOJ argued that the PCA was not justified. On behalf of long-distance competitors, it argued that AT&T provided discriminatory access to various parts of its network, including the local exchange. In addition, it argued that AT&T was engaging in predatory

---

* *Use of the Carterfone Device in Message Toll Tel. Serv.*, 13 F.C.C.2d 420 (1968).

[†] *Microwave Communications Inc.*, 18 F.C.C.2d 953 (1969).

[‡] MCI Telecommunications Corp. v. FCC, 561 F.2d 365 (D.C. Cir. 1977) (Execunet I); *see also* MCI Telecommunications Corp. v. FCC, 580 F.2d 590 (D.C. Cir.) (Execunet II), *cert. denied*, 439 U.S. 980 (1978).

pricing through cross subsidization. After some initial procedural skirmishes in front of Judge Harold Greene of the DC district court, AT&T agreed to a settlement in the form of a consent decree called the "Modified Final Judgment."

Act IV: The Breakup. In 1982, the Bell System and the DOJ entered into a consent decree, which was approved by the district court, and implemented finally in 1984. A key element of the Modified Final Judgment was divestiture. If control over the local loop allowed power to be abused both upstream and downstream, divestiture would strip away the local loop from the Bell System. Here's a summary from commentator:

> The "bottleneck theory" dictated a separation of the bottleneck monopoly from all competitive services, including transmission services... and equipment supply. Inasmuch as local exchange service was regarded as a "natural" monopoly (at least in terms of current technology, and economic and political circumstance) while long distance service was now regarded as competitive, it followed that the twenty-two Bell Operating Companies (BOCs) should be severed from AT&T long lines and made independent. By the logic of the bottleneck theory it also followed that the BOCs should not be authorized to enter those markets considered competitive lest as independent bottleneck monopolies they revive AT&T's anticompetitive strategies. So it seemed at the time. The BOCs were reorganized as subsidiaries of seven new regional holding companies (RHCs) and authorized to provide service only within defined "local access and transport areas" (LATAs); the LATA is an area larger than the old local exchange area and generally coextensive with a defined metropolitan area (in exceptional instances a LATA embraces the entire state). The RHCs were forbidden to provide interLATA service which was reserved for long distance carriers such as AT&T, MCI, US Sprint, and others. The RHC/BOCs were also prohibited from providing information services (such as videotext, voice storage/retrieval, electronic mail), and from manufacturing CPE, though they were allowed to supply CPE made by others.[*]

As explained in CHAPTER 3: PRICING, a new entity, called a local exchange carrier (LEC) would provide local exchange services, within a new political geography called a LATA. By contrast, any calls crossing LATA boundaries would have to be carried by a new entity called an interexchange carrier (IXC), which would provide transport services. What was formerly known as AT&T was broken up into seven regional Bell Operating Companies, each of which would only serve as a LEC. The long lines department of AT&T would keep the

[*] Glen O. Robinson, *The Titanic Remembered: AT&T and the Changing World of Telecommunications*, 5 YALE J. REG. 517, 531-32 (1988).

brand "AT&T" and provide only interexchange transport services, in competition with firms like MCI and Sprint.

After the MFJ, federal regulators focused on nurturing competition in the interexchange market (long-distance). Later, starting in the 1990s, federal regulators began encouraging competition in the local loop, not only in exchange service (connecting one end-user through a local switch to another end-user within the same LATA) but also exchange access (connecting the end-user to an IXC point-of-presence by bypassing the incumbent local exchange carrier).

From our study in CHAPTER 3: PRICING, we also know that in the early 1990s, the FCC changed its rate regulation methodology from rate-of-return to price caps. Many state regulators followed suit regarding intrastate pricing. As of 1995, based on AT&T's diminished market share, the FCC deemed AT&T a non-dominant carrier and removed all rate regulation of interexchange services.

Finally, the RBOCs labored to wiggle out of the MFJ quarantines, invoking complex legal fights with well-paid experts. In addition, RBOCs aggressively pursued individual "waivers" permitted by the MFJ. Judge Harold Greene maintained continual oversight over the consent decree. Thus, from 1984 (when the consent decree was effected) to 1996 (when the Telecommunications Act was passed), an elaborate administrative-law-like jurisprudence interpreting the MFJ and sometimes permitting waivers developed before Judge Greene.

2. ACCESS TO THE LOCAL EXCHANGE

a. PROMOTING LOCAL EXCHANGE COMPETITION

Among other things, the Telecommunications Act of 1996 repealed the MFJ.* The Act replaced it with a new part, "Special Provisions concerning Bell Operating Companies," to be appended to Title II (Common Carriage) of the 1934 Communications Act. *See* 47 U.S.C. §§ 271–275. These provisions allowed regional BOCs (RBOCs) to provide out-of-region interexchange services immediately. But in order to provide in-region interexchange service (i.e. service in areas where the RBOC was also providing local exchange service), it had to receive FCC approval through a complex two-track process, which prompted enormously complex litigation. The details are not discussed here, but you should know that all the RBOCs satisfied the required processes as of 2003.

---

* *See* § 601(a)(1) of Act (not codified in Title 47).

Why did Congress want to even allow RBOCs into long distance given the lessons of the breakup of AT&T? One reason was to use the possibility of entering long distance as a carrot to entice the RBOCs to interconnect with competitors in the local exchange.

Imagine that you are the incumbent local exchange carrier (ILEC).[*] An ILEC is any local exchange carrier that was in operation when the Telecommunications Act was passed, or its successor. It is the dominant local telephone company in the region, which is the legacy of the original RBOC serving the territory when AT&T was broken up. Suppose that an upstart competitor wants to provide local exchange service in the same geographical area that you serve. As the ILEC, you own the wires connecting 99 percent of the homes in the area; by contrast, your competitor owns only 1 percent. Assume further that your telephone network and your competitor's telephone network do not interconnect. In other words, homes connected to your network cannot call homes connected to your competitor's network, and vice versa.

Now, suppose that a new home is built in your service area. The new homeowner must decide between your telephone company or your competitor's. Which company will that homeowner select? The answer is obvious: Yours. Your company allows calling to 99 percent of the other homes in the area, not just 1 percent. This is an example of the network effect (or network externality) originally introduced when we studied natural monopoly in CHAPTER 2: ENTRY. The more homes that use your network, the more valuable your network becomes. The fewer homes that use your competitor's network, the less valuable that network becomes.

Your competitor quickly recognizes that it cannot compete for any new customers because of this network externality, so it approaches you and asks for interconnection—a simple agreement that each network will transport and terminate calls originating from the other network. Would you voluntarily agree to this proposal? Not if you're rational in the economist's sense of maximizing self-interest. Interconnection would obliterate your network externality advantage. With interconnection, a subscriber to your competitor's network would be able to telephone everyone on your network seamlessly.

Now, put yourself in the shoes of a federal policymaker trying to promote competition in the local exchange, a central goal of the Telecommunications Act of 1996. What essential steps would you have to take?

First, to the extent that state regulators granted a monopoly franchise for the local exchange, thereby legally prohibiting competition, you as a federal regulator

---

[*] *See* 47 U.S.C. § 251(h)(1).

would have to preempt those state laws. This is precisely what Congress did in § 253.

> 47 U.S.C. § 253. Removal of barriers to entry
>
> (a). In general. No State or local statute or regulation, or other State or local legal requirement, may prohibit or have the effect of prohibiting the ability of any entity to provide interstate or intrastate telecommunications service.

Second, to deal with the network externality advantage, you would have to force interconnection. Otherwise, no competitor would be able to compete successfully against the incumbent. Congress did this too, generally for all telecommunications carriers in § 251(a) and more specifically for incumbent local exchange carriers (ILECs) in § 251(c)(2).

> 47 U.S.C. § 251. Interconnection
>
> (a) General duty of telecommunications carriers. Each telecommunications carrier has the duty—
>
>> (1) to interconnect directly or indirectly with the facilities and equipment of other telecommunications carriers; and
>
> (c) Additional obligations of incumbent local exchange carriers. . . . [E]ach incumbent local exchange carrier has the following duties:
>
>> (2) Interconnection. The duty to provide, for the facilities and equipment of any requesting telecommunications carrier, interconnection with the local exchange carrier's network—
>>
>>> (A) for the transmission and routing of telephone exchange service and exchange access;
>>>
>>> (B) at any technically feasible point within the carrier's network;
>>>
>>> (C) that is at least equal in quality to that provided by the local exchange carrier to itself or to any subsidiary, affiliate, or any other party to which the carrier provides interconnection; and
>>>
>>> (D) on rates, terms, and conditions that are just, reasonable, and nondiscriminatory, in accordance with the terms and conditions of the agreement and the requirements of this section and section 252.

With these two fundamental changes, Congress envisioned three different paths by which competitors might enter the market.

Facilities. One, there could be head-to-head facilities-based competition. In other words, a competitive local exchange carrier (CLEC) would build its own physical telephone network in the same area served by the ILEC. With interconnection, the CLEC would have a fighting economic chance.

Resale. Two, Congress envisioned the possibility of resale. In other words, a CLEC would buy local telephone service from the ILEC at wholesale prices and then sell them to its customers at retail prices.

> 47 U.S.C. § 251. Interconnection
>
> (b) Obligations of all local exchange carriers. Each local exchange carrier has the following duties:

> (1) Resale. The duty not to prohibit, and not to impose unreasonable or discriminatory conditions or limitations on, the resale of its telecommunications services.
>
> (c) Additional obligations of incumbent local exchange carriers.
>
> > (4) Resale. The duty—
> >
> > > (A) to offer for resale at wholesale rates any telecommunications service that the carrier provides at retail to subscribers who are not telecommunications carriers; and
> > >
> > > (B) not to prohibit, and not to impose unreasonable or discriminatory conditions or limitations on, the resale of such telecommunications service, except that a State commission may, consistent with regulations prescribed by the Commission under this section, prohibit a reseller that obtains at wholesale rates a telecommunications service that is available at retail only to a category of subscribers from offering such service to a different category of subscribers.

Unbundled Network Elements (UNEs). Three, Congress envisioned the possibility of a CLEC adopting a mix-and-match technique by combining its own network elements with network elements provided by the ILEC on an unbundled basis, at a reasonable cost.[*] In this manner, the CLEC could pick and choose which elements of the local network it could provide itself, through its own facilities (such as switches), and which other network elements (such as the copper wires connecting the household to the local exchange) it could more efficiently purchase from the incumbent.

> 47 U.S.C. § 251. Interconnection
>
> (c) Additional obligations of incumbent local exchange carriers.
>
> > (3) Unbundled access. The duty to provide, to any requesting telecommunications carrier for the provision of a telecommunications service, nondiscriminatory access to network elements on an unbundled basis at any technically feasible point on rates, terms, and conditions that are just, reasonable, and nondiscriminatory in accordance with the terms and conditions of the agreement and the requirements of this section and section 25. An incumbent local exchange carrier shall provide such unbundled network elements in a manner that allows requesting carriers to combine such elements in order to provide such telecommunications service.

How would the details be worked out? Section 252 envisions CLECs entering into private interconnection agreements with ILECs through voluntary negotiation.[†] If the carriers cannot agree,[‡] state PUCs have the power to mediate the negotiations,[§] as well as to conduct compulsory arbitration.[**] Not

---

[*] *See* § 251(c)(3).

[†] *See* § 252(a)(1).

[‡] Congress dangled a carrot in front of the BOCs: if competition was found in their local exchange (according to a complicated competitive checklist), the BOC could provide interexchange service (crossing the LATA barrier) within their region of service. *See* § 271. By the end of 2003, the RBOCS—BellSouth, Qwest, SBC, and Verizon—had received § 271 authority for all the states in which they provided local exchange service.

[§] *See* § 252(a)(2).

surprisingly, these provisions have generated enormous complexity, controversy, and litigation on matters ranging from FCC power to implement such rules to the correct pricing formulas for resale and unbundled network elements.* The details are beyond the scope of this text.

b. INTERCARRIER COMPENSATION

This is as good a place as any to discuss the financial implications of forcing access. Just because the law requires access doesn't mean that it has to be for free. For instance, leased access in cable TV may be required, but the cable operator is permitted to charge some fee.

With this insight, let's return to the telephone network. Recall our careful study of interstate access charges in CHAPTER 3: PRICING. Well, these particular access charges are just a subset of the more general problem of *intercarrier compensation.* Back when AT&T was effectively a monopoly, things were so much simpler. Now, the modern "telephone" environment comprises heterogeneous networks owned by different firms. Therefore, completing a simple phone call often requires networks to hand off traffic to other networks. When those bits of information exchange, are pennies exchanged as well? And if so, who or what sets the prices?

LEC ←→ IXC: Access Charges. We have already learned that LECs provide exchange access to interexchange carriers (IXCs) to originate and terminate calls. For such services, IXCs have to pay LECs *access charges.* As we have already discussed, the FCC has regulated the rates of interstate access charges.

You might assume that the FCC treats incumbent LECs (ILECs) differently from competitive LECs (CLECs): after all, CLECs are newer entrants in the local telephone business, and they lack the historical market dominance of the incumbent. But this misunderstands the nature of the power wielded by all LECs, whether they be incumbents or new entrants. Even CLECs enjoy a terminating access monopoly (what we've called *last-leg connection*) for all its subscribers. Put another way, suppose that a long-distance caller wants to contact someone who subscribes to a CLEC with tiny market share. Regardless of how small the CLEC's market share, the caller's IXC must still pay access charges to that terminating CLEC—there's no way to avoid this party if the call is to be completed. In the 1990s, some CLECs tariffed exorbitant fees for

---

** *See* § 252(b)(1).

* *See, e.g.,* AT&T v. Iowa Util. Bd., 525 U.S. 366 (1998) (vacating certain FCC unbundling requirements but upholding FCC jurisdictional authority to set prices for unbundled network elements).

terminating long distance calls and insisted that IXCs pay the filed rates. The FCC adjudicated some of these rates as unjust and unreasonable under 47 U.S.C. § 201.* To avoid similar ploys, in 2001, the FCC adopted a general rule that capped CLEC interstate access charges to the price charged by ILECs.†

Finally, don't forget the federalism wrinkles. Although the FCC sets interstate access charges, the state PUCs have historically set *intrastate* access charges. Since 1996, the FCC has tried aggressively to push down interstate access charges to their actual cost. By comparison, states generally have been much slower to follow suit. That's why interstate access charges tend to be lower than intrastate access charges.

LEC ←→ LEC: Reciprocal Compensation. Now suppose you live in a downtown loft and are calling a nearby office building. Your wireline telephone provider is Verizon, but the office building is serviced by a competitive LEC (CLEC) called TelePacific. In order to complete the call, somehow the signal must traverse Verizon's network onto TelePacific's. Are there access charges here too?

Although this handoff between LECs seems technologically and conceptually similar to the IXC-LEC handoff inherent in long distance, the access charge regime does not apply. Instead, in the parlance of the 1996 Telecommunications Act, it's called "reciprocal compensation." Section 251(b)(5) specifically requires all LECs to establish "reciprocal compensation arrangements for the transport and termination of telecommunications." The rates that LECs might charge each other is governed by private negotiated agreement between the carriers or set by state PUCs, which must regulate in a manner consistent with the FCC's pricing methodology. In magnitude, these reciprocal compensation payments tend to be lower than either intra- or interstate access charges.

At this point, you can already see the potential arbitrariness of intercarrier compensation. Access charges arose from the break-up of AT&T, and are different depending on whether they are intra- or interstate. By contrast, reciprocal compensation agreements arose from the Telecommunications Act of 1996, as it tried to induce competition in the local loop. Things get even crazier if we add cell phones (CMRS)‡ and the Internet. As the FCC recently put it:

---

* *See, e.g.,* In the Matters of AT&T Corp., Complainant, v. Business Telecom, Inc., MO&O, 16 FCC Rcd. 12312 (2001) (holding that BTI's rate of 7.18 cents per minute violated § 201(b)).

† *See* 47 CFR § 61.26(b).

‡ Roughly speaking, CMRS providers cannot demand "access charges" from IXCs who terminate long distance calls to cell phones. They are, of course, free to negotiate private agreements if they can do so. *See In the Matter of Petitions of Sprint PCS and AT&T Corp., For Declaratory Ruling Regarding CMRS Access*

As a result of this long history, today, there are two primary types of intercarrier compensation regulation: (1) access charges; and (2) reciprocal compensation. However, the rates that apply to traffic under these systems continue to depend on a number of factors including: (1) where the call begins and ends (interstate, intrastate, or "local"); (2) what types of carriers are involved (incumbent LECs, competitive LECs, interexchange carriers (IXCs), wireless); and (3) the type of traffic (wireline voice, wireless voice, ISP-bound, data). The resulting patchwork of rates and regulations is inefficient, wasteful and slowing the evolution to IP [Internet Protocol] networks.*

Gaming the system. This crazy patchwork has led to gaming and arbitrage. Consider for example "access stimulation" where the goal is to drive calls to a terminating LEC that can charge high interstate access charges. Various "free" services such as "free telephone conference" numbers and adult chat lines are free to end-users like you and me because they're making a killing from our IXCs who have to pay per minute access charges. As the FCC explains:

> [A]ccess stimulation [involves] arrangements in which carriers, often competitive carriers, profit from revenue-sharing agreements by operating in an area where the incumbent carrier has a relatively high per-minute interstate access rate. Under our existing rules, the competitive carrier benchmarks its rate to that of the incumbent rural carrier, but the revenue-sharing arrangement results in a volume of traffic that is more consistent with a larger carrier. A competitive carrier could, for example, generate millions of dollars in revenues each month from other carriers simply by entering into a revenue sharing arrangement with a company that operates a chat line.†

Or consider "phantom traffic," which is a call whose true origin is unknown or disguised in order to avoid various intercarrier connection charges. For example, if intrastate access charges (historically set by the state PUC) are higher than interstate access charges (set by the FCC), an IXC will have the incentive to make an intrastate long distance call appear as an interstate long distance call. In FCC filings, various parties have complained that phantom traffic is a substantial problem, with estimates suggesting that anywhere from 3 to 20% of all traffic is "phantom."‡

Charges, 17 FCC Rcd. 13192, ¶¶ 8-9 (2002). If a CMRS terminates "local" traffic from a nearby LEC (or vice versa) in the same Metropolitan Trading Area (MTA), then the reciprocal compensation regime applies. Any such compensation, if there is any, must involve the sending network paying the receiving network for terminating calls. *See* 47 C.F.R. § 20.11(a)(b) (principle of "mutual compensation"). Don't fret over the details since the FCC is in the process of revamping all these rules.

* *In the Matter of Connect America Fund,* NPRM & Further NPRM, 26 FCC Rcd. 4554, 4707 ¶ 502 (2011).

† *Id.* at ¶ 36.

‡ 26 FCC Rcd. at ¶ 703.

Intercarrier Compensation Reform 2011. You should now have a sense of why intercarrier compensation has to be comprehensively overhauled. In the same Order that restructured universal service and created the Connect American Fund, the FCC adopted just such an overhaul and embraced a unified intercarrier compensation regime. The FCC took immediate steps to end access stimulation (by creating clear conditions for what counts as stimulation, e.g., a revenue sharing agreement, or a 3-to-1 interstate terminating-to-originating traffic ratio within a calendar month)[*] and phantom traffic (by modifying call signaling rules to require the calling party number).

Next, it adopted a uniform "bill-and-keep" framework for all telecommunications traffic exchanged with a LEC, including access charges paid by IXCs and reciprocal compensation payments paid by other LECs or CMRS providers. "Bill-and-keep" means that a carrier does not charge another carrier for sending or receiving traffic. Instead, a carrier recovers costs solely by billing its own subscriber. This approach differs substantially from the more traditional calling-party-network-pays model.

To charge subscribers (instead of other carriers), the Commission authorized LECs to initiate a new limited monthly charge, called the Access Recovery Charge (ARC) on wireline telephony service, with various caps to protect consumers. If subscriber revenue isn't enough, the LEC can then look to the Universal Service Fund as well as state universal service funds for further subsidies. Given the enormous change, the FCC has planned the transition in multiple steps, over a six to nine year glide path, depending on the circumstances. In justifying this framework, the FCC repeatedly pointed out that a bill-and-keep framework would ease the transition to more modern phone networks based on Internet Protocol (the language of the Internet), promote competitive discipline (since the subscriber has a direct contractual relationship with the carrier), decrease arbitrage opportunities, and promote administrative simplicity.

The FCC located its legal authority to adopt the bill-and-keep framework in various statutory provisions, including 47 U.S.C. §§ 251(b)(5). Recall that § 251(b)(5) required LECs to establish reciprocal compensation agreements. Although the FCC in the past had interpreted this provision to cover only LEC-to-LEC transfers within the same local area, the FCC has since then interpreted the section more broadly, to include exchanges of all telecommunications traffic, including LEC-IXC handoffs. Importantly, under the FCC's interpretation, this includes not only interstate but also intrastate exchanges of telecommunications.

---

[*] *Id.* at ¶ 667.

This is why the FCC felt comfortable adopting the unified framework of bill-and-keep not only for interstate access charges, which the FCC has always controlled, *but also intrastate access charges, which has historically been set by state PUCs.*[*] This ambitious attempt to reform intercarrier compensation will spawn extensive litigation in the coming years.

To be sure, this has been extremely dense technical material. But the history of the AT&T breakup and its regulatory aftermath still informs our communications law and policy today.

In this chapter, we have examined the fourth concept essential to understanding communications law and policy: *access.* Access is important because, in many industries, a few firms come to control key choke points in the network. In broadcast TV, it could be the station itself or the broadcast network, who can exercise power in vertically related markets. In cable TV, it could be the local cable operator or the MSOs, who can discriminate against unaffiliated programmers. In telephony and internet, it is largely although not entirely the last-leg connection linking end users to the service provider. Sometimes society imposes legal requirements that mandate access. Why and how we do so are the crucial policy questions. And depending on the policies adopted, courts may overturn or uphold the rules under the Administrative Procedure Act or the First   Amendment.

---

[*] Another source of power claimed by the FCC was 47 U.S.C. § 332, which governs mobile telephony. *See id.* at ¶ 779.

CHAPTER 5

CLASSIFICATION

Now that we've studied the four major communication services—broadcast, cable TV, telephony, and internet—it is natural to consider how new and emerging services might fit into the existing regulatory structure. For example, what about video streaming services? On the one hand, like both cable and broadcast, some streaming services provide access to television programs, so maybe they should be treated in the same way. But while broadcast stations and cable operators "own" the last-leg connection to your home, video streaming services do not. Instead, they ride "over the top" on the on the broadband internet service that you already have. Should that matter?

Such questions pose the general problem of "classification," our next key concept. When a seemingly novel communications service comes online, the first question will be whether it should be classified into some existing set of known and well-established categories. If the answer is yes, then we can apply the standard set of existing legal requirements, licensing schemes, and regulations. But what if the answer is no? What should be done then? And, as important, by whom? We start to study these questions by discussing the advent of cable television—a technology that was cutting-edge six decades ago.

A. CABLE TELEVISION

> ### UNITED STATES V. MIDWEST VIDEO CORP.
> ### (MIDWEST VIDEO I)
> 406 U.S. 649 (1972)

Mr. Justice BRENNAN announced the judgment of the Court, and an opinion in which Mr. Justice WHITE, Mr. Justice MARSHALL, and Mr. Justice BLACKMUN join.

Community antenna television (CATV) was developed long after the enactment of the Communications Act of 1934 as an auxiliary to broadcasting through the retransmission by wire of intercepted television signals to viewers otherwise unable to receive them because of distance or local terrain. In *United States v. Southwestern Cable Co.* (1968), where we sustained the jurisdiction of the Federal Communications Commission to regulate the new industry, at least to the extent 'reasonably ancillary to the effective performance of the Commission's various responsibilities for the regulation of television broadcasting,' we observed that the growth of CATV since the establishment of the first commercial system in 1950 has been nothing less than "explosive." The potential of the new industry to augment communication services now available is equally phenomenal.

[T]he Commission on October 24, 1969, adopted a rule providing that 'no CATV system having 3,500 or more subscribers shall carry the signal of any television broadcast station unless the system also operates to a significant extent as a local outlet by cablecasting and has available facilities for local production and presentation of programs other than automated services.' 47 CFR § 74.1111(a).

[T]he United States Court of Appeals for the Eighth Circuit set aside the regulation on the ground that the Commission 'is without authority to impose' it.

I

In 1966 the Commission promulgated regulations that, in general, required CATV systems (1) to carry, upon request and in a specified order of priority within the limits of their channel capacity, the signals of broadcast stations into whose service area they brought competing signals; (2) to avoid, upon request, the duplication on the same day of local station programming; and (3) to refrain from bringing new distant signals into the 100 largest television markets except upon a prior showing that that service would be consistent with the public interest. In assessing the Commission's jurisdiction over CATV against the backdrop of these regulations, we focused in *Southwestern* chiefly on § 2(a) of the Communications Act, 47 U.S.C. § 152(a), which provides in pertinent part: 'The provisions of this [Act] shall apply to all interstate and foreign communication by wire or radio . . ., which originates and/or is received within the United States, and to all persons engaged within the United States in such communication . . . .' In view of the Act's definitions of 'communication by wire' and 'communication by radio,' the interstate character of CATV services, and the evidence of congressional intent that '[t]he Commission was expected to serve as the 'single Government agency' with 'unified jurisdiction' and 'regulatory power over all forms of electrical communication, whether by telephone, telegraph, cable, or radio," we held that § 2(a) amply covers CATV systems and operations.

This conclusion, however, did not end the analysis, for § 2(a) does not in and of itself prescribe any objectives for which the Commission's regulatory power over CATV might properly be exercised. We accordingly went on to evaluate the reasons for which the Commission had asserted jurisdiction and found that 'the Commission has reasonably concluded that regulatory authority over CATV is imperative if it is to perform with appropriate effectiveness certain of its other responsibilities.' In particular, we found that the Commission had reasonably determined that "the unregulated explosive growth of CATV," especially through 'its importation of distant signals into the service areas of local stations' and the resulting division of audiences and revenues, threatened to 'deprive the public of the various benefits of [the] system of local broadcasting stations' that the Commission was charged with developing and overseeing under § 307(b) of the Act. We therefore concluded . . . that the Commission does have jurisdiction over CATV 'reasonably ancillary to the effective performance of (its) various responsibilities for the regulation of television broadcasting . . . [and] may, for these purposes, issue 'such rules and regulations and prescribe such restrictions and conditions, not inconsistent with law,' as 'public convenience, interest, or necessity requires.'" (quoting 47 U.S.C. s 303(r)).

The controversy [in this case] centers on whether the Commission's program-origination rule is 'reasonably ancillary to the effective performance of [its] various responsibilities for the regulation of television broadcasting.' We hold that it is.

[T]he critical question . . . is whether the Commission has reasonably determined that its origination rule will 'further the achievement of long-established regulatory goals in the field of television broadcasting by increasing the number of outlets for community self-expression and augmenting the public's choice of programs and types of services . . ..' We find that it has.

The goals specified are plainly within the Commission's mandate for the regulation of television broadcasting. In *National Broadcasting Co. v. United States* (1943), for example, we sustained Commission regulations governing relations between broadcast stations and network organizations for the purpose of preserving the stations' ability to serve the public interest through their programming.

Equally plainly the broadcasting policies the Commission has specified are served by the program-origination rule under review. To be sure, the cablecasts required may be transmitted without use of the broadcast spectrum. But the regulation is not the less, for that reason, reasonably ancillary to the Commission's jurisdiction over broadcast services. The effect of the regulation, after all, is to assure that in the retransmission of broadcast signals viewers are provided suitably diversified programming the same objective underlying regulations sustained in *National Broadcasting Co. v. United States*, as well as the local-carriage rule reviewed in *Southwestern* and subsequently upheld. In essence the regulation is no different from Commission rules governing the technological quality of CATV broadcast carriage.... In sum, the regulation preserves and enhances the integrity of broadcast signals and therefore is 'reasonably ancillary to the effective performance of the Commission's various responsibilities for the regulation of television broadcasting.'

Respondent, nevertheless, maintains that just as the Commission is powerless to require the provision of television broadcast services where there are no applicants for station licenses... it cannot require CATV operators unwillingly to engage in cablecasting. In our view, the analogy... is misconceived. The Commission is not attempting to compel wire service where there has been no commitment to undertake it. CATV operators to whom the cablecasting rule applies have voluntarily engaged themselves in providing that service, and the Commission seeks only to ensure that it satisfactorily meets community needs within the context of their undertaking.

For these reasons we conclude that the program-origination rule is within the Commission's authority recognized in Southwestern. *Reversed.*

Mr. Chief Justice BURGER, concurring in the result.

Congress could not anticipate the advent of CATV when it enacted the regulatory scheme nearly 40 years ago. Yet that statutory scheme plainly anticipated the need for comprehensive regulation as pervasive as the reach of the instrumentalities of broadcasting.

In the four decades spanning the life of the Communications Act, the courts have consistently construed the Act as granting pervasive jurisdiction to the Commission to meet the expansion and development of broadcasting.

Concededly, the Communications Act did not explicitly contemplate either CATV or the jurisdiction the Commission has now asserted. However, Congress was well aware in the 1930's that broadcasting was a dynamic instrumentality, that its future could not be predicted, that scientific developments would inevitably enlarge the role and scope of broadcasting, and that, in consequence, regulatory schemes must be flexible and virtually open-ended.

Candor requires acknowledgment, for me at least, that the Commission's position strains the outer limits of even the open-ended and pervasive jurisdiction that has evolved by decisions of the Commission and the courts. The almost explosive development of CATV suggests the need of a comprehensive re-examination of the statutory scheme as it relates to this new development, so that the basic policies are considered by Congress and not left entirely to the Commission and the courts.

I am not fully persuaded that the Commission has made the correct decision in this case . . . . But the scope of our review is limited and does not permit me to resolve this issue as perhaps I would were I a member of the Federal Communications Commission. . . . [U]ntil Congress acts, the Commission should be allowed wide latitude and I therefore concur in the result reached by this Court.

Mr. Justice DOUGLAS, with whom Mr. Justice STEWART, Mr. Justice POWELL, and Mr. Justice REHNQUIST concur, dissenting.

The policies reflected in the plurality opinion may be wise ones. But whether CATV systems should be required to originate programs is a decision that we certainly are not competent to make and in my judgment the Commission is not authorized to make. Congress is the agency to make the decision and Congress has not acted.

Compulsory origination of programs is, however, a far cry from the regulation of communications approved in *Southwestern Cable.* Origination requires new investment and new and different equipment, and an entirely different cast of personnel.

'Essentially a CATV system no more than enhances the viewer's capacity to receive the broadcaster's signals; it provides a well-located antenna with an efficient connection to the viewer's television set. It is true that a CATV system plays an 'active' role in making reception possible in a given area, but so do ordinary television sets and antennas. CATV equipment is powerful and sophisticated, but the basic function the equipment serves is little different from that served by the equipment generally furnished by a television viewer. If an individual erected an antenna on a hill, strung a cable to his house, and installed the necessary amplifying equipment, he would not be 'performing' the programs he received on his television set. The result would be no different if several people combined to erect a cooperative antenna for the same purpose. The only difference in the case of CATV is that the antenna system is erected and owned not by its users but by an entrepreneur.

[N]owhere in the [Communications] Act is there the slightest suggestion that a person may be compelled to enter the broadcasting or cablecasting field.

The idea that a carrier or any other person can be drafted against his will to become a broadcaster is completely foreign to the history of the Act, as I read it.

CATV is simply a carrier having no more control over the message content than does a telephone company. A carrier may, of course, seek a broadcaster's license; but there is not the slightest suggestion in the Act or in its history that a carrier can be bludgeoned into becoming a broadcaster while all other broadcasters live under more lenient rules. There is not the slightest clue in the Act that CATV carriers can be compulsorily converted into broadcasters.

The plurality opinion performs the legerdemain by saying that the requirement of CATV origination is 'reasonably ancillary' to the Commission's power to regulate television broadcasting. That requires a brand-new amendment to the broadcasting provisions of the Act, which only the Congress can effect. The Commission is not given carte blanche to initiate broadcasting stations; it cannot force people into the business.

NOTES & QUESTIONS

1. *Capture the zeitgeist.* Make sure you situate yourself in the proper time. This case takes place before Congress created Title VI of the Communications Act in 1984. The Court is talking about cable TV in ways reminiscent of how courts have recently talked about the internet. Here's more from the majority opinion:

> As we said in *Southwestern,* CATV '[promises] for the future to provide a national communications system, in which signals from selected broadcasting centers would be transmitted to metropolitan areas throughout the country.' Moreover, as the Commission has noted, 'the expanding multichannel capacity of cable systems could be utilized to provide a variety of new communications services to homes and businesses within a community,' such as facsimile reproduction of documents, electronic mail delivery, and information retrieval.

2. *Regulations at issue.* There's no point to studying closely the regulations that were being challenged because they have long been replaced. Roughly speaking, they were program-origination requirements. The policy motivation went something like this: Cable TV operators, for example by importing distant signals, were acting more like broadcasters. If broadcast TV stations were obliged to produce local content, then to be fair, shouldn't cable TV have to do the same?

3. *Legal standard.* So, how do we know whether the FCC has power to issue the challenged regulations? The Supreme Court had provided a two-step process in *United States v. Southwestern Cable Co.** Explain what those steps were, and how they were applied to the facts of *Midwest Video I.*

---

* 392 U.S. 157 (1968).

4. *Framing the technology.* The different opinions characterize cable TV in different ways. If Justice Brennan highlights "facsimile reproduction of documents, electronic mail delivery, and information retrieval," Justice Douglas highlights "an antenna on a hill, strung [with] a cable." Do these different understandings of technology matter to the legal question?

5. *Gone too far.* Chief Justice Burger is concerned that this might have gone too far in stretching the idea of what's "reasonably ancillary." Seven years later, the Supreme Court found a case that did go too far.

FCC v. MIDWEST VIDEO CORP.
(MIDWEST VIDEO II)
440 U.S. 689 (1979)

Mr. Justice WHITE delivered the opinion of the Court.

In May 1976, the Federal Communications Commission promulgated rules requiring cable television systems that have 3,500 or more subscribers and carry broadcast signals to develop, at a minimum, a 20-channel capacity by 1986, to make available certain channels for access by third parties, and to furnish equipment and facilities for access purposes. The issue here is whether these rules are "reasonably ancillary to the effective performance of the Commission's various responsibilities for the regulation of television broadcasting," *United States v. Southwestern Cable Co.* (1968), and hence within the Commission's statutory authority.

I

[The challenged] rules prescribe a series of interrelated obligations ensuring public access to cable systems of a designated size and regulate the manner in which access is to be afforded and the charges that may be levied for providing it. Under the rules, cable systems must possess a minimum capacity of 20 channels .... Moreover, to the extent of their available activated channel capacity, cable systems must allocate four separate channels for use by public, educational, local governmental, and leased-access users, with one channel assigned to each.

Under the rules, cable operators are deprived of all discretion regarding who may exploit their access channels and what may be transmitted over such channels. System operators are specifically enjoined from exercising any control over the content of access programming except that they must adopt rules proscribing the transmission on most access channels of lottery information and commercial matter. The regulations also instruct cable operators to issue rules providing for first-come, nondiscriminatory access on public and leased channels.

The Commission's capacity and access rules were challenged on jurisdictional grounds.... The Commission did not find persuasive the contention that "the access requirements are in effect common carrier obligations which are beyond our authority to impose." The explanation was:

> "So long as the rules adopted are reasonably related to achieving objectives for which the Commission has been assigned jurisdiction we do not think they can be held beyond our authority merely by denominating them as somehow 'common carrier' in nature. The proper question, we believe, is not whether they fall in one category or another of regulation—whether they are more akin to obligations imposed on common carriers or obligations imposed on broadcasters to operate in the public interest—but whether the rules adopted promote statutory objectives."

On petition for review, the Eighth Circuit set aside the Commission's [rules. ... W]e now affirm.

II

A

The Commission derives its regulatory authority from the Communications Act of 1934. The Act preceded the advent of cable television and understandably does not expressly provide for the regulation of that medium. But it is clear that Congress meant to confer "broad authority" on the Commission, so as "to maintain, through appropriate administrative control, a grip on the dynamic aspects of radio transmission." *FCC v. Pottsville Broadcasting Co.* (1940). To that end, Congress subjected to regulation "all interstate and foreign communication by wire or radio." 47 U.S.C. § 152(a). In *United States v. Southwestern Cable Co.*, we construed § 2(a) [codified at 47 U.S.C. § 152(a)] as conferring on the Commission a circumscribed range of power to regulate cable television, and we reaffirmed that determination in *United States v. Midwest Video Corp.* (1972) [*Midwest Video I*]. The question now before us is whether the Act, as construed in these two cases, authorizes the capacity and access regulations that are here under challenge.

B

[A]gency jurisdiction to promulgate the access rules would require an extension of this Court's prior decisions. Our holding in *Midwest Video* sustained the Commission's authority to regulate cable television with a purpose affirmatively to promote goals pursued in the regulation of television broadcasting; and the plurality's analysis of the origination requirement stressed the requirement's nexus to such goals. But the origination rule did not abrogate the cable operators' control over the composition of their programming, as do the access rules. It compelled operators only to assume a more positive role in that regard, one comparable to that fulfilled by television broadcasters.

With its access rules, however, the Commission has transferred control of the content of access cable channels from cable operators to members of the public who wish to communicate by the cable medium. Effectively, the Commission has relegated cable systems, pro tanto, to common-carrier status.

Congress, however, did not regard the character of regulatory obligations as irrelevant to the determination of whether they might permissibly be imposed in the context of broadcasting itself. The Commission is directed explicitly by § 3(h) of the Act not to treat persons engaged in broadcasting as common carriers.

The language of § 3(h) is unequivocal; it stipulates that broadcasters shall not be treated as common carriers. . . . We now reaffirm that view of § 3(h): The purpose of the provision and its mandatory wording preclude Commission discretion to compel broadcasters to act as common carriers, even with respect to a portion of their total services. As we demonstrate in the following text, that same constraint applies to the regulation of cable television systems.

Of course, § 3(h) does not explicitly limit the regulation of cable systems. But without reference to the provisions of the Act directly governing broadcasting, the Commission's jurisdiction under § 2(a) would be unbounded. *See United States v. Midwest Video Corp.* (opinion of Brennan, J.). Though afforded wide latitude in its supervision over communication by wire, the Commission was not delegated unrestrained authority. The Court regarded the Commission's regulatory effort at issue in *Southwestern* as consistent with the Act because it had been found necessary to ensure the achievement of the Commission's statutory responsibilities. Specifically, regulation was imperative to prevent interference with the Commission's work in the broadcasting area. And in *Midwest Video* the Commission had endeavored to promote long-established goals of broadcasting regulation.

In determining, then, whether the Commission's assertion of jurisdiction is "reasonably ancillary to the effective performance of [its] various responsibilities for the regulation of television broadcasting," *United States v. Southwestern Cable Co.*, we are unable to ignore Congress' stern disapproval—evidenced in § 3(h)—of negation of the editorial discretion otherwise enjoyed by broadcasters and cable operators alike. Though the lack of congressional guidance has in the past led us to defer—albeit cautiously—to the Commission's judgment regarding the scope of its authority, here there are strong indications that agency flexibility was to be sharply delimited.

The exercise of jurisdiction in *Midwest Video*, it has been said, "strain[ed] the outer limits" of Commission authority. (Burger, C. J., concurring in result). . . . [T]he Commission exceeded those limits in promulgating its access rules. The Commission may not regulate cable systems as common carriers, just as it may not impose such obligations on television broadcasters. We think authority to compel cable operators to provide common carriage of public-originated transmissions must come specifically from Congress. *Affirmed.*

Mr. Justice STEVENS, with whom Mr. Justice BRENNAN and Mr. Justice MARSHALL join, dissenting.

In my opinion the Court's holding in *Midwest Video [I]* . . . requires a like holding with respect to the less burdensome access rules at issue here. The Court's contrary conclusion is based on its reading of § 3(h) of the Act . . . [but] the Court has misread the statute.

Section 3 is the definitional section of the Act. It does not purport to grant or deny the Commission any substantive authority. Section 3(h) makes it clear that every broadcast station is not to be deemed a common carrier, and therefore subject to common-carrier regulation under Title II of the Act, simply because it is engaged in radio broadcasting. But nothing in the words of the statute or its legislative history suggests that § 3(h) places limits on the Commission's exercise of powers otherwise within its statutory authority because lawfully imposed requirement might be termed a "common carrier obligation."

The Commission here has exercised its "flexibility to experiment" . . . . I have no reason to doubt its conclusion that these rules . . . promote the statutory objectives of "increasing the number of outlets for community self-expression and augmenting the public's choice of programs and types of services." And under this Court's holding in *Midwest Video [I]*, this is all that is required . . . .

NOTES & QUESTIONS

1. *Regulations at issue.* Again, there's no need to parse the regulations at issue with precision because they've been replaced. Roughly speaking, these regulations required commercial leased access channels (which we've already studied in CHAPTER 4: ACCESS).

2. *Clarifying the standard?* Does *Midwest Video II* clarify the legal standard provided by *Midwest Video I*, which in turn was interpreting what the Court did in *Southwestern Cable?*

3. *Application.* Why are the access regulations in *Midwest Video II*, but not the program origination requirements in *Midwest Video I*, beyond the ancillary

jurisdiction of the FCC? What role does § 3(h), codified currently at 47 U.S.C. § 153(10), play in this analysis?

> 47 U.S.C. § 153(10). Common carrier.
>
> The term "common carrier" or "carrier" means any person engaged as a common carrier for hire, in interstate or foreign communication by wire or radio or in interstate or foreign radio transmission of energy, except where reference is made to common carriers not subject to this Act; but a person engaged in radio broadcasting shall not, insofar as such person is so engaged, be deemed a common carrier.

4. *Reverse transmutation?* In *Midwest Video I,* Justice Douglas in dissent complained that the origination rules were transmutating a common carrier into a broadcaster (speaker). In *Midwest Video II,* the Court complains about just the reverse—that cable TV is being transmutated back into a common carrier. What's really going on in this alchemy? By the way, should it be any easier to convert in one direction versus the reverse?

5. *Cleaning up the mess.* Anytime there is uncertainty about agency power, Congress can step in and clarify. And in 1984 and 1992, Congress did just that, giving us Title VI of the Communications Act. Now, we don't have to struggle over ancillary jurisdiction doctrine; instead, we get to struggle over the meaning of the words in Title VI.

6. *Ancillary jurisdiction.* These cable TV cases serve as the foundation for the ancillary jurisdiction doctrine, which becomes important whenever a new communications technology comes online and doesn't seem to fit within any specific "family" of services in the Communications Act. Right now, that's the internet.

B. DIAL-UP INTERNET

The internet started to become a communications service to reckon with in the mid-1990s. But *who* should regulate the internet and *how* presented difficult questions. Indeed, many commentators questioned whether the internet could be regulated at all, by any government or agency. In retrospect, these claims might seem quaint or naïve given that internet has since matured and become domesticated. Still, it's fascinating to see how slowly and reluctantly the FCC moved in its initial attempts to grapple with the internet's development. We start the story, even before the internet, when technological advancements in telephony raised classification questions that foreshadowed internet puzzles to come.

1. TELECOMMUNICATIONS SERVICE OR INFORMATION SERVICE

Way back in 1966, far before the internet, the FCC initiated an inquiry to examine the marriage between computing and communications. On the one hand, the computing industry was beginning to grow, largely unregulated. On the other hand, common carriage (provided by AT&T) was highly regulated. As common carriers began to offer computing services, regulators began to have the standard fears associated with a regulated monopoly entering adjacent unregulated markets: cross-subsidization and discrimination.

In an inquiry known as *Computer I*, the FCC decided that the answer would be maximum structural separation. If common carriers wanted to enter the computing business, they would have to do so using a separate affiliate. This required federal regulators to distinguish between the traditional common carriage business and the new computing business, for which a separate affiliate would be necessary. The FCC devised three terms: data processing, communications, and hybrid services. Data processing would *not* be regulated by the FCC; communications would be regulated; hybrid services would be decided on a case-by-case basis.[*]

In *Computer II*, the FCC addressed the increasing difficulties of distinguishing between simple communications and data processing in a time of technological flux and convergence.[†] It also altered the vocabulary. Roughly speaking, standard common carriage or transport was called "basic services." Everything else, such as database access and voicemail, was renamed "enhanced services."[‡] What is the difference between the two? Here's a useful analogy:

> A useful way to think about the distinction between basic and enhanced services is an analogy to the nation's oil pipelines, storage facilities, and the refineries that rely on pipelines to transport oil. Oil pipelines are bare transport mechanisms that carry oil from, for example, ship to storage facility, often across great distances. The pipelines take oil in at one end, and transport that oil to the destination of the customer's choosing. The pipeline is a "dumb" transmission mechanism that does not interact with its cargo.
>
> In the case of a data service, like a dial-up Internet access service, for example, there are two components involved. First, the consumer purchases local telephone service, the equivalent of the empty pipeline, from the phone

---

[*] *See Regulatory and Policy Problems Presented by the Interdependence of Computer and Communications Services and Facilities,* Final Decision and Order, 28 F.C.C.2d 267 (1971).

[†] Recall from CHAPTER 1: POWER that the microprocessor was invented in 1971.

[‡] *See In re of Section 64.702 of the Commission's Rules and Regulations* (Second Computer Inquiry), 77 F.C.C.2d 384 (1980).

company. This purchase entitles the customer to put its "oil," i.e., voice or data, into the pipeline, and the telephone company will transport it to the user's chosen destination. Second, the consumer purchases Internet access from an Internet Service Provider (ISP). The ISP takes data placed in the pipeline by the end user and performs computer processing on that data. Using the oil analogy, imagine a pipeline that has a ship at one end (the end user), a storage facility at the other end (the Internet), and a refinery in the middle. Oil is transported via the pipeline from ship to refinery, where the pipeline offloads the oil; the refinery transforms the oil into gasoline; and the pipeline then carries the processed oil to the storage facility. The pipeline still performs no more of a function than the transmission of its cargo: it is not responsible for the changes the cargo has undergone.

The ISP is the equivalent of the refinery. Thus, when the user dials in to the ISP and establishes a modem connection, the telephone line is the transmission path. The end user transmits data over the telephone line to the ISP, the ISP modifies that data, and the telephone line carries that data to its destination. When the data reaches its destination, the telephone line "unloads" it, and prepares to carry back to the end user whatever data has been requested. In the case of Internet access, the end user utilizes two different and distinct services. One is the transmission pathway, a telecommunications service that the end user purchases from the telephone company. The second is the Internet access service, which is an enhanced service provided by an ISP. The telephone service is the basic service; the Internet access service, offered over the telephone service, is the "basic service plus" protocol processing and other computer offerings, so it is an enhanced service. The ISP provides the end user the capability of sending, retrieving, and storing data, as well as transforming data to different protocols to allow the end user to interact with other computer networks that speak other "languages." These functions are separate from the transmission pathway over which that data travels. The pathway is a regulated telecommunications service; the enhanced service offered over it is not.[*]

As before, enhanced services would not be regulated. In addition, the structural separation requirement was lifted for non-AT&T firms.

In the break-up of AT&T, the Modified Final Judgment (MFJ) introduced yet another pair of terms: *telecommunications service* and *information service*. The local telephone companies were originally prohibited from providing any service besides basic telecommunications service, but that prohibition was eventually partially lifted.[†] As used in the MFJ, the term "information service" strongly resembled the FCC's term "enhanced service." Finally, Congress in

---

[*] Jason Oxman, *The FCC and the Unregulation of the Internet*, OPP Working Paper No. 31, FCC Office of Policy & Planning 12–13 (July 1999).

[†] *See* United States v. Western Electric, 993 F.2d 1572 (D.C. Cir. 1993).

the 1996 Telecommunications Act codified the terms *telecommunications service* and *information service.* The FCC interpreted "telecommunications service" to be functionally identical to the prior FCC term "basic service." Similarly, "information service" was interpreted to be fully inclusive of and slightly broader than the term "enhanced service."*

In sum, as telephone companies began to offer services that merged computing and communications, the FCC created and Congress subsequently codified a set of mutually exclusive categories called "telecommunications service" and "information service." The former would be regulated like telephony, the latter would be barely regulated at all.

2. DIAL-UP INTERNET AS INFORMATION SERVICE

Starting in the mid-1990s, people got exposed to the Internet for the first time through dial-up access. Using a home computer, an end-user used her modem, which plugged into a standard telephone jack, to dial a phone number for her Internet Service Provider (ISP). After a bunch of screeching sounds, which represented the modem establishing a data connection with the ISP, the end user had access to an online service like America Online or CompuServ, or the entire unrestricted internet.

Not surprisingly, as this new communication service caught on in popularity, incumbent industries started to complain. To see why, compare an e-mail sent from Los Angeles to New York over dial-up internet with a telephone call between the same locations. For the e-mail, the sender's local exchange carrier (LEC) carries the data from the sender's home to the ISP point-of-presence (POP), after which point the message is carried through the internet. For the phone call, the sender's LEC carries the voice from the sender's home to the IXC POP, at which point the message is carried through the IXC's long distance network and ultimately dropped off at the receiver's LEC. In CHAPTER 3: PRICING, we learned that in the case of the telephone call, the IXC must pay the originating and terminating LECs access charges for their help in making the long distance call possible. Should ISPs have to pay similar access charges?

LECs thought they should, and so argued in front of the FCC. Why? Well, LECs viewed themselves as potential competitors to ISPs. After all, if you can't send an email, you might have to make a phone call. They also complained that

---

* *See Implementation of the Non-Accounting Safeguards of Sections 271 and 272 of the Communications Act of 1934,* 1st R&O and FNPRM, 11 FCC Rcd. 21905, 21955-56, ¶ 102 (1996).

internet users would stay on-line for hours at a time, creating network congestion on the local exchange. Recall that state public utilities commissions (PUCs) generally require flat rates for local residential service. Thus, if you are calling a nearby ISP point of presence (POP), within your local calling area, it didn't matter in terms of price whether you connected for one minute or one hour. In sum, LECs claimed that the combination of relieving ISPs from access charges coupled with flat-rate billing underpriced internet access. Accordingly, there was over-consumption of internet access.

The FCC was not persuaded.[*] It held that ISPs were not acting like long distance companies (IXCs). Instead, they were acting as "enhanced service providers," which were exempted from interstate access charges. Consistent with this characterization, the FCC excused ISPs from certain taxes to support universal service programs that telecommunications carriers, including long distance companies, had to pay.[†] In sum, with the advent of dial-up internet access, the FCC was pressed to make a classification choice. It could have treated ISPs like IXCs. But the FCC chose not to. In its view, the internet was not a telecommunications service provided by a new kind of long distance company. Instead, it was an information service that could only be lightly regulated.

---

[*] *See* Access Charge Reform, 1st R&O, 12 FCC Rcd. 15982 (1997).

[†] *See In re Federal-State Joint Board on Universal Service*, Report to Congress, 13 FCC Rcd. 11501, ¶ 66 (1998).

C. BROADBAND INTERNET

1. TECHNOLOGY AND CONTEXT

Dial-up telephone connections to the internet are cumbersome and slow compared to broadband internet. Given the huge advantages of broadband, there was a race to deliver fast, always-on internet access at home. In the United States, cable operators were first to market, with what was called "cable modem service." Local telephone carriers came next with their "digital subscriber lines" (DSL). Even satellite companies entered the business and began to target underserved areas. We start with a technological introduction.

ADVANCED TELECOMMUNICATIONS CAPABILITY
3rd Report, 17 FCC Rcd. 2844 (2002)

Introduction

1. Cable modem service provides high-speed access to the Internet . . . over cable system facilities. . . .

10. [C]able modem technologies rely on the same basic network architecture used for many years to provide multichannel video service, but with upgrades and enhancements to support a variety of advanced services.

13. The typical upgrade employs a hybrid fiber-coaxial (HFC) architecture. Most HFC systems utilize fiber between the cable operators' offices (the headend) and the neighborhood "nodes." Between the nodes and the individual end-user homes, signals travel over traditional coaxial cable infrastructure. Part of the cable system, typically a 6 MHz channel, is dedicated to cable modem service. At each subscriber's home or office, a splitter and a high-speed cable modem are installed. The splitter separates signals and sends them to different cables going to the subscriber's television and computer. The cable that goes to the computer connects with a high-speed cable modem and an Ethernet card that are attached to the computer. This modem and card enable the cable system to communicate with the subscriber's computer, and vice versa.

18. Cable networks transport data signals over infrastructure that serves numerous users simultaneously, i.e., a "shared network", rather than providing a dedicated link or "local loop" between the provider and each home, as does DSL technology.

23. [H]igh-speed cable modem service is primarily available to the residential market, rather than the business market. Cable networks were originally deployed to provide video programming and other programming services to residences throughout the United States. While some residences are located in

areas where there are large and small businesses alike, most businesses were originally, and still are, not wired for cable service.

2. DSL and other LEC-Provided Services

24. Since 1996, local telephone carriers have offered consumers high-speed data service through their digital subscriber line (DSL) service offerings. With the addition of certain electronics to the telephone line, carriers can transform the copper loop that already provides voice service into a conduit for high-speed data traffic. . . . With most DSL technologies today, a high-speed signal is sent from the end-user's terminal through the last 100 feet and the last mile (sometimes a few miles) consisting of the copper loop until it reaches a Digital Subscriber Line Access Multiplexer (DSLAM), usually located in the carrier's central office. At the DSLAM, the end-user's signal is combined with the signals of many other customers and forwarded though a switch to middle mile facilities.

25. The most common form of DSL used by residential customers is asymmetric DSL, or ADSL. As its name suggests, ADSL provides speeds in one direction (usually downstream) that are greater than the speeds in the other direction. ADSL permits the customer to have both conventional voice and high-speed data carried on the same line simultaneously because it segregates the high frequency data traffic from the voice traffic. This segregation allows customers to have an "always on" connection for the data traffic and an open path for telephone calls over a single line. Thus a single line can be used for both a telephone conversation and for Internet access at the same time.

27. DSL service is subject to certain limitations that currently prevent it from being deployed as a last mile facility to all potential end-users. First, it is distance sensitive. Currently, an ADSL customer must be within approximately 15,000 feet of the Digital Subscriber Line Access Multiplexer (DSLAM), usually located in the carrier's central office . . . . Eighty percent of the subscriber loop plant falls within these distance limitations, and thus is capable of supporting DSL service, but this factor remains an impediment to DSL deployment in more sparsely populated and remote locations.

28. The second factor limiting the deployment of DSL to some potential customers is the presence on their loops of load coils and bridged taps, devices that were used to enhance the quality of voice traffic over the copper. While they improve the quality of voice transmission, these devices prevent the deployment of DSL service over a line on which they are installed. Thus, in contrast to an upgraded cable network, which can offer upgraded service to all homes it passes, LECs must "condition" each end-user's line by removing the load coils and bridged taps while increasing the strength of the signal to maintain the quality of the line's voice traffic.

5. Satellite Service

45. Satellite service provides another option for last mile facilities with its own set of unique characteristics. Two companies, StarBand and Hughes Network Systems, which provides a high-speed service with the brand name DIRECTWAY, now provides residential satellite-based last mile facilities in the United States. Both can provide a service in which both the downstream and upstream signal is provided by satellite.... [T]he downstream signals for current residential satellite offerings are capable of providing speeds in excess of 200 kbps, but the upstream signals are generally much slower and therefore do not meet the definition of advanced telecommunications capability.

Satellite-based last mile facilities have some limitations. Consumers must have a clear line of sight to the south in order to access satellite-based services. Areas subject to extreme rain or snow may have difficulty receiving satellite signals in those conditions.

NOTES & QUESTIONS

1. *Technical review.* The technical appendix reveals the importance of understanding basic communications technologies. By drawing on the technological background in this section and in CHAPTER 1: POWER, you should be able to understand the analysis of comparative bandwidths, wireless versus wireline channels, line of sight limitations, etc. Can you explain the key technological differences between cable and DSL broadband services?

2. *By the way, what did we just read?* It's a Report by the FCC that was mandated by § 706 of the Telecommunications Act of 1996 (later codified in 47 U.S.C. § 1302). The 1996 Act was drafted before most people had any idea about the internet. Not surprisingly, it does not have any specific sections that address the internet. That said, there was some language that encouraged the FCC and state agencies to promote investment in infrastructure for "advanced telecommunications capability." Specifically, Congress instructed:

> 47 U.S.C. § 1302. Advanced telecommunications incentives.
>
> (a) In general
>
> The Commission and each State commission with regulatory jurisdiction over telecommunications services shall encourage the deployment on a reasonable and timely basis of advanced telecommunications capability to all Americans (including, in particular, elementary and secondary schools and classrooms) by utilizing, in a manner consistent with the public interest, convenience, and necessity, price cap regulation, regulatory forbearance, measures that promote competition in the local telecommunications market, or other regulating methods that remove barriers to infrastructure investment.

The law offered a functional, rather than technological definition of these new, advanced services:

(d) Definition

   (1) Advanced telecommunications capability

The term "advanced telecommunications capability" is defined, without regard to any transmission media or technology, as high-speed, switched, broadband telecommunications capability that enables users to originate and receive high-quality voice, data, graphics, and video telecommunications using any technology.

Congress also ordered the FCC to "initiate a notice of inquiry" and provide annual reports on the "availability of advanced telecommunications capability to all Americans" and to determine whether those services were being "deployed to all Americans in a reasonable and timely fashion." The FCC completed the first inquiry in 1998 and issued a report in 1999, in which it identified the key classification challenge of two competing broadband offerings: "cable modem service" and "digital subscriber line (DSL) service." The agency's review of those services in its third report was what was excerpted above. What's a notice of inquiry?

Notice of Inquiry (NOI): The Commission releases an NOI for the purpose of gathering information about a broad subject or as a means of generating ideas on a specific issue. NOIs are initiated either by the Commission or an outside request.

3. *Defining broadband.* In 2010 the FCC reported that only 5% of the U.S. population lacked access to broadband. But by 2015, that number had *increased* significantly, and the agency found that 17% of Americans (55 million people), and over half of all rural Americans, lacked access to broadband. Did we technologically regress? No. Instead, the FCC had updated its "benchmark" definition of broadband:

Congress directed us to evaluate annually "whether advanced telecommunications capability is being deployed to all Americans in a reasonable and timely fashion." For a service to be considered advanced, it must enable Americans "to originate and receive high-quality voice, data, graphics, and video telecommunications." We can no longer conclude that broadband at speeds of 4 megabits per second (Mbps) download and 1 Mbps upload (4 Mbps/1 Mbps)—a benchmark established in 2010 and relied on in the last three Reports—supports the "advanced" functions Congress identified. Trends in deployment and adoption, the speeds that providers are offering today, and the speeds required to use high-quality video, data, voice, and other broadband applications all point at a new benchmark. . . . [W]e [now] find that, having "advanced telecommunications capability" requires access to actual download speeds of at least 25 Mbps and actual upload speeds of at least 3 Mbps (25 Mbps/3 Mbps).

Do you think the FCC's decision to increase the benchmark was a reasonable one? What factors would you weigh when considering such a change? What do you think Congress intended when it defined the term in the 1996 Act?

4. *Moving the chains.* Recall from our discussion in Chapter 3: Pricing that the FCC has again revisited its definition of broadband in the most recent report. The Commission continued to recognize the importance of mobile broadband deployment, but modified its definition of fixed terrestrial to included satellite internet services (which had previously been excluded from the measurement due to their high latency). Using this new definition, the FCC concluded that approximately 25 million Americans still lack access to both fixed broadband at 25 Mbps/3 Mbps and mobile LTE at speeds of 5 Mbps/1 Mbps (approx. 8%). In rural areas 68.6% of the population has access to both, and for tribal lands that drops to 63.9%.

Do you agree with the FCC that satellite internet access should be considered advanced capability or broadband? How often do you think the Commission will need to update this definition going forward? What will be the impact of the law that Congress recently passed demanding more accurate and granular broadband deployment maps?[*] Who will ultimately get to decide?

2. Broadband Internet as Information Service

If dial-up internet is an information service, is there any reason to think that broadband internet should be treated differently? The mere facts that broadband is always on and that it is faster don't seem to be a reason to change its classifications. But there is one important difference between dial-up and broadband: vertical integration.

Dial-up internet access always involved two parties—the Internet Service Provider (e.g., America Online) and the telephone company (e.g., Pacific Bell), since you had to "call" AOL with your screeching modem. From the consumer's perspective, the phone company had no more to do with that internet access than the phone company had to do with your call to Grandma or your pizza order to Domino's. The phone company provided the service to transport your voice to whomever you chose to call.

But when cable modem service rolled out, cable operators pursued a very different business model: vertically integrated the transport with the internet

---

[*] *See* Broadband Deployment Accuracy and Technological Availability (DATA) Act, Pub. L. No. 116-130, 134 Stat. 228 (2020) (codified at 47 U.S.C. §§ 641-646).

access services. In other words, instead of two players, Pacific Bell + AOL, you now just needed one, Time Warner, who provided you both the fat pipe and internet access over that pipe.

Not surprisingly, this terrified ISPs that did not own any fat pipes. How could they possibly compete against firms like Time Warner when they couldn't provide broadband speeds? So, these ISPs demanded "open access" to the cable operator's pipe. Should government force such access? More important, could government do so? This question turned on the classification of broadband internet service.

NOTE: CABLE MODEM SERVICE AS HYBRID SERVICE?

In 1999, AT&T sought to merge with TCI, a large cable company, which controlled a cable modem service called @Home. Because the merger would require transfer of common carriage and spectrum licenses, AT&T needed approval from the FCC under 47 U.S.C. § 214(a) (common carriage) and § 310(d) (spectrum).[*] Opponents of the merger sought to impose open access conditions on AT&T such that other ISPs could provide internet access services over the TCI cable infrastructure (the fat pipes). After all, similar open access requirements had been placed on another cable company, Time Warner, when it merged with AOL (an internet service provider). The FCC, however, declined to do so.

AT&T v. Portland (2000):[†] *Switching regulators.* In order to offer television service, cable operators have to obtain a franchise license from their state regulatory agency. Accordingly, when AT&T wanted to merge with TCI, it also had to request franchise transfers from approximately 940 different local franchising authorities.[‡] Having failed to persuade the FCC, "open access" proponents switched levels (from federal to state) and lobbied these local authorities and persuaded, for example, the City of Portland, Oregon to condition the franchise transfer on open access. AT&T sued the city and lost in the federal district court.

On appeal, the Ninth Circuit had to address a classification question— whether cable modem service was a "cable service" for which Portland could

---

[*] *See Section 214 Authorizations From TCI to AT&T,* MO&O, 14 FCC Rcd. 3160 (1999)

[†] AT&T Corp. v. City of Portland, 216 F.3d 871 (9th Cir. 2000)

[‡] *See* 47 U.S.C. § 537 (requiring approval of local franchising authority for sale or transfer of franchise if such approval is written into the franchise contract).

legally insist on a franchise.* The Communications Act defines "cable service" as "(A) the one-way transmission to subscribers of (i) video programming, or (ii) other programming service, and (B) subscriber interaction, if any, which is required for the selection or use of such video programming or other programming service."† According to the court, this definition covered cable TV as conventionally understood but did not cover broadband internet access.

Portland, however, had a back-up argument. Even if cable modem service is not "cable service," certainly the rest of TCI's business was cable service (standard cable television). Thus, Portland could simply condition the transfer of the cable television business (a "cable service") on accepting open access conditions on the broadband internet side of the business (not a "cable service").

But this back-up argument potentially ran into a federal preemption problem. Congress had made clear that if a cable operator wanted to start offering *telecommunications services*, it would not need the permission of a local franchising authority. *See* 47 U.S.C. § 541(b)(3). The purpose of this rule was to increase local telephone competition by encouraging cable operators to compete against the incumbent local exchange carriers (ILECs). Therefore, if cable modem service were classified as a telecommunications service, then Portland could not obstruct AT&T's launching this service.

> 47 U.S.C. § 541. General franchise requirements
>
> (b) No cable service without franchise; exception under prior law
>
>> (3)(B) A franchising authority may not impose any requirement under this title that has the purpose or effect of prohibiting, limiting, restricting, or conditioning the provision of a telecommunications service by a cable operator or an affiliate thereof.

By contrast, if cable modem service were classified as an *information service*, then § 541(b)(3) would not apply, and Portland could attach the "open access" strings to the transfer of the cable television business.

So, which one was it—telecommunications service or information service? In the end, the Ninth Circuit concluded that cable modem service was a *hybrid fusion*, both partly telecommunications service (the broadband pipe) *and* partly information service (conventional ISP services). This meant the preemption provision § 541(b)(3)(B) *did* apply. Accordingly, the Portland franchising authority was preempted and had to get out of the way. This was a pyrrhic victory for AT&T, which had not argued in favor of this result; in fact, no party argued in this vein. By being classified a telecommunications service, even if the

---

* *See* 47 U.S.C. § 541(b)(1) ("[A] cable operator may not provide cable service without a franchise.")
† 47 U.S.C. § 522(6).

cable franchising authority was pushed out of the picture, both local and federal regulations governing common carriers would presumptively apply.

Now, the FCC was in a quandary. It had intentionally avoided classifying broadband internet in any definitive manner. Indeed, although the FCC filed an amicus brief in the *AT&T v. Portland* case, it did not take a firm stance on the correct regulatory classification. But the U.S. Court of Appeals for the Ninth Circuit had just gone ahead and classified cable modem service as hybrid, as a little bit of both telecommunications service and information service. Two years later, in March 2002, the FCC tried to clean up the mess by issuing a declaratory ruling. What's a declaratory ruling?

> 47 C.F.R. § 1.2. Declaratory Rulings.
>
> The Commission may, in accordance with section 5(d) of the Administrative Procedure Act, on motion or on its own motion issue a declaratory ruling terminating a controversy or removing uncertainty.

HIGH-SPEED ACCESS TO THE INTERNET
OVER CABLE
Declaratory Ruling & NPRM, 17 FCC Rcd. 4798 (2002)

III. DECLARATORY RULING: STATUTORY CLASSIFICATION OF CABLE MODEM SERVICE

B. "Information Service" or "Telecommunications Service" Classification

34. Because the classification of cable modem service turns on statutory interpretation, we begin with a review of relevant statutory definitions. The 1996 Act defines "telecommunications service" as "the offering of telecommunications for a fee directly to the public, or to such classes of users as to be effectively available directly to the public, regardless of the facilities used."[137] "Telecommunications" is defined in turn as "the transmission, between or among points specified by the user, of information of the user's choosing, without change in the form or content of the information as sent and received."[138] The Act defines "information service" as "the offering of a capability for generating, acquiring, storing, transforming, processing, retrieving, utilizing, or making available information via telecommunications, and includes electronic publishing, but does not include any use of any such capability for the

---

[137] Communications Act § 3(46), 47 U.S.C. § 153(46).
[138] Communications Act § 3(43), 47 U.S.C. § 153(43).

management, control, or operation of a telecommunications system or the management of a telecommunications service."[139]

35. None of the foregoing statutory definitions rests on the particular types of facilities used. Rather, each rests on the function that is made available.

36. In the *Universal Service Report*, the Commission found that Internet access service is appropriately classified as an information service, because the provider offers a single, integrated service, Internet access, to the subscriber. The service combines computer processing, information provision, and computer interactivity with data transport, enabling end users to run a variety of applications.

38. Consistent with the analysis in the *Universal Service Report*, we conclude that the classification of cable modem service turns on the nature of the functions that the end user is offered. We find that cable modem service is an offering of Internet access service, which combines the transmission of data with computer processing, information provision, and computer interactivity, enabling end users to run a variety of applications. . . . As currently provisioned, cable modem service is a single, integrated service that enables the subscriber to utilize Internet access service through a cable provider's facilities and to realize the benefits of a comprehensive service offering.

39. Cable modem service is not itself and does not include an offering of telecommunications service to subscribers. We disagree with commenters that urge us to find a telecommunications service inherent in the provision of cable modem service. Consistent with the statutory definition of information service, cable modem service provides the capabilities described above "via telecommunications."[155] That telecommunications component is not, however, separable from the data-processing capabilities of the service. As provided to the end user the telecommunications is part and parcel of cable modem service and is integral to its other capabilities.

40. As stated above, the Act distinguishes "telecommunications" from "telecommunications service." The Commission has previously recognized that "[a]ll information services require the use of telecommunications to connect customers to the computers or other processors that are capable of generating, storing, or manipulating information." Although the transmission of information to and from these computers may constitute "telecommunications," that transmission is not necessarily a separate "telecommunications service."

---

[139] Communications Act § 3(20), 47 U.S.C. § 153(20).

[155] *See* 47 U.S.C. § 153(20).

42. *Computer II Requirements.* EarthLink argues that it is irrelevant whether cable operators in fact offer transmission service on a stand-alone basis. Instead, EarthLink contends that cable modem service providers must create a stand-alone transmission service and offer it to ISPs and other information service providers on a tariffed basis pursuant to the Commission's *Computer II* requirements. EarthLink maintains *Computer II* applies to cable modem service because cable operators offer it on an indiscriminate and standardized basis to the public and because they do so using their own facilities.

43. These decisions are inapposite.... The Commission has never before applied *Computer II* to information services provided over cable facilities. Indeed, for more than twenty years, *Computer II* obligations have been applied exclusively to traditional wireline services and facilities. We decline to extend *Computer II* here.

44. EarthLink further contends that the fact that some cable operators offer local exchange service as competitive LECs in some markets "using the same cable facilities that are at issue in this proceeding" establishes that these cable operators are common carriers and therefore must abide by the requirements of *Computer II* with respect to their offerings of cable modem service.... We disagree.... As noted above, the Commission has applied these obligations only to traditional wireline services and facilities, and has never applied them to information services provided over cable facilities.

45. Even if *Computer II* were to apply, however, we waive on our own motion the requirements of *Computer II* in situations where the cable operator additionally offers local exchange service.

46. If we were to require cable operators to unbundle cable modem service merely because they also provide cable telephony service, we would in essence create an open access regime for cable Internet service applicable only to some operators.

47. Also, we believe that many, if not most, such cable operators would stop offering telephony if such an offering triggered a multiple ISP access obligation for the cable modem service. [This] would undermine the long-delayed hope of creating facilities based competition in the telephony marketplace and thereby seriously undermine the goal of the 1996 Act to open all telecommunications markets to competition. It would also disserve the goal of Section 706 that we "encourage the deployment on a reasonable and timely basis of advanced telecommunications capability to all Americans ...."

52. *Cable Operators' Relationships With ISPs - Potential Private Carriage Offering.* AOL Time Warner recently has begun offering multiple brands of cable modem service to subscribers on all of its major systems pursuant to the

FTC AOL Time Warner Merger Order. AOL Time Warner describes its arrangements with EarthLink and the unaffiliated ISPs as a kind of partnership . . . .

54. It is possible, however, that when EarthLink or other unaffiliated ISPs offer service to cable modem subscribers, they receive from AOL Time Warner an "input" that is a stand-alone transmission service, making the ISP an end-user of "telecommunications," as that term is defined in the Act. . . . To the extent that AOL Time Warner is providing a stand-alone telecommunications offering to EarthLink or other ISPs, we conclude that the offering would be a private carrier service and not a common carrier service . . . .

55. The Commission and courts have long distinguished between common carriage[205] and private carriage by examining the particular service at issue. As the D.C. Circuit has stated, "the primary sine qua non of common carrier status is a quasi-public character, which arises out of the undertaking to carry for all people indifferently."[207] In contrast, an entity is a private carrier for a particular service when a carrier "chooses its clients on an individual basis and determines in each particular case 'whether and on what terms to serve' and there is no specific regulatory compulsion to serve all indifferently."[208] The record indicates that AOL Time Warner is determining on an individual basis whether to deal with particular ISPs and is in each case deciding the terms on which it will deal with any particular ISP. . . . Thus, such an offering would be a private carrier service, not a "telecommunications service."

56. *AT&T v. City of Portland.* We recognize that the United States Court of Appeals for the Ninth Circuit considered issues related to the classification of cable modem service in *AT&T v. City of Portland.*[211] . . . In that case, the court held that the cable modem service at issue, @Home, was not a "cable service." The court further concluded that [@Home provides a combination of information and telecommunications services.]

57. The Ninth Circuit's decision was based on a record that was less than comprehensive. The parties proceeded on the assumption that the cable modem service at issue was a cable service and therefore did not brief the regulatory

---

[205] The Commission has repeatedly found in various contexts that the definition of "telecommunications service" under the Act is equivalent to "common carrier" service. Moreover, the D.C. Circuit has held that the FCC's interpretation of "telecommunications service" as common carrier service is reasonable and permissible. Virgin Islands Tel. Co. v. FCC (D.C. Cir. 1999).

[207] [NARUC v. FCC, 533 F.2d 601 (D.C. Cir. 1976) (NARUC II).]

[208] Southwestern Bell Tel. Co. v. FCC (D.C. Cir. 1994).

[211] AT&T v. City of Portland, 216 F.3d 871 (9th Cir. 2000) ("Portland"), *reversing* 43 F. Supp. 2d 1146 (D. Ore. 1999).

classification issue. Notably, the Commission, filing as amicus curiae, was not a party to the case and did not provide its expert opinion on this issue. In contrast, the record in this proceeding, developed over the course of a year through written comments and replies and meetings with interested parties, has fully addressed the classification issue and explored the characteristics of cable modem service as it is now provided.

59. *Commission Authority.* Having concluded that cable modem service is an information service, we clarify that it is an interstate information service. The Commission has found that "traffic bound for information service providers (including Internet access traffic) often has an interstate component."[220] The Commission concluded that although such traffic is both interstate and intrastate in nature, it "is properly classified as interstate and it falls under the Commission's ... jurisdiction."[221] The jurisdictional analysis rests on an end-to-end analysis, in this case on an examination of the location of the points among which cable modem service communications travel. These points are often in different states and countries. Accordingly, cable modem service is an interstate information service.

Separate Statement of Chairman Michael K. Powell

The Commission is not left powerless to protect the public interest by classifying cable modem service as an information service. Congress invested the Commission with ample authority under Title I. That provision has been invoked consistently by the Commission to guard against public interest harms and anti-competitive results.

It was this Commission that promulgated *Computer I, Computer II* and, *Computer III,* (all under Title I) in an effort to protect against public interest harms, all with the blessing of judicial review and court sanction of its ancillary authority. Additionally, Title VI is a direct progeny of the Commission's assertion of jurisdiction over cable services under its Title I authority and has regulated cable extensively for a number of years under that authority. This exercise, too, was approved by the Supreme Court as within the congressional scheme.[3]

There is no basis to conclude that Title I is inadequate to strike the right regulatory balance. The Commission's willingness to ask searching questions about competitive access, universal service and other important policy issues

---

[220] *Implementation of the Local Competition Provisions in the Telecommunications Act of 1996* ("Intercarrier Compensation Order") FCC 01-131 p 52 (rel. Apr. 27, 2001).

[221] *Intercarrier Compensation Order,* supra note 220 at p 52 (footnote omitted).

[3] United States v. Southwestern Cable Co., 392 U.S. 157 (1968).

demonstrates its commitment to explore, evaluate and make responsible judgments about the regulatory framework.

Dissenting Statement of Commissioner Michael J. Copps

The Ruling will force cable modem services into the generally deregulated information services category, subject only to the Commission's ancillary jurisdiction of Title I. I cannot conceive that Congress intended to remove from its statutory framework core communications services such as the one at issue in this proceeding. I cannot imagine that it envisioned its statutory handiwork being made obsolete by a new service offering.

But make no mistake—today's decision places these services outside any viable and predictable regulatory framework.

[W]e are... told not to worry—the Commission can build its own regulatory framework under its ancillary jurisdiction. Years ago, when I worked on Capitol Hill, we used to worry about legislation on an appropriations bill. Down here, I'm learning that I have to look out for legislation on an NPRM.

Today we take a gigantic leap down the road of removing core communications services from the statutory frameworks established by Congress, substituting our own judgment for that of Congress and playing a game of regulatory musical chairs by moving technologies and services from one statutory definition to another.

Let me repeat my serious misgivings about not just the propriety, but the wisdom of the Commission proceeding directly from a general Notice of Inquiry to the adoption of such far-reaching conclusions in so important an area of national policy. How America deploys broadband is the central infrastructure challenge our country faces. It is a public policy matter of enormous implications. How we get it done affects not only how many megabytes of information our computers can download, but what kinds of options consumers will be able to choose from, what kinds of protections they will have against misguided or fraudulent business practices, and what kinds of opportunities will be available to those in our society who do not share fully in our general prosperity. With so much at stake, I would have hoped for a little more modesty and measured pace on our part.

NOTES & QUESTIONS

1. *Not cable service.* In agreement with the Ninth Circuit, the FCC concluded in this Declaratory Ruling that cable modem service was not a "cable service." Although the intricacies of that argument were important back in

2002, subsequent regulatory and judicial actions make that conclusion no longer controversial.

2. *Information service vs. telecommunications service?* This classification question has a long regulatory history with significant consequences even today. Walk through the FCC's analysis. In particular, explain how the FCC addressed the vertical integration complexity, and explain how the difference between "telecommunications" and "telecommunications service" mattered.

3. *Regulatory consequences.* After all this taxonomy, what is the end result in terms of regulatory consequences? In other words, who (federal, state, or local government) can exercise what kinds of power (e.g., under which titles)?

4. *Moving too fast?* Commissioner Copps worries that the FCC is moving too quickly, without adequate time for analysis and public comment. Are you persuaded by his dissent, or do Chairman Powell's comments assuage your concerns?

5. *The Ninth Circuit Strikes Back:* Brand X. The FCC's declaratory ruling was quickly appealed. Seven different petitions for review were filed in various circuits, and the cases were randomly consolidated in the Ninth Circuit.[*] Different stakeholders sought different rulings. For example, certain ISPs, such as Brand X and EarthLink, wanted cable modem service to be classified as both an information and a telecommunication service. By contrast, state regulators wanted the service to be classified as both information and cable services, giving power to local franchising authorities.[†]

    a. *No* Chevron *deference.* The Ninth Circuit held that *Chevron* deference was inappropriate because it had already decided this specific issue in *AT&T v. City of Portland,* before the FCC had acted. That *Portland* decision was binding as a matter of *stare decisis* on the court. Accordingly, the FCC's ruling was partially vacated.

    b. *Beating the FCC to the punch.* Judge Diarmuid F. O'Scannlain, in a concurring opinion raised misgivings. He wrote:

> Our *Portland* decision, in essence, beat the FCC to the punch, leading to the strange result we are compelled to reach today: three judges telling an agency acting within the area of its expertise that its interpretation of the statute it is charged with administering cannot stand—and that *our* interpretation of how the Act should be applied to a "quicksilver technological environment," is the correct, indeed the only, interpretation.[‡]

---

[*] *See* Brand X Internet Services v. FCC, 345 F.3d 1120 (9th Cir. 2003).

[†] *Cf.* MediaOne Group, Inc. v. County of Henrico, 97 F. Supp. 2d 712 (E.D. Va. 2000), aff'd, 257 F.3d 356 (4th Cir. 2001) (concluding that cable modem services involved both telecommunications and cable service).

[‡] *Brand X,* 345 F.3d at 1133-34.

With this regrettably lengthy background, we are now prepared for the Supreme Court's decision in *Brand X*.

| NCTA v. BRAND X |
| 545 U.S. 967 (2005) |

Justice THOMAS delivered the opinion of the Court.

II

At issue in these cases is the proper regulatory classification under the Communications Act of broadband cable Internet service. The Act . . . defines two categories of regulated entities relevant to these cases: telecommunications carriers and information-service providers. The Act regulates telecommunications carriers, but not information-service providers, as common carriers. Telecommunications carriers, for example, must charge just and reasonable, nondiscriminatory rates to their customers, 47 U.S.C. §§ 201-209, design their systems so that other carriers can interconnect with their communications networks, § 251(a)(1), and contribute to the federal 'universal service' fund, § 254(d). These provisions are mandatory, but the Commission must forbear from applying them if it determines that the public interest requires it. §§ 160(a), (b). Information-service providers, by contrast, are not subject to mandatory common-carrier regulation under Title II, though the Commission has jurisdiction to impose additional regulatory obligations under its Title I ancillary jurisdiction to regulate interstate and foreign communications, see §§ 151-161.

These two statutory classifications originated in the late 1970's, as the Commission developed rules to regulate data-processing services offered over telephone wires. That regime, the '*Computer II*' rules, distinguished between 'basic' service (like telephone service) and 'enhanced' service (computer-processing service offered over telephone lines). *In re Amendment of Section 64.702 of the Commission's Rules and Regulations (Second Computer Inquiry)*, 77 F.C.C.2d 384 (1980) (hereinafter *Computer II Order*). The *Computer II* rules defined both basic and enhanced services by reference to how the consumer perceives the service being offered.

In particular, the Commission defined 'basic service' as 'a pure transmission capability over a communications path that is virtually transparent in terms of its interaction with customer supplied information.' By 'pure' or 'transparent' transmission, the Commission meant a communications path that enabled the consumer to transmit an ordinary-language message to another point, with no computer processing or storage of the information, other than the processing or storage needed to convert the message into electronic form and then back into ordinary language for purposes of transmitting it over the network—such as via a telephone or a facsimile. Basic service was subject to common-carrier regulation.

'[E]nhanced service,' however, was service in which 'computer processing applications [were] used to act on the content, code, protocol, and other aspects of the subscriber's information,' such as voice and data storage services, as well as 'protocol conversion' (*i.e.*, ability to communicate between networks that employ different data-transmission formats). By contrast to basic service, the Commission decided not to subject providers of enhanced service, even enhanced service offered via transmission wires, to Title II common-carrier regulation. The Commission explained that it was unwise to subject enhanced service to common-carrier regulation given the 'fast-moving, competitive market' in which they were offered.

The definitions of the terms 'telecommunications service' and 'information service' established by the 1996 Act are similar to the *Computer II* basic- and enhanced-service classifications. 'Telecommunications service'—the analog to basic service—is 'the offering of telecommunications for a fee directly to the public ... regardless of the facilities used.' 47 U.S.C. § 153(46). 'Telecommunications' is 'the transmission, between or among points specified by the user, of information of the user's choosing, without change in the form or content of the information as sent and received.' § 153(43). 'Telecommunications carrier[s]'—those subjected to mandatory Title II common-carrier regulation—are defined as 'provider[s] of telecommunications services.' § 153(44). And 'information service'—the analog to enhanced service—is 'the offering of a capability for generating, acquiring, storing, transforming, processing, retrieving, utilizing, or making available information via telecommunications ... .' § 153(20).

In the [FCC's March 2002] *Declaratory Ruling*, the Commission concluded that broadband Internet service provided by cable companies is an 'information service' but not a 'telecommunications service' under the Act, and therefore not subject to mandatory Title II common-carrier regulation. In support of this conclusion, the Commission relied heavily on its *Universal Service Report*.

[On appeal,] the Court of Appeals ... vacated the ruling to the extent it concluded that cable modem service was not 'telecommunications service' under the Communications Act. ... Rather than analyzing the permissibility of that construction under the deferential framework of *Chevron*, however, the Court of Appeals grounded its holding in the *stare decisis* effect of *AT&T Corp. v. Portland* (CA9 2000).

III

We first consider whether we should apply *Chevron*'s framework to the Commission's interpretation of the term 'telecommunications service.' We conclude that we should. We also conclude that the Court of Appeals should have done the same, instead of following the contrary construction it adopted in *Portland.*

B

A court's prior judicial construction of a statute trumps an agency construction otherwise entitled to *Chevron* deference only if the prior court decision holds that its construction follows from the unambiguous terms of the statute and thus leaves no room for agency discretion. This principle follows from *Chevron* itself. *Chevron* established a 'presumption that Congress, when it left ambiguity in a statute meant for implementation by an agency, understood that the ambiguity would be resolved, first and foremost, by the agency, and desired the agency (rather than the courts) to possess whatever degree of discretion the ambiguity allows.' Yet allowing a judicial precedent to foreclose an agency from interpreting an ambiguous statute, as the Court of Appeals assumed it could, would allow a court's interpretation to override an agency's. *Chevron*'s premise is that it is for agencies, not courts, to fill statutory gaps. The better rule is to hold judicial interpretations contained in precedents to the same demanding *Chevron* step one standard that applies if the court is reviewing the agency's construction on a blank slate: Only a judicial precedent holding that the statute unambiguously forecloses the agency's interpretation, and therefore contains no gap for the agency to fill, displaces a conflicting agency construction.

A contrary rule would produce anomalous results. It would mean that whether an agency's interpretation of an ambiguous statute is entitled to *Chevron* deference would turn on the order in which the interpretations issue: If the court's construction came first, its construction would prevail, whereas if the agency's came first, the agency's construction would command *Chevron* deference. Yet whether Congress has delegated to an agency the authority to interpret a statute does not depend on the order in which the judicial and administrative constructions occur.

[T]he Court of Appeals erred in refusing to apply *Chevron* to the Commission's interpretation of the definition of 'telecommunications service,' 47 U.S.C. § 153(46). Its prior decision in *Portland* held only that the *best* reading of § 153(46) was that cable modem service was a 'telecommunications service,' not that it was the *only permissible* reading of the statute. Nothing in *Portland* held that the Communications Act unambiguously required treating cable Internet providers as telecommunications carriers.

IV

We next address whether the Commission's construction of the definition of 'telecommunications service,' 47 U.S.C. § 153(46), is a permissible reading of the Communications Act under the *Chevron* framework. *Chevron* established a familiar two-step procedure for evaluating whether an agency's interpretation of a statute is lawful. At the first step, we ask whether the statute's plain terms 'directly addres[s] the precise question at issue.' If the statute is ambiguous on the point, we defer at step two to the agency's interpretation so long as the construction is 'a reasonable policy choice for the agency to make.' The Commission's interpretation is permissible at both steps.

A

We first set forth our understanding of the interpretation of the Communications Act that the Commission embraced. The issue before the Commission was whether cable companies providing cable modem service are providing a 'telecommunications service' in addition to an 'information service.'

The Commission first concluded that cable modem service is an 'information service,' a conclusion unchallenged here.

At the same time, the Commission concluded that cable modem service was not 'telecommunications service.' 'Telecommunications service' is 'the offering of telecommunications for a fee directly to the public.' 47 U.S.C. § 153(46). 'Telecommunications,' in turn, is defined as 'the transmission, between or among points specified by the user, of information of the user's choosing, without change in the form or content of the information as sent and received.' § 153(43). The Commission conceded that, like all information-service providers, cable companies use 'telecommunications' to provide consumers with Internet service; cable companies provide such service via the high-speed wire that transmits signals to and from an end user's computer. For the Commission, however, the question whether cable broadband Internet providers 'offer' telecommunications involved more than whether telecommunications was one necessary component of cable modem service. Instead, whether that service also includes a telecommunications 'offering' 'tur[ned] on the nature of the functions the *end user* is offered,' for the statutory definition of 'telecommunications service' does not 'res[t] on the particular types of facilities used'.

Seen from the consumer's point of view, the Commission concluded, cable modem service is not a telecommunications offering because the consumer uses the high-speed wire always in connection with the information-processing capabilities provided by Internet access, and because the transmission is a necessary component of Internet access: 'As provided to the end user the telecommunications is part and parcel of cable modem service and is integral to its other capabilities.'

B

This construction passes *Chevron*'s first step. Respondents argue that it does not, on the ground that cable companies providing Internet service necessarily 'offe[r]' the underlying telecommunications used to transmit that service. The word 'offering' as used in § 153(46), however, does not unambiguously require that result. Instead, 'offering' can reasonably be read to mean a 'stand-alone' offering of telecommunications, *i.e.*, an offered service that, from the user's perspective, transmits messages unadulterated by computer processing. That conclusion follows not only from the ordinary meaning of the word 'offering,' but also from the regulatory history of the Communications Act.

1

It is common usage to describe what a company 'offers' to a consumer as what the consumer perceives to be the integrated finished product, even to the exclusion of discrete components that compose the product, as the dissent concedes. One might well say that a car dealership 'offers' cars, but does not 'offer' the integrated major inputs that make purchasing the car valuable, such as the engine or the chassis. It would, in fact, be odd to describe a car dealership as 'offering' consumers the car's components in addition to the car itself.

The question, then, is whether the transmission component of cable modem service is sufficiently integrated with the finished service to make it reasonable to describe the two as a single, integrated offering. We think that they are sufficiently integrated . . . .

2

The Commission's traditional distinction between basic and enhanced service also supports the conclusion that the Communications Act is ambiguous about whether cable companies 'offer' telecommunications with cable modem service. Congress passed the definitions in the Communications Act against the background of this regulatory history, and we may assume that the parallel terms 'telecommunications service' and 'information service' substantially incorporated their meaning, as the Commission has held. The regulatory history in at least two respects confirms that the term 'telecommunications service' is ambiguous.

First, in the *Computer II Order* that established the terms 'basic' and 'enhanced' services, the Commission defined those terms functionally, based on how the consumer interacts with the provided information, just as the Commission did in the order below.... It was therefore consistent with the statute's terms for the Commission to assume that the parallel term 'telecommunications service' in 47 U.S.C. § 153(46) likewise describes a 'pure' or 'transparent' communications path ....

The Commission's application of the basic/enhanced service distinction to non-facilities-based ISPs also supports this conclusion. The Commission has long held that 'all those who provide some form of transmission services are not necessarily common carriers.' *Computer II Order.* For example, the Commission did not subject to common-carrier regulation those service providers that offered enhanced services over telecommunications facilities, but that did not themselves own the underlying facilities—so-called 'non-facilities-based' providers. Examples of these services included database services in which a customer used telecommunications to access information, such as Dow Jones News and Lexis .... Following this traditional distinction, the Commission in the *Universal Service Report* classified ISPs that leased rather than owned their transmission facilities as pure information-service providers.

Respondents' statutory arguments conflict with this regulatory history. They claim that the Communications Act unambiguously classifies as telecommunications carriers all entities that use telecommunications inputs to provide information service. [T]his argument would subject to mandatory common-carrier regulation all information-service providers that use telecommunications as an input to provide information service to the public.

Respondents' analogy between cable companies that provide cable modem service and facilities-based enhanced-service providers—that is, enhanced-service providers who own the transmission facilities used to provide those services—fares no better. Respondents stress that under the *Computer II* rules the Commission regulated such providers more heavily than non-facilities-based providers. The Commission required, for example, local telephone companies that provided enhanced services to offer their wires on a common-carrier basis to competing enhanced-service providers. See, *e.g., In re Amendment of Sections 64.702 of the Commission's Rules and Regulations (Third Computer Inquiry)*, 104 F. C. C. 2d 958, 964, ¶ 4 (1986) (hereinafter *Computer III Order*). Respondents argue that the Communications Act unambiguously requires the same treatment for cable companies because cable companies also own the facilities they use to provide cable modem service (and therefore information service).

We disagree. We think it improbable that the Communications Act unambiguously freezes in time the *Computer II* treatment of facilities-based information-service providers. The Act's definition of 'telecommunications service' says nothing about imposing more stringent regulatory duties on facilities-based information-service providers. . . . In the *Computer II* rules, the Commission subjected facilities-based providers to common-carrier duties not because of the nature of the 'offering' made by those carriers, but rather because of the concern that local telephone companies would abuse the monopoly power they possessed by virtue of the 'bottleneck' local telephone facilities they owned. The differential treatment of facilities-based carriers was therefore a function not of the definitions of 'enhanced-service' and 'basic service,' but instead of a choice by the Commission to regulate more stringently, in its discretion, certain entities that provided enhanced service. The Act's definitions, however, parallel the definitions of enhanced and basic service, not the facilities-based grounds on which that policy choice was based, and the Commission remains free to impose special regulatory duties on facilities-based ISPs under its Title I ancillary jurisdiction. In fact, it has invited comment on whether it can and should do so.

[T]he relevant definitions do not distinguish facilities-based and non-facilities-based carriers. That silence suggests, instead, that the Commission has the discretion to fill the consequent statutory gap.

C

We also conclude that the Commission's construction was 'a reasonable policy choice for the [Commission] to make' at *Chevron*'s second step.

Respondents argue that the Commission's construction is unreasonable because it allows any communications provider to 'evade' common-carrier regulation by the expedient of bundling information service with telecommunications. Respondents argue that under the Commission's construction a telephone company could, for example, offer an information service like voice mail together with telephone service, thereby avoiding common-carrier regulation of its telephone service.

[T]he Commission did not say that any telecommunications service that is priced or bundled with an information service is automatically unregulated under Title II.

'It is plain,' for example, that a local telephone company 'cannot escape Title II regulation of its residential local exchange service simply by packaging that service with voice mail.' *Universal Service Report*. That is because a telephone company that packages voice mail with telephone service offers a transparent transmission path—telephone service—that transmits information independent of the information-storage capabilities provided by voice mail. For instance, when a person makes a telephone call, his ability to convey and receive information using the call is only trivially affected by the additional voice-mail capability. Equally, were a telephone company to add a time-of-day announcement that played every time the user picked up his telephone, the 'transparent' information transmitted in the ensuing call would be only trivially dependent on the information service the announcement provides. By contrast, the high-speed transmission used to provide cable modem service is a functionally integrated component of that service because it transmits data only in connection with the further processing of information and is necessary to provide Internet service. The Commission's construction therefore was more limited than respondents assume.

Respondents answer that cable modem service does, in fact, provide 'transparent' transmission from the consumer's perspective, but this argument, too, is mistaken. . . . When a consumer goes beyond those offerings and accesses content provided by parties other than the cable company, respondents argue, the consumer uses 'pure transmission' no less than a consumer who purchases phone service together with voice mail.

This argument . . . conflicts with the Commission's understanding of the nature of cable modem service, an understanding we find to be reasonable. . . [P]art of the information service cable companies provide is access to DNS [Domain Name Server] service. A user cannot reach a third-party's Web site without DNS, which (among other things) matches the Web site address the end user types into his browser (or 'clicks' on with his mouse) with the IP address of the Web page's host server. It is at least reasonable to think of DNS as a 'capability for ... acquiring ... retrieving, utilizing, or making available' Web site addresses and therefore part of the information service cable companies provide. 47 U.S.C. § 153(20).[3] Similarly, the Internet service provided by cable companies . . . 'cache[]' popular content on local computer servers. Cacheing obviates the need for the end user to download anew information from third-party Web sites each time the consumer attempts to access them, thereby increasing the speed of information retrieval. . . .

---

[3] The dissent claims that access to DNS does not count as use of the information-processing capabilities of Internet service because DNS is 'scarcely more than routing information, which is expressly excluded from the definition of 'information service.' ' But the definition of information service does not exclude 'routing information.' Instead, it excludes 'any use of any such capability for the management, control, or operation of a telecommunications system or the management of a telecommunications service.' 47 U.S.C. § 153(20). The dissent's argument therefore begs the question because it assumes that Internet service is a 'telecommunications system' or 'service' that DNS manages (a point on which, contrary to the dissent's assertion, we need take no view for purposes of this response).

V

Respondent MCI, Inc., urges that the Commission's treatment of cable modem service is inconsistent with its treatment of DSL service, and therefore is an arbitrary and capricious deviation from agency policy. MCI points out that when local telephone companies began to offer Internet access through DSL technology in addition to telephone service, the Commission applied its *Computer II* facilities-based classification to them and required them to make the telephone lines used to transmit DSL service available to competing ISPs on nondiscriminatory, common-carrier terms. See *In re Deployment of Wireline Services Offering Advanced Telecommunications Capability*, 13 FCC Rcd. 24011 (1998) (hereinafter *Wireline Order*) (classifying DSL service as a telecommunications service). MCI claims that the Commission's decision not to regulate cable companies similarly under Title II is inconsistent with its DSL policy.

We conclude, however, that the Commission provided a reasoned explanation for treating cable modem service differently from DSL service. [T]he Commission is free within the limits of reasoned interpretation to change course if it adequately justifies the change.[4] The traditional reason for its *Computer II* common-carrier treatment of facilities-based carriers (including DSL carriers)... was 'that the *telephone network* [was] the primary, if not exclusive, means through which information service providers can gain access to their customers.' *Declaratory Ruling* 4825. The Commission applied the same treatment to DSL service based on that history, rather than on an analysis of contemporaneous market conditions.

The Commission in the order under review, by contrast, concluded that changed market conditions warrant different treatment of facilities-based cable companies providing Internet access. Unlike at the time of *Computer II*, substitute forms of Internet transmission exist today: '[R]esidential high-speed access to the Internet is evolving over multiple electronic platforms, including wireline, cable, terrestrial wireless and satellite.' *Declaratory Ruling*.... We find nothing arbitrary about the Commission's providing a fresh analysis of the problem as applied to the cable industry, which it has never subjected to these rules. This is adequate rational justification for the Commission's conclusions.

Respondents argue... that the Commission's justification for exempting cable modem service providers from common-carrier regulation applies with

---

[4] Respondents vigorously argue that the Commission's purported inconsistent treatment is a reason for holding the Commission's construction impermissible under *Chevron*. Any inconsistency bears on whether the Commission has given a reasoned explanation for its current position, not on whether its interpretation is consistent with the statute.

similar force to DSL providers. We need not address that argument. The Commission's decision appears to be a first step in an effort to reshape the way the Commission regulates information-service providers; that may be why it has tentatively concluded that DSL service provided by facilities-based telephone companies should also be classified solely as an information service. *See In re Appropriate Framework for Broadband Access to the Internet over Wireline Facilities*, 17 FCC Rcd. 3019 (2002). The Commission need not immediately apply the policy reasoning in the *Declaratory Ruling* to all types of information-service providers. It apparently has decided to revisit its longstanding *Computer II* classification of facilities-based information-service providers incrementally. Any inconsistency between the order under review and the Commission's treatment of DSL service can be adequately addressed when the Commission fully reconsiders its treatment of DSL service and when it decides whether, pursuant to its ancillary Title I jurisdiction, to require cable companies to allow independent ISPs access to their facilities. We express no view on those matters.

Justice SCALIA, with whom Justice SOUTER and Justice GINSBURG join as to Part I, dissenting.

The Federal Communications Commission has once again attempted to concoct 'a whole new regime of regulation (or of free-market competition)' under the guise of statutory construction. Actually, in these cases, it might be more accurate to say the Commission has attempted to establish a whole new regime of *non*-regulation, which will make for more or less free-market competition, depending upon whose experts are believed. The important fact, however, is that the Commission has chosen to achieve this through an implausible reading of the statute, and has thus exceeded the authority given it by Congress.

I

The first sentence of the FCC ruling under review reads as follows: 'Cable modem service provides high-speed access to the Internet, *as well as* many applications or functions that can be used with that access, over cable system facilities.' *Declaratory Ruling* (emphasis added). Does this mean that cable companies 'offer' high-speed access to the Internet? Surprisingly not, if the Commission and the Court are to be believed.

It happens that cable-modem service is popular precisely because of the high-speed access it provides, and that, once connected with the Internet, cable-modem subscribers often use Internet applications and functions from providers other than the cable company. Nevertheless, for purposes of classifying what the cable company does, the Commission (with the Court's approval) puts all the emphasis on the rest of the package (the additional 'applications or functions').

'[T]elecommunications service' ' is defined as 'the offering of telecommunications for a fee directly to the public ... regardless of the facilities used.' § 153(46). The question here is whether cable-modem-service providers 'offe[r] ... telecommunications for a fee directly to the public.'

The Court concludes that the word 'offer' is ambiguous in the sense that it has "alternative dictionary definitions" that might be relevant. It seems to me, however, that the analytic problem pertains not really to the meaning of 'offer,' but to the identity of what is offered. The relevant question is whether the individual components in a package being offered still possess sufficient identity to be described as separate objects of the offer, or whether they have been so changed by their combination with the other components that it is no longer reasonable to describe them in that way.

Thus, I agree that it would be odd to say that a car dealer is in the business of selling steel or carpets because the cars he sells include both steel frames and carpeting. Nor does the water company sell hydrogen, nor the pet store water (though dogs and cats are largely water at the molecular level). But what is sometimes true is not, as the Court seems to assume, *always* true. There are instances in which it is ridiculous to deny that one part of a joint offering is being offered merely because it is not offered on a "stand-alone" basis.

If, for example, I call up a pizzeria and ask whether they offer delivery, both common sense and common 'usage' would prevent them from answering: 'No, we do not offer delivery—but if you order a pizza from us, we'll bake it for you and then bring it to your house.' The logical response to this would be something on the order of, 'so, you *do* offer delivery.' But our pizza-man may continue to deny the obvious and explain, paraphrasing the FCC and the Court: "No, even though we bring the pizza to your house, we are not actually 'offering' you delivery, because the delivery that we provide to our end users is 'part and parcel' of our pizzeria-pizza-at-home service and is 'integral to its other capabilities.'"[1] Any reasonable customer would conclude at that point that his interlocutor was either crazy or following some too-clever-by-half legal advice.

In short, for the inputs of a finished service to qualify as the objects of an 'offer' (as that term is reasonably understood), it is perhaps a sufficient, *but*

---

[1] The myth that the pizzeria does not offer delivery becomes even more difficult to maintain when the pizzeria advertises quick delivery as one of its advantages over competitors. That, of course, is the case with cable broadband.

surely not a necessary, condition that the seller offer separately 'each discrete input that is necessary to providing … a finished service'. The pet store may have a policy of selling puppies only with leashes, but any customer will say that it *does* offer puppies—because a leashed puppy is still a puppy, even though it is not offered on a 'stand-alone' basis.

Despite the Court's mighty labors to prove otherwise, the telecommunications component of cable-modem service retains such ample independent identity that it must be regarded as being on offer—especially when seen from the perspective of the consumer or the end user, which the Court purports to find determinative.

The consumer's view of the matter is best assessed by asking what other products cable-modem service substitutes for in the marketplace. Broadband Internet service provided by cable companies is one of the three most common forms of Internet service, the other two being dial-up access and broadband Digital Subscriber Line (DSL) service. In each of the other two, the physical transmission pathway to the Internet is sold—indeed, *is legally required* to be sold—separately from the Internet functionality. With dial-up access, the physical pathway comes from the telephone company and the Internet service provider (ISP) provides the functionality.

As the Court acknowledges, DSL service has been similar to dial-up service in the respect that the physical connection to the Internet must be offered separately from Internet functionality. Thus, customers shopping for dial-up or DSL service will not be able to use the Internet unless they get both someone to provide them with a physical connection and someone to provide them with applications and functions such as e-mail and Web access. It is therefore inevitable that customers will regard the competing cable-modem service as giving them *both* computing functionality *and* the physical pipe by which that functionality comes to their computer—both the pizza and the delivery service that nondelivery pizzerias require to be purchased from the cab company.[4]

Since the delivery service provided by cable (the broad-band connection between the customer's computer and the cable company's computer-processing facilities) is downstream from the computer-processing facilities,

---

[4] The Court contends that this analogy is inapposite because one need not have a pizza delivered, whereas one must purchase the cable connection in order to use cable's ISP functions. But the ISP functions provided by the cable company *can* be used without cable delivery—by accessing them from an Internet connection other than cable. The merger of the physical connection and Internet functions in cable's offerings has nothing to do with the "inextricably intertwined," nature of the two (like a car and its carpet), but is an artificial product of the cable company's marketing decision not to offer the two separately, so that the Commission could (by the *Declaratory Ruling* under review here) exempt it from common-carrier status.

there is no question that it merely serves as a conduit for the information services that have already been 'assembled' by the cable company in its capacity as ISP. This is relevant because of the statutory distinction between an 'information service' and 'telecommunications.' The former involves the capability of getting, processing, and manipulating information. § 153(20). The latter, by contrast, involves no 'change in the form or content of the information as sent and received.' § 153(43). When cable-company-assembled information enters the cable for delivery to the subscriber, the information service is already complete. The information has been (as the statute requires) generated, acquired, stored, transformed, processed, retrieved, utilized, or made available. All that remains is for the information in its final, unaltered form, to be delivered (via telecommunications) to the subscriber.

This reveals the insubstantiality of the fear invoked by both the Commission and the Court: the fear of what will happen to ISPs that do not provide the physical pathway to Internet access, yet still use telecommunications to acquire the pieces necessary to assemble the information that they pass back to their customers. According to this *reductio,* if cable-modem-service providers are deemed to provide 'telecommunications service,' then so must *all* ISPs because they all 'use' telecommunications in providing Internet functionality (by connecting to other parts of the Internet, including Internet backbone providers, for example). In terms of the pizzeria analogy, this is equivalent to saying that, if the pizzeria 'offers' delivery, *all* restaurants 'offer' delivery, because the ingredients of the food they serve their customers have come from other places; no matter how their customers get the food (whether by eating it at the restaurant, or by coming to pick it up themselves), they still consume a product for which delivery was a necessary 'input.' This is nonsense. Concluding that delivery of the finished pizza constitutes an 'offer' of delivery does not require the conclusion that the serving of prepared food includes an 'offer' of delivery. And that analogy does not even do the point justice, since "'telecommunications service' ' is defined as 'the offering of telecommunications for a fee *directly to the public.*" 47 U.S.C. § 153(46) (emphasis added). The ISPs' use of telecommunications in their processing of information is not offered directly to the public.

The 'regulatory history' on which the Court depends so much provides another reason why common-carrier regulation of all ISPs is not a worry. Under its *Computer Inquiry* rules, which foreshadowed the definitions of 'information' and 'telecommunications' services, the Commission forbore from regulating as common carriers 'value-added networks'—non-facilities-based providers who leased basic services from common carriers and bundled them with enhanced services; it said that they, unlike facilities-based providers, would be deemed to provide only enhanced services.[5] That same result can be achieved today under the Commission's statutory authority to forbear from imposing most Title II regulations. 47 U.S.C. § 160. In fact, the statutory criteria for forbearance—which include what is 'just and reasonable,' 'necessary for the protection of consumers,' and 'consistent with the public interest,' §§ 160(a)(1), (2), (3)—correspond well with the kinds of policy reasons the Commission has invoked to justify its peculiar construction of 'telecommunications service' to exclude cable-modem service.

The Court also puts great stock in its conclusion that cable-modem subscribers cannot avoid using information services provided by the cable company in its ISP capacity, even when they only click-through to other ISPs . . . . [H]e will still be using the cable company's Domain Name System (DNS) server and, when he goes to popular Web pages, perhaps versions of them that are stored in the cable company's cache. This argument suffers from at least two problems. First, in the context of telephone services, the Court recognizes a *de minimis* exception to contamination of a telecommunications service by an information service. A similar exception would seem to apply to the functions in question here. DNS, in particular, is scarcely more than routing information, which is expressly excluded from the definition of 'information service.' 47 U.S.C. § 153(20).[6] Second, it is apparently possible to sell a telecommunications service separately from, although in conjunction with, ISP-like services; that is precisely what happens in the DSL context, and the Commission does not contest that it *could* be done in the context of cable. The

---

[5] The Commission says forbearance cannot explain why value-added networks were not regulated as basic-service providers because it was not given the power to forbear until 1996. It is true that when the Commission ruled on value-added networks, the statute did not explicitly provide for forbearance—any more than it provided for the categories of basic and enhanced services that the *Computer Inquiry* rules established, and through which the forbearance was applied. The D. C. Circuit, however, had long since recognized the Commission's discretionary power to 'forbear from Title II regulation.' *Computer & Communications Industry Assn. v. FCC* (1982).

The Commission also says its *Computer Inquiry* rules should not apply to cable because they were developed in the context of telephone lines. But to the extent that the statute imported the *Computer Inquiry* approach, there is no basis for applying it differently to cable than to telephone lines, since the definition of 'telecommunications service' applies 'regardless of the facilities used.' 47 U.S.C. § 153(46).

[6] The Court says that invoking this explicit exception from the definition of information services, which applies only to the 'management, control, or operation of a telecommunications system or the management of a telecommunications service,' 47 U.S.C. § 153(20), begs the question whether cable-modem service includes a telecommunications service. I think not, and cite the exception only to demonstrate that the incidental functions do not *prevent* cable from including a telecommunications service *if it otherwise qualifies.* It is rather the Court that begs the question, saying that the exception cannot apply because cable is not a telecommunications service.

only impediment appears to be the Commission's failure to require from cable companies the unbundling that it required of facilities-based providers under its *Computer Inquiry*.

Finally, I must note that, notwithstanding the Commission's self-congratulatory paean to its deregulatory largesse, it concluded the *Declaratory Ruling* by asking, as the Court paraphrases, 'whether under its Title I jurisdiction [the Commission] should require cable companies to offer other ISPs access to their facilities on common-carrier terms.' In other words, what the Commission hath given, the Commission may well take away—unless it doesn't. This is a wonderful illustration of how an experienced agency can (with some assistance from credulous courts) turn statutory constraints into bureaucratic discretions. The main source of the Commission's regulatory authority over common carriers is Title II, but the Commission has rendered that inapplicable in this instance by concluding that the definition of 'telecommunications service' is ambiguous and does not (in its current view) apply to cable-modem service. It contemplates, however, altering that (unnecessary) outcome, not by changing the law (*i.e.,* its construction of the Title II definitions), but by reserving the right to change the facts. Under its undefined and sparingly used 'ancillary' powers, the Commission might conclude that it can order cable companies to 'unbundle' the telecommunications component of cable-modem service.[7] And presto, Title II will then apply to them, because they will finally be 'offering' telecommunications service! Of course, the Commission will still have the statutory power to forbear from regulating them under § 160 (which it has already tentatively concluded it would do, *Declaratory Ruling* 4847-4848, ¶¶ 94-95). Such Möbius-strip reasoning mocks the principle that the statute constrains the agency in any meaningful way.

After all is said and done, after all the regulatory cant has been translated, and the smoke of agency expertise blown away, it remains perfectly clear that someone who sells cable-modem service is 'offering' telecommunications. For that simple reason set forth in the statute, I would affirm the Court of Appeals.

---

[7] Under the Commission's assumption that cable-modem-service providers are not providing 'telecommunications services,' there is reason to doubt whether it can use its Title I powers to impose common-carrier-like requirements, since 47 U.S.C. § 153(44) specifically provides that a 'telecommunications carrier shall be treated as a common carrier under this chapter *only to the extent* that it is engaged in providing telecommunications services' (emphasis added), and 'this chapter' includes Titles I and II.

NOTES & QUESTIONS

1. *Chevron v. stare decisis.* The Supreme Court clarified a difficult question of administrative law. What should a court do when judicial precedent points in the opposite direction of a subsequent agency clarification?

2. *Sharpening the conflict.* A "telecommunications service" is the offering of telecommunications directly to the public for a fee. Both majority and dissenting opinions seem to suggest that if the broadband pipe is fully integrated with the internet access, then cable modem services are not telecommunications services. By contrast, if the broadband pipe is severable, then cable modem services count as both telecommunications services and information services. But what does it mean to be fully integrated or severable? Why is telephony with voicemail severable because the voicemail is "trivial," but not a fast pipe with DNS and caching?

3. *Consumer expectations.*

    a. *Arbitrary anchoring.* Both sides suggest that what is being offered turns on consumer expectations. Is this a sensible way to make regulatory decisions about a huge chunk of our economy? After all, aren't consumer expectations arbitrary given that whatever comes first will anchor expectations? Those who were introduced first to the internet through dial-up will tend to see the internet access component as separate from the pipe component. By contrast, those who first experienced cable broadband will tend to think of it as one indivisible package. Isn't this encouraging a sort of arbitrary path dependence in regulation?

    b. *Circular standard.* If the courts say the law requires X, then firms will comply, and consumers will come to expect X. By contrast, if the courts say that no such requirement is necessary, then expectations will readjust accordingly. Law drives norms, which in turn drive the law. Compare your study of what counts as a "reasonable expectation of privacy" under Fourth Amendment law.

4. *Warring analogies.* Is cable modem service like a car, leashed puppy, or delivered pizza? Who has the best analogy? Does it really matter in a *Chevron* framework? Does deference make the difference?

5. *Computer Inquiries.* Both majority and dissent draw different lessons from the *Computer Inquiries.* Try to explain how the majority uses them to support its view. How does Justice Scalia make use of the exact same regulatory precedents to support his dissent?

6. *Consequences.* What precisely are the regulatory consequences? Cable modem services do not fall under Title II. They do fall under Title I.

a. *Title II and opt-out.* Falling into Title II is something like an opt-out regime: lots of default regulations that the FCC can opt out of. Recall that in 1996 Congress explicitly granted forbearance authority to the FCC as long as certain conditions are satisfied.[*] This means that the FCC could have opted out of open access conditions.

b. *Title I and opt-in.* Falling into Title I is like entering an opt-in regime: no default regulations, which means that the FCC must adopt new ones on a regulation-by-regulation basis. Recall Chairman Powell's statements about Title I authority in the *Cable Modem Declaratory Ruling.* After reading *Brand X,* what sort of regulations do you think the Supreme Court might countenance on cable modem services under Title I authority?

7. *Regulatory parity between cable modem service and DSL.*

a. *Information service. Brand X* affirmed the FCC's classification of cable modem service as an information service. What about DSL, which is the way that broadband is delivered over telephone lines? (To be more careful, instead of *DSL,* we could use the term *wireline broadband internet access service* which is defined as "a service that uses existing or future wireline facilities of the telephone network to provide subscribers with Internet access capabilities."[†]) In the 2005 *Wireline Broadband Order,* the FCC established regulatory parity between cable modem service and wireline broadband Internet access service by classifying the latter also an "information service" as well.

b. *Lifting legacy regulations: the Computer Inquiries.* Recall our discussion of the "Computer Inquiries" earlier in this chapter. By the end of *Computer II* and *Computer III,* all common carriers that owned their own transmission facilities and also provided enhanced services (which includes internet access) had to provide that same transmission capacity to other enhanced service providers on an unbundled, nondiscriminatory basis. In the 2005 *Wireline Broadband Order,* the FCC lifted these requirements as unnecessary legacy regulations. The Commission wrote:

> BOCs are immediately relieved of the separate subsidiary, CEI, and ONA obligations with respect to wireline broadband Internet access services. In addition, subject to a one-year transition period for existing wireline broadband transmission services, all wireline broadband Internet access service providers are no longer subject to the *Computer II* requirement to separate out the underlying transmission from wireline broadband Internet access service and offer it on a common carrier basis.[‡]

---

[*] *See* 47 U.S.C. § 160.

[†] *Appropriate Framework for Broadband Access to the Internet over Wireline Facilities,* R&O and NPRM, 20 FCC Rcd. 14853, ¶ 9 (2005) [hereinafter *Wireline Broadband Order*].

c. *Putting it all together.* So, if you are an independent ISP that does not own any transmission facilities, is it still possible to provide broadband internet access to end-users over telephone lines? In the past, because of the *Computer Inquiries*, you could have purchased the broadband transmission capacity *directly* from the ILEC on a common carriage basis. But in 2005, the *Computer Inquiries* obligations were lifted. In the past, because of unbundling requirements, you could have accessed the broadband transmission capacity as a UNE, by becoming a data CLEC. But since 2003, line sharing is no longer a requirement either. Therefore, independent ISPs are out of luck, besides whatever a voluntary contract with ILECs might produce.[*]

3. UNINTENDED CONSEQUENCES: ACCESS

As of 2005, the FCC had made its classification decision that broadband internet was an information service confirmed by the Supreme Court in *Brand X.* One would expect that to be the end of the matter. But the story hardly ends there. In particular, as we studied in the prior chapter, starting around 2005, the FCC increasingly urged the importance of net neutrality, with open access to the last-leg connection. In other words, just as it had locked down that broadband internet was *not* a telecommunications service, it was simultaneously insisting on the importance of preserving certain common carriage-like features, such as carrying all traffic without discrimination. Could the FCC have its cake and eat it too?

The three most serious attempts by the FCC to enforce access came in a 2008 adjudication against Comcast; a 2010 rulemaking; and most recently a 2015 rulemaking. We start with *Comcast*, in which the FCC adjudicated a complaint that alleged that Comcast was violating net neutrality principles by suppressing the packets of a popular file-sharing application, BitTorrent. The FCC decided that Comcast had violated these principles, but on judicial review, the Commission first had to address whether it even had the power to enforce open access principles on an "information service" provider.

[‡] *Id.* ¶ 41

[*] To complicate matters, there is another arrangement called *line splitting.* In that case, the ILEC leases the entire local loop to a CLEC. That CLEC provides retail analog voice service to the end user. In addition, that CLEC splits off the high frequency portion and makes that capacity available to another data CLEC. (Engineering this split requires the cooperation of the ILEC.) A data CLEC would much rather engage in line sharing than in line splitting. The details are beyond the scope of this text.

COMCAST V. FCC
600 F.3d 642 (D.C. Cir. 2010)

TATEL, Circuit Judge:

In this case we must decide whether the [FCC] has authority to regulate an Internet service provider's network management practices. . . . The Commission has failed to make that showing.

II.

The Commission . . . rests its assertion of authority over Comcast's network management practices on the broad language of section 4(i) of the Act: "The Commission may perform any and all acts, make such rules and regulations, and issue such orders, not inconsistent with this chapter, as may be necessary in the execution of its functions," 47 U.S.C. § 154(i).

Courts have come to call the Commission's section 4(i) power its "ancillary" authority, a label that derives from three foundational Supreme Court decisions: *Southwestern Cable Co. (1968)*, *Midwest Video Corp., (1972) (Midwest Video I)*, and *Midwest Video Corp. (1979) (Midwest Video II)*.

We recently distilled the holdings of these three cases into a two-part test. In *American Library Ass'n v. FCC [(D.C. Cir. 2005)]*, we wrote: "The Commission . . . may exercise ancillary jurisdiction only when two conditions are satisfied: (1) the Commission's general jurisdictional grant under Title I [of the Communications Act] covers the regulated subject and (2) the regulations are reasonably ancillary to the Commission's effective performance of its statutorily mandated responsibilities." Comcast concedes that the Commission's action here satisfies the first requirement because the company's Internet service qualifies as "interstate and foreign communication by wire" within the meaning of Title I of the Communications Act. 47 U.S.C. § 152(a). Whether the Commission's action satisfies *American Library's* second requirement is the central issue in this case.

IV.

The Commission argues that the *Order* satisfies *American Library's* second requirement because it is "reasonably ancillary to the Commission's effective performance" of its responsibilities under several provisions of the Communications Act. These provisions fall into two categories: those that the parties agree set forth only congressional policy and those that at least arguably delegate regulatory authority to the Commission. We consider each in turn.

A.

The Commission relies principally on section 230(b), [which] states, in relevant part, that "[i]t is the policy of the United States . . . to promote the continued development of the Internet and other interactive computer services" and "to encourage the development of technologies which maximize user control over what information is received by individuals, families, and schools who use the Internet."

In addition, the Commission relies on section 1, in which Congress set forth its reasons for creating the Commission in 1934: "For the purpose of regulating interstate and foreign commerce in communication by wire and radio so as to make available, so far as possible, to all the people of the United States . . . a rapid, efficient, Nation-wide, and world-wide wire and radio communication service . . . at reasonable charges, . . . there is created a commission to be known as the 'Federal Communications Commission' . . . ." 47 U.S.C. § 151.

The Commission acknowledges that [these sections] are statements of policy that themselves delegate no regulatory authority. Still, the Commission maintains that the two provisions, like all provisions of the Communications Act, set forth "statutorily mandated responsibilities" that can anchor the exercise of ancillary authority.

In support of its reliance on congressional statements of policy, the Commission points out that in both *Southwestern Cable* and *Midwest Video I* the Supreme Court linked the challenged Commission actions to the furtherance of various congressional "goals," "objectives," and "policies."

We read *Southwestern Cable* and *Midwest Video I* quite differently. In those cases, the Supreme Court relied on policy statements not because, standing alone, they set out "statutorily mandated responsibilities," but rather because they did so in conjunction with an express delegation of authority to the Commission, i.e., Title III's authority to regulate broadcasting.

The teaching of [these and other related cases]—that policy statements alone cannot provide the basis for the Commission's exercise of ancillary authority—derives from the "axiomatic" principle that "administrative agencies may [act] only pursuant to authority delegated to them by Congress." *Am. Library.* Policy statements are just that—statements of policy. They are not delegations of regulatory authority.

B.

This brings us to the second category of statutory provisions the Commission relies on to support its exercise of ancillary authority. Unlike section 230(b) and section 1, each of these provisions could at least arguably be read to delegate regulatory authority to the Commission.

We begin with section 706 of the Telecommunications Act of 1996, which provides that "[t]he Commission . . . shall encourage the deployment on a reasonable and timely basis of advanced telecommunications capability to all Americans . . . by utilizing . . . price cap regulation, regulatory forbearance, measures that promote competition in the local telecommunications market, or other regulating methods that remove barriers to infrastructure investment." 47 U.S.C. § 1302(a). As the Commission points out, section 706 does contain a direct mandate—the Commission "shall encourage . . . ." In an earlier, still-binding order, however, the Commission ruled that section 706 "does not constitute an independent grant of authority." *In re Deployment of Wireline Servs. Offering Advanced Telecomms. Capability (1998)* (Wireline Deployment Order). Instead, the Commission explained, section 706 "directs the Commission to use the authority granted in other provisions . . . to encourage the deployment of advanced services."

Because the Commission has never questioned, let alone overruled, that understanding of *section 706*, and because agencies "may not . . . depart from a prior policy *sub silentio*," *FCC v. Fox Television Stations, Inc.(2009)*, the Commission remains bound by its earlier conclusion that section 706 grants no regulatory authority.

The Commission's attempt to tether its assertion of ancillary authority to section 256 of the Communications Act suffers from the same flaw. Section 256 directs the Commission to "establish procedures for . . . oversight of coordinated network planning . . . for the effective and efficient interconnection of public telecommunications networks." 47 U.S.C. § 256(b)(1). In language unmentioned by the Commission, however, section 256 goes on to state that "[n]othing in this section shall be construed as expanding . . . any authority that the Commission" otherwise has under law—precisely what the Commission seeks to do here.

The Commission next cites section 257. Enacted as part of the Telecommunications Act of 1996, that provision gave the Commission fifteen months to "complete a proceeding for the purpose of identifying and eliminating . . . market entry barriers for entrepreneurs and other small businesses in the provision and ownership of telecommunications services and information services." 47 U.S.C. § 257(a). Although the section 257 proceeding is now complete, that provision also directs the Commission to report to Congress every three years on any remaining barriers. . . . We readily accept that certain assertions of Commission authority could be "reasonably ancillary" to the Commission's statutory responsibility to issue a report to Congress. . . . But the Commission's attempt to dictate the operation of an otherwise unregulated service based on nothing more than its obligation to issue a report defies any plausible notion of "ancillariness."

Next the Commission argues that its exercise of authority over Comcast's network management practices is ancillary to its section 201 common carrier authority—though the section 201 argument the Commission sets forth in its brief is very different from the one appearing in the *Order*. As indicated above, section 201 provides that "[a]ll charges, practices, classifications, and regulations for and in connection with [common carrier] service shall be just and reasonable." 47 U.S.C. § 201(b). In the *Order*, the Commission found that by blocking certain traffic on Comcast's Internet service, the company had effectively shifted the burden of that traffic to other service providers, some of which were operating their Internet access services on a common carrier basis subject to Title II. By marginally increasing the variable costs of those providers, the Commission maintained, Comcast's blocking of peer-to-peer transmissions affected common carrier rates.

Instead, the Commission now argues that voice over Internet Protocol (VoIP) services—in essence, telephone services using Internet technology— affect the prices and practices of traditional telephony common carriers subject to section 201 regulation. According to the Commission, some VoIP services were disrupted by Comcast's network management practices. We have no need to examine this claim, however, for the Commission must defend its action on the same grounds advanced in the Order. *SEC v. Chenery Corp. (1943)*.

The same problem undercuts the Commission's effort to link its regulation of Comcast's network management practices to its Title III authority over broadcasting. The Commission contends that Internet video "has the potential to affect the broadcast industry" by influencing "local origination of programming, diversity of viewpoints, and the desirability of providing service in certain markets." But the Commission cites no source for this argument in the *Order*, nor can we find one.

[The court's analysis why 47 U.S.C. § 543, which addresses cable television rates, did not provide ancillary jurisdiction has been omitted.—ED.]

V.

"[T]he allowance of wide latitude in the exercise of delegated powers is not the equivalent of untrammeled freedom to regulate activities over which the statute fails to confer . . . Commission authority." *NARUC II [(D.C. Cir. 1989)]*. Because the Commission has failed to tie its assertion of ancillary authority over

Comcast's Internet service to any "statutorily mandated responsibility," *Am. Library,* we grant the petition for review and vacate the *Order.*

So ordered.

NOTES & QUESTIONS

1. *What* Brand X *decided.* In an omitted portion of the opinion, the court addressed how the FCC had read the Supreme Court's opinion in *Brand X.* In its *Comcast* Order, the FCC wrote:

> [A]ny assertion the Commission lacks the requisite statutory authority over providers of Internet broadband access services, such as Comcast, has been flatly rejected by the U.S. Supreme Court. In *Brand X . . .* the Court specifically stated that "the Commission has jurisdiction to impose additional regulatory obligations [on information service providers] under its Title I ancillary jurisdiction to regulate interstate and foreign communications" and that "the Commission remains free to impose special regulatory duties on facilities-based ISPs under its Title I ancillary jurisdiction."

In response, the D.C. Circuit pointed out, first, that the Supreme Court's discussion of ancillary jurisdiction was dicta. The court conceded that even if technically dicta, Supreme Court statements can nevertheless be "authoritative." But any such hard question did not have to be answered because "the Commission stretche[d] the Court's words too far. By leaping from *Brand X's* observation that the Commission's ancillary authority may allow it to impose *some* kinds of obligations on cable internet providers to a claim of plenary authority over such providers, the Commission runs afoul of *Southwestern Cable* and *Midwest Video I.*"[*]

2. *Easy first step.* What is step 1 of the ancillary jurisdiction inquiry, and how is it connected to the following section?

> § 152. Application of chapter
>
> (a) The provisions of this Act shall apply to all interstate and foreign communication by wire or radio and all interstate and foreign transmission of energy by radio, which originates and/or is received within the United States . . . and to the licensing and regulating of all radio stations as hereinafter provided. . . . The provisions of this Act shall apply with respect to cable service, to all persons engaged within the United States in providing such service, and to the facilities of cable operators. . . .

Why was step one easily satisfied?

3. *Harder second step.* What is step two, and how is it connected to the following section?

---

[*] 600 F.3d at 650.

§ 154. Federal Communications Commission

(i) Duties and powers. The Commission may perform any and all acts, make such rules and regulations, and issue such orders, not inconsistent with this Act, as may be necessary in the execution of its functions.

4. *Powerless provisions.* In the step two analysis, certain provisions were seen as not delegating any actual power to the FCC. Explain how and why §§ 230, 151, 706, and 256 fall into this category.

5. *Ancillary gone too far.* Even if a provision does delegate some power, open access might be too distantly connected to that power to fall within the Commission's ancillary jurisdiction. Recall *Midwest Video II.* Explain how § 257 falls into this category.

6. *Paradise lost.* The court holds that the FCC waived some of its best arguments either because it had taken a contrary stance in a prior ruling or because it had failed to make specific arguments in the *Comcast* adjudication. Explain how and why § 706 and various Title II and Title III arguments fall into this category. By the way, do you think that the waiver is somehow permanent? Or could the FCC change its mind and try again?

7. *The FCC response.* The FCC decided not to file for cert. review with the Supreme Court. Instead, it went back to the drawing board and pivoted away from adjudication and opted instead for a rulemaking, and issued a revised *Report & Order* in 2010.[*] After the Commission issued its rules, Verizon and other providers immediately sued. But, this time around, the FCC didn't rely purely on its ancillary jurisdiction; the Commission argued that Congress had granted explicit authority in § 706 to regulate broadband providers. Judge Tatel was on the panel again, and this time around he reached a different conclusion about the scope of the Commission's authority.

VERIZON v. FCC
740 F.3d 623 (D.C. Cir. 2014)

TATEL, Circuit Judge:

I.

Four major participants in the Internet marketplace are relevant to the issues before us: backbone networks, broadband providers, edge providers, and end users. Backbone networks are interconnected, long-haul fiber-optic links and high-speed routers capable of transmitting vast amounts of data. . . . To pull the whole picture together with a slightly oversimplified example: when an edge

---

[*] Preserving the Open Internet, 25 FCC Rcd. 17905 (2010).

provider such as YouTube transmits some sort of content—say, a video of a cat—to an end user, that content is broken down into packets of information, which are carried by the edge provider's local access provider to the backbone network, which transmits these packets to the end user's local access provider, which, in turn, transmits the information to the end user, who then views and hopefully enjoys the cat.

As authority for the adoption of these rules, the Commission invoked a plethora of statutory provisions. In particular, the Commission relied on section 706 of the 1996 Telecommunications Act, which directs it to encourage the deployment of broadband telecommunications capability. *See* 47 U.S.C. § 1302(a), (b). According to the Commission, the rules furthered this statutory mandate by preserving unhindered the "virtuous circle of innovation" that had long driven the growth of the Internet. Internet openness, it reasoned, spurs investment and development by edge providers, which leads to increased end-user demand for broadband access, which leads to increased investment in broadband network infrastructure and technologies, which in turn leads to further innovation and development by edge providers. If, the Commission continued, broadband providers were to disrupt this "virtuous circle" by "[r]estricting edge providers' ability to reach end users, and limiting end users' ability to choose which edge providers to patronize," they would "reduce the rate of innovation at the edge and, in turn, the likely rate of improvements to network infrastructure."

II.

The Commission cites numerous statutory provisions it claims grant it the power to promulgate the *Open Internet Order* rules. But we start and end our analysis with section 706 of the 1996 Telecommunications Act, which, as we shall explain, furnishes the Commission with the requisite affirmative authority to adopt the regulations.

Verizon contends that neither subsection (a) nor (b) of section 706 confers any regulatory authority on the Commission. As Verizon sees it, the two subsections amount to nothing more than congressional statements of policy. Verizon further contends that even if either provision grants the Commission substantive authority, the scope of that grant is not so expansive as to permit the Commission to regulate broadband providers in the manner that the *Open Internet Order* rules do. In addressing these questions, we apply the familiar two-step analysis of [*Chevron*]. As the Supreme Court has recently made clear, *Chevron* deference is warranted even if the Commission has interpreted a statutory provision that could be said to delineate the scope of the agency's jurisdiction. *See City of Arlington v. FCC* (2013). Thus, if we determine that the

Commission's interpretation of section 706 represents a reasonable resolution of a statutory ambiguity, we must defer to that interpretation. The *Chevron* inquiry overlaps substantially with that required by the Administrative Procedure Act (APA), pursuant to which we must also determine whether the Commission's actions were "arbitrary, capricious, an abuse of discretion, or otherwise not in accordance with law." 5 U.S.C. § 706(2)(A).

A

This is not the first time the Commission has asserted that section 706(a) grants it authority to regulate broadband providers. Advancing a similar argument in *Comcast,* the Commission contended that section 706(a) provided a statutory hook for its exercise of ancillary jurisdiction. Although we thought that section 706(a) might "arguably be read to delegate regulatory authority to the Commission," we concluded that the Commission could not rely on this provision . . . because it had previously determined, in the still-binding *Advanced Services Order,*[*] that the provision "does not constitute an independent grant of authority."

But the Commission need not remain *forever* bound by the *Advanced Services Order* 's restrictive reading of section 706(a). . . . The APA's requirement of reasoned decision-making ordinarily demands that an agency acknowledge and explain the reasons for a changed interpretation. [S]o long as an agency "adequately explains the reasons for a reversal of policy," its new interpretation of a statute cannot be rejected simply because it is new. *Brand X.*

In the *Open Internet Order,* however, the Commission has offered a reasoned explanation for its changed understanding of section 706(a).

[S]etting forth those "reasons" at some length, the Commission analyzed the statute's text, its legislative history, and the resultant scope of the Commission's authority, concluding that each of these considerations supports the view that section 706(a) constitutes an affirmative grant of regulatory authority. In these circumstances, and contrary to Verizon's contentions, we have no basis for saying that the Commission "casually ignored prior policies and interpretations or otherwise failed to provide a reasoned explanation" for its changed interpretation.

The question, then, is this: Does the Commission's current understanding of section 706(a) as a grant of regulatory authority represent a reasonable interpretation of an ambiguous statute? We believe it does.

---

[*] *In re Deployment of Wireline Services Offering Advanced Telecommunications Capability,* 13 FCC Rcd. 24012 (1998).

Recall that the provision directs the Commission to "encourage the deployment ... of advanced telecommunications capability ... by utilizing ... price cap regulation, regulatory forbearance, measures that promote competition in the local telecommunications market, or other regulating methods that remove barriers to infrastructure investment." 47 U.S.C. § 1302(a). As Verizon argues, this language could certainly be read as simply setting forth a statement of congressional policy, directing the Commission to employ "regulating methods" already at the Commission's disposal in order to achieve the stated goal of promoting "advanced telecommunications" technology. But the language can just as easily be read to vest the Commission with actual authority to utilize such "regulating methods" to meet this stated goal. As the Commission put it in the *Open Internet Order*, one might reasonably think that Congress, in directing the Commission to undertake certain acts, "necessarily invested the Commission with the statutory authority to carry out those acts."

This case, moreover, is a far cry from *FDA v. Brown & Williamson Tobacco Corp.*,* on which Verizon principally relies. There, the Supreme Court held that "Congress ha[d] clearly precluded the [Food and Drug Administration] from asserting jurisdiction to regulate tobacco products." The Court emphasized that the FDA had not only completely disclaimed any authority to regulate tobacco products, but had done so for more than eighty years, and that Congress had repeatedly legislated against this background. The Court also observed that the FDA's newly adopted conclusion that it did in fact have authority to regulate this industry would, given its findings regarding the effects of tobacco products and its authorizing statute, logically require the agency to ban such products altogether, a result clearly contrary to congressional policy. Furthermore, the Court reasoned, if Congress had intended to "delegate a decision of such economic and political significance" to the agency, it would have done so far more clearly.

The circumstances here are entirely different. Although the Commission once disclaimed authority to regulate under section 706(a), it never disclaimed authority to regulate the Internet or Internet providers altogether, nor is there any similar history of congressional reliance on such a disclaimer. [W]hen Congress passed section 706(a) in 1996, it did so against the backdrop of the Commission's long history of subjecting to common carrier regulation the entities that controlled the last-mile facilities over which end users accessed the Internet. Indeed, one might have thought, as the Commission originally concluded, that Congress clearly contemplated that the Commission would

---

* 529 U.S. 120 (2000).

continue regulating Internet providers in the manner it had previously. In fact, section 706(a)'s legislative history suggests that Congress may have, somewhat presciently, viewed that provision as an affirmative grant of authority to the Commission whose existence would become necessary if other contemplated grants of statutory authority were for some reason unavailable. The Senate Report describes section 706 as a "necessary fail-safe" "intended to ensure that one of the primary objectives of the [Act]—to accelerate deployment of advanced telecommunications capability—is achieved." As the Commission observed in the *Open Internet Order*, it would be "odd ... to characterize Section 706(a) as a 'fail-safe' that 'ensures' the Commission's ability to promote advanced services if it conferred no actual authority."

Thus, although regulation of broadband Internet providers certainly involves decisions of great "economic and political significance," we have little reason given this history to think that Congress could not have delegated some of these decisions to the Commission. To be sure, Congress does not, as Verizon reminds us, "hide elephants in mouseholes."[*] But FCC regulation of broadband providers is no elephant, and section 706(a) is no mousehole.

Of course, we might well hesitate to conclude that Congress intended to grant the Commission substantive authority in section 706(a) if that authority would have no limiting principle. But we are satisfied that the scope of authority granted to the Commission by section 706(a) is not so boundless as to compel the conclusion that Congress could never have intended the provision to set forth anything other than a general statement of policy. The Commission has identified at least two limiting principles inherent in section 706(a). First, the section must be read in conjunction with other provisions of the Communications Act, including, most importantly, those limiting the Commission's subject matter jurisdiction to "interstate and foreign communication by wire and radio." 47 U.S.C. § 152(a). Any regulatory action authorized by section 706(a) would thus have to fall within the Commission's subject matter jurisdiction over such communications—a limitation whose importance this court has recognized in delineating the reach of the Commission's ancillary jurisdiction. Second, any regulations must be designed to achieve a particular purpose: to "encourage the deployment on a reasonable and timely basis of advanced telecommunications capability to all Americans." 47 U.S.C. § 1302(a). Section 706(a) thus gives the Commission authority to promulgate only those regulations that it establishes will fulfill this specific

---

[*] Whitman v. American Trucking Ass'ns, Inc., 531 U.S. 457, 468 (2001).

statutory goal—a burden that, as we trust our searching analysis below will demonstrate, is far from "meaningless."

NOTES & QUESTIONS

1. *The § 706 arguments.* The D.C. Circuit had suggested that the FCC was bound by a prior order, which had rejected the notion that § 706 granted any substantive power. How does the FCC respond to this argument? And if that response is persuasive, how precisely does § 706 give the FCC power to enact net neutrality regulations?

2. *Towards a new title?* The D.C. Circuit found in *Verizon* that the FCC has broad, but not unlimited, power to regulate service providers under § 706. How would you define this authority? Does the court view it as 'ancillary' to some other power, or is it essentially a separate *classification* similar to Title II authority used to regulate common carriers or Title VI authority to regulate cable providers? Could it also be used to regulate edge providers?

3. *Pyrrhic victory.* Although the D.C. Circuit agreed that the FCC had authority to regulate broadband providers under § 706, it nevertheless vacated many of the Open Internet rules because they conflicted with other federal statutes that required, in rough terms, that only common carriers could be treated like common carriers:

> We think it obvious that the Commission would violate the Communications Act were it to regulate broadband providers as common carriers. Given the Commission's still-binding decision to classify broadband providers not as providers of "telecommunications services" but instead as providers of "information services," such treatment would run afoul of section 153(51): "A telecommunications carrier shall be treated as a common carrier under this [Act] only to the extent that it is engaged in providing telecommunications services." 47 U.S.C. § 153(51); Likewise, because the Commission has classified mobile broadband service as a "private" mobile service, and not a "commercial" mobile service, treatment of mobile broadband providers as common carriers would violate section 332: "A person engaged in the provision of a service that is a private mobile service shall not, insofar as such person is so engaged, be treated as a common carrier for any purpose under this [Act]." 47 U.S.C. § 332(c)(2).

The court went on to review the proposed Open Internet rules, and determined whether they "subject broadband providers to common carrier treatment." In particular, the court looked to the definition of common carrier outlined in the *Midwest Video II* decision that we read earlier. The court rejected the FCC's argument that broadband providers are not "carriers":

It is true, generally speaking, that the "customers" of broadband providers are end users. But that hardly means that broadband providers could not also be carriers with respect to edge providers. "Since it is clearly possible for a given entity to carry on many types of activities, it is at least logical to conclude that one may be a common carrier with regard to some activities but not others." Because broadband providers furnish a service to edge providers, thus undoubtedly functioning as edge providers' "carriers," the obligations that the Commission imposes on broadband providers may well constitute common carriage per se regardless of whether edge providers are broadband providers' principal customers. This is true whatever the nature of the preexisting commercial relationship between broadband providers and edge providers. In contending otherwise, the Commission appears to misunderstand the nature of the inquiry in which we must engage. The question is not whether, absent the Open Internet Order, broadband providers would or did act as common carriers with respect to edge providers; rather, the question is whether, given the rules imposed by the Open Internet Order, broadband providers are now obligated to act as common carriers.

The court ultimately held that the "anti-discrimination" and "anti-blocking" rules imposed by the FCC—which we discussed in CHAPTER 4: ACCESS— were equivalent to common carrier obligations and could not be imposed on non common carrier providers.

4. *Hitting the regulatory reset button.* The FCC had to go back to the drawing board yet again. Through painful litigation, it had been vindicated that the internet, whether via dial-up or broadband, was indeed an information service. It had also been vindicated that the FCC had power to adopt open internet rules under § 706. Nevertheless, the FCC was still blocked because the Communications Act prevented anything but telecommunications services from being treated like common carriers. What could the FCC do at that point? Well, it finally pulled the trigger and reclassified internet service providers as common carriers.

4. BROADBAND INTERNET AS TELECOMMUNICATIONS SERVICE

In 2015, the FCC officially hit "reset" and issued a new Open Internet order. This time, the Commission did not rely solely on its Title I ancillary jurisdiction or on its § 706 authority. Instead, the FCC redefined broadband internet access service as a Title II common carriage service ("telecommunications service"). That order was upheld by the D.C. Circuit on review in *USTA v. FCC*, 825 F.3d 674 (D.C. Cir. 2016). Then, as we learned in

CHAPTER 4: ACCESS, everything changed after the 2016 Election and the appointment of Chairman Pai.

In 2018, the Commission decided to hit "undo" and classify broadband internet service as an information service again (not subject to Title II). But even though the 2015 reclassification order was nullified, we will still review its reasoning because the courts reviewing the 2018 Order will have to decide whether the FCC's decision to undo its reclassification order was arbitrary and capricious.

**PROTECTING AND PROMOTING
THE OPEN INTERNET**
R&O, 30 FCC Rcd. 5601 (2015)

42. The *Verizon* decision thus made clear that section 706 affords the Commission substantive authority, and that open Internet protections are within the scope of that authority. And this Order relies on section 706 for the open Internet rules. But, in light of *Verizon*, absent a classification of broadband providers as providing a "telecommunications service," the Commission could only rely on section 706 to put in place open Internet protections that steered clear of regulating broadband providers as common carriers *per se*. Thus, in order to bring a decade of debate to a certain conclusion, we conclude that the best path is to rely on all available sources of legal authority—while applying them with a light touch consistent with further investment and broadband deployment. Taking the *Verizon* decision's implicit invitation, we revisit the Commission's classification of the retail broadband Internet access service as an information service and clarify that this service encompasses the so-called "edge service."

43. Exercising our delegated authority to interpret ambiguous terms in the Communications Act, as confirmed by the Supreme Court in *Brand X*, today's Order concludes that the facts in the market today are very different from the facts that supported the Commission's 2002 decision to treat cable broadband as an information service and its subsequent application to fixed and mobile broadband services. Those prior decisions were based largely on a factual record compiled over a decade ago, during an earlier time when, for example, many consumers would use homepages supplied by their broadband provider. In fact, the *Brand X* Court explicitly acknowledged that the Commission had previously classified the transmission service, which broadband providers offer, as a telecommunications service and that the Commission could return to that classification if it provided an adequate justification. . . . As the record reflects, times and usage patterns have changed and it is clear that broadband providers

are offering both consumers and edge providers straightforward transmission capabilities that the Communications Act defines as a "telecommunications service."

44.   The *Brand X* decision made famous the metaphor of pizza delivery. Justice Scalia, in dissent, concluded that the Commission had exceeded its legal authority by classifying cable-modem service as an "information service." To make his point, Justice Scalia described a pizzeria offering delivery services as well as selling pizzas and concluded that, similarly—broadband providers were offering "telecommunications services" even if that service was not offered on a "stand-alone basis."

45.   To take Justice Scalia's metaphor a step further, suppose that in 2014, the pizzeria owners discovered that other nearby restaurants did not deliver their food and thus concluded that the pizza-delivery drivers could generate more revenue by delivering from any neighborhood restaurant (including their own pizza some of the time). Consumers would clearly understand that they are being offered a delivery service.

46.   Today, broadband providers are offering stand-alone transmission capacity and that conclusion is not changed even if, as Justice Scalia recognized, other products may be offered at the same time. The trajectory of technology in the decade since the *Brand X* decision has been towards greater and greater modularity. For example, consumers have considerable power to combine their mobile broadband connections with the device, operating systems, applications, Internet services, and content of their choice. Today, broadband Internet access service is fundamentally understood by customers as a transmission platform through which consumers can access third-party content, applications, and services of their choosing.

47.   Based on this updated record, this Order concludes that the retail broadband Internet access service available today is best viewed as separately identifiable offers of (1) a broadband Internet access service that is a telecommunications service (including assorted functions and capabilities used for the management and control of that telecommunication service) and (2) various "add-on" applications, content, and services that generally are information services. This finding more than reasonably interprets the ambiguous terms in the Communications Act, best reflects the factual record in this proceeding, and will most effectively permit the implementation of sound policy consistent with statutory objectives, including the adoption of effective open Internet protections.

48.   This Order also revisits the Commission's prior classification of mobile broadband Internet access service as a private mobile service, which cannot be

subject to common carrier regulation, and finds that it is best viewed as a commercial mobile service or, in the alternative, the functional equivalent of commercial mobile service. Under the statutory definition, commercial mobile services must be "interconnected with the public switched network (as such terms are defined by regulation by the Commission)."[44] Consistent with that delegation of authority to define these terms, and with the Commission's previous recognition that the public switched network will grow and change over time, this Order updates the definition of public switched network to reflect current technology, by including services that use public IP addresses. Under this revised definition, the Order concludes that mobile broadband Internet access service is interconnected with the public switched network. In the alternative, the Order concludes that mobile broadband Internet access service is the functional equivalent of commercial mobile service because, like commercial mobile service, it is a widely available, for profit mobile service that offers mobile subscribers the capability to send and receive communications, including voice, on their mobile device.

49. By classifying broadband Internet access service under Title II of the Act, in our view the Commission addresses any limitations that past classification decisions placed on the ability to adopt strong open Internet rules, as interpreted by the D.C. Circuit in the *Verizon* case.

50. Having classified broadband Internet access service as a telecommunications service, we respond to the *Verizon* court's holding, supporting our open Internet rules under the Commission's Title II authority and removing any common carriage limitation on the exercise of our section 706 authority. For mobile broadband services, we also ground the open Internet rules in our Title III authority to protect the public interest through the management of spectrum licensing.

D. Broad Forbearance

51. In finding that broadband Internet access service is subject to Title II, we simultaneously exercise the Commission's forbearance authority to forbear from 30 statutory provisions and render over 700 codified rules inapplicable, to establish a light-touch regulatory framework tailored to preserving those provisions that advance our goals of more, better, and open broadband. We thus forbear from the vast majority of rules adopted under Title II. We do not, however, forbear from sections 201, 202, and 208 . . . which are necessary to support adoption of our open Internet rules.

---

[44] 47 U.S.C. § 332(d)(2).

52. In addition, we do not forbear from a limited number of sections necessary to ensure consumers are protected, promote competition, and advance universal access, all of which will foster network investment, thereby helping to promote broadband deployment.

*　　*　　*

IV. DECLARATORY RULING: CLASSIFICATION OF BROADBAND INTERNET ACCESS SERVICES

B. Rationale for Revisiting the Commission's Classification of Broadband Internet Access Services

329. The *Brand X* Court emphasized that the Commission has an obligation to consider the wisdom of its classification decision on a continuing basis. An agency's evaluation of its prior determinations naturally includes consideration of the law affecting its ability to carry out statutory policy objectives. As discussed above, the record in the *Open Internet* proceeding demonstrates that broadband providers continue to have the incentives and ability to engage in practices that pose a threat to Internet openness, and as such, rules to protect the open nature of the Internet remain necessary. To protect the open Internet, and to end legal uncertainty, we must use multiple sources of legal authority . . . . Thus, we now find it appropriate to examine how broadband Internet access services are provided today.

330. Changed factual circumstances cause us to revise our earlier classification of broadband Internet access service based on the voluminous record developed in response to the *2014 Open Internet NPRM*. In the 2002 *Cable Modem Declaratory Ruling*, the Commission observed that "the cable modem service business is still nascent, and the shape of broadband deployment is not yet clear. Business relationships among cable operators and their service offerings are evolving." [T]he premises underlying that decision have changed. As the record demonstrates and we discuss in more detail below, we are unable to maintain our prior finding that broadband providers are offering a service in which transmission capabilities are "inextricably intertwined" with various proprietary applications and services. Rather, it is more reasonable to assert that the "indispensable function" of broadband Internet access service is "the connection link that in turn enables access to the essentially unlimited range of Internet-based services." This is evident, as discussed below, from: (1) consumer conduct, which shows that subscribers today rely heavily on third-party services, such as email and social networking sites, even when such services are included as add-ons in the broadband Internet access provider's service; (2) broadband providers' marketing and pricing strategies, which

emphasize speed and reliability of transmission separately from and over the extra features of the service packages they offer; and (3) the technical characteristics of broadband Internet access service. We also note that the predictive judgments on which the Commission relied in the *Cable Modem Declaratory Ruling* anticipating vibrant intermodal competition for fixed broadband cannot be reconciled with current marketplace realities.

C. Classification of Broadband Internet Access Service

331. [We] conclude that broadband Internet access service is a telecommunications service subject to our regulatory authority under Title II of the Communications Act regardless of the technological platform over which the service is offered. We both revise our prior classifications of wired broadband Internet access service and wireless broadband Internet access service, and classify broadband Internet access service provided over other technology platforms. In doing so, we exercise the well-established power of federal agencies to interpret ambiguous provisions in the statutes they administer.

332. The Court's application of this *Chevron* test in *Brand X* makes clear our delegated authority to revisit our prior interpretation of ambiguous statutory terms and reclassify broadband Internet access service as a telecommunications service[.]

333. Furthermore, reading the *Brand X* majority, concurring, and dissenting opinions together, it is apparent that most, and perhaps all, of the nine Justices believed that it would have been at least permissible under the Act to have classified the transmission service included with wired Internet access service as a telecommunications service[.]

334. It is also well settled that we may reconsider, on reasonable grounds, the Commission's earlier application of the ambiguous statutory definitions of "telecommunications service" and "information service[."]

3. Broadband Internet Access Service Is a Telecommunications Service

355. We now turn to applying the statutory terms at issue in light of our updated understanding of how both fixed and mobile broadband Internet access services are offered. Three definitional terms are critical to a determination of the appropriate classification of broadband Internet access service. First, the Act defines "telecommunications" as "the transmission, between or among points specified by the user, of information of the user's choosing, without change in the form or content of the information as sent and received." Second, the Act defines "telecommunications service" as "the offering of telecommunications for a fee directly to the public, or to such classes of users as to be effectively available directly to the public, regardless of the facilities used."[967] Finally,

"information service" is defined in the Act as "the offering of a capability for generating, acquiring, storing, transforming, processing, retrieving, utilizing, or making available information via telecommunications . . . , but does not include any use of any such capability for the management, control, or operation of a telecommunications system or the management of a telecommunications service."[968]   We observe that the critical distinction between a telecommunications and an information service turns on what the provider is "offering." If the offering meets the statutory definition of telecommunications service, then the service is also necessarily a common carrier service.[969]

356. In reconsidering our prior decisions and reaching a different conclusion, we find that this result best reflects the factual record in this proceeding, and will most effectively permit the implementation of sound policy consistent with statutory objectives. [W]e find that broadband Internet access service, as offered by both fixed and mobile providers, is best seen, and is in fact most commonly seen, as an offering (in the words of Justice Scalia, dissenting in *Brand X*) "consisting of two separate things": "*both* 'high-speed access to the Internet' *and* other 'applications and functions.'" . . . We also find that domain name service (DNS)[972] and caching,[973] when provided with broadband Internet access services, fit squarely within the telecommunications systems management exception to the definition of "information service."[974]   Thus, when provided with broadband Internet access services, these integrated services do not convert broadband Internet access service into an information service.

---

[967] Id. § 153(53).

[968] Id. § 153(24).

[969] See Universal Service First Report and Order, 12 FCC Rcd. at 9177, para. 785 ("We find that the definition of 'telecommunications services' in which the phrase 'directly to the public' appears is intended to encompass only telecommunications provided on a common carrier basis."); U.S. Telecom Ass'n v. FCC, 295 F.3d at 1328-29 (telecommunications carriers limited to common carriers); Cable & Wireless, PLC, Order, 12 FCC Rcd. 8516, 8521, para. 13 (1997) ("[T]he definition of telecommunications services is intended to clarify that telecommunications services are common carrier services.").

[972] DNS is most commonly used to translate domain names, such as "nytimes.com," into numerical IP addresses that are used by network equipment to locate the desired content. See Cable Modem Declaratory Ruling, 17 FCC Rcd. at 4810, para. 17 n.74; see also Brand X, 545 U.S. at 987, 999.

[973] Caching is the storing of copies of content at locations in a network closer to subscribers than the original source of the content. This enables more rapid retrieval of information from websites that subscribers wish to see most often. See Cable Modem Declaratory Ruling, 17 FCC Rcd. at 4810, para. 17 n.76.

[974] See 47 U.S.C. § 153(24) ("The term 'information service' . . . does not include any use of any such capability for the management, control, or operation of a telecommunications system of the management of a telecommunications service."). Hereinafter, we refer to this exception as the "telecommunications systems management" exception.

357. *The Commission Does Not Bear a Special Burden in This Proceeding.* Opponents of classifying broadband Internet access service as a telecommunications service advocate a narrow reading of the Supreme Court's decision in *Brand X.* They contend that the Court's decision to affirm the classification of cable modem service as an information service was driven by specific factual findings concerning DNS and caching, and argue that the Commission may not revisit its decision unless it can show that the facts have changed. Opponents also cite a passage from the Supreme Court's *Fox [v. FCC]* decision suggesting that an agency must provide "a more detailed justification than what would suffice for a new policy on a blank slate" where the agency's "new policy rests upon factual findings that contradict those which underlay its prior policy," or "when its prior policy has engendered serious reliance interests that must be taken into account."

358. We disagree with these commenters on both counts. The *Fox* court explained that in these circumstances, "it is not that further justification is demanded by the mere fact of policy change; but that a reasoned explanation is needed for disregarding facts and circumstances that underlay or were engendered by the prior policy." As the D.C. Circuit more recently confirmed, "[t]his does not . . . equate to a 'heightened standard' for reasonableness." The Commission need only show "that the new policy is permissible under the statute, that there are good reasons for it, and that the agency *believes* it to be better.

360. In *Fox,* the Supreme Court also suggested that an agency may need to provide "a more detailed justification" for a change in policy when the prior policy "has engendered serious reliance interests." Opponents of reclassification contend that broadband providers have invested billions of dollars to deploy new broadband network facilities in reliance on the Title I classification decisions and it would be unreasonable to change course now. We disagree. As a factual matter, the regulatory status of broadband Internet access service appears to have, at most, an indirect effect (along with many other factors) on investment. [T]he history of the *Computer Inquiries* indicates that, at a minimum the regulatory status of these or similar offerings involved a highly regulated activity for many years. . . . The legal status of the information service classification [has] been called into question too consistently to have engendered such substantial reliance interests that our reclassification decision cannot now be sustained absent extraordinary justifications. Finally, the forbearance relief we grant in the accompanying order in conjunction with our reclassification decision keeps the scope of our proposed regulatory oversight within the same

general boundaries that the Commission earlier anticipated drawing under its Title I authority.

a. Broadband Internet Access Service Involves Telecommunications

361. *Broadband Internet Access Service Transmits Information of the User's Choosing Between Points Specified by the User.* [I]t is clear that broadband Internet access service is providing "telecommunications." Users rely on broadband Internet access service to transmit "information of the user's choosing," "between or among points specified by the user." Time Warner Cable asserts that broadband Internet access service cannot be a telecommunications service because—as end users do not know where online content is stored—Internet communications allegedly do not travel to "points specified by the user" within the statutory definition of "telecommunications." We disagree. We find that the term "points specified by the user" is ambiguous, and conclude that uncertainty concerning the geographic location of an endpoint of communication is irrelevant for the purpose of determining whether a broadband Internet access service is providing "telecommunications." Although Internet users often do not know the geographic location of edge providers or other users, there is no question that users specify the end points of their Internet communications. . . . Likewise, numerous forms of telephone service qualify as telecommunications even though the consumer typically does not know the geographic location of the called party. . . . More generally, we have never understood the definition of "telecommunications" to require that users specify—or even know—information about the routing or handling of their transmissions along the path to the end point, nor do we do so now.

362. *Information is Transmitted Without Change in Form or Content.* Broadband Internet access service may use a variety of protocols to deliver content from one point to another. However, the packet payload (*i.e.,* the content requested or sent by the user) is not altered by the variety of headers that a provider may use to route a given packet. The information that a broadband provider places into a packet header as part of the broadband Internet access service is for the management of the broadband Internet access service and it is removed before the packet is handed over to the application at the destination.[1003] Broadband providers thus move packets from sender to recipient without any change in format or content, and "merely transferring a packet to its intended recipient does not by itself involve generating, acquiring, transforming, processing, retrieving, utilizing, or making available information." Rather, "it is

---

[1003] See Internet Engineering Task Force, Requirements for Internet Hosts – Communications Layers, RFC 1122 (Oct. 1989), https://tools.ietf.org/html/rfc1122.

the nature of [packet delivery] that the 'form and content of the information' is precisely the same when an IP packet is sent by the sender as when that same packet is received by the recipient."

b. Broadband Internet Access Service is a "Telecommunications Service"

363. Having affirmatively determined that broadband Internet access service involves "telecommunications," we also find that broadband Internet access service is a "telecommunications service." A "telecommunications service" is the "offering of telecommunications for a fee directly to the public,. . . regardless of the facilities used."[1006] We find that broadband Internet access service providers offer broadband Internet access service "directly to the public." [T]he record indicates that broadband providers routinely market broadband Internet access services widely and to the general public. Because a provider is a common carrier "by virtue of its functions," we find that such offerings are made directly to the public within the Act's definition of telecommunications service. . . . Further, that some broadband providers require potential broadband customers to disclose their addresses and service locations before viewing such an offer does not change our conclusion. The Commission has long maintained that offering a service to the public does not necessarily require holding it out to all end users. Some individualization in pricing or terms is not a barrier to finding that a service is a telecommunications service.

364. [B]roadband providers hold themselves out to carry all edge provider traffic to the broadband provider's end user customers regardless of source and regardless of whether the edge provider itself has a specific arrangement with the broadband provider. . . . We recognize that there are some interconnection agreements that do contain more individualized terms and conditions. However, this circumstance is not inherently different from similarly individualized commercial agreements for certain enterprise broadband services, which the Commission has long held to be common carriage telecommunications services subject to Title II. That the individualized terms may be negotiated does not change the underlying fact that a broadband provider holds the *service* out directly to the public.

c. Broadband Internet Access Service is Not an "Information Service"

365. We further find that broadband Internet access service is not an information service. The Act defines "information service" as "the offering of a capability for generating, acquiring, storing, transforming, processing, retrieving, utilizing, or making available information via telecommunications . . .

[1006] 47 U.S.C. § 153(53).

but does not include any use of any such capability for the management, control, or operation of a telecommunications system or the management of a telecommunications service."[1023] To the extent that broadband Internet access service is offered along with some capabilities that would otherwise fall within the information service definition, they do not turn broadband Internet access service into a functionally integrated information service. To the contrary, we find these capabilities either fall within the telecommunications systems management exception or are separate offerings that are not inextricably integrated with broadband Internet access service, or both.

366. *DNS Falls Within the Telecommunications Systems Management Exception to the Definition of Information Services.* As the Supreme Court spotlighted in *Brand X,* the Commission predicated its prior conclusion that cable modem service was an integrated information service at least in part on the view that it "transmits data *only* in connection with the further processing of information." That was so, under the theory of the *Cable Modem Declaratory Ruling,* because "[a] user cannot reach a third-party's Web site without DNS, which (among other things) matches the Web site address the end user types into his browser (or 'clicks' on with his mouse) with the IP address of the Web page's host server." The Commission had assumed without analysis that DNS, when provided with Internet access service, is an information service. The Commission credited record evidence that DNS "enable[s] routing" and that "*[w]ithout this service, Internet access would be impractical for most users.*" In his *Brand X* dissent, however, Justice Scalia correctly observed that DNS "is scarcely more than *routing* information, which is expressly excluded from the definition of 'information service'" by the telecommunications systems management exception set out in the last clause of section 3(24) of the Act.

367. Although the Commission assumed in the *Cable Modem Declaratory Ruling—sub silentio—*that DNS fell outside the telecommunications systems management exception,[1028] Justice Scalia's assessment finds support both in the language of section 3(24), and in the Commission's consistently held view that "adjunct-to-basic" functions fall within the telecommunications systems management exception to the "information service" definition. Such functions, the Commission has held: (1) must be "incidental" to an underlying

---

[1023] 47 U.S.C. § 153(24).

[1028] See Cable Modem Declaratory Ruling, 17 FCC Rcd. at 4822, para. 38 n.150 (containing a passing reference to the telecommunications systems management exception). The Commission's subsequent conclusions that wireline broadband services offered by telephone companies and broadband offered over power lines were unitary information services followed the same theory, also without any analysis of the telecommunications systems management exception. See Wireline Broadband Classification Order, 20 FCC Rcd. at 14864, para. 15; BPL-Enabled Broadband Order, 21 FCC Rcd. at 13284-87, paras. 5-9.

telecommunications service—*i.e.*, "'basic' in purpose and use" in the sense that they facilitate use of the network; and (2) must "not alter the fundamental character of [the telecommunications service]." By established Commission precedent, they include "speed dialing, call forwarding, [and] computer-provided directory assistance," each of which shares with DNS the essential characteristic of using computer processing to convert the number or keystroke that the end user enters into another number capable of routing the communication to the intended recipient. Similarly, traditional voice telephone calls to toll free numbers, pay-per-call numbers, and ported telephone numbers require a database query to translate the dialed telephone number into a different telephone number and/or to otherwise determine how to route the call properly, and there is no doubt that the inclusion of that functionality does not somehow convert the basic telecommunications service offering into an information service.[1033]

368. [AT&T] argues that DNS must fall outside of the telecommunications systems management exception because "Internet access providers use DNS functionality not merely (or even primarily) to 'manage' their networks more efficiently, but to make the Internet as a whole easily accessible and convenient *for their subscribers.*" We disagree. [DNS] allows more efficient use of the telecommunications network by facilitating accurate and efficient routing from the end user to the receiving party.

370. Although we find that DNS falls within the telecommunications systems management exception, even if did not, DNS functionality is not so inextricably intertwined with broadband Internet access service so as to convert the entire service offering into an information service. First, the record indicates that "IP packet transfer does work just as well without DNS, but is simply less useful, just as a telephone system is less useful without a phone book." Indeed, "[t]here is little difference between DNS support offered by a broadband Internet access provider and the 411 directory service offered by many providers of telephone service. Both allow a user to discover how to reach another party, but no one argued that telephone companies were not providing a telecommunications service because they offered 411." Second, the factual assumption that DNS lookup necessarily is provided *by the broadband Internet access provider* is no longer true today, if it ever was. While most users rely on their broadband providers to provide DNS lookup, the record indicates that

---

[1033] Consider also the role that telephone operators traditionally played in routing telephone calls. Traditional telephony required a telephone operator to route and place calls requested by the customer. We do not believe that anyone would argue that such arrangements would turn traditional telephone service into an information service.

third-party-provided-DNS is now widely available, and the availability of the service from third parties cuts against a finding that Internet transmission and DNS are inextricably intertwined[.]

371. Accordingly, we now reconsider our prior analysis and conclude for two reasons that the bundling of DNS by a provider of broadband Internet access service does not convert the broadband Internet access service offering into an integrated information service. This is both because DNS falls within the telecommunications systems management exception to the definition of information service and because, regardless of its classification, it does not affect the fundamental nature of broadband Internet access service as a distinct offering of telecommunications.

372. *Caching Falls Within the Telecommunications Systems Management Exception.* Opponents of revisiting the Commission's earlier classification decisions also point to caching as another feature of broadband Internet access service packages that the Commission relied upon to find such packages to be information services. When offered as part of a broadband Internet access service, caching, like DNS, is simply used to facilitate the transmission of information so that users can access other services, in this case by enabling the user to obtain "more rapid retrieval of information" through the network. Thus, it falls easily within the telecommunications systems management exception to the information service definition. We observe that this caching function provided by broadband providers as part of a broadband Internet service, is distinct from third party caching services provided by parties other than the provider of Internet access service (including content delivery networks, such as Akamai), which are separate information services.

NOTES & QUESTIONS

1. *Now Chevron step two is on the other foot.* How does the FCC leverage the Supreme Court's decision in *Brand X* to its advantage in this order? Recall when open access advocates argued in *Brand X* that the text of the Communications Act was unambiguous. Does the FCC agree? If not, why?

2. *How to deal with a regulatory flip-flop.* What justifications does the agency provide for reversing its prior classification decisions? Can you articulate precisely what changed and why that is relevant to the Title II classification? Was the change based on new facts, new values, politics, or some combination of the three? Imagine you are the FCC defending this decision before the Supreme Court. What would offer as the lead argument in support of the order?

a. *What matters is indispensible.* What does the FCC identify as the "indispensible function" of broadband internet access service? What are the three types of evidence that the agency uses to support this conclusion?

b. *Protecting "edge service" providers.* What is an example of an "edge service" and how does the FCC classify those services? Does it matter that some edge providers negotiate individual deals with broadband providers? What happens when a broadband provider also provides edge services?

c. *An "offering" to the mass market.* The definition of a "telecommunications service" is the "offering of telecommunications for a fee directly to the public."* How does the FCC interpret the term "directly to the public"? What if a company offers different prices and options in different cities? Does the size of the market matter?

3. *All about the deference.* Does the FCC have the power to change the classification of broadband internet services? What standard should a court apply when reviewing the agency's decision? Do you think that any special burden should apply when an agency reverses course in this way? Does it help that the FCC reads the D.C. Circuit decision as an "implicit invitation" to reclassify?

4. *Finding a new analogy.* You have already seen the warring analogies in *Brand X*—is cable modem service more like a car, a leashed puppy, or pizza delivery? What analogy does the FCC focus on in this order? How did the FCC classify services like DNS and Caching? How does the evolution of the internet ecosystem support the agency's analysis?

5. *Where the rubber hits the road.* The FCC's definition of "broadband Internet access service" is a "mass market retail service by wire or radio that provides the capability to transmit data to and receive data from all or substantially all Internet endpoints" including services provided "over any technology platform" and any "functional equivalent."[†] That sounds pretty comprehensive. But can you imagine a future scenario where the FCC might grapple with the question of what qualifies as a functional equivalent to broadband service?

6. *Embracing regulatory opt-out.* While a Title II classification would traditionally have triggered hundreds of additional regulatory obligations, the FCC made a point of embracing a "light touch" approach by using forbearance to limit the rules for broadband providers. Why do you think the agency chose to emphasize the use of forbearance? How does forbearance of these Title II regulations serve the agency's broader purposes of promoting broadband access?

---

* 47 U.S.C. § 153(53).
† 30 FCC Rcd. 5745–46 (internal footnotes omitted).

7. *Judicial review.* As we learned in CHAPTER 4: ACCESS, the D.C. Circuit upheld the FCC's 2015 Open Internet Rules in *USTA v. FCC,* and the court also upheld the Commission's decision to reclassify broadband internet access service as a telecommunications service (and thus a common carrier). But after the 2016 Election and appointment of Chairman Pai, the FCC changed course yet again and "declassified" broadband internet to remove all Title II obligations. As you read the 2018 Order, consider what evidence the Commission uses to support its conclusion that broadband internet is not a telecommunications service. Did something change between 2015 and 2018? Did the Commission just get it wrong the last time? If so, should their interpretation be entitled to any deference?

| RESTORING INTERNET FREEDOM |
| DR, R&O, and O, FCC 17-166 (2018) |

2.   We take several actions in this Order to restore Internet freedom. First, we end utility-style regulation of the Internet in favor of the market-based policies necessary to preserve the future of Internet freedom. In the 2015 *Title II Order,* the Commission abandoned almost twenty years of precedent and reclassified broadband Internet access service as a telecommunications service subject to myriad regulatory obligations under [Title II]. We reverse this misguided and legally flawed approach and restore broadband Internet access service to its Title I information service classification. We find that reclassification as an information service best comports with the text and structure of the Act, Commission precedent, and our policy objectives. We thus return to the approach to broadband Internet access service affirmed as reasonable by the U.S. Supreme Court. We also reinstate the private mobile service classification of mobile broadband Internet access service and return to the Commission's definition of "interconnected service" that existed prior to 2015. We determine that this light-touch information service framework will promote investment and innovation better than applying costly and restrictive laws of a bygone era to broadband Internet access service. Our balanced approach also restores the authority of the nation's most experienced cop on the privacy beat—the Federal Trade Commission—to police the privacy practices of Internet Service Providers (ISPs).

*   *   *

III. ENDING PUBLIC-UTILITY REGULATION OF THE INTERNET

20.   [B]ased on the record before us, we conclude that the best reading of the relevant definitional provisions of the Act supports classifying broadband

Internet access service as an information service. Having determined that broadband Internet access service, regardless of whether offered using fixed or mobile technologies, is an information service under the Act, we also conclude that as an information service, mobile broadband Internet access service should not be classified as a commercial mobile service or its functional equivalent. We find that it is well within our legal authority to classify broadband Internet access service as an information service, and reclassification also comports with applicable law governing agency decisions to change course. While we find our legal analysis sufficient on its own to support an information service classification of broadband Internet access service, strong public policy considerations further weigh in favor of an information service classification. Below, we find that economic theory, empirical data, and even anecdotal evidence also counsel against imposing public-utility style regulation on ISPs. The broader Internet ecosystem thrived under the light-touch regulatory treatment of Title I, with massive investment and innovation by both ISPs and edge providers, leading to previously unimagined technological developments and services. We conclude that a return to Title I classification will facilitate critical broadband investment and innovation by removing regulatory uncertainty and lowering compliance costs.

A. Reinstating the Information Service Classification of Broadband Internet Access Service

1. Scope

21. We continue to define "broadband Internet access service" as a mass-market retail service by wire or radio that provides the capability to transmit data to and receive data from all or substantially all Internet endpoints, including any capabilities that are incidental to and enable the operation of the communications service, but excluding dial-up Internet access service. . . .

2. Broadband Internet Access Service Is an Information Service Under the Act

26. In deciding how to classify broadband Internet access service, we find that the best reading of the relevant definitional provisions of the Act supports classifying broadband Internet access service as an information service. . . . Our action here simply returns to that prior approach.

27. When interpreting a statute it administers, the Commission, like all agencies, "must operate 'within the bounds of reasonable interpretation.' And reasonable statutory interpretation must account for both 'the specific context in which . . . language is used' and 'the broader context of the statute as a whole.'" Below, we first explore the meaning of the "capability" contemplated in the

statutory definition of "information service," and find that broadband Internet access service provides consumers the "capability" to engage in all of the information processes listed in the information service definition. We also find that broadband Internet access service likewise provides information processing functionalities itself, such as DNS and caching, which satisfy the capabilities set forth in the information service definition. We then address what "capabilities" we believe are being "offered" by ISPs, and whether these are reasonably viewed as separate from or inextricably intertwined with transmission, and find that broadband Internet access service offerings inextricably intertwine these information processing capabilities with transmission.

28. . . . . [B]roadband Internet access service offerings still involve a number of "capabilities" within the meaning of the section 3 definition of information services, including critical capabilities that all ISP customers must use for the service to work as it does today. While many popular uses of the Internet have shifted over time, the record reveals that broadband Internet access service continues to offer information service capabilities that typical users both expect and rely upon. Indeed, the basic nature of Internet service— "[p]rovid[ing] consumers with a comprehensive capability for manipulating information using the Internet via high-speed telecommunications"—has remained the same since the Supreme Court upheld the Commission's similar classification of cable modem service as an information service twelve years ago.

29. A body of precedent from the courts and the Commission served as the backdrop for the 1996 Act and informed the Commission's original interpretation . . . . The classification decisions in the *Title II Order* discounted or ignored much of that precedent. Without viewing ourselves as formally bound by that prior precedent, we find it eminently reasonable, as a legal matter, to give significant weight to that pre-1996 Act precedent . . . .

a. *Broadband Internet Access Service Information Processing Capabilities*

30. . . . In other contexts, the Commission has looked to dictionary definitions and found the term "capability" to be "broad and expansive," including the concepts of "potential ability" and "the capacity to be used, treated, or developed for a particular purpose." Because broadband Internet access service necessarily has the capacity or potential ability to be used to engage in the activities within the information service definition . . . we conclude that it is best understood to have those "capabilit[ies]." The record reflects that fundamental purposes of broadband Internet access service are for its use in "*generating*" and "*making available*" information to others, for example through social media and file sharing; "*acquiring*" and "*retrieving*" information from sources such as websites and online streaming and audio applications,

gaming applications, and file sharing applications; "*storing*" information in the cloud and remote servers, and via file sharing applications; "*transforming*" and "*processing*" information such as by manipulating images and documents, online gaming use, and through applications that offer the ability to send and receive email, cloud computing and machine learning capabilities; and "*utilizing*" information by interacting with stored data.... These are not merely incidental uses of broadband Internet access service—rather, because it not only has "the capacity to be used" for these "particular purpose[s]" but was designed and intended to do so, we find that broadband Internet access is best interpreted as providing customers with the "capability" for such interactions with third party providers.

31.   We also find that broadband Internet access is an information service irrespective of whether it provides the *entirety* of any end user functionality or whether it provides end user functionality in tandem with edge providers. We do not believe that Congress, in focusing on the "offering of a capability," intended the classification question to turn on an analysis of which capabilities the end user selects. Further, we are unpersuaded by commenters who assert that in order to be considered an "information service," an ISP must not only offer customers the "capability" for interacting with information that may be offered by third parties ("click-through"), but must also provide the ultimate content and applications themselves. Although there is no dispute that many edge providers likewise perform functions to facilitate information processing capabilities, they *all* depend on the combination of information-processing and transmission that ISPs make available through broadband Internet access service. The fundamental purpose of broadband Internet access service is to "enable a constant flow of computer-mediated communications between end-user devices and various servers and routers to facilitate interaction with online content."

32.   . . .   When the *Title II Order* attempted to evaluate customer perception based on their usage of broadband Internet access service, it failed to persuasively grapple with the relevant implications of prior Commission classification precedent. The *Title II Order* argued that broadband Internet access service primarily is used to access content, applications, and services from third parties unaffiliated with the ISP in support of the view that customers perceive it as a separate offering of telecommunications. The *Title II Order* offers no explanation as to why its narrower view of "capability" was more reasonable than the Commission's previous, long-standing view (other than seeking to advance the classification outcome that *Order* was driving towards)...

.

33. But even if "capability" were understood as requiring more of the information processing to be performed by the classified service itself, we find that broadband Internet access service meets that standard. Not only do ISPs offer end users the capability to interact with information online in each and every one of the ways set forth above, they also do so through a variety of functionally integrated information processing components that are part and parcel of the broadband Internet access service offering itself. In particular, we conclude that DNS and caching functionalities, as well as certain other information processing capabilities offered by ISPs, are integrated information processing capabilities offered as part of broadband Internet access service to consumers today.

34. *DNS.* We find that DNS is an indispensable functionality of broadband Internet access service. . . . DNS is used to facilitate the information retrieval capabilities that are inherent in Internet access. DNS allows "'click through' access from one web page to another, and its computer processing functions analyze user queries to determine which website (and server) would respond best to the user's request." And "[b]ecause it translates human language (*e.g.*, the name of a website) into the numerical data (i.e., an IP address) that computers can process, it is indispensable to ordinary users as they navigate the Internet." Without DNS, a consumer would not be able to access a website by typing its advertised name (*e.g.*, fcc.gov or cnn.com). . . . While ISPs are not the sole providers of DNS services, the vast majority of ordinary consumers rely upon the DNS functionality provided by their ISP, and the absence of ISP-provided DNS would fundamentally change the online experience for the consumer. We also observe that DNS, as it is used today, provides more than a functionally integrated address-translation capability, but also enables other capabilities critical to providing a functional broadband Internet access service to the consumer, including for example, a variety of underlying network functionality information associated with name service, alternative routing mechanisms, and information distribution. . . .

36. We thus find that the *Title II Order* erred in finding that DNS functionalities fell within the telecommunications systems management exception to the definition of "information service." That exception from the statutory information service definition was drawn from the language of the MFJ, and was understood as "directed at internal operations, not at services for customers or end users." We interpret the concepts of "management, control, or operation" in the telecommunications management exception consistent with that understanding. . . .

39.   The *Title II Order* also put misplaced reliance on *Computer Inquiries* adjunct-to-basic precedent from the traditional telephone service context as a comparison when evaluating broadband Internet access service functionalities. Because broadband Internet access service was not directly addressed in pre-1996 Act *Computer Inquiries* and MFJ precedent, analogies to functions that were classified under that precedent must account for potentially distinguishing characteristics not only in terms of technical details but also in terms of the regulatory backdrop.   The 1996 Act enunciates a policy for the Internet that distinguishes broadband Internet access from legacy services like traditional telephone service.   The 1996 Act explains that it is federal policy "to preserve the vibrant and competitive free market that presently exists for the Internet and other interactive computer services, unfettered by Federal or State regulation." The application of potentially ambiguous precedent to broadband Internet access service should be informed by how well—or how poorly—it advances that deregulatory statutory policy.   We find that our approach to that precedent, which results in an information service classification of broadband Internet access service, better advances that deregulatory policy than the approach in the *Title II Order*, which led to the imposition of utility-style regulation under Title II.

40.   The regulatory history of traditional telephone service also informs our understanding of *Computer Inquiries* precedent, further distinguishing it from broadband Internet access service.   Given the long history of common carriage offering of that service by the time of the *Computer Inquiries*, it is understandable that some precedent started with a presumption that the underlying service was a "basic service."   But similar assumptions would not be warranted in the case of services other than traditional telephone service for which there was no similar longstanding history of common carriage.   Thus, not only did the *Title II Order* rely on specific holdings that are at best ambiguous in their analogy to technical characteristics of broadband Internet access service, but it failed to adequately appreciate key regulatory distinctions between traditional telephone service and broadband Internet access service.

41.   *Caching.*   We also conclude that caching, a functionally integrated information processing component of broadband Internet access service, provides the capability to perform functions that fall within the information service definition.   As the record reflects, "[c]aching does much more than simply enable the user to obtain more rapid retrieval of information through the network; caching depends on complex algorithms to determine what information to store where and in what format."   This requires "extensive information processing, storing, retrieving, and transforming for much of the

most popular content on the Internet," and as such, caching involves storing and retrieving capabilities required by the "information service" definition. . . .

42. We find that ISP-provided caching does not merely "manage" an ISP's broadband Internet access service and underlying network, it enables and enhances consumers' access to and use of information online. . . . DNS and Web caching are functions provided as part and parcel of the broadband Internet access service. When ISPs cache content from across the Internet, they are not performing functions, like switching, that are instrumental to pure transmission, but instead storing third party content they select in servers in their own networks to enhance access to information. The record reflects that without caching, broadband Internet access service would be a significantly inferior experience for the consumer, particularly for customers in remote areas, requiring additional time and network capacity for retrieval of information from the Internet. Thus, because caching is useful to the consumer, we conclude that the *Title II Order* erred in incorrectly categorizing caching as falling within the telecommunications system management exception to the definition of "information service." . . .

44. . . . That category of activity relied upon in the *Title II Order* thus actually appears to be barely or not at all analogous to caching. We instead find more persuasive the MFJ court's information service treatment of BOC provision of "storage space in their gateways for databases created by others" such as "information service providers and end users"—a distinct category of storage and retrieval functionality that is a close fit to caching.

b. ISPs' Service Offerings Inextricably Intertwine Information Processing Capabilities with Transmission

45. Having established that broadband Internet access service has the information processing capabilities outlined in the definition of "information service," the relevant inquiry is whether ISPs' broadband Internet access service offerings make available information processing technology inextricably intertwined with transmission. Below we examine both how consumers perceive the offer of broadband Internet access service, as well as the nature of the service actually offered by ISPs, and conclude that ISPs are best understood as offering a service that inextricably intertwines the information processing capabilities described above and transmission.

46. We begin by considering the ordinary customer's perception of the ISP's offer of broadband Internet access service. As *Brand X* explained, "[i]t is common usage to describe what a company 'offers' to a consumer as what the consumer perceives to be the integrated finished product." ISPs generally market and provide information processing capabilities and transmission

capability together as a single service. Therefore, it is not surprising that consumers perceive the offer of broadband Internet access service to include more than mere transmission, and that customers want and pay for functionalities that go beyond mere transmission. . . .

47.   This view also accords with the Commission's historical understanding that "[e]nd users subscribing to . . . broadband Internet access service expect to receive (and pay for) a finished, functionally integrated service that provides access to the Internet. End users do not expect to receive (or pay for) two distinct services—both Internet access service and a distinct transmission service, for example." While the *Title II Order* dwells at length on the prominence of transmission speed in ISP marketing, it makes no effort to compare that emphasis to historical practice. In fact, ISPs have been highlighting transmission speed in their marketing materials since long before the *Title II Order.* The very first report on advanced telecommunication capability pursuant to section 706(b) of the 1996 Act, released in 1999, cited ISPs' marketing of their Internet access service speed. ISPs' inclusion of speed information in their marketing also was acknowledged by the Court in *Brand X,* which nonetheless upheld the Commission's information service classification as reasonable. Indeed, consideration of ISP marketing practices has been part of the backdrop of all of the Commission's decisions classifying broadband Internet access service as an information service and thus cannot justify a departure from the historical classification of broadband Internet access service as an information service.

48. . . . [A]ll broadband Internet access services rely on DNS and commonly also rely on caching by ISPs, to the extent that those capabilities, in themselves, do not provide a point of differentiation among services or providers, it would be unsurprising that ISPs did not feature them prominently in their marketing or advertising, particularly to audiences already familiar with broadband Internet access service generally. Indeed, speed and reliability are not exclusive to telecommunications services; rather, the record reflects that speed and reliability are crucial attributes of an information service. Consequently, the mere fact that broadband Internet access service marketing often focuses on characteristics, such as transmission speed, by which services and providers can be differentiated sheds little to no light on whether consumers perceive broadband Internet access service as inextricably intertwining that data transmission with information service capabilities.[172]

---

[172] Neither the discussion of the consumer's perspective by Justice Scalia nor that in the *Title II Order* identifies good reasons to depart from the Commission's prior understanding that broadband Internet access is a single, integrated information service. Justice Scalia contended

49. Separate and distinct from our finding that an ISP "offers" an information service from the consumer's perspective, we find that as a factual matter, ISPs offer a single, inextricably intertwined information service. The record reflects that information processes must be combined with transmission in order for broadband Internet access service to work, and it is the combined information processing capabilities and transmission functions that an ISP offers with broadband Internet access service. Thus, even assuming that any individual consumer could perceive an ISP's offer of broadband Internet access service as akin to a bare transmission service, the information processing capabilities that are actually offered as an integral part of the service make broadband Internet access service an information service as defined by the Act. As such, we reject commenters' assertions that the primary function of ISPs is to simply transfer packets and not process information.

50. The inquiry called for by the relevant classification precedent focuses on the nature of the service offering the provider makes, rather than being limited to the functions within that offering that particular subscribers do, in fact, use or that third parties also provide. The *Title II Order* erroneously contended that, because functions like DNS and caching potentially could be provided by entities other than the ISP itself, those functions should not be understood as part of a single, integrated information service offered by ISPs. However, the fact that some consumers obtain these functionalities from third-party alternatives is not a basis for ignoring the capabilities that a broadband provider actually "offers." The *Title II Order* gave no meaningful explanation why a contrary, narrower interpretation of "offer" was warranted other than, implicitly, its seemingly end-results driven effort to justify a telecommunications service classification of broadband Internet access service.

51. Our findings today are consistent with classification precedent prior to the *Title II Order*, which consistently found that ISPs offer a single, integrated service.... The core, essential elements of these prior analyses of the functional nature of Internet access remain persuasive as to broadband Internet access

---

that how customers perceive cable modem service is best understood by considering the services for which it would be a substitute—in his view at the time, dial-up Internet access and digital subscriber line (DSL) service over telephone networks[.] However, dial-up Internet access has substantially diminished in marketplace significance in the subsequent years[.] In addition, the legal compulsion for facilities-based carriers to offer broadband transmission on a common carrier basis was eliminated in 2005.... Consequently, whatever might have been arguable at the time of *Brand X*, the service offerings in the marketplace as it developed thereafter provide no reason to expect that consumers "inevitabl[y]" would view broadband Internet access service as involving "*both* computing functionality *and* the physical pipe" as separate offerings based on comparisons to the likely alternatives[.]

service today. We adhere to that view notwithstanding arguments that some subset of the array of Internet access uses identified in the *Stevens Report* or subsequent decisions either are no longer as commonly used, or occur more frequently today.

52. We disagree with commenters who assert that ISPs necessarily offer both an information service and a telecommunications service because broadband Internet access service includes a transmission component. In providing broadband Internet access service, an ISP *makes use* of telecommunications—i.e., it provides information-processing capabilities "via telecommunications"—but does not separately *offer* telecommunications on a stand-alone basis to the public. By definition, *all* information services accomplish their functions "via telecommunications," and as such, broadband Internet access service has always had a telecommunications component intrinsically intertwined with the computer processing, information provision, and computer interactivity capabilities an information service offers. Indeed, service providers, who are in the best position to understand the inputs used in broadband Internet access service, do not appear to dispute that the "via telecommunications" criteria is satisfied even if also arguing that they are *not providing* telecommunications to end-users. For example, ISPs typically transmit traffic between aggregation points on their network and the ISPs' connections with other networks. Whether self-provided by the ISP or purchased from a third party, that readily appears to be transmission between or among points selected by the ISP of traffic that the ISP has chosen to have carried by that transmission link. Such inclusion of a transmission component does not render broadband Internet access services telecommunications services; if it did, the entire category of information services would be narrowed drastically. Because we find it more reasonable to conclude that at least some telecommunications is being used as an input into broadband Internet access service—thereby satisfying the "via telecommunications" criteria—we need not further address the scope of the "telecommunications" definition in order to justify our classification of broadband Internet access service as an information service. We thus do not comprehensively address other criticisms of the *Title II Order*'s interpretation and applications of the "telecommunications" definition, which potentially could have implications beyond the scope of issues we are considering in this proceeding.

53. The approach we adopt today best implements the Commission's long-standing view that Congress intended the definitions of "telecommunications service" and "information service" to be mutually exclusive ways to classify a given service. . . .

54. The *Title II Order* interpretation stands in stark contrast to the Commission's historical classification precedent and the views of all Justices in *Brand X.* . . . the fact that its view of telecommunications services sweeps so much more broadly than previously considered possible provides significant support for our reading of the statute and the classification decision we make today.

55. In contrast, our approach leaves ample room for a meaningful range of "telecommunications services." . . . The Commission's historical interpretation thus gives full meaning to both "information service" and "telecommunications service" categories in the Act.

56. We reject assertions that the analysis we adopt today would necessarily mean that standard telephone service is likewise an information service. The record reflects that broadband Internet access service is categorically different from standard telephone service in that it is "*designed with* advanced features, protocols, and security measures so that it can integrate directly into electronic computer systems and enable users to electronically create, retrieve, modify and otherwise manipulate information stored on servers around the world." Further, "[t]he dynamic network functionality enabling the Internet connectivity provided by [broadband Internet access services] is fundamentally different from the largely static one dimensional, transmission oriented Time Division Multiplexing (TDM) voice network." . . .

* * *

C. Public Policy Supports Classifying Broadband Internet Access Service As An Information Service

86. While our legal analysis concluding that broadband Internet access service is best classified as an information service under the Act is sufficient grounds alone on which to base our classification decision, the public policy arguments advanced in the record and economic analysis reinforce that conclusion. We find that reinstating the information service classification for broadband Internet access service is more likely to encourage broadband investment and innovation, furthering our goal of making broadband available to all Americans and benefitting the entire Internet ecosystem. For almost 20 years, there was a bipartisan consensus that broadband should remain under Title I, and ISPs cumulatively invested $1.5 trillion in broadband networks between 1996 and 2015. During that period of intense investment, broadband deployment and adoption increased dramatically, as the combined number of fixed and mobile Internet connections increased from 50.2 million to 355.2 million from 2005 to 2015, and even as early as 2011, a substantial majority of Americans had access to broadband at home. As of 2016, roughly 91 percent of

homes had access to networks offering 25 Mbps, and there were 395.9 million wireless connections, twenty percent more than the U.S. population. Mobile data speeds have also dramatically increased, with speeds increasing 40-fold from the 3G speeds of 2007. Cable broadband speeds increased 3,200 percent between 2005 and 2015, while prices per Mbps fell by more than 87 percent between 1996 and 2012.

87.   Based on the record in this proceeding, we conclude that economic theory, empirical studies, and observational evidence support reclassification of broadband Internet access service as an information service rather than the application of public-utility style regulation on ISPs. We find the Title II classification likely has resulted, and will result, in considerable social cost, in terms of foregone investment and innovation. At the same time, classification of broadband Internet access service under Title II has had no discernable incremental benefit relative to Title I classification. The regulations promulgated under the Title II regime appear to have been a solution in search of a problem. Close examination of the examples of harm cited by proponents of Title II to justify heavy-handed regulation reveal that they are sparse and often exaggerated. Moreover, economic incentives, including competitive pressures, support Internet openness. We find that the gatekeeper theory, the bedrock of the *Title II Order*'s overall argument justifying its approach, is a poor fit for the broadband Internet access service market. Further, even if there may be potential harms, we find that pre-existing legal remedies, particularly antitrust and consumer protection laws, sufficiently address such harms so that they are outweighed by the well-recognized disadvantages of public utility regulation. As such, we find that public policy considerations support our legal finding that broadband Internet access service is an information service under the Act.

NOTES & QUESTIONS

1. *Back to basics – the definitions.* Take a moment to go back and review the definitions at issue here (telecommunications, telecommunications service, and information service), which are found in 47 U.S.C. § 153. You have now heard from three different sets of FCC Commissioners and two different courts grapple with applying these definitions to broadband internet service. Do you feel confident that there is a clear answer? If not, who do you think is in the best position to make the classification decision?

2. *Who speaks for the Commission?* This Order makes clear at the outset that the current Commission does not agree with the interpretations put forward by the FCC in the 2015 Order. But who ultimately speaks for the Commission? In one sense, the current Commissioners have significant power to dictate

outcomes, vote for or against judgments or rules, and draft or edit the final statements as they see fit. But as we have seen already, Courts will give weight to the prior statements of an agency when considering whether an order is arbitrary and capricious. Courts have also grown increasingly skeptical in recent years to the broader interpretations of the *Chevron* doctrine and the degree of deference given to agency interpretations. How would you view the Commission's new order in light of those trends? Should a court be more or less skeptical of the FCC's conclusions given the immediate reversal under Chairman Pai?

3. *What is on the menu?* Set aside for a moment the dispute over deference and the standard of review. How does the FCC interpret the relevant definitions differently in this Order as compared to the 2015 Order? Do they disagree on certain facts relevant to the definition of "telecommunications service?" Do they consider the same functions to be "indispensable?" What types of evidence does the agency provide to support this conclusion?

a. *The entrée is the same.* Notice that the FCC has chosen to maintain the same definition of the service at issue—"broadband Internet access service." They don't disagree about the thing to be categorized, only its proper classification. Yet the emphasize a "return" to their "prior approach." So are they saying that a BIAS service in 2018 is the same as cable modem service in 2003?

b. *All about the toppings.* The Commission begins by focusing on the "capabilities" offered as part of the BIAS service, which it ties to the definition of information service. What are those capabilities? How are they different from pure transmission of data? Does it matter if the user actually uses these capabilities? Does the Commission believe that consumer perceptions have changed over time or can change over time?

4. *Pulling back the curtain.* Recall again the warring analogies in *Brand X*— cable modem service is like a car, a leashed puppy, or pizza delivery service. Those analogies were discussed as part of an analytical exercise and dispute, one that centered on the meaning of the terms that Congress chose when it drafted the Telecommunications Act. But ultimately the Court concluded that the terms were ambiguous. What to do? Well, the FCC's answer in the new Order is that the interpretation of an ambiguous term "should be informed by how well—or how poorly—it advances the deregulatory statutory policy." How do you think that fits with the Supreme Court's view in *Brand X*? Is the current Commission disagreeing with the 2015 Commission about the statutory policy in the 1996 law? Or are they disagreeing about how to achieve that policy? Do courts have a role in mediating such disputes?

5. *First essential, now intertwined.* The FCC explains in the Order how the "information processing" capabilities that BIAS providers offer are "inextricably intertwined" with their transmission service. Can you explain why this is so? As an internet subscriber, can you choose to use a different DNS service? A different caching service? Would you? If you were an ISP that didn't want to be regulated as a common carrier, would you see an advantage to adding packaged "information services" to your offering? What if you were a telephone service provider? Could you also avoid Title II regulation?

6. *The DC Circuit Provides a Recap.* As you might expect, the D.C. Circuit was again called upon to grade the FCC's homework. Petitions for Review of the Commission's Order were filed by public interest groups, State Attorneys General, and others. The cases were consolidated in the D.C. Circuit, and a three judge panel of the court issued its decision in October 2019 and upheld the FCC's 2018 Order in part, with an important twist. The decision begins by walking through the regulatory and litigation history that led to this point, and goes on to again consider the FCC and challengers' warring analogies.

MOZILLA V. FCC
940 F.3d 1 (D.C. Cir. 2019)

PER CURIAM:

In 2018, the Federal Communications Commission adopted an order classifying broadband Internet access service as an information service under Title I of the Communications Act of 1934. In so doing, the agency pursued a market-based, "light-touch" policy for governing the Internet and departed from its 2015 order that had imposed utility-style regulation under Title II of the Act.

Petitioners--an array of Internet companies, non-profits, state and local governments, and other entities--bring a host of challenges to the 2018 Order. We find their objections unconvincing for the most part, though we vacate one portion of the 2018 Order and remand for further proceedings on three discrete points.

The 2018 Order and today's litigation represent yet another iteration of a long-running debate regarding the regulation of the Internet. We rehearsed much of this complex history in [*USTA v. FCC*], and see no need to recapitulate here what was so well and thoroughly said there. In the interest of reader-friendliness, though, we briefly review certain highlights necessary to understand this opinion.

As relevant here, the 1996 Telecommunications Act creates two potential classifications for broadband Internet: "telecommunications services" under Title II of the Act and "information services" under Title I. These similar-sounding terms carry considerable significance: Title II entails common carrier status . . . and triggers an array of statutory restrictions and requirements (subject to forbearance at the Commission's election). For example, Title II "declar[es] . . . unlawful" "any . . . charge, practice, classification or regulation that is unjust or unreasonable." By contrast, "information services" are exempted from common carriage status and, hence, Title II regulation.

An analogous set of classifications applies to mobile broadband: A "commercial mobile service" is subject to common carrier status, whereas a "private mobile service" is not.

The Commission's authority under the Act includes classifying various services into the appropriate statutory categories. *See* [*Brand X*]. In the years since the Act's passage, the Commission has exercised its classification authority with some frequency.

Initially, in 1998, the Commission classified broadband over phone lines as a "telecommunications service." *See In re Deployment of Wireline Services Offering Advanced Telecommunications Capability*, 13 FCC Rcd. 24012 (1998).

Just four years later, though, the Commission determined that cable broadband was an "information service," a choice that the Supreme Court upheld in *Brand X*. The agency then applied a similar classification to wireline and wireless broadband.

But in 2015 the Commission took the view that broadband Internet access is, in fact, a "telecommunications service" and that mobile broadband is a "commercial mobile service." In USTA, this court upheld that classification as reflecting a reasonable interpretation of the statute under *Chevron*'s second step.

Once again, the Commission has switched its tack. In 2017, the Commission issued a notice of proposed rulemaking seeking to revert to its pre-2015 position[,] and released the final order at issue in this case in January 2018.

The 2018 Order accomplishes a number of objectives. First, and most importantly, it classifies broadband Internet as an "information service," and mobile broadband as a "private mobile service." Second, relying on Section 257 of the Act (located in Title II but written so as to apply to Titles I through VI), the Commission adopts transparency rules intended to ensure that consumers have adequate data about Internet Service Providers' network practices. Third, the Commission undertakes a cost-benefit analysis, concluding that the benefits of a market-based, "light-touch" regime for Internet governance outweigh those of common carrier regulation under Title II, resting heavily on the combination of the transparency requirements imposed by the Commission under Section 257 with enforcement of existing antitrust and consumer protection laws. The Commission likewise finds that the burdens of the Title II Order's conduct rules exceed their benefits.

We uphold the 2018 Order, with two exceptions. First, the Court concludes that the Commission has not shown legal authority to issue its Preemption Directive, which would have barred states from imposing any rule or requirement that the Commission "repealed or decided to refrain from imposing" in the Order or that is "more stringent" than the Order. *2018 Order* ¶ 195. The Court accordingly vacates that portion of the Order. Second, we remand the Order to the agency on three discrete issues: (1) The Order failed to examine the implications of its decisions for public safety; (2) the Order does not sufficiently explain what reclassification will mean for regulation of pole attachments; and (3) the agency did not adequately address Petitioners' concerns about the effects of broadband reclassification on the Lifeline Program.

I. BROADBAND INTERNET CLASSIFICATION

The central issue before us is whether the Commission lawfully applied the statute in classifying broadband Internet access service as an "information service." We approach the issue through the lens of the Supreme Court's decision in *Brand X*, which upheld the Commission's 2002 refusal to classify cable broadband as a "telecommunications service." The Commission's classification of cable modem as an "information service" was not challenged in *Brand X*, but, given that "telecommunications service" and "information service" have been treated as mutually exclusive by the Commission since the late 1990s, a premise Petitioners do not challenge, we view *Brand X* as binding precedent in this case.

*   *   *

The Commission appears to make two arguments for its classification. It states first that "broadband Internet access service necessarily has the capacity or potential ability to be used to engage in the activities within the information service definition—'generating, acquiring, storing, transforming, processing, retrieving, utilizing, or making available information via telecommunications,'" and on that basis alone merits an "information service" classification.

The Commission then goes on to say: "But even if 'capability' were understood as requiring more of the information processing to be performed by the classified service itself, we find that broadband Internet access service meets that standard." *2018 Order* ¶ 33. As we will see, the Commission regards this requirement as being met by specific information-processing features that are, in its view, functionally integrated with broadband service, particularly Domain Name Service ("DNS") and caching, about which more later. (Petitioners themselves treat the Commission's DNS/caching argument as "an alternative ground" for the Commission's classification.)

Our review is governed by the familiar *Chevron* framework in which we defer to an agency's construction of an ambiguous provision in a statute that it administers if that construction is reasonable. By the same token, if "Congress has directly spoken to an issue then any agency interpretation contradicting what Congress has said would be unreasonable."

At *Chevron* Step One, we ask "whether Congress has directly spoken to the precise question at issue." Where "the intent of Congress is clear, that is the end of the matter; for [we], as well as the agency, must give effect to the unambiguously expressed intent of Congress." But if "the statute is silent or ambiguous with respect to the specific issue," we proceed to *Chevron* Step Two, where "the question for the court is whether the agency's answer is based on a permissible construction of the statute." However, we do not apply *Chevron* reflexively, and we find ambiguity only after exhausting ordinary tools of the judicial craft. All this of course proceeds in the shadow of *Brand X*, which itself applied *Chevron* to a similar issue.

Applying these principles here, we hold that classifying broadband Internet access as an "information service" based on the functionalities of DNS and caching is "'a reasonable policy choice for the [Commission] to make' at *Chevron*'s second step." As we said in USTA, "Our job is to ensure that an agency has acted 'within the limits of [Congress's] delegation' of authority," and "we do not 'inquire as to whether the agency's decision is wise as a policy matter; indeed, we are forbidden from substituting our judgment for that of the agency.'"

A. The Supreme Court's Decision in *Brand X*

Brand X held that, by virtue of the ambiguity of the word "offering," the FCC could permissibly choose not to classify cable modem service as a "telecommunications service." As to DNS and caching, the *Brand X* Court endorsed the Commission's argument that those functionalities can be relied on to classify cable modem service as an "information service." Challengers opposing the FCC had argued that when consumers "go[ ] beyond" certain Internet services offered by cable modem companies themselves—for example, beyond access to proprietary e-mail and Web pages (commonly referred to as the cable modem companies' "walled gardens")—the companies were "offering" a "telecommunications service" rather than an "information service." The Court rejected this claim. It found that such a view "conflicts with the Commission's understanding of the nature of cable modem service," which the Court deemed "reasonable." The Court explained that—when a user accesses purely third-party content online—"he is *equally using* the information service provided by the cable company that offers him Internet access as when he accesses the company's own Web site, its e-mail service, or his personal Web page," i.e., "walled garden" services. Why so?

Brand X's answer, as relevant here, lay in DNS and caching. The argument proceeded in two steps—first, showing that DNS and caching themselves can properly fall under the "information service" rubric; second, showing that these "information services" are sufficiently integrated with the transmission element of broadband that it is reasonable to classify cable modem service as an "information service."

As to the first step, the Court observed that "[a] user cannot reach a third party's Web site without DNS," which "among other things, matches the Web page addresses that end users type into their browsers (or 'click' on) with the Internet Protocol (IP) addresses of the servers containing the Web pages the users wish to access." It therefore saw it as "at least reasonable" to treat DNS *itself* "as a 'capability for acquiring . . . retrieving, utilizing, or making available' Web site addresses and therefore part of the information service cable companies provide." The Court applied a cognate analysis to caching, which "facilitates access to third-party Web pages by offering consumers the ability to store, or 'cache' popular content on local computer servers," . . . "obviat[ing] the need for the end user to download anew information from third-party Web sites each time the consumer attempts to access them." Thus the Court found "reasonable" the FCC's position that "subscribers can reach third-party Web sites via 'the World Wide Web, and browse their contents, [only] because their service provider offers the capability for . . . acquiring, [storing] . . . retrieving [and] utilizing . . . information.'"

As to the second step, the *Brand X* Court endorsed the FCC's position that—because DNS and caching are "inextricably intertwined" with high-speed transmission—it was reasonable for the Commission *not* to treat the resulting package as an "offering" of a standalone "telecommunications service." "[H]igh-speed transmission used to provide cable modem service is a *functionally integrated* component of [cable modem] service because it transmits data only in connection with the further processing of information and is necessary to provide Internet service." DNS and caching, in turn, are two examples of such "further processing" integrated with the data transmission aspect of cable modem service. "[A] consumer cannot purchase Internet service without also purchasing a connection to the Internet and the transmission always occurs in connection with information processing," in the form of (for example) DNS or caching. Thus, according to the Supreme Court, the Commission reasonably concluded that cable modem service is not an offering of a standalone "telecommunications service," but, rather, an "information service"—which by definition is offered "via telecommunications."

B. DNS and Caching in the 2018 Order

The reasoning in the 2018 Order tallies with the line of argument in *Brand X* described above. The Commission's principal claim is that "ISPs offer end users the capability to interact with information online . . . through a variety of functionally integrated information processing components that are part and parcel of the broadband Internet access service offering itself"—including DNS and caching. The Commission describes DNS and caching as "integrated information processing capabilities offered as part of broadband Internet access service to consumers today." We hold that under *Brand X* this conclusion is reasonable.

We note that the 2018 Order alluded to several "information processing functionalities inextricably intertwined with the underlying service" besides DNS and caching, such as "email, speed test servers, backup and support services, geolocation-based advertising, data storage, parental controls, unique programming content, spam protection, pop-up blockers, instant messaging services, on-the-go access to Wi-Fi hotspots, and various widgets, toolbars, and applications." *2018 Order* ¶ 33 n.99. Although the 2018 Order states that these "further support the 'information service' classification," it did not find them "determinative," and mentioned them only briefly in a footnote. Thus we address DNS and caching only.

In passages echoing *Brand X*, the Commission characterized the essential roles of DNS and caching. As to DNS, it observed that DNS is "indispensable to ordinary users as they navigate the Internet." . . . "[T]he absence of ISP-provided DNS would fundamentally change the online experience for the consumer." This formulation is actually a good deal more cautious than that of the Court in *Brand X*, which declared that without DNS a "user cannot reach a third party's Web site[."] In fact users who know the necessary IP addresses could enter them for each relevant server. But the Commission and the Court (the latter more emphatically) are making an undeniable pragmatic point—that use of the Web would be nightmarishly cumbersome without DNS.

As to caching, the Commission explained that it "provides the capability to perform functions that fall within the information service definition," including, but not limited to, "enabl[ing] the user to obtain more rapid retrieval of information through the network." Operating a caching service entails running "complex algorithms to determine what information to store where and in what format," . . . so that "caching involves storing and retrieving capabilities required by the 'information service' definition." Thus the Commission added technical detail reinforcing the *Brand X* Court's statements as to caching.

The Commission then summarized these points, again in terms resonating with those in which *Brand X* had endorsed the 2002 Cable Modem Order. It argued that "ISPs offer a single, inextricably intertwined information service," based in part on the functionalities of DNS and caching. It said that "all broadband Internet access services rely on DNS and commonly also rely on caching by ISPs," and contended that DNS and caching should be "understood as part of a single, integrated information service offered by ISPs." It then maintained, drawing on *Brand X*, that "[w]here . . . a service involving transmission inextricably intertwines that transmission with information service capabilities—in the form of an integrated information service—there cannot be 'a "stand-alone" offering of telecommunications . . .,'" in line with the Commission's stance in *Brand X*. "[A]n offering like broadband Internet access service that 'always and necessarily' includes integrated transmission and information service capabilities . . . [is] an information service."

C. Objections to the Classification

Petitioners raise numerous objections aimed to show that the Commission's reliance on DNS and caching for classifying broadband as an "information service" is unreasonable at *Chevron*'s second step. We find them unconvincing.

1. "Walled Garden" Reading of Brand X

First, to short-circuit the Commission's reliance on *Brand X*, Petitioners try to characterize the Court's reasoning in that case as dependent on a vision of Internet providers as offering mainly access to their "walled gardens." They assert that in *Brand X* "the Court was focused on the [Broadband Internet Access Service ("BIAS")] providers' add-on information services, such as ISP-provided e-mail," and that "the Court had no occasion to consider the proper classification of a service combining telecommunications with nothing more than DNS and caching." Mozilla Br. 42. This reading is unpersuasive because it airbrushes out the lengthy discussion summarized above in which the Court finds "reasonable" the Commission's "information-service" classification even where "a consumer goes beyond [walled garden] offerings and accesses content provided by parties other than the cable company[,"]—by virtue of the functionalities of DNS and caching. We thus reject Petitioners' attempt to discredit the Commission's sensible reliance on *Brand X*'s treatment of DNS and caching. *See, e.g., 2018 Order* ¶¶ 10, 34, 41, 51; *see also* Part I.C.4 *infra* (addressing Petitioners' related claims in functional integration context).

2. *"Telecommunications Management" Exception*

Petitioners assert that DNS and caching fall under the "telecommunications management" exception ("TME") and so cannot be relied on to justify an "information service" classification. We find that Petitioners' arguments do not hold up, either because they rest on a misreading of *Brand X* and USTA or do not adequately grapple with the Commission's reasonable explanation as to why DNS and caching fall outside that exception. Our discussion here will be quite involved in part because *Brand X* did not directly confront whether DNS and caching may fall within the TME.

In deciding whether to slot DNS and caching under the TME the Commission confronted "archetypal *Chevron* questions[ ] about how best to construe an ambiguous term in light of competing policy interests." . . . . "[I]f the implementing agency's construction is reasonable, *Chevron* requires a federal court to accept the agency's construction of the statute, even if the agency's reading differs from what the court believes is the best statutory interpretation." And when an agency changes course, as it did here, it "must show that there are good reasons for the new policy," but "it need not demonstrate to a court's satisfaction that the reasons for the new policy are *better* than the reasons for the old one." The Commission clears this bar.

a. *The Commission's Interpretation*

To begin with, Petitioners misconstrue USTA. As they do persistently, they gloss passages that find parts of the Title II Order to be *permissible* readings of the statute as *mandating* those readings—when the passages plainly do not do so. A case in point is the treatment of the TME. Petitioners say that "[t]his Court has *already agreed* that DNS and caching fall within the terms of the telecommunications management exception." Yet all we said in USTA was that we were "unpersuaded" that the FCC's "use of the telecommunications management exception was . . . unreasonable." The Title II Order, in other words, adopted a permissible reading, though not a required one. This holding in no way bars the Commission from adopting a contrary view now—so long as it adequately justifies that view, as we find it has.

Despite Petitioners' objections, we find that the 2018 Order engages in reasonable line-drawing for purposes of administering this amorphous exception. Relying on judicial precedent, Department of Justice policy (developed pursuant to its duty to see that the settlement of its antitrust suit against AT&T was lawfully implemented), and prior Commission statements, the 2018 Order seems to envision a continuum with two poles: a user-centered pole and network management-centered pole. It locates a given service on the continuum and classifies it as falling within or outside the TME according to which pole it appears closest to. If a service is "directed at . . . customers or end users," *2018 Order* ¶ 36 (quoting *United States v. Western Elec. Co.*, No. 82-0192, 1989 WL 119060, at *1 (D.D.C. Sept. 11, 1989)), or benefits users "in significant part," *id.* ¶ 38, or "predominantly," *id.* ¶ 42, it does not call for TME classification. We view this construction as an adequately justified departure from the Title II Order's understanding of the TME in the face of a dauntingly ambiguous provision with inevitably fuzzy borderline cases and complex and possibly inconsistent (or at least orthogonal) policy implications.

Given the Commission's approach, it need not—and does not—deny that even those services properly classed under the TME benefit end users *in some respect*. It would be folly to deny as much given that the raison d'être of ISPs is to serve their customers. As one commenter notes, "To maintain . . . that something that is 'useful' to an end user cannot fall under the management exception is absurd, as the entire purpose of broadband is to be useful to end users."

But a rule involving a spectrum or continuum commonly requires a decider to select a point where both ends are in play. Night and day are distinguishable, however difficult classification may be at dawn and dusk. The Commission's way of construing the TME and applying its continuum-based approach is not inconsistent with Public Knowledge's point that "the entire purpose of broadband is to be useful to end users." The Commission notes that its "focus remains on the purpose or use of the specific function in question and not merely whether the resulting service, as a whole, is useful to end-users." *2018 Order* ¶ 38 n.135. While DNS might play a role in managing a network, the Commission reasonably concluded that DNS "is a function that is useful and essential to providing Internet access for the ordinary consumer," and that these benefits to the end user predominate over any management function DNS might serve. The Commission says that caching "benefits" users through "rapid retrieval of information from a local cache," and can also be used "as part of a service, such as DNS, which is *predominantly* to the benefit of the user (DNS caching)." And it gives examples of services that in its view are genuine TME services: Simple Network Management Protocol ("SNMP"), Network Control Protocol ("NETCONF"), or Data Over Cable Service Interface Specification ("DOCSIS") bootfiles for controlling the configuration of cable modems. *Id.* ¶ 36 (quoting Sandvine Comments at 5, WC Dkt. No. 17-108 (July 14, 2017)). It observes that the Title II Order had essentially proceeded in a contrary manner, finding that the management-centered functionality of DNS predominated, so as to render it TME-worthy. "Although confronted with claims that DNS is, *in significant part*, designed to be useful to end-users rather than providers, the *Title II Order* nonetheless decided that it fell within the [TME]." The Commission reasonably declined to follow this route (partly, as we shall see below, because it believed that it would cause the exception to swallow the rule in ways antithetical to its reading of Commission precedent and the Act's goals). It chose a different, and reasonable, alternative.

b. Modification of Final Judgment Precedent

In adopting its approach to the TME, the Commission rested on precedent from a line of judicial decisions interpreting the Modification of Final Judgment ("MFJ"), a consent decree entered into between the Department of Justice and AT&T in 1982 as part of the breakup of the AT&T monopoly to create a set of independent regional Bell Operating Companies ("BOCs"). This decree, which modified a 1956 consent decree and final judgment, spawned a long line of cases in which District Court Judge Harold Greene resolved conflicts over the decree's limits on the BOCs' permissible business ventures. The cases interpreted a broad array of terms of the consent decree, entered many modifications, and granted waivers, balancing a need to "avoid anticompetitive effects" (which might flow from BOC exploitation of their monopolies in telecommunications to dominate related services) with a hope of "bring[ing] th[e] nation closer to enjoyment of the full benefits of the information age" by facilitating "the efficient, rapid, and inexpensive dissemination of . . . information." *United States v. Western Elec. Co.*, 714 F. Supp. 1, 3, 5 (D.D.C. 1988), *aff'd in part, rev'd in part*, 900 F.2d 283 (D.C. Cir. 1990).

The Commission makes a good case for the persuasiveness of this precedent. First, the definition of "information service" in the 1996 Act—including the TME—is lifted nearly verbatim from the 1982 consent decree. Second, in the case on which the Commission principally relies, the court was interpreting the MFJ's TME equivalent and adopted a reading in keeping with its understanding of Department of Justice policy at the time.

In *Western Electric*, Judge Greene addressed the question whether the consent decree permitted the BOCs to offer relay services for customers who use "telecommunications devices for the deaf" ("TDDs"). The court held that, because TDD services involve "transformation of information"—"the very crux and purpose of the TDD relay services"—they "f[e]ll squarely" within the definition of "information services," which covers the capability to "transform[ ] . . . information." Accordingly offering the service ran afoul of Section II(D)(1) of the decree, banning the BOCs from providing information services. The

BOCs argued as a fallback position that TDD services fell within the TME. Judge Greene made quick work of this, finding it "patently obvious that what is being sought . . . does not involve the internal management of Bell Atlantic" and hence was not TME-eligible. In support of this conclusion the court explained, relying on the Department of Justice *Competitive Impact Statement*, that the TME "was *directed at* internal operations, not at services for customers or end users."

It is this language that the Commission expressly invokes to ground its interpretation of the TME, stating that it (the Commission) "interpret[s] the concepts of 'management, control, or operation' in the [TME] consistent with" Judge Greene's analysis. And as we have noted above, the Commission rightly acknowledges that being "directed at" one end of a spectrum does not rule out embodying certain aspects from the other end. The agency was within its rights to treat Judge Greene's analysis--which in essence interpreted the statutory provision at issue and squared with the government's position supporting enforcement of the antitrust decree—as support for its construction of the TME. (As no party objected to the BOCs' offering of TDD services, and BOC entry into this activity posed no anticompetitive risk, the court granted a waiver for their provision.)

The Commission offers an added reason to put stock in the MFJ precedent: It believed that Petitioners' approach risked causing the TME exception to swallow the "information services" category. It said, plausibly, that such an "expansive view" of the TME assigns it an outsized role, thereby "narrowing . . . the scope of information services" in a way that clashes with the Commission's pre-1996 Act approach to cabining the "basic services" category, and the 1996 Act's imperative to "preserve the vibrant and competitive free market . . . for the Internet . . . unfettered by Federal or State regulation," which the Commission permissibly uses as a rationale to interpret a vague provision in a way that limits regulatory burdens. In sum, the Commission lawfully construed an ambiguous statutory phrase in a way that tallies with its policy judgment, as is its prerogative.

Petitioners' objections to the Commission's classification of DNS and reliance on the MFJ do not convince us.

Many of Petitioners' objections pillory a straw man. They state that "[t]he statute asks whether a function is used 'for the management, control, or operation of a telecommunications system,' not whether the function also benefits consumers." But, as noted before, the Commission need not deny, for example, that "configuration management"--a function it slots under the TME—benefits end users in some respect. It can simply say that DNS/caching and (for example) configuration management, respectively, adjoin opposite ends of the spectrum, one meriting inclusion in the TME and the other not.

Petitioners observe that DNS renders broadband Internet access "more efficient in ways that are generally invisible to users," a point that misses its mark entirely, or at best equivocates on the key point at issue. While DNS is "invisible" in the sense that it is "under the hood," so to speak, it remains "essential to providing Internet access for the ordinary consumer." Using a certain "configuration" tool or protocol might, say, make Internet traffic a bit faster or slower in the way that a metro's use of varying rail technologies might influence train speeds. But an absence of DNS would be something different altogether, hobbling ordinary users in navigating the Web, akin to a total absence of signage in a metro. Signage, unlike DNS, is of course quite apparent, but their user-centered purposes are alike for all practical purposes. (We address in Part I.C.4 Petitioners' separate argument that users' ability to obtain DNS from providers other than their ISPs precludes a finding of functional integration.) So the sense in which DNS is "invisible" to many end users is fully consistent with the agency's rationale for locating it nearer to the user-centric pole—and hence beyond the TME.

Finally, an argument made by amici on behalf of Petitioners as to DNS arguably aligns with claims made by the Commission's amici and so may work in the agency's favor. Petitioners' amici assert in the context of functional integration (an issue to which we turn in Part I.C.4) that broadband Internet access is not functionally integrated with DNS because broadband access works perfectly well *without* DNS. "Internet architects deliberately created DNS to be entirely independent from the IP packet transfer function," Jordan/Peha Amicus Br. 17, and "a BIAS provider's DNS is an *extraneous capability* . . . not required for the core service," *id.* at 17–18 (emphasis added). But if DNS is "extraneous" to operating the network, it is at least debatable whether DNS is used in "the management, control, or operation of a telecommunications system or the management of a telecommunications service." Amici for the Commission make related points, observing that "[a]n app's DNS translation transaction ends before the BIAS transmission begins," "DNS transactions do not provide the BIAS provider with information about the best path to the destination," and they "do not have the power to either optimize or impair the BIAS provider network." Bennett *et al.*, Amicus Br. 13. Thus it is at least reasonable not to view DNS as a network management tool. *Id.* at 13–14. Granted, Jordan and Peha remark that running DNS helps an ISP "reduce[ ] the volume of DNS queries passing through its network." Jordan/Peha Amicus Br. 18. But in the deferential posture of *Chevron* the points quoted above by

Jordan/Peha seem in part to support the Commission's reading of the record (consistent with Bennett *et al.*) as showing that, whereas "little or nothing in the DNS look-up process is designed to help an ISP 'manage' its network," DNS is "essential to providing Internet access for the ordinary consumer," for whom "DNS is a must."

The Commission extends the same logic to caching, though matters here are less obvious. It explains that caching "does not merely 'manage' an ISP's broadband Internet access service and underlying network," but "enables and enhances consumers' access to and use of information online." It makes clear that ISP caching service is not just "instrumental to pure transmission" but, rather, "enhances access to information" by consumers by facilitating "rapid retrieval of information from a local cache or repository." As the Title II Order had put it (albeit drawing a different lesson), "caching . . . provide[s] a benefit to subscribers in the form of faster, more efficient service," by "enabling the user to obtain 'more rapid retrieval of information' through the network."

Granted, some ISPs describe caching in terms indicating that it is a network management practice, and caching can help reduce ISPs' costs. *See* Jordan/Peha Amicus Br. 20–21. But these facts are not determinative. The Commission is entitled to draw its own conclusions based on its (permissible) interpretation of the TME, so long as consistent with the record. Here it has done that. The Commission found (without contradiction in the record) that caching "enables and enhances consumers' access to and use of information online." In particular, "[t]he record reflects that without caching, broadband Internet access service would be a significantly inferior experience for the consumer, particularly for customers in remote areas, requiring additional time and network capacity for retrieval of information from the Internet." That is so, the Commission maintains, even though encrypted traffic does not use caching, because "truly pervasive encryption on the Internet is still a long way off[ ] and . . . many sites still do not encrypt."

3. Adjunct-to-Basic Precedent

Finally, Petitioners raise a host of objections arising from the Commission's "adjunct-to-basic" precedent, developed in the *Computer Inquiries* orders issued by the Commission.

Because in our view the precedents in this area are murky, raising convoluted questions of grafting older Commission interpretations onto the "information services" definition as applied to broadband Internet service, we find neither side's recounting of adjunct-to-basic precedent fully compelling. Even though Congress's creation of the TME may fairly be said to have "[t]rack[ed]" adjunct-to-basic in certain respects, the Commission reasonably refused to be bound by facets of the analogy filtered through the lens of the Title II Order. The Commission's chief task was to interpret the TME's statutory text in a coherent, workable fashion and offer a reasonable rationale for altering its course, not to demonstrate that its reading is a tight fit with every aspect of adjunct-to-basic precedent. In fact, as we will see, that precedent is not the seamless web of Petitioners' vision.

Petitioners try to catch the Commission in a contradiction in a two-step approach. The agency, as we have seen, locates DNS and caching outside the TME. First, Petitioners invoke Commission precedent seeming to suggest that all or most adjunct-to-basic services would fall under the TME. Second, they observe that—whereas paradigmatic examples of adjunct-to-basic services such as speed dialing and call forwarding are undeniably useful to consumers and, per step one, belong under the TME—the Commission can give no satisfactory explanation for excluding DNS and caching from the TME. In particular, Petitioners and commenters analogize DNS to ordinary directory assistance, which the Commission has dubbed adjunct-to-basic, since both services help direct users to their chosen endpoints. Whence the difference?

To make sense of these claims and the Commission's response, we need to review the basic terms. To preview, even if there are incongruities in the Commission's treatment of the TME vis-à-vis the adjunct-to-basic idea, we see them as byproducts of drawing imperfect analogies.

The FCC created a distinction between "basic services" and "enhanced services" in its *Second Computer Inquiry*, with the latter concept defined as follows:

> [T]he term "enhanced service" shall refer to services[ ] offered over common carrier transmission facilities used in interstate communications, which employ computer processing applications that act on the format, content, code, protocol or similar aspects of the subscriber's transmitted information; provide the subscriber additional, different, or restructured information; or involve subscriber interaction with stored information. Enhanced services are not regulated under Title II of the Act.[*]

In contrast,

> In offering a basic transmission service . . . a carrier essentially offers a pure transmission capability over a communications path that is virtually transparent in terms of its interaction with customer supplied information.[†]

The most contested category is a third: adjunct-to-basic. It arose to accommodate the reality that providers of ordinary telephone services wished to

---

[*] *Second Computer Inquiry*, 77 F.C.C.2d at 498.
[†] *Second Computer Inquiry*, 77 F.C.C.2d at 420 ¶ 96.

offer new technologies facilitating that service—technologies that would quite plainly fall under the "enhanced services" definition, though ordinary phone service was indisputably a "basic service." To square the circle and avoid complexities of hybrid treatment, the Commission created an adjunct-to-basic bucket:

> In the [1985] *NATA Centrex* proceeding, the Commission defined adjunct services as services that 'facilitate the provision of basic services without altering their fundamental character,' and determined that such services should be treated as basic services for purposes of the *Computer II* rules, even though they might fall within possible literal readings of the definition of enhanced services.[*]

The Commission has set out two necessary criteria for a service to qualify as adjunct-to-basic:

> [C]arriers may use some of the processing and storage capabilities within their networks to offer optional tariffed features as 'adjunct to basic' services, if the features: (1) are intended to facilitate the use of traditional telephone service; and (2) do not alter the fundamental character of telephone service.[†]

Which services qualify as adjunct-to-basic? The answer covers a remarkably wide gamut, including "*inter alia*, speed dialing, call forwarding, computer-provided directory assistance, call monitoring, caller i.d., call tracing, call blocking, call return, repeat dialing, and call tracking, as well as certain Centrex features."[‡] The same goes for "communications between a subscriber and the network itself for call setup, call routing, call cessation, calling or called party identification, billing, and accounting,"[§] and prepaid calling cards with built-in advertisements—though not "talking yellow pages" with advertisements.[**]

Having laid out the key terms, we return to the parties' claims. We are satisfied with the Commission's prioritization of the MFJ precedent and its way of squaring the adjunct-to-basic precedent with its treatment of DNS and caching.

---

[*] *In re Bell Operating Companies, Petitions for Forbearance from the Application of Section 272 of the Commc'ns Act of 1934, as Amended, to Certain Activities*, 13 FCC Rcd. 2627, 2639 ¶ 18 (CCB 1998) ("*272 Forbearance Order*") (citation omitted).

[†] *In re Establishment of a Funding Mechanism for Interstate Operator Servs. for the Deaf*, 11 FCC Rcd. 6808, 6816–6817 ¶ 16 (1996) ("*Operator Services Order*").

[‡] *In re Implementation of the Non-Accounting Safeguards of Sections 271 and 272 of the Commc'ns Act of 1934, as Amended*, 11 FCC Rcd. 21905, 21958 ¶ 107 n.245 (1996) ("*Non-Accounting Safeguards Order*").

[§] *In re N. Am. Telecommunications Ass'n Petition for Declaratory Ruling Under Section 64.702 of the Commission's Rules Regarding the Integration of Centrex, Enhanced Servs., and Customer Premises Equip.*, 3 FCC Rcd. 4385, 4386 ¶ 11 (1988) ("*Centrex Order*") (citation omitted).

[**] *See* American Tel. & Tel. Co. v. FCC, 454 F.3d 329, 331 (D.C. Cir. 2006).

First, as explained above, the Commission had adequate grounds to focus on the 1982 MFJ's definition of "information service," which the 1996 Act took over virtually word for word.

Second, devising a coherent and workable test for applying the statutory TME permissibly takes precedence in the Commission's analysis over attempts to reach synthetic conformity between adjunct-to-basic precedent and the 1996 Act's terms. As the Court said in *Brand X*, we should "leav[e] federal telecommunications policy in this technical and complex area to be set by the Commission, not by warring analogies," whether crafted by courts, litigants, or Commissions past.

Third, the Commission's historical approach to adjunct-to-basic has hardly been clear-cut in its own right. As we have previously said, "it is difficult to discern any clear policy" in the Commission's application of its "various formulations" of what counts as adjunct-to-basic, so that "[t]he Commission's rulings reflect a highly fact-specific, case-by-case style of adjudication." Given this lack of cohesion, we can hardly fault the current Commission for discounting the persuasive force of adjunct-to-basic analogies in interpreting and applying the 1996 Act's TME in light of its policy views.

Furthermore, the Commission's definition of adjunct-to-basic services does not, as a linguistic matter, force the Commission's hand in interpreting the TME. Just because an adjunct-to-basic service like speed dialing or directory assistance "facilitate[s]" telephone service, it hardly follows automatically that it also qualifies under the text of the TME, since it requires no contortion of English to say that (for example) directory assistance is, by and large, not used to "manage[ ]" or "control" or "operat[e]" a telecommunications system or service, 47 U.S.C. § 153(24).

So the Commission had ample basis to dub the adjunct-to-basic line of analysis "potentially ambiguous precedent," and depart from what it regarded as "loose analogies" devised in the Title II Order. "Because broadband Internet access service was not directly addressed in pre-1996 Act *Computer Inquiries* and MFJ precedent, analogies to functions that were classified under that precedent must account for potentially distinguishing characteristics" as they relate to "technical details" and "regulatory backdrop." These claims are not unreasonable. Whatever the Commission's prior views on the relationship between basic services and *their* adjuncts, it is reasonable for the Commission to say that that rubric need not transfer over neatly to what it claims *is not* a basic service—broadband Internet access. Hence there is little basis for the claim that adjunct-to-basic lore requires the Commission to jettison the lesson of Judge Greene's TDD ruling.

Fourth, the Commission identifies precedent from the *Computer Inquiries* themselves to support a reading of the TME as requiring location of particular services on a spectrum running between utility to carriers and utility to end users. A ruling invoked by the 2018 Order allowed BOCs to enable the tracing of Emergency 911 ("E911") calls to the right location. The FCC's Common Carrier Bureau said:

> Although the "telecommunications management exception" encompasses adjunct services, the storage and retrieval functions associated with the BOCs' automatic location identification databases provide information that is useful to end users, rather than carriers. As a consequence, those functions are not adjunct services and cannot be classified as telecommunications services on that basis.[*]

While the Title II Order had sought to distinguish this precedent on the ground that the benefit of E911 service was "unrelated to telecommunications," it does not seem unreasonable for the current 2018 Order to assume a broader view of telecommunications in its invocation of this precedent.

Fifth, in any case, we are satisfied with the agency's refusal to treat DNS like speed dialing, call forwarding, and directory assistance.

As already noted, the Commission has adequate grounds not to hold its interpretation of the TME hostage to a chimerical hope for a perfect match-up with adjunct-to-basic precedent, in part because the regulatory history is so convoluted as to render the likelihood of a "perfect" matchup remote. So even if the Commission's interpretation of the TME comes at the cost of certain incongruities with the concept of adjunct-to-basic services, it reasonably regards alignment with the text and purposes of the 1996 Act, and the unifying policy vision animating the 2018 Order, as more weighty factors.

Moreover, implicit in the Commission's analysis is a recognition of a key difference between the above services and, at the least, DNS. Those other services are plausibly described as *adjunct*-to-basic, i.e., "ancillary" and "optional" in relation to telephone service. Not so, the Commission says, for DNS, which "[f]or an Internet user . . . is a *must.*" So DNS might well be seen to "alter the fundamental character of [the] service," and would thus fail to satisfy one of the two criteria *specified* by the Commission (and quoted above) for a service to qualify as adjunct-to-basic. This seems to distinguish DNS from such functions as speed dialing, call forwarding, and directory assistance, and thus square the Commission's current treatment of DNS with the Commission's prior treatment of those services as adjunct-to-basic, consistent

---

[*] *272 Forbearance Order*, 13 FCC Rcd. at 2639 ¶ 18.

with Judge Greene's treatment of a certain type of directory assistance as falling within the TME. (While some adjunct-to-basic services seem non-optional in certain respects, like "communications between a subscriber and the network itself for call setup . . . [and] call cessation," this point simply reinforces the miscellaneous nature of the adjunct-to-basic category, where "it is difficult to discern any clear policy.")

We find the above considerations sufficient to uphold the agency's position and hence do not address analogies to other MFJ precedents on technologies and services. Even if Petitioners offer plausible interpretations of rulings on address translation and third-party storage services provided by the BOCs, we believe the Commission has given a sufficiently sturdy justification for treating DNS and caching as non-TME services apart from other MFJ-linked analogies. It has set forth a plausible reading of the highly ambiguous TME, adequately explained its basis for giving more credence to judicial MFJ precedent than to the *Computer Inquiries* in this context, and made a reasonable case as to why DNS and caching need not be classed under the TME.

4. Functional Integration

Petitioners then open a new—and final—line of attack: *Even if* DNS and caching are "information services," the Commission's reliance on them to classify broadband as an "information service" was still unreasonable. They make three arguments in support of this thesis, but none holds water. As a threshold matter, we note that *Brand X* already held it reasonable for the Commission to conclude that DNS and caching are information services functionally integrated with the offering of "Internet access [service]" "to members of the public."

Petitioners first play up the facts that users may obtain DNS from providers other than their ISPs and that caching is not utterly indispensable. According to them, because "a user can easily configure her computer to use a third-party DNS server and content can be delivered even without caching," especially in the context of encrypted communications that occur without caching, it follows that DNS and caching are not "inextricably intertwined with the transmission component" of broadband. These facts ostensibly yield a "contradict[ion]" in the agency's position, since one's ISP-provided DNS and caching are not "indispensable" after all.

We find the objection misguided. As the Commission explained, "[T]he fact that some consumers obtain [DNS and caching] from third-party alternatives is not a basis for ignoring the capabilities that a broadband provider actually 'offers.'" Given the ambiguity in the term "offe[r]," the Commission's preferred reading of that term rather than the Title II Order's "narrower interpretation,"—which would foreclose the Commission's view quoted above—is permissible. In elucidating the ambiguity, *Brand X* said that "[t]he entire question is whether the products here are functionally integrated (like the components of a car) or functionally separate (like pets and leashes). That question turns not on the language of the Act, but on the factual particulars of how Internet technology works and how it is provided, questions *Chevron* leaves to the Commission to resolve in the first instance." The agency reasonably concluded that, notwithstanding the availability of alternative sources of DNS, a market where "the vast majority of ordinary consumers"—"[a]pproximately 97 percent"—"rely upon the DNS functionality provided by their ISP," as "part and parcel of the broadband Internet access service," meets *Brand X*'s requirements for functional integration. *Chevron* licenses these interpretive steps.

Second, Petitioners focus on what they dub the "relative importance" of the "inextricably intertwined" components at play—DNS/caching and high-speed transmission. The transmission aspect, they say, overshadows DNS and caching in "importance," where that concept is understood in terms of what "consumers focus on," and what aspect has "dominance in the broadband experience." The supposedly miniscule "importance" of DNS and caching in consumers' minds when using the Web means that those functionalities cannot be "inextricably intertwined" with high-speed transmission—and hence broadband cannot be an "information service" based on DNS and caching services.

These claims are unavailing. To begin with, Petitioners' invocation of USTA is yet again misplaced. There we said simply that the Commission *reasonably* determined what "consumers focus on," without holding that that is the only permissible view. Moreover, nowhere does *Brand X* say that a finding of "functional integration" requires a finding as to "dominance" or "relative importance" in the sense Petitioners imply. Average consumers, presumably, are no less in the dark now about the inner workings of DNS and caching than they were in 2005 when the Court decided *Brand X*. Yet that did not keep the Court from finding reasonable the FCC's position that DNS and caching were functionally integrated with high-speed transmission. However "consumer perception" might be understood, it is not unreasonable to interpret it as reflected in a consumer's *use* of the offered service as a whole and the functionalities that make that possible, even if the consumer has no inkling of what is "under the hood." As *Brand X* said, "Seen from the consumer's point of view, the Commission concluded, cable modem service is not a telecommunications offering because the consumer *uses* the high-speed wire

Chapter 5: Classification

always in connection with the information-processing capabilities provided by Internet access . . . ." So it is perfectly sensible for the agency to retort that "[w]hile the typical broadband subscriber may know little or nothing about DNS or caching, that subscriber would keenly feel the absence of those functions" in everyday Web use.

Petitioners reply that the argument proves too much, as Web browsers and search engines are also essential to the consumer's Internet experience. But quite apart from the fact that the role of ISP-provided browsers and search engines appears very modest compared to that of DNS and caching in ISPs' overall provision of Internet access, Petitioners are in a weak posture to deny that inclusion of "search engines and web browsers" could support an "information service" designation, since those appear to be examples of the "walled garden" services that Petitioners hold up as models of "information service"-eligible offerings in their gloss of *Brand X.*

Finally, Petitioners contend that even if DNS and caching *were* functionally integrated with transmission, that "does not automatically lead to an information service classification." . . . "The FCC could not have reasonably concluded that a drop of DNS and caching in a sea of transmission transformed the service into something that could properly be called an information service." The idea seems to be that ISPs now offer fewer "walled garden" services of the kind consumers mostly care about than they did in the era of the 2002 Cable Modem Order and *Brand X,* so that basing an "information service" designation on DNS and caching alone is currently as dubious as saying that a few golden threads interwoven in an ordinary sweater turn the sweater into a golden garment. "Congress could not have intended inclusion of two minor auxiliary information services to transform the classification of what is otherwise overwhelmingly telecommunications."

But the Supreme Court has never imposed or even hinted at such a quantitative standard to determine whether inextricably intertwined functionalities can justify an "information service" classification. We see no basis for launching such a notion on our own. Had the Court thought along Petitioners' lines, it could have sided with challengers in *Brand X* by saying that—when users wander beyond ISPs' proprietary services—the quantum of ISP-offered "information services" shrinks so greatly in proportion to the transmission aspect that in that realm they are accepting an "offering" of standalone telecommunications service. The Court took the opposite tack, marshaling DNS and caching as examples of "information services" operative when users "access[ ] content provided by parties other than the cable company," thereby rendering the Commission's classification "reasonable."

Petitioners try to get mileage from a hypothetical in *Brand X* involving the bundling of telephone service with voicemail, but the attempt falls far short. Challengers in *Brand X* had argued that, on the FCC's theory in that case, a telephone-plus-voicemail bundle would have to be classified as an "information service," making it far too easy to evade the reach of Title II. The Court declined to "decide whether a construction that resulted in these consequences would be unreasonable"—because the hypothetical misfired. Its result "d[id] not follow from the construction the Commission adopted," which was "more limited than respondents [had] assume[d]." That is, the FCC's position "*d[id] not* leave all information-service offerings exempt from mandatory Title II regulation." A landline telephone service provider could not—on the FCC's theory as interpreted by the Court—get away with "packag[ing] voice mail [or a time-of-day announcement] with telephone service" and on that basis take landline service out of Title II. That gimmick must fail because add-ons like voicemail and time-of-day announcements are separable from "pure transmission" in a way that is not true for DNS and caching in relation to broadband. Whereas landline service "transmits information independent of the information-storage capabilities provided by voice mail," and is "only trivially dependent on the information service the [time-of-day] announcement provides," broadband involves "functional[ ] integrat[ion]" between "high-speed transmission," which is "necessary to provide Internet service," with "further processing of information," e.g., in the form of DNS and caching. The *Brand X* Court, in short, made plain that the challengers' hypothetical was simply irrelevant. Since Petitioners develop no credible explanation as to why the current Commission's theory is any more vulnerable to the hypothetical discredited by *Brand X*, we can see no merit in their criticism.

To summarize, just as the USTA petitioners "fail[ed] to provide an unambiguous answer to" whether "broadband providers make a standalone offering of telecommunications," Petitioners have not done so here. Nor have they shown the Commission's stance to be unreasonable. We conclude, under the guidance of *Brand X*, that the Commission permissibly classified broadband Internet access as an "information service" by virtue of the functionalities afforded by DNS and caching.

NOTES & QUESTIONS

1. *A curious byline.* This decision is huge and complex in many ways (just like our telecommunications network . . .), but let's start at the beginning. Notice that no judge is listed as an author. "Per Curiam" is a decision issued in the name of the court, not the name of any individual judge. In most cases, per

curiam decisions are short and deal with issues that are procedural or non-controversial. The decision in this case runs more than 145 pages and concerns one of the most controversial issues in telecommunications law. What's more, all three judges wrote separate opinions. Judges Millett wrote a concurring opinion that Judge Wilkins endorsed, and Judge Williams wrote an opinion concurring in part and dissenting in part. So what is going on? Let's unpack it a bit.

a. *Judge Millett wants an upgrade.* Throughout her concurrence, Judge Millett makes it very clear that she is not happy with the outcome here but feels bound by the Supreme Court's decision in *Brand X.* Specifically, the 2018 Order survives (in her view) "because it hewed closely to the portions of *Brand X* that discuss DNS and caching as information services." But she is not enthusiastic about the Commission's decision:

> *Brand X* allows that approach. The Supreme Court picked out DNS and caching to explain why the consumer continues to make use of a functionally integrated information service, even when she "goes beyond [the walled garden] and accesses content provided by third parties other than the cable company[.]" In so doing, the Supreme Court implied that DNS and caching were themselves information services.

> From our limited institutional perch as a lower court, that conclusion controls our decision. "[W]e must follow the binding Supreme Court precedent."

Indeed, she takes the time to closely analyze the current state of broadband technology and the marketplace to question the wisdom of this outcome, noting that she is "deeply concerned that the result is unhinged from the realities of modern broadband service." She doesn't take issue with the Court's understanding of broadband technology in *Brand X*; instead, she distinguishes it:

> But that was then, and this is now. *Brand X* was decided almost fifteen years ago, during the bygone era of iPods, AOL, and Razr flip phones. The market for broadband access has changed dramatically in the interim. *Brand X* faced a "walled garden" reality, in which broadband was valued not merely as a means to access third-party content, but also for its bundling of then-nascent information services like private email, user newsgroups, and personal webpage development. Today, none of those add-ons occupy the significance that they used to. Now it is impossible "to deny [the] dominance of [third-party content] in the broadband experience." *USTA*, 825 F.3d at 698. "[C]onsumers use broadband principally to access third-party content, *not* [ISP-provided] email and other add-on applications." *Id.* (emphasis added). In a nutshell, a speedy pathway to content is what consumers value. It is what broadband providers advertise and compete over. And so, under any natural reading of the statute, the technological mechanism for accessing third-party content is what broadband providers "offer."

As our opinion today recognizes, auxiliary services like DNS and caching remain in the broadband bundle. But their salience has waned significantly since *Brand X* was decided. DNS is readily available, free of charge, and at a remarkably high quality, from upwards of twenty different third-party providers. And caching has been fundamentally stymied by the explosion of Internet encryption. For these accessories to singlehandedly drive the Commission's classification decision is to confuse the leash for the dog. In 2005, the Commission's classification decision was "just barely" permissible. *Brand X*, 545 U.S. at 1003, 125 S.Ct. 2688 (Breyer, J., concurring). Almost fifteen years later, hanging the legal status of Internet broadband services on DNS and caching blinks technological reality.

Judge Millett is also not afraid to spell out what she thinks should happen next:

The Supreme Court, however, is not so constrained. It is freer than we are to conclude that the "factual particulars of how Internet technology works," *Brand X*, 545 U.S. at 991, 125 S.Ct. 2688, have changed so materially as to undermine the reasonableness of the agency's judgments and in particular its "determinative" reliance on DNS and caching, *2018 Order* ¶ 33 n.99. Or Congress could bring its own judgment to bear by updating the statute's governance of telecommunications and information services to match the rapid and sweeping developments in those areas. Either intervention would avoid trapping Internet regulation in technological anachronism.

And she flexes her literary acumen in her criticism of the Commission's analysis, quoting from T.S. Elliot's *Burnt Norton*:

The Commission's decision to cling to DNS and caching as the acid test for its regulatory classification "cannot bear very much reality." Today, the typical broadband offering bears little resemblance to its *Brand X* version. The walled garden has been razed and its fields sown with salt. The add-ons described in *Brand X*—"a cable company's e-mail service, its Web page, and the ability it provides consumers to create a personal Web page," 545 U.S. at 998, 125 S.Ct. 2688—have dwindled as consumers routinely deploy "their high-speed Internet connections to take advantage of competing services offered by third parties." *Title II Order* ¶ 347. That is why the Commission today makes no effort to rely on those ancillary services. *2018 Order* ¶ 33 n.99.

. . .

With the Commission now having abandoned its reliance on any additional technologies provided by broadband, *see 2018 Order* ¶ 33 n.99, the question is whether the combination of transmission with DNS and caching *alone* can justify the information service classification. If we were writing on a clean slate, that question would seem to have only one answer given the current state of technology: No. . . . Not only does the walled garden lay in ruin, but the roles of DNS and caching themselves have changed dramatically since *Brand X* was decided. And they have done so in ways that strongly favor classifying broadband as a telecommunications service, as Justice Scalia had originally advocated. *Brand X*, 545 U.S. at 1012–1014, 125 S.Ct. 2688 (Scalia, J., dissenting).

Judge Millett offers three reasons why the Commission's classification decision should be rejected: (1) because DNS and caching services are freely available from third parties in the Internet marketplace and, thus, are not an essential part of the BIAS offering, (2) classifying BIAS as a telecommunications service is consistent with the structure and purpose of the Communications Act, which was enacted to "correct for the problems of monopoly power in the telecommunications industry," and (3) while the telecommunications management exception is ambiguous, its application should turn on "the 'relative importance' of the different capabilities in the marketplace."

   b. *Judge Wilkins makes it a majority in all but name.* With two short sentences, Judge Wilkins gives significant weight to Judge Millett's analysis. He joins the Per Curiam opinion "in full" but also emphasizes how Judge Millett's concurrence "persuasively explains" the reason for the outcome: *Brand X* precedent. Why do you think that Judge Millett and Judge Wilkins presented their conclusions in this way? If they both agree on Judge Millett's analysis, why not simply put that in the majority opinion under her name? It only takes two votes to author a majority opinion in a three-judge panel. What signal are they trying to send? And who are they trying to send it to? Is there some other tactic at play?

   c. *Judge Williams sees this as a tragedy.* If you thought Judge Millett's quotation of Elliot was a flourish, wait until you see Judge Williams' decision concurring in part and dissenting in part; he goes straight for The Bard:

> *And be these juggling fiends no more believed,*
> *That palter with us in a double sense;*
> *That keep the word of promise to our ear,*
> *And break it to our hope.*

So says Macbeth, finding that the witches' assurances were sheer artifice and that his life is collapsing around him. The enactors of the *2018 Order*, though surely no Macbeths, might nonetheless feel a certain kinship, being told that they acted lawfully in *rejecting* the heavy hand of Title II for the Internet, but that each of the 50 states is free to impose just that. (Many have already enacted such legislation. *See, e.g.*, Cal. S. Comm. on Judiciary, SB 822 Analysis 1 (2018) (explaining that California has expressly "codif[ied] portions of the recently-rescinded . . . rules").) If Internet communications were tidily divided into federal markets and readily severable state markets, this might be no problem. But no modern user of the Internet can believe for a second in such tidy isolation; indeed, the Commission here made an uncontested finding that it would be "impossible" to maintain the regime it had adopted under Title I in the face of inconsistent state regulation. On my colleagues' view, state policy trumps federal; or, more precisely, the most draconian state policy trumps all else. "The Commission may lawfully decide to free the Internet from Title II," we say, "It just can't give its decision any effect in the real world."

The part of the majority opinion that Judge Williams takes issue with is one that we have not yet covered: preemption. We will discuss this part of the opinion in more detail in CHAPTER 7: PRIVACY, but for now it is sufficient to understand the bottom line and the point he is making about the likely impact of the decision. Here is the key sentence from the Majority's conclusion:

> But because the Commission's Preemption Directive, *see 2018 Order* ¶¶ 194–204, lies beyond its authority, we vacate the portion of the 2018 Order purporting to preempt "any state or local requirements that are inconsistent with [the Commission's] deregulatory approach[,]" *see id.* ¶ 194.

So what is Judge Williams saying? That the Commission has been handed a pyrrhic victory. The court upheld their decision not to regulate BIAS providers, but simultaneously held that states can enter that regulatory vacuum. How do you think the BIAS providers feel about this outcome? If you were an attorney at a broadband company like Comcast or Verizon, would you prefer the regulatory world after the *USTA* decision or after the *Mozilla* decision?

2. *Death of analogies?* There seem to be an endless stream of analogies in the Commission's and the courts' classification decisions. Is broadband Internet more like pizza delivery or a car or a leashed puppy? Are DNS and caching more like speed dialing and directory assistance (adjunct-to-basic) or configuration settings on cable modems (TME)? But is the court convinced by these analogies? Or do they just create ambiguity that leads to deference under *Chevron* Step 2? Take a moment to re-read the court's analysis of TME and the adjunct-to-basic precedents. What purpose do these analogies serve? Do you have any guesses about which of the three judges authored those portions of the Per Curiam opinion?

3. *Birds of a feather.* The court also upheld the Commission's classification of mobile broadband as a "private mobile service" rather than a "commercial mobile service" subject to Title II common carriage regulations. Ultimately, the court simply deferred to the Commission's judgment under the *Chevron* framework, citing the "compelling policy grounds to ensure consistent treatment of the two varieties of broadband Internet access."

4. *The elephant in the room.* If we take a step back and think about the series of Internet classification decisions from *Brand X* to *Mozilla*, what is the central thread that ties them all together? Clearly it is the two-step *Chevron* framework and the concept of deference to agency interpretations of ambiguous provisions.

No matter what the Commission or the challengers argue, the courts have all agreed that the definitions for these key classification terms in the Communications act are ambiguous. But in the years since *Brand X* was decided, the Supreme Court has become less enthusiastic about citing to or relying upon *Chevron.* Judge Millett's concurrence encourages the Court or Congress to step in and update the record on broadband classification. Do you think she expects them to apply *Chevron?*

D. CROSS PLATFORM SERVICES

For modern users, classifying services based on the particular method of delivery can seem blurry and somewhat arbitrary. Most services are now made available via broadband, including Digital Voice and Digital Television, and all that matters from the user's perspective is whether they can gain quick and reliable access. But for the providers it still matters what statutory *classification* the FCC chooses to impose—different services are subject to very different regulations. So the question is how will the Commission view a particular service delivered over a particular channel. Is this just a minor variation of a known service? If not, does it belong to an existing family of regulated services that fit under a current Title of the Communications Act? If not, does it fall under the FCC's generic Title I authority? If so, finally, what regulatory powers does the FCC actually have and what rules will apply? We can see these questions play out in recent disputes over new services.

1. VoIP

We start with voice over IP or "VoIP." The beauty of the internet is its flexibility. It's almost like a stem cell that can take on different functional forms as necessary. Companies first began to offer VoIP services in the mid-1990s, but now these services are commonplace—users can subscribe directly through their ISP or can purchase equipment from a third party vendor and use their existing broadband access to connect. But the widespread adoption of VoIP has presented a number of regulatory questions.

The FCC first addressed in 1998 the question of whether VoIP should be classified as a "telecommunications service" and subject to Title II common carrier and Universal Service Fund obligations.[*] The Commission found that

---

[*] Universal Service Report, 13 FCC Rcd. 11501 (1998).

companies who only provide hardware and software ("consumer premises equipment") and companies that facilitate computer-to-computer VoIP calls were not providing a "telecommunications service." But the Commission deferred its decision as to phone-to-phone VoIP services. It did suggest that providers could be regulated under Title II and be required to contribute to the Universal Service Fund if their services are "interstate" and offered "to the public for a fee."

In February 2004, the FCC held that computer-to-computer VoIP was indeed an "information service."* At issue was the on-line messaging service called Free World Dial Up (also known as "Pulver"). This service did not resemble everyday use of the public switched telephone network (PSTN). It was instead computer-to-computer, and did not involve telephone numbers from the North American Numbering Plan (NANP) (standard 10 digit American dialing). The Commission asserted federal jurisdiction, and suggested that contrary treatment by state regulators would be inconsistent with federal policy.

In March 2004, the FCC launched the *IP-enabled Services* NPRM.† In that NPRM, the Commission asked for broad ranging feedback on how the FCC should respond to new communications services provided over IP networks. Although phrased broadly to cover any type of service, most of the questions focused on VoIP and its variants. The Commission floated various characteristics that could potentially be relevant to the classification question. They included: functional equivalence to telephony; substitutability; interconnection with the PSTN (public switched telephone network) and use of the NANP (North American numbering plan); decentralized peer-to-peer communications versus network services that rely on some centralized server.‡

If *Pulver* was an easy example of an information service, AT&T's bypass was a relatively easy example of VoIP as a telecommunications service. AT&T's long-distance service allowed customers to make long-distance calls from their standard phones, dialing standard 10 digit North America Numbering Plan (NANP) numbers, without any requirement of internet access. The originating LEC would carry the call over the local loop to AT&T's point of presence, where the call would then be converted to VoIP and sent over the public internet to the destination. But instead of handing off the call to the terminating LEC, which would generate termination access charges, AT&T converted the call back into a format suitable for the PSTN, then funneled it through a local

---

* See Petition for Declaratory Ruling that Pulver.com's Free World Dialup is Neither Telecommunications nor a Telecommunications Service, MO&O, 19 FCC Rcd. 3307 (2004).

† IP-Enabled Services, 19 FCC Rcd. 4863 (2004).

‡ See id. at ¶ 37.

business line. From the terminating LEC's perspective, it was switching local calls, not terminating long distance ones. Applying the logic of the "Stevens" report, this service looked too much like traditional telephone service from the customer's perspective and made substantial use of the PSTN. Accordingly, it was classified as a telecommunications service.* This classification prompted suits by LECs against AT&T for hundreds of millions of dollars in access charges.

Having resolved easier classification questions in *Pulver* and *AT&T bypass*, the FCC faced a much harder set of questions related to Vonage's *DigitalVoice* service.† Vonage petitioned the FCC after the Minnesota Public Utilities Commission sought to apply traditional local "telephone company" regulations to the VoIP service provider. In response to the petition, the Commission had to decide whether *state* or *federal* law should apply to a service like Vonage, which could be used to place both intrastate and interstate calls. This also implicated the question of whether Vonage was providing an "information service" because, if so, the Minnesota ruling would conflict with the FCC's "national policy of nonregulation of information services." In order to resolve these questions, the FCC looked to the underlying functionality of Vonage's service from the perspective of the users.

VONAGE PETITION

Vonage Holdings Corporation Petition for Declaratory Ruling,
MO&O, 19 FCC Rcd. 22404 (2004)

II. BACKGROUND

A. Vonage's DigitalVoice Service

4. DigitalVoice is a service[9] that enables subscribers to originate and receive voice communications and provides a host of other features.... DigitalVoice resembles the telephone service provided by the circuit-switched network. But as described in detail here, there are fundamental differences between the two types of service.

5. First, Vonage customers must have access to a broadband connection to the Internet.... DigitalVoice customers must obtain a broadband connection to the Internet from another provider.... [I]t is not relevant where that broadband

---

* *See AT&T's Phone-to-Phone IP Telephony Services,* Order, 19 FCC Rcd. 7457 (2004).

† *Vonage Holdings Corporation Petition for Declaratory Ruling,* 19 FCC Rcd. 22404 (2004).

[9] DigitalVoice provides VoIP, among other capabilities. Although the Commission has adopted no formal definition of "VoIP," we use the term generally to include any IP-enabled services offering real-time, multidirectional voice functionality, including, but not limited to, services that mimic traditional telephony. *See IP-Enabled Services Proceeding,* 19 FCC at 4866, ¶ 3 n.7.

connection is located or even whether it is the same broadband connection every time the subscriber accesses the service. Rather, Vonage's service is fully portable; customers may use the service anywhere in the world where they can find a broadband connection to the Internet.

6. Second, Vonage . . . requires customers to use specialized customer premises equipment (CPE). Customers may choose among several different types of specialized CPE[, such as] a Multimedia Terminal Adapter (MTA), which contains a digital signal processing unit that performs digital-to-audio and audio-to-digital conversion and has a standard telephone jack connection . . . . [A] conventional telephone alone will not work with Vonage's service.

8. DigitalVoice provides the capability to originate and terminate real-time voice communications. Once the CPE and software are installed and configured, the customer may place or receive calls over the Internet to or from anyone with a telephone number—including another Vonage customer, a customer of another VoIP provider, a customer of a commercial mobile radio service (CMRS) provider, or a user reachable only through the public switched telephone network (PSTN). In any case, the subscriber's outgoing calls originate on the Internet and are routed over the Internet to Vonage's servers. If the destination is another Vonage customer or a user on a peered service, the server routes the packets to the called party over the Internet and the communication also terminates via the Internet.[24] If the destination is a telephone attached to the PSTN, the server converts the IP packets into appropriate digital audio signals and connects them to the PSTN using the services of telecommunications carriers interconnected to the PSTN. If a PSTN user originates a call to a Vonage customer, the call is connected, using the services of telecommunications carriers interconnected to the PSTN, to the Vonage server, which then converts the audio signals into IP packets and routes them to the Vonage user over the Internet.

9. [A]lthough Vonage's service uses North American Numbering Plan (NANP) numbers as the identification mechanism for the user's IP address, the NANP number is not necessarily tied to the user's physical location for either assignment or use, in contrast to most wireline circuit-switched calls. Rather, as Vonage explains, the number correlates to the user's digital signal processor to facilitate the exchange of calls between the Internet and the PSTN using a

---

[24] Vonage-to-Vonage calls are not transmitted over the PSTN. Calls from Vonage customers to customers of certain other IP service providers with which Vonage has a peering arrangement also are not transmitted over the PSTN, but solely over the Internet. . . . If Vonage does not have a peering arrangement with a particular VoIP provider, calls between users of the two services are routed in part over the PSTN but originate and terminate via the Internet.

convenient mechanism with which users are familiar to identify the user's IP address. In other words . . . a call to a Vonage customer's NANP number can reach that customer anywhere in the world and does not require the user to remain at a single location.

B. History of Vonage's Petition

10. In July 2003, the Minnesota Department of Commerce filed an administrative complaint against Vonage with the Minnesota Commission, asserting that Vonage was providing telephone exchange service in Minnesota and was thus subject to state laws and regulations governing a "telephone company."

11. In September 2003, the Minnesota Commission issued an order asserting regulatory jurisdiction over Vonage and ordering the company to comply with all state statutes and regulations relating to the offering of telephone service in Minnesota. . . . In response, Vonage filed suit against the Minnesota Commission in the U.S. District Court for the District of Minnesota. In October 2003, the district court entered a permanent injunction in favor of Vonage.[31] The court determined that Vonage is providing an information service under the Act and that the Act preempts the Minnesota Commission's authority to subject such a service to common carrier regulation. . . . The appeal [in the 8th Circuit] remains pending.

12. At the same time that it filed suit in the district court in Minnesota, Vonage filed the instant petition with the Commission.

III. DISCUSSION

14. We grant Vonage's petition in part and preempt the *Minnesota Vonage Order.*

A. Preemption of the Minnesota Vonage Order

1. Commission Jurisdiction over DigitalVoice

16. In the absence of a specific statutory provision regarding jurisdiction over services like DigitalVoice, we begin with section 2 of the Act. In 1934, Congress set up a dual regulatory regime for communications services. In section 2(a) of the Act, Congress has given the Commission exclusive jurisdiction over "all interstate and foreign communication" and "all persons engaged . . . in such communication."[52] Section 2(b) of the Act reserves to the states jurisdiction "with respect to intrastate communication service . . . of any carrier."[53]

---

[31] *See* Vonage Holding Corp. v. Minnesota Pub. Utils. Comm'n, 290 F. Supp. 2d 993 (D. Minn. 2003), *appeal pending*, Vonage Holdings Corp. v. Minnesota Pub. Utils. Comm'n, No. 04-1434 (8th Cir.).

[52] 47 U.S.C. § 152(a).

17. In applying section 2 to specific services and facilities, the Commission has traditionally applied its so-called "end-to-end analysis" based on the physical end points of the communication. Under this analysis, the Commission considers the "continuous path of communications," beginning with the end point at the inception of a communication to the end point at its completion, and has rejected attempts to divide communications at any intermediate points.

18. Thus, our threshold determination must be whether DigitalVoice is purely intrastate (subject only to state jurisdiction) or jurisdictionally mixed (subject also to federal jurisdiction). The nature of DigitalVoice precludes any suggestion that the service could be characterized as a purely intrastate service. As Vonage has indicated, it has over 275,000 subscribers located throughout the United States, each with the ability to communicate with anyone in the world from anywhere in the world. While DigitalVoice clearly enables intrastate communications, it also enables interstate communications. It is therefore a jurisdictionally mixed service, and this Commission has exclusive jurisdiction under the Act to determine the policies and rules, if any, that govern the interstate aspect of DigitalVoice service.

2. Commission Authority To Preempt State Regulations

19. Where separating a service into interstate and intrastate communications is impossible or impractical, the Supreme Court has recognized the Commission's authority to preempt state regulation that would thwart or impede the lawful exercise of federal authority over the interstate component of the communications.[66]

3. Conflict With Commission Rules and Policies

20. Regardless of the definitional classification of DigitalVoice under the Communications Act, the *Minnesota Vonage Order* directly conflicts with our pro-competitive deregulatory rules and policies governing entry regulations, tariffing, and other requirements arising from these regulations for services such as DigitalVoice.[69] Were DigitalVoice to be classified a telecommunications

---

[53] 47 U.S.C. § 152(b).

[66] *See Louisiana Pub. Serv. Comm'n....* As summarized by the Supreme Court, federal law and policy preempt state action in several circumstances: (1) where compliance with both federal and state law is in effect physically impossible; (2) when there is outright or actual conflict between federal and state law; (3) where the state law stands as an obstacle to the accomplishment and execution of the full objectives of Congress; (4) when Congress expresses a clear intent to preempt state law; (5) where there is implicit in federal law a barrier to state regulation; and (6) where Congress has legislated comprehensively, thus occupying an entire field of regulation. Additionally, the Supreme Court has held that preemption may result not only from action taken by Congress but also from a federal agency action that is within the scope of the agency's congressionally delegated authority. *Louisiana Pub. Serv. Comm'n.*

[69] While we do not rely on it as a basis for our action in this Order, we also note that section 253 of the Act

service, Vonage would be considered a nondominant, competitive telecommunications provider for which the Commission has eliminated entry and tariff filing requirements with respect to services like DigitalVoice.[70] In particular, in completely eliminating interstate market entry requirements, the Commission reasoned that retaining entry requirements could stifle new and innovative services whereas blanket entry authority, *i.e.,* unconditional entry, would promote competition. State entry and certification requirements, such as the Minnesota Commission's, require the filing of an application which must contain detailed information regarding all aspects of the qualifications of the would-be service provider, including public disclosure of detailed financial information, operational and business plans, and proposed service offerings. The application process can take months and result in denial of a certificate, thus preventing entry altogether. Similarly, when the Commission ordered the mandatory detariffing of most interstate, domestic interexchange services (including services like DigitalVoice), the Commission found that prohibiting such tariffs would promote competition and the public interest, and that tariffs for these services *may actually harm consumers* by impeding the development of vigorous competition. Tariffs and "price lists," such as those required by Minnesota's statutes and rules, are lengthy documents subject to specific filing and notice requirements that must contain every rate, term, and condition of service offered by the provider, including terms and conditions to which the provider may be subject in its certificate of authority. The Minnesota Commission may also require the filing of cost-justification information or order a change in a rate, term or condition set forth in the tariff. The administrative process involved in entry certification and tariff filing requirements, alone, introduces substantial delay in time-to-market and ability to respond to changing consumer demands, not to mention the impact these processes have on how an entity subject to such requirements provides its service.

21. On the other hand, if DigitalVoice were to be classified as an information service, it would be subject to the Commission's long-standing national policy of nonregulation of information services, particularly regarding economic regulation such as the type imposed on Vonage in the *Minnesota Vonage Order.*

---

provides the Commission additional preemption authority over state regulations that "prohibit or have the effect of prohibiting the ability of an entity to provide any interstate or intrastate telecommunications service." 47 U.S.C. § 253.

[70] *See, e.g., Implementation of Section 402(b)(2)(A) of the Telecommunications Act of 1996,* 14 FCC Rcd. 11364, 11372-75, paras. 12-16 (1999) (*Section 214 Order*) (granting blanket section 214 authority for new lines of all domestic carriers including dominant carriers like the Bell operating companies (BOCs)); *Policy and Rules Concerning the Interstate, Interexchange Marketplace,* 11 FCC Rcd. 20730 (1996) (*Interexchange Detariffing Order*) (adopting mandatory detariffing of most domestic interstate, interexchange services) . . . .

In a series of proceedings beginning in the 1960's, the Commission issued orders finding that economic regulation of information services would disserve the public interest because these services lacked the monopoly characteristics that led to such regulation of common carrier services historically. The Commission found the market for these services to be competitive and best able to "burgeon and flourish" in an environment of "free give-and-take of the market place without the need for and possible burden of rules, regulations and licensing requirements."

22. Thus . . . regardless of its definitional classification . . . Minnesota's order produces a direct conflict with our federal law and policies. . . . This notwithstanding, some commenters argue that the traditional dual regulatory scheme must nevertheless apply to DigitalVoice *because it is functionally similar* to traditional local exchange and long distance voice service. Were it appropriate to base our decision today . . . solely on the functional similarities between DigitalVoice and other existing voice services (as the Minnesota Commission appears to have done), we would find DigitalVoice *far more similar* to CMRS, which provides mobility, is often offered as an all-distance service, and needs uniform national treatment on many issues. Indeed, in view of these differences, CMRS, including IP-enabled CMRS, is expressly exempt from the type of state economic regulation Minnesota seeks to impose on DigitalVoice.[83]

4. Preemption Based on "Impossibility"

23. In this section, we examine whether there is any plausible approach to separating DigitalVoice into interstate and intrastate components for purposes of enabling dual federal and state regulations to coexist without "negating" federal policy and rules. We find none.

24. DigitalVoice harnesses the power of the Internet to enable its users to establish a virtual presence in multiple locations simultaneously, to be reachable anywhere they may find a broadband connection, and to manage their communications needs from any broadband connection. The Internet's inherently global and open architecture obviates the need for any correlation between Vonage's DigitalVoice service and its end users' geographic locations. As we noted above, however, the Commission has historically applied the geographic "end-to-end" analysis to distinguish interstate from intrastate communications. . . . [T]he Commission has increasingly acknowledged the difficulty of using an end-to-end analysis when the services at issue involve the

---

[83] *See* 47 U.S.C. § 332(c)(3)(A). Pursuant to section 332 of the Act, state and local governments are specifically preempted from regulating the "*entry of or the rates charged* by any commercial mobile service or any private mobile service." *Id.* (emphasis added).

Internet.[89] DigitalVoice shares many of the same characteristics as these other services involving the Internet, thus making jurisdictional determinations about particular DigitalVoice communications based on an end-point approach difficult, if not impossible.

25. In fact, the geographic location of the end user at any particular time is only one clue to a jurisdictional finding under the end-to-end analysis. The geographic location of the "termination" of the communication is the other clue; yet this is similarly difficult or impossible to pinpoint. This "impossibility" results from the inherent capability of IP-based services to enable subscribers to utilize multiple service features that access different websites or IP addresses during the same communication session and to perform different types of communications simultaneously, none of which the provider has a means to separately track or record. For example, a DigitalVoice user checking voicemail or reconfiguring service options would be communicating with a Vonage server. A user forwarding a voicemail via e-mail to a colleague using an Internet-based e-mail service would be "communicating" with a different Internet server or user. An incoming call to a user invoking forwarding features could "terminate" anywhere the DigitalVoice user has programmed. A communication from a DigitalVoice user to a similar IP-enabled provider's user would "terminate" to a geographic location unknown either to Vonage or to the other provider. These functionalities in all their combinations form an integrated communications service designed to overcome geography, not track it. Indeed, it is the total lack of dependence on *any* geographically defined location that most distinguishes DigitalVoice from other services whose federal or state jurisdiction is determined based on the geographic end points of the communications. Consequently, Vonage has no service-driven reason to know users' locations, and Vonage asserts it presently has no way to know.[95] Furthermore, to require Vonage to attempt to incorporate geographic "end-point" identification

---

[89] For example, in attempting to apply an end-to-end analysis to an incumbent LEC's digital subscriber line (DSL) telecommunications service to determine whether federal or state tariffing requirements should attach, the Commission noted that "an Internet communication does not necessarily have a point of 'termination' in the traditional sense." *GTE ADSL Order*, 13 FCC Rcd. at 22478-79, para. 22. . . . In *Pulver*, the Commission concluded that the concept of "end points" and an end-to-end analysis were not relevant to Pulver's Internet-based VoIP information service. *See Pulver*, 19 FCC Rcd. at 3316-23, paras. 15-25.

[95] We acknowledge that certain geolocation products may be capable of identifying, to some degree, the geographic location of a Vonage user in the future, *see, e.g.,* Sprint Reply at 7, but the record does not reflect that such information is readily obtainable at this time. *See, e.g.,* 8x8 Comments at 14-15. Should Vonage decide in the future to incorporate geolocation capabilities into its service to facilitate additional features that may be dependent on reliable location determining capabilities, *e.g.,* E911-type features or law enforcement surveillance capabilities, this would not alter the fact that the service enables the user's location to change continually.

capabilities into its service solely to facilitate the use of an end-to-end approach would serve no legitimate policy purpose. Rather than encouraging and promoting the development of innovative, competitive advanced service offerings, we would be taking the opposite course, molding this new service into the same old familiar shape.

26. In the absence of a capability to identify *directly* DigitalVoice communications that originate and terminate within the boundaries of Minnesota, we still consider whether some method exists to identify such communications *indirectly*, such that Minnesota's regulations could nonetheless apply to only that "intrastate" usage such as voice calls between persons located in the same state. For example, assume Minnesota were to use DigitalVoice subscribers' NPA/NXXs as a proxy for those subscribers' geographic locations when making or receiving calls. If a subscriber's NPA/NXX were associated with Minnesota under the NANP, Minnesota's telephone company regulations would attach to every DigitalVoice communication that occurred between that subscriber and any other party having a Minnesota NPA/NXX. But because subscribers residing anywhere could obtain a Minnesota NPA/NXX, a subscriber may never be present in Minnesota when communicating with another party that is, yet Minnesota would treat those calls as subject to its jurisdiction.

28. We further consider whether Minnesota could assert jurisdiction over DigitalVoice communications based on whether the subscriber's billing address or address of residence are in Minnesota. This too fails. When a subscriber with a Minnesota billing address or address of residence uses DigitalVoice from any location outside the state to call a party located in Minnesota, Minnesota would treat that communication as "intrastate" based on the address proxy for that subscriber's location, yet in actuality it would be an interstate call.

29. These proxies are very poor fits, yet even their implementation would impose substantial costs retrofitting DigitalVoice into a traditional voice service model for the sole purpose of making it easier to apply traditional voice regulations to only a small aspect of Vonage's integrated service.

30. In the case of DigitalVoice, Vonage could not even avoid violating Minnesota's order by trying *not* to provide intrastate communications in that state. For the same reasons that Vonage cannot identify a communication that occurs within the boundaries of a single state, it cannot prevent its users from making such calls by attempting to block any calls between people in Minnesota. Indeed, Vonage could not avoid similar "intrastate" regulations if imposed by any of the other more than 50 separate jurisdictions. Due to the intrinsic ubiquity of the Internet, *nothing short of Vonage ceasing to offer its service entirely* could

guarantee that any subscriber would not engage in some communications where a state may deem that communication to be "intrastate" thereby subjecting Vonage to its economic regulations absent preemption.

31. [B]ecause of the impossibility of separating out [an intrastate] component, we must preempt the *Minnesota Vonage Order* because it outright conflicts with federal rules and policies governing interstate DigitalVoice communications.

5. Policies and Goals of the 1996 Act Consistent With Preemption of Minnesota's Regulations

33. We find that Congress's directives in sections 230 and 706 of the 1996 Act are consistent with our decision to preempt Minnesota's order.

34. In addition to defining the Internet in section 230 of the Act, Congress used section 230 to articulate its national Internet policy. There, Congress stated that "it is the policy of the United States - to preserve the vibrant and competitive free market that presently exists for the Internet and other interactive computer services, unfettered by Federal or State regulation."[116]

35. While the majority of those commenting on the applicability of section 230 in this proceeding share this view, others claim that section 230 relates only to content-based services.... While we acknowledge that the title of section 230 refers to "offensive material," the general policy statements regarding the Internet and interactive computer services contained in the section are not similarly confined to offensive material. In the case of section 230, Congress articulated a very broad policy regarding the "Internet and other interactive computer services" without limitation to content-based services. Through codifying its Internet policy in the Commission's organic statute, Congress charges the Commission with the ongoing responsibility to advance that policy consistent with our other statutory obligations. Accordingly, in interpreting section 230's phrase "unfettered by Federal or State regulation," we cannot permit more than 50 different jurisdictions to impose traditional common carrier economic regulations such as Minnesota's on DigitalVoice and still meet our responsibility to realize Congress's objective.

36. We are also guided by section 706 of the 1996 Act, which directs the Commission (and state commissions with jurisdiction over telecommunications services) to encourage the deployment of advanced telecommunications capability to all Americans by using measures that "promote competition in the local telecommunications market" and removing "barriers to infrastructure investment."[125] Internet-based services such as DigitalVoice are capable of being

---

[116] 47 U.S.C. § 230(b)(2).

[125] *47 U.S.C. § 157* nt. Section 706 of the 1996 Act is located in the notes of section 7 of the Communication

accessed only via broadband facilities, *i.e.,* advanced telecommunications capabilities under the 1996 Act, thus driving consumer demand for broadband connections, and consequently encouraging more broadband investment and deployment consistent with the goals of section 706.

37. Allowing Minnesota's order to stand would invite similar imposition of 50 or more additional sets of different economic regulations on DigitalVoice, which could severely inhibit the development of this and similar VoIP services.

IV. CONCLUSION

46. For the reasons set forth above, we preempt the *Minnesota Vonage Order.* As a result, the Minnesota Commission may not require Vonage to comply with its certification, tariffing or other related requirements as conditions to offering DigitalVoice in that state. Moreover, for services having the same capabilities as DigitalVoice, the regulations of other states must likewise yield to important federal objectives. To the extent other entities, such as cable companies, provide VoIP services, we would preempt state regulation to an extent comparable to what we have done in this Order.

NOTES & QUESTIONS

1. *Distinguishing technologies.* Vonage's DigitalVoice is what the FCC calls "interconnected VoIP."

> 47 C.F.R. § 9.3. Interconnected VoIP service.
>
> An interconnected Voice over Internet protocol (VoIP) service is a service that:
>> (1) Enables real-time, two-way voice communications;
>> (2) Requires a broadband connection from the user's location;
>> (3) Requires Internet protocol-compatible customer premises equipment (CPE); and
>> (4) Permits users generally to receive calls that originate on the public switched telephone network and to terminate calls to the public switched telephone network.

How does Vonage's service differ from pulver.com or AT&T's bypass? Why is Vonage a harder case than the other two?

2. *Not what but who.* The *Vonage Order* does not so much decide *what* should be done, if anything, to VoIP. Rather, it's deciding *who* should do it—the states, the feds, or both. The *what* is supposed to be addressed comprehensively in a separate proceeding.[*] On this point, what is Commissioner Copps' concern?

3. *Does the FCC have the power?* In the preemption analysis, the first question to ask is whether the FCC has any power to regulate VoIP in the first

---

Act.

[*] *See IP-Enabled Services,* NPRM, 19 FCC Rcd. 4863 (2004).

place. What does the FCC say? Does it matter whether VoIP is an intra or inter-state service?

4. *The conflict.* Supposing that the FCC has the power to regulate VoIP, in what ways does federal law or policy conflict with Minnesota's attempted regulation of Vonage? Note how the Commission elaborates two scenarios—depending on whether VoIP is categorized as a "telecommunications service" or an "information service." In each scenario, what's the conflict?

5. *Avoiding conflict.* Even if there seems to be a conflict, can't it be resolved by distinguishing purely intrastate from interstate domains? After all, that is precisely what is done with wireline telephony. To be sure, the federalism issues are tricky, but we have over one hundred years experience of sharing power between state and federal governments in telecommunications. According to the FCC, why is it so difficult to carve VoIP along intrastate and interstate jurisdictional lines?

6. *Knowing geography.* The FCC points out that with VoIP, it is difficult to know the geographical points of origination and termination. Even if this were so, can't governments nudge the technology toward geolocation? As you will learn in the next chapter, the Supreme Court ruled that so-called "dial-a-porn" operators had to abide by local indecency laws even if required identifying the caller's location, which was simply the cost of doing business.[*]

7. *E-911.* Since the *Vonage* Order, the FCC has required all interconnected VoIP service providers to provide enhanced 911 (E911) capabilities to their customers as a standard feature.[†] The FCC concluded that it had power under Title I of the Communications Act to impose these requirements.[‡] The Commission gave the industry 120 days to set up a system that must "transmit all 911 calls, as well as a call back number and the caller's 'Registered Location' for each call, to . . . [an] appropriate local emergency authority that serves the caller's Registered Location."[§] VoIP providers must obtain location information from their customers and provide easy ways for customers to update this information.[**]

---

[*] *See* Sable Communications of CA, Inc. v. FCC, 492 US 115, 125-26 (1989) ("While Sable may be forced to incur some costs in developing and implementing a system for screening the locale of incoming calls, there is no constitutional impediment to enacting a law which may impose such costs on a medium electing to provide these messages. . . . If Sable's audience is comprised of different communities with different local standards, Sable ultimately bears the burden of complying with the prohibition on obscene messages.").

[†] *See In the Matters of IP-Enabled Services; E911 Requirements for IP-Enabled Service Providers,* 1st R&O and NPRM, 2005 FCC LEXIS 3209 (2005).

[‡] *Id.* at ¶ 26.

[§] *Id.* at ¶ 37.

[**] *See id.* at ¶ 46.

8. *On judicial review.* Numerous petitions for review were consolidated in the U.S. Court of Appeals for the Eighth Circuit. At issue were various arguments that the Vonage pre-emption order was arbitrary and capricious under the Administrative Procedure Act. The court was exceedingly deferential. The toughest argument was based on the E911 Order. Here's the court's analysis:

> The *911 Order* does not provide a basis for concluding the order before us is arbitrary and capricious. Contrary to the assertions of the state public utilities commissions, the *911 Order* also recognizes the practical difficulties of accurately determining the geographic location of VoIP customers when they place a phone call. Recognizing this practical difficulty, the FCC devised a temporary solution requiring VoIP service providers to have their customers register the physical location at which they would first utilize VoIP service, and to also provide a means for customers to update these registered locations. Under this temporary fix, responses to 911 calls would be routed to the registered location, which may not be the same as the actual location where the call was placed. Thus, in both the order before us and the *911 Order*, the FCC recognized the practical difficulties of determining the geographic location of nomadic VoIP phone calls.

> Moreover, subsequent to issuing the order we are reviewing, the FCC recognized the potentially limited temporal scope of its preemption of state regulation in this area in the event technology is developed to identify the geographic location of nomadic VoIP communications.

> Similarly, we emphasize the limited scope of our review of the FCC's decision. Our review is limited to the issue whether the FCC's determination was reasonable based on the record existing before it at the time. If, in the future, advances in technology undermine the central rationale of the FCC's decision, its preemptive effect may be reexamined.[*]

9. *More recent VoIP action: contributing to universal service.*

a. *USF squeeze.* The FCC is engaged in a lengthy and difficult reconsideration of Universal Service fundamentals.[†] In the meantime, the fund is being squeezed, as traditional wireline interstate long distance revenues decrease (displaced by CMRS and VoIP traffic)[‡] and as claims on the high cost fund dramatically increase.[§] As the taxable revenue base has shrunk, the FCC

---

[*] Minn. PUC v. FCC, 483 F.3d 570, 579-80 (8th Cir. 2007).

[†] *See generally In the Matter of Federal-State Joint Board on Universal Service,* Further NPRM and R&O, 17 FCC Rcd. 3752 (2002).

[‡] The FCC points out that from Dec. 2000 to Dec. 2004 wireless subscribers increased in number from 101 million to 181 million and from the end of 2003 to the end of 2005 the number of VoIP subscribers grew from 150,000 to 4.2 million. *See In the Matter of Universal Service Contribution Methodology,* R&O and NPRM, FCC 06-94, 2006 FCC LEXIS 3668 (June 27, 2006), ¶ 3.

has responded by increasing the tax rate (known as the "contribution factor"). For example, back in 2000 Q1, the contribution factor was 5.9%; by 2011 Q3, the rate was raised to 14.4%. In 2006, the FCC adopted two further kludges. First, the Commission raised the percentage of revenue that CMRS providers had to classify as *inter*state revenue (The "safe harbor" percentage—the percentage that a CMRS provider could allocate as interstate without providing any specific evidence that could be audited for accuracy—had been 28.5% since 2002, but was raised to 37.1%). More interestingly, the Commission concluded that interconnected VoIP providers must start contributing to the USF.

b.   *Taxing VoIP—the legal authority.* On what legal grounds did the FCC impose this tax on interconnected VoIP service providers? If they were classified as "telecommunications service" providers, they would have to pay into the fund in accordance with the first sentence of 47 U.S.C. § 254(d): "Every telecommunications carrier that provides interstate telecommunications services *shall* contribute . . . ." But the FCC was extremely wary of classifying anything internet-related as a telecommunications service. Therefore, the Commission declined to classify interconnected VoIP as either telecommunications or information service, and instead invoked the permissive authority granted in the last sentence of § 254(d): "Any other provider of interstate telecommunications *may* be required to contribute . . . if the public interest so requires." (emphasis added). In addition, the FCC claimed authority under its general Title I ancillary jurisdiction.[*] This regulation was largely upheld by the D.C. Circuit.[†] As a matter of power, the court held that VoIP providers could reasonably be defined, under *Chevron* deference, as "provider[s] of interstate telecommunications"; accordingly, the FCC had the power to force contributions under § 254(d). The court did not have to reach the Title I question and declined to do so.[‡]

c.   *Knowing geography redux.* What percentage of VoIP revenues should be considered interstate, so as to fall into the revenue base for the universal service tax? Isn't this an impossible question to answer, given the reasoning in the *Vonage Order?* The Commission said that it would be reasonable to set the safe harbor at 100%, but drew the line at 64.9%. (Vonage had suggested a mere 23%). The FCC invited VoIP providers to depart from the safe harbor and provide more precise, individualized data, by either (i) conducting a

---

[§] *See In the Matter of High Cost Universal Service Support,* Recommended Decision, FCC 07J-1, May 1, 2007 (recommending "that the Commission take immediate action to rein in the explosive growth in high-cost universal service support disbursements.")

[*] *See In the Matter of Universal Service Contribution Methodology,* ¶¶ 38-49.

[†] Vonage Holdings Corp. v. FCC, 489 F.3d 1232 (D.C. Cir. 2007).

[‡] *See id. at* 1241.

traffic study or (ii) calculating actual interstate revenues. But any traffic study methodology would first have to be vetted by the FCC—no easy matter. And the FCC (almost mischievously) observed that if the provider could identify actual interstate revenues, then it must be able to distinguish between intra- and interstate traffic, in which case the federal preemption outlined in the *Vonage Order* would no longer apply.* In other words, if interconnected VoIP providers did not want to accept the federal government's safe harbor percentage, it could be inviting state-by-state regulation.

        d. *Potential legislative action.* At some point, there may be legislative clarification. For instance, the Senate's *Communications, Consumer's Choice, and Broadband Deployment Act of 2006* would have required all "communications service providers" to contribute to universal service. This new term included "telecommunications service, broadband service, or IP-enabled voice service."[†] The proposed legislation also would have limited the methodology that the FCC could use to calculate universal service contributions. Also, some states are legislating on this front. California recently enacted a law that prohibits its PUC from regulating VoIP until Jan. 2020.[‡]

        10. *Domesticating VoIP?* We may not know definitively what VoIP is. That said, the FCC has incrementally applied certain obligations associated with common carriers. To summarize:

- May 2005: 911 emergency calling requirements (issued under Title I and § 251(e));[§]

- June 2006: USF contributions (issued under Title I and § 254(d));[**]

- March 2007: Customer Proprietary Network Information (privacy) obligations (issued under Title I);[††]

- June 2007: disability access requirements under 47 U.S.C. §255 (issued under Title I);[‡‡]

---

* *See id.* ¶ 56.

[†] *See* S. 2686, 109th Cong. (2006), § 211.

[‡] *See* Act of September 28, 2012, ch. 733, 2012 Cal. Legis. Serv. 6011 (West) (codified at Cal. Pub. Util. § 239).

[§] *See* VoIP 911 Order, 20 FCC Rcd. at 10246, ¶ 1.

[**] *See* Universal Service Contribution Methodology, Report and Order and Notice of Proposed Rulemaking, 21 FCC Rcd. 7518, 7538-43, ¶¶ 38-49 (rel. June 27, 2006), *aff'd in relevant part,* Vonage Holdings Corp., v. FCC, 489 F.3d 1232 (D.C. Cir. 2007).

[††] *See* Implementation of the Telecommunications Act of 1996, Report and Order and Further Notice of Proposed Rulemaking, FCC 07-22 (rel. April 2, 2007) (CPNI Order).

[‡‡] *See* Implementation of Sections 255 and 251(a)(2) of The Communications Act of 1934, Report and Order, FCC 07-110 (rel. June 15, 2007).

- November 2007: portability of local phone numbers to and from VoIP providers (issued under § 251(e) authority regarding FCC jurisdiction over North American Numbering Plan);[*]
- May 2009: mandatory notice from VoIP providers before disconnection (issued under Title I);[†]
- Feb. 2012: reporting of network outages (issued under various sections, including Title I).[‡]

But in addition to these regulatory obligations, VoIP providers also benefit from more traditional common carrier treatment. In June 2015, the Commission issued a Report and Order that established a process for VoIP providers to obtain North American Numbering Plan (NANP) telephone numbers[§] directly from the Numbering Administrators, rather than through intermediaries.[**] The order also established rules for VoIP Positioning Center (VPC) providers to obtain pseudo-Automatic Number Identification (p-ANI) codes directly from the Numbering Administrators for purposes of providing E911 services.[††]

Can we now say that if it "quacks" like a duck, it will be regulated like a duck?

11. *Pointless classification?* Recall the huge fight over the proper classification of cable modem service as either Title I or Title II in *Brand X.* Was that classification battle largely pointless? Here, even though VoIP seems not to be a Title II service, it is subject to many of the identical Title II requirements

---

[*] *See In the Matter of Tel. No. Requirements for Ip-Enabled Servs. Providers Local No. Portability,* 22 FCC Rcd. 19531, 19548-49, ¶ 32 (2007).

[†] See *In the Matter of IP-Enabled Servs.,* 24 FCC Rcd. 6039, 6039-40 ¶ 2 (2009).

[‡] *See The Proposed Extension of Part 4 of the Commission's Rules Regarding Outage Reporting To Interconnected Voice Over Internet Protocol Service Providers and Broadband Internet Service Providers,* Report and Order, 27 FCC Rcd. 2650, 2651, ¶ 1 (2012).

[§] The NANP is the basic numbering scheme for telecommunications networks located in the United States and its territories, Canada, and parts of the Caribbean. *See* 47 C.F.R. § 52.5(c). NANP telephone numbers are ten-digit numbers consisting of a three-digit area code, followed by a seven-digit local number. In order to provide interconnected VoIP service, a provider must offer customers NANP telephone numbers; otherwise, a customer on the public switched telephone network (PSTN) would not have a way to dial the interconnected VoIP customer using his PSTN service.

[**] *Numbering Policies for Modern Communications,* 30 FCC Rcd. 6839 (2015).

[††] VPC providers are entities that help interconnected VoIP providers deliver 911 calls to the appropriate public safety answering point (PSAP). Among other things, VPCs provide such capabilities as location-based call routing and real-time delivery to the PSAP of the caller's location information. A p-ANI is a number, consisting of the same number of digits as an Automatic Number Identification (ANI), that is not a NANP telephone directory number and may be used in place of an ANI to convey special meaning to the selective router, PSAP, and other elements of the 911 system. P-ANI codes are a numbering resource administered by the Routing Number Administrator (RNA).

under Title I authority. So, what's the point of the classification battle? Is it really a question about *who* gets to decide—Congress or the FCC?

2. NEXT GENERATION VIDEO PROGRAMMING

VoIP offers a traditional "telephone" services, but over the internet (at least in part), not over the public switched telephone network (PSTN). But what about the offering of traditional TV services over the internet, rather than through a cable or broadcast TV system? What about the offering of non-traditional, non-linear, on demand video services over the internet? How should we classify these internet TV (IPTV) services? As with any new service or technology, be cautious about how folks are using the term, which can be quite ambiguous.

Even as early as 1996, telephone companies were exploring various technologies to provide video programming. In the 1996 Telecommunications Act, Congress provided specific options for these firms.

> § 571. Regulatory treatment of video programming services
>
> (a) Limitations on cable regulation.
>
> > (1) Radio-based systems. To the extent that a common carrier (or any other person) is providing video programming to subscribers using radio communication, such carrier (or other person) shall be subject to the requirements of title III and [47 USC § 572], but shall not otherwise be subject to the requirements of this title.
> >
> > (2) Common carriage of video traffic. To the extent that a common carrier is providing transmission of video programming on a common carrier basis, such carrier shall be subject to the requirements of title II and [47 USC § 572], but shall not otherwise be subject to the requirements of this title. This paragraph shall not affect the treatment under [47 USC § 522(7)(C)] of a facility of a common carrier as a cable system.
> >
> > (3) Cable systems and open video systems. To the extent that a common carrier is providing video programming to its subscribers in any manner other than that described in paragraphs (1) and (2)—
> >
> > > (A) such carrier shall be subject to the requirements of this title, unless such programming is provided by means of an open video system for which the Commission has approved a certification under [47 USC § 573]; or
> > >
> > > (B) if such programming is provided by means of an open video system for which the Commission has approved a certification under [47 USC § 573], such carrier shall be subject to the requirements of this part, but shall be subject to parts I through IV of this title [47 USC §§ 521 et seq. through §§ 551 et seq.] only as provided in [47 USCS § 573(c)].
> >
> > (4) Election to operate as open video system. A common carrier that is providing video programming in a manner described in paragraph (1) or (2), or a combination thereof, may elect to provide such programming by means of an open video system that complies with section [47 USCS § 573]. If the Commission approves such carrier's certification . . . such carrier shall be subject to the requirements of

> this part, but shall be subject to parts I through IV of this title [47 USC §§ 521 et seq. through §§ 551 et seq.] only as provided in [47 USC § 573(c)].

If we parse this provision, we can see three vectors of entry, as:

- *common carriers* under Title II of the Communications Act,
- *cable television service* under Title VI, or
- *open video systems* (OVS), a new, hybrid category created by the Act.

So far, telephone companies have demonstrated no interest in delivering video as either a common carrier or OVS. So, the real question is whether they will be treated as a provider of cable television service (regulated under Title VI) or something else entirely, such as information service (regulated under Title I). More recently, there's been some settling on the vocabulary used to describe various video services. In 2012, the FCC started to chunk the entire market for delivered video programming into three strategic groups.

First, there are the venerable *broadcast TV stations*. You might be surprised that this type of video is even counted given that it's "free" TV that is advertiser supported. But with the rise of retransmission consent fees, broadcast TV stations are now getting "paid" in ways that resemble the business model of cable programming networks.

Second, there are MVPDs (Multichannel Video Programming Distributors), a term we've seen many times before.[*] This term is broad and includes all entities that sell subscriptions to multiple channels of video programming. It specifically includes cable operators (about 60% of the market), DBS operators (33%), and the video services offered by recent entrants Verizon and AT&T through their FiOS and U-Verse video products ("telephone MVPDs") (7%).[†]

Third, the FCC has introduced a new term, "Online Video Distributors" (OVDs), which describes services such as Netflix, Hulu, and YouTube. "An 'OVD' is any entity that offers video content by means of the internet or other Internet Protocol (IP)-based transmission path provided by a person or entity other than the OVD."[‡] Roughly speaking, OVDs provide the content, but you the customer must BYOB (bring your own broadband).

---

[*] *See* 47 U.S.C. § 522(13) ("a person such as, but not limited to, a cable operator, a multichannel multipoint distribution service, a direct broadcast satellite service, or a television receive-only satellite program distributor, who makes available for purchase, by subscribers or customers, multiple channels of video programming.").

[†] The market percentages come from the FCC's 14th Video Competition report. *In the Matter of Annual Assessment of the Status of Competition in the Mkt. for the Delivery of Video Programming*, 27 FCC Rcd. 8610, 8611, ¶¶ 3-5 (2012).

[‡] *Application of Comcast Corporation, General Electric Company and NBC Universal, Inc. for Consent to Assign Licenses and Transfer Control of Licenses*, Memorandum Opinion and Order, 26 FCC Rcd. 4238,

The two most prominent telephone MVPD offerings are Verizon's FiOS TV and AT&T's U-verse, which were launched in 2005 and 2006 respectively. As of 2014, telephone MVPD providers had approximately 13 million subscribers (in comparison to 34 million for DBS and 54 million for cable TV).[*] AT&T carries its video over a 100% Internet Protocol (IP) network; by contrast, Verizon combines both IP carriage and video transport technologies historically used by cable television systems. Verizon has conceded that its FiOS should be regulated as a cable service. But AT&T has been more resistant. Its position is that it is providing an information service. Courts[†] and state public utilities commissions have responded differently to this claim.

What follows is the most extensive federal court discussion of how to classify AT&T's U-verse service. Full disclosure: Due to subsequent action by the State of Connecticut legislature,[‡] this opinion was vacated as moot by the U.S. Court of Appeals for the Second Circuit. Accordingly, it lacks legal precedential value. However, after the City of Hopkinsville, Kentucky, brought a complaint against AT&T in 2009 for offering U-verse without obtaining a cable franchise, AT&T again argued that it could provide the video service under its existing state telephone franchise agreement. The district court dismissed a third party challenge in a short opinion granting AT&T's motion to dismiss. But the U.S. Court of Appeals disagreed, relying on the Connecticut court's analysis in *Office of Consumer Counsel*, and finding that while "the line between television and telephone service was once quite concrete; it is now rather fuzzy."[§]

4358, App. A (2011) ("Comcast-NBCU Order") (defining "OVD").

[*] *See* Seventeenth Report, *Annual Assessment of the Status of Competition in the Market for the Delivery of Video Programming*, 2016 WL 2691126 ¶ 3 (May 6, 2016).

[†] *Compare* Pacific Bell Telephone Company v. City of Walnut Creek, 428 F. Supp. 2d 1037 (N.D. Cal. 2006) (dismissing for failure to state a claim AT&T's request for declaratory judgment that franchise conditions are federally preempted, and declining to assert supplemental jurisdiction over the question whether state law requires a separate franchise for AT&T's service) *with* Illinois Bell Telephone Co. v. Village of Itasca, Illinois, 503 F. Supp. 2d 928 (N.D. Il. 2007) (denying most of the city's motion to dismiss AT&T's claims, which included federal preemption and violation of the First Amendment).

[‡] *See* Act of Oct. 1, 2007, No. 07-253, § 1, 2007 Conn. Acts 1294 (Reg. Sess.) ("An Act Concerning Certified Competitive Video Service").

[§] Mediacom Southeast LLC v. BellSouth Telecommunications, Inc., 672 F.3d 396, 401 (6th Cir. 2012).

OFFICE OF CONSUMER COUNSEL V. AT&T

515 F. Supp. 2d 269 (D. Conn. 2007), *vacated as moot,*
368 Fed. Appx. 244 (2nd Cir. 2010)

JANET BOND ARTERTON, U.S.D.J.

II. FACTUAL BACKGROUND

"Project Lightspeed" [is] a network upgrade project which would allow AT&T to provide video programming and other applications in Connecticut.... AT&T's network uses Internet Protocol ("IP") packetization for its digital video signals transmitted over its network.... AT&T's service transmits to customers prescheduled video programming (*e.g.,* ABC, CBS, ESPN, CNN, HBO) at the same time and on the same schedule as the programming is being transmitted from the programming provider. In addition, the service also makes available Video on Demand ("VOD") content, which is video programming that is stored on central computers/servers and which can be chosen using on-screen menus and viewed by subscribers at a selected time, rather than a prescheduled time; subscribers are charged for VOD programs on a pay-per-view basis.

When a subscriber wants to view prescheduled programming (such as on ABC, CNN, *et cetera*), the subscriber uses his or her remote control and set-top box to initiate a request to change the video stream, and that request (*i.e.,* channel change) will send a signal from the remote control/set-top box upstream to the "node," intermediate network office, or video hub office; in response to the subscriber's "request," AT&T's network will then transmit video programming to that subscriber. Thus, when an AT&T subscriber wishes to watch a particular program on a particular channel, there will be a flow of information in both directions, including the request sent upstream from the set-top box to the network, IP packets carrying the requested video information sent downstream from the network to the set-top box, and IP packets carrying error correction and other information concerning authentication (*i.e.,* making sure the particular subscriber is entitled to view the requested programming) traveling in both directions. When an AT&T subscriber wants to switch to a different channel, he or she will push a button on the remote control and, after the intermediate communications/signaling described above, the video programming received by the subscriber on his or her television monitor will change.[2] Thus, while communication/signaling takes place upstream from the

---

[2] This is in contrast to traditional CATV (Cable Antenna Television) programming where the video programming is automatically sent to all subscribers' set-top boxes, and the set-top boxes then decode the programming on the basis of the particular selections of the subscriber (including whether the subscriber is

subscriber's set-top box to the network, the actual video programming runs in only one direction—downstream from the network to the customer premises; AT&T admits that no video programming is transmitted from the customer premises. Notwithstanding the internal signaling occurring between the subscriber's set-top box, triggered by a subscriber changing the channel or making a VOD selection on his or her remote, the result (the requested channel change/delivery of selected video programming) is the same as a subscriber to traditional CATV changing a channel on his or her remote— that is, the push of the button changes the video programming displayed on the screen.

AT&T's U-verse programming includes three primary packages of programming (named "U200," "U300," and "U400"). Each of these packages will offer different varieties of video programming and will carry different prices, but each provides a certain number of channels showing prescheduled programming. These channels include local broadcast networks (*e.g.*, ABC, CBS, NBC), cable channels (*e.g.*, ESPN, CNN), premium cable channels (*e.g.*, HBO), and also the aforementioned VOD/pay-per-view services. With the exception of VOD/pay-per-view, the programming on U-verse is linear—it is prescheduled by the programming provider, transmitted to AT&T on a schedule set by the provider, and made available to all subscribers on the tier. Every U-verse subscriber that selects a particular programming package will have the ability to request transmission of the same video programming (*i.e.*, channels, VOD) as every other U-verse subscriber that subscribes to that same programming package.

The [Connecticut] DPUC proceeding [addressed] whether AT&T's video programming service constitutes a "cable service" under the Act.... As the DPUC noted at the time, this issue appears to be one of first impression among both courts and regulatory commissions. *See Ill. Bell Tel. Co. v. Vill. of Itasca, Ill.* (N.D. Ill. May 25, 2007) (slip op.) (leaving the issue of whether "plaintiff's IP-based services" were "outside the definition of 'cable services' in the Cable Act" "to another day," citing *Pac. Bell Tel. Co. v. City of Walnut Creek* (N.D. Cal. 2006), which also did not decide the issue but held "[w]hether AT&T's video programming in fact is a two-way interactive service is an evidentiary matter to be addressed in future proceedings"). The DPUC ultimately concluded that "IPTV service, as proposed by [AT&T], is fundamentally two-way in nature, and as such, does not meet the federal or state definition of 'cable service' despite the apparent similarity in images that may appear on end users' screens in IPTV and CATV households."

authorized to view the selected channel/programming).

"In essence," the DPUC found, "[AT&T's] planned IPTV service is merely another form of data byte stream transmitted like other data over the Internet, and as such it is not subject to legacy franchising requirements." It is this conclusion that plaintiffs challenge as preempted.

IV. DISCUSSION

B. Statutory Definitions

[T]he Cable Act defines "cable service" as "(A) the one-way transmission to subscribers of (i) video programming, or (ii) other programming service, and (B) subscriber interaction, if any, which is required for the selection or use of such video programming or other programming service." 47 U.S.C. § 522(6). The words "or use" in part (B) were added by amendment in 1996. "Video programming" is defined as "programming provided by, or generally considered comparable to programming provided by, a television broadcast station," *id.* § 522(20).... It does not appear to be disputed that AT&T is providing "video programming"....

C. Legislative History

The August 1, 1984 Cable Act House Report explains... that "th[e] distinction between cable services and other services offered over cable systems is based upon *the nature of the service provided*, not upon a technological evaluation of the two-way transmission capabilities of cable systems. For instance, any service that allows customers to buy a product by sending a signal over cable facilities, regardless of the precise mechanism to provide this signal, would not be a cable service." But the report clarifies that "[s]ubscribers to video programming offered over cable systems have the capacity to select which programs they want to receive. Sometimes—as in some ways of providing pay-per-view service—the selection involves sending a signal from the subscriber premises to the cable operator over the cable system. Such interaction to select video programming is permitted in a cable service."

With respect to subscriber interaction, the Report states "[t]he Committee intends that the interaction permitted in a cable service shall be that required for the retrieval of information from among a specific number of options or categories delineated by the cable operator or the programming service provider. Such options or categories must themselves be created by the cable operator or programming service provider and made generally available to all subscribers. By contrast, interaction that would enable a particular subscriber to engage in the off-premises creation and retrieval of a category of information would not fall under the definition of cable service...."

As noted above, in 1996 the definition of "cable service" was amended to add the words "or use" to the subscriber interaction element of the definition. The House Conference Report explained that the amendment was included to "reflect[] the evolution of video programming toward interactive services." 1996 U.S.C.C.A.N. 10. More specifically, the Report stated that the amendment was intended to reflect "the evolution of cable to include interactive services such as game channels and information services made available to subscribers by the cable operator, as well as enhanced services."

D. "Cable Service"

AT&T's video programming service . . . constitute[s] a "cable service," as defined by the Cable Act. . . . AT&T acknowledges that the flow of its video programming will be one-way, downstream, from the network to subscribers, and that video programming will not be transmitted upstream from the customer's premises. The . . . two-way transmission of data/signals between the subscribers' set-top boxes and the network is not excluded by the statutory definition referencing only "one-way transmission to subscribers *of . . . video programming*" (emphasis added).

[T]he legislative history of the Cable Act is not inconsistent with this conclusion. . . . The examples of "non-cable services" given in the Report ("shop-at-home and bank-at-home services, electronic mail, one-way and two-way transmission of non-video data and information not offered to all subscribers, data processing, video-conference, and all voice communications") involve the back-and-forth of the actual programming (or other target service), rather than just the back-and-forth of signals necessary to obtain the programming. By contrast, the examples given of "cable services" include programming that would be transmitted in only one direction but the selection and retrieval of which might involve upstream transmission of signaling or other data (*e.g.*, pay-per-view, voter preference polls and video rating services, stock market information, *id.*).

As to the subscriber interaction component of the "cable service" definition, the statute covers "subscriber interaction, if any, which is required for the selection or use of such video programming or other programming service." *47 U.S.C. § 522(6)(B)*. . . . [The] 1984 House Report . . . explained that subscriber interaction required for selection of "which programs they want to receive" . . . "is permitted in a cable service." H.R. Rep. No. 98-934.

As described above, the record shows that AT&T's U-verse makes available sets of channels to all subscribers to a particular "tier" and that a U-verse subscriber will "interact" only as is required to turn the set-top box "on" and "off," change channels on the remote, and select pay-per-view/VOD

CHAPTER 5: CLASSIFICATION

programming. Thus, although an AT&T subscriber's set-top box will be engaged in signaling back and forth with the network to retrieve content and engage in error correction, the subscriber him- or herself will do no more than turn the box "on" and "off" and select channels or pay-per-view/VOD programming, just as would a subscriber to traditional CATV. This level of required subscriber interaction does not "enable a particular subscriber to engage in the off-premises creation and retrieval of a category of information." *Id.*

Defendants, relying on the so-called "Cable Modem Ruling," *In re Inquiry Concerning High-Speed Access to Internet Over Cable and Other Facilities, 17 F.C.C.R. 4798* (2002) . . . argue that "[t]he phrase 'one-way transmission to subscribers' in the definition reflects the traditional view of cable as primarily a medium of mass communication, with the same package or packages of video programming transmitted from the cable operator and available to all subscribers," and contend that AT&T's service constitutes one "offering a high degree of interactivity," taking it outside of the "cable service" definition in the Cable Act. However, notwithstanding the [technological] differences . . . , the video programming (both prescheduled broadcast programming and VOD) is generally available to all subscribers within a particular tier, and the fact that the programming is not transmitted to a particular subscriber from the network until that subscriber tunes to that channel or selects that particular VOD program does not change this fact. . . . [T]he level of interactivity required exactly fits into the FCC's own characterization of what Congress intended by its "cable service" definition: "[t]he legislative history states that Congress intended 'simple menu-selection' or searches of pre-sorted information from an index of keywords that would not activate a sorting program and 'would not produce a subset of data individually tailored to the subscriber's request' to be cable services."[6]

Defendants' other arguments supporting its interpretation of the "cable service" definition are not persuasive. First, defendants argue that AT&T's service does not constitute "cable service" because, unlike traditional CATV, all programming is not delivered to all subscribers' set-top boxes all of the time, but rather only following upstream signaling from the subscriber's set-top box.

---

[6] For this reason, AT&T's claim that plaintiffs' characterization of "cable service" would mean that streaming of Internet video would qualify as a "cable service" is not persuasive - streaming of Internet video does not involve packages of video programming, largely prescheduled by the programming provider and made available to all subscribers to that programming; for this reason, streaming of video from the Internet has the capability of "produc[ing] a subset of data individually tailored to the subscriber's request," which degree of subscriber interactivity - unlike that implicated by U-verse - appears to take it outside of plaintiffs' and the Court's interpretation of the "cable service" definition.

However, the Cable Act does not, by its terms, specify [this requirement]. Rather . . . programming simply must be made "generally available to all subscribers," and must be limited to "a specific number of options or categories delineated [and] created by the cable operator or programming service provider." H.R. Rep. No. 98-934.

Defendants also argue, relying on the *Cable Modem Ruling*, that AT&T's service creates programming tailored to the individual subscriber and that it thus falls outside of the "cable service" definition. However, as described above . . . the programming is not in fact "tailored" . . . . Rather, AT&T's service consists of at least three different programming packages (or "tiers"), each of which provides all subscribers in that particular tier with identical programming.

Lastly, defendants argue that their service constitutes an "information service," as defined in *47 U.S.C. § 153(20)*, and not a "cable service." Defendants rely on the FCC's decision in *Pulver.com, 19 F.C.C.R. 3307* (F.C.C. 2004), in which the FCC determined that pulver.com's Free World Dialup ("FWD") was an unregulated information service. Defendants' contention that FWD and AT&T's video product are "indistinguishable" because both use telecommunications to transmit Internet Protocol packets between a server and a customer's premises, with the only differentiation occurring after these packets are reassembled into voice communication or video offering, is not persuasive. The FCC determined that pulver.com's FWD fit the definition of "information service" because it "enables its members to 'acquire' information about other members' online presence at any particular time," it "'stores' both member information . . . and, if a member opts-in, voicemail messages on its server, that are accessible to other members," it 'provides members with certain information . . . that they 'utilize' first to register for the FWD service and then to contact other members who are online," it "'processes' the [information an initiating member sends to the FWD server indicating it wishes to communicate with a recipient member] by determining both the recipient member's Internet addresses and online availability," and "makes available [that information] to that recipient member," and "[m]aking available the Internet addresses of the intended recipient member enables the initiating member to 'retrieve' this information;" lastly, "if a member's equipment generates a private Internet address that interferes with the ability of the user's CPE to determine public Internet addresses, FWD will 'transform' or repair the addressing information and will relay the 'signaling and media stream via a protocol conversion solution to facilitate delivery." Thus, in contrast to AT&T's video service, which provides packets of video programming content from AT&T's network to subscribers' set-top boxes, FWD only provides information to "facilitate[] peer-to-peer communication" over the Internet without any "geographic correlation to any particular underlying physical transmission facilities." Further, while AT&T's service transmits video programming one-way (from private network to set-top box on subscribers' premises), FWD facilitates the two-way exchange of information/content/ideas/*et cetera* between peers over the public Internet. In short, FWD did not fit the definition of telecommunications service of cable service, and U-verse does.[8]

* * *

[T]he DPUC's conclusions in its June 7, 2006 Decision . . . , and its related determination that AT&T need not comply with the franchising requirement in 47 U.S.C. § 541 and the regulations promulgated thereunder, are in conflict with and are thus preempted by federal law.

NOTES & QUESTIONS

1. *What difference does technology make?* In some sense, this is a boring, typical statutory interpretation case. There's a definition of "cable service." Just interpret the statute. In another sense, the task is more unusual and interesting because technology seems to play such a crucial role in the definition. Consider the following.

a. *IP or not IP.* The fact that telephone MVPDs deliver their video programming via Internet Protocol might be exciting to technology geeks. Is it at all interesting to lawyers trying to interpret "cable service"?

b. *The whole freeway or just one lane.* Recall our pick-up truck analogy, when we discussed frequency division multiplexing. Review footnotes 2 and 6 of the opinion, and try to determine whether the entire freeway or just the selected lane arrives at the set-top box for AT&T's U-verse and plain old cable service. Does this technological difference make any legal difference in the opinion? Should it?

c. *Interactivity.* Obviously differences in interactivity seem to be crucial in the court's discussion. Is "interactivity" a technological question (to be answered by network gurus), or a user interface question (to be answered by

---

[8] Moreover, the FCC specifically limited its holding regarding FWD and "information service" to "FWD" and "only to the extent it facilities free communications over the Internet between one on-line FWD member using a broadband connection and other on-line FWD members using a broadband connection," and "decline[d] to extend [its] classification holdings to the legal status of FWD to the extent it is involved in any way in communications that originate or terminate on the public switched telephone network, or that may be made via dial-up access." This limitation counsels against applying the FCC's reasoning here, in a context even further removed from the FWD at issue in the decision, that is, the transmission of packetized video programming over a private network to subscribers.

software designers), or maybe a consumer usage question (to be answered by watching how average consumers actually use the technology)? What's the court's ultimate conclusion on the amount of interactivity and its legal significance?

2. *Harder cases.* If AT&T's U-verse is a "cable service," what are the following: mlb.com (major league baseball), YouTube, Netflix (streaming), iTunes, Amazon Instant Video, Hulu? They differ from Verizon's FiOS and AT&T's U-verse in that these sites and services don't own any last mile pipe that connects them to the viewer. In other words, they all require the viewer to already have a broadband Internet connection provided by someone else. Does this matter?

3. *Consequences.* What practically turns on whether a telephone MVPD is regulated as cable TV (Title VI) versus information service (Title I)? If AT&T is offering cable TV service, how are various cable regulations going to be applied? Think about leased "access channels"? Are we going to partition off some percentage of a media hub's hard drive? Would it be different for Netflix, Amazon, or any other OVD?

4. *Is an MVPD an OVD?* Many MVPDs have launched "TV Everywhere" initiatives, to make their video content available on laptops, tablets, and phones, delivered over the public internet. Some MVPDs provide this service only to subscribers of their traditional services, whereas other MVPDs are allowing even non-subscribers to purchase limited access. According to the FCC, "[a]n OVD does not include an MVPD inside its MVPD footprint or an MVPD to the extent it is offering Online Video Programming as a component of an MVPD subscription to customers whose homes are inside its MVPD footprint."[*] In other words, as long as the MVPD is operating within its footprint, the delivered video remains within the service category of MVPD even if it's being offered over the internet, over facilities that are not owned by the MVPD. So does that mean HBO's new streaming service "HBO GO" is an OVD or an MVPD? How about HBO's new streaming service "HBO NOW"?[†]

5. *Is an OVD an MVPD?* For various reasons, it seems clear that an OVD is *not* a cable operator. By tracing the definition of a "cable operator," can you explain why? The harder question is whether an OVD counts as an MVPD. If so, then an OVD would be subject to various regulations. On the one hand, some regulations would be beneficial. For example, the OVD would then be able to

---

[*] *Id.*

[†] You can read a description of the difference between the two offerings here: HBO, "Differences between HBO NOW and HBO GO," https://help.hbonow.com/app/answers/detailHBO/a_id/125.

insist on "program access" rights* as well as good faith negotiations in garnering retransmission consent rights from broadcast stations.† What might Netflix do with such rights? On the other hand, some regulations would exact costs. For example, the OVD would be subject to "program carriage" claims,‡ which could be asserted by unaffiliated video programming vendors. This difficult question of whether an OVD is an MVPD has been raised in pending program access complaints.§

In this chapter, we have examined a concept essential to understanding communications law and policy: *classification*. As new communications services come online, there is a predictable process of classification that takes place. The service may not actually be new; or it could be new, but fall within an existing "family" of services; or it could not be part of any such "family" but nevertheless fall within the general jurisdiction of the FCC because it involves interstate communications via wire or radio. What the Commission can do with this general authority, under Title I of the Communications Act, is an open question. And this entire classification process involves not only the FCC, but also the courts, state regulators, and eventually the Congress. Understanding this process, and how it might be influenced, is an important aspect of practicing communications   law   and   policy.

---

* *See* 47 U.S.C. § 548 (limiting cable operators who own video content from preventing other MVPD reasonable access to that content).

† *See* 47 U.S.C. §§ 325(b)(3)(C)(ii)-(iii); 47 C.F.R. § 76.65.

‡ *See* 47 U.S.C. § 536.

§ *See, e.g.,* VDC Corp. v. Turner Network Sales, Inc., et al., Program Access Complaint (Jan. 18, 2007); Sky Angel U.S., LLC v. Discovery Communications LLC, et al., Program Access Complaint, MB Docket No. 12-80, CSR-8605-P (Mar. 24, 2010). The FCC is currently seeking comment on the interpretation of the terms "MVPD" and "channel." *See Media Bureau Seeks Comment On Interpretation of the Terms "Multichannel Video Programming Distributor" and "Channel" as Raised in Pending Program Access Complaint Proceeding,* MB Docket No. 12-83, Public Notice, 27 FCC Rcd. 3079 (2012).

INDECENT CONTENT

So far, we have discussed what it takes to *enter* various communication industries that provide and transport information. We have also examined how and why society might *price* these services outside the default framework of the marketplace, why we have regulated *access* to certain services in order to limit control over choke points, and how the *classification* process proceeds when a new service is introduced. We now turn our focus directly to the bits of information themselves—the *content*.

Various types of information—such as genuine threats, defamation of character, releases of military secrets, fraudulent claims of medical cures, or racial epithets—can cause great harm if published, distributed, or used. From a policy perspective, it shouldn't be surprising that the government may seek to restrict the flow of information—at least as an experiment—to limit such harms. However, from a legal perspective, some of these restrictions would violate the U.S. Constitution's First Amendment, which protects freedom of expression.

Since CHAPTER 1: POWER, we have studied how communication technologies make it easier to create, search, and distribute information—in some sense, how technology makes information flow more easily. But these technologies do not distinguish between content that human beings judge to be good or bad. As far as these networks and systems are concerned, content is content, bits are bits.

But to policy makers, not all bits are created equal. Congress has imposed regulations on both the content that users of these services seek to access and on the collection and disclosure of information about users by their service providers. The first type of content regulations that we will study are indecency laws, which restrict access to certain types of indecent content. The second type of content regulations, which we will study in the next chapter, are communications privacy laws. These laws restrict the collection and use of personal information by service providers.

* * *

The basic policy underling indecency laws is simple. Some sexual content should almost never be exposed to children, at least not without the consent of their parents. Also, some content should not even be exposed to adults unless they consent in advance. As the flow of this "offensive" content increases and barriers to access are removed by new technologies, what can and should the government do to limit the flow? Can it apply some legal or technological filter to block or shunt it off? We will look at the way indecency has been regulated in each industry because the law has developed differently for each new service. Throughout our study, we question whether such disparate treatment can be justified.

A. BROADCAST

Imagine that you are driving your 6 year-old nephew back from school one afternoon and you turn on your car radio and hear the following:

> I was thinking one night about the words you couldn't say on the public, ah, airwaves, um, the ones you definitely wouldn't say, ever.... [I]t came down to seven but the list is open to amendment.... The... words were, shit, piss, fuck, cunt, cocksucker, motherfucker, and tits. Those are the ones that will curve your spine, grow hair on your hands and (laughter) maybe, even bring us, God help us, peace without honor (laughter) um, and a bourbon. (laughter).... *

FCC v. PACIFICA
438 U.S. 726 (1978)

Mr. Justice STEVENS delivered the opinion of the Court.

I

A satiric humorist named George Carlin recorded a 12-minute monologue entitled "Filthy Words" before a live audience in a California theater.

At about 2 o'clock in the afternoon on Tuesday, October 30, 1973, a New York radio station, owned by respondent Pacifica Foundation, broadcast the "Filthy Words" monologue. A few weeks later a man, who stated that he had heard the broadcast while driving with his young son, wrote a letter complaining to the Commission.

In its response, Pacifica explained that the monologue had been played during a program about contemporary society's attitude toward language and

---

* George Carlin, Seven Dirty Words Monologue, FCC v. Pacifica, Appendix, 438 U.S. 726 (1978).

CHAPTER 6: INDECENT CONTENT

that, immediately before its broadcast, listeners had been advised that it included "sensitive language which might be regarded as offensive to some." Pacifica characterized George Carlin as "a significant social satirist" who "like Twain and Sahl before him, examines the language of ordinary people. . . . Carlin is not mouthing obscenities, he is merely using words to satirize as harmless and essentially silly our attitudes towards those words." Pacifica stated that it was not aware of any other complaints about the broadcast.

On February 21, 1975, the Commission [held] that Pacifica "could have been the subject of administrative sanctions." The Commission did not impose formal sanctions, but it did state that the order would be "associated with the station's license file. . . ."

The Commission characterized the language used in the Carlin monologue as "patently offensive," though not necessarily obscene, and expressed the opinion that it should be regulated by principles analogous to those found in the law of nuisance where the "law generally speaks to channeling behavior more than actually prohibiting it. . . . [T]he concept of 'indecent' is intimately connected with the exposure of children to language that describes, in terms patently offensive as measured by contemporary community standards for the broadcast medium, sexual or excretory activities and organs at times of the day when there is a reasonable risk that children may be in the audience." 56 F.C.C.2d, at 98.[5] . . . In summary, the Commission stated: "We therefore hold that the language as broadcast was indecent and prohibited by 18 U.S.C. [§] 1464."

The United States Court of Appeals for the District of Columbia Circuit reversed. . . .

IV

C

We have long recognized that each medium of expression presents special First Amendment problems. *Joseph Burstyn, Inc. v. Wilson.* And of all forms of communication, it is broadcasting that has received the most limited First Amendment protection. Thus, although other speakers cannot be licensed except under laws that carefully define and narrow official discretion, a broadcaster may be deprived of his license and his forum if the Commission decides that such an action would serve "the public interest, convenience, and necessity." Similarly, although the First Amendment protects newspaper

---

[5] Thus, the Commission suggested, if an offensive broadcast had literary, artistic, political, or scientific value, and were preceded by warnings, it might not be indecent in the late evening, but would be so during the day, when children are in the audience.

publishers from being required to print the replies of those whom they criticize, *Miami Herald Publishing Co. v. Tornillo*, it affords no such protection to broadcasters; on the contrary, they must give free time to the victims of their criticism. *Red Lion Broadcasting Co. v. FCC.*

The reasons for these distinctions are complex, but two have relevance to the present case. First, the broadcast media have established a uniquely pervasive presence in the lives of all Americans. Patently offensive, indecent material presented over the airwaves confronts the citizen, not only in public, but also in the privacy of the home, where the individual's right to be left alone plainly outweighs the First Amendment rights of an intruder. *Rowan v. Post Office Dept.* Because the broadcast audience is constantly tuning in and out, prior warnings cannot completely protect the listener or viewer from unexpected program content. To say that one may avoid further offense by turning off the radio when he hears indecent language is like saying that the remedy for an assault is to run away after the first blow. One may hang up on an indecent phone call, but that option does not give the caller a constitutional immunity or avoid a harm that has already taken place.[27]

Second, broadcasting is uniquely accessible to children, even those too young to read. Although Cohen's written message[, "Fuck the Draft," in *Cohen v. California*] might have been incomprehensible to a first grader, Pacifica's broadcast could have enlarged a child's vocabulary in an instant. Other forms of offensive expression may be withheld from the young without restricting the expression at its source. Bookstores and motion picture theaters, for example, may be prohibited from making indecent material available to children. We held in *Ginsberg v. New York*, that the government's interest in the "well-being of its youth" and in supporting "parents' claim to authority in their own household" justified the regulation of otherwise protected expression.[28] The ease with which

---

[27] Outside the home, the balance between the offensive speaker and the unwilling audience may sometimes tip in favor of the speaker, requiring the offended listener to turn away. *See Erznoznik v. Jacksonville.* As we noted in *Cohen v. California*:

> While this Court has recognized that government may properly act in many situations to prohibit intrusion into the privacy of the home of unwelcome views and ideas which cannot be totally banned from the public dialogue . . . , we have at the same time consistently stressed that 'we are often "captives" outside the sanctuary of the home and subject to objectionable speech.'

[28] The Commission's action does not by any means reduce adults to hearing only what is fit for children. *Cf.* Butler v. Michigan. Adults who feel the need may purchase tapes and records or go to theaters and nightclubs to hear these words. In fact, the Commission has not unequivocally closed even broadcasting to speech of this sort; whether broadcast audiences in the late evening contain so few children that playing this monologue would be permissible is an issue neither the Commission nor this Court has decided.

children may obtain access to broadcast material, coupled with the concerns recognized in *Ginsberg*, amply justify special treatment of indecent broadcasting.

It is appropriate, in conclusion, to emphasize the narrowness of our holding. This case does not involve a two-way radio conversation between a cab driver and a dispatcher, or a telecast of an Elizabethan comedy. We have not decided that an occasional expletive in either setting would justify any sanction or, indeed, that this broadcast would justify a criminal prosecution. The Commission's decision rested entirely on a nuisance rationale under which context is all-important. The concept requires consideration of a host of variables. The time of day was emphasized by the Commission. The content of the program in which the language is used will also affect the composition of the audience, and differences between radio, television, and perhaps closed-circuit transmissions, may also be relevant. As Mr. Justice Sutherland wrote, a "nuisance may be merely a right thing in the wrong place,—like a pig in the parlor instead of the barnyard." *Euclid v. Ambler Realty Co.* We simply hold that when the Commission finds that a pig has entered the parlor, the exercise of its regulatory power does not depend on proof that the pig is obscene.

The judgment of the Court of Appeals is reversed. It is so ordered.

Mr. Justice POWELL, with whom Mr. Justice BLACKMUN joins, concurring in part and concurring in the judgment.

The Commission's primary concern was to prevent the broadcast from reaching the ears of unsupervised children who were likely to be in the audience at that hour.... In my view, this consideration provides strong support for the Commission's holding.

In most instances, the dissemination of this kind of speech to children may be limited without also limiting willing adults' access to it. Sellers of printed and recorded matter and exhibitors of motion pictures and live performances may be required to shut their doors to children, but such a requirement has no effect on adults' access. The difficulty is that such a physical separation of the audience cannot be accomplished in the broadcast media. During most of the broadcast hours, both adults and unsupervised children are likely to be in the broadcast audience, and the broadcaster cannot reach willing adults without also reaching children.

A second difference, not without relevance, is that broadcasting—unlike most other forms of communication—comes directly into the home.... *Rowan v. Post Office Dept.*

In short, I agree that on the facts of this case, the Commission's order did not violate respondent's First Amendment rights.

Mr. Justice BRENNAN, with whom Mr. Justice MARSHALL joins, dissenting.

I find the Court's misapplication of fundamental First Amendment principles so patent, and its attempt to impose its notions of propriety on the whole of the American people so misguided, that I am unable to remain silent.

I

A

[A]n individual's actions in switching on and listening to communications transmitted over the public airways and directed to the public at large do not implicate fundamental privacy interests, even when engaged in within the home. Instead, because the radio is undeniably a public medium, these actions are more properly viewed as a decision to take part, if only as a listener, in an ongoing public discourse. Although an individual's decision to allow public radio communications into his home undoubtedly does not abrogate all of his privacy interests, the residual privacy interests he retains vis-à-vis the communication he voluntarily admits into his home are surely no greater than those of the people present in the corridor of the Los Angeles courthouse in *Cohen* who bore witness to the words "Fuck the Draft" emblazoned across Cohen's jacket.

[Furthermore,] unlike other intrusive modes of communication, such as sound trucks, "[t]he radio can be turned off," *Lehman v. Shaker Heights* (1974)—and with a minimum of effort....

The Court's balance, of necessity, fails to accord proper weight to the interests of listeners who wish to hear broadcasts the FCC deems offensive. It permits majoritarian tastes completely to preclude a protected message from entering the homes of a receptive, unoffended minority. No decision of this Court supports such a result. Where the individuals constituting the offended majority may freely choose to reject the material being offered, we have never found their privacy interests of such moment to warrant the suppression of speech on privacy grounds. *Cf. Lehman v. Shaker Heights.*

Rowan v. Post Office Dept. relied on by the FCC and by the opinions of my Brothers POWELL and STEVENS, confirms rather than belies this conclusion. In *Rowan,* the Court upheld a statute permitting householders to require that mail advertisers stop sending them lewd or offensive materials and remove their names from mailing lists. Unlike the situation here, householders who wished to receive the sender's communications were not prevented from doing so. Equally important, the determination of offensiveness vel non under the statute involved in *Rowan* was completely within the hands of the individual householder; no governmental evaluation of the worth of the mail's content stood between the mailer and the householder. In contrast, the visage of the censor is all too discernible here.

B

[The majority opinion] violates in spades the principle of *Butler v. Michigan.* *Butler* involved a challenge to a Michigan statute that forbade the publication, sale, or distribution of printed material "tending to incite minors to violent or depraved or immoral acts, manifestly tending to the corruption of the morals of youth." ... [T]his Court found the statute unconstitutional. Speaking for the Court, Mr. Justice Frankfurter reasoned:

> "The incidence of this enactment is to reduce the adult population of Michigan to reading only what is fit for children. It thereby arbitrarily curtails one of those liberties of the individual, now enshrined in the Due Process Clause of the Fourteenth Amendment, that history has attested as the indispensable conditions for the maintenance and progress of a free society."

[T]he opinions of my Brother POWELL and my Brother STEVENS both stress the time-honored right of a parent to raise his child as he sees fit—a right this Court has consistently been vigilant to protect. *See Wisconsin v. Yoder* (1972); *Pierce v. Society of Sisters* (1925). Yet this principle supports a result directly contrary to that reached by the Court. *Yoder* and *Pierce* hold that parents, not the government, have the right to make certain decisions regarding the upbringing of their children. As surprising as it may be to individual Members of this Court, some parents may actually find Mr. Carlin's unabashed attitude towards the seven "dirty words" healthy, and deem it desirable to expose their children to the manner in which Mr. Carlin defuses the taboo surrounding the words. Such parents may constitute a minority of the American public, but the absence of great numbers willing to exercise the right to raise their children in this fashion does not alter the right's nature or its existence. Only the Court's regrettable decision does that.[4]

C

These two asserted justifications[—the intrusive nature of radio and the presence of children in the listening audience—] are further plagued by a common failing: the lack of principled limits on their use as a basis for FCC censorship.... Taken to their logical extreme, these rationales would support the cleansing of public radio of any "four-letter words" whatsoever, regardless of their context. The rationales could justify the banning from radio of a myriad

---

[4] The opinions of my Brothers POWELL and STEVENS rightly refrain from relying on the notion of "spectrum scarcity" to support their result. As Chief Judge Bazelon noted below, "although scarcity has justified increasing the diversity of speakers and speech, it has never been held to justify censorship."

of literary works, novels, poems, and plays by the likes of Shakespeare, Joyce, Hemingway, Ben Jonson, Henry Fielding, Robert Burns, and Chaucer; they could support the suppression of a good deal of political speech, such as the Nixon tapes; and they could even provide the basis for imposing sanctions for the broadcast of certain portions of the Bible.[5]

<h2 style="text-align:center">II</h2>

My Brother STEVENS . . . finds relevant to his First Amendment analysis the fact that "[a]dults who feel the need may purchase tapes and records or go to theaters and nightclubs to hear [the tabooed] words." . . . The opinions of my Brethren display both a sad insensitivity to the fact that these alternatives involve the expenditure of money, time, and effort that many of those wishing to hear Mr. Carlin's message may not be able to afford, and a naive innocence of the reality that in many cases the medium may well be the message.

The Court apparently believes that the FCC's actions here can be analogized to the zoning ordinances upheld in *Young v. American Mini Theatres, Inc.* (1976). For two reasons, it is wrong. First, the zoning ordinances found to pass constitutional muster in *Young* had valid goals other than the channeling of protected speech. No such goals are present here. Second . . . the ordinances did not restrict the access of distributors or exhibitors to the market or impair the viewing public's access to the regulated material. Again, this is not the situation here. Both those desiring to receive Carlin's message over the radio and those wishing to send it to them are prevented from doing so by the Commission's actions.

<h2 style="text-align:center">III</h2>

[I]n our land of cultural pluralism, there are many who think, act, and talk differently from the Members of this Court, and who do not share their fragile sensibilities. It is only an acute ethnocentric myopia that enables the Court to approve the censorship of communications solely because of the words they contain.

The words that the Court and the Commission find so unpalatable may be the stuff of everyday conversations in some, if not many, of the innumerable subcultures that compose this Nation. Academic research indicates that this is

---

[5] *See, e.g.*, I Samuel 25:22: "So and more also do God unto the enemies of David, if I leave of all that pertain to him by the morning light any that pisseth against the wall"; II Kings 18:27 and Isaiah 36:12: "[H]ath he not sent me to the men which sit on the wall, that they may eat their own dung, and drink their own piss with you?"; Ezekiel 23:3: "And they committed whoredoms in Egypt; they committed whoredoms in their youth; there were their breasts pressed, and there they bruised the teats of their virginity."; Ezekiel 23:21: "Thus thou calledst to remembrance the lewdnes of thy youth, in bruising thy teats by the Egyptians for the paps of thy youth." THE HOLY BIBLE (KING JAMES VERSION) (OXFORD 1897).

indeed the case. *See* B. JACKSON, "GET YOUR ASS IN THE WATER AND SWIM LIKE ME" (1974); J. DILLARD, BLACK ENGLISH (1972); W. LABOV, LANGUAGE IN THE INNER CITY: STUDIES IN THE BLACK ENGLISH VERNACULAR (1972). As one researcher concluded "[w]ords generally considered obscene like 'bullshit' and 'fuck' are considered neither obscene nor derogatory in the [black] vernacular except in particular contextual situations and when used with certain intonations." C. Bins, "*Toward an Ethnography of Contemporary African American Oral Poetry*," LANGUAGE AND LINGUISTICS WORKING PAPERS No. 5, p. 82 (Georgetown Univ. Press 1972). *Cf.* Keefe v. Geanakos (CA1 1969) (finding the use of the word "motherfucker" commonplace among young radicals and protesters).

Today's decision will thus have its greatest impact on broadcasters desiring to reach, and listening audiences composed of, persons who do not share the Court's view as to which words or expressions are acceptable and who, for a variety of reasons, including a conscious desire to flout majoritarian conventions, express themselves using words that may be regarded as offensive by those from different socio-economic backgrounds. In this context, the Court's decision may be seen for what, in the broader perspective, it really is: another of the dominant culture's inevitable efforts to force those groups who do not share its mores to conform to its way of thinking, acting, and speaking.

NOTES & QUESTIONS

1. *Legal categories.* In bad content analysis, it is important to categorize the type of information considered harmful. More specifically, whenever analyzing forms of sexual speech, carefully distinguish obscenity from indecency.

a. *Obscenity.* "Obscenity" is not considered to be protected speech and therefore restrictions on obscene material do not implicate the First Amendment. The Supreme Court defines obscenity according to the three-prong *Miller* test established in 1973:

(a) whether the average person, applying contemporary community standards would find that the work, taken as a whole, appeals to the prurient interest;

(b) whether the work depicts or describes, in a patently offensive way, sexual conduct specifically defined by the applicable state law; and

(c) whether the work, taken as a whole, lacks serious literary, artistic, political, or scientific value.[*]

---

[*] Miller v. California, 413 U.S. 15 (1973) (internal citations omitted).

Under this definition, what do you think is "obscene"? For example, do you think your community would consider hard-core pornography displaying explicit acts of consensual sex "obscene"? In *United States v. Various Articles of Obscene Merchandise*,* the U.S. Court of Appeals for the Second Circuit concluded that hard-core pornography, including movies such as "Deep Throat" and "Debbie Does Dallas," was not obscene because it was not patently offensive according to the community standards of New York City.

b. *Indecency.* In contrast to obscenity, indecency counts as protected speech and thus receives First Amendment protections. Although the Supreme Court has sometimes suggested that sexual or profane speech is less protected than, say, pure political speech, such as the Federalist Papers, the orthodox First Amendment line is that indecent speech should not be given weaker First Amendment protections. According to the *Pacifica* Court, what is the operational definition of indecency? What are the principal differences between indecency and obscenity? Should such large constitutional consequences flow from these differences?

2. *Threshold statutory questions.* Before reaching the First Amendment analysis excerpted above, the Court had to address threshold statutory questions.

a. *Indecency.* In response to the complaint against the Pacifica radio station, the FCC enforced 18 U.S.C. § 1464, which criminalizes the broadcast of "obscene, indecent, or profane" content. Note that this section is not codified in Title 47 of the U.S. Code, but in Title 18 (Crimes and Criminal Procedure), Part I (Crimes), Chapter 71 (Obscenity). The DOJ prosecutes criminal violations of this statute, but the FCC sanctions stations for broadcasting indecency.†

> 18 U.S.C. § 1464. Broadcasting obscene language
>
> Whoever utters any obscene, indecent, or profane language by means of radio communication shall be fined under this title or imprisoned not more than two years, or both.

Pacifica argued that "indecent" in this statute should be interpreted as having the same meaning as "obscene," which the Carlin monologue was not. (Why not?) The Court majority disagreed and held that the term "indecent" was intended to cover content that was offensive for reasons different from obscenity. Specifically, it was intended to refer to "nonconformance with accepted standards of morality." The Court emphasized that the FCC had long interpreted § 1464 to prohibit more than the obscene.

---

* 709 F.2d 132 (2d Cir. 1983).

† *See* FCC v. Pacifica Foundation, 438 U.S. 726, 739, n.13 (1978).

b. *Censorship.* Pacifica also argued that the FCC's action violated the anti-censorship provision.

> 47 U.S.C. § 326. Censorship
>
> Nothing in this chapter shall be understood or construed to give the Commission the power of censorship over the radio communications or signals transmitted by any radio station, and no regulation or condition shall be promulgated or fixed by the Commission which shall interfere with the right of free speech by means of radio communication.

Rejecting this argument, the majority explained that since the Radio Act of 1927, the FCC and the courts had consistently interpreted § 326 as only prohibiting censorship of programming *in advance of* broadcast. The provision, however, did not prevent the FCC from taking into consideration past programming in renewing licenses or in enforcing the ban against "obscene, indecent, or profane language."

3. *First Amendment standard of review.*

a. *Content neutrality.* As we have already seen, selecting the standard of review is critical (at least formally) to First Amendment analysis. Obviously, the FCC's action here turned on the "content" of Pacifica's speech; accordingly, the government sanction is content-based, and strict scrutiny is appropriate. (If the speech regulation were content-neutral, courts would apply "intermediate scrutiny," often called "time, place, manner" scrutiny.)

b. *Medium warp.* Recall our study of *Red Lion* in CHAPTER 2: ENTRY. Does it make a difference that Carlin's monologue took place over the radio and not in a magazine (or on http://georgecarlin.com, or in this casebook)? If so, why? Is it the "scarcity" justification we saw in *Red Lion*, which the majority cites early in its opinion? Or is there some other technological aspect of broadcasting that poses a greater indecency threat, which justifies greater government regulation?

4. *Cultural power.* Are you concerned about whom the law empowers to make indecency classifications? As Justice Brennan argues in his dissent, certain groups in America probably make use of Carlin's seven dirty words far more casually than FCC Commissioners and Supreme Court Justices. Through indecency regulations, do we privilege prudish, majoritarian social norms enacted through legal power? (By the way, according to Justice Brennan, which groups are more likely to talk in this manner? Do you agree? How appropriate are such generalizations in a judicial opinion?) What if it's not just majoritarian social norms but raw political power? Shock Jock Howard Stern, who in 2004 left broadcast radio for less regulated Sirius satellite radio, insisted that his indecency fines came down as soon as he started railing against President George W. Bush.

5. *Filter.*

a. *Comparing real space to broadcast space.* According to Justice Powell, why is filtering indecency away from minors so much easier in real space—at the record store, movie theater, or concert hall—than in broadcast space?

b. *The futility?* Is it realistic anymore to try to shield children from indecency? Should the goal be perfect protection or just slowing down such information flows?

c. *The alternative?* It is always easier to criticize than to propose a constructive solution. If you dislike the FCC's informal sanctions, what is your alternative? Many adults prefer not to be exposed to "indecent" speech through broadcast. Moreover, many prefer that their young children not be exposed to such content, notwithstanding their children's curiosity or willingness. How might we design a system that perfectly filters away such content for children but allows total access by willing adults?

6. *Time-channeling.* After *Pacifica*, the FCC enforced its indecency powers very narrowly. Only material closely resembling Carlin's monologue was frowned upon; material shown after 10 p.m. enjoyed a safe harbor. Indeed, from 1975 to 1987, the FCC found no broadcasts actionable for indecency. That changed in 1987, in what is known as the *Infinity Order,*[*] with specific enforcement actions against three stations (including 2 broadcasts aired *after* 10 p.m.) and an announcement that indecency would be interpreted more generically, not just as derivatives of Carlin's particular dirty words.

This prompted litigation, in which the D.C. Circuit affirmed the FCC's decision to apply a more generic definition of indecency (instead of just a seven "dirty words" approach). But the court vacated the FCC's shift away from the bright-line 10 p.m. safe harbor towards potential enforcement even late at night.[†] Before the FCC could respond on remand, Congress passed a law that commanded the FCC to enforce § 1464 (the indecency ban at issue in *Pacifica*) on a 24-hour basis, without any safe harbor.[‡] The FCC complied, was sued, and the D.C. Circuit struck down the 24-hour ban.[§] Shortly afterwards, in 1992, Congress intervened again,[**] and passed the time-channeling provisions at issue in the opinion we read next.

---

[*] *See In the Matter of Infinity Broadcasting,* 3 FCC Rcd. 930, ¶ 4 (1987).

[†] *See* Action for Children's Television v. FCC, 852 F.2d 1332, 1338–42 (D.C. Cir. 1988) (ACT I).

[‡] *See* Pub. L. No. 100-459, § 608, 102 Stat. 2228 (1988) (rider on 1989 appropriations bill).

[§] Action for Children's Television v. FCC, 932 F.2d 1504, 1509 (D.C. Cir. 1991) ("ACT II").

[**] *See* § 16(a) of the Public Telecommunications Act of 1992, Pub. L. 102-356, 106 Stat. 949 (1992).

ACTION FOR CHILDREN'S TELEVISION V. FCC

58 F.3d 654 (D.C. Cir. 1995) ("ACT III")

BUCKLEY, Circuit Judge

I. BACKGROUND

[At issue was the Commission's enforcement actions in three cases. As the court summarized, they involved radio broadcasts that included "explicit references to masturbation, ejaculation, breast size, penis size, sexual intercourse, nudity, urination, oral-genital contact, erections, sodomy, bestiality, menstruation and testicles."—ED.]

Section 16(a) of the [Public Telecommunications Act of 1992] requires the Commission to promulgate regulations to prohibit the broadcasting of indecent programming—

(1) between 6 a.m. and 10 p.m. on any day by any public radio station or public television station that goes off the air at or before 12 midnight. . . .

(2) between 6 a.m. and 12 midnight on any day for any radio or television broadcasting station not described in paragraph (1).

47 U.S.C. § 303 note. Pursuant to this congressional mandate, the Commission . . . issued regulations implementing section 16(a). These are challenged in the petition now before us.

II. DISCUSSION

A. The first amendment challenge

It is common ground that "sexual expression which is indecent but not obscene is protected by the First Amendment." [*FCC v. Sable* (1989)]. The Government may, however,

regulate the content of constitutionally protected speech in order to promote a compelling interest if it chooses the least restrictive means to further the articulated interest.

Id.

The Supreme Court has "long recognized that each medium of expression presents special First Amendment problems. . . . Of all forms of communication, it is broadcasting that has received the most limited First Amendment protection." *Pacifica.*

Unlike cable subscribers, who are offered such options as "pay-per-view" channels, broadcast audiences have no choice but to "subscribe" to the entire output of traditional broadcasters. Thus they are confronted without warning with offensive material. *See Pacifica.*

In light of these differences, radio and television broadcasts may properly be subject to different—and often more restrictive—regulation than is permissible for other media under the First Amendment. While we apply strict scrutiny to regulations of this kind regardless of the medium affected by them, our assessment . . . must necessarily take into account the unique context of the broadcast medium.

1.   The compelling Government interests

The Commission identifies three compelling Government interests . . . support for parental supervision of children, a concern for children's well-being, and the protection of the home against intrusion by offensive broadcasts. Because we find the first two sufficient to support such regulation, we will not address the third.

Petitioners do not contest that the Government has a compelling interest in supporting parental supervision of what children see and hear on the public airwaves.

Although petitioners disagree, we believe the Government's own interest in the well-being of minors provides an independent justification for the regulation of broadcast indecency. The Supreme Court has described that interest as follows:

> It is evident beyond the need for elaboration that a State's interest in safeguarding the physical and psychological well-being of a minor is compelling. A democratic society rests, for its continuance, upon the healthy, well-rounded growth of young people into full maturity as citizens. Accordingly, we have sustained legislation aimed at protecting the physical and emotional well-being of youth even when the laws have operated in the sensitive area of constitutionally protected rights.

New York v. Ferber (1982).

While conceding that the Government has an interest in the well-being of children, petitioners argue that because "no causal nexus has been established between broadcast indecency and any physical or psychological harm to minors," that interest is "too insubstantial to justify suppressing indecent material at times when parents are available to supervise their children." That statement begs two questions: The first is how effective parental supervision can actually be expected to be even when parent and child are under the same roof; the second, whether the Government's interest in the well-being of our youth is limited to protecting them from clinically measurable injury.

As Action for Children's Television argued in an earlier FCC proceeding, "parents, no matter how attentive, sincere or knowledgeable, are not in a position to really exercise effective control" over what their children see on television. *In re Action for Children's Television*, 50 F.C.C.2d 17, 26 (1974). [A survey commissioned by Children Now] found that 54 percent of the 750 children questioned had a television set in their own rooms and that 55 percent of them usually watched television alone or with friends, but not with their families. Sixty-six percent of them lived in a household with three or more television sets. Studies described by the FCC in its 1989 Notice of Inquiry suggest that parents are able to exercise even less effective supervision over the radio programs to which their children listen. According to these studies, each American household had, on average, over five radios, and up to 80 percent of children had radios in their own bedrooms, depending on the locality studied; two-thirds of all children ages 6 to 12 owned their own radios, more than half of whom owned headphone radios.

With respect to the second question begged by petitioners, the Supreme Court has never suggested that a scientific demonstration of psychological harm is required in order to establish the constitutionality of measures protecting minors from exposure to indecent speech. In *Ginsberg*, the Court considered a New York State statute forbidding the sale to minors under the age of 17 of literature displaying nudity even where such literature was "not obscene for adults. . . ." The Court observed that while it was "very doubtful" that the legislative finding that such literature impaired "the ethical and moral development of our youth" was based on "accepted scientific fact," a causal link between them "had not been disproved either." The Court then stated that it "did not demand of legislatures scientifically certain criteria of legislation. . . ."

[In addition,] the Supreme Court has recognized that the Government's interest in protecting children extends beyond shielding them from physical and psychological harm. The statute that the Court found constitutional in *Ginsberg* sought to protect children from exposure to materials that would "impair[] [their] ethical and moral development."

> The Court noted, in the context of obscenity, that
>
> if we accept the well nigh universal belief that good books, plays, and art lift the spirit, improve the mind, enrich the human personality, and develop character, can we then say that a . . . legislature may not act on the corollary assumption that commerce in obscene books, or public exhibitions focused on obscene conduct, have a tendency to exert a corrupting and debasing impact leading to antisocial behavior. . . . The sum of experience . . . affords an ample basis for legislatures to conclude that a sensitive, key relationship of human existence, central to family life, community welfare, and the development of human personality, can be debased and distorted by crass commercial exploitation of sex.

Paris Adult Theatre I v. Slaton (1973).

Congress does not need the testimony of psychiatrists and social scientists in order to take note of the coarsening of impressionable minds that can result from a persistent exposure to sexually explicit material just this side of legal obscenity. The Supreme Court has reminded us that society has an interest not only in the health of its youth, but also in its quality. As Irving Kristol has observed, it follows "from the proposition that democracy is a form of self-government, . . . that if you want it to be a meritorious polity, you have to care about what kind of people govern it." IRVING KRISTOL, ON THE DEMOCRATIC IDEA IN AMERICA 41–42 (1972).

2. Least restrictive means

Petitioners argue that . . . the "safe harbor" is not narrowly tailored because it fails to take proper account of the First Amendment rights of adults and because of the chilling effect of the 6:00 a.m. to midnight ban on the programs aired during the evening "prime time" hours.

In *Pacifica*, the Supreme Court found that it was constitutionally permissible for the Government to place restrictions on the broadcast of indecent speech in order to protect the well-being of our youth. We have since acknowledged that such restrictions may take the form of channeling provided "that the Commission . . . identify some reasonable period of time during which indecent material may be broadcast. . . . " *ACT II*.*

The data on broadcasting that the FCC has collected reveal that large numbers of children view television or listen to the radio from the early morning until late in the evening, that those numbers decline rapidly as midnight approaches, and that a substantial portion of the adult audience is tuned into television or radio broadcasts after midnight. We find this information sufficient to support the safe harbor parameters that Congress has drawn.

The data collected by the FCC . . . indicate that while 4.3 million, or approximately 21 percent, of "teenagers" (defined as children ages 12 to 17) watch broadcast television between 11:00 and 11:30 p.m., the number drops to 3.1 million (15.2 percent) between 11:30 p.m. and 1:00 a.m. and to less than 1 million (4.8 percent) between 1:45 and 2:00 a.m.

Concerning the morning portion of the broadcast restriction, the FCC has produced studies which suggest that significant numbers of children aged 2 through 17 watch television in the early morning hours. In the case of Seattle, one of two medium-sized media markets surveyed, an average of 102,200 minors watched television between the hours of 6:00 a.m. and 8:00 a.m., Monday

---

* The procedural history of this litigation is complicated. Suffice it to say that the D.C. Circuit had seen this case twice before, in *ACT I* and *ACT II*. The opinion you are now reading is referred to as *ACT III*.—ED.

through Friday; in Salt Lake City, the average was 28,000 for the period from 6:00 a.m. to 10:00 a.m.

The statistical data on radio audiences also demonstrate that there is a reasonable risk that significant numbers of children would be exposed to indecent radio programs if they were broadcast in the hours immediately before midnight. According to the FCC, there is an average quarter-hour radio audience of 2.4 million teenagers, or 12 percent, between 6:00 a.m. and midnight. Just over half that number, 1.4 million teenagers, listen to the radio during the quarter hour between midnight and 12:15 a.m. on an average night.

It is apparent, then, that of the approximately 20.2 million teenagers and 36.3 million children under 12 in the United States, a significant percentage watch broadcast television or listen to radio from as early as 6:00 a.m. to as late as 11:30 p.m.; and in the case of teenagers, even later. We conclude that there is a reasonable risk that large numbers of children would be exposed to any indecent material broadcast between 6:00 a.m. and midnight.

The remaining question, then, is whether Congress, in enacting section 16(a), and the Commission, in promulgating the regulations, have taken into account the First Amendment rights of the very large numbers of adults who wish to view or listen to indecent broadcasts. We believe they have. The data indicate that significant numbers of adults view or listen to programs broadcast after midnight. Based on information provided by Nielsen indicating that television sets in 23 percent of American homes are in use at 1:00 a.m., the Commission calculated that between 21 and 53 million viewers were watching television at that time. Comments submitted to the FCC by petitioners indicate that approximately 11.7 million adults listen to the radio between 10:00 p.m. and 11:00 p.m., while 7.4 million do so between midnight and 1:00 a.m. With an estimated 181 million adult listeners, this would indicate that approximately 6 percent of adults listen to the radio between 10:00 p.m. and 11:00 p.m. while 4 percent of them do so between midnight and 1:00 a.m.

While the numbers of adults watching television and listening to radio after midnight are admittedly small, they are not insignificant. Furthermore, as we have noted above, adults have alternative means of satisfying their interest in indecent material at other hours in ways that pose no risk to minors. We therefore believe that a midnight to 6:00 a.m. safe harbor takes adequate account of adults' First Amendment rights.

Petitioners argue, nevertheless, that delaying the safe harbor until midnight will have a chilling effect on the airing of programs during the evening "prime time" hours that are of special interest to adults. They cite, as examples, news and documentary programs and dramas that deal with . . . sexual harassment and the AIDS epidemic.... Whatever chilling effects may be said to inhere in the regulation of indecent speech, these have existed ever since the Supreme Court first upheld the FCC's enforcement of section 1464 of the Radio Act. The enactment of section 16(a) does not add to such anxieties; to the contrary, the purpose of channeling... is to provide a period in which radio and television stations may let down their hair without worrying whether they have stepped over any line other than that which separates protected speech from obscenity. Thus, section 16(a) has ameliorated rather than aggravated whatever chilling effect may be inherent in section 1464.

Petitioners also argue that section 16(a)'s midnight to 6:00 a.m. channeling provision is not narrowly tailored because, for example, Congress has failed to take into consideration the fact that it bans indecent broadcasts during school hours when children are presumably subject to strict adult supervision.... The Government's concerns, of course, extend to children who are too young to attend school. But more to the point, even if such fine tuning were feasible, we do not believe that the First Amendment requires that degree of precision.

In this case, determining the parameters of a safe harbor involves a balancing of irreconcilable interests. It is, of course, the ultimate prerogative of the judiciary to determine whether an act of Congress is consistent with the Constitution. Nevertheless, we believe that deciding where along the bell curves of declining adult and child audiences it is most reasonable to permit indecent broadcasts is the kind of judgment that is better left to Congress, so long as there is evidence to support the legislative judgment. Extending the safe harbor for broadcast indecency to an earlier hour involves "a difference only in degree, not a less restrictive alternative in kind." *Burson v. Freeman* (1992) (reducing campaign-free boundary around entrances to polling places from 100 feet to 25 feet is a difference in degree, not a less restrictive alternative in kind); *see also Buckley v. Valeo* (1976) (if some limit on campaign contributions is necessary, court has no scalpel to probe whether $ 2,000 ceiling might not serve as well as $ 1,000). It follows, then, that in a case of this kind, which involves restrictions in degree, there may be a range of safe harbors, each of which will satisfy the "narrowly tailored" requirement of the First Amendment. We are dealing with questions of judgment; and here, we defer to Congress's determination of where to draw the line....

We thus conclude that, standing alone, the midnight to 6:00 a.m. safe harbor is narrowly tailored to serve the Government's compelling interest in the well-being of our youth.*

---

* The dissenting opinion of Chief Judge Edwards has been omitted.—ED.

WALD, Circuit Judge, with whom R**OGERS** and T**ATEL**, Circuit Judges, join, dissenting:

[P]resumptively, expression that many or even most of us find deeply reprehensible may not be, on that basis alone, proscribed. In *R.A.V. v. City of St. Paul* (1992), for instance, the Court held that racist fighting words could not be penalized on the basis of the hatred they expressed. Thus, whatever our collective interests in a "meritorious polity" and the moral development of the "people [who] govern it," *Majority Opinion*, governmental enforcement of those interests is radically constrained by the First Amendment's guarantee of freedom of expression.

Because the Commission insists that indecency determinations must be made on a case-by-case basis and depend upon a multi-faceted consideration of the context of allegedly indecent material, broadcasters have next-to-no guidance in making complex judgment calls.

When, for instance, radio station hosts read over the air from a PLAYBOY MAGAZINE interview of Jessica Hahn about her alleged rape by the Reverend Jim Bakker, they did not regard the material as indecent because it involved matters of obvious public concern. The Commission, however, issued a notice of apparent liability for a forfeiture of $2,000, explaining that, "while the newsworthy nature of broadcast material and its presentation in a serious, newsworthy manner would be relevant contextual considerations in an indecency determination, they are not, in themselves, dispositive factors." KSD-FM, Notice of Apparent Liability, 6 F.C.C.R. 3689, 3689 (1990). . . . Although in reading the interview, the hosts had said that the account made them "sick," that it described rape rather than consensual sex, and that they regretted their earlier jokes about the incident, the Commission concluded, without elaboration, that the presentation was "pandering."

As this one case exemplifies so well . . . the Commission takes upon itself a delicate and inevitably subjective role of drawing fine lines between "serious" and "pandering" presentations.

Because of this potential for significant incursion into the First Amendment rights . . . it is particularly important that the channelling "balance" . . . preserve a meaningful place on the spectrum for adult rights to hear and view controversial or graphic nonobscene material. . . . Thus, I cannot agree with the majority that determining the perimeter of the safe harbor can be relegated to the category of discretionary line-drawing akin to the distance from polls at which electioneering is allowed and so largely shielded from judicial review. God or the Devil (pick your figure of speech) is in the details.

Recent Supreme Court cases have made clear that "when the Government defends a regulation on speech as a means to . . . prevent anticipated harms, it . . . must demonstrate that the recited harms are real, not merely conjectural, and that the regulation will in fact alleviate these harms in a direct and material way." *Turner* [*Broadcasting v. FCC* (1994) (*Turner I*)].

[I]n the record before Congress, there is as little evidence regarding the magnitude of psychological or moral harm, if any, to children and teenagers who see and hear indecency. . . . We have not a scintilla of evidence as to how many allegedly indecent programs have been either aired or seen or heard by children inside or outside the safe harbor.

I do not believe that [the government] can impose a valid ban during any hours it pleases solely because some children are in the audience. Nor do I believe that we can throw up our hands at the assumed impossibility of parental supervision simply because large numbers of children have television sets in their own room. Either or both of these excuses would justify a 24-hour ban as easily as the current 18-hour ban.

Instead, the scope of any safe harbor can only be responsibly justified . . . by identifying for parents a reasonable time period during which they must exert their supervisory function.

Despite the majority's valiant effort to extract evidence for the government's position from the sparse record before us, the pickings are too slim for constitutional legitimacy. There is no evidence at all of psychological harm from exposure to indecent programs aired inside the current safe harbor. There is no evidence either that parents cannot supervise their children in those safe harbor hours or that "grazing" is leading to any significant viewing of indecency. Finally, the imminence of "V-chip" technology to enable parental control of all violence-and indecency-viewing suggests that a draconian ban from 6 a.m. to midnight is decidedly premature.

In spite of this evidentiary black hole, we have a broadside ban on vaguely defined indecency during all hours when most working people are awake. . . . The net effect of the majority's decision is a gratuitous grant of power allowing casual and lightly reviewed administrative decisionmaking about fundamental liberties. I respectfully dissent.

NOTES & QUESTIONS

1. *Categories.* Society has categorized a type of information called "indecency" as bad. By the way, how clear is the definition of indecency? Would you be able to give concrete advice to a client about what is indecent? What does Judge Wald say in her dissent?

2. *First Amendment standard of review.* Recall that the first step in selecting the appropriate First Amendment standard of review is determining whether the regulation is content-neutral or content-based. Because this regulation, as in *Pacifica*, is targeting a specific type of speech—indecent speech—it is clearly content-based. Thus strict scrutiny is appropriate. However, as we saw in *Red Lion* and *Pacifica*, "strict scrutiny" as applied to the broadcast medium can differ substantially from "strict scrutiny" as applied to the print medium. One might call this a sort of medium warp. So beware of equivocation: Strict scrutiny comes in multiple flavors, some sharper than others.

3. *Ends analysis.* Under strict scrutiny, the government must demonstrate that it is pursuing *compelling* interests. The majority focuses on two interests: (a) facilitation of parental supervision of children, and (b) government concern for children's well-being.

    a. *Parental supervision.* Why can't parents control the situation themselves? For instance, is it inevitable that children must have television sets in their bedrooms? Do you think this is true across all socio-economic classes and ethnic groups in America?

    b. *Children's well-being.* Which interests are we discussing—physical, psychological, or moral? These distinctions are significant because different types of evidence are necessary, depending on the harm. For instance, if the claim is of psychological harm, one would expect the Court to evaluate the conclusions of dueling mass media psychologists. By contrast, if the claim is of moral harm, would you expect the Court to evaluate the debates of moral philosophers or religious leaders? To avoid controversy on matters of "morality," should the Court defer to the legislative branch on such questions? Or would doing so guarantee that a multicultural society gets flattened by the tyranny of the moralistic majority?

    c. *Proof of harm?* According to Judge Wald in dissent, has the government made its case on the magnitude of the harm suffered without time-channeling?

4. *Means analysis.* Applying strict scrutiny, the restraint on speech must be *narrowly tailored* to advancing the compelling government interest.

    a. *Understanding narrow tailoring.* What does it mean to be "narrowly tailored"? Recall what the goal of the legislation is. Indecency is bad. But it is not so "bad" that it should be banned across the board, as obscenity or child pornography are. Instead, certain individuals (e.g., willing adults) should have unfettered access to indecency. Even if it might be socially stigmatized, it should be legally unconstrained. By contrast, other individuals (e.g., minors without parental consent) should be protected from exposure and prevented from access.

To the extent that the FCC regulations prevent willing adults from accessing indecency, the regulations are *over-inclusive*. To the extent that the FCC regulations allow unsupervised minors to access indecency, the regulations are *under-inclusive*. By being over-inclusive and/or under-inclusive, a statute or regulation may not be well tailored to further the government's goal while respecting the First Amendment.

      b.   *Narrowly tailored?* Judge Wald did not believe this requirement was met. Why not? Why was time-channeling inadequate? Try to identify carefully what evidence the government provided and what further evidence Judge Wald would have required before signing off on the constitutionality of this section. Is Judge Wald being unreasonable in demanding perfection, or is she asking for only what the First Amendment requires?

      5. *Tricky result.* The opinion as excerpted focused on the 12 a.m. to 6 a.m. safe harbor for commercial broadcast stations, as required by § 16(a)(2) of the Public Telecommunications Act of 1992. The majority concluded that when analyzed alone, this section was constitutional. But there was a (2-hour) longer safe harbor, between 10 p.m. to 6 a.m., granted to public broadcast stations. *See* § 16(a)(1). In omitted sections of the opinion, the court thought that this preferential treatment was unwarranted. Moreover, it thought that Congress' willingness to have a longer safe harbor period for public broadcast stations undermined the argument that commercial broadcast stations' safe harbor had to start two hours later, at midnight. Accordingly, the court actually struck down the § 16(a)(2) safe harbor requirement and instructed the FCC to reestablish a uniform safe harbor for all broadcast stations—commercial and noncommercial alike. On remand, the FCC created these uniform rules with the safe harbor starting at 10 p.m.:

> 47 C.F.R. § 73.3999. Enforcement of 18 U.S.C. 1464 (restrictions on the transmission of obscene and indecent material)
>
> (a) No licensee of a radio or television broadcast station shall broadcast any material which is obscene.
>
> (b) No licensee of a radio or television broadcast station shall broadcast on any day between 6 a.m. and 10 p.m. any material which is indecent.

      6. *The new trend.* The broadcast indecency landscape has changed significantly since *ACT III*, in terms of the numbers of both complaints and enforcement actions. In 2000, the FCC received only 111 complaints regarding 111 different programs. The Notice of Apparent Liability (NAL) amount (fines) summed to a paltry $48,000. By contrast, in 2004, the FCC received 1,405,419 complaints on 314 different programs (more than half a million complaints pertaining to Janet Jackson's Superbowl "wardrobe malfunction" discussed *infra* p.410). The NALs summed to a whopping $7.9M.[*]

7. *Parents Television Council.* Most of the complaints came from the Parent Television Council (PTC), which leverages the Internet to generate mass filings of indecency complaints. By one journalist's count, the PTC was responsible for 99.8% of the 2003 complaints; in 2004, the PTC was responsible for 99.9% of all non-Superbowl-related complaints.[*] In 2009, the PTC helped generate approximately 180,000 complaints because of a *Family Guy* episode aired on FOX. A PTC advisory asked "Should a Sunday night cartoon show YOUR children bestiality, gay orgies and babies eating sperm? Fox thinks so."[†]

8. *Cultural power.* Recall in *Pacifica* Justice Brennan's fear of privileging majoritarian sensibilities. Was Brennan envisioning groups like the Parents Television Council? Consider also why we worry about eroticism (and to a lesser extent violence) on television, but not racial, gender, or sexual orientation stereotypes, which may be just as harmful to inculcating virtue in children.

NOTE: SHIFTING INDECENCY POLICIES

Recall that after the Court issued its decision in *Pacifica* in 1978, the Commission left most broadcasts untouched because the definition of "indecency" was seen as quite narrow. That all changed in 1987 with the *Infinity Order,* where the FCC put forth a more general definition of indecency and brought enforcement actions against three stations. The D.C. Circuit vacated this in part in *ACT I,* and the saga that we just studied ensued.

Then in 2001, the FCC issued a new *Industry Guidance Policy Statement* to provide better notice as to what it would deem indecent. The Commission clarified that indecency findings involve a two-step process: (i) determine whether the material falls within the subject matter (re "sexual or excretory organs or activities"), and (ii) determine whether it is "patently offensive as measured by contemporary community standards for the broadcast medium" (a national standard).[‡] The *Policy Statement* provides numerous transcripts of examples of very indecent, mostly indecent, just barely indecent, and not quite (but awfully close to) indecent broadcasts.

The Commission's interpretation of indecency shifted *again* in 2004 when it issued a "fleeting expletives" order. At the 2003 *Golden Globes,* U2 singer and

---

[*] *See* FCC, Indecency Complaints Chart, http://www.fcc.gov/eb/broadcast/ichart.pdf.

[*] *See* Todd Shields, *Activists Dominate Content Complaints,* MEDIAWEEK, December 06, 2004; *see also* Chris Baker, *TV Complaints to FCC Soar as Parents Lead the Way,* WASH. TIMES, May 24, 2004, at A01.

[†] *See* http://www.parentstv.org/ptc/action/familyguy/Content.asp (last visited September 21, 2011).

[‡] *See In the Matter of Industry Guidance On the Commission's Case Law Interpreting 18 U.S.C. § 1464 and Enforcement Policies Regarding Broadcast Indecency,* Policy Statement, 16 FCC Rcd. 7999, ¶¶ 7-8 (2001).

social activist Bono accepted his award with the words "this is really, really, fucking brilliant. Really, really, great." As could be predicted, many viewers filed complaints. The FCC's enforcement bureau denied them, partly on the grounds that a mere fleeting expletive did not amount to "indecency." Months later, the full Commission reversed and put the broadcast industry on notice.[*] In 2006, after complex procedural maneuvers, the FCC issued an Order holding that various broadcasts had violated the standard announced in the *Golden Globes Order*. (The broadcasters, however, were not required to pay a fine.) On appeal, the Second Circuit held that the FCC's decision was arbitrary and capricious because it had changed indecency policy in the *Golden Globes Order* without providing adequate explanation.[†] The Supreme Court agreed to hear the case in 2008.

FCC v. FOX (2D CIR. 2007): FLEETING EXPLETIVES

In *FCC v. Fox Television Stations, Inc.*,[‡] the Court upheld the FCC's new fleeting expletive policy, finding that the agency's "reasons for expanding the scope of its enforcement activity were entirely rational" and that it was "reasonable to determine that it made no sense to distinguish between literal and nonliteral uses of offensive words, requiring repetitive use to render only the latter indecent." The Court emphasized that the decision was consistent with the "context-based approach" established in *Pacifica* and with the Commission's prior refusal to create "safe harbors for particular types of broadcasts." Justice Scalia, writing for the majority, rejected all three of the lower court's rationales for overturning the order. First, he found that the Commission need not provide empirical data to support the conclusion that fleeting expletives are harmful because "Congress has made the determination that indecent material is harmful to children." Second, he found that "the agency's decision to retain some discretion" did not render the order arbitrary because the context of the use matters (comparing use in a violent film like Saving Private Ryan to use in a family-oriented awards show). And finally, he found "logical" the agency's prediction that a *per se* exemption for fleeting expletives "would lead to increased use of expletives one at a time."

Both Justice Stevens and Justice Breyer filed dissenting opinions in the case, criticizing the FCC's rule on First Amendment grounds. Justice Breyer also focused on the inadequacy of the Commission's explanation for the change in policy. In Justice Breyer's view "To explain a change requires more than setting

---

[*] *Golden Globes Order*, 19 FCC Rcd. 4975 (2004).

[†] Fox Television Stations, Inc. v. FCC, 489 F.3d 444 (2d Cir. 2007).

[‡] 556 U.S. 502 (2009).

forth reasons why the new policy is a good one." In particular, he focused on the fact that the FCC's previous decision to exempt fleeting expletives was based on "the need to avoid treading too close to the constitutional line" and the Commission's understanding of Justice Powell's concurring opinion in *Pacifica*. Justice Breyer was also concerned about the impact that a "bleeping" mandate would have on "smaller, independent broadcasters," especially given the uncertainty regarding the FCC's use of fines.

The Court made clear that the case was being decided on statutory grounds. On remand, however, the Second Circuit addressed the constitutional question. *See* Fox v. FCC, 613 F.3d 317 (2d Cir. 2010). The court held that the FCC's indecency policy, as set forth in its 2001 *Industry Guidance*, violated the First Amendment by being vague and chilling speech. It provided numerous examples of vagueness, and asked, for instance, why "bullshitter" should be deemed indecent but not "dickhead." It also noted that the two exceptions to the presumptive rule against "fuck" or "shit"—bona fide news, and artistic necessity—were themselves vague. The court also cataloged numerous examples of chilled speech.

The Supreme Court granted cert. again, but managed to avoid the direct First Amendment issue. Instead, in *FCC v. Fox, Inc.* (*Fox II*),[*] the Court decided the case on Fifth Amendment vagueness grounds. The Court first explained the void-for-vagueness doctrine:

> Even when speech is not at issue, the void for vagueness doctrine addresses at least two connected but discrete due process concerns: first, that regulated parties should know what is required of them so they may act accordingly; second, precision and guidance are necessary so that those enforcing the law do not act in an arbitrary or discriminatory way. *Grayned v. City of Rockford* (1972). When speech is involved, rigorous adherence to those requirements is necessary to ensure that ambiguity does not chill protected speech.[†]

Applying this standard to the facts, the Court concluded that the broadcasters were not granted "fair notice . . . that fleeting expletives and momentary nudity could be found actionably indecent."[‡] The majority opinion, authored by Justice Kennedy, made explicit that it was not addressing the First Amendment argument or reconsidering *Pacifica*. Justice Ginsburg, who concurred in the judgment, specifically stated that *Pacifica* was wrongly decided. Justice Sotomayor did not participate in the deliberations.

---

[*] 132 S. Ct. 2307 (2012).

[†] *Id.* at 2317.

[‡] *Id.* at 2320.

CBS v. FCC (3D CIR. 2008): FLEETING BODY PARTS

In addition to Bono, Cher, Nicole, Paris, and their fleeting expletives, there's also Justin, Janet, and their wardrobe malfunctions. At the 2004 Superbowl halftime show, Justin Timberlake exposed Janet Jackson's breast during their dance routine. This prompted a huge protest, and a severe FCC fine in 2006.* The ensuing litigation produced CBS Corp. v. FCC, 535 F.3d 167 (3d Cir. 2008).

During oral argument before the appellate court in the *Fox* case that we just read, the FCC conceded that the *Golden Globes* Order, issued in March 2004, did indeed represent a change in policy on fleeting expletives. Because the Superbowl aired in February 2004—*before* that policy change—the new policy could not be applied to the wardrobe malfunction. Any retroactive application would be arbitrary and capricious.

But the FCC had another argument, based on a distinction between fleeting expletives and fleeting images. Even though the FCC conceded a policy change with respect to expletives, it contended that there was no such change with respect to images. In other words, the broadcast of indecent images, even if fleeting, was always potentially sanctionable—both before and after the *Golden Globes* Order. The U.S. Court of Appeals for the Third Circuit was not impressed by this hair-splitting and criticized the FCC's lack of forthrightness:

> When confronted with these troublesome revisionist arguments, the FCC conceded the existence of its prior policy [to the 2nd Circuit in *Fox*]. . . . But it has made no such concession here. Faced with extensive evidence to the contrary, the Commission nevertheless continues to assert that its fleeting material policy was limited to words and did not exclude fleeting images from the scope of actionable indecency.†

Rejecting the FCC's position, the court determined that there never was any distinct policy for images (as opposed to words). It then concluded:

> Because the Commission fails to acknowledge that it has changed its policy on fleeting material, it is unable to comply with the requirement .... that an agency supply a reasoned explanation for its departure from prior policy.‡

Having decided that the FCC's enforcement was arbitrary and capricious, the court could have stopped. But it went on to explain that even if the *Golden Globes* order had issued before the Superbowl, CBS could not be held

---

* *See Complaints Against Various Television Licensees Concerning Their February 1, 2004 Broad. of the Super Bowl XXXVIII Halftime Show*, Notice of Apparent Liability for Forfeiture, 19 FCC Rcd. 19230 (2004).

† 535 F.3d at 188.

‡ Id.

vicariously liable for the gyrating actions of Timberlake and Jackson. First, the entertainers were independent contractors, not employees, and therefore CBS could not be held liable under the theory of *respondeat superior.* Second, the court rejected on First Amendment grounds the notion that CBS, as a broadcaster, had a non-delegable duty and was strictly liable for what was broadcast. It wrote:

> [The] First Amendment precludes a strict liability regime for broadcast indecency. The First Amendment requires that the FCC prove scienter when it seeks to hold a broadcaster liable for indecent material. In the case of scripted or pre-recorded indecent material, the scienter element likely would be satisfied. But when the indecent material is unscripted and occurs during a live broadcast, as in the Halftime Show, a showing of scienter must be made on the evidence.[*]

Accordingly, the court read into the indecency statute and regulation a scienter requirement that was inconsistent with FCC's "non-delegable duty" theory.

B. TELEPHONY

We return to indecent speech, but now communicated through a different channel, the telephone. At the outset, ask yourself: In what ways does this communication technology differ from broadcast? Should such differences matter constitutionally?

FCC v. SABLE COMMUNICATIONS OF CALIFORNIA
492 U.S. 115 (1989)

Justice WHITE delivered the opinion of the Court.

I

In 1983, Sable Communications, Inc. . . . began offering sexually oriented prerecorded telephone messages (popularly known as "dial-a-porn"). . . .

In 1988, Sable brought suit in District Court seeking declaratory and injunctive relief against enforcement of the recently amended § 223(b) [of the Communications Act of 1934].

The District Court denied Sable's request for a preliminary injunction against enforcement of the statute's ban on obscene telephone messages, rejecting the argument that the statute was unconstitutional because it created a

---

[*] *Id.* at 200.

national standard of obscenity. The District Court, however, struck down the "indecent speech" provision of § 223(b), holding that in this respect the statute was overbroad and unconstitutional and that this result was consistent with *FCC v. Pacifica Foundation* (1978).

II

[In this Part, the Court explained the long, convoluted procedural history of this litigation. Initially, Congress passed 47 U.S.C. § 223(b), which prohibited dial-a-porn to unconsenting adults or to youths.[*] The statute required the FCC to create defenses, which it did originally in the form of time-channeling (9 p.m. to 8 a.m. EST), but the FCC regulations were struck down in 1984.[†] The FCC amended the regulations (e.g., by including credit card authorization defenses), which were struck down again by the Second Circuit Court of Appeals in 1986.[‡] Finally, in 1988 a newly revised set of regulations (including credit card, access codes, and scrambling defenses) seemed acceptable to the Second Circuit; however, the court then proceeded to invalidate the *statute* (not the regulations) as applied to indecent (nonobscene) speech.[§] At this point, in April 1988, a frustrated Congress amended § 223(b) to ban totally all dial-a-porn, *even to consenting adults*. This is the statute challenged here.—ED.][4]

III

In its facial challenge to the statute, Sable argues that the legislation creates an impermissible national standard of obscenity, and that it places message senders in a "double bind" by compelling them to tailor all their messages to the least tolerant community.

Section 223(b) no more establishes a "national standard" of obscenity than do federal statutes prohibiting the mailing of obscene materials, 18 U.S.C.

---

[*] *See* Federal Communications Commission Authorization Act of 1983, Pub. L. 98-214, § 8(b), 97 Stat. 1470.

[†] *See* Carlin Communications, Inc. v. FCC, 749 F.2d 113 (2d Cir. 1984) (Carlin I).

[‡] *See* Carlin Communications, Inc. v. FCC, 787 F.2d 846 (2d Cir. 1986) (Carlin II)

[§] *See* Carlin Communications, Inc. v. FCC, 837 F.2d 546 (2d Cir.) (Carlin III), *cert. denied*, 488 U.S. 924 (1988),

[4] "(b)(1) Whoever knowingly—

"(A) in the District of Columbia or in interstate or foreign communication, by means of telephone, makes (directly or by recording device) any obscene or indecent communication for commercial purposes to any person, regardless of whether the maker of such communication placed the call; or

"(B) permits any telephone facility under such person's control to be used for an activity prohibited by subparagraph (A),

"shall be fined not more than $50,000 or imprisoned not more than six months, or both." [This footnote has been moved.—ED.]

§ 1461, *see Hamling v. United States* (1974), or the broadcasting of obscene messages, 18 U.S.C. § 1464.

[T]he fact that "distributors of allegedly obscene materials may be subjected to varying community standards in the various federal judicial districts into which they transmit the materials does not render a federal statute unconstitutional because of the failure of application of uniform national standards of obscenity." *Hamling.*

Furthermore, Sable is free to tailor its messages, on a selective basis, if it so chooses, to the communities it chooses to serve. While Sable may be forced to incur some costs in developing and implementing a system for screening the locale of incoming calls, there is no constitutional impediment to enacting a law which may impose such costs on a medium electing to provide these messages. Whether Sable chooses to hire operators to determine the source of the calls or engages with the telephone company to arrange for the screening and blocking of out-of-area calls or finds another means for providing messages compatible with community standards is a decision for the message provider to make. There is no constitutional barrier under *Miller* to prohibiting communications that are obscene in some communities under local standards even though they are not obscene in others. If Sable's audience is comprised of different communities with different local standards, Sable ultimately bears the burden of complying with the prohibition on obscene messages.

IV

[T]he District Court [also] concluded that while the Government has a legitimate interest in protecting children from exposure to indecent dial-a-porn messages, § 223(b) was not sufficiently narrowly drawn to serve that purpose and thus violated the First Amendment. We agree.

In attempting to justify the complete ban and criminalization of the indecent commercial telephone communications with adults as well as minors, the federal parties rely on . . . *Pacifica.* . . .

Pacifica is readily distinguishable from these cases, most obviously because it did not involve a total ban on broadcasting indecent material.

The *Pacifica* opinion also relied on the "unique" attributes of broadcasting, noting that broadcasting is "uniquely pervasive," can intrude on the privacy of the home without prior warning as to program content, and is "uniquely accessible to children, even those too young to read." The private commercial telephone communications at issue here are substantially different from the public radio broadcast at issue in *Pacifica.* In contrast to public displays, unsolicited mailings and other means of expression which the recipient has no meaningful opportunity to avoid, the dial-it medium requires the listener to take affirmative steps to receive the communication. There is no "captive audience" problem here; callers will generally not be unwilling listeners. The context of dial-in services, where a caller seeks and is willing to pay for the communication, is manifestly different from a situation in which a listener does not want the received message. Placing a telephone call is not the same as turning on a radio and being taken by surprise by an indecent message. Unlike an unexpected outburst on a radio broadcast, the message received by one who places a call to a dial-a-porn service is not so invasive or surprising that it prevents an unwilling listener from avoiding exposure to it.

The federal parties nevertheless argue that the total ban on indecent commercial telephone communications is justified because nothing less could prevent children from gaining access to such messages. We find the argument quite unpersuasive. The FCC, after lengthy proceedings, determined that its credit card, access code, and scrambling rules were a satisfactory solution to the problem of keeping indecent dial-a-porn messages out of the reach of minors. The Court of Appeals, after careful consideration, agreed that these rules represented a "feasible and effective" way to serve the Government's compelling interest in protecting children.

The federal parties now insist that the rules would not be effective enough— that enterprising youngsters could and would evade the rules and gain access to communications from which they should be shielded. There is no evidence in the record before us to that effect.... [T]he federal parties assert that in amending § 223(b) in 1988, Congress expressed its view that there was not a sufficiently effective way to protect minors short of the total ban that it enacted. The federal parties claim that we must give deference to that judgment.

To the extent that the federal parties suggest that we should defer to Congress' conclusion about an issue of constitutional law, our answer is that while we do not ignore it, it is our task in the end to decide whether Congress has violated the Constitution. This is particularly true where the Legislature has concluded that its product does not violate the First Amendment.

[T]he congressional record presented to us contains no evidence as to how effective or ineffective the FCC's most recent regulations were or might prove to be. It may well be that there is no fail-safe method of guaranteeing that never will a minor be able to access the dial-a-porn system. The bill that was enacted, however, was introduced on the floor; nor was there a committee report on the bill from which the language of the enacted bill was taken. No Congressman or Senator purported to present a considered judgment with respect to how often or to what extent minors could or would circumvent the rules and have access to dial-a-porn messages.

For all we know from this record, the FCC's technological approach to restricting dial-a-porn messages to adults who seek them would be extremely effective.... If this is the case, it seems to us that § 223(b) is not a narrowly tailored effort to serve the compelling interest of preventing minors from being exposed to indecent telephone messages. Under our precedents, § 223(b), in its present form, has the invalid effect of limiting the content of adult telephone conversations to that which is suitable for children to hear. It is another case of "burn[ing] the house to roast the pig." *Butler v. Michigan.*

Accordingly, we affirm the judgment of the District Court.[*]

Justice BRENNAN, with whom Justice MARSHALL and Justice STEVENS join, concurring in part and dissenting in part.

In my view ... 47 U.S.C. § 223(b)(1)(A)'s parallel criminal prohibition with regard to obscene commercial communications likewise violates the First Amendment. I have long been convinced that the exaction of criminal penalties for the distribution of obscene materials to consenting adults is constitutionally intolerable. In my judgment, "the concept of 'obscenity' cannot be defined with sufficient specificity and clarity to provide fair notice to persons who create and distribute sexually oriented materials, to prevent substantial erosion of protected speech as a byproduct of the attempt to suppress unprotected speech, and to avoid very costly institutional harms." *Paris Adult Theatre I v. Slaton* (1973) (BRENNAN, J., dissenting).... [A] complete criminal ban on obscene telephonic messages for profit is "unconstitutionally overbroad, and therefore invalid on its face," as a means for achieving this end.

Accordingly, I dissent....

NOTES & QUESTIONS

1. *Legal category of "obscenity."*

   a. *Line-drawing.* Notwithstanding Justice Brennan's dissent, the majority repeats standard First Amendment orthodoxy that "obscenity" does not count as protected speech and therefore can be banned without First Amendment objections. What do you think of Justice Brennan's argument, however? Should we be so comfortable in giving something called "obscenity" zero First Amendment protections? Who ultimately decides what counts as obscene versus merely indecent? Where should the line be drawn?

---

[*] Justice Scalia's concurring opinion is omitted.—ED.

b. *National standard.* What is the complaint about creating a "national standard" of obscenity? What is wrong with doing so? Recall that the FCC enforces a national broadcast viewer standard for what counts as "patently offensive" in its indecency analysis. Keep these examples in mind when we study the internet.

2. *Comparison: broadcast versus telephone.* Broadcast and telephony technologies differ in many ways. Consider which, if any, of the following distinctions should affect your policy and legal analysis. Further, does the Court agree?

a. *Potency.* Imagine yourself as a parent. What are you most concerned about: indecent print (image only), radio (audio only), or indecent television (audio and video)? Where does telephony fit into this spectrum? Does interactivity matter? Is there any discussion of comparative potency in the above opinion? Should there be?

b. *Technology: the channel.* Recall that one justification for regulating broadcast entry was spectrum scarcity. Standard wireline telephony does not use the e-m spectrum as a channel; instead, it uses wires (such as twisted-pair, coaxial cable, and optical fiber). That said, over some links there may be some wireless communications, such as point-to-point microwave connections (although these have been largely replaced by optical fiber). And, of course, there is wireless telephony, which makes extensive use of the e-m spectrum as a channel. Does any of this matter to the Court? If not, why not?

c. *A pervasive flow.* In the previous section, we examined the attempts to control indecency in broadcasting. Because broadcast is pervasive/intrusive and uniquely accessible to children, it is treated differently from print. *See Pacifica.* Is the telephone any different from broadcasting? Being so common, are telephones as pervasive and accessible to children as the broadcast media? What about the possibility of unwanted exposure or surprise for both children and adults? What impact does this have on the First Amendment standard of review?

3. *Unconstitutionality.* State succinctly why the total ban on dial-a-porn violated the First Amendment. Was the government not pursuing a compelling interest? Or were the means adopted not narrowly tailored?

NOTE: DIAL-A-PORN REGULATIONS

In response to *Sable*, Congress once again rewrote § 223. Here are the relevant portions. Please read them carefully.

47 U.S.C. § 223

(b). Prohibited acts for commercial purposes; defense to prosecution

(1) Whoever knowingly—

(A) within the United States, by means of telephone, makes (directly or by recording device) any obscene communication for commercial purposes to any person, regardless of whether the maker of such communication placed the call; or

(B) permits any telephone facility under such person's control to be used for an activity prohibited by subparagraph (A), shall be fined in accordance with title 18, United States Code, or imprisoned not more than two years, or both.

(2) Whoever knowingly—

(A) within the United States, by means of telephone, makes (directly or by recording device) any indecent communication for commercial purposes which is available to any person under 18 years of age or to any other person without that person's consent, regardless of whether the maker of such communication placed the call; or

(B) permits any telephone facility under such person's control to be used for an activity prohibited by subparagraph (A), shall be fined not more than $50,000 or imprisoned not more than six months, or both.

(3) It is a defense to prosecution under paragraph (2) of this subsection that the defendant restricted access to the prohibited communication to persons 18 years of age or older in accordance with subsection (c) of this section and with such procedures as the Commission may prescribe by regulation.

(c). Restriction on access to subscribers by common carriers; judicial remedies respecting restrictions.

(1) A common carrier within the District of Columbia or within any State, or in interstate or foreign commerce, shall not, to the extent technically feasible, provide access to a communication specified in subsection (b) from the telephone of any subscriber who has not previously requested in writing the carrier to provide access to such communication if the carrier collects from subscribers an identifiable charge for such communication that the carrier remits, in whole or in part, to the provider of such communication.

Note that Congress placed two different sets of restrictions on two different sets of players, who cooperate to provide indecent content. The first player is the dial-a-porn provider, which is prohibited from providing its services to minors. *See* §§ 223(b)(1) (obscenity), (b)(2) (indecency). Congress also allowed for an FCC-designated safe harbor, which would create some bright lines by which the dial-a-porn provider could avoid prosecution. *See* § 223(b)(3).

But Congress did not stop there. The second player is the local telephone company, which connects the caller to porn provider and sometimes provides special billing services. *See* § 223(c). Congress imposed on them a blocking requirement under certain circumstances.

In 1990, the FCC issued implementing regulations on dial-a-porn.[*] First, in terms of the safe harbor, the FCC told the dial-a-porn industry that they would be safe from prosecution if they used credit card authorization, access codes

---

[*] *See Regulations Concerning Indecent Communications by Telephone*, R&O, 5 FCC Rcd. 4926 (1990).

(passwords mailed to home), or scrambling (physical device that only adults could use) to check that the caller wasn't a minor. Second, the Commission codified in regulation the blocking requirement. In explaining and justifying its regulations, the FCC was mindful of the First Amendment. For example, in defending the reverse blocking requirement[*] the Commission explained:

> 18. The First Amendment does not preclude Congress from imposing a burden on message providers. *See Sable v. FCC.* Regulations need not be so weak that they are completely useless. It was reasonable for Congress to conclude that its reverse blocking scheme would be considerably more effective than a voluntary scheme in preventing children from accessing indecent material. A voluntary blocking scheme would be far less effective in protecting children from exposure to indecent material because it is likely that most parents would not realize the need for blocking until their children had already obtained access to indecent messages. Nor would neighbors or relatives where children are only occasional visitors recognize the need to, nor act to, have access blocked. It is reasonable, therefore, to implement a reverse blocking scheme that brings the potential problem to the attention of parents before the damage to children has occurred, rather than waiting until the damage has been done.

> 22. To the extent that message providers are arguing that the Congress' reverse blocking requirement will drive them out of business, and is therefore unconstitutional, we disagree. Reverse blocking, together with the Commission's regulations, constitute a regulatory approach that is narrowly tailored to address a compelling need. This approach may cause message providers to incur additional costs, and perhaps to raise their prices, but the Supreme Court has said that raising the cost of providing a service is not unconstitutional. *Sable.* In addition, the statute requires reverse blocking only if the telephone company performs certain billing and collection services for the message provider. The record does not show message providers cannot feasibly arrange for independent billing for their services. We see no reason why adult message providers cannot continue to operate under the statutory scheme.

The revised § 223 and the FCC's implementing rules, 47 C.F.R. § 64.201, were challenged on both constitutional and Administrative Procedure Act grounds. Both the Ninth Circuit and the Second Circuit Courts of Appeal[†] sided with the FCC. Here's what the Ninth Circuit had to say:

> We hold that the term "indecent" as used in section 223 of the Act and defined in the FCC rules is not void for vagueness, that the statute and the FCC's

---

[*] "Reverse blocking" requires the caller to explicitly opt into dial-a-porn by asking for it in writing. By contrast, "voluntary blocking" requires the caller to explicitly opt out of the possibility of dial-a-porn by asking the telephone company not to make such connections.

[†] *See* Dial Information Servs. Corp. of N.Y. v. Thornburgh, 938 F.2d 1535 (2d Cir. 1991), *cert. denied,* 502 U.S. 1072 (1992) (upholding statute and regulations).

implementing regulations are narrowly tailored to promote the compelling government interest of protecting the physical and psychological well-being of minors, that section 223 is not a prior restraint on speech, that substantial evidence supports the agency findings and that the FCC did not act arbitrarily or capriciously, abuse its discretion, or act otherwise not in accordance with the law in promulgating its rules.[*]

Make sure you understand what this really means. In order to access dial-a-porn, adults can be forced to request access in writing to their telephone company (to lift the reverse blocking) and also use their credit card. In other words, you can effectively obliterate anonymity. Keep these rulings in mind when we study indecency on the internet.

C. CABLE

We now turn to indecency regulations for cable television. While you consider these regulations, think about whether cable makes this bad content more or less accessible than through broadcast or telephone? Do you imagine constitutional analysis of cable television indecency will resemble more our analysis of indecency on broadcast or telephone?

	CRUZ V. FERRE
	755 F.2d 1415 (11th Cir. 1985)

STAFFORD, District Judge:

FACTS AND PROCEDURAL HISTORY

[City of Miami Ordinance No. 9538] . . . is intended to regulate "indecent" and "obscene" material on cable television. The relevant portions of this ordinance provide:

Section 1. No person shall by means of a cable television system knowingly distribute by wire or cable any obscene or indecent material.

Section 2. The following words have the following meanings: . . .

(g) "Indecent material" means material which is a representation or description of a human sexual or excretory organ or function which the average person, applying contemporary community standards, would find to be patently offensive.

---

[*] Information Providers' Coalition v. FCC, 928 F.2d 866, 879 (9th Cir. 1991).

Plaintiff-appellee Ruben Cruz is a Cablevision subscriber. The complaint sought a judgment declaring the ordinance void on its face and an injunction restraining the enforcement of the ordinance.

[On a motion for summary judgment, t]he city was permanently enjoined from enforcing... Ordinance No. 9538, which regulate[s] "indecent material" on cable television.

FIRST AMENDMENT

Appellants' primary argument on appeal is that authority for the city's regulation is found in the Supreme Court decision *FCC v. Pacifica Foundation* (1978).

[W]e are persuaded that *Pacifica* cannot be extended to cover the particular facts of this case. *Pacifica*, it must be remembered, focused upon broadcasting's "pervasive presence," and the fact that broadcasting "is uniquely accessible to children, even those too young to read." *Id.* The Court's concern with the pervasiveness of the broadcast media can best be seen in its description of broadcasted material as an "intruder" into the privacy of the home. Cablevision, however, does not "intrude" into the home. The Cablevision subscriber must affirmatively elect to have cable service come into his home. Additionally, the subscriber must make the additional affirmative decision whether to purchase any "extra" programming services, such as HBO. The subscriber must make a monthly decision whether to continue to subscribe to cable, and if dissatisfied with the cable service, he may cancel his subscription. The Supreme Court's reference to "a nuisance rationale," is not applicable to the Cablevision system, where there is no possibility that a non-cable subscriber will be confronted with materials carried only on cable. One of the keys to the very existence of cable television is the fact that cable programming is available only to those who have the cable attached to their television sets.[6]

Probably the more important justification recognized in *Pacifica* for the FCC's authority to regulate the broadcasting of indecent materials was the accessibility of broadcasting to children.... This interest, however, is significantly weaker in the context of cable television because parental manageability of cable television greatly exceeds the ability to manage the broadcast media. Again, parents must decide whether to allow Cablevision into the home. Parents decide whether to select supplementary programming

---

[6] Appellants seem to want to extend Justice Stevens' "pig in the parlor" analogy. See Brief of Appellants at 16 ("it makes no difference whether the pig enters the parlor through the door of broadcast, cable, or amplified speech: government is entitled to keep the pig out of the parlor"). It seems to us, however, that if an individual voluntarily opens his door and allows a pig into his parlor, he is in less of a position to squeal.

services such as HBO. These services publish programming guides which identify programs containing "vulgarity," "nudity," and "violence." Additionally, parents may obtain a "lockbox" or "parental key" device enabling parents to prevent children from gaining access to "objectionable" channels of programming. Cablevision provides these without charge to subscribers.

Pacifica represents a careful balancing of the first amendment rights of broadcasters and willing adult listeners against the FCC's interests in protecting children and unwilling adults. The Court held that, under the particular facts of *Pacifica*, the balance weighed in favor of the FCC. Because we determine that under the facts of the instant case the interests of the City of Miami are substantially less strong than those of the FCC in *Pacifica*, we believe that we must hold *Pacifica* to be inapplicable to this case.[9]

Even if we were to find the rationale of *Pacifica* applicable to this case, we would still be compelled to strike the ordinance as facially overbroad. As the district judge noted, the ordinance "prohibits far too broadly the transmission of indecent materials through cable television. The ordinance's prohibition is wholesale, without regard to the time of day or other variables indispensable to the decision in Pacifica." The ordinance totally fails to account for the variables identified in *Pacifica*: the time of day; the context of the program in which the material appears; the composition of the viewing audience. In ignoring these variables, the ordinance goes far beyond the realm of permissible regulation envisioned by the *Pacifica* Court.

NOTES & QUESTIONS

1. *Filter.* In studying broadcast, we saw the technique of time-channeling. With telephony, we saw that a complete ban was unconstitutional; however, a blocking scheme was constitutional. (Note how the block could be lifted by someone authenticated as an adult through credit cards, access codes, or possession of a scrambler.) In *Cruz v. Ferre*, what technique did the city adopt?

2. *Comparison.*

   a. *Potency.* How does cable indecency compare to indecency on radio broadcast, television broadcast, telephony, and print? What are the causes of such differences? Are they due to the different senses that are titillated or provoked by audio, still image, video? Are they due to different business models that encourage different levels of hardcore? Are they due to historical or

---

[9] Appellants ... argue that the limited number of stations on cable television somehow gives the city an interest in regulating indecency on cable television. This argument, however, misconstrues the rationale in *Pacifica* and in other Supreme Court cases such as *Red Lion* (1969).

sociological factors pertaining to the different industries? Is any of this discussed in the opinion?

b. *Technology: the channel.* Cable television does not use the e-m spectrum directly as a channel; instead, it uses a mix of coaxial cable and fiber optics to deliver television signals from the cable system's head end to the home. (In fact, this is only partly true. How do the video signals arrive at the head end in the first place?) Recall that cable TV *entry* has never been justified on spectrum-scarcity grounds. Is this technological difference discussed by the court? (*See* footnote 9.) Should it be relevant?

c. *Push versus pull?* In comparing and contrasting accessibility of bad content, the following concepts of "push" and "pull" may be useful:

> "Push" communications arrive at the receiver without any special effort on the part of the receiver to obtain that particular communication item. E-mail is a good example. Once one has established an account and publicized the address, e-mails will arrive without any special effort by the receiver. By contrast, "pull" communications require more focused effort by the receiver to retrieve particular information. Surfing the Web is a common example of pull technology.*

Many forms of communication have both push and pull aspects. For example, one can configure Web browsers to receive channels of information automatically. After the initial specification of channels (akin to "pull"), data are periodically delivered to the individual without a specific request for that information (akin to "push").

Is the Eleventh Circuit suggesting that broadcast television is a push technology, which can be quite intrusive and pervasive, whereas cable is a pull technology, with little chance of receiving undesired content? Where do dial-a-porn and print fit in?

d. *Assumption of risk?* Instead of "push" or "pull," perhaps the central difference between the communication technologies is the tort law concept of *assumption of risk.* For example, the court writes that one must invite cable television into one's home, including programming tiers more likely to feature indecent content. Indeed, the choice to keep cable television is reaffirmed monthly. Is this persuasive? After all, as Justice Brennan argued in his *Pacifica* dissent, one can say the same thing about broadcast television or radio: It too must be purchased and invited home. What about telephone? Print? By the way, who should be allowed to assume the risk? If protecting children is an

---

* Jerry Kang, *Cyber-Race*, 113 HARV. L. REV. 1130, 1147 (2000).

independent goal, separate from the objective of furthering parental supervision, should parents be able to assume the risk on behalf of their children?

3. *Standard of review: Does the medium matter?* The city ordinance is clearly content-based; thus strict scrutiny is appropriate. However, in *Pacifica*, the Court took into account how broadcast technologies allow for easier access to indecent materials. (Thus the Court applied a diluted form of strict scrutiny.) Given the comparison just made, what is the appropriate standard of review for cable television?

4. *Better filter techniques?* In contrast to broadcast television, how might indecent content be blocked on cable television, with only the parents (properly authenticated) able to remove the block? In this way, is cable TV more like telephony or broadcast TV? Is there something intrinsic about the architecture of these technologies that mandates this difference? Does analog versus digital TV matter? Or is this all just historical accident? And how might historical accidents respond to swiftly-changing technologies?

5. *Federal statutes and regulation. Cruz* addressed a *constitutional* challenge to a local franchising authority's attempt to ban indecency. What is the federal statutory and regulatory regime? As always, obscenity is proscribed.

> 47 U.S.C. § 559. Obscene programming
>
> Whoever transmits over any cable system any matter which is obscene or otherwise unprotected by the Constitution of the United States shall be fined under Title 18 or imprisoned not more than 2 years, or both.
>
> 18 U.S.C. § 1468. Distributing obscene material by cable or subscription television
>
> (a) Whoever knowingly utters any obscene language or distributes any obscene matter by means of cable television or subscription services on television, shall be punished by imprisonment for not more than 2 years or by a fine in accordance with this title, or both.

As for indecency, the indecency statute we studied earlier, 18 U.S.C. § 1464, requires use of "radio communication" and does not apply to cable television. (More generally, subscription services, which require the end-user to pay for video, is not considered to be "broadcasting" within the FCC's regulations.[*]) This means that the time channeling regulations promulgated under § 1464 also do not apply to cable television.

There are, however, specific statutes and implementing regulations that target indecency on cable television. For example, the 1984 Cable Act promoted end-user filtering by requiring that the cable operator make available a lock-box upon subscriber request and to be notified of any free "give aways" of premium channels that might have adult content.

---

[*] *See generally Subscription Video*, R&O, 2 FCC Rcd. 1001 (1987).

> 47 U.S.C. § 544(d) Cable service unprotected by Constitution; blockage of premium channel upon request
>
> (1) Nothing in this subchapter shall be construed as prohibiting a franchising authority and a cable operator from specifying, in a franchise or renewal thereof, that certain cable services shall not be provided or shall be provided subject to conditions, if such cable services are obscene or are otherwise unprotected by the Constitution of the United States.
>
> (2) In order to restrict the viewing of of of [sic] programming which is obscene or indecent, upon the request of a subscriber, a cable operator shall provide (by sale or lease) a device by which the subscriber can prohibit viewing of a particular cable service during periods selected by that subscriber.
>
> (3)(A) If a cable operator provides a premium channel without charge to cable subscribers who do not subscribe to such premium channel, the cable operator shall, not later than 30 days before such premium channel is provided without charge—
>
> > (i) notify all cable subscribers that the cable operator plans to provide a premium channel without charge;
> >
> > (ii) notify all cable subscribers when the cable operator plans to offer a premium channel without charge;
> >
> > (iii) notify all cable subscribers that they have a right to request that the channel carrying the premium channel be blocked; and
> >
> > (iv) block the channel carrying the premium channel upon the request of a subscriber.

Other provisions require filtering (scrambling) of adult channels by the cable operator.[*]

UNITED STATES v. PLAYBOY ENTERTAINMENT GROUP

529 U.S. 803 (2000)

Justice KENNEDY delivered the opinion of the Court.[†]

This case presents a challenge to § 505 of the Telecommunications Act of 1996, 47 U.S.C. § 561. Section 505 requires cable television operators who provide channels "primarily dedicated to sexually-oriented programming" either to "fully scramble or otherwise fully block" those channels or to limit their transmission to hours when children are unlikely to be viewing, set by administrative regulation as the time between 10 p.m. and 6 a.m. 47 U.S.C. § 561(a); 47 CFR § 76.227.

I

Cable operators transmit Playboy's signal, like other premium channel signals, in scrambled form. . . . The statute was enacted because not all scrambling technology is perfect. Analog cable television systems may use either

---

[*] *See* 47 U.S.C. § 560 (scrambling of cable channels for nonsubscribers), § 561 (scrambling of sexually explicit adult video service programming).

[†] This opinion was joined by Justices Stevens, Souter, Thomas, and Ginsburg. The concurring opinions by Justice Stevens and Justice Thomas are omitted. The dissenting opinion of Justice Scalia is omitted. —ED.

"RF" or "baseband" scrambling systems, which may not prevent signal bleed, so discernible pictures may appear from time to time on the scrambled screen. Furthermore, the listener might hear the audio portion of the program.

These imperfections are not inevitable.... Digital technology may one day provide another solution, as it presents no [signal] bleed problem at all.

When [§ 505, codified at 47 U.S.C. § 561] became operative, most cable operators had "no practical choice but to curtail [the targeted] programming during the [regulated] sixteen hours or risk the penalties imposed ... if any audio or video signal bleed occurred during [those] times." 30 F. Supp. 2d at 711. The majority of operators—"in one survey, 69%"—complied with § 505 by time channeling the targeted programmers. *Ibid.* Since "30 to 50% of all adult programming is viewed by households prior to 10 p.m.," the result was a significant restriction of communication, with a corresponding reduction in Playboy's revenues. *Ibid.*

II

This is the essence of content-based regulation.

Not only does § 505 single out particular programming content for regulation ... [o]ne sponsor of the measure even identified appellee by name.

Since § 505 is a content-based speech restriction, it can stand only if it satisfies strict scrutiny. *Sable* (1989). If a statute regulates speech based on its content, it must be narrowly tailored to promote a compelling Government interest. If a less restrictive alternative would serve the Government's purpose, the legislature must use that alternative.

Cable television, like broadcast media, presents unique problems, which inform our assessment of the interests at stake, and which may justify restrictions that would be unacceptable in other contexts. *See Denver Area* (1996); *Pacifica* (1978). No one suggests the Government must be indifferent to unwanted, indecent speech that comes into the home without parental consent.... [But,] even where speech is indecent and enters the home, the objective of shielding children does not suffice to support a blanket ban if the protection can be accomplished by a less restrictive alternative.

There is, moreover, a key difference between cable television and the broadcasting media, which is the point on which this case turns: Cable systems have the capacity to block unwanted channels on a household-by-household basis. [T]argeted blocking enables the Government to support parental authority without affecting the First Amendment interests of speakers and willing listeners—listeners for whom, if the speech is unpopular or indecent, the privacy of their own homes may be the optimal place of receipt. Simply put, targeted blocking is less restrictive than banning, and the Government cannot ban speech if targeted blocking is a feasible and effective means of furthering its compelling interests.

III

The District Court concluded that a less restrictive alternative is available: § 504 [codified at 47 U.S.C. § 560], with adequate publicity.

[I]t is the Government's obligation to prove that the alternative will be ineffective.... The Government has not met that burden here. In support of its position, the Government cites empirical evidence showing that § 504... generated few requests for household-by-household blocking. Between March 1996 and May 1997... fewer than 0.5% of cable subscribers requested full blocking during that time. The uncomfortable fact is that § 504 was the sole blocking regulation in effect for over a year; and the public greeted it with a collective yawn.

[T]he District Court explored three explanations for the lack of individual blocking requests. First, individual blocking might not be an effective alternative, due to technological or other limitations. Second, although an adequately advertised blocking provision might have been effective, § 504 as written did not require sufficient notice to make it so. Third, the actual signal bleed problem might be far less of a concern than the Government at first had supposed.

To sustain its statute, the Government was required to show that the first was the right answer. According to the District Court, however, the first and third possibilities were "equally consistent" with the record before it.... The case, then, was at best a draw. Unless the District Court's findings are clearly erroneous, the tie goes to free expression.

The District Court began with the problem of signal bleed itself, concluding "the Government has not convinced us that [signal bleed] is a pervasive problem." ... There is little hard evidence of how widespread or how serious the problem of signal bleed is. Indeed, there is no proof as to how likely any child is to view a discernible explicit image, and no proof of the duration of the bleed or the quality of the pictures or sound.... Although the parties have taken the additional step of lodging with the Court an assortment of videotapes, some of which show quite explicit bleeding and some of which show television static or snow, there is no attempt at explanation or context; there is no discussion, for instance, of the extent to which any particular tape is representative of what appears on screens nationwide.

Accordingly, the District Court... made this finding: "The Government presented no evidence on the number of households actually exposed to signal bleed and thus has not quantified the actual extent of the problem of signal bleed." The finding is not clearly erroneous; indeed it is all but required.

In addition, market-based solutions such as programmable televisions, VCR's, and mapping systems (which display a blue screen when tuned to a scrambled signal) may eliminate signal bleed at the consumer end of the cable. . . . Without some sort of field survey, it is impossible to know how widespread the problem in fact is, and the only indicator in the record is a handful of complaints. If the number of children transfixed by even flickering pornographic television images in fact reached into the millions we, like the District Court, would have expected to be directed to more than a handful of complaints.

Nor did the District Court err in its second conclusion. The Government also failed to prove § 504 with adequate notice would be an ineffective alternative to § 505. . . . There is no evidence that a well-promoted voluntary blocking provision would not be capable at least of informing parents about signal bleed (if they are not yet aware of it) and about their rights to have the bleed blocked (if they consider it a problem and have not yet controlled it themselves).

It is no response that voluntary blocking requires a consumer to take action, or may be inconvenient, or may not go perfectly every time. A court should not assume a plausible, less restrictive alternative would be ineffective; and a court should not presume parents, given full information, will fail to act. If unresponsive operators are a concern, moreover, a notice statute could give cable operators ample incentive, through fines or other penalties for noncompliance, to respond to blocking requests in prompt and efficient fashion.

[U]nder a voluntary blocking regime, even with adequate notice, some children will be exposed to signal bleed; and . . . a graphic image could have a negative impact on a young child. It must be remembered, however, that children will be exposed to signal bleed under time channeling as well. Time channeling, unlike blocking, does not eliminate signal bleed around the clock. Just as adolescents may be unsupervised outside of their own households, it is hardly unknown for them to be unsupervised in front of the television set after 10 p.m. The record is silent as to the comparative effectiveness of the two alternatives. . . .

Basic speech principles are at stake in this case. . . . We cannot be influenced . . . by the perception that the regulation in question is not a major one because the speech is not very important. The history of the law of free expression is one of vindication in cases involving speech that many citizens may find shabby, offensive, or even ugly. It follows that all content-based restrictions on speech must give us more than a moment's pause. If television broadcasts can expose children to the real risk of harmful exposure to indecent materials, even in their own home and without parental consent, there is a problem the Government can address. It must do so, however, in a way consistent with First Amendment principles. Here the Government has not met the burden the First Amendment imposes.

Justice BREYER, with whom THE CHIEF JUSTICE, Justice O'CONNOR, and Justice SCALIA join, dissenting.

I

At the outset, I would describe the statutory scheme somewhat differently than does the majority.

The statute ... creat[es] two "default rules" applicable unless the subscriber decides otherwise. Section 504 requires a cable operator to "fully scramble" any channel (whether or not it broadcasts adult programming) if a subscriber asks not to receive it. Section 505 requires a cable operator to "fully scramble" every adult channel unless a subscriber asks to receive it.... [E]ach law creates a different "default" assumption about silent subscribers. Section 504 assumes a silent subscriber wants to see the ordinary (non adult) channels that the cable operator includes in the paid-for bundle sent into the home. Section 505 assumes that a silent subscriber does not want to receive adult channels. Consequently, a subscriber wishing to view an adult channel must "opt in," and specifically request that channel. A subscriber wishing not to view any other channel (sent into the home) must "opt out."

II

The majority first concludes that the Government failed to prove the seriousness of the problem.... This claim is flat-out wrong. For one thing, the parties concede that basic RF scrambling does not scramble the audio portion of the program. For another, Playboy itself conducted a survey of cable operators who were asked: "Is your system in full compliance with Section 505 (no discernible audio or video bleed)?" To this question, 75% of cable operators answered "no." Further, the Government's expert ... found 29 million children are potentially exposed to audio and video bleed from adult programming. Even discounting by 25% for systems that might be considered in full compliance, this left 22 million children in homes with faulty scrambling systems.

I would add to this empirical evidence the majority's own statement that "most cable operators had 'no practical choice but to curtail' " adult programming by switching to nighttime only transmission of adult channels. If signal bleed is not a significant empirical problem, then why, in light of the cost of its cure, must so many cable operators switch to night time hours?

If, as the majority suggests, the signal bleed problem is not significant, then there is also no significant burden on speech created by § 505. The majority cannot have this evidence both ways.

III

The majority's second claim—that the Government failed to demonstrate the absence of a "less restrictive alternative"—presents a closer question. The specific question is whether § 504's "opt-out" amounts to a "less restrictive," but *similarly* practical and *effective*, way to accomplish § 505's child-protecting objective.

The words I have just emphasized, "similarly" and "effective," are critical.

These words imply a degree of leeway, however small, for the legislature when it chooses among possible alternatives in light of predicted comparative effects. Without some such empirical leeway, the undoubted ability of lawyers and judges to imagine some kind of slightly less drastic or restrictive an approach would make it impossible to write laws that deal with the harm that called the statute into being.

Unlike the majority, I believe the record makes clear that § 504's opt-out is not a similarly effective alternative. . . . Section 505 does more.

As the majority observes, during the 14 months the Government was enjoined from enforcing § 505, "fewer than 0.5% of cable subscribers requested full blocking" under § 504. The majority describes this public reaction as "a collective yawn," adding that the Government failed to prove that the "yawn" reflected anything other than the lack of a serious signal bleed problem or a lack of notice which better information about § 504 might cure. The record excludes the first possibility—at least in respect to exposure, as discussed above. And I doubt that the public . . . would "yawn" when the exposure in question concerns young children. . . .

Neither is the record neutral in respect to the curative power of better notice. Section 504's opt-out right works only when parents (1) become aware of their § 504 rights, (2) discover that their children are watching sexually-explicit signal "bleed," (3) reach their cable operator and ask that it block the sending of its signal to their home, (4) await installation of an individual blocking device, and, perhaps (5) (where the block fails or the channel number changes) make a new request. Better notice of § 504 rights does little to help parents discover their children's viewing habits (step two). And it does nothing at all in respect to steps three through five. Yet the record contains considerable evidence that those problems matter, i.e., evidence of endlessly delayed phone call responses, faulty installations, blocking failures, and other mishaps, leaving those steps as significant § 504 obstacles. *See, e.g.,* Deposition of J. Cavalier in Civ. Action No. 96-94, pp. 17–18 (D. Del., Dec. 5, 1997) ("It's like calling any utilities; you sit there, and you wait and wait on the phone. . . . [It took] three weeks, numerous phone calls. . . . Every time I call Cox Cable. . . . I get different stories"); Telephonic Deposition of M. Bennett, at 10–11 (D. Del., Dec. 9, 1997) ("After two [failed installations,] no, I don't recall calling them again. I just said well, I guess this is something I'm going to have to live with").

Further, the District Court's actual plan for "better notice"—the only plan that makes concrete the majority's "better notice" requirement—is fraught with difficulties. The District Court ordered Playboy to insist that cable operators place notice of § 504 "inserts in monthly billing statements, barker channels . . . and on-air advertising." But how can one say that placing one more insert in a monthly billing statement stuffed with others, or calling additional attention to adult channels through a "notice" on "barker" channels, will make more than a small difference? More importantly, why would doing so not interfere to some extent with the cable operators' own freedom to decide what to broadcast?

All these considerations show that § 504's opt-out, even with the Court's plan for "better notice," is not similarly effective in achieving the legitimate goals that the statute was enacted to serve.

IV

Congress has taken seriously the importance of maintaining adult access to the sexually explicit channels here at issue. It has tailored the restrictions to minimize their impact upon adults while offering parents help in keeping unwanted transmissions from their children. By finding "adequate alternatives" where there are none, the Court reduces Congress' protective power to the vanishing point. That is not what the First Amendment demands. I respectfully dissent.

NOTES & QUESTIONS

1. *Standard of review.* We start again with the standard of review. We know that this is content-based regulation, but is there something special about cable television? For example, do the *Pacifica* factors warp the standard of review for cable? Four years before *Playboy,* in *Denver Area Educational Telecommunications Consortium v. FCC* (1996), the Court per Justice Breyer struck down some cable indecency regulations[*] but declined to answer cleanly

whether *Pacifica* applied.* Does Justice Kennedy provide a more definitive answer in *Playboy*?

2. *Can't stop the flow.*

a. *Is cable like broadcast?* Various opinions have distinguished cable from broadcast television on the grounds that cable TV provides greater control over the types of content displayed. Now we see that the blocking that exists on cable (in the form of signal scrambling) may not be so effective. Should this make us rethink the analysis in *Cruz v. Ferre* (11th Cir. 1985)?

b. *Analog versus digital.* The court is confident that digital cable will not have any signal bleed problem (in contrast to analog cable television with RF scrambling). Why would this be so?

3. *Empirical proof.* The Court emphasizes that Congress had not provided enough evidence of a genuine problem with signal bleed. How much proof is necessary, especially if we are concerned about the moral impact on our children? (Compare what the D.C. Circuit required in *ACT III* or what Justice Scalia wrote about fleeting expletives in *Fox v. FCC*.) Moreover, as Justice Breyer asks in his dissent, if there were no problem, why did a majority of cable operators decide to comply with the time-channeling regulations? Is the majority trying to have it both ways? In response, the majority wrote:

> Once § 505 [codified as 47 U.S.C. § 561] went into effect, of course, a significant percentage of cable operators felt it necessary to time channel their sexually explicit programmers. This is an indication that scrambling technology is not yet perfected. That is not to say, however, that scrambling is completely ineffective. . . . A rational cable operator, faced with the possibility of sanctions for intermittent bleeding, could well choose to time channel even if the bleeding is too momentary to pose any concern to most households. To affirm that the Government failed to prove the existence of a problem, while at the same time observing that the statute imposes a severe burden on speech, is consistent with the analysis our cases require.†

Are you satisfied?

4. *Filter alternatives.* A central dispute between the majority and Justice Breyer in his dissent is whether § 504 of the Telecommunications Act of 1996,

---

* 518 U.S. 727 (1996). At issue were requirements that cable operators must segregate adult content transmitted by third-parties (via both commercial leased access and Public, Educational, and Governmental channels) and also block that channel unless subscribers opted-in. A majority struck down the segregate-and-block provision as unconstitutional. For further discussion of *Denver Area*, see *infra* p.556.

* *See Denver Area*, 518 U.S. at 755 ("Nor need we here determine whether, or the extent to which, *Pacifica* does, or does not, impose some lesser standard of review where indecent speech is at issue.").

† 529 U.S. at 821.

codified at 47 U.S.C. § 560, is a less restrictive alternative that achieves the government's goals similarly well. Who has the better argument?

5. *Default rules.* In his dissent, Justice Breyer describes the two statutory provisions at issue as different default rules. Make sure you understand the vocabulary.

   a. *Related terms.* What is the relationship between default rules and the concepts of "opting in" or "opting out"? How do these concepts compare to voluntary and reverse blocking, which we saw with dial-a-porn?

   b. *"Sticky" versus "Teflon" rules.* An important aspect of default rules is their "stickiness." To grasp this idea, consider airline meals. Suppose that the meal that is served always features some form of meat. If this is only a default rule, then a customer should be able to "flip out" of the default and choose a vegetarian dish. However, it may be very difficult to make that change. For example, you may not be aware that there are vegetarian options, or the procedures to select a vegetarian dish may be elaborate, requiring you to stay on hold listening to annoying elevator music for hours or provide certification from a medical professional (health vegetarian) or an affidavit (ethical vegetarian). Because it is such a hassle to flip out of the default, the default rule is "sticky," and passengers will end up eating meat (or nothing at all), even if many of them prefer a vegetarian meal. By contrast, one could imagine procedures that make it very easy to flip out of the default rule. If you want a vegetarian dish, simply mention it when you check in at the gate—no questions asked, no 24-hour advance reservation necessary. In this case, the default rule is more like "Teflon," and passengers will get what they want. According to Justice Breyer, is § 504 [a.k.a. 47 U.S.C. § 560] a "sticky" or a "Teflon" default rule? How does this affect the constitutional analysis?

6. *A technological conundrum.* The majority thinks that 47 U.S.C. § 560 is more narrowly tailored than § 561. But if cable operators cannot fully scramble adult channels per § 561, how are they going to do any better when a subscriber requests scrambling under § 560?

D. INTERNET

We now turn to the newest and most powerful communications medium ever created: the internet. Back in 1996, the fear of indecency prompted Congress to pass the Communications Decency Act (CDA), the first federal statute regulating the internet. However, in the first Supreme Court pronouncement on this new medium, the CDA was struck down as unconstitutional. What follows is a necessarily long excerpt from the first Supreme Court opinion to ever discuss the internet.

RENO V. ACLU
521 U.S. 844 (1997)

Justice STEVENS delivered the opinion of the Court.[*]

I

The Internet

The Internet is "a unique and wholly new medium of worldwide human communication."[†]

The best known category of communication over the Internet is the World Wide Web. . . .

The Web is thus comparable, from the readers' viewpoint, to both a vast library including millions of readily available and indexed publications and a sprawling mall offering goods and services.

From the publishers' point of view, it constitutes a vast platform from which to address and hear from a world-wide audience of millions of readers, viewers, researchers, and buyers. Any person or organization with a computer connected to the Internet can "publish" information. "No single organization controls any membership in the Web, nor is there any centralized point from which individual Web sites or services can be blocked from the Web."

Sexually Explicit Material

Sexually explicit material on the Internet . . . "extends from the modestly titillating to the hardest-core." These files . . . may be accessed either deliberately or unintentionally during the course of an imprecise search. "Once a provider posts its content on the Internet, it cannot prevent that content from entering any community."

Though such material is widely available, users seldom encounter such content accidentally. . . . Unlike communications received by radio or television, "the receipt of information on the Internet requires a series of affirmative steps more deliberate and directed than merely turning a dial. A child requires some sophistication and some ability to read to retrieve material and thereby to use the Internet unattended."

---

[*] The opinion was joined by Justices Scalia, Kennedy, Souter, Thomas, Ginsburg, and Breyer. —ED.

[†] The quotations describing the Internet come from the district court's findings of fact. —ED.

Systems have been developed to help parents control the material that may be available on a home computer with Internet access.... "Although parental control software currently can screen for certain suggestive words or for known sexually explicit sites, it cannot now screen for sexually explicit images." Nevertheless, the evidence indicates that "a reasonably effective method by which parents can prevent their children from accessing sexually explicit and other material which parents may believe is inappropriate for their children will soon be available."

Age Verification

The District Court categorically determined that there "is no effective way to determine the identity or the age of a user who is accessing material through e-mail, mail exploders, newsgroups or chat rooms."

Technology exists by which an operator of a Web site may condition access on the verification of requested information such as a credit card number or an adult password. Credit card verification is only feasible, however, either in connection with a commercial transaction in which the card is used, or by payment to a verification agency. Using credit card possession as a surrogate for proof of age would impose costs on non-commercial Web sites that would require many of them to shut down.... Moreover, the imposition of such a requirement "would completely bar adults who do not have a credit card...."

Commercial pornographic sites that charge their users for access have assigned them passwords as a method of age verification. The record does not contain any evidence concerning the reliability of these technologies. Even if passwords are effective for commercial purveyors of indecent material, the District Court found that an adult password requirement would impose significant burdens on noncommercial sites....

II

The Telecommunications Act of 1996 was an unusually important legislative enactment.... The Act includes seven Titles, six of which are the product of extensive committee hearings and the subject of discussion in Reports prepared by Committees of the Senate and the House of Representatives. By contrast, Title V—known as the "Communications Decency Act of 1996" (CDA)—contains provisions that were either added in executive committee after the hearings were concluded or as amendments offered during floor debate on the legislation. An amendment offered in the Senate was the source of the two statutory provisions challenged in this case. They are informally described as the "indecent transmission" provision and the "patently offensive display" provision.

The first, 47 U.S.C.A. § 223(a), prohibits the knowing transmission of obscene or indecent messages to any recipient under 18 years of age. It provides in pertinent part:

"(a) Whoever—

"(1) in interstate or foreign communications—

"(B) by means of a telecommunications device knowingly—

"(i) makes, creates, or solicits, and

"(ii) initiates the transmission of,

"any comment, request, suggestion, proposal, image, or other communication which is obscene or indecent, knowing that the recipient of the communication is under 18 years of age, regardless of whether the maker of such communication placed the call or initiated the communication;

"(2) knowingly permits any telecommunications facility under his control to be used for any activity prohibited by paragraph (1) with the intent that it be used for such activity,

"shall be fined under Title 18, or imprisoned not more than two years, or both."

The second provision, § 223(d), prohibits the knowing sending or displaying of patently offensive messages in a manner that is available to a person under 18 years of age. It provides:

"(d) Whoever—

"(1) in interstate or foreign communications knowingly—

"(A) uses an interactive computer service to send to a specific person or persons under 18 years of age, or

"(B) uses any interactive computer service to display in a manner available to a person under 18 years of age,

"any comment, request, suggestion, proposal, image, or other communication that, in context, depicts or describes, in terms patently offensive as measured by contemporary community standards, sexual or excretory activities or organs, regardless of whether the user of such service placed the call or initiated the communication; or

"(2) knowingly permits any telecommunications facility under such person's control to be used for an activity prohibited by paragraph (1) with the intent that it be used for such activity,

"shall be fined under Title 18, or imprisoned not more than two years, or both."

The breadth of these prohibitions is qualified by two affirmative defenses. One covers those who take "good faith, reasonable, effective, and appropriate actions" to restrict access by minors to the prohibited communications. § 223(e)(5)(A). The other covers those who restrict access to covered material by requiring certain designated forms of age proof, such as a verified credit card or an adult identification number or code. § 223(e)(5)(B).

IV

In arguing for reversal, the Government contends that the CDA is plainly constitutional under . . . our prior decisions: (1) *Ginsberg v. New York* (1968) [and] (2) *FCC v. Pacifica Foundation* (1978) . . . . A close look at these cases, however, raises—rather than relieves—doubts concerning the constitutionality of the CDA.

In *Ginsberg*, we upheld the constitutionality of a New York statute that prohibited selling to minors under 17 years of age material that was considered obscene as to them even if not obscene as to adults. [W]e relied not only on the State's independent interest in the well-being of its youth, but also on our consistent recognition of the principle that "the parents' claim to authority in their own household to direct the rearing of their children is basic in the structure of our society."

In four important respects, the statute upheld in *Ginsberg* was narrower than the CDA. First, we noted in *Ginsberg* that "the prohibition against sales to minors does not bar parents who so desire from purchasing the magazines for their children." Under the CDA, by contrast, neither the parents' consent—nor even their participation—in the communication would avoid the application of the statute. Second, the New York statute applied only to commercial transactions, whereas the CDA contains no such limitation. Third, the New York statute cabined its definition of material that is harmful to minors with the requirement that it be "utterly without redeeming social importance for minors." The CDA fails to provide us with any definition of the term "indecent" as used in § 223(a)(1) and, importantly, omits any requirement that the "patently offensive" material covered by § 223(d) lack serious literary, artistic, political, or scientific value. Fourth, the New York statute defined a minor as a person under the age of 17, whereas the CDA, in applying to all those under 18 years, includes an additional year of those nearest majority.

[T]here are [also] significant differences between the order upheld in *Pacifica* and the CDA. First, the order in *Pacifica*, issued by an agency that had been regulating radio stations for decades, targeted a specific broadcast that represented a rather dramatic departure from traditional program content in order to designate when—rather than whether—it would be permissible to air such a program in that particular medium. The CDA's broad categorical prohibitions are not limited to particular times and are not dependent on any evaluation by an agency familiar with the unique characteristics of the Internet. Second, unlike the CDA, the Commission's declaratory order was not punitive; we expressly refused to decide whether the indecent broadcast "would justify a criminal prosecution." Finally, the Commission's order applied to a medium which as a matter of history had "received the most limited First Amendment protection," in large part because warnings could not adequately protect the listener from unexpected program content. The Internet, however, has no comparable history. Moreover, the District Court found that the risk of encountering indecent material by accident is remote because a series of affirmative steps is required to access specific material.

These precedents . . . do not require us to uphold the CDA and are fully consistent with the application of the most stringent review of its provisions.

V

[S]ome of our cases have recognized special justifications for regulation of the broadcast media that are not applicable to other speakers, *see Red Lion* (1969); *Pacifica* (1978). In these cases, the Court relied on the history of extensive government regulation of the broadcast medium, *Red Lion*; the scarcity of available frequencies at its inception, *Turner Broadcasting System, Inc. v. FCC* (1994); and its "invasive" nature, *Sable* (1989).

Those factors are not present in cyberspace. Neither before nor after the enactment of the CDA have the vast democratic fora of the Internet been subject to the type of government supervision and regulation that has attended the broadcast industry.[33] Moreover, the Internet is not as "invasive" as radio or television. The District Court specifically found that "[c]ommunications over the Internet do not 'invade' an individual's home or appear on one's computer screen unbidden. Users seldom encounter content 'by accident.' " It also found that "[a]lmost all sexually explicit images are preceded by warnings as to the content. . . ."

We distinguished *Pacifica* in *Sable* on just this basis. . . . We explained that "the dial-it medium requires the listener to take affirmative steps to receive the communication." "Placing a telephone call," we continued, "is not the same as turning on a radio and being taken by surprise by an indecent message."

Finally, unlike the conditions that prevailed when Congress first authorized regulation of the broadcast spectrum, the Internet can hardly be considered a "scarce" expressive commodity. It provides relatively unlimited, low-cost capacity for communication of all kinds. . . . Through the use of chat rooms, any person with a phone line can become a town crier with a voice that resonates farther than it could from any soapbox. Through the use of Web pages, mail exploders, and newsgroups, the same individual can become a pamphleteer. As the District Court found, "the content on the Internet is as diverse as human thought." We agree with its conclusion that our cases provide no basis for

---

[33] When *Pacifica* was decided, given that radio stations were allowed to operate only pursuant to federal license, and that Congress had enacted legislation prohibiting licensees from broadcasting indecent speech, there was a risk that members of the radio audience might infer some sort of official or societal approval of whatever was heard over the radio. No such risk attends messages received through the Internet, which is not supervised by any federal agency.

qualifying the level of First Amendment scrutiny that should be applied to this medium.

VI

[T]he many ambiguities concerning the scope of its coverage render it problematic for purposes of the First Amendment. For instance, each of the two parts of the CDA uses a different linguistic form. The first uses the word "indecent," 47 U.S.C.A. § 223(a), while the second speaks of material that "in context, depicts or describes, in terms patently offensive as measured by contemporary community standards, sexual or excretory activities or organs," § 223(d). Given the absence of a definition of either term,[35] this difference in language will provoke uncertainty . . . about how the two standards relate to each other and just what they mean.[37] Could a speaker confidently assume that a serious discussion about birth control practices, homosexuality, the First Amendment issues raised by the Appendix to our *Pacifica* opinion, or the consequences of prison rape would not violate the CDA? This uncertainty undermines the likelihood that the CDA has been carefully tailored. . . .

The Government argues that the statute is no more vague than the obscenity standard this Court established in Miller v. California (1973). . . . [W]e set forth in *Miller* the test for obscenity that controls to this day:

> "(a) whether the average person, applying contemporary community standards would find that the work, taken as a whole, appeals to the prurient interest; (b) whether the work depicts or describes, in a patently offensive way, sexual conduct specifically defined by the applicable state law; and (c) whether the work, taken as a whole, lacks serious literary, artistic, political, or scientific value."

Because the CDA's "patently offensive" standard (and, we assume *arguendo*, its synonymous "indecent" standard) is one part of the three-prong *Miller* test, the Government reasons, it cannot be unconstitutionally vague.

The Government's assertion is incorrect as a matter of fact. The second prong of the *Miller* test—the purportedly analogous standard—contains a critical requirement that is omitted from the CDA: that the proscribed material be "specifically defined by the applicable state law." This requirement reduces

---

[35] "Indecent" does not benefit from any textual embellishment at all. "Patently offensive" is qualified only to the extent that it involves "sexual or excretory activities or organs" taken "in context" and "measured by contemporary community standards."

[37] The statute does not indicate whether the "patently offensive" and "indecent" determinations should be made with respect to minors or the population as a whole. The Government asserts that the appropriate standard is "what is suitable material for minors." But the Conferees expressly rejected amendments that would have imposed such a "harmful to minors" standard. The Conferees also rejected amendments that would have limited the proscribed materials to those lacking redeeming value.

the vagueness inherent in the open-ended term "patently offensive" as used in the CDA. Moreover, the *Miller* definition is limited to "sexual conduct," whereas the CDA extends also to include (1) "excretory activities" as well as (2) "organs" of both a sexual and excretory nature.

The Government's reasoning is also flawed. Just because a definition including three limitations is not vague, it does not follow that one of those limitations, standing by itself, is not vague. Each of *Miller*'s additional two prongs—(1) that, taken as a whole, the material appeal to the "prurient" interest, and (2) that it "lac[k] serious literary, artistic, political, or scientific value"—critically limits the uncertain sweep of the obscenity definition. The second requirement is particularly important because, unlike the "patently offensive" and "prurient interest" criteria, it is not judged by contemporary community standards. This "societal value" requirement, absent in the CDA, allows appellate courts to impose some limitations and regularity on the definition by setting, as a matter of law, a national floor for socially redeeming value.

In contrast to *Miller* . . . the CDA thus presents a greater threat of censoring speech that, in fact, falls outside the statute's scope. Given the vague contours of the coverage of the statute, it unquestionably silences some speakers whose messages would be entitled to constitutional protection.

VII

We are persuaded that the CDA lacks the precision that the First Amendment requires when a statute regulates the content of speech. In order to deny minors access to potentially harmful speech, the CDA effectively suppresses a large amount of speech that adults have a constitutional right to receive and to address to one another. That burden on adult speech is unacceptable if less restrictive alternatives would be at least as effective in achieving the legitimate purpose that the statute was enacted to serve.

The District Court was correct to conclude that the CDA effectively resembles the ban on "dial-a-porn" invalidated in *Sable*.

In arguing that the CDA does not so diminish adult communication, the Government relies on the incorrect factual premise that prohibiting a transmission whenever it is known that one of its recipients is a minor would not interfere with adult-to-adult communication. The findings of the District Court make clear that this premise is untenable.

The District Court found that at the time of trial existing technology did not include any effective method for a sender to prevent minors from obtaining access to its communications on the Internet without also denying access to adults. The Court found no effective way to determine the age of a user who is accessing material through e-mail, mail exploders, newsgroups, or chat rooms.

The breadth of the CDA's coverage is wholly unprecedented. Unlike the regulations upheld in *Ginsberg* and *Pacifica*, the scope of the CDA is not limited to commercial speech or commercial entities. Its open-ended prohibitions embrace all nonprofit entities and individuals posting indecent messages or displaying them on their own computers in the presence of minors. The general, undefined terms "indecent" and "patently offensive" cover large amounts of nonpornographic material with serious educational or other value. Moreover, the "community standards" criterion as applied to the Internet means that any communication available to a nation-wide audience will be judged by the standards of the community most likely to be offended by the message. The regulated subject matter includes any of the seven "dirty words" used in the *Pacifica* monologue . . . and arguably the card catalogue of the Carnegie Library.

Under the CDA, a parent allowing her 17-year-old to use the family computer to obtain information on the Internet that she, in her parental judgment, deems appropriate could face a lengthy prison term. Similarly, a parent who sent his 17-year-old college freshman information on birth control via e-mail could be incarcerated even though neither he, his child, nor anyone in their home community, found the material "indecent" or "patently offensive," if the college town's community thought otherwise.

The breadth of this content-based restriction of speech imposes an especially heavy burden on the Government to explain why a less restrictive provision would not be as effective as the CDA. It has not done so. The arguments in this Court have referred to possible alternatives such as requiring that indecent material be "tagged" in a way that facilitates parental control of material coming into their homes, making exceptions for messages with artistic or educational value, providing some tolerance for parental choice, and regulating some portions of the Internet—such as commercial web sites—differently than others, such as chat rooms. Particularly in the light of the absence of any detailed findings by the Congress, or even hearings addressing the special problems of the CDA, we are persuaded that the CDA is not narrowly tailored if that requirement has any meaning at all.

VIII

The Government . . . asserts that the "knowledge" requirement of both §§ 223(a) and (d), especially when coupled with the "specific child" element found in § 223(d), saves the CDA from overbreadth. Because both sections prohibit the dissemination of indecent messages only to persons known to be under 18, the Government argues, it does not require transmitters to "refrain from communicating indecent material to adults; they need only refrain from disseminating such materials to persons they know to be under 18."

This argument ignores the fact that most Internet fora—including chat rooms, newsgroups, mail exploders, and the Web—are open to all comers. . . . Even the strongest reading of the "specific person" requirement of § 223(d) cannot save the statute. It would confer broad powers of censorship, in the form of a "heckler's veto," upon any opponent of indecent speech who might simply log on and inform the would-be discoursers that his 17-year-old child—a "specific person . . . under 18 years of age"—would be present.

IX

The Government's three remaining arguments focus on the defenses provided in § 223(e)(5). First, relying on the "good faith, reasonable, effective, and appropriate actions" provision, the Government suggests that "tagging" provides a defense that saves the constitutionality of the Act. The suggestion assumes that transmitters may encode their indecent communications in a way that would indicate their contents, thus permitting recipients to block their reception with appropriate software. It is the requirement that the good faith action must be "effective" that makes this defense illusory. The Government recognizes that its proposed screening software does not currently exist. Even if it did, there is no way to know whether a potential recipient will actually block the encoded material. Without the impossible knowledge that every guardian in America is screening for the "tag," the transmitter could not reasonably rely on its action to be "effective."

For its second and third arguments concerning defenses—which we can consider together—the Government relies on the latter half of § 223(e)(5), which applies when the transmitter has restricted access by requiring use of a verified credit card or adult identification. . . . Under the findings of the District Court, however, it is not economically feasible for most noncommercial speakers to employ such verification. . . . Even with respect to the commercial pornographers that would be protected by the defense, the Government failed to adduce any evidence that these verification techniques actually preclude minors from posing as adults.

We agree with the District Court's conclusion that the CDA places an unacceptably heavy burden on protected speech, and that the defenses do not constitute the sort of "narrow tailoring" that will save an otherwise patently invalid unconstitutional provision. In *Sable*, we remarked that the speech restriction at issue there amounted to " 'burn[ing] the house to roast the pig.' " The CDA, casting a far darker shadow over free speech, threatens to torch a large segment of the Internet community.

[T]he judgment of the district court is affirmed. *It is so ordered.*

Justice O'CONNOR, with whom THE CHIEF JUSTICE joins, concurring in the judgment in part and dissenting in part.

I write separately to explain why I view the Communications Decency Act of 1996 (CDA) as little more than an attempt by Congress to create "adult zones" on the Internet.

I

Our cases make clear that a "zoning" law is valid only if adults are still able to obtain the regulated speech. . . . In Ginsberg v. New York (1968), for example, the Court sustained a New York law that barred store owners from selling pornographic magazines to minors in part because adults could still buy those magazines.

The Court in *Ginsberg* concluded that the New York law created a constitutionally adequate adult zone simply because, on its face, it denied access only to minors. The Court did not question—and therefore necessarily assumed—that an adult zone, once created, would succeed in preserving adults' access while denying minors' access to the regulated speech. Before today, there was no reason to question this assumption, for the Court has previously only considered laws that operated in the physical world, a world that with two characteristics that make it possible to create "adult zones": geography and identity. *See* Lessig, *Reading the Constitution in Cyberspace*, 45 EMORY L.J. 869, 886 (1996). A minor can see an adult dance show only if he enters an establishment that provides such entertainment. And should he attempt to do so, the minor will not be able to conceal completely his identity (or, consequently, his age). Thus, the twin characteristics of geography and identity enable the establishment's proprietor to prevent children from entering the establishment, but to let adults inside.

The electronic world is fundamentally different. Because it is no more than the interconnection of electronic pathways, cyberspace allows speakers and listeners to mask their identities. Cyberspace undeniably reflects some form of geography; chat rooms and Web sites, for example, exist at fixed "locations" on the Internet. Since users can transmit and receive messages on the Internet without revealing anything about their identities or ages, however, it is not currently possible to exclude persons from accessing certain messages on the basis of their identity.

Cyberspace differs from the physical world in another basic way: Cyberspace is malleable. Thus, it is possible to construct barriers in cyberspace and use them to screen for identity, making cyberspace more like the physical world and, consequently, more amenable to zoning laws. This transformation of cyberspace is already underway. Internet speakers (users who post material on the Internet) have begun to zone cyberspace itself through the use of "gateway" technology. Such technology requires Internet users to enter information about themselves—perhaps an adult identification number or a credit card number—before they can access certain areas of cyberspace, much like a bouncer checks a person's driver's license before admitting him to a nightclub. Internet users who access information have not attempted to zone cyberspace itself, but have tried to limit their own power to access information in cyberspace, much as a parent controls what her children watch on television by installing a lock box. This user-based zoning is accomplished through the use of screening software (such as Cyber Patrol or SurfWatch) or browsers with screening capabilities, both of which search addresses and text for keywords that are associated with "adult" sites and, if the user wishes, blocks access to such sites. The Platform for Internet Content Selection (PICS) project is designed to facilitate user-based zoning by encouraging Internet speakers to rate the content of their speech using codes recognized by all screening programs.

Despite this progress, the transformation of cyberspace is not complete. Although gateway technology has been available on the World Wide Web for some time now, it is not available to all Web speakers, and is just now becoming technologically feasible for chat rooms and USENET newsgroups, Gateway technology is not ubiquitous in cyberspace, and because without it "there is no means of age verification," cyberspace still remains largely unzoned—and unzoneable. [District court opinion.] User-based zoning is also in its infancy.

Given the present state of cyberspace, I agree with the Court that the "display" provision[, § 223(d)(1)(B),] cannot pass muster. Until gateway technology is available throughout cyberspace, and it is not in 1997, a speaker cannot be reasonably assured that the speech he displays will reach only adults because it is impossible to confine speech to an "adult zone." Thus, the only way for a speaker to avoid liability under the CDA is to refrain completely from using indecent speech.

The "indecency transmission"[, § 223(a)(1)(B),] and "specific person"[, § 223(d)(1)(A)] provisions present a closer issue, for they are not unconstitutional in all of their applications. [Justice O'Connor continued by reading these provisions as requiring the sender's actual knowledge that each recipient is a minor. Reading the statute this way, Justice O'Connor saw a clear analogy with *Ginsberg*.]

I would therefore sustain the "indecency transmission" and "specific person" provisions to the extent they apply to the transmission of Internet communications where the party initiating the communication knows that all of the recipients are minors.

NOTES & QUESTIONS

1. *Framing the problem.* Drawing upon Justice O'Connor's opinion, try to frame the problem in terms of power. The technological power of the internet increases the free flow of sexually explicit content. At the same time, the architecture of a cyberspace interaction often masks identity. In real space, it is difficult for a child to walk into an adults-only bookstore because the child is immediately identifiable as a child. But in cyberspace, because identity is not authenticated, it is difficult—although not impossible—to distinguish between an adult (who seeks to browse anonymously) and a child. The CDA is an attempt to exercise legal power in response to the harms caused by increased technological power.

2. *CDA terminology.* Since the statutory provisions at issue are complicated, make sure to develop a consistent vocabulary to talk about each of the relevant sections. The different provisions of the CDA were given names by the court, such as the "indecent transmission" provision or the "specific person" provision. These names refer to specific parts of 47 U.S.C. § 223.

- Section 223(a)(1) refers to the "indecent transmission" provision, which criminalizes the "knowing" transmission of "obscene or indecent" material to any recipient known to be under 18 years of age.

- Section 223(d) is the "patently offensive display" provision, which prohibits the "knowin[g]" sending or displaying of any material "that, in context, depicts or describes, in terms patently offensive as measured by contemporary community standards, sexual or excretory activities or organs" to a minor. The text of the statute does not require the sender of the message to *know* that the recipient is a minor.[*]

Also incorporated into the statute are affirmative defenses (or safe harbors) for those who take "good faith ... effective ... actions" to restrict access by minors to the prohibited communications, § 223(e)(5)(A), and those who restrict such access by requiring certain designated forms of age proof, such as a verified credit card or an adult identification number, § 223(e)(5)(B).

> 47 U.S.C. § 223(e). Defenses
>
> (5). It is a defense to a prosecution under subsection (a)(1)(B) or (d) of this section, or under subsection (a)(2) of this section with respect to the use of a facility for an activity under subsection (a)(1)(B) of this section that a person—

---

[*] The full text of these sections appears in the opinion itself.

CHAPTER 6: INDECENT CONTENT

> (A) has taken, in good faith, reasonable, effective, and appropriate actions under the circumstances to restrict or prevent access by minors to a communication specified in such subsections, which may involve any appropriate measures to restrict minors from such communications, including any method which is feasible under available technology; or
>
> (B) has restricted access to such communication by requiring use of a verified credit card, debit account, adult access code, or adult personal identification number.

3. *Comparison.*

a. *Potency.* How might one compare the potency of the indecent content available on the internet with that on broadcast, telephony, and cable television? Consider not only the level of media richness, such as multimedia versus audio only, but also the degree of hard-core available.

b. *Technology: channel.* Obviously, the government would like to analogize the internet to broadcast so that a diluted form of strict scrutiny would apply and *Pacifica*-like regulations will be upheld. On factors such as scarcity and a history of regulation, how does the internet compare to broadcast, according to the Court? Are you persuaded?

c. *Flow.* Recall the central justification in *Pacifica* for treating broadcast television differently from print. Broadcast somehow made indecent content flow more to unsupervised children and created the possibility of accidental exposure even to adults. How does the internet compare in terms of accessibility of indecent content? Must one "pull" such content into one's computer screen, or is indecency "pushed" into our e-mail boxes by adult e-mail spammers? Has one assumed the risk of accessing such material by inviting a computer (or tablet or smartphone) and the internet into one's home?

4. *Standard of review.* In the end, based on such comparisons, what is the appropriate standard of review for content-based regulations of the internet? Is it more like print or like broadcast? In answering this question, consider the analogies invoked by the Court in describing the internet at the beginning of the opinion.

5. *Reconciling* Sable *with* Reno. Much of the Communications Decency Act should look familiar to you. Recall the regulatory framework adopted by Congress and the FCC for dial-a-porn after *Sable.* Are there any material differences between the regime governing the telephone and this one governing the internet? If there is little difference, why should post-*Sable* dial-a-porn laws and regulations be upheld, but the CDA be struck down?

6. *Narrow tailoring.* What were some of the reasons why the Court thought the CDA was not narrowly tailored? In particular, what alternative constraint techniques could have been used? By the way, must these alternatives be exactly

as effective as the CDA, or do the offsetting benefits found in freedom of expression allow the alternatives to be almost (but not quite) as good?*

7. *Contradictions in code.* Does the *Reno* majority have two different attitudes towards the possibility that software will solve the problem? On the one hand, the Court seems to have great faith in parental control software, which, although imperfect now, will soon improve to the point that legal intervention will be unnecessary. On the other hand, the Court seems to have little faith that code can or soon will be able to authenticate age so as to distinguish between adults and children. Are these views of technology internally consistent?

8. *Justice O'Connor's "zones."* Justice O'Connor frames the policy problem and solution in terms of establishing adult "cyberzones." When the zoning technology improves sufficiently, Justice O'Connor seems to suggest that a version of the CDA will become constitutional. This opinion was written based on facts found in 1997. Has the technology changed sufficiently such that creating adult zones is now feasible? (After an initial approval in 2005, ICANN rejected a proposal to create a top level domain name .xxx for sex-related entertainment Web sites in 2007. Following an independent internal panel review of its 2007 decision, ICANN in March 2011 finally approved .xxx).[†] Do you feel comfortable with the idea that constitutional jurisprudence should change as technology advances? What would this methodology of constitutional interpretation do to the "scarcity" justification for regulating broadcast entry? How might this approach be implemented if technology changes so quickly such that cyberspace looks materially different at the time of appeal as compared to the time of trial?[‡]

9. *The dormant commerce clause.* After the federal government's attempt to regulate indecency on the internet failed, several states attempted to fill that void with state regulation. For example, the New York legislature passed N.Y. PENAL LAW § 235.21(3), and the New Mexico legislature passed N.M STAT.

---

[*] *See generally* Eugene Volokh, *Freedom of Speech, Shielding Children, and Transcending Balancing,* 1997 SUP. CT. REV. 141 (criticizing the Court for adopting an "at least as effective" standard for narrow tailoring, which avoids resolving the genuine tension between adult speech benefits and children harms and thus risks under-protecting speech).

[†] *See* http://www.icann.org/en/minutes/resolutions-18mar11-en.htm#5. An agreement between ICANN and ICM Registry, the entity that petitioned ICANN to approve .xxx, puts ICM in charge of administering the new top level domain. The agreement mandates that .xxx only host "sexually-oriented Adult Entertainment" sites. Further, ICM must ensure that these sites abide by guidelines determined by the International Foundation for Online Responsibility, a non-profit organization tasked with creating best practices for the .xxx top level domain. These best practices include measures to safeguard children and to promote content labeling and meta-tagging.

[‡] *See generally* Stuart Benjamin, *Stepping into the Same River Twice: Rapidly Changing Facts and the Appellate Process,* 78 TEX. L. REV. 269 (1999).

ANN. § 30-37-3.2(A). These laws were immediately challenged, and preliminary injunctions against their enforcement were granted and sustained.* In addition to the First Amendment concerns just addressed, the states confronted another problem: the dormant commerce clause. For example, in *Pataki* the court wrote:

> The unique nature of the Internet highlights the likelihood that a single actor might be subject to haphazard, uncoordinated, and even outright inconsistent regulation by states that the actor never intended to reach and possibly was unaware were being accessed.

> The menace of inconsistent state regulation invites analysis under the Commerce Clause of the Constitution, because that clause represented the framers' reaction to overreaching by the individual states that might jeopardize the growth of the nation—and in particular, the national infrastructure of communications and trade—as a whole.†

10. *Not "protected speech."* It is important to emphasize again what falls outside the bounds of "protected speech" and is therefore regulable without First Amendment concerns. As we have seen repeatedly, obscenity is not protected speech and is criminalized. Child pornography is not protected speech, nor is using the internet to threaten or lure minors. For example, parts of New York and New Mexico statutes that criminalized the luring of children through the internet were not challenged.‡

11. *Upgrading to CDA version 2.0: COPA.* The original CDA, version 1.0, failed to receive a "seal of approval" by the Supreme Court. The Supreme Court found too many *bugs* (bad code) that needed to be fixed before the statute could be certified as Constitution-compliant. After extensive legislative hearings, Congress came up with CDA version 2.0, the Child Online Protection Act (COPA). Please read 47 U.S.C. § 231 in the Statutory Appendix now (it's too long to excerpt here). Here are "bullet points" of important upgrades. Try to fill in the details of each upgrade and decide whether it is a constitutional improvement:

- World Wide Web only
- Commercial only
- New and improved definition of "minor"

---

* *See* American Libraries Association v. Pataki, 969 F. Supp. 160 (S.D.N.Y. 1997); ACLU v. Johnson, 194 F.3d 1149 (10th Cir. 1999).

† 969 F. Supp. 160 at 169.

‡ *See* N.Y. PENAL LAW § 235.21(2); N.M. STAT. ANN. § 30-37-3.2(B). "B. Child luring consists of a person knowingly and intentionally inducing a child under sixteen years of age, by means of computer, to engage in sexual intercourse, sexual contact or in a sexual or obscene performance, or to engage in any other sexual conduct when the perpetrator is at least three years older than the child. Whoever commits child luring is guilty of a fourth degree felony." N.M. STAT. ANN § 30-37-3.2

- New and improved definition of "material harmful to minors"
- Improved privacy protections

12. *The litigation.* Not surprisingly, various groups immediately sued to enjoin COPA. Applying strict scrutiny, the district court granted the preliminary injunction because COPA was not narrowly tailored given the alternative technologies of blocking and filtering. After being affirmed by the Third Circuit on unusual grounds,[*] which were reversed by the Supreme Court,[†] then being reaffirmed again by the Third Circuit on more conventional grounds,[‡] the case returned back to the Supreme Court.

ASHCROFT V. ACLU
542 U.S. 656 (2004)

Justice KENNEDY delivered the opinion of the Court.[§]

II

A

The District Court, in deciding to grant the preliminary injunction, concentrated primarily on the argument that there are plausible, less restrictive alternatives to COPA.

In considering this question, a court assumes that certain protected speech may be regulated, and then asks what is the least restrictive alternative that can be used to achieve that goal. The purpose of the test is not to consider whether the challenged restriction has some effect in achieving Congress' goal, regardless of the restriction it imposes. The purpose of the test is to ensure that speech is restricted no further than necessary to achieve the goal, for it is important to assure that legitimate speech is not chilled or punished. For that reason, the test does not begin with the status quo of existing regulations, then ask whether the challenged restriction has some additional ability to achieve Congress' legitimate interest. Any restriction on speech could be justified under that analysis. Instead, the court should ask whether the challenged regulation is the least restrictive means among available, effective alternatives.

---

[*] ACLU v. Reno, 217 F.3d 162 (3d Cir. 2000) (affirming on grounds that *Miller* definition of obscenity cannot function on the Internet because it would force use of national standards).

[†] Ashcroft v. ACLU, 535 U.S. 564, 585 (2002) (holding that "COPA's reliance on 'community standards' to identify what material 'is harmful to minors' does not *by itself* render the statute substantially overbroad for First Amendment purposes") (emphasis added).

[‡] ACLU v. Reno, 322 F.3d 240 (3d Cir. 2003).

[§] STEVENS, SOUTER, THOMAS, and GINSBURG, JJ., joined. —ED.

The primary alternative considered by the District Court was blocking and filtering software. Blocking and filtering software is an alternative that is less restrictive than COPA, and, in addition, likely more effective as a means of restricting children's access to materials harmful to them.

Filters are less restrictive than COPA. They impose selective restrictions on speech at the receiving end, not universal restrictions at the source. Under a filtering regime, adults without children may gain access to speech they have a right to see without having to identify themselves or provide their credit card information. Even adults with children may obtain access to the same speech on the same terms simply by turning off the filter on their home computers. Above all, promoting the use of filters does not condemn as criminal any category of speech, and so the potential chilling effect is eliminated, or at least much diminished. All of these things are true, moreover, regardless of how broadly or narrowly the definitions in COPA are construed.

Filters also may well be more effective than COPA. First, a filter can prevent minors from seeing all pornography, not just pornography posted to the Web from America. The District Court noted in its factfindings that one witness estimated that 40% of harmful-to-minors content comes from overseas. COPA does not prevent minors from having access to those foreign harmful materials. That alone makes it possible that filtering software might be more effective in serving Congress' goals. Effectiveness is likely to diminish even further if COPA is upheld, because the providers of the materials that would be covered by the statute simply can move their operations overseas. It is not an answer to say that COPA reaches some amount of materials that are harmful to minors; the question is whether it would reach more of them than less restrictive alternatives. In addition, the District Court found that verification systems may be subject to evasion and circumvention, for example by minors who have their own credit cards. Finally, filters also may be more effective because they can be applied to all forms of Internet communication, including e-mail, not just communications available via the World Wide Web.

That filtering software may well be more effective than COPA is confirmed by the findings of the Commission on Child Online Protection, a blue-ribbon commission created by Congress in COPA itself. Congress directed the Commission to evaluate the relative merits of different means of restricting minors' ability to gain access to harmful materials on the Internet. It unambiguously found that filters are more effective than age-verification requirements. See Commission on Child Online Protection (COPA), Report to Congress, at 19-21, 23-25, 27 (Oct. 20, 2000) (assigning a score for "Effectiveness" of 7.4 for server-based filters and 6.5 for client-based filters, as compared to 5.9 for independent adult-id verification, and 5.5 for credit card verification). Thus, not only has the Government failed to carry its burden of showing the District Court that the proposed alternative is less effective, but also a Government Commission appointed to consider the question has concluded just the opposite. That finding supports our conclusion that the District Court did not abuse its discretion in enjoining the statute.

Filtering software, of course, is not a perfect solution .... [H]owever, the Government failed to introduce specific evidence proving that existing technologies are less effective than the restrictions in COPA.... The Government's burden is not merely to show that a proposed less restrictive alternative has some flaws; its burden is to show that it is less effective. It is not enough for the Government to show that COPA has some effect. Nor do respondents bear a burden to introduce, or offer to introduce, evidence that their proposed alternatives are more effective. The Government has the burden to show they are less so. The Government having failed to carry its burden, it was not an abuse of discretion for the District Court to grant the preliminary injunction.

One argument to the contrary is worth mentioning—the argument that filtering software is not an available alternative because Congress may not require it to be used. That argument carries little weight, because Congress undoubtedly may act to encourage the use of filters. We have held that Congress can give strong incentives to schools and libraries to use them. *United States v. American Library Assn., Inc.* (2003).[*] It could also take steps to promote their development by industry, and their use by parents. It is incorrect, for that reason, to say that filters are part of the current regulatory status quo. The need for parental cooperation does not automatically disqualify a proposed less restrictive alternative. *Playboy.* COPA presumes that parents lack the ability, not the will, to monitor what their children see. By enacting programs to promote use of filtering software, Congress could give parents that ability without subjecting protected speech to severe penalties.

The closest precedent on the general point is our decision in *Playboy....* The choice was between a blanket speech restriction and a more specific technological solution that was available to parents who chose to implement it.

* * *

The District Court did not abuse its discretion when it entered the preliminary injunction. The judgment of the Court of Appeals is affirmed, and the case is remanded for proceedings consistent with this opinion.

---

[*] The opinion appears *infra.*—ED.

It is so ordered.[*]

Justice BREYER, with whom THE CHIEF JUSTICE and Justice O'CONNOR join, dissenting.

I cannot accept [the Court's] conclusion that Congress could have accomplished its statutory objective—protecting children from commercial pornography on the Internet—in other, less restrictive ways.

I

[T]he term "less restrictive alternative" is a comparative term. An "alternative" is "less restrictive" only if it will work less First Amendment harm than the statute itself, while at the same time similarly furthering the "compelling" interest that prompted Congress to enact the statute.

A

The Act's definitions limit the material it regulates to material that does not enjoy First Amendment protection, namely legally obscene material, and very little more.

The only significant difference between the present statute and *Miller*'s definition [of obscenity] consists of the addition of the words "with respect to minors," § 231(e)(6)(A), and "for minors," § 231(e)(6)(C). But the addition of these words to a definition that would otherwise cover only obscenity expands the statute's scope only slightly.

The "lack of serious value" requirement narrows the statute yet further— despite the presence of the qualification "for minors." That is because one cannot easily imagine material that has serious literary, artistic, political, or scientific value for a significant group of adults, but lacks such value for any significant group of minors. Thus, the statute, read literally, insofar as it extends beyond the legally obscene, could reach only borderline cases. And to take the words of the statute literally is consistent with Congress' avowed objective in enacting this law; namely, putting material produced by professional pornographers behind screens that will verify the age of the viewer.

Respondents fear prosecution for the Internet posting of material that does not fall within the statute's ambit . . . for example: an essay about a young man's experience with masturbation and sexual shame; "a serious discussion about birth control practices, homosexuality, ... or the consequences of prison rape"; . . . Aldous Huxley's Brave New World, J.D. Salinger's Catcher in the Rye, or, as

---

[*] The concurring opinion of Justice Stevens, joined by Justice Ginsburg, and the dissenting opinion of Justice Scalia have been omitted. Justice Scalia wrote that "commercial pornography covered by COPA . . . could, consistent with the First Amendment, be banned entirely . . . ."—ED.

the complaint would have it, "Ken Starr's report on the Clinton-Lewinsky scandal."

These materials are *not* both (1) "designed to appeal to, or ... pander to, the prurient interest" of significant groups of minors *and* (2) lacking in "serious literary, artistic, political, or scientific value" for significant groups of minors. §§ 231(e)(6)(A), (C). Thus, they fall outside the statute's definition of the material that it restricts, a fact the Government acknowledged at oral argument.

B

The Act does not censor the material it covers. Rather, it requires providers of the "harmful to minors" material to restrict minors' access to it by verifying age.... In this way, the Act requires creation of an internet screen that minors, but not adults, will find difficult to bypass.

I recognize that the screening requirement imposes some burden on adults who seek access to the regulated material, as well as on its providers. The cost is, in part, monetary. The parties agreed that a Web site could store card numbers or passwords at between 15 and 20 cents per number. And verification services provide free verification to Web site operators, while charging users less than $20 per year. According to the trade association for the commercial pornographers who are the statute's target, use of such verification procedures is "standard practice" in their online operations.

In addition to the monetary cost, and despite strict requirements that identifying information be kept confidential, see 47 U.S.C. §§ 231(d)(1), 501, the identification requirements inherent in age-screening may lead some users to fear embarrassment. Both monetary costs and potential embarrassment can deter potential viewers and, in that sense, the statute's requirements may restrict access to a site. But this Court has held that in the context of congressional efforts to protect children, restrictions of this kind do not automatically violate the Constitution. And the Court has approved their use. *See, e.g., American Library Assn.* (2003). *Cf. Reno* (O'CONNOR, J., concurring in judgment in part and dissenting in part) (calling the age-verification requirement similar to "a bouncer [who] checks a person's driver's license before admitting him to a nightclub").

II

I turn next to the question of "compelling interest," that of protecting minors from exposure to commercial pornography. No one denies that such an interest is "compelling." Rather, the question here is whether the Act, given its restrictions on adult access, significantly advances that interest. In other words, is the game worth the candle?

The majority argues that it is not, because of the existence of "blocking and filtering software." The majority refers to the presence of that software as a "less restrictive alternative." But that is a misnomer—a misnomer that may lead the reader to believe that all we need do is look to see if the blocking and filtering software is less restrictive . . . .

But such reasoning has no place here. Conceptually speaking, the presence of filtering software is not an *alternative* legislative approach to the problem of protecting children from exposure to commercial pornography. Rather, it is part of the status quo, *i.e.,* the backdrop against which Congress enacted the present statute. It is always true, by definition, that the status quo is less restrictive than a new regulatory law. It is always less restrictive to do *nothing* than to do *something.* But "doing nothing" does not address the problem Congress sought to address—namely that, despite the availability of filtering software, children were still being exposed to harmful material on the Internet.

Thus, the relevant constitutional question is not the question the Court asks: Would it be less restrictive to do nothing? Of course it would be. Rather, the relevant question posits a comparison of (a) a status quo that includes filtering software with (b) a change in that status quo that adds to it an age-verification screen requirement. Given the existence of filtering software, does the problem Congress identified remain significant? Does the Act help to address it? These are questions about the relation of the Act to the compelling interest. Does the Act, compared to the status quo, significantly advance the ball?

The answers to these intermediate questions are clear: Filtering software, as presently available, does not solve the "child protection" problem. It suffers from four serious inadequacies that prompted Congress to pass legislation instead of relying on its voluntary use. First, its filtering is faulty, allowing some pornographic material to pass through without hindrance.

Second, filtering software costs money. Not every family has the $40 or so necessary to install it. By way of contrast, age screening costs less.

Third, filtering software depends upon parents willing to decide where their children will surf the Web and able to enforce that decision. As to millions of American families, that is not a reasonable possibility.

Fourth, software blocking lacks precision, with the result that those who wish to use it to screen out pornography find that it blocks a great deal of material that is valuable.

Nothing in the District Court record suggests the contrary.

The Court's response—that 40% of all pornographic material may be of foreign origin—is beside the point. Even assuming (I believe unrealistically) that *all* foreign originators will refuse to use screening, the Act would make a difference in respect to 60% of the Internet's commercial pornography. I cannot call that difference insignificant.

The upshot is that Congress could reasonably conclude that, despite the current availability of filtering software, a child protection problem exists. It also could conclude that a precisely targeted regulatory statute, adding an age-verification requirement for a narrow range of material, would more effectively shield children from commercial pornography.

Is this justification sufficient? The lower courts thought not. But that is because those courts interpreted the Act as imposing far more than a modest burden. They assumed an interpretation of the statute in which it reached far beyond legally obscene and borderline-obscene material, affecting material that, given the interpretation set forth above, would fall well outside the Act's scope. But we must interpret the Act to save it, not to destroy it. So interpreted, the Act imposes a far lesser burden on access to protected material. Given the modest nature of that burden and the likelihood that the Act will significantly further Congress' compelling objective, the Act may well satisfy the First Amendment's stringent tests. *Cf. Sable.* Indeed, it does satisfy the First Amendment unless, of course, there is a genuine alternative, "less restrictive" way similarly to further that objective.

III

I turn, then, to the actual "less restrictive alternatives" that the Court proposes. The Court proposes two real alternatives, *i.e.,* two potentially less restrictive ways in which Congress might alter the status quo in order to achieve its "compelling" objective.

First, the Government might "act to encourage" the use of blocking and filtering software. The problem is that any argument that rests upon this alternative proves too much. If one imagines enough government resources devoted to the problem and perhaps additional scientific advances, then, of course, the use of software might become as effective and less restrictive. Obviously, the Government could give all parents, schools, and Internet cafes free computers with filtering programs already installed, hire federal employees to train parents and teachers on their use, and devote millions of dollars to the development of better software. The result might be an alternative that is extremely effective.

But the Constitution does not, because it cannot, require the Government to disprove the existence of magic solutions, *i.e.,* solutions that, put in general terms, will solve any problem less restrictively but with equal effectiveness. Otherwise, "the undoubted ability of lawyers and judges," who are not constrained by the budgetary worries and other practical parameters within which Congress must operate, "to imagine *some* kind of slightly less drastic or restrictive an approach would make it impossible to write laws that deal with the harm that called the statute into being." *Playboy* (BREYER, J., dissenting). As Justice Blackmun recognized, a "judge would be unimaginative indeed if he could not come up with something a little less 'drastic' or a little less 'restrictive' in almost any situation, and thereby enable himself to vote to strike legislation down." *Illinois Bd. of Elections v. Socialist Workers Party* (1979) (concurring opinion). Perhaps that is why no party has argued seriously that additional expenditure of government funds to encourage the use of screening is a "less restrictive alternative."

Second, the majority suggests decriminalizing the statute, noting the "chilling effect" of criminalizing a category of speech. To remove a major sanction, however, would make the statute less effective, virtually by definition.

IV

My conclusion is that the Act, as properly interpreted, risks imposition of minor burdens on some protected material—burdens that adults wishing to view the material may overcome at modest cost. At the same time, it significantly helps to achieve a compelling congressional goal, protecting children from exposure to commercial pornography. There is no serious, practically available "less restrictive" way similarly to further this compelling interest. Hence the Act is constitutional.

V

[W]hat has happened to the "constructive discourse between our courts and our legislatures" that "is an integral and admirable part of the constitutional design"? *Blakely v. Washington* (2004) (KENNEDY, J., dissenting). After eight years of legislative effort, two statutes, and three Supreme Court cases the Court sends this case back to the District Court for further proceedings. What proceedings? I have found no offer by either party to present more relevant evidence. What remains to be litigated?

Moreover, Congress passed the current statute "[i]n response to the Court's decision in *Reno*.... Congress read *Reno* with care. It dedicated itself to the task of drafting a statute that would meet each and every criticism of the predecessor statute that this Court set forth in *Reno*. It incorporated language from the Court's precedents, particularly the *Miller* standard, virtually verbatim. And it created what it believed was a statute that would protect children from exposure to obscene professional pornography without obstructing adult access to material that the First Amendment protects. What else was Congress supposed to do?

If this statute does not pass the Court's "less restrictive alternative" test, what does? If nothing does, then the Court should say so clearly.

For these reasons, I dissent.

NOTES & QUESTIONS

1. *Agreement.* Focus on the majority opinion, per Justice Kennedy, and the dissent by Justice Breyer. There are broad areas of agreement. Strict scrutiny is appropriate, and protecting kids is a compelling interest. The only dispute is whether COPA is "narrowly tailored" to the task.

2. *An algorithm.* To answer the "narrow tailoring" question, one could follow this algorithm. First, identify options that might solve the problem. The state action that is being constitutionally challenged is always one option; so is doing nothing—the status quo. Second, assess the efficacy of these options both in terms of benefits to child welfare and the costs to adult freedom of expression. Third, make some constitutional value judgment on the basis of these factual assessments. The majority and dissent differ at each step of the algorithm.

3. *Step one: Identify options.* As explained, COPA and the status quo are obviously two options to be evaluated against each other. But what about alternative options? Can or must they be considered? What other options does the majority specifically consider? Does Justice Breyer accept this methodology, and if so, what about his observation that any competent lawyer could fabricate "magic solutions" coupled with infinite resources and political will that would better solve any given problem?

4. *Step two: Assess efficacy.* In assessing the efficacy of the options, the court must make factual assessments about how each option will benefit child welfare *and* hurt adult speech interests. Let's focus on (a) COPA, which strong-arms commercial pornographers into the age-verification safe harbor, and (b) the alternative option of filters. According to the majority and dissent, what are the benefits and costs of each option?

    a.   *COPA.* The majority does not think that COPA will benefit children much; Justice Breyer thinks COPA will benefit them greatly. Why? The majority thinks that COPA will harm adult speech freedoms substantially; Justice Breyer thinks little speech worthy of constitutional concern will be chilled. Why? On this point, Justice Stevens in his omitted concurrence wrote:

> I wish to underscore just how restrictive COPA is. COPA is a content-based restraint on the dissemination of constitutionally protected speech. It enforces its prohibitions by way of the criminal law, threatening noncompliant Web

speakers with a fine of as much as $50,000, and a term of imprisonment as long as six months, for each offense. 47 U.S.C. § 231(a). Speakers who "intentionally" violate COPA are punishable by a fine of up to $50,000 for each day of the violation. *Ibid.* And because implementation of the various adult-verification mechanisms described in the statute provides only an affirmative defense, § 231(c)(1), even full compliance with COPA cannot guarantee freedom from prosecution. Speakers who dutifully place their content behind age screens may nevertheless find themselves in court, forced to prove the lawfulness of their speech on pain of criminal conviction.[*]

Who has the better factual argument?

b. *Filters.* Do the same analysis for filters. The majority thinks that filters can benefit children greatly; Justice Breyer says they do not work well at all. Why? The majority thinks that filters do not harm adults; again, Justice Breyer suggests that the filter approach could boomerang against adult speech interests. Why? Which side has the better factual argument?

5. *Step three: Make constitutional judgment.* At the conclusion of the prior step, a judge will come to some rough assessment about the benefits and costs of COPA, the status quo, and any other potential options considered. Under what findings should the challenged option be struck down as unconstitutional? For example, what if a judge makes the following assessment?

	COPA	Filters
Benefit to Children	++ (big benefit)	de minimis
Cost to Adults	de minimis	de minimis

Is this how Justice Breyer sees things? What if the assessment matrix looked like this?

	COPA	Filters
Benefit to Children	de minimis	++ (big benefit)
Cost to Adults	-- (big cost)	de minimis

Is this how Justice Kennedy sees things? Finally, what about a harder case?

---

[*] 542 U.S. at 674 (Stevens, J., concurring).

	COPA	Filters
Benefit to Children	++ (big benefit)	+ (some benefit)
Cost to Adults	- (some cost)	de minimis

If both Justices Kennedy and Breyer came to this last factual assessment, would they come out the same way in terms of constitutional value judgment? Put another way, does their disagreement arise from differences in the way they see "the facts" or their constitutional "values"?

6. *Uncertainty.* Uncertainty appears in every step of this algorithm: Which options can be considered? What are the benefits and costs? How do we make value judgments on incommensurable tradeoffs between child welfare and adult freedom? In addition, rapidly changing technologies exacerbate the uncertainty. Under such conditions of imperfect knowledge, how should courts decide cases? Does the idea of burden of proof help? What about the relative institutional competencies between court and legislature?

7. *On remand.* Remember that this opinion addressed the preliminary injunction granted by the trial court. On remand, the district court conducted a full bench trial on the merits. The district court found COPA unconstitutional, especially given the alternative of software filters, and issued a permanent injunction, which was affirmed by the Third Circuit.[*] The Supreme Court denied cert.

8. *Filtering generally.* From reading the CDA and COPA opinions, we can see how the state of technological code (technological power) alters the constitutional analysis of statutory code (legal power). Specifically, the efficacy of software filtering technologies seems critical. In the ideal world, each content provider would label her content accurately and each household computer would have easy-to-use software that screens content based on that accurate rating. But in the real world, content providers don't voluntarily rate their own content and just as families don't know how to use their V-Chip, they don't know how to program content filters on their computers.

9. *Other internet pornography legislation.* A few other pieces of internet indecency legislation bear mention.

a. *Child Pornography Prevention Act* (CPPA). Enacted in 1996, the CPPA redefined child pornography not only to include pornography created by using actual minors but also:

---

[*] *See* ACLU v. Mukasey, 478 F. Supp. 2d 775 (E.D. Pa. 2007), *aff'd*, 534 F.3d 181 (3d Cir. 2008), *cert. denied*, 555 U.S. 1137 (2009).

- "morphed" child pornography: where innocent pictures of actual children are doctored so as to appear that "an identifiable minor is engaging in sexually explicit conduct," 18 U.S.C. § 2256(8)(C);

- "virtual" child pornography: pornography that seems to portray minors engaging in sexual acts, but in no way uses actual minors (high-tech version could be created completely through computer animation; low-tech version could use youthful-looking adults who would "act" like minors), § 2256(8)(B); and

- "pandered as" child pornography: material that is advertised in a way that "conveys the impression" that it contains "a minor engaging in sexually explicit conduct." § 2256(8)(D).

The "virtual" and "pandered as" definitions (but not the "morphed" category) were challenged on First Amendment grounds. In *Ashcroft v. The Free Speech Coalition* (2002),[*] the Supreme Court struck down both provisions as unconstitutional. The Court reasoned that these materials do not make use of actual children; therefore, they fall outside the category of child pornography defined in *New York v. Ferber*.[†] Accordingly, these materials were protected speech and could be prohibited only if they violated the obscenity test stated in *Miller v. California*.[‡]

     b. *Dot kids domain.* Enacted in 2002, the Dot Kids Implementation and Efficiency Act commands the National Telecommunications and Information Administration (NTIA) to require the registry selected to operate the United States top-level country code internet domain to establish a second-level domain (e.g. *.kids.us) that would host only material suitable for minors and not harmful to minors.[§] Minors are defined as under 13 years of age. You might be curious about how many sites exist under ".kids.us" subdomain. As of late 2011 (after almost a decade of operation), there were approximately 5 sites (Nickelodeon, Smithsonian, PBS, and a trampoline store).[**]

---

[*] 535 U.S. 234 (2002).

[†] 458 U.S. 747 (1982).

[‡] 413 U.S. 15 (1973). For repeals and modifications of these provisions, see generally PROTECT Act of 2003, P.L. 108-21, 117 Stat. 678 (Apr. 30, 2003).

[§] *See* 47 U.S.C.A. § 941(a) (Supp. 2004).

[**] The domain was suspended by NTIA in 2012 because the agency determined that it was "not serving its intended purpose as per the Dot Kids Act." *See* Amendment of Solicitation/Modification of Contract (June 27, 2012), *available at* https://www.ntia.doc.gov/files/ntia/publications/ustld_27_jun_2012_mod_012-1.pdf. An archived copy of the kids.com page is available at https://web.archive.org/web/20110901221738/http://www.cms.kids.us/.

c. *Misleading domain names.* Enacted in 2003, this statute criminalizes the knowing use of a misleading domain name to intentionally deceive adults into viewing obscene material or minors into viewing "material that is harmful to minors."[*] The statute creates a sort of safe harbor by noting explicitly that a domain name that includes words that "indicate the sexual content of the site, such as 'sex' or 'porn', is not misleading."[†] 10. *Recent push to expand liability for platforms that facilitate sex trafficking.* After a prolonged period of minimal activity on indecency, Congress recently enacted a new law to impose liability on providers that facilitate prostitution and sex trafficking.[‡] Shortly after the law went into effect, Craigslist eliminated its "personals" listings and Reddit banned several subreddits. Some outlets also voiced concern that the law could expose sex workers to increased risks by taking away online platforms that provide a means to screen potential customers from a safe distance. We will discuss the law more in CHAPTER 8: INTERMEDIARY LIABILITY.

NOTE: CHILDREN'S INTERNET PROTECTION ACT

By now, you might think that no serious attempt at regulating internet indecency can withstand judicial scrutiny. But there is one act that has done so: the Children's Internet Protection Act (CIPA), upheld by the Supreme Court in 2003. According to the Court,

> [CIPA] provides that a library may not receive E-rate or LSTA assistance unless it has "a policy of Internet safety for minors that includes the operation of a technology protection measure ... that protects against access" by all persons to "visual depictions" that constitute "obscen[ity]" or "child pornography," and that protects against access by minors to "visual depictions" that are "harmful to minors." 20 U.S.C. §§ 9134(f)(1)(A)(i) and (B)(i); 47 U.S.C. §§ 254(h)(6)(B)(i) and (C)(i). The statute defines a "[t]echnology protection measure" as "a specific technology that blocks or filters Internet access to material covered by" CIPA. § 254(h)(7)(I). CIPA also permits the library to "disable" the filter "to enable access for bona fide research or other lawful purposes." 20 U.S.C. § 9134(f)(3); 47 U.S.C. § 254(h)(6)(D). Under the E-rate program, disabling is permitted "during use by an adult." § 254(h)(6)(D). Under the LSTA program, disabling is permitted during use by any person. 20 U.S.C. § 9134(f)(3).[§]

---

[*] 18. U.S.C. § 2252B(a) and (b) (Supp. 2004).

[†] *Id.* at § 2252B(c).

[‡] *See* Allow States and Victims to Fight Online Sex Trafficking Act of 2017, Pub. L. 115-164 (2018).

[§] U.S. v. American Library Assoc., Inc, 539 U.S. 194 (2003).

Why did this law survive, when the CDA failed in 1996 and the much-improved COPA failed in 2004? A critical difference is that CIPA was merely a filtering requirement and, more importantly, it was tied to receiving federal dollars. Whenever the federal government uses dollars to manipulate behavior, two doctrines come into play, the Spending Clause and Unconstitutional Conditions.

Spending clause. Under *South Dakota v. Dole* (1987), the leading spending clause[*] case, Congress has substantial flexibility to condition federal spending. The minor limitations on the spending power are:

- the spending must be imposed in pursuit of the general welfare;
- the "strings" attached to the funding must be stated explicitly;
- the condition must be germane to (or "related to") the goals pursued; and finally,
- the action necessary to receive federal funding cannot itself be unconstitutional when performed by the recipient.[†]

The last requirement is what was at issue. In other words, could a public library, on its own accord, install filters on its Internet access computers, consistent with the First Amendment?

In order to determine the standard of review, the Court had to analyze public forum doctrine. This doctrine addresses what happens when government regulates expressive activity on its own property. Can it do whatever it feels like, as a property owner with dominion over its territory? Or must government abide by the First Amendment without regard to the fact that the speech is taking place on its property? Current First Amendment public forum doctrine answers this question by dividing up government property into three categories: traditional public forum, designated public forum (unlimited and limited), and nonpublic forum.

"Traditional" public fora such as streets, sidewalks, and parks are said to have a long-standing tradition of expressive activity as a principal purpose. On these fora, government restraints on speech are given no greater leeway because the speech takes place on government property. For instance, a content-based regulation of speech on traditional public fora must satisfy strict scrutiny.

By contrast, "designated" public fora obtain their status not from history but by purposeful action by the government. If the government designates an "unlimited" public forum, then that forum is to be treated no differently from a traditional public forum. By contrast, if the government designates a "limited"

---

[*] U.S. Const., Art. I, sec. 8.

[†] *See* South Dakota v. Dole, 483 U.S. 203, 207-08 (1987).

public forum (e.g., a theater for live performances of Shakespeare), then content-based distinctions seem to be acceptable (e.g., allowing only Shakespeare plays, not rock musicals) to the extent that they are consistent with the reasons why the forum was "limited" in the first place. This area of law remains poorly developed.

Finally, the category of "nonpublic" fora covers the rest of government property. In these properties, reasonable regulation of speech is acceptable, as long as there is no viewpoint discrimination (e.g., allowing pro-Republican speech but not pro-Democrat).

Why is this categorization of government property important? To repeat, if Internet access at a library is deemed a public forum, then the mere fact that it is government subsidized "property" does not excuse greater speech regulation.

The Court held that internet access in a library was neither a traditional nor a designated public forum. After all, the internet is new, hardly in existence since "time immemorial" and thus cannot be a traditional public forum. Also, "[a] public library does not acquire internet terminals in order to create a public forum for Web publishers to express themselves, any more than it collects books in order to provide a public forum for the authors of books to speak."

Since internet access at libraries wasn't a public forum, no heightened scrutiny was necessary.[*] To the majority, it was reasonable for a library not to carry pornography in its print collection and there should be no difference for online porn. Moreover, the Court emphasized the ease with which adults could ask librarians to turn off filters and did not think that potential embarrassment was too burdensome.

Unconstitutional conditions. The other principal argument was based on the doctrine of unconstitutional conditions, which holds that the government cannot deny a benefit to a person on a basis that infringes his constitutionally protected freedom of speech even if he has no entitlement to that benefit. The leading case is *Rust v. Sullivan* (1991),[†] which more-or-less turned on a penalty/subsidy distinction. A penalty for exercising a constitutional right would be unconstitutional, but a mere lack of subsidy would be fine. The Court explained:

---

[*] In dissent, Justice Souter invoked a different framing, based on *Board of Education v. Pico*, 457 U.S. 853 (1982). That case addressed the constitutionality of book removal from a school library. In a highly fragmented opinion, four Justices of the Supreme Court (in a 4-4-1 breakdown) drew a distinction between book removal (which would warrant strict scrutiny because it was more likely to reflect a desire to suppress ideas) and book acquisition (which would warrant intermediate scrutiny because it was more likely to reflect general standards of suitability and quality for a school system). Justice Souter likened the Internet filters to book removal (not failure to acquire books) and called for the application of strict scrutiny.

[†] 500 U.S. 173 (1991).

CIPA does not "penalize" libraries that choose not to install such software, or deny them the right to provide their patrons with unfiltered Internet access. Rather, CIPA simply reflects Congress' decision not to subsidize their doing so. To the extent that libraries wish to offer unfiltered access, they are free to do so without federal assistance. "'A refusal to fund protected activity, without more, cannot be equated with the imposition of a 'penalty' on that activity.'" *Rust.* "'[A] legislature's decision not to subsidize the exercise of a fundamental right does not infringe the right.

End result. Since libraries of their own volition could install filters, it did not violate the Spending Clause for Congress to condition receipt of federal funds on libraries doing so. Also, since the funds were more a subsidy than a penalty, no unconstitutional   conditions   were   attached.

CHAPTER 7

PRIVACY

Unlike indecency laws, communications privacy laws do not focus on limiting the flow of information *to* users, but instead on limiting the flow of information *about* users from service providers to third parties. Most of these laws have the same basic structure—limit the collection or disclosure of a user's personal information without their consent—and some laws also prohibit specific uses of telephone numbers, e-mail addresses, or other information by third parties. A comprehensive overview of privacy laws is beyond the scope of this text and should be studied in a separate class. However, this brief study of communications privacy laws will introduce you to many of the same principles that underlie privacy laws in other domains, both statutory and constitutional.

A. TELEPHONY

Modern communications privacy law can be traced back to the Communications Act of 1934 and the creation of the FCC,[*] which were passed in the wake of the Supreme Court's decision in *Olmstead v. United States*.[†] In *Olmstead*, the Court allowed the government to introduce evidence obtained through an illegal wiretap. While the *Olmstead* decision, which concerned Fourth Amendment principles that we will not be covering in detail in this text, was not overturned for nearly 40 years, Congress sought to limit the interception and use of private telephone communications after *Olmstead*, providing that:

> no person not being authorized by the sender shall intercept any communication and divulge or publish the existence, contents, substance, purport, effect, or meaning of such intercepted communication to any person ; and no person not being entitled thereto shall receive or assist in receiving any interstate or foreign communication by wire or radio and use the same or any information therein contained for his own benefit or for the benefit of another not entitled thereto; and no person having received such intercepted

---

[*] A more limited prohibition on interception was included in the Radio Act of February 23, 1927, c. 169, s 27. 44 Stat. 1162, 1172 (47 USCA s 107).

[†] 277 U.S. 438 (1928).

communication or having become acquainted with the contents, substance, purport, effect, or meaning of the same or any part thereof, knowing that such information was so obtained, shall divulge or publish the existence, contents, substance, purport, effect, or meaning of the same or any part thereof, or use the same or any information therein contained for his own benefit or for the benefit of another not entitled thereto: Provided, That this section shall not apply to the receiving, divulging, publishing, or utilizing the contents of any radio communication broadcast, or transmitted by amateurs or others for the use of the general public, or relating to ships in distress.[*]

This law created such a strong prohibition on the interception and use of communications content that the Supreme Court ruled in *Nardone v. United States*[†] that government officers could not even use wiretaps in criminal investigations. The Court later held in *Weiss v. United States* that "there is no constitutional requirement that the scope of the statute be limited so as to exclude intrastate communications."[‡] Congress subsequently created special rules for government wiretapping in Title III of the Omnibus Crime Control and Safe Streets Act of 1968.[§] But the prohibitions on interception, use, and disclosure of private communications content remained. During the intervening decades, the Court considered many cases related to government surveillance; but the Court did not have occasion to address the prohibition on use and disclosure of private communications by third parties until 2001.

BARTNICKI V. VOPPER
532 U.S. 514 (2001)

Justice Stevens delivered the opinion of the Court.[**]

These cases raise an important question concerning what degree of protection, if any, the First Amendment provides to speech that discloses the contents of an illegally intercepted communication. That question is both novel and narrow. Despite the fact that federal law has prohibited such disclosures since 1934, this is the first time that we have confronted such an issue.

The suit at hand involves the repeated intentional disclosure of an illegally intercepted cellular telephone conversation about a public issue. The persons who made the disclosures did not participate in the interception, but they did know—or at least had reason to know—that the interception was unlawful.

---

[*] Pub. L. 73-416, 48 Stat. 1064, 1104, codified at 47 U.S.C. § 605 (1934).

[†] 302 U.S. 379 (1937).

[‡] 308 U.S. 321, 237 (1939).

[§] Pub. L. 90-351, 82 Stat. 97 (1968).

[**] The opinion was joined by Justices O'Connor, Kennedy, Souter, Ginsburg, and Breyer.—ED.

Accordingly, these cases present a conflict between interests of the highest order—on the one hand, the interest in the full and free dissemination of information concerning public issues, and, on the other hand, the interest in individual privacy and, more specifically, in fostering private speech. The Framers of the First Amendment surely did not foresee the advances in science that produced the conversation, the interception, or the conflict that gave rise to this action. It is therefore not surprising that Circuit judges, as well as the Members of this Court, have come to differing conclusions about the First Amendment's application to this issue. Nevertheless, having considered the interests at stake, we are firmly convinced that the disclosures made by respondents in this suit are protected by the First Amendment.

I

During 1992 and most of 1993, the Pennsylvania State Education Association, a union representing the teachers at the Wyoming Valley West High School, engaged in collective-bargaining negotiations with the school board. Petitioner Kane, then the president of the local union, testified that the negotiations were "contentious" and received "a lot of media attention." In May 1993, petitioner Bartnicki, who was acting as the union's "chief negotiator," used the cellular phone in her car to call Kane and engage in a lengthy conversation about the status of the negotiations. An unidentified person intercepted and recorded that call.

In their conversation, Kane and Bartnicki discussed the timing of a proposed strike, difficulties created by public comment on the negotiations and the need for a dramatic response to the board's intransigence. At one point, Kane said: " 'If they're not gonna move for three percent, we're gonna have to go to their, their homes .... To blow off their front porches, we'll have to do some work on some of those guys. (PAUSES). Really, uh, really and truthfully because this is, you know, this is bad news. (UNDECIPHERABLE).' "

In the early fall of 1993, the parties accepted a nonbinding arbitration proposal that was generally favorable to the teachers. In connection with news reports about the settlement, respondent Vopper, a radio commentator who had been critical of the union in the past, played a tape of the intercepted conversation on his public affairs talk show. Another station also broadcast the tape, and local newspapers published its contents. After filing suit against Vopper and other representatives of the media, Bartnicki and Kane (hereinafter petitioners) learned through discovery that Vopper had obtained the tape from respondent Jack Yocum, the head of a local taxpayers' organization that had opposed the union's demands throughout the negotiations. Yocum, who was added as a defendant, testified that he had found the tape in his mailbox shortly after the interception and recognized the voices of Bartnicki and Kane. Yocum played the tape for some members of the school board, and later delivered the tape itself to Vopper.

II

In their amended complaint, petitioners alleged that their telephone conversation had been surreptitiously intercepted by an unknown person using an electronic device, that Yocum had obtained a tape of that conversation, and that he intentionally disclosed it to Vopper, as well as other individuals and media representatives. Thereafter, Vopper and other members of the media repeatedly published the contents of that conversation. The amended complaint alleged that each of the defendants "knew or had reason to know" that the recording of the private telephone conversation had been obtained by means of an illegal interception[.]

Respondents contended that they had not violated the statute because (a) they had nothing to do with the interception, and (b) in any event, their actions were not unlawful since the conversation might have been intercepted inadvertently. Moreover, even if they had violated the statute by disclosing the intercepted conversation, respondents argued, those disclosures were protected by the First Amendment. The District Court rejected the first statutory argument because, under the plain statutory language, an individual violates the federal Act by intentionally disclosing the contents of an electronic communication when he or she "know[s] or ha[s] reason to know that the information was obtained" through an illegal interception.[3] Accordingly, actual involvement in the illegal interception is not necessary in order to establish a violation of that statute. . . . [T]he District Court rejected respondents' First Amendment defense because the statutes were content-neutral laws of general applicability that contained "no indicia of prior restraint or the chilling of free speech."

One of the stated purposes of [Title III] was "to protect effectively the privacy of wire and oral communications." In addition to authorizing and regulating electronic surveillance for law enforcement purposes, Title III also regulated private conduct. One part of those regulations, § 2511(1), defined five offenses punishable by a fine of not more than $10,000, by imprisonment for not more than five years, or by both. Subsection (a) applied to any person who "willfully intercepts . . . any wire or oral communication." Subsection (b)

---

[3] Title 18 U.S.C. § 2511(1)(c) provides that any person who "intentionally discloses, or endeavors to disclose, to any other person the contents of any wire, oral, or electronic communication, knowing or having reason to know that the information was obtained through the interception of a wire, oral, or electronic communication in violation of this subsection; . . . shall be punished. . . ." The Pennsylvania Act contains a similar provision.

applied to the intentional use of devices designed to intercept oral conversations; subsection (d) applied to the use of the contents of illegally intercepted wire or oral communications; and subsection (e) prohibited the unauthorized disclosure of the contents of interceptions that were authorized for law enforcement purposes. Subsection (c), the original version of the provision most directly at issue in this suit, applied to any person who "willfully discloses, or endeavors to disclose, to any other person the contents of any wire or oral communication, knowing or having reason to know that the information was obtained through the interception of a wire or oral communication in violation of this subsection." The oral communications protected by the Act were only those "uttered by a person exhibiting an expectation that such communication is not subject to interception under circumstances justifying such expectation."

As enacted in 1968, Title III did not apply to the monitoring of radio transmissions. In the Electronic Communications Privacy Act of 1986, however, Congress enlarged the coverage of Title III to prohibit the interception of "electronic" as well as oral and wire communications. By reason of that amendment, as well as a 1994 amendment which applied to cordless telephone communications, Title III now applies to the interception of conversations over both cellular and cordless phones.[7] Although a lesser criminal penalty may apply to the interception of such transmissions, the same civil remedies are available whether the communication was "oral," "wire," or "electronic," as defined by 18 U.S.C. § 2510.

IV

The constitutional question before us concerns the validity of the statutes as applied to the specific facts of these cases. Because of the procedural posture of these cases, it is appropriate to make certain important assumptions about those facts. We accept petitioners' submission that the interception was intentional, and therefore unlawful, and that, at a minimum, respondents "had reason to know" that it was unlawful. Accordingly, the disclosure of the contents of the intercepted conversation by Yocum to school board members and to representatives of the media, as well as the subsequent disclosures by the media defendants to the public, violated the federal and state statutes. Under the provisions of the federal statute, as well as its Pennsylvania analogue, petitioners are thus entitled to recover damages from each of the respondents. The only question is whether the application of these statutes in such circumstances violates the First Amendment.

---

[7] See, *e.g., Nix v. O'Malley,* 160 F.3d 343, 346 (C.A.6 1998); *McKamey v. Roach,* 55 F.3d 1236, 1240 (C.A.6 1995).

In answering that question, we accept respondents' submission on three factual matters that serve to distinguish most of the cases that have arisen under § 2511. First, respondents played no part in the illegal interception. Rather, they found out about the interception only after it occurred, and in fact never learned the identity of the person or persons who made the interception. Second, their access to the information on the tapes was obtained lawfully, even though the information itself was intercepted unlawfully by someone else. Third, the subject matter of the conversation was a matter of public concern. If the statements about the labor negotiations had been made in a public arena—during a bargaining session, for example—they would have been newsworthy. This would also be true if a third party had inadvertently overheard Bartnicki making the same statements to Kane when the two thought they were alone.

V

We agree with petitioners that [Title III] is in fact a content-neutral law of general applicability[.]

In this suit, the basic purpose of the statute at issue is to "protec[t] the privacy of wire[, electronic,] and oral communications." The statute does not distinguish based on the content of the intercepted conversations, nor is it justified by reference to the content of those conversations. Rather, the communications at issue are singled out by virtue of the fact that they were illegally intercepted—by virtue of the source, rather than the subject matter.

On the other hand, the naked prohibition against disclosures is fairly characterized as a regulation of pure speech. Unlike the prohibition against the "use" of the contents of an illegal interception in § 2511(1)(d),[10] subsection (c) is not a regulation of conduct. It is true that the delivery of a tape recording might be regarded as conduct, but given that the purpose of such a delivery is to provide the recipient with the text of recorded statements, it is like the delivery of a handbill or a pamphlet, and as such, it is the kind of "speech" that the First Amendment protects[.]

---

[10] The Solicitor General has cataloged some of the cases that fall under subsection (d): "[I]t is unlawful for a company to use an illegally intercepted communication about a business rival in order to create a competing product; it is unlawful for an investor to use illegally intercepted communications in trading in securities; it is unlawful for a union to use an illegally intercepted communication about management (or vice versa) to prepare strategy for contract negotiations; it is unlawful for a supervisor to use information in an illegally recorded conversation to discipline a subordinate; and it is unlawful for a blackmailer to use an illegally intercepted communication for purposes of extortion. See, *e.g.,* 1968 Senate Report 67 (corporate and labor-management uses); *Fultz v. Gilliam,* 942 F.2d 396, 400 n. 4 (6th Cir. 1991) (extortion); *Dorris v. Absher,* 959 F.Supp. 813, 815–817 (M.D. Tenn.1997) (workplace discipline), aff'd. in part, rev'd in part, 179 F.3d 420 (6th Cir. 1999). The statute has also been held to bar the use of illegally intercepted communications for important and socially valuable purposes. See *In re Grand Jury,* 111 F.3d 1066, 1077–1079 (3d Cir.1997)."

VI

As a general matter, "state action to punish the publication of truthful information seldom can satisfy constitutional standards." More specifically, this Court has repeatedly held that "if a newspaper lawfully obtains truthful information about a matter of public significance then state officials may not constitutionally punish publication of the information, absent a need ... of the highest order."

Accordingly, in *New York Times Co. v. United States*, the Court upheld the right of the press to publish information of great public concern obtained from documents stolen by a third party. In so doing, that decision resolved a conflict between the basic rule against prior restraints on publication and the interest in preserving the secrecy of information that, if disclosed, might seriously impair the security of the Nation[.]

However, *New York Times v. United States* raised, but did not resolve, the question "whether, in cases where information has been acquired *unlawfully* by a newspaper or by a source, government may ever punish not only the unlawful acquisition, but the ensuing publication as well." The question here, however, is a narrower version of that still-open question. Simply put, the issue here is this: "Where the punished publisher of information has obtained the information in question in a manner lawful in itself but from a source who has obtained it unlawfully, may the government punish the ensuing publication of that information based on the defect in a chain?"

The Government identifies two interests served by the statute—first, the interest in removing an incentive for parties to intercept private conversations, and second, the interest in minimizing the harm to persons whose conversations have been illegally intercepted. We assume that those interests adequately justify the prohibition in § 2511(1)(d) against the interceptor's own use of information that he or she acquired by violating § 2511(1)(a), but it by no means follows that punishing disclosures of lawfully obtained information of public interest by one not involved in the initial illegality is an acceptable means of serving those ends.

The normal method of deterring unlawful conduct is to impose an appropriate punishment on the person who engages in it. If the sanctions that presently attach to a violation of § 2511(1)(a) do not provide sufficient deterrence, perhaps those sanctions should be made more severe. But it would be quite remarkable to hold that speech by a law-abiding possessor of information can be suppressed in order to deter conduct by a non-law-abiding third party. Although there are some rare occasions in which a law suppressing one party's speech may be justified by an interest in deterring criminal conduct by another, this is not such a case.

With only a handful of exceptions, the violations of § 2511(1)(a) that have been described in litigated cases have been motivated by either financial gain or domestic disputes. In virtually all of those cases, the identity of the person or persons intercepting the communication has been known. Moreover, petitioners cite no evidence that Congress viewed the prohibition against disclosures as a response to the difficulty of identifying persons making improper use of scanners and other surveillance devices and accordingly of deterring such conduct, and there is no empirical evidence to support the assumption that the prohibition against disclosures reduces the number of illegal interceptions.

Although this suit demonstrates that there may be an occasional situation in which an anonymous scanner will risk criminal prosecution by passing on information without any expectation of financial reward or public praise, surely this is the exceptional case. Moreover, there is no basis for assuming that imposing sanctions upon respondents will deter the unidentified scanner from continuing to engage in surreptitious interceptions. Unusual cases fall far short of a showing that there is a "need ... of the highest order" for a rule supplementing the traditional means of deterring antisocial conduct. The justification for any such novel burden on expression must be "far stronger than mere speculation about serious harms." Accordingly, the Government's first suggested justification for applying § 2511(1)(c) to an otherwise innocent disclosure of public information is plainly insufficient.

The Government's second argument, however, is considerably stronger. Privacy of communication is an important interest,[20] and Title III's restrictions are intended to protect that interest, thereby "encouraging the uninhibited exchange of ideas and information among private parties. . . ." Moreover, the fear of public disclosure of private conversations might well have a chilling effect on private speech.

"In a democratic society privacy of communication is essential if citizens are to think and act creatively and constructively. Fear or suspicion that one's speech is being monitored by a stranger, even without the reality of such activity, can have a seriously inhibiting effect upon the willingness to voice critical and constructive ideas."

Accordingly, it seems to us that there are important interests to be considered on *both* sides of the constitutional calculus. In considering that

---

[20] "The essential thrust of the First Amendment is to prohibit improper restraints on the *voluntary* public expression of ideas; it shields the man who wants to speak or publish when others wish him to be quiet. There is necessarily, and within suitably defined areas, a concomitant freedom *not* to speak publicly, one which serves the same ultimate end as freedom of speech in its affirmative aspect." *Harper & Row, Publishers, Inc. v. Nation Enterprises,* 471 U.S., 539, 559 (1985).

balance, we acknowledge that some intrusions on privacy are more offensive than others, and that the disclosure of the contents of a private conversation can be an even greater intrusion on privacy than the interception itself. As a result, there is a valid independent justification for prohibiting such disclosures by persons who lawfully obtained access to the contents of an illegally intercepted message, even if that prohibition does not play a significant role in preventing such interceptions from occurring in the first place.

We need not decide whether that interest is strong enough to justify the application of § 2511(c) to disclosures of trade secrets or domestic gossip or other information of purely private concern. In other words, the outcome of these cases does not turn on whether § 2511(1)(c) may be enforced with respect to most violations of the statute without offending the First Amendment. The enforcement of that provision in these cases, however, implicates the core purposes of the First Amendment because it imposes sanctions on the publication of truthful information of public concern.

In these cases, privacy concerns give way when balanced against the interest in publishing matters of public importance. As Warren and Brandeis stated in their classic law review article: "The right of privacy does not prohibit any publication of matter which is of public or general interest." One of the costs associated with participation in public affairs is an attendant loss of privacy.

We think it clear that [the reasoning in *New York Times v. Sullivan*] requires the conclusion that a stranger's illegal conduct does not suffice to remove the First Amendment shield from speech about a matter of public concern. The months of negotiations over the proper level of compensation for teachers at the Wyoming Valley West High School were unquestionably a matter of public concern, and respondents were clearly engaged in debate about that concern.

Chief Justice Rehnquist, with whom Justice Scalia and Justice Thomas join, dissenting

Technology now permits millions of important and confidential conversations to occur through a vast system of electronic networks. These advances, however, raise significant privacy concerns. We are placed in the uncomfortable position of not knowing who might have access to our personal and business e-mails, our medical and financial records, or our cordless and cellular telephone conversations. In an attempt to prevent some of the most egregious violations of privacy, the United States, the District of Columbia, and 40 States have enacted laws prohibiting the intentional interception and knowing disclosure of electronic communications. The Court holds that all of these statutes violate the First Amendment insofar as the illegally intercepted conversation touches upon a matter of "public concern," an amorphous concept that the Court does not even attempt to define. But the Court's decision diminishes, rather than enhances, the purposes of the First Amendment, thereby chilling the speech of the millions of Americans who rely upon electronic technology to communicate each day.

[T]here is no intimation that these laws seek "to suppress unpopular ideas or information or manipulate the public debate" or that they "distinguish favored speech from disfavored speech on the basis of the ideas or views expressed." The antidisclosure provision is based solely upon the manner in which the conversation was acquired, not the subject matter of the conversation or the viewpoints of the speakers. The same information, if obtained lawfully, could be published with impunity. As the concerns motivating strict scrutiny are absent, these content-neutral restrictions upon speech need pass only intermediate scrutiny.

[T]he Court places an inordinate amount of weight upon the fact that the receipt of an illegally intercepted communication has not been criminalized. But this hardly renders those who knowingly receive and disclose such communications "law-abiding," . . . . The transmission of the intercepted communication from the eavesdropper to the third party is itself illegal; and where, as here, the third party then knowingly discloses that communication, another illegal act has been committed. The third party in this situation cannot be likened to the reporters in the *Daily Mail* cases, who lawfully obtained their information through consensual interviews or public documents.

[C]ongress and the overwhelming majority of States reasonably have concluded that sanctioning the knowing disclosure of illegally intercepted communications will deter the initial interception itself, a crime which is extremely difficult to detect. It is estimated that over 20 million scanners capable of intercepting cellular transmissions currently are in operation, notwithstanding the fact that Congress prohibited the marketing of such devices eight years ago. As Congress recognized, "[a]ll too often the invasion of privacy itself will go unknown. Only by striking at all aspects of the problem can privacy be adequately protected."

Nonetheless, the Court faults Congress for providing "no empirical evidence . . . ."

The "quantum of empirical evidence needed to satisfy heightened judicial scrutiny of legislative judgments will vary up or down with the novelty and plausibility of the justification raised." "[C]ourts must accord substantial deference to the predictive judgments of Congress." This deference recognizes that, as an institution, Congress is far better equipped than the judiciary to evaluate the vast amounts of data bearing upon complex issues and that "[s]ound policymaking often requires legislators to forecast future events and to anticipate the likely impact of these events based on deductions and inferences for which complete empirical support may be unavailable." Although we must nonetheless independently evaluate such congressional findings in performing our constitutional review, this "is not a license to reweigh the evidence *de novo,* or to replace Congress' factual predictions with our own."

The "dry-up-the-market" theory, which posits that it is possible to deter an illegal act that is difficult to police by preventing the wrongdoer from enjoying the fruits of the crime, is neither novel nor implausible. It is a time-tested theory that undergirds numerous laws, such as the prohibition of the knowing possession of stolen goods.

These statutes also protect the important interests of deterring clandestine invasions of privacy and preventing the involuntary broadcast of private communications. Over a century ago, Samuel Warren and Louis Brandeis recognized that "[t]he intensity and complexity of life, attendant upon advancing civilization, have rendered necessary some retreat from the world, and man, under the refining influence of culture, has become more sensitive to publicity, so that solitude and privacy have become more essential to the individual."*

These statutes undeniably protect this venerable right of privacy. Concomitantly, they further the First Amendment rights of the parties to the conversation. "At the heart of the First Amendment lies the principle that each person should decide for himself or herself the ideas and beliefs deserving of expression, consideration, and adherence."

Although the Court recognizes and even extols the virtues of this right to privacy, these are "mere words," overridden by the Court's newfound right to publish unlawfully acquired information of "public concern." The Court concludes that the private conversation between Gloria Bartnicki and Anthony Kane is somehow a "debate . . . . worthy of constitutional protection." Perhaps the Court is correct that "[i]f the statements about the labor negotiations had been made in a public arena—during a bargaining session, for example—they would have been newsworthy." The point, however, is that Bartnicki and Kane had no intention of contributing to a public "debate" at all, and it is perverse to hold that another's unlawful interception and knowing disclosure of their conversation is speech "worthy of constitutional protection." The Constitution

---

* The Right to Privacy, 4 Harv. L.Rev. 193, 196 (1890).

should not protect the involuntary broadcast of personal conversations. Even where the communications involve public figures or concern public matters, the conversations are nonetheless private and worthy of protection. Although public persons may have forgone the right to live their lives screened from public scrutiny in some areas, it does not and should not follow that they also have abandoned their right to have a private conversation without fear of it being intentionally intercepted and knowingly disclosed.

Surely "the interest in individual privacy," at its narrowest, must embrace the right to be free from surreptitious eavesdropping on, and involuntary broadcast of, our cellular telephone conversations. The Court subordinates that right, not to the claims of those who themselves wish to speak, but to the claims of those who wish to publish the intercepted conversations of others. Congress' effort to balance the above claim to privacy against a marginal claim to speak freely is thereby set at naught.

NOTES & QUESTIONS

1. *Sweeping snooper statute.* Start at the beginning. What did Congress choose to prohibit in Title III, and who was the target of the prohibition? Why did Congress believe that it was important to prohibit interception? Do you think the prohibition on disclosure was included for the same reason? Does the Court believe that the law serves a compelling governmental interest?

2. *First Amendment brush clearing.* The court begins by calibrating the statutory provision in Title III in order to review the defendant's First Amendment challenge. Did the Court decide that the statute regulates speech? If so, does the entire statute regulate speech, or are some of the provisions not implicated? Did the Court find that the statute is content-neutral? If so, does that matter?

3. *Shielding the professionals.* What was Mr. Vopper's profession? Did that help him win this case? Do you have a sense of what motivated him to play the tape? Should that matter?

    a. *Publisher's prerogative.* Did the Court feel bound by the prior decisions in *New York Times* and *Daily Mail?* If so, why? Would the Court have reached a different conclusion if Vopper had not been a member of the media? Why did Chief Justice Rehnquist argue that Mr. Vopper's profession should not matter in this case? Would Rehnquist have reached a different conclusion if the Daily Mail or New York Times were the defendant instead?

b. *The truth shall set you free?* The Court underscores that "publication of truthful information seldom can satisfy constitutional standards." Based on the cases that you have read so far, do you agree? Think back to our review of indecency regulations. Were those indecent broadcasts truthful or untruthful? Did it matter? Would the court reach a different conclusion if Mr. Vopper played an edited version of the tape that included false information? What if Mr. Vopper had recorded the call himself?

c. *A content-based protection.* The Court found that one of the reasons the law was unconstitutional as applied to Mr. Vopper was because "the subject matter of the conversation was a matter of public concern." What test did the Court use to determine the 'newsworthiness' of Bartnicki's conversation? Do you think that test creates a workable distinction between protected and unprotected speech?

Justice Breyer certainly did. In his concurring opinion, he sought to sharpen the distinction between "public" and "private" speech and to clarify the interaction between the different statutory and constitutional interests at stake:

> As a general matter, despite the statutes' direct restrictions on speech, the Federal Constitution must tolerate laws of this kind because of the importance of these privacy and speech-related objectives. Rather than broadly forbid this kind of legislative enactment, the Constitution demands legislative efforts to tailor the laws in order reasonably to reconcile media freedom with personal, speech-related privacy.

> Nonetheless, looked at more specifically, the statutes, as applied in these circumstances, do not reasonably reconcile the competing constitutional objectives. Rather, they disproportionately interfere with media freedom. For one thing, the broadcasters here engaged in no unlawful activity other than the ultimate publication of the information another had previously obtained. They "neither encouraged nor participated directly or indirectly in the interception." No one claims that they ordered, counseled, encouraged, or otherwise aided or abetted the interception, the later delivery of the tape by the interceptor to an intermediary, or the tape's still later delivery by the intermediary to the media. And, as the Court points out, the statutes do not forbid the receipt of the tape itself. The Court adds that its holding "does not apply to punishing parties for obtaining the relevant information *unlawfully*."

> For another thing, the speakers had little or no *legitimate* interest in maintaining the privacy of the particular conversation. That conversation involved a suggestion about "blow[ing] off ... front porches" and "do[ing] some work on some of those guys," thereby raising a significant concern for the safety of others. Where publication of private information constitutes a wrongful act, the law recognizes a privilege allowing the reporting of threats to public safety. Even where the danger may have passed by the time of publication, that fact

cannot legitimize the speaker's earlier privacy expectation. Nor should editors, who must make a publication decision quickly, have to determine present or continued danger before publishing this kind of threat.

Can you articulate the difference between public and private speech as Justice Breyer explained it? How about the difference between legitimate interests in maintaining privacy and non-legitimate interests? If you were an editor for the legal blog *Above the Law*, would you feel comfortable making the decision to post an audio clip of a recorded conversation between two partners at a major law firm concerning staffing and management issues? What factors would you consider when making your decision?

   d. *More empirical battles.* Justice Stevens and Chief Justice Rehnquist disagree on the impact that liability would have on the prevalence of unlawful interceptions. Explain the "dry-up-the-market" theory. Who has the better argument? Do either of them offer evidence to support their view? How do we know who is right? How should we decide?

   4. *First Amendment and Privacy.* The Justices acknowledge conflicting concepts of both free speech and privacy. Does Justice Stevens believe that these two values are necessarily at odds? Does Chief Justice Rehnquist? Is one more interested in protecting speech than in privacy (or vice versa)?

   5. *Not all communications are created equal.* Notice that the prohibited conduct described by the Court depends on the type of communication at issue. As the statute makes clear, different standards apply to *oral* and *wire* communications. Take a look at the definitions:

> 18 U.S.C. § 2510
>
> (1) "wire communication" means any aural transfer made in whole or in part through the use of facilities for the transmission of communications by the aid of wire, cable, or other like connection between the point of origin and the point of reception (including the use of such connection in a switching station) furnished or operated by any person engaged in providing or operating such facilities for the transmission of interstate or foreign communications or communications affecting interstate or foreign commerce;
>
> (2) "oral communication" means any oral communication uttered by a person exhibiting an expectation that such communication is not subject to interception under circumstances justifying such expectation, but such term does not include any electronic communication;

Why do you think Congress chose to give different levels of protection to these different types of communications? Does the distinction make sense? Do you think the definitions were drafted with a case like *Bartnicki* in mind?

   6. *The exception explains the rule.* As Justice Stevens makes clear at the outset, many cases have been brought under Title III and similar privacy provisions without much fanfare. What set *Bartnicki* apart from the others was the fact that the defendant was a member of the media and the subject matter an

issue of public concern. The Court also noted that the prohibition on 'use' of unlawfully intercepted communications does not trigger the same First Amendment scrutiny. Many different uses of intercepted communications are prohibited: corporate and labor-management uses, extortion, workplace discipline, and even "important and socially valuable purposes." Many states have even enacted more restrictive rules regulating the interception or recording of conversations.

Of course, communications themselves are not the only private information created and stored by telephone networks. The service providers also have access to a great deal of private information about their subscribers: name and address, billing information, call records, and even location information. This type of information can sometimes be just as sensitive and revealing as the calls themselves. Congress recognized as much when it passed the Telecommunications Act of 1996, adding a provision to protect the "privacy of customer information."[*] In particular, the statute restricted the use and disclosure of "consumer proprietary network information." After several rounds of rulemakings, the Commission issued a modified rule in 2007 that required express consumer consent prior to the disclosure of such customer information. A group of telecommunications carriers challenged that ruling in the D.C. Circuit.

NCTA v. FCC
555 F.3d 996 (2009)

RANDOLPH, Circuit Judge

Whenever someone makes a call on a telephone or a cell phone, that person's telecommunications carrier receives information about who was called, when, and for how long. Carriers also have records about the kinds of services and features their customers purchase. More than twenty years ago, the Federal Communications Commission required carriers to maintain the confidentiality of such information if their customers so requested.[†] The Telecommunications Act of 1996 also imposed on carriers a "duty to protect the confidentiality of proprietary information of ... consumers."[‡] Although § 222 permitted carriers to use customer information within the confines of the existing service relationship, it prohibited carriers from otherwise using, disclosing or allowing access to such

---

[*] 47 U.S.C. § 222.

[†] *In re Furnishing of Customer Premises Equipment And Enhanced Services By American Telephone & Telegraph Co.,* 102 F.C.C.2d 655, ¶¶ 64-67 (1985).

[‡] 47 U.S.C. § 222(a).

information except "as required by law" or "with the approval of the customer."* The issues presented in this petition for judicial review deal with the validity of the Commission's latest order specifying how carriers are to obtain their customers' approval.

I

Under the 1996 Act, "customer proprietary network information" consists of information relating to the "quantity, technical configuration, type, destination, location, and amount of use of a telecommunications service subscribed to by any customer of a telecommunications carrier."† This statutory definition of what we will refer to as "customer information" encompasses customers' particular calling plans and special features, the pricing and terms of their contracts for those services, and details about who they call and when. Some carriers may use this information to market specific services or upgrades to their customers, tailored to individual usage patterns. Other carriers, especially smaller ones and new market entrants, may find it more efficient to enter into agreements with joint venturers or independent contractors to conduct such targeted marketing.

In its 1998 Order implementing the confidentiality mandate of the 1996 Act, the Commission interpreted § 222 as setting out two categories of uses of customer information: those uses to which customers implicitly consent simply by subscribing to a carrier's services, and those for which the carrier would have to obtain express customer approval.‡ ... The 1998 Order provided that carriers could infer customer approval within the confines of existing service . . . . Implicit approval also extended to customer information sharing with carriers' affiliates [w]ithin the existing service relationship between the customer and the carrier. But if carriers wished to use or disclose customer information outside of the existing relationship, even in communications with their customers, the Commission determined that customers had to consent, affirmatively and explicitly, ahead of time. This approach became known as the "opt-in" method.

In *U.S. West, Inc. v. FCC*,§ the court of appeals held that the 1998 Order's opt-in consent requirement amounted to an unconstitutional restriction on the carriers' First Amendment right to speak to their customers. [T]he court ruled that the Commission had not satisfied "its burden of showing that the customer

---

* *Id.* § 222(c)(1).

† *Id.* § 222(h)(1).

‡ *Implementation of the Telecommunications Act of 1996: Telecommunications Carriers' Use of Customer Proprietary Network Information and Other Customer Information,* 13 FCC Rcd. 8061, ¶ 23 (1998) ("1998 Order").

§182 F.3d 1224 (10th Cir. 1999),

approval regulations restrict no more speech than necessary to serve the asserted state interests." The court cited a lack of evidence that "customers do not want carriers to use their" information; even if there were such evidence, the court thought the Commission had failed to show "that an opt-out strategy would not sufficiently protect consumer privacy."

In response to the Tenth Circuit's decision, the Commission initiated a new rulemaking proceeding and issued an order modifying its regulations. The Commission stated that "in light of *U.S. West* we now conclude that an opt-in rule for intra-company use [between a carrier and its affiliates] cannot be justified based on the record we have before us." The Commission took into account customers' interest in learning of their carriers' service offerings and what it perceived as a lower risk of infringement of personal privacy when customer information is shared within an organization. The Commission therefore required only opt-out approval for the sharing of customer information between a carrier and its affiliates for communications-related purposes. The Commission prescribed the content, form, and frequency of the notice and opt-out process, pursuant to which the approval of customers would be presumed unless they specifically told their carriers not to share the information.

The 2002 Order also allowed carriers to share customer information with joint venture partners or independent contractors for marketing communications-related services. But the Commission recognized a heightened personal privacy risk associated with these third parties because they did not qualify as "carriers" under the Telecommunications Act and thus were not subject to § 222's confidentiality requirements. The Commission therefore ordered carriers and their joint venture partners or independent contractors to enter into confidentiality agreements to safeguard customer information, in addition to the opt-out notices sent to customers. Carriers were apparently content with this state of affairs; no challenges were mounted against the 2002 Order.

The Electronic Privacy Information Center petitioned in 2005 for further rulemaking to modify the Commission's customer information sharing rules. The petition noted the increasing number of "data brokers"-organizations that sell private information about individuals online-and expressed concern about how easily these organizations are able to obtain the information from carriers and other entities. The petition suggested that data brokers might obtain the information from customer service representatives by pretending to have proper authority to receive it (known as "pretexting"), by gaining unauthorized access to consumers' online accounts with carriers (by hacking, for example), or through "dishonest insiders" working for the carriers. Concerned that inadequate privacy protections contributed to the data broker problem, the Commission initiated a new rulemaking proceeding, received comments, and issued the Order at issue in this case.[*]

Two months before the Commission adopted the 2007 Order, Congress passed the Telephone Records and Privacy Protection Act of 2006.[†] The statute imposed criminal penalties for pretexting, unauthorized access to consumer accounts online, selling or transferring customer information, presumably by either data brokers or dishonest company insiders, and knowing purchase or receipt of fraudulently obtained customer information. Congress found that unauthorized disclosure of customer information "not only assaults individual privacy but, in some instances, may further acts of domestic violence or stalking, compromise the personal safety of law enforcement officers, their families, victims of crime, witnesses, or confidential informants, and undermine the integrity of law enforcement investigations."

In its 2007 Order the Commission changed, for the third time, its requirements for the form of customer approval necessary to satisfy [Section] 222. Relying on "new circumstances" to justify its altered approach, the Commission now required carriers to "obtain opt-in consent from a customer before disclosing that customer's [information] to a carrier's joint venture partner or independent contractor for the purpose of marketing communications-related services to that customer." The Commission distinguished joint venture partners and independent contractors from affiliates for two reasons. First, it determined that information shared with third-party marketers is subject to a greater risk of loss once out of the carrier's actual control; and second, it determined that those third parties would not likely be subject to the confidentiality requirements of § 222 because they are not themselves carriers. It would not sufficiently protect consumer privacy, the Commission found, for carriers simply to terminate their relationships with third parties who lose customer information, or for the Commission to rely on enforcement proceedings in the case of unauthorized disclosure: at that point, the damage has already been done. The Commission also found, based on studies brought to its attention during the rulemaking process, that consumers were less amenable to the sharing of their private information with third parties without their express prior authorization. It thus concluded that before carriers

---

[*] *See Implementation of the Telecommunications Act of 1996: Telecommunications Carriers' Use of Customer Proprietary Network Information and Other Customer Information*, 22 FCC Rcd. 6927 (2007) ("2007 Order").

[†] Pub. L. No. 109-476, 120 Stat. 3568 (codified at 18 U.S.C. § 1039).

could share customer information with joint venture partners or independent contractors, the customers had to consent expressly to such sharing.

II

Petitioner and intervenors (collectively, "petitioners") think the 2007 Order violates the First Amendment to the Constitution, or is arbitrary in violation of the Administrative Procedure Act, or both. Whatever the heading, their argument is basically the same-that the administrative record does not support the Commission's Order. There is nothing to this.

Before we get to the record we need to be precise about petitioners' position. They have not even attempted to mount an argument that the 2007 Order misinterprets § 222 and so we will assume that the Commission has faithfully adhered to the statute. Nor have they claimed that § 222 violates the First Amendment, or that it is arbitrary or capricious. The question naturally arises: if the First Amendment did not bar Congress (in § 222) from requiring carriers to obtain their customers' consent, how can it be that the First Amendment bars the Commission from implementing § 222 by requiring customer consent? Petitioners give this answer: "Both the First Amendment and the Administrative Procedure Act ... require that the Commission ... support its assertions with *evidence* before it may restrict the communication of truthful, lawfully obtained information between carriers and their marketing partners, and the ways that carriers may communicate with their existing customers." They say this evidence is needed because the "selective opt-in requirement" is more restrictive than the opt-out system it replaced.

It is true that in some First Amendment cases the Supreme Court has demanded an evidentiary showing in support of a state's law. It is also true that in other First Amendment cases the Supreme Court has found "various unprovable assumptions" sufficient to support the constitutionality of state and federal laws, particularly laws regulating business. But this case comes to us in a different posture. By conceding the constitutionality of § 222, petitioners necessarily concede at least two factual predicates underlying both the statute and the Commission's Order-namely, that the government has a substantial interest in protecting the privacy of customer information and that requiring customer approval advances that interest. We put the matter in these terms because all parties proceed on the basis that what we have here is a regulation of commercial speech, and that the validity of the regulation must therefore be tested according to the standards set forth in *Central Hudson*: the speech must "at least concern lawful activity and not be misleading"; the "governmental interest [must be] substantial"; the regulation must "directly advance[ ] the governmental interest asserted"; and the regulation must not be "more extensive than is necessary to serve that interest." We too will assume that *Central Hudson* controls.

The first part of *Central Hudson* is not in play so we turn to the second-is there a "substantial" governmental interest? Petitioners seem to recognize that they cannot contest the point in light of their agreement that § 222 is constitutional. Still, we think it important-particularly in light of the Tenth Circuit's opinion in *U.S. West*-to spell out the nature of the governmental interest at stake. The Tenth Circuit supposed that § 222 sought to promote a governmental interest in protecting against the disclosure of "information [that] could prove embarrassing," and it doubted whether this interest could be deemed "substantial." We do not share the Tenth Circuit's doubt. For one thing, we have already held, in an analogous context, that "protecting the privacy of consumer credit information" is a "substantial" governmental interest, as *Central Hudson* uses the term.[*] For another thing, we do not agree that the interest in protecting customer privacy is confined to preventing embarrassment as the Tenth Circuit thought. There is a good deal more to privacy than that. It is widely accepted that privacy deals with determining for oneself when, how and to whom personal information will be disclosed to others. The Supreme Court knows this as well as Congress: "both the common law and the literal understandings of privacy encompass the individual's control of information concerning his or her person."

The next question that must be posed under *Central Hudson* is whether the Commission's 2007 Order "directly advances" the governmental interest just identified. Here again petitioners' agreement that § 222 complies with the First Amendment all but settles the issue. The privacy of customer information cannot be preserved unless there are restrictions on the carrier's disclosure of it. And the restriction Congress imposed was customer approval. But petitioners say the Commission violated the First Amendment by implementing this congressional requirement with an opt-in system. According to petitioners, the record does not indicate that joint venturers or independent contractors have disclosed customer information to others. This argument, by focusing on what happens after a joint venturer or independent contractor receives the information, performs a sort of sleight of hand. It diverts attention from the fact that the carrier's sharing of customer information with a joint venturer or an independent contractor without the customer's consent is itself an invasion of the customer's privacy-the very harm the regulation targets. In addition, common sense supports the Commission's determination that the risk of

---

[*]Trans Union Corp. v. FTC, 245 F.3d 809, 818 (D.C. Cir. 2001).

unauthorized disclosure of customer information increases with the number of entities possessing it. The Commission therefore reasonably concluded that an opt-in consent requirement directly and materially advanced the interests in protecting customer privacy and in ensuring customer control over the information[.]

This brings us to *Central Hudson*'s final requirement that the restriction on commercial speech must be "no more broad or no more expansive than necessary to serve its substantial interests." The government does not have to show that it has adopted the least restrictive means for bringing about its regulatory objective; it does not have to demonstrate a perfect means-ends fit; and it does not have to satisfy a court that it has chosen the best conceivable option. The only condition is that the regulation be proportionate to the interests sought to be advanced. The 2007 Order easily meets this standard.

The Commission's opt-in consent scheme presumes that consumers do not want their information shared unless they expressly indicate otherwise; an opt-out scheme, which is what petitioners want, presumes the opposite. Confronted with a challenge analogous to this one, we held that opt-out is only "marginally less intrusive" than opt-in for First Amendment purposes and so upheld a nearly identical regime requiring opt-in consent for the sharing of customer credit information. In that case we did not require exhaustive evidence documenting the necessity of opt-in over opt-out; we relied on Congress's reasonable, commonsense determination that express customer consent was required. In any event, here the Commission carefully considered the differences between these two regulatory approaches, and the evidence supports the Commission's decision to prefer opt-in consent. Unlike the 1998 Order at issue in *U.S. West*, the 2007 Order required opt-in consent only with respect to a carrier's sharing of customer information with third-party marketers. The evidence showed that customers were less willing to have their information shared with third parties as opposed to affiliated entities. And the Commission reasonably concluded that customer information would be at a greater risk of disclosure once out of the control of the carriers and in the hands of entities not subject to § 222. Contractual safeguards requiring the carrier to terminate its relationship with the third party after a breach-a solution carriers favored-would not sufficiently protect customer privacy because, the Commission stated, "the damage is already inflicted upon the customer."

III

Petitioners' claim under the Administrative Procedure Act fails for the same reasons we reject their First Amendment claim: substantial evidence supported the Commission's 2007 Order and its reasoning cannot be faulted. There is one wrinkle in administrative law that petitioners seek to use to their advantage. When an agency departs from its previous policy, it must give a "reasoned analysis" for the change. The argument is that the Commission acted arbitrarily when, in light of evidence of unauthorized disclosures by *carriers,* it reversed the policy of its 2002 Order and imposed greater restrictions on the carriers' sharing of customer information with third-party marketing partners.

[H]ere the governmental interest and potential harms are the same for customer information in the hands of carriers, affiliates, or third-party marketing partners. The Commission explained that customer information could be illegally obtained by the same methods from any organization, regardless of the nature of the entity.

Accordingly, because the Commission returned to a limited opt-in consent requirement in response to the increasing activity of data brokers, and because it gave sufficient reasons for singling out the relationships between carriers and third-party marketing partners, we hold that the Commission adequately provided the reasoned analysis *State Farm* requires.

NOTES & QUESTIONS

1. *Different shades of speech.* The petitioners in this case sought to overturn a privacy regulation based on their First Amendment interest. Why did they fail where the defendant in *Bartnicki* succeeded? Explain what "speech" the petitioners argue is being regulated. Recall that the Court in *Bartnicki* emphasized that the statute at issue restricted *truthful* speech. Is the speech at issue in this case truthful? If so, why did the court reach a different conclusion?

2. *Confidentiality versus control.* How would you distinguish the privacy interest at stake in this case, embodied in Section 222, from the privacy interest at stake in *Bartnicki*? Whom did Congress intend to protect when they enacted Section 222 and why? Do you share Congress' concern about the nonconsensual use of customer data? If not, why not? Sometimes it is helpful to frame the privacy interest in terms of *control* rather than secrecy or confidentiality. Why did Congress believe that it was important to give consumers control over the collection, use, and disclosure of their information?

3. *Evidence or deference.* The petitioners in this case argued, as we have seen in many other cases, that the Commission did not have sufficient "evidence" to support the regulation. Based on the court's opinion, how much evidence do you think is required for the regulation to survive First Amendment scrutiny? How much is required to survive an APA challenge? Are Congressional findings more or less persuasive than surveys or other evidence cited in the agency record?

4. *Marketers, beware.* The CPNI rules at issue in this case limit the ability of telecommunications providers to disclose or use a customer's information without their consent. One of the most tempting uses of this data, as the court mentioned at the outset, is for cross marketing. If you are a long distance provider, you likely see local telephone customers as your main target market and want to get your hands on customer lists to send targeted ads. The CPNI rules prohibit carriers from disclosing that information without affirmative, opt-in consent from their customers.

a. *Chasing after your customers.* There are some cases where a carrier's disclosure of customer information is necessary to provide the service. The D.C. Circuit addressed such a case just a few days before it issued the decision in *NCTA*. In *Verizon v. FCC,*[*] the court reviewed a cease and desist order issued by the Commission to Verizon in response to complaints filed by competitors (cable companies providing VoIP services). These competitors challenged Verizon's practice of targeting outbound customers with "retention marketing" solicitations. Verizon was using the telephone number porting requests (called "Local Service Requests") sent by their competitors to target "defecting" customers. Verizon conceded that "that advance notice of a carrier change that one carrier is required to submit to another is carrier 'proprietary information' under section 222(b)." But Verizon argued that the statute only protected information provided for the purpose of the "receiving carrier's provision of a telecommunications service."

The court rejected Verizon's claim under the APA, deferring to the FCC's interpretation of the statute, and also rejected Verizon's First Amendment challenge, focusing on the *Central Hudson* factors as above. The court was not persuaded by an argument about ensuring the *confidentiality* of customer information, but by the argument that this rule helps to "make sure that Verizon's incentive on receiving an LSR is unambiguously to complete it promptly and effectively" and to "avoid the 'two-masters problem.'"

5. *Welcome to the Cyber Age.* While the privacy protections established in the Fourth Amendment to the U.S. Constitution are not a central concern of many Communications Law practitioners, the Supreme Court has recently issued a landmark opinion that will ensure the two legal fields become closely intertwined in the years to come. The case concerned the constitutionality of the warrantless collection of nearly six months of "cell site location information" (CSLI) from MetroPCS and Sprint.[†] The Government ultimately "obtained

---

[*] 555 F.3d 270 (D.C. Cir. 2009).
[†] Carpenter v. United States, 138 S. Ct. 2206 (2018).

12,898 location points cataloging Carpenter's [the petitioner's] movements—an average of 101 data points per day."[*] The Court ultimately held that "when the Government accessed CSLI from the wireless carriers, it invaded Carpenter's reasonable expectation of privacy in the whole of his physical movements."[†]

The Court's decision marks a doctrinal inflection point for Fourth Amendment privacy rights. Prior to *Carpenter* the federal courts refused to hold that the seizure of location data held by a telecommunications carrier (a "third party") could be limited by the Fourth Amendment. This "third-party doctrine" was rooted in a pair of cases from the 1970s, one about telephone call records (*Smith v. Maryland*) and the other about bank checks, deposit slips, and statements (*Miller v. United States*). But the Court in *Carpenter* declined to extend the rationale of *Smith* and *Miller* to modern cell phone location data, finding that "[s]uch a chronicle implicates privacy concerns far beyond those considered in *Smith* and *Miller*."[‡]

The four of the Justices who dissented in *Carpenter* each presented distinct views as to why the case should have come out differently and how they would approach similar cases in the future. But they all took seriously one of the arguments presented by Carpenter's attorneys in the case: that location data should be entitled to special constitutional protection because Congress recognized its sensitivity in the CPNI provision (47 U.S.C. § 222). Justice Gorsuch, in particular, keyed in on the significance of the rights granted to telecommunications subscribers under the FCC rules:

> It seems to me entirely possible a person's cell-site data could qualify as his papers or effects under existing law. Yes, the tele-phone carrier holds the information. But 47 U. S. C. § 222 designates a customer's cell-site location information as "customer proprietary network information" (CPNI), § 222(h)(1)(A), and gives customers certain rights to control use of and access to CPNI about themselves.

Not only did Justice Gorsuch express interest in analyzing the "positive law" protections given to personal data under the CPNI rules, he viewed those (underdeveloped) points as "perhaps his most promising line of argument."[§]

Justices Kennedy, Thomas, and Alito all expressed greater skepticism of the impact of the CPNI provision on the Fourth Amendment protections for cell phone location data. But now that the Court has held that such data are protected, it is likely that both Congress and the FCC will step in to provide

---

[*] Id. (slip op. at 3).

[†] Id. (slip op. at 15).

[‡] Id. (slip op. at 17).

[§] Id. (Gorsuch, J, dissenting) (slip op. at 20-21).

greater clarity to both law enforcement and to carriers about their obligations in protecting personal data.

| NOTE: LIMITING UNWANTED CALLS |

Most cell phone users have become keenly aware in recent years of a scourge that Congress first tried to address more than twenty-five years ago: unwanted phone calls. The Telephone Consumer Protection Act of 1991[*]was enacted to address the widespread problem of automated and prerecorded calls and faxes. As Justice Ginsburg recently described in a decision upholding the right to bring private suits to enforce its rules, the TCPA was a response to "[v]oluminous consumer complaints about abuses of telephone technology—for example, computerized calls dispatched to private homes."[†] In particular, "Congress determined that federal legislation was needed because telemarketers, by operating interstate, were escaping state-law prohibitions on intrusive nuisance calls." Congress found that "Unrestricted telemarketing," can be "an intrusive invasion of privacy" and that "[m]any consumers are outraged over the proliferation of intrusive, nuisance [telemarketing] calls to their homes." This was especially true for "automated or prerecorded telephone calls" made to private residences.

Congress made four practices unlawful under the TCPA:

- (1) use of an "automatic telephone dialing system or an artificial or prerecorded voice message," without the prior express consent of the called party, to call any emergency telephone line, hospital patient, pager, cellular telephone, or other service for which the receiver is charged for the call;[‡]

- (2) use of "artificial or prerecorded voice messages" to call residential telephone lines without prior express consent;[§]

- (3) sending "unsolicited advertisements" to fax machines;[**] and

- (4) using "automatic telephone dialing systems" to engage two or more of a business' telephone lines simultaneously.[††]

Congress also added a new prohibition on manipulating caller identification information ("spoofing") in 2010.[‡‡] The law gives the FCC the authority to ban

---

[*] 47 U.S.C. § 227

[†] 132 S. Ct. 740, 744 (2012).

[‡] 47 U.S.C. § 227(b)(1)(A).

[§] *Id.* § 227(b)(1)(B).

[**] *Id.* § 227(b)(1)(C).

[††] *Id.* § 227(b)(1)(D).

or exempt certain types of prerecorded calls and directed the Commission to proscribe regulations to protect the privacy of residential telephone numbers. The Federal Trade Commission also manages a "do not call" system that compliments these TCPA restrictions by providing consumers with a mechanism to opt-out of all telemarketing calls (even those that do not violate the TCPA).

As cell phones have become more commonplace than residential telephones, many businesses now use automated systems to push out marketing calls and SMS messages at a huge scale. As a result, the TCPA has become one of the most active litigation areas in Communications Law. The U.S. Chamber of Commerce (which represents many companies that have been subject to liability for unauthorized calls under the TCPA) reported in 2017 that the number of suits brought under the law "spiked" by 50 percent in the period between August 2015 and the end of 2016.

Why did the Chamber select August 2015 as the starting point? Shortly before that date the FCC issued a declaratory ruling, in response to 21 separate petitions requesting clarification, on the scope of the TCPA. The Commission in the Order (1) expanded the definition of "automatic telephone dialing system," (2) found that when a number has been reassigned, the caller must obtain consent of the current provider for any autodialed or prerecorded call (though the Commission provided a "one call safe harbor" for reassigned numbers), (3) provided that consumers may revoke consent through "any reasonable means," and clarified the emergency and healthcare exemptions.[*] Many companies challenged the FCC order under the APA, and those petitions for review were considered by the D.C. Circuit in a consolidated case.[†] The court rejected the FCC Order in part, finding that the proposed definition of ATDS was too broad because it could be read to include conventional smartphones and that the "one call safe harbor" for reassigned numbers had no statutory basis. But the court did uphold the Commission's rule permitting revocation of consent and clarification of the healthcare exemption.

After the D.C. Circuit's decision in *ACA International*, several different groups began pursuing a different strategy to reduce their liability under the TCPA: they challenged the constitutionality of the statute's cellphone call ban on First Amendment grounds. These legal issues should be familiar to you now after reading *Bartnicki* and *NCTA*, but there was another important wrinkle that

---

‡ *Id.* § 227(e).

In The Matter Of Rules And Regulations Implementing The Telephone Consumer Protection Act Of 1991, 30 FCC Rcd. 7961 (2015).

† ACA Int'l v. FCC, 885 F.3d 687 (D.C. Cir. 2018).

made these challenges particularly complicated. In 2015 Congress amended the TCPA to provide a specific exception for calls made to collect debts owed to or guaranteed by the federal government. So a number of groups, including defendants in civil TCPA lawsuits and plaintiffs bringing constitutional claims against the government, argued that this exemption made the TCPA a content-based speech restriction and that the law could not survive strict scrutiny. All the lower courts that have considered this issue have held that the TCPA itself is constitutional, but some courts have ruled that the government debt collection exception is unconstitutional and must be severed from the statute. One such case made it all the way up to the U.S. Supreme Court.

BARR V. AMERICAN ASSOCIATION OF POLITICAL CONSULTANTS
140 S. Ct. 2335 (2020)

Justice Kavanaugh announced the judgment of the Court and delivered an opinion.[*]

Americans passionately disagree about many things. But they are largely united in their disdain for robocalls. The Federal Government receives a staggering number of complaints about robocalls—3.7 million complaints in 2019 alone. The States likewise field a constant barrage of complaints.

For nearly 30 years, the people's representatives in Congress have been fighting back. As relevant here, the Telephone Consumer Protection Act of 1991, known as the TCPA, generally prohibits robocalls to cell phones and home phones. But a 2015 amendment to the TCPA allows robocalls that are made to collect debts owed to or guaranteed by the Federal Government, including robocalls made to collect many student loan and mortgage debts.

This case concerns robocalls to cell phones. Plaintiffs in this case are political and nonprofit organizations that want to make political robocalls to cell phones. Invoking the First Amendment, they argue that the 2015 government-debt exception unconstitutionally favors debt-collection speech over political and other speech. As relief from that unconstitutional law, they urge us to invalidate the entire 1991 robocall restriction, rather than simply invalidating the 2015 government-debt exception.

---

[*] Justice Kavanaugh's opinion was joined by the Chief Justice, Justice Alito, and Justice Thomas as to Parts I and II. So his opinion had plurality support for the First Amendment analysis. Justice Breyer wrote an opinion concurring in the judgment and dissenting in part, which was joined by Justices Kagan and Ginsburg. Justice Sotomayor wrote separately concurring in the judgment but agreeing with Justice Breyer that intermediate scrutiny should apply. Justice Gorsuch wrote an opinion, joined in part by Justice Thomas, dissenting in part from the judgment with respect to severability.—ED.

Six Members of the Court today conclude that Congress has impermissibly favored debt-collection speech over political and other speech, in violation of the First Amendment. Applying traditional severability principles, seven Members of the Court conclude that the entire 1991 robocall restriction should not be invalidated, but rather that the 2015 government-debt exception must be invalidated and severed from the remainder of the statute. As a result, plaintiffs still may not make political robocalls to cell phones, but their speech is now treated equally with debt-collection speech. The judgment of the U. S. Court of Appeals for the Fourth Circuit is affirmed.

I

A

In 1991, Congress passed and President George H. W. Bush signed the Telephone Consumer Protection Act. The Act responded to a torrent of vociferous consumer complaints about intrusive robocalls. A growing number of telemarketers were using equipment that could automatically dial a telephone number and deliver an artificial or prerecorded voice message. At the time, more than 300,000 solicitors called more than 18 million Americans every day. Consumers were "outraged" and considered robocalls an invasion of privacy "regardless of the content or the initiator of the message."

A leading Senate sponsor of the TCPA captured the zeitgeist in 1991, describing robocalls as "the scourge of modern civilization. They wake us up in the morning; they interrupt our dinner at night; they force the sick and elderly out of bed; they hound us until we want to rip the telephone right out of the wall."

In enacting the TCPA, Congress found that banning robocalls was "the only effective means of protecting telephone consumers from this nuisance and privacy invasion." To that end, the TCPA imposed various restrictions on the use of automated telephone equipment. As relevant here, one restriction prohibited "any call (other than a call made for emergency purposes or made with the prior express consent of the called party) using any automatic telephone dialing system or an artificial or prerecorded voice" to "any telephone number assigned to a paging service, *cellular telephone service*, specialized mobile radio service, or other radio common carrier service, or any service for which the called party is charged for the call." That provision is codified in § 227(b)(1)(A)(iii) of Title 47 of the U. S. Code.

In plain English, the TCPA prohibited almost all robocalls to cell phones.

Twenty-four years later, in 2015, Congress . . . carved out a new government-debt exception to the general robocall restriction.

. . .

B

Plaintiffs in this case are the American Association of Political Consultants and three other organizations that participate in the political system. Plaintiffs and their members make calls to citizens to discuss candidates and issues, solicit donations, conduct polls, and get out the vote. Plaintiffs believe that their political outreach would be more effective and efficient if they could make robocalls to cell phones. But because plaintiffs are not in the business of collecting government debt, § 227(b)(1)(A)(iii) prohibits them from making those robocalls.

. . .

II

Ratified in 1791, the First Amendment provides that Congress shall make no law "abridging the freedom of speech." Above "all else, the First Amendment means that government" generally "has no power to restrict expression because of its message, its ideas, its subject matter, or its content."

The Court's precedents allow the government to "constitutionally impose reasonable time, place, and manner regulations" on speech, but the precedents restrict the government from discriminating "in the regulation of expression on the basis of the content of that expression." Content-based laws are subject to strict scrutiny. By contrast, content-neutral laws are subject to a lower level of scrutiny.

Section 227(b)(1)(A)(iii) generally bars robocalls to cell phones. Since the 2015 amendment, the law has exempted robocalls to collect government debt. The initial First Amendment question is whether the robocall restriction, with the government-debt exception, is content-based. The answer is yes.

As relevant here, a law is content-based if "a regulation of speech 'on its face' draws distinctions based on the message a speaker conveys." That description applies to a law that "singles out specific subject matter for differential treatment." For example, "a law banning the use of sound trucks for political speech—and only political speech—would be a content-based regulation, even if it imposed no limits on the political viewpoints that could be expressed."

Under § 227(b)(1)(A)(iii), the legality of a robocall turns on whether it is "made solely to collect a debt owed to or guaranteed by the United States." A robocall that says, "Please pay your government debt" is legal. A robocall that says, "Please donate to our political campaign" is illegal. That is about as content-based as it gets. Because the law favors speech made for collecting government debt over political and other speech, the law is a content-based restriction on speech.

The Government advances three main arguments for deeming the statute content-neutral, but none is persuasive.

First, the Government suggests that § 227(b)(1)(A)(iii) draws distinctions based on speakers (authorized debt collectors), not based on content. But that is not the law in front of us. This statute singles out calls "made solely to collect a debt owed to or guaranteed by the United States," not all calls from authorized debt collectors.

In any event, "the fact that a distinction is speaker based" does not "automatically render the distinction content neutral."* Indeed, the Court has held that "'laws favoring some speakers over others demand strict scrutiny when the legislature's speaker preference reflects a content preference.'"

Second, the Government argues that the legality of a robocall under the statute depends simply on whether the caller is engaged in a particular economic activity, not on the content of speech. We disagree. The law here focuses on whether the caller is *speaking* about a particular topic. In *Sorrell,* this Court held that a law singling out pharmaceutical marketing for unfavorable treatment was content-based. So too here.

Third, according to the Government, if this statute is content-based because it singles out debt-collection speech, then so are statutes that *regulate* debt collection, like the Fair Debt Collection Practices Act. That slippery-slope argument is unpersuasive in this case. As we explained in *Sorrell,* "the First Amendment does not prevent restrictions directed at commerce or conduct from imposing incidental burdens on speech." The law here, like the Vermont law in *Sorrell,* "does not simply have an effect on speech, but is directed at certain content and is aimed at particular speakers." The Government's concern is understandable, but the courts have generally been able to distinguish impermissible content-based speech restrictions from traditional or ordinary economic regulation of commercial activity that imposes incidental burdens on speech. The issue before us concerns only robocalls to cell phones. Our decision today on that issue fits comfortably within existing First Amendment precedent. Our decision is not intended to expand existing First Amendment doctrine or to otherwise affect traditional or ordinary economic regulation of commercial activity.

---

* Reed v. Town of Gilbert, 576 U.S. 155, 170 (2015); Sorrell v. IMS Health Inc., 564 U.S. 552, 563–564 (2011).

In short, the robocall restriction with the government-debt exception is content-based. Under the Court's precedents, a "law that is content based" is "subject to strict scrutiny." *Reed*, 576 U.S., at 165, 135 S.Ct. 2218. The Government concedes that it cannot satisfy strict scrutiny to justify the government-debt exception. We agree. The Government's stated justification for the government-debt exception is collecting government debt. Although collecting government debt is no doubt a worthy goal, the Government concedes that it has not sufficiently justified the differentiation between government-debt collection speech and other important categories of robocall speech, such as political speech, charitable fundraising, issue advocacy, commercial advertising, and the like.

III

Having concluded that the 2015 government-debt exception created an unconstitutional exception to the 1991 robocall restriction, we must decide whether to invalidate the entire 1991 robocall restriction, or instead to invalidate and sever the 2015 government-debt exception. Before we apply ordinary severability principles, we must address plaintiffs' broader initial argument for why the entire 1991 robocall restriction is unconstitutional.

A

Plaintiffs correctly point out that the Government's asserted interest for the 1991 robocall restriction is consumer privacy. But according to plaintiffs, Congress's willingness to enact the government-debt exception in 2015 betrays a newfound lack of genuine congressional concern for consumer privacy. As plaintiffs phrase it, the 2015 exception "undermines the credibility" of the Government's interest in consumer privacy. Plaintiffs further contend that if Congress no longer has a genuine interest in consumer privacy, then the underlying 1991 robocall restriction is no longer justified (presumably under any level of heightened scrutiny) and is therefore now unconstitutional.

Plaintiffs' argument is not without force, but we ultimately disagree with it. It is true that the Court has recognized that exceptions to a speech restriction "may diminish the credibility of the government's rationale for restricting speech in the first place." But here, Congress's addition of the government-debt exception in 2015 does not cause us to doubt the credibility of Congress's continuing interest in protecting consumer privacy.

After all, the government-debt exception is only a slice of the overall robocall landscape. This is not a case where a restriction on speech is littered with exceptions that substantially negate the restriction. On the contrary, even after 2015, Congress has retained a very broad restriction on robocalls. The pre-1991 statistics on robocalls show that a variety of organizations collectively made a huge number of robocalls. And there is no reason to think that the incentives for those organizations—and many others—to make robocalls has diminished in any way since 1991. The continuing robocall restriction proscribes *tens of millions* of would-be robocalls that would otherwise occur *every day*. Congress's continuing broad prohibition of robocalls amply demonstrates Congress's continuing interest in consumer privacy.

The simple reality, as we assess the legislative developments, is that Congress has competing interests. Congress's growing interest (as reflected in the 2015 amendment) in collecting government debt does not mean that Congress suddenly lacks a genuine interest in restricting robocalls. Plaintiffs seem to argue that Congress must be interested either in debt collection or in consumer privacy. But that is a false dichotomy, as we see it. As is not infrequently the case with either/or questions, the answer to this either/or question is "both." Congress is interested both in collecting government debt and in protecting consumer privacy.

Therefore, we disagree with plaintiffs' broader initial argument for holding the entire 1991 robocall restriction unconstitutional.

B

Plaintiffs next focus on ordinary severability principles. Applying those principles, the question before the Court is whether (i) to invalidate the entire 1991 robocall restriction, as plaintiffs want, or (ii) to invalidate just the 2015 government-debt exception and sever it from the remainder of the statute, as the Government wants.

We agree with the Government that we must invalidate the 2015 government-debt exception and sever that exception from the remainder of the statute.

. . .

3

One final severability wrinkle remains. This is an equal-treatment case, and equal-treatment cases can sometimes pose complicated severability questions.

The "First Amendment is a kind of Equal Protection Clause for ideas."* And Congress violated that First Amendment equal-treatment principle in this case by favoring debt-collection robocalls and discriminating against political and other robocalls.

---

* Williams-Yulee v. Florida Bar, 575 U.S. 433, 470 (2015) (Scalia, J., dissenting).

When the constitutional violation is unequal treatment, as it is here, a court theoretically can cure that unequal treatment either by extending the benefits or burdens to the exempted class, or by nullifying the benefits or burdens for all. Here, for example, the Government would prefer to cure the unequal treatment by extending the robocall restriction and thereby proscribing nearly all robocalls to cell phones. By contrast, plaintiffs want to cure the unequal treatment by nullifying the robocall restriction and thereby allowing all robocalls to cell phones.

When, as here, the Court confronts an equal-treatment constitutional violation, the Court generally applies the same commonsense severability principles described above. If the statute contains a severability clause, the Court typically severs the discriminatory exception or classification, and thereby extends the relevant statutory benefits or burdens to those previously exempted, rather than nullifying the benefits or burdens for all. In light of the presumption of severability, the Court generally does the same even in the absence of a severability clause. The Court's precedents reflect that preference for extension rather than nullification.

To be sure, some equal-treatment cases can raise complex questions about whether it is appropriate to extend benefits or burdens, rather than nullifying the benefits or burdens. For example, there can be due process, fair notice, or other independent constitutional barriers to extension of benefits or burdens. There also can be knotty questions about what is the exception and what is the rule. But here, we need not tackle all of the possible hypothetical applications of severability doctrine in equal-treatment cases. The government-debt exception is a relatively narrow exception to the broad robocall restriction, and severing the government-debt exception does not raise any other constitutional problems.

Plaintiffs insist, however, that a *First Amendment* equal-treatment case is different. According to plaintiffs, a court should not cure "a First Amendment violation by outlawing more speech." The implicit premise of that argument is that extending the robocall restriction to debt-collection robocalls would be unconstitutional. But that is wrong. A generally applicable robocall restriction would be permissible under the First Amendment. Extending the robocall restriction to those robocalls raises no First Amendment problem. So the First Amendment does not tell us which way to cure the unequal treatment in this case. Therefore, we apply traditional severability principles. And as we have explained, severing the 2015 government-debt exception cures the unequal treatment and constitutes the proper result under the Court's traditional severability principles. In short, the correct result in this case is to sever the 2015 government-debt exception and leave in place the longstanding robocall restriction.

...

*   *   *

In 1991, Congress enacted a general restriction on robocalls to cell phones. In 2015, Congress carved out an exception that allowed robocalls made to collect government debt. In doing so, Congress favored debt-collection speech over plaintiffs' political speech. We hold that the 2015 government-debt exception added an unconstitutional exception to the law. We cure that constitutional violation by invalidating the 2015 government-debt exception and severing it from the remainder of the statute. The judgment of the U. S. Court of Appeals for the Fourth Circuit is affirmed.

It is so ordered.

NOTES & QUESTIONS

1. *Privacy rules for thee not for me.* On one level, the challenge in this case is straightforward. Congress created a special exception to the general privacy rule protecting individuals from unwanted calls to their cell phones. That exception gave government debt collectors the unique privilege of making unwanted robocalls without prior written consent. And the rule certainly did not serve the statutes underlying purpose of protecting privacy. So what was the Government's defense?

2. *A Judgment is more than one man's opinion.* Notice the unusual byline on this decision. Justice Kavanaugh announced "the Judgment" of the Court and delivered "an Opinion." What is the difference? Well that last paragraph at the end (before "it is so ordered") is the Judgment of the Court. The bottom line? The government-debt exception is unconstitutional and is severed from the TCPA. Four other Justices concur in the full judgment—Chief Justice Roberts, Justice Alito, Justice Thomas, and Justice Sotomayor. But the four remaining Justices also concurred in *parts* of the Judgment (just not the same parts). Justice Gorsuch concurred in the part of the Judgment that the exception was unconstitutional, but disagreed that it should be severed. Justices Breyer, Kagan, and Ginsburg disagreed with the Court's conclusion that the exception was unconstitutional, but agreed that if it was unconstitutional it should be severed. So what is the significance of Kavanaugh's "Opinion" and what controls?

a. *Essential elements of the plurality.* Justice Kavanaugh's plurality opinion follows a simple logical structure. The government-debt exception is a content-based restriction on speech. Content-based restrictions are subject to strict scrutiny. The Government concedes the exception cannot survive strict scrutiny. Thus the exception is unconstitutional. When part of a statute is unconstitutional, it should be severed if Congress said so in the statute or if the presumption in favor of severability applies. Both are true in this case, so the unconstitutional exception should be severed. Seems straightforward enough. Except that more than four justices disagree with different links in that logical chain. So Justice Kavanaugh could not garner a majority for his Opinion.

b. *Justice Sotomayor to the rescue.* Without the concurrence by Justice Sotomayor there might have been even more uncertainty as to the majority result in this case. Her opinion straddles Justice Kavanaugh's plurality and Justice Breyer's partial dissent. She agrees with Justice Kavanaugh that the exception is unconstitutional and must be severed, but also agrees with Justice Breyer that not all content-based speech restrictions must survive strict scrutiny. She writes:

> I agree with much of the partial dissent's explanation that strict scrutiny should not apply to all content-based distinctions. In my view, however, the government-debt exception in 47 U.S.C. § 227(b) still fails intermediate scrutiny because it is not "narrowly tailored to serve a significant governmental interest." Even under intermediate scrutiny, the Government has not explained how a debt-collection robocall about a government-backed debt is any less intrusive or could be any less harassing than a debt-collection robocall about a privately backed debt. As the Fourth Circuit noted, the government-debt exception is seriously underinclusive because it permits "many of the intrusive calls that the automated call ban was enacted to prohibit." The Government could have employed far less restrictive means to further its interest in collecting debt, such as "secur[ing] consent from the debtors to make debt-collection calls" or "plac[ing] the calls itself." Nor has the Government "sufficiently justified the differentiation between government-debt collection speech and other important categories of robocall speech, such as political speech, charitable fundraising, issue advocacy, commercial advertising, and the like."

> Nevertheless, I agree that the offending provision is severable.

> With those understandings, I concur in the judgment.

c. *Justice Breyer scrutinizes the level of scrutiny.* In his partial dissent joined by Justices Kagan and Ginsburg (and, in a way, by Justice Sotomayor), Justice Breyer challenges the assumption that all content-based speech restrictions should be subject to strict scrutiny:

I recognize that the underlying cell phone robocall restriction primarily concerns a means of communication. And that fact, as I discuss below, triggers some heightened scrutiny, reflected in an intermediate scrutiny standard. Strict scrutiny and its strong presumption of unconstitutionality, however, have no place here.The plurality claims that its approach, which categorically applies strict scrutiny to content-based distinctions, will not "affect traditional or ordinary economic regulation of commercial activity." But how is that so? Much of human life involves activity that takes place through speech. And much regulatory activity turns upon speech content. Consider, for example, the regulation of securities sales, drug labeling, food labeling, false advertising, workplace safety warnings, automobile airbag instructions, consumer electronic labels, tax forms, debt collection, and so on. All of those regulations necessarily involve content-based speech distinctions. What are the differences between regulatory programs themselves other than differences based on content? After all, the regulatory spheres in which the Securities and Exchange Commission or the Federal Trade Commission operate are defined by content. Put simply, treating all content-based distinctions on speech as presumptively unconstitutional is unworkable and would obstruct the ordinary workings of democratic governance.

That conclusion is true here notwithstanding the plurality's effort to bring political speech into the First Amendment analysis. It is true that the underlying cell phone robocall restriction generally prohibits political speakers from making robocalls. But that has little to do with the government-debt exception or *its* practical effect. Nor does it justify the application of strict scrutiny.

Consider prescription drug labels, securities forms, and tax statements. A government agency might reasonably specify just what information the form or label must contain and further provide that the form or label may not contain other information (thereby excluding political statements). No one would think that the exclusion of political speech, say, from a drug label, means that courts must examine all other regulatory exceptions with strict scrutiny. Put differently, it is hard to imagine that such exceptions threaten political speech in the marketplace of ideas, or have any significant impact on the free exchange of ideas. To treat those exceptions as presumptively unconstitutional would work a significant transfer of authority from legislatures and agencies to courts, potentially inhibiting the creation of the very government programs for which the people (after debate) have voiced their support, despite those programs' minimal speech-related harms. Given the values at the heart of the First Amendment, that interpretation threatens to stand that Amendment on its head. It could also lead the Court to water down the strict scrutiny standard, which would limit speech protections in situations where strict scrutiny's strong protections should properly apply.

What do you think is animating Justice Breyer's concern with applying strict scrutiny in this case? What does he think might happen as a result? Do you agree?

d. *Which rule hits the Mark?* When the Supreme Court reviews a case, it generally adjudicates by majority rule. Five or more Justices make a majority, and the decision of the majority becomes binding precedent in future cases. But when a majority of Justices agree on an outcome but cannot agree on the specific reasoning, the precedential status of the opinions is less clear. The Supreme Court held in a 1977 case called *Marks v. United States* that "when a fragmented Court decides a case and no single rationale explaining the result enjoys the assent of five Justices, 'the holding of the Court may be viewed as that position taken by those Members who concurred in the judgments on the narrowest grounds.'" But this "*Marks* rule" can be more easily stated than applied. What is the narrowest grounds for concurring in the Judgment in *Barr v. AAPC*?

3. *Winning the battle but losing the war.* The Plaintiffs in this case did not want to block government debt collectors from robocalling them. They wanted to make their own robocalls for political campaigns. Did they get what they wanted? Why not? If they were right that the statute was unconstitutional, doesn't that mean that they won? If they won but did not get what they wanted, doesn't that mean that they didn't have standing? This all turns on the issue of severability. Note Justice Kavanaugh's acknowledgment of the thorny issues that severability can cause in First Amendment cases.

B. CABLE TV

Most of the communications privacy legislation and litigation in the 1990s was focused on the privacy of wire communications and telephone customer data, but even before Congress enacted the TCPA and the CPNI rules, it included provisions to protect the privacy of cable subscribers in the Cable Communications Policy Act of 1984.[*] The law not only limits collection and disclosure of personal information, but also requires cable companies to provide customers with access to the information collected about them and requires the companies to delete personal information that is no longer needed. The law also requires cable providers to give subscribers notice of their privacy practices, the subscriber's rights, the provider's duties under the law, and the subscriber's ability to enforce those rights. The U.S. Court of Appeals for the Tenth Circuit

---

[*]47 U.S.C. § 551.

explained these requirements and the basis of the law in a 1992 case brought by subscribers who challenged the sufficiency of their provider's privacy notices.

SCOFIELD V. TELECABLE OF OVERLANDPARK, INC.
973 F.2d 874 (10th Cir. 1992)

In 1984, Congress enacted the Cable Act to establish national policy and guidelines for the cable television industry. Section 551 of this Act establishes a self-contained and privately enforceable scheme for the protection of cable subscriber privacy. The section was included in the Act in response to Congress' observation that: "Cable systems, particularly those with a 'two-way' capability, have an enormous capacity to collect and store personally identifiable information about each cable subscriber." "Subscriber records from interactive systems," Congress noted, "can reveal details about bank transactions, shopping habits, political contributions, viewing habits and other significant personal decisions."

Consequently, Section 551 regulates four types of cable company practices involving "personally identifiable information." Most importantly, it limits the cable company's ability to use its system to "peer in" on the cable viewer and collect personally identifiable information such as the subscriber's viewing habits or the nature of transactions made by the subscriber over the cable system, and it limits the types of third-party disclosure that can be made of information the cable company has collected. Section 551 also requires that cable operators provide subscribers access to personally identifiable information collected and maintained by them . . . and it mandates that operators destroy personally identifiable information that is no longer necessary for the purpose for which it was collected.

In addition, section 551(a) establishes a set of subscriber notice requirements designed to inform subscribers of (1) the operator's information practices that affect subscriber privacy, (2) the subscriber's rights to limit the collection and disclosure of information, (3) the operator's legal duties, and (4) the subscriber's right to enforce those duties. These requirements do not themselves create a class of protected privacy interests. That is, subscribers have no privacy interest in receiving a notice itself. Nor can one infer from the failure to provide a privacy notice that an operator's practices in any way intrude upon subscriber privacy. Instead, the notice requirements provide "procedural safeguards to consumers for the protection of their privacy interests."

NOTES & QUESTIONS

1. *Nitpicking about notice.* The plaintiffs in *Scofield* sought to challenge the privacy notices provided by their local cable company. The statute requires the company to provide "clear and conspicuous" notice of:

> 47 U.S.C. § 551(a)(1)
>
> (A) the nature of personally identifiable information collected or to be collected with respect to the subscriber and the nature of the use of such information;
>
> (B) the nature, frequency, and purpose of any disclosure which may be made of such information, including an identification of the types of persons to whom the disclosure may be made;
>
> (C) the period during which such information will be maintained by the cable operator;
>
> (D) the times and place at which the subscriber may have access to such information in accordance with subsection (d) of this section; and
>
> (E) the limitations provided by this section with respect to the collection and disclosure of information by a cable operator and the right of the subscriber under subsections (f) and (h) of this section to enforce such limitations.

Ultimately the court was not convinced that the notices provided by the cable company were insufficient under the statute. In deciding whether the notices were clear, the court looked to the degree of precision and detail of the information provided in the notices, as well as the underlying interest that the statute promotes. As the court found:

> in determining whether a disclosure is sufficiently precise or detailed, we must consider the statute's aim of protecting subscriber privacy. Logically, a disclosure is not sufficiently "clear and conspicuous" or "meaningful," if it is couched in terms so broad that it fails to warn an ordinary subscriber of practices that materially affect his privacy interests. Conversely, unless a guideline specifically requires it, "meaningful" disclosure does not require the addition of information that is redundant or marginally useful to a person of ordinary sensibilities.

Notice is a common issue in privacy law because it is inherent to the opt-out model used in some of the laws and regulations limiting the use or disclosure of customer data. However, many people are critical of the "notice and choice" framing of privacy law in the United States because they feel that consumers are not in a position to bargain with these companies or to meaningfully control what information is collected about them. The companies, in contrast, do not want to implement an opt-in model because they feel that consumers will most likely not choose to be tracked, and companies fear diminished access to valuable customer data that they want for marketing purposes. This is why we saw such a contentious fight in the *NCTA* case over whether opt-in or opt-out rules would apply to the disclosure of telephone customer information for marketing purposes.

2. *Picking your speech battles.* Unlike in the telephone context, we have not seen a company bring a First Amendment challenge to the Cable Act privacy requirements. Why do you think that is? Do you think that a provider would have success with such a challenge? If not, why not?

3. *Towards data minimization.* More recently, the focus has shifted away from notice to challenges concerning the underlying privacy practices of cable companies. Recall that the statute requires providers to "destroy personally identifiable information if the information is no longer necessary for the purpose for which it was collected" and there are no pending requests for the data.[*] This is part of a set of pro-privacy practices generally known as "data minimization." A group of plaintiffs in Wisconsin brought suit against Time Warner Cable in 2015, alleging that the company routinely failed to delete subscriber data as required under the statute.[†] The case was initially dismissed by the district court on Article III standing grounds, and the Seventh Circuit affirmed that decision in 2017. The court found that the plaintiff had not established that violation of privacy rights granted under the Cable Act invaded a "concrete interest." This case is one example of a larger trend, as federal courts are increasingly blocking privacy suits on "jurisdictional" grounds. If individuals cannot sue when their rights under privacy laws have been violated, how do you think that will impact compliance with those rules?

4. *Invasion of the data collectors.* You might think that cable companies are much less likely to collect or disclose their subscribers' personal information than, say, a telephone company or internet service provider. After all, how much data can the cable companies really collect? Many of you are familiar with the standard "set top" boxes that cable companies provide in order to decode digital channels, and you might think that those devices seem outdated and incapable of doing much of anything, let alone track your TV viewing habits. That is all likely to change sooner than you might think.

In February 2016 the FCC issued a Notice of Proposed Rulemaking aimed at promoting "innovation in the display, selection, and use of this programming and of other video programming available to consumers" by opening up the standards for set top boxes.[‡] This means that, in theory, companies like Google, Apple, Amazon, Roku, and others could offer devices capable of decoding cable

---

[*] 47 U.S.C. § 551(e).

[†] *See* Gubala v. Time Warner Cable, Inc., 846 F.3d 909 (7th Cir. 2017).

[‡] *Expanding Consumers' Video Navigation Choices*, 31 FCC Rcd. 2070 (2016).

channels for subscribers. A number of different industry groups, including the cable companies, have opposed elements of the proposal. But privacy advocates have also expressed reservations, arguing that the FCC needs to ensure that the Cable Act's privacy rules are enforced against any new companies that seek to provide cable-type services via open set top boxes.[*]

C. INTERNET

The internet has caused major upheavals in most, if not all, areas of communications law. But the privacy rules limiting disclosure of electronic communications were put in place years before the internet as we know it existed. Congress proscribed unauthorized access to and disclosure of digital messages in the Electronic Communications Privacy Act of 1986 ("ECPA").[†] When Congress passed ECPA, it amended Title III to include protections against "interception" of electronic communications and also prohibited the disclosure of stored communications and subscriber information by service providers.[‡] These provisions not only established a similar degree of protection for electronic and telephonic communications but also created new categories of protected personal information, recognizing that digital networks necessarily generate and store far more than analog telephone networks.

The principles underlying internet privacy laws are the same as those that animated the original privacy protections in the Communications Act of 1934, Title III, the Cable Act, and other privacy laws. Yet the application of these privacy rules is much broader in the internet context. Every service provider collects information about their users, and almost every company with a website acts as a service provider in some way. The development of wireless networking has complicated the matter further, and the application of traditional interception prohibitions to modern networks raises complicated definitional questions. For example, a few years ago the Ninth Circuit had to address the legality of the interception of unencrypted Wi-Fi data after Google was caught using its "Street View" vehicles to collect data from nearby private networks.

---

[*] *See, e.g.,* Comments of the Electronic Privacy Information Center (Apr. 22, 2016), https://epic.org/apa/comments/EPIC-FCC-Set-Top-Box-Comments.pdf.

[†] 18 U.S.C. § 2510.

[‡] 18 U.S.C. § 2702.

JOFFE V. GOOGLE
746 F.3d 920 (2013)

BYBEE, CIRCUIT JUDGE:

In the course of capturing its Street View photographs, Google collected data from unencrypted Wi-Fi networks. Google publicly apologized, but plaintiffs brought suit under federal and state law, including the Wiretap Act.[*] Google argues that its data collection did not violate the Act because data transmitted over a Wi-Fi network is an "electronic communication" that is "readily accessible to the general public" and exempt under the Act.[†] The district court rejected Google's argument. We affirm.

I. BACKGROUND

A. Facts and History

Google launched its Street View feature in the United States in 2007 to complement its Google Maps service by providing users with panoramic, street-level photographs. Street View photographs are captured by cameras mounted on vehicles owned by Google that drive on public roads and photograph their surroundings. Between 2007 and 2010, Google also equipped its Street View cars with Wi-Fi antennas and software that collected data transmitted by WiFi networks in nearby homes and businesses. The equipment attached to Google's Street View cars recorded basic information about these Wi-Fi networks, including the network's name (SSID), the unique number assigned to the router transmitting the wireless signal (MAC address), the signal strength, and whether the network was encrypted. Gathering this basic data about the Wi-Fi networks used in homes and businesses enables companies such as Google to provide enhanced "location-based" services, such as those that allow mobile phone users to find nearby restaurants and attractions or receive driving directions.

But the antennas and software installed in Google's Street View cars collected more than just the basic identifying information transmitted by Wi-Fi networks. They also gathered and stored "payload data" that was sent and received over unencrypted Wi-Fi connections at the moment that a Street View car was driving by.[1] Payload data includes everything transmitted by a device connected to a Wi-Fi network, such as personal emails, usernames, passwords, videos, and documents.

---

[*] 18 U.S.C. § 2511.
[†] 18 U.S.C. § 2511(2)(g)(i).

Google acknowledged in May 2010 that its Street View vehicles had been collecting fragments of payload data from unencrypted Wi-Fi networks. The company publicly apologized, grounded its vehicles, and rendered inaccessible the personal data that had been acquired. In total, Google's Street View cars collected about 600 gigabytes of data transmitted over Wi-Fi networks in more than 30 countries.

[J]offe seeks to represent a class comprised of all persons whose electronic communications were intercepted by Google Street View vehicles since May 25, 2007.

Google moved to dismiss Joffe's consolidated complaint. The district court declined to grant Google's motion to dismiss Joffe's federal Wiretap Act claims. *In re Google Inc. St. View Elec. Commc'n Litig.,* 794 F.Supp.2d at 1084. On Google's request, the court certified its ruling for interlocutory appeal under 28 U.S.C. § 1292(b) because the district court resolved a novel question of statutory interpretation. We granted Google's petition, and we have jurisdiction under 28 U.S.C. § 1292(b).

Google maintained before the district court that it should have dismissed Joffe's Wiretap Act claims because data transmitted over unencrypted Wi-Fi networks falls under the statutory exemption that makes it lawful to intercept "electronic communications" that are "readily accessible to the general public." The question was whether payload data transmitted on an unencrypted WiFi network is "readily accessible to the general public," such that the [exemption] applies to Google's conduct.

II. OVERVIEW OF THE WIRETAP ACT

The Wiretap Act imposes liability on a person who "intentionally intercepts ... any wire, oral, or electronic communication," subject to a number of exemptions. There are two exemptions that are relevant to our purposes. First, the Wiretap Act exempts intercepting "an electronic communication made through an electronic communication system" if the system is configured so that it is "readily accessible to the general public." "Electronic communication" includes communication by radio,[*] and "'readily accessible to the general public' means, with respect to a radio communication" that the communication is "not ... scrambled or encrypted."[†] Second, the Act exempts intercepting "radio communication" by "any station for the use of the general public;" by certain governmental communication systems "readily accessible to the general public," including police, fire, and civil defense agencies; by a station operating

---

[*] 18 U.S.C. § 2510(12).
[†] 18 U.S.C. § 2510(16)(A).

on an authorized frequency for "amateur, citizens band, or general mobile radio services;" or by a marine or aeronautical communications system.[*]

Google only argues, as it did before the district court, that it is exempt from liability under the Act because data transmitted over a Wi-Fi network is an "electronic communication ... readily accessible to the general public" under § 2511(2)(g)(i). It concedes that it does not qualify for any of the exemptions for specific types of "radio communication" under § 2511(2)(g)(ii). Joffe, however, argues that if data transmitted over a Wi-Fi network is not exempt as a "radio communication" under § 2511(2)(g)(ii), it cannot be exempt as a radio communication under the broader exemption for "electronic communication" in § 2511(2)(g)(i). This argument has some force, and we wish to address it before we consider Google's claims.

Joffe contends that the definition of "readily accessible to the general public" in § 2510(16) does not apply to the § 2511(2)(g)(i) exemption. Instead, Joffe argues, the § 2510(16) definition applies exclusively to § 2511(2)(g)(ii)(II), which exempts specifically enumerated types of "radio communication" when they are "readily accessible to the general public." We ultimately reject Joffe's alternative reading of the statute, although—as we will explain—we find § 2511(2)(g)(ii) useful as a lexigraphical aid to understanding the phrase "radio communication."

As noted, § 2510(16) defines "readily accessible to the general public" solely with respect to a "radio communication," and not with respect to other types of "electronic communication." Although § 2511(2)(g)(i) does not use the words "radio communication," the statute nevertheless directs us to apply the § 2510(16) definition to the § 2511(2)(g)(i) exemption. First, "radio communication" is a subset of "electronic communication." Second, the statute directs us to apply § 2510(16) to the entire chapter. The definition[s] are prefaced with the phrase, "As used in this chapter." We cannot disregard this command by holding that the definition of " 'readily accessible to the general public' [ ] with respect to a radio communication" applies to § 2511(2)(g)(ii), but not § 2511(2)(g)(i).

Admittedly, following the plain language of the statute creates some tension with § 2511(2)(g)(ii)(II), which provides an exemption for intercepting "any radio communication which is transmitted ... by any governmental, law enforcement, civil defense, private land mobile, or public communications system, including police and fire, readily accessible to the general public." Under our reading of the statute—which is the same reading adopted by the

---

[*] 18 U.S.C. § 2511(2)(g)(ii)(I)-(IV).

district court, Google, and Joffe in his lead argument— § 2511(2)(g)(i) exempts all electronic communications (including radio communications) that are "readily accessible to the general public" as the phrase is defined in § 2510(16). This reading likely renders § 2511(2)(g)(ii)(II) superfluous. As discussed, that section exempts specific kinds of radio communications that are "readily accessible to the general public," such as those transmitted by a law enforcement communications system. But this exemption is unnecessary when § 2511(2)(g)(i) already exempts all radio communications that are "readily accessible to the general public."

Although our reading may render § 2511(2)(g)(ii)(II) superfluous or at least redundant, we understand that Congress "sometimes drafts provisions that appear duplicative of others—simply in Macbeth's words, 'to make assurance double sure.' That is, Congress means to clarify what might be doubtful—that the mentioned item is covered." This interpretation is especially plausible given that Congress was concerned that radio hobbyists not face liability for intercepting readily accessible broadcasts, such as those covered by § 2511(2)(g)(ii)(II), which can be picked up by a police scanner.*

In short, we agree with Google that the definition of "readily accessible to the general public" in § 2510(16) applies to the § 2511(2)(g)(i) exemption when the communication in question is a "radio communication." With that understanding, we now turn to whether data transmitted over a Wi–Fi network is a "radio communication" exempt from the Wiretap Act as an "electronic communication" under § 2511(2)(g)(i).

III. ANALYSIS

Google contends that data transmitted over a Wi–Fi network is a "radio communication" and that the Act exempts such communications by defining them as "readily accessible to the general public," so long as "such communication is not ... scrambled or encrypted." We reject this claim. We hold that the phrase "radio communication" in 18 U.S.C. § 2510(16) excludes payload data transmitted over a Wi–Fi network. As a consequence, the definition of "readily accessible to the general public [ ] with respect to a radio communication" set forth in § 2510(16) does not apply to the exemption for an "electronic communication" that is "readily accessible to the general public" under 18 U.S.C. § 2511(2)(g)(i).

---

* See 132 Cong. Rec. S7987-04 (1986) ("In order to address radio hobbyists' concerns, we modified the original language of S. 1667 to clarify that intercepting traditional radio services is not unlawful.").

A. The Ordinary Meaning of "Radio Communication" Does Not Include Data Transmitted over a Wi-Fi Network

The Wiretap Act does not define the phrase "radio communication" so we must give the term its ordinary meaning.

According to Google, radio communication "refers to any information transmitted using radio waves, *i.e.,* the radio frequency portion of the electromagnetic spectrum." The radio frequency portion of the spectrum is "the part of the spectrum where electromagnetic waves have frequencies in the range of about 3 kilohertz to 300 gigahertz."

Google's technical definition does not conform with the common understanding held contemporaneous with the enacting Congress. The radio frequency portion of the electromagnetic spectrum covers not only WiFi transmissions, but also television broadcasts, Bluetooth devices, cordless and cellular phones, garage door openers, avalanche beacons, and wildlife tracking collars. One would not ordinarily consider, say, television a form of "radio communication." Not surprisingly, Congress has not typically assumed that the term "radio" encompasses the term "television."

The Wiretap Act itself does not assume that the phrase "radio communication" encompasses technologies like satellite television that are outside the scope of the phrase as it is ordinarily defined. . . . Rather, it uses "radio" to refer to traditional radio technologies, and then separately describes other modes of communication that are not ordinarily thought of as radio, but that nevertheless use the radio spectrum.

Google's proposed definition is in tension with how Congress—and virtually everyone else—uses the phrase. In common parlance, watching a television show does not entail "radio communication." Nor does sending an email or viewing a bank statement while connected to a Wi-Fi network. There is no indication that the Wiretap Act carries a buried implication that the phrase ought to be given a broader definition than the one that is commonly understood.

Importantly, Congress provided definitions for many other similar terms in the Wiretap Act, but refrained from providing a technical definition of "radio communication" that would have altered the notion that it should carry its common, ordinary meaning. As Google writes in its brief, "[t]he fact that the Wiretap Act provides specialized definitions for certain compound terms—but not for 'radio communication'—is powerful evidence that the undefined term was not similarly intended [to] be defined in a specialized or narrow way" but rather "according to its ordinary meaning." We agree and, accordingly, we reject Google's proposed definition of "radio communication" in favor of one that better reflects the phrase's ordinary meaning.

B. A "Radio Communication" is a Predominantly Auditory Broadcast, Which Excludes Payload Data Transmitted over Wi-Fi Networks

There are two telltale indicia of a "radio communication." A radio communication is commonly understood to be (1) predominantly auditory, and (2) broadcast. Therefore, television—whether connected via an indoor antenna or a satellite dish—is not radio, by virtue of its visual component. A land line phone does not broadcast, and, for that reason, is not radio. On the other hand, AM/FM, Citizens Band (CB), 'walkie-talkie,' and shortwave transmissions are predominantly auditory, are broadcast, and are, not coincidentally, typically referred to as "radio" in everyday parlance. Thus, we conclude that "radio communication" should carry its ordinary meaning: a predominantly auditory broadcast.

The payload data transmitted over unencrypted Wi-Fi networks that was captured by Google included emails, usernames, passwords, images, and documents that cannot be classified as predominantly auditory. They therefore fall outside of the definition of a "radio communication" as the phrase is used in 18 U.S.C. § 2510(16).

C. Defining "Radio Communication" to Include Only Predominantly Auditory Broadcasts is Consistent with the Rest of the Wiretap Act

Crucially, defining "radio communication" as a predominantly auditory broadcast yields a coherent and consistent Wiretap Act. Google's overly broad definition does not.

Throughout the Wiretap Act, Congress used the phrase "radio communication"—which is at issue here—and the similar phrase "communication by radio." Even within the very provision that we are construing—18 U.S.C. § 2510(16)—Congress used both phrases. We must ascribe to each phrase its own meaning. The phrase "communication by radio" is used more expansively: it conjures an image of all communications using radio *waves* or a radio *device*.

NOTES & QUESTIONS

1. *Protecting hobbyists.* Recall that the interception provision, which was discussed briefly in *Bartnicki*, is intended to protect the privacy of individuals' communications. But in this case the court is focused on an *exception* to that general prohibition, which was adopted in part to protect "radio hobbyists" as we can see from the congressional record. Describe how the statute protects hobbyists and what Congress thought might happen if they had not adopted this

exception in ECPA. Do you think the exception serves the purpose that Congress intended?

2. *An audio-only exception.* Explain why the court decided that "radio communications" must be "predominantly auditory." Do you agree? Do you think that Congress anticipated a technology that would allow individuals to send electronic communications wirelessly? If so, do you think that they intended to exempt those communications from the privacy protections of Title III?

3. *Shifting technologies vs. stiff definitions.* How does the court go about applying a definition written in 1986 to technologies that were invented and deployed many years later? Notice that this is similar to the problem we studied in CHAPTER 5: CLASSIFICATION. Do you think that Congress could have done a better job of making these definitions "future proof"? What alternative did they have? As you consider these questions, put yourself in the shoes of a congressional staffer who is asked to draft a bill to regulate an evolving communications technology.

4. *Authority over interceptions.* Notice that this case was brought by a group of private plaintiffs, not the FCC. The FCC did conduct an investigation into Google's conduct, and ultimately issued a Notice of Apparent Liability for Forfeiture, fining the company $25,000 for noncompliance with the investigation. But the FCC did not issue an order against the company, in part because the Commission does not have jurisdiction to enforce the Title III provisions at issue in *Joffe*. Instead, the FCC looked to the Communications Act privacy provisions, 47 U.S.C. § 605, which prohibits the "unauthorized publication or use of communications." In response to the Commission's inquiry, Google made the same arguments that it later made in *Joffe* (the Communications Act privacy provision cross references the Wiretap Act provisions that the court considered above). In concluding the investigation, the FCC said the following (a year before the court ruled in *Joffe*):

> After thoroughly reviewing the existing record in this investigation and applicable law, the Bureau has decided not to take enforcement action against Google for violation of Section 705(a). There is no Commission precedent addressing the application of Section 705(a) in connection with Wi-Fi communications. The available evidence, moreover, suggests that Google collected payload data only from unencrypted Wi-Fi networks, not from encrypted ones. Google argues that the Wiretap Act permits the interception of unencrypted Wi-Fi communications, and some case law suggests that Section 705(a)'s prohibition on the interception or unauthorized reception of interstate radio communications excludes conduct permitted (if not expressly authorized) under the Wiretap Act. Although Google also collected and stored encrypted

communications sent over unencrypted Wi-Fi networks, the Bureau has found no evidence that Google accessed or did anything with such encrypted communications. The Bureau's inability to compel an interview of Engineer Doe made it impossible to determine in the course of our investigation whether Google did make any use of any encrypted communications that it collected. For all these reasons, we do not find sufficient evidence that Google has violated Section 705(a) to support a finding of apparent liability under that provision in the context of this case.

After reading the Ninth Circuit's decision and the FCC's reasoning, are you convinced that the agency was right to close the investigation? How much weight do you think the agency gave to Google's representation that it not make use of the intercepted WiFi data?

5. *Giving, and then taking back, telecommunications privacy rules for the internet.* Back in CHAPTER 4: ACCESS and CHAPTER 5: CLASSIFICATION we learned about the FCC's 2015 Order reclassifying broadband providers as Title II common carriers, subject to the same access and other rules that the agency imposes on telephone companies and other providers. After the D.C. Circuit upheld the FCC's reclassification order, the Commission initiated a new rulemaking to impose the CPNI privacy rules on broadband providers.[*] But after the 2016 Election both Chairman Pai and the Republicans in Congress were opposed to the new rules. They argued that broadband providers should not be subject to more restrictive rules than the internet giants like Google and Facebook. And because the Republicans had control of the House, the Senate, and the Presidency, they were able to use a special tool to eliminate the new FCC rules: the Congressional Review Act.[†]

The CRA, which was passed in 1996, gives Congress the power to invalidate agency rules within the first 60 days after they are published in the Federal Register. If both houses of Congress pass a joint resolution of disapproval, and the President does not veto the resolution, then the rule (1) does not take effect and (2) cannot be "reissued in substantially the same form" without authorization by Congress. Part of the logic behind this provision is that it prevents a President or Agency leader from enacting "midnight rules" at the end of a term (and on their way out the door).

After the FCC's new Broadband Privacy Rules were published in the Federal Register and after the 2016 Election, Republicans in Congress passed a joint resolution of disapproval, which was then signed by President Trump.[‡] The

---

[*] Protecting the Privacy of Customers of Broadband and Other Telecommunications Services, 31 FCC Rcd. 3943 (2016).

[†] 5 U.S.C. §§ 801 et seq.

resolution ensured that the broadband privacy rules did not go into effect and cannot be reinstated without new legislative authority from Congress.

Many groups opposed the resolution of disapproval, and there were widespread criticisms that Congress was allowing companies to "sell your browsing history." Lawmakers at the state level even began drawing up their own plans to reinstate broadband privacy rules under state law. But the issue at that time was even more interesting and complicated than many realized. The invalidation of the broadband privacy rule did not eliminate the existing statutory and regulatory CPNI obligations that apply to common carriers. And, at the time, the 2015 Net Neutrality Order was still in effect and broadband providers were still subject to common carrier obligations (including the CPNI rules). It wasn't until the FCC Order repealing the Title II reclassification went into effect in June 2018 that the CPNI burden was officially lifted from the broadband providers.

6. *Are states the new masters of privacy?* Recall that in CHAPTER 5: CLASSIFICATION we read the recent decision by the D.C. Circuit upholding the FCC's declassification of broadband internet services. As a result of that decision, broadband providers are no longer subject to Title II requirements like the CPNI rules. But there was a twist. In most cases, FCC regulations *preempt* state law. That means that if there is a conflict between a state law and an FCC law or regulation, the Commission usually wins. But not in the *Mozilla* case. The FCC included in its 2018 declassification order an explicit discussion of the preemptive effect that the order would have on state law—the Commission believed that no states would be able to impose net neutrality obligations on BIAS providers. Not so fast, the D.C. Circuit said:

> We vacate the portion of the 2018 Order that expressly preempts "any state or local requirements that are inconsistent with [its] deregulatory approach." The Commission ignored binding precedent by failing to ground its sweeping Preemption Directive—which goes far beyond conflict preemption—in a lawful source of statutory authority. That failure is fatal.

> The relevant portion of the Order provides that "regulation of broadband Internet access service should be governed principally by a uniform set of federal regulations," and not "by a patchwork that includes separate state and local requirements." *2018 Order* ¶ 194. In service of that goal, the 2018 Order expressly "preempt[s] any state or local measures that would effectively impose rules or requirements that we have repealed or decided to refrain from imposing in this order or that would impose more stringent requirements for any aspect of broadband service that we address in this order." *Id.* ¶ 195. In other words,

‡ Pub. L. 115-22 (2017).

the Preemption Directive invalidates all state and local laws that the Commission deems to "interfere with federal regulatory objectives" or that involve "any aspect of broadband service * * * address[ed]" in the Order. *Id.* ¶¶ 195–196.

The Preemption Directive conveys more than a mere intent for the agency to preempt state laws in the future if they conflict with the 2018 Order. As the Commission confirmed at oral argument, it is not just a "heads up that ordinary conflict preemption principles are going to apply." The Order was meant to have independent and far-reaching preemptive effect from the moment it issued. And the Commission meant for that preemptive effect to wipe out a broader array of state and local laws than traditional conflict preemption principles would allow.

The Governmental Petitioners challenge the Preemption Directive on the ground that it exceeds the Commission's statutory authority. They are right.

So what does that mean for state privacy laws? The FCC can no longer rely on the 2018 Preemption Directive to argue that any state law imposing CPNI-like privacy obligations on BIAS providers is necessarily preempted. The Commission would have to prove that the state law actually *conflicts* with federal law and regulation. The court in *Mozilla* directly rejected the Commission's argument that its "policy of nonregulation" justified preempting new state regulations. Given this decision, any state could pass legislation mirroring the broadband privacy rules (or an even broader version of those rules) without a serious threat of a preemption challenge.

7. *A new acronym emerges to change the landscape of digital privacy.* At the same time that the FCC was creating new rules for broadband privacy, and then watching those rules get taken away by Congress, a much broader regulatory effort was underway across the Atlantic. Europeans have been proactive about privacy and "data protection" rules since the founding of the EU in 1994. The European Data Protection Directive (95/46/EC) provided a comprehensive framework for the protection of personal information, in contrast with the "sectoral" and ad-hoc approach taken in the United States during the 1980s and 1990s. But in 2012 the EU undertook the most substantial overhaul of privacy regulation in history. The result was the EU General Data Protection Directive (GDPR), which was finalized on April 14, 2016, and went into effect on May 25, 2018.

NOTE: GDPR AND GLOBAL PRIVACY REGULATION ON THE INTERNET

The GDPR has a broad material and territorial scope. It applies to any "processing of personal data" and covers actions by data "controllers" and "processors" in the EU and of similar entities that offer goods or services to "data subjects" in the EU.

Article 1

Subject-matter and objectives

1.   This Regulation lays down rules relating to the protection of natural persons with regard to the processing of personal data and rules relating to the free movement of personal data.

2.   This Regulation protects fundamental rights and freedoms of natural persons and in particular their right to the protection of personal data.

3.   The free movement of personal data within the Union shall be neither restricted nor prohibited for reasons connected with the protection of natural persons with regard to the processing of personal data.

Article 2

Material scope

1.   This Regulation applies to the processing of personal data wholly or partly by automated means and to the processing other than by automated means of personal data which form part of a filing system or are intended to form part of a filing system.

2.   This Regulation does not apply to the processing of personal data:

    (a) in the course of an activity which falls outside the scope of Union law;

    (b) by the Member States when carrying out activities which fall within the scope of Chapter 2 of Title V of the TEU;

    (c) by a natural person in the course of a purely personal or household activity;

    (d) by competent authorities for the purposes of the prevention, investigation, detection or prosecution of criminal offences or the execution of criminal penalties, including the safeguarding against and the prevention of threats to public security.

3.   For the processing of personal data by the Union institutions, bodies, offices and agencies, Regulation (EC) No 45/2001 applies. Regulation (EC) No 45/2001 and other Union legal acts applicable to such processing of personal data shall be adapted to the principles and rules of this Regulation in accordance with Article 98.

4.   This Regulation shall be without prejudice to the application of Directive 2000/31/EC, in particular of the liability rules of intermediary service providers in Articles 12 to 15 of that Directive.

Article 3

Territorial scope

1.   This Regulation applies to the processing of personal data in the context of the activities of an establishment of a controller or a processor in the Union, regardless of whether the processing takes place in the Union or not.

2.   This Regulation applies to the processing of personal data of data subjects who are in the Union by a controller or processor not established in the Union, where the processing activities are related to:

> (a) the offering of goods or services, irrespective of whether a payment of the data subject is required, to such data subjects in the Union; or
>
> (b) the monitoring of their behaviour as far as their behaviour takes place within the Union.
>
> 3. This Regulation applies to the processing of personal data by a controller not established in the Union, but in a place where Member State law applies by virtue of public international law.

Businesses around the world were keenly interested in the rollout of this new regulation because of its broad scope. The EU itself encompasses a significant portion of the world's population (the third largest population after China and India). And most large companies that operate on the internet target users around the globe (including in the EU).

Two of the key terms in the GDPR, "personal data" and "processing," are broad enough to implicate the activities of most companies that use communications systems.

> Article 4
>
> **Definitions**
>
> For the purposes of this Regulation:
>
> (1) 'personal data' means any information relating to an identified or identifiable natural person ('data subject'); an identifiable natural person is one who can be identified, directly or indirectly, in particular by reference to an identifier such as a name, an identification number, location data, an online identifier or to one or more factors specific to the physical, physiological, genetic, mental, economic, cultural or social identity of that natural person;
>
> (2) 'processing' means any operation or set of operations which is performed on personal data or on sets of personal data, whether or not by automated means, such as collection, recording, organisation, structuring, storage, adaptation or alteration, retrieval, consultation, use, disclosure by transmission, dissemination or otherwise making available, alignment or combination, restriction, erasure or destruction;1. This Regulation applies to the processing of personal data wholly or partly by automated means and to the processing other than by automated means of personal data which form part of a filing system or are intended to form part of a filing system.

The GDPR therefore applies to most businesses online (assuming those businesses operate in or target data subjects in the EU). The core framework of the regulation incorporates the "Fair Information Practices" that were first developed in the United States in the 1970s[*] and later adopted by the Organization for Economic Cooperation and Development (OECD).[†] These

---

[*] U.S. PRIVACY PROTECTION STUDY COMM'N, PERSONAL PRIVACY IN AN INFORMATION SOCIETY (1977), *available at* https://epic.org/privacy/ppsc1977report/.

[†] OECD, Guidelines on the Protection of Privacy and Transborder Flows of Personal Data, http://www.oecd.org/sti/ieconomy/oecdguidelinesontheprotectionofprivacyandtransborderflowsofpersonal data.htm (last visited July 12, 2018).

FIPs allocate rights and responsibilities for data processors and data subjects respectively.

Article 5

Principles relating to processing of personal data

1. Personal data shall be:

    (a) processed lawfully, fairly and in a transparent manner in relation to the data subject ('lawfulness, fairness and transparency');

    (b) collected for specified, explicit and legitimate purposes and not further processed in a manner that is incompatible with those purposes; further processing for archiving purposes in the public interest, scientific or historical research purposes or statistical purposes shall, in accordance with Article 89(1), not be considered to be incompatible with the initial purposes ('purpose limitation');

    (c) adequate, relevant and limited to what is necessary in relation to the purposes for which they are processed ('data minimisation');

    (d) accurate and, where necessary, kept up to date; every reasonable step must be taken to ensure that personal data that are inaccurate, having regard to the purposes for which they are processed, are erased or rectified without delay ('accuracy');

    (e) kept in a form which permits identification of data subjects for no longer than is necessary for the purposes for which the personal data are processed; personal data may be stored for longer periods insofar as the personal data will be processed solely for archiving purposes in the public interest, scientific or historical research purposes or statistical purposes in accordance with Article 89(1) subject to implementation of the appropriate technical and organisational measures required by this Regulation in order to safeguard the rights and freedoms of the data subject ('storage limitation');

    (f) processed in a manner that ensures appropriate security of the personal data, including protection against unauthorised or unlawful processing and against accidental loss, destruction or damage, using appropriate technical or organisational measures ('integrity and confidentiality').

2. The controller shall be responsible for, and be able to demonstrate compliance with, paragraph 1 ('accountability').

The GDPR implements these privacy principles through a series of articles in the regulation that concern "lawfulness of processing" (Article 6), "conditions for consent" (Article 7), and other rules for special categories of personal data. The Regulation also enumerates the "rights of the data subject" (Chapter III) including "transparency (Article 12), "access" to information about data processing (Articles 13-15), "rectification and erasure" and portability (Articles 16–20), and the right to "object" to processing (Articles 21 and 22).

Under the GDPR, the data controllers and processors bear the responsibility of safeguarding and properly handling personal data. This responsibility extends to the design of data collection systems as well as the maintenance and security of those systems. Violations of GDPR can result in administrative fines imposed by data protection authorities in EU member states (Article 83). These fines can be as high as 20 million euros or 4% of a company's total global turnover for certain offenses (whichever is higher), though there are 10 factors that the Regulation requires be taken into account (Article 83.2).

With the potential for billions or hundreds of millions of dollars in fines, it should be no surprise that major internet companies are investing heavily in their systems to ensure they are GDPR compliant. This renewed focus on data protection will likely have a significant impact on how personal information is handled by all companies and for all users, not just those in the EU.

NOTES & QUESTIONS

1. *Comparing privacy protections.* The GDPR imposes new privacy rules on internet companies. How does this new regulation compare to the other privacy regimes we have studied? Can you give examples of how U.S. laws already impose data protection principles to other types of communications services? To the extent that the GDPR rules are different, is that difference justified by the unique nature of personal data processing on the internet?

2. *The one-way ratchet.* All laws are limited in both subject matter and territorial scope; the GDPR is no exception. But in an increasingly global and interconnected economy, regulations in one field or in one territory can have spillover effects. If you were working for the General Counsel of Facebook, how would you recommend the company handle the data of users from different countries. Would you recommend a system for complying with GDPR for EU users and a separate system for US users? What are the costs and benefits associated with those systems? Why might it be better for Facebook to treat all users alike and comply with GDPR globally?

3. *Looking forward.* The impact of GDPR is only now starting to be felt by companies and by users. But the implementation of GDPR has already had a marked effect on lawmakers in the United States. California also recently adopted a new data privacy law. Many other legislative proposals have been introduced in the U.S. Congress, and Facebook and others have been summoned to Capitol Hill numerous times to answer questions about the U.S. privacy regime and their collection and use of users' personal information. It remains to be seen how Congress will react to GDPR and other shifts in privacy law over the last few years. But there is certainly an appetite to update the current laws to reflect the changes in technology and the economy that the internet has wrought over the last 20 years.

In this chapter, we have examined the regulatory responses to modern communications systems that enable the collection, disclosure, and processing of personal data. These services have generated new threats to communications privacy, and it is the work of lawmakers and regulators to allocate rights and assign responsibilities to ensure that data is properly safeguarded.

CHAPTER 8

INTERMEDIARY LIABILITY

In modern communications, no one speaks alone. For example, in a long distance telephone call, you often need the assistance of a local exchange carrier and an interexchange carrier to transport your speech to the person you called. If you say something "harmful," should the telephone companies be held morally or legally responsible? What about a broadcast licensee? May a television station owner or broadcast licensee respond to criticism about too much TV violence by pointing her finger at the studios that produced the television shows? (Who chose to show the program anyway?)

As new communication industries come into being, new intermediaries that facilitate communications also come into existence, fulfilling new roles. Accordingly, new questions are asked about their responsibility, social as well as legal, for the content that they help distribute. Consider, for instance, the internet. To what extent should Google, YouTube, Twitter, Instagram, Snapchat and Facebook bear responsibility for the indecent content, the "fake news," and the sensitive personal information that they help distribute? We will begin by looking at how courts approached this issue in defamation cases brought before Congress passed the Communications Decency Act (which was part of the Telecommunications Act of 1996).

A. BEFORE 47 U.S.C. § 230

NOTE: DEFAMATION LAW

Defamation is a false statement of fact that injures a person's reputation. According to the Restatement (Second) on Torts §558, the elements of the defamation cause of action are:

(a) a false and defamatory statement concerning another;

(b) an unprivileged *publication* to a third party;

(c) fault amounting at least to negligence on the part of the *publisher*; and

(d) either actionability of the statement irrespective of special harm or the existence of special harm caused by the publication.[*]

"Publication" is a term of art. It means the intentional or negligent communication to any person who is not the person defamed.[†] Thus, scribbling a message on a napkin, and leaving it on a table for others to see can count as publication.

Historically, one's sincere but mistaken belief in the truth of the statement was no defense to a defamation suit. If the statement turned out to be false, the defendant was strictly liable. Obviously, such laws inhibited the flow of information in a free society. Thus, the common law managed numerous, complex privileges that insulated parties from liability. Matters grew still more complicated by the 1960s, as defamation law became significantly constitutionalized.

Like obscenity and child pornography, defamation is not protected speech; however, because of the fear of chilling non-defamatory speech at the margins, a complex set of constitutional defenses have come into being. For example, in order to hold a defendant liable for defamation of a public figure on a matter of public concern, the plaintiff must show "actual malice" (that the defendant knew of the falsity or acted in reckless disregard of the truth).[‡] By contrast, a statement about a private figure on a matter of public concern requires only a showing of "negligence."[§] Due to these constitutional defenses as well as changes in state defamation law, strict liability for false but defamatory statements is rarely the appropriate standard. These constitutional doctrines should be studied carefully in your First Amendment class. Here, we focus on whether intermediaries, such as ISPs, should be held liable for the defamation they help distribute.

Let's explore intermediary liability using an age-old technology, the book. Suppose that an author ("Ann") writes a false and defamatory statement in a book manuscript. Let's say it concerns a matter of private concern,[**] and she knows that the defamatory statement ("Bill is a sodomizing felon") is false.

---

[*] Restatement of Torts, Second § 558 (Elements Stated) (emphasis added).

[†] *See* § 577(1) (What Constitutes Publication).

[‡] *See* New York Times Co. v Sullivan, 376 U.S. 254 (1964).

[§] *See* Gertz v Robert Welch, Inc., 418 U.S. 323 (1974).

[**] The Supreme Court has suggested, although not ruled explicitly, that false statements of purely private concern could be subject to strict liability. *See* Dun & Bradstreet, Inc. v Greenmoss Builders, Inc., 472 U.S. 749 (1985). Many states have nonetheless imposed negligence requirements in this situation.

When she emails that manuscript to her publishing house ("Fair Press"), she has—for purposes of the tort—"published" the defamation. On these facts, Ann is liable to Bill.

What happens when the Fair Press prints 10,000 copies of the book? Can Bill go after the publisher too? (Be wary about how the word "publisher "is used in this area of law. Sometimes, it is a tort term of art—one who has engaged in a publication of a defamation. Other times, it is used in an everyday, business parlance to refer to publishing houses, magazines, and newspapers.) What if Fair Press defended with the claim that "We did not write the book. It was written by Ann, who is not an employee."

A careful review of the elements of the defamation cause of action suggests that this defense fails: the defamation tort does not apply only to the original author ("Ann") or first publication (the e-mail transmission to Fair Press). Republishing creates the same liability.[*] Fair Press re-"published" (i.e. intentionally communicated via reproduction of the book) a false and defamatory statement. As long as Fair Press has the requisite amount of fault, it will be held liable as a repeater or republisher of the defamation. Suppose that under the applicable state law, defamation on a matter of private concern requires a showing of negligence. If Bill could demonstrate that Fair Press was negligent in failing to fact-check Ann's allegation, then Fair Press could also be held liable.

Once the books are manufactured, they are distributed through outlets such as libraries, newsstands, and bricks-and-mortar bookstores (e.g. BARNES & NOBLE). Could Bill also sue BARNES & NOBLE (B&N)? Again, if we parse literally the elements of the cause of action, it seems plausible to view B&N as republishing the defamation by selling a hardcopy of Ann's book. If B&N has the requisite fault—negligence, in our case—then it could be liable for defamation. What counts as negligent behavior for a bookstore? Do they have a duty of care that includes checking each book proactively for defamation? Any such obligation would create ridiculous burdens on distributors.

The common law recognized this impracticality, and thus created a conditional privilege for those who only deliver or transmit defamation published by a third person.[†] These distributors (sometimes called "secondary publishers") could not be subject to liability unless they *knew or had reason to know* of the defamatory content.[‡] Thus, in order for B&N even to be potentially

[*] *See* § 578 (Liability of Republisher).

[†] *See* § 581(1) ("[O]ne who only delivers or transmits defamatory matter published by a third person *is subject to liability* if, but only if, he knows or has reason to know of *its defamatory character*.") (emphasis added). These actors are sometimes called "secondary publishers."

[‡] *See* § 581(1) Comment (c):

liable, Bill would have to get past a threshold obstacle by showing that B&N knew or had reason to know of the defamation. Moreover, the mere act of selling the book would not be enough to show knowledge or reason to know. Otherwise, this would impose a general duty to monitor all texts—precisely, the burdensome result that the conditional privilege was meant to avoid.

Knowledge or reason to know goes not to the mere existence of the statement, but to its *defamatory* character. Further, such a showing merely extinguishes the privilege and makes the distributor *subject to* liability. This is not the same as making the distributor liable. Instead, the basic elements of the defamation cause of action would also have to be satisfied, including meeting the relevant fault standard.

With this simplified background to defamation law,[*] we turn to the two critical cases that addressed ISP liability for defamation before Congress radically altered the terrain with § 230 of the Communications Decency Act.

CUBBY V. COMPUSERVE
776 F. Supp. 135 (S.D.N.Y. 1991)

LEISURE, District Judge:

BACKGROUND

CompuServe develops and provides computer-related products and services, including CompuServe Information Service ("CIS"), an on-line general information service or "electronic library" that subscribers may access from a personal computer or terminal.... Subscribers may ... obtain access to

---

The composer or original publisher of a defamatory statement, such as the author, printer or publishing house, usually knows or can find out whether a statement in a work produced by him is defamatory or capable of a defamatory import. If his publication defames a private person he is subject to liability for negligence in failing to ascertain its falsity or defamatory character. (See § 580B). If his publication defames a public official or public figure he is subject to liability only if he knew of the falsity or acted recklessly regarding it. (See § 580A). Under the rule stated in this Section, one who only delivers or transmits matter first published by a third person does not do so at the peril of liability for defamatory imputations unknown to him and which he had no reason to know.

[*] The law of defamation is both complicated and often internally inconsistent. Take this summary as only a first-order approximation of the law. Additional sources worth consulting include: W. PAGE KEETON ET AL., PROSSER AND KEETON ON THE LAW OF TORTS § 113 (5th ed. 1984); RODNEY A. SMOLLA, LAW OF DEFAMATION (2d ed. 1999); KENT D. STUCKEY, INTERNET AND ONLINE LAW, CHAPTER 2: DEFAMATION (2005) (defamation chapter originally authored by Robert W. Hamilton). *See also* Susan Freiwald, *Comparative Institutional Analysis in Cyberspace: The Case of Intermediary Liability for Defamation,* 14 Harv. J. L. & Tech. 569 (2001).

over 150 special interest "forums," which are comprised of electronic bulletin boards, interactive online conferences, and topical databases.

One forum available is the Journalism Forum, which focuses on the journalism industry. Cameron Communications, Inc. ("CCI"), which is independent of CompuServe, has contracted to "manage, review, create, delete, edit and otherwise control the contents" of the Journalism Forum "in accordance with editorial and technical standards and conventions of style as established by CompuServe." Affidavit of Jim Cameron.

One publication available as part of the Journalism Forum is Rumorville USA ("Rumorville"), a daily newsletter that provides reports about broadcast journalism and journalists. Rumorville is published by Don Fitzpatrick Associates of San Francisco ("DFA"), which is headed by defendant Don Fitzpatrick. CompuServe has no employment, contractual, or other direct relationship with either DFA or Fitzpatrick; DFA provides Rumorville to the Journalism Forum under a contract with CCI. The contract between CCI and DFA provides that DFA "accepts total responsibility for the contents" of Rumorville. The contract also requires CCI to limit access to Rumorville to those CIS subscribers who have previously made membership arrangements directly with DFA.

CompuServe has no opportunity to review Rumorville's contents before DFA uploads it into CompuServe's computer banks, from which it is immediately available to approved CIS subscribers. CompuServe receives no part of any fees that DFA charges for access to Rumorville, nor does CompuServe compensate DFA for providing Rumorville to the Journalism Forum; the compensation CompuServe receives for making Rumorville available to its subscribers is the standard online time usage and membership fees charged to all CIS subscribers, regardless of the information services they use. CompuServe maintains that, before this action was filed, it had no notice of any complaints about the contents of the Rumorville publication or about DFA.

In 1990, plaintiffs Cubby, Inc. ("Cubby") and Robert Blanchard ("Blanchard") (collectively, "plaintiffs") developed Skuttlebut, a computer database designed to . . . compete with Rumorville. . . .

Plaintiffs claim that . . . Rumorville published false and defamatory statements relating to Skuttlebut and Blanchard[:] . . . Skuttlebut gained access to information first published by Rumorville "through some back door"; a statement that Blanchard was "bounced" from his previous employer, WABC; and a description of Skuttlebut as a "new start-up scam."

Plaintiffs have asserted claims against CompuServe and Fitzpatrick under New York law for libel of Blanchard, business disparagement of Skuttlebut, and unfair competition as to Skuttlebut.... CompuServe has moved... for summary judgment on all claims against it. CompuServe does not dispute, solely for the purposes of this motion, that the statements relating to Skuttlebut and Blanchard were defamatory; rather, it argues that it acted as a distributor, and not a publisher, of the statements, and cannot be held liable for the statements because it did not know and had no reason to know of the statements.

DISCUSSION

II. LIBEL CLAIM

A. The Applicable Standard of Liability

CompuServe argues that ... as a distributor of Rumorville, it cannot be held liable on the libel claim because it neither knew nor had reason to know of the allegedly defamatory statements. Plaintiffs, on the other hand, argue that the Court should conclude that CompuServe is a publisher of the statements and hold it to a higher standard of liability.

Ordinarily, "'one who repeats or otherwise republishes defamatory matter is subject to liability as if he had originally published it.'" With respect to entities such as news vendors, book stores, and libraries, however, "New York courts have long held that vendors and distributors of defamatory publications are not liable if they neither know nor have reason to know of the defamation."

The requirement that a distributor must have knowledge of the contents of a publication before liability can be imposed for distributing that publication is deeply rooted in the First Amendment.... "[T]he constitutional guarantees of the freedom of speech and of the press stand in the way of imposing" strict liability on distributors for the contents of the reading materials they carry. Smith v. California (1959). In *Smith*, the Court struck down an ordinance that imposed liability on a bookseller for possession of an obscene book, regardless of whether the bookseller had knowledge of the book's contents. The Court reasoned that

> "Every bookseller would be placed under an obligation to make himself aware
> of the contents of every book in his shop. It would be altogether unreasonable to
> demand so near an approach to omniscience." And the bookseller's burden
> would become the public's burden, for by restricting him the public's access to
> reading matter would be restricted. If the contents of bookshops and periodical
> stands were restricted to material of which their proprietors had made an
> inspection, they might be depleted indeed.

Id. (citation and footnote omitted).

CompuServe's CIS product is in essence an electronic, for-profit library.... While CompuServe may decline to carry a given publication altogether, in reality, once it does decide to carry a publication, it will have little or no editorial control over that publication's contents. This is especially so when CompuServe carries the publication as part of a forum that is managed by a company unrelated to CompuServe.

With respect to the Rumorville publication, the undisputed facts are that DFA uploads the text of Rumorville into CompuServe's data banks and makes it available to approved CIS subscribers instantaneously. CompuServe has no more editorial control over such a publication than does a public library, book store, or newsstand, and it would be no more feasible for CompuServe to examine every publication it carries for potentially defamatory statements than it would be for any other distributor to do so. "First Amendment guarantees have long been recognized as protecting distributors of publications. . . . Obviously, the national distributor of hundreds of periodicals has no duty to monitor each issue of every periodical it distributes. Such a rule would be an impermissible burden on the First Amendment." Lerman v. Flynt Distributing Co. (2d Cir. 1984).

Technology is rapidly transforming the information industry. A computerized database is the functional equivalent of a more traditional news vendor, and the inconsistent application of a lower standard of liability to an electronic news distributor such as CompuServe than that which is applied to a public library, book store, or newsstand would impose an undue burden on the free flow of information. Given the relevant First Amendment considerations, the appropriate standard of liability to be applied to CompuServe is whether it knew or had reason to know of the allegedly defamatory Rumorville statements.

B. CompuServe's Liability as a Distributor

CompuServe contends that it is undisputed that it had neither knowledge nor reason to know of the allegedly defamatory Rumorville statements, especially given the large number of publications it carries and the speed with which DFA uploads Rumorville into its computer banks and makes the publication available to CIS subscribers. . . .

Plaintiffs have not set forth any specific facts showing that there is a genuine issue as to whether CompuServe knew or had reason to know of Rumorville's contents. Because CompuServe, as a news distributor, may not be held liable if it neither knew nor had reason to know of the allegedly defamatory Rumorville statements, summary judgment in favor of CompuServe on the libel claim is granted.*

---

* Plaintiffs also tried to argue that CompuServe was vicariously liable because CCI and DFA were agents, not independent contractors. Applying New York agency law, the court held that all three parties are independent of each other. Accordingly, there would be no vicarious liability.—ED.

NOTES & QUESTIONS

1. *The difference that internet makes.* The problem of defamation has been with us for as long as human beings have used language. What, if anything, is different about defamation on the internet?

2. *The specific players.* Make sure you understand the business relationships between CompuServe, Cameron Communications Inc. (CCI), and Don Fitzpatrick Associates (DFA). Which relationships were connected by contract? Which relationships were connected by oversight or control? Do these questions matter?

3. *Categories.* The allegedly defamatory statement took place in Rumorville USA. The parties disagree whether CompuServe should be considered a publisher or distributor of that statement.

    a. *Value of distributor status.* Why does CompuServe want to be deemed a "distributor"? What additional legal benefit does it gain from this status?

    b. *Making the call.* The court categorizes CompuServe as a distributor. Why? Which factors were important in the court's reasoning? What is the implicit definition of "distributor" that the court employs?

    c. *The consequence.* Because CompuServe is categorized as a distributor, it is ultimately held not liable for defamation on the facts provided. But why precisely? Is it because the four elements of the defamation action articulated by the Restatement (Second) § 558 (provided in the introductory materials) were not satisfied? Or was it because of the conditional privilege?

STRATTON OAKMONT V. **PRODIGY**
SERVICES CO.
1995 WL 323710 (N.Y. Sup. Ct.)

STUART L. AIN, Justice.

At issue in this case are [allegedly libelous] statements about Plaintiffs made by an unidentified bulletin board user or "poster" on PRODIGY's "Money Talk" computer bulletin board. . . .

PRODIGY's computer network has at least two million subscribers who communicate with each other and with the general subscriber population on PRODIGY's bulletin boards. "Money Talk" . . . is allegedly the leading and most widely read financial computer bulletin board in the United States, where members can post statements regarding stocks, investments and other financial matters. PRODIGY contracts with bulletin Board Leaders, who, among other things, participate in board discussions and undertake promotional efforts to encourage usage and increase users. The Board Leader for "Money Talk" at the time the alleged libelous statements were posted was Charles Epstein.

PRODIGY commenced operations in 1990. Plaintiffs base their claim that PRODIGY is a publisher in large measure on PRODIGY's stated policy, starting in 1990, that it was a family oriented computer network. In various national newspaper[s] . . . PRODIGY held itself out as an online service that exercised editorial control over the content of messages posted on its computer bulletin boards, thereby expressly differentiating itself from its competition and expressly likening itself to a newspaper.

In opposition, PRODIGY insists that its policies have changed and evolved since 1990 . . . [to] 1994, when the allegedly libelous statements were posted.

Plaintiffs further rely upon the following additional evidence in support of their claim that PRODIGY is a publisher:

(A) promulgation of "content guidelines" in which, inter alia, users are requested to refrain from posting notes that are "insulting" and are advised that "notes that harass other members or are deemed to be in bad taste or grossly repugnant to community standards, or are deemed harmful to maintaining a harmonious online community, will be removed when brought to PRODIGY's attention"; the Guidelines all expressly state that although "Prodigy is committed to open debate and discussion on the bulletin boards, . . . this doesn't mean that 'anything goes'";

(B) use of a software screening program which automatically prescreens all bulletin board postings for offensive language;

(C) the use of Board Leaders such as Epstein whose duties include enforcement of the Guidelines, according to Jennifer Ambrozek, the Manager of Prodigy's bulletin boards and the person at PRODIGY responsible for supervising the Board Leaders; and

(D) testimony by Epstein as to a tool for Board Leaders known as an "emergency delete function" pursuant to which a Board Leader could remove a note and send a previously prepared message of explanation. . . .

A finding that PRODIGY is a publisher is the first hurdle for Plaintiffs to overcome in pursuit of their defamation claims, because one who repeats or otherwise republishes a libel is subject to liability as if he had originally published it. In contrast, distributors such as book stores and libraries may be liable for defamatory statements of others only if they knew or had reason to know of the defamatory statement at issue. [*Cubby Inc. v. CompuServe Inc.*]* . . . In short, the critical issue to be determined by this Court is whether . . . PRODIGY

---

* The court used brackets around its citations. The citations appeared in the original. —ED.

exercised sufficient editorial control over its computer bulletin boards to render it a publisher with the same responsibilities as a newspaper.

Again, PRODIGY insists that its former policy of manually reviewing all messages prior to posting was changed "long before the messages complained of by Plaintiffs were posted". However, no documentation or detailed explanation of such a change, and the dissemination of news of such a change, has been submitted. In addition, PRODIGY argues that in terms of sheer volume— currently 60,000 messages a day are posted on PRODIGY bulletin boards— manual review of messages is not feasible. While PRODIGY admits that Board Leaders may remove messages that violate its Guidelines, it claims in conclusory manner that Board Leaders do not function as "editors".

As for legal authority, PRODIGY relies on the *Cubby* case.... The key distinction between CompuServe and PRODIGY is two fold. First, PRODIGY held itself out to the public and its members as controlling the content of its computer bulletin boards. Second, PRODIGY implemented this control through its automatic software screening program, and the Guidelines which Board Leaders are required to enforce. By actively utilizing technology and manpower to delete notes from its computer bulletin boards on the basis of offensiveness and "bad taste", for example, PRODIGY is clearly making decisions as to content and such decisions constitute editorial control. That such control is not complete and is enforced both as early as the notes arrive and as late as a complaint is made, does not minimize or eviscerate the simple fact that PRODIGY has uniquely arrogated to itself the role of determining what is proper for its members to post and read on its bulletin boards. Based on the foregoing, this Court is compelled to conclude that for the purposes of Plaintiffs' claims in this action, PRODIGY is a publisher rather than a distributor.

An interesting comparison may be found in *Auvil v. CBS 60 Minutes*, where apple growers sued a television network and local affiliates because of an allegedly defamatory investigative report generated by the network and broadcast by the affiliates. The record established that the affiliates exercised no editorial control over the broadcast although they had the power to do so by virtue of their contract with CBS, they had the opportunity to do so by virtue of a three hour hiatus for the west coast time differential, they had the technical capability to do so, and they in fact had occasionally censored network programming in the past, albeit never in connection with "60 Minutes". The *Auvil* court found:

> It is argued that these features, coupled with the power to censor, triggered the duty to censor. That is a leap which the Court is not prepared to join in.

* * *

[P]laintiffs' construction would force the creation of full time editorial boards at local stations throughout the country which possess sufficient knowledge, legal acumen and access to experts to continually monitor incoming transmissions and exercise on-the-spot discretionary calls or face $75 million dollar lawsuits at every turn. That is not realistic.

* * *

More than merely unrealistic in economic terms, it is difficult to imagine a scenario more chilling on the media's right of expression and the public's right to know.

Consequently, the court dismissed all claims against the affiliates on the basis of "conduit liability", which could not be established therein absent fault, which was not shown.

In contrast, here PRODIGY has virtually created an editorial staff of Board Leaders who have the ability to continually monitor incoming transmissions and in fact do spend time censoring notes. Indeed, it could be said that PRODIGY's current system of automatic scanning, Guidelines and Board Leaders may have a chilling effect on freedom of communication in Cyberspace, and it appears that this chilling effect is exactly what PRODIGY wants, but for the legal liability that attaches to such censorship.

Let it be clear that this Court is in full agreement with *Cubby* and *Auvil.* Computer bulletin boards should generally be regarded in the same context as bookstores, libraries and network affiliates. It is PRODIGY's own policies, technology and staffing decisions which have altered the scenario and mandated the finding that it is a publisher.

PRODIGY's conscious choice, to gain the benefits of editorial control, has opened it up to a greater liability than CompuServe and other computer networks that make no such choice. For the record, the fear that this Court's finding of publisher status for PRODIGY will compel all computer networks to abdicate control of their bulletin boards, incorrectly presumes that the market will refuse to compensate a network for its increased control and the resulting increased exposure. Presumably PRODIGY's decision to regulate the content of its bulletin boards was in part influenced by its desire to attract a market it perceived to exist consisting of users seeking a "family-oriented" computer service. This decision simply required that to the extent computer networks provide such services, they must also accept the concomitant legal consequences.[*]

---

[*] Like in *Cubby,* plaintiffs argued for vicarious liability based on agency. Specifically, they argued that Epstein was PRODIGY's agent. Applying New York agency law, the court examined the contractual agreement between Prodigy and bulletin board leaders. Notwithstanding language within the contract that seemed to

[On this reasoning, the court granted partial summary judgment on the issue of whether PRODIGY was a "publisher" of the statements in question.—ED.]

NOTES & QUESTIONS

1. *The specific players.* Again, make sure that you understand the contractual and supervisory relationships among Prodigy, Epstein, and the bulletin board user who allegedly defamed Stratton Oakmont. How do these relationships compare among the players in the CompuServe case?

2. *Categorizing PRODIGY.* According to the court, the question presented is:

> whether ... PRODIGY exercised sufficient editorial control over its computer bulletin boards to render it a publisher with the same responsibilities as a newspaper.

Because the term "publisher" invites equivocation—are we talking about publishing in a business sense, or in the tort sense (as one who has committed a "publication")—a clearer way to pose the question is to ask whether PRODIGY, by its advertisements and actions, lost its distributor conditional privilege. If it retained its privilege, then Stratton Oakmont would have to demonstrate, as a threshold matter, that PRODIGY knew or had reason to know of the defamatory character of the statements. Since PRODIGY knew nothing about the post when the anonymous poster made it, PRODIGY could not be held liable.

3. *Comparison with* Cubby. The court finds, however, that PRODIGY is *not* a distributor, whereas the *Cubby* court found CompuServe to be a distributor. Do the different results come from different implicit definitions of "distributor." Or did the two courts use the same definition, but apply them to materially different facts?

4. *Network affiliate analogy.* In deciding whether PRODIGY should remain in the distributor category, the court compared PRODIGY to a broadcast TV network affiliate and quoted from *Auvil v. CBS 60 Minutes.** In an abstract sense, *Auvil* posed the same question as PRODIGY. A new intermediary (the television affiliate) helps facilitate the distribution of defamation (video produced by the CBS network). The affiliate has both the legal right and technological ability to edit or censor feeds it does not like. Does this mean the affiliate loses the privileges that it might have as a mere conduit (e.g., UPS) or even as a

---

deny a principal-agent relationship the Court refused to give such language "talismanic" effect. Instead, it probed the substance of the relationship, and found that "PRODIGY directed and controlled Epstein's actions." Thus he was an agent.—ED.

* 800 F. Supp. 928 (E.D.Wa. 1992).

distributor (e.g., BARNES AND NOBLE)? The court concluded no. Further, the affiliates had no reason to know of the defamation, and therefore there could be no liability.

5. *Quid pro quo.* The opinion suggests that PRODIGY cannot have it both ways. PRODIGY held itself out as intentionally chilling certain types of impolite, family-unfriendly speech. For this *benefit* of generating a pleasant environment, the court suggests that PRODIGY must also accept the *cost*—losing distributor status and its conditional privilege. Does that seem like a fair trade-off?

6. *The real cost.* How costly is it to lose distributor status and its conditional privilege? At one time the cost was very high. Before the constitutionalization of defamation law, parties could be held liable for defamation without fault. In other words, authors as well as publishing houses, magazines, and newspapers (often called "primary publishers") could be held strictly liable for defamatory statements that turned out to be false, even if they were sincerely and non-negligently believed to be true. In sharp contrast, distributors enjoyed the conditional privilege that required actual knowledge or reason to know, which is effectively a negligence standard. Thus, at one time, the cost of losing distributor status was the cost of shifting from negligence to strict liability. But these days, strict liability for defamation is rare (constitutionally, it could only be on matters of private concern). So, the cost of losing distributor status is much less than it once was.[*]

The real cost comes from whether a court imposes a duty to monitor. The conditional privilege enjoyed by distributors means that they have no general duty to monitor proactively the contents of what they distribute. Bookstores don't have to read every book in advance of selling the first copy. But if you are not a distributor, the failure to monitor proactively *could* be evidence of negligent behavior. In contrast to a bookstore, a publishing house's failure to read a book that it publishes *could* be evidence of negligence.

7. *In-house response.* If *Stratton Oakmont* were the law of the land and you were advising an ISP, what recommendations would you make about editing or filtering obnoxious or potentially defamatory content? In other words, if you were keen on maintaining the conditional privilege enjoyed by distributors, what would you recommend? One creative approach would be to tell Congress in the middle of drafting the Communications Decency Act that *Stratton Oakmont* chills any family-friendly editing (by using such editing as grounds for removing

---

[*] *See* Eugene Volokh, *Freedom of Speech in Cyberspace from the Listener's Perspective: Private Speech Restrictions, Libel, State Action, Harassment, and Sex,* 1996 UNIVERSITY OF CHICAGO LEGAL FORUM 377, at § I.D.

the distributor conditional privilege). Congress was persuaded and passed 47 U.S.C. § 230.

> 47 U.S.C. § 230. Protection for private blocking and screening of offensive material
>
> (c) Protection for "good samaritan" blocking and screening of offensive material
>
> > (1) *Treatment of publisher or speaker.* No provider or user of an interactive computer service shall be treated as the publisher or speaker of any information provided by another information content provider.
> >
> > (2) *Civil liability.* No provider or user of an interactive computer service shall be held liable on account of—
> >
> > > (A) any action voluntarily taken in good faith to restrict access to or availability of material that the provider or user considers to be obscene, lewd, lascivious, filthy, excessively violent, harassing, or otherwise objectionable, whether or not such material is constitutionally protected; or
> > >
> > > (B) any action taken to enable or make available to information content providers or others the technical means to restrict access to material described in paragraph (1). [FN1: So in original. Probably should be "subparagraph (A)".]
>
> (e) Effect on other laws
>
> > (1) *No effect on criminal law.* Nothing in this section shall be construed to impair the enforcement of section 223 or 231 of this title, chapter 71 (relating to obscenity) or 110 (relating to sexual exploitation of children) of Title 18, or any other Federal criminal statute.
> >
> > (2) *No effect on intellectual property law.* Nothing in this section shall be construed to limit or expand any law pertaining to intellectual property.
> >
> > (3) *State law.* Nothing in this section shall be construed to prevent any State from enforcing any State law that is consistent with this section. No cause of action may be brought and no liability may be imposed under any State or local law that is inconsistent with this section.
> >
> > (4) *No effect on Communications Privacy law.* Nothing in this section shall be construed to limit the application of the Electronic Communications Privacy Act of 1986 or any of the amendments made by such Act, or any similar State law.
>
> (f) Definitions
>
> As used in this section:
>
> > (1) *Internet.* The term "Internet" means the international computer network of both Federal and non-Federal interoperable packet switched data networks.
> >
> > (2) *Interactive computer service.* The term "interactive computer service" means any information service, system, or access software provider that provides or enables computer access by multiple users to a computer server, including specifically a service or system that provides access to the Internet and such systems operated or services offered by libraries or educational institutions.
> >
> > (3) *Information content provider.* The term "information content provider" means any person or entity that is responsible, in whole or in part, for the creation or development of information provided through the Internet or any other interactive computer service.

B. AFTER 47 U.S.C. § 230

1. EXPANSION

	ZERAN V. AMERICA ONLINE
	129 F.3d 327 (4th Cir. 1997)

WILKINSON, Chief Judge:

I.

The instant case comes before us on a motion for judgment on the pleadings, see Fed. R. Civ. P. 12(c), so we accept the facts alleged in the complaint as true. On April 25, 1995, an unidentified person posted a message on an AOL bulletin board advertising "Naughty Oklahoma T-Shirts." The posting described the sale of shirts featuring offensive and tasteless slogans related to the April 19, 1995, bombing of the Alfred P. Murrah Federal Building in Oklahoma City. Those interested in purchasing the shirts were instructed to call "Ken" at Zeran's home phone number in Seattle, Washington. As a result of this anonymously perpetrated prank, Zeran received a high volume of calls, comprised primarily of angry and derogatory messages, but also including death threats. Zeran could not change his phone number because he relied on its availability to the public in running his business out of his home. Later that day, Zeran called AOL and informed a company representative of his predicament. The employee assured Zeran that the posting would be removed from AOL's bulletin board but explained that as a matter of policy AOL would not post a retraction. The parties dispute the date that AOL removed this original posting from its bulletin board.

On April 26, the next day, an unknown person posted another message advertising additional shirts with new tasteless slogans related to the Oklahoma City bombing. Again, interested buyers were told to call Zeran's phone number, to ask for "Ken," and to "please call back if busy" due to high demand. The angry, threatening phone calls intensified. Over the next four days, an unidentified party continued to post messages on AOL's bulletin board, advertising additional items including bumper stickers and key chains with still more offensive slogans. During this time period, Zeran called AOL repeatedly and was told by company representatives that the individual account from which the messages were posted would soon be closed. Zeran also reported his case to

Seattle FBI agents. By April 30, Zeran was receiving an abusive phone call approximately every two minutes.*

On April 23, 1996, [Zeran] filed this separate suit against AOL. . . . Zeran did not bring any action against the party who posted the offensive messages.[1] AOL answered Zeran's complaint and interposed 47 U.S.C. § 230 as an affirmative defense. AOL then moved for judgment on the pleadings pursuant to Fed. R. Civ. P. 12(c). The district court granted AOL's motion, and Zeran filed this appeal.

II.

A.

The relevant portion of § 230 states: "No provider or user of an interactive computer service shall be treated as the publisher or speaker of any information provided by another information content provider." 47 U.S.C. § 230(c)(1). By its plain language, § 230 creates a federal immunity to any cause of action that would make service providers liable for information originating with a third-party user of the service. Specifically, § 230 precludes courts from entertaining claims that would place a computer service provider in a publisher's role. Thus, lawsuits seeking to hold a service provider liable for its exercise of a publisher's traditional editorial functions—such as deciding whether to publish, withdraw, postpone or alter content—are barred.

The purpose of this statutory immunity is not difficult to discern. Congress recognized the threat that tort-based lawsuits pose to freedom of speech in the new and burgeoning Internet medium. The imposition of tort liability on service providers for the communications of others represented, for Congress, simply another form of intrusive government regulation of speech. Section 230 was enacted, in part, to maintain the robust nature of Internet communication and, accordingly, to keep government interference in the medium to a minimum.

None of this means, of course, that the original culpable party who posts defamatory messages would escape accountability. . . . Congress made a policy choice, however, not to deter harmful online speech through the separate route of imposing tort liability on companies that serve as intermediaries for other parties' potentially injurious messages.

Congress' purpose in providing the § 230 immunity was thus evident. Interactive computer services have millions of users. The amount of information

---

* The court explained how things got worse for Zeran as local radio stations and newspapers spread news about Zeran's alleged advertisements—ED.

[1] Zeran maintains that AOL made it impossible to identify the original party by failing to maintain adequate records of its users. The issue of AOL's record keeping practices, however, is not presented by this appeal.

communicated via interactive computer services is therefore staggering. The specter of tort liability in an area of such prolific speech would have an obvious chilling effect. It would be impossible for service providers to screen each of their millions of postings for possible problems. Faced with potential liability for each message republished by their services, interactive computer service providers might choose to severely restrict the number and type of messages posted. Congress considered the weight of the speech interests implicated and chose to immunize service providers to avoid any such restrictive effect.

Another important purpose of § 230 was to encourage service providers to self-regulate the dissemination of offensive material over their services. In this respect, § 230 responded to a New York state court decision, Stratton Oakmont, Inc. v. Prodigy Servs. Co. (N.Y. Sup. Ct. May 24, 1995). . . . Congress enacted § 230 to remove the disincentives to self-regulation created by the *Stratton Oakmont* decision. Under that court's holding, computer service providers who regulated the dissemination of offensive material on their services risked subjecting themselves to liability, because such regulation cast the service provider in the role of a publisher. Fearing that the specter of liability would therefore deter service providers from blocking and screening offensive material, Congress enacted § 230's broad immunity "to remove disincentives for the development and utilization of blocking and filtering technologies that empower parents to restrict their children's access to objectionable or inappropriate online material." 47 U.S.C. § 230(b)(4). In line with this purpose, § 230 forbids the imposition of publisher liability on a service provider for the exercise of its editorial and self-regulatory functions.

B.

Zeran argues, however, that the § 230 immunity eliminates only publisher liability, leaving distributor liability intact. Publishers can be held liable for defamatory statements contained in their works even absent proof that they had specific knowledge of the statement's inclusion. W. Page Keeton et al., Prosser and Keeton on the Law of Torts § 113, at 810 (5th ed. 1984). . . . Distributors cannot be held liable for defamatory statements contained in the materials they distribute unless it is proven at a minimum that they have actual knowledge of the defamatory statements upon which liability is predicated. Id. at 811.

Because of the difference between these two forms of liability, Zeran contends that the term "distributor" carries a legally distinct meaning from the term "publisher." Accordingly, he asserts that Congress' use of only the term "publisher" in § 230 indicates a purpose to immunize service providers only from publisher liability. He argues that distributors are left unprotected by § 230 and, therefore, his suit should be permitted to proceed against AOL. We disagree. [Distributor] liability is merely a subset, or a species, of publisher liability, and is therefore also foreclosed by § 230.

The terms "publisher" and "distributor" derive their legal significance from the context of defamation law. Although Zeran attempts to artfully plead his claims as ones of negligence, they are indistinguishable from a garden variety defamation action. Because the publication of a statement is a necessary element in a defamation action, only one who publishes can be subject to this form of tort liability. Restatement (Second) of Torts § 558(b) (1977); Keeton et al., supra, § 113, at 802. Publication does not only describe the choice by an author to include certain information. In addition, both the negligent communication of a defamatory statement and the failure to remove such a statement when first communicated by another party—each alleged by Zeran here under a negligence label—constitute publication. Restatement (Second) of Torts § 577; see also Tacket v. General Motors Corp., 836 F.2d 1042, 1046-47 (7th Cir. 1987). In fact, every repetition of a defamatory statement is considered a publication. Keeton et al., supra, § 113, at 799.

In this case, AOL is legally considered to be a publisher.... Even distributors are considered to be publishers for purposes of defamation law:

> Those who are in the business of making their facilities available to disseminate the writings composed, the speeches made, and the information gathered by others may also be regarded as participating to such an extent in making the books, newspapers, magazines, and information available to others as to be regarded as publishers. They are intentionally making the contents available to others, sometimes without knowing all of the contents—including the defamatory content—and sometimes without any opportunity to ascertain, in advance, that any defamatory matter was to be included in the matter published.

Id. at 803. AOL falls squarely within this traditional definition of a publisher and, therefore, is clearly protected by § 230's immunity.

Zeran contends that decisions like *Stratton Oakmont* and *Cubby* recognize a legal distinction between publishers and distributors.... It is undoubtedly true that mere conduits, or distributors, are subject to a different standard of liability. As explained above, distributors must at a minimum have knowledge of the existence of a defamatory statement as a prerequisite to liability. But this distinction signifies only that different standards of liability may be applied within the larger publisher category, depending on the specific type of publisher concerned. To the extent that decisions like *Stratton* and *Cubby* utilize the terms "publisher" and "distributor" separately, the decisions correctly describe two different standards of liability. *Stratton* and *Cubby* do not, however, suggest that distributors are not also a type of publisher for purposes of defamation law.

Zeran simply attaches too much importance to the presence of the distinct notice element in distributor liability. The simple fact of notice surely cannot transform one from an original publisher to a distributor in the eyes of the law. To the contrary, once a computer service provider receives notice of a potentially defamatory posting, it is thrust into the role of a traditional publisher. The computer service provider must decide whether to publish, edit, or withdraw the posting. In this respect, Zeran seeks to impose liability on AOL for assuming the role for which § 230 specifically proscribes liability—the publisher role.

If computer service providers were subject to distributor liability, they would face potential liability each time they receive notice of a potentially defamatory statement—from any party, concerning any message. Each notification would require a careful yet rapid investigation of the circumstances surrounding the posted information, a legal judgment concerning the information's defamatory character, and an on-the-spot editorial decision whether to risk liability by allowing the continued publication of that information. Although this might be feasible for the traditional print publisher, the sheer number of postings on interactive computer services would create an impossible burden in the Internet context. Because service providers would be subject to liability only for the publication of information, and not for its removal, they would have a natural incentive simply to remove messages upon notification, whether the contents were defamatory or not. Thus, like strict liability, liability upon notice has a chilling effect on the freedom of Internet speech.

Similarly, notice-based liability would deter service providers from regulating the dissemination of offensive material over their own services. Any efforts by a service provider to investigate and screen material posted on its service would only lead to notice of potentially defamatory material more frequently and thereby create a stronger basis for liability. Instead of subjecting themselves to further possible lawsuits, service providers would likely eschew any attempts at self-regulation.

More generally, notice-based liability for interactive computer service providers would provide third parties with a no-cost means to create the basis for future lawsuits. Whenever one was displeased with the speech of another party conducted over an interactive computer service, the offended party could simply "notify" the relevant service provider, claiming the information to be legally defamatory.... Because the probable effects of distributor liability on the vigor of Internet speech and on service provider self-regulation are directly contrary to § 230's statutory purposes, we will not assume that Congress intended to leave liability upon notice intact.

For the foregoing reasons, we affirm the judgment of the district court. AFFIRMED.

NOTES & QUESTIONS

1. *Parsing the statute carefully.*

    a. *Core provision.* Section 230(c)(1) reads: "No provider or user of an interactive computer service shall be treated as the publisher or speaker of any information provided by another information content provider."

    b. *Interactive computer service.* An interactive computer service is defined as: "any information service, system, or access software provider that provides or enables computer access by multiple users to a computer server, including specifically a service or system that provides access to the internet and such systems operated or services offered by libraries or educational institutions." § 230(f)(2). There is no dispute that AOL is a provider of an "interactive computer service."

    c. *Another information content provider.* This term is defined as: "any person or entity that is responsible, in whole or in part, for the creation or development of information provided through the internet or any other interactive computer service." § 230(f)(3). There is no dispute that the anonymous poster is the "information content provider."

2. *Reading the law carefully.* In the first paragraph in Part II.B of the opinion, the court sets out the law as follows:

> Publishers can be held liable for defamatory statements contained in their works even absent proof that they had specific knowledge of the statement's inclusion. . . . Distributors cannot be held liable for defamatory statements contained in the materials they distribute unless it is proven at a minimum that they have actual knowledge of the defamatory statements upon which liability is predicated.

The court's authorities are citations to the well-known Prosser & Keeton tort treatise.[*] But this paragraph invites misreading.

First, as for publishers, it is true that they may be held liable without specific knowledge of the statement, but this should not be mistaken for a strict vicarious liability between author and publisher. As the treatise clarifies:

> Prior to *New York Times* [v. Sullivan] and its progeny, the primary publisher was strictly liable in the same way as the author. Today, the primary publisher as a public medium will not be subject to liability except on proof of fault of an authorized agent.[†]

---

[*] *See* W. PAGE KEETON ET AL., PROSSER AND KEETON ON THE LAW OF TORTS § 113, at 810-11 (5th ed. 1984).

Second, as for distributors, the court articulates the conditional privilege far more strongly than it in fact is. The privilege does not mandate a showing of "actual knowledge". Rather, in order to be subject to liability, there must be a showing of knowledge *or* "reason to know." The treatise makes this clear on the same pages the court cites.

3. *Equivocating publisher.* This case turns on the meaning of "publisher" in § 230(c)(1). What precisely does it mean that AOL cannot be deemed a publisher of the anonymous comments? On the one hand, Congress might have used "publisher" in a commercial sense, to refer to the kind of firm that is a publishing house, in contrast to a bookstore which is a mere "distributor." Read this way and in light of the legislative history to overturn *Stratton Oakmont*, § 230(c)(1) could just mean that a provider of an interactive computer service should not be stripped of its distributor status (and deemed a speaker or publisher) simply because it edits obnoxious content. This would mean that AOL could still be held liable if it knew or had reason to know (which gets us past the conditional privilege), and AOL satisfied the other elements of the defamation tort (including the requisite amount of fault).

On the other hand, "publisher" might be used in a defamation tort sense, to refer to anyone who has engaged in the act of "publication"—an intentional or negligent indication of a defamatory statement. If Congress intended this meaning, then AOL cannot be held liable for defamation regardless of knowledge or fault since publication is an element of the defamation cause of action, and the statute declares that AOL has not published these anonymous comments. Which interpretation of "publisher" does the court adopt? Which is correct?

4. *Cheapest cost avoider analysis.* The person truly culpable for this tort cannot be found because of anonymity. (Even if the person were found, she may be judgment-proof.) As between Zeran and AOL, who is more innocent? Consider applying standard economic justifications for strict liability in tort law. Who is the cheaper cost-avoider for these defamation "accidents"? Who is better able to create architecture that might avoid such problems in the future?

5. *Ending anonymity.* Isn't the simplest solution to end anonymity on bulletin boards and threaded discussions and the like on the internet? Can this be done technologically? Do you think it would be constitutional to do so? Finally, would this be a bad social policy, even if it were technologically and legally possible? Could AOL or a similar Internet Service Provider face liability for sharing the identities of their anonymous users?

---

† *Id.* at 810.

BLUMENTHAL V. DRUDGE
992 F. Supp. 44 (D.D.C. 1998)

PAUL L. FRIEDMAN, District Judge.

I. BACKGROUND

In early 1995, defendant Drudge created an electronic publication called the Drudge Report, a gossip column focusing on gossip from Hollywood and Washington, D.C. Mr. Drudge's base of operations for writing, publishing and disseminating the Drudge Report has been an office in his apartment in Los Angeles, California.

Access to defendant Drudge's world wide web site is available at no cost to anyone who has access to the Internet at the Internet address of "www.drudgereport.com." ... In addition, during the time period relevant to this case, Drudge had developed a list of regular readers or subscribers to whom he e-mailed each new edition of the Drudge Report. . . . [P]laintiffs allege that by 1997 Drudge had 85,000 subscribers to his e-mail service.

In late May or early June of 1997 . . . Drudge entered into a written license agreement with AOL. The agreement made the Drudge Report available to all members of AOL's service for a period of one year. . . . Drudge transmits new editions of the Drudge Report by e-mailing them to AOL. AOL then posts the new editions on the AOL service. Drudge also has continued to distribute each new edition of the Drudge Report via e-mail and his own web site.

Late at night on the evening of Sunday, August 10, 1997, defendant Drudge wrote and transmitted the edition of the Drudge Report that contained the alleged defamatory statement about [domestic violence by Sidney Blumenthal, a White House aide].

After receiving a letter from plaintiffs' counsel on Monday, August 11, 1997, Drudge retracted the story through a special edition of the Drudge Report posted on his web site and e-mailed to his subscribers. At approximately 2:00 a.m. on Tuesday, August 12, 1997, Drudge e-mailed the retraction to AOL which posted it on the AOL service. Defendant Drudge later publicly apologized to the Blumenthals.

II. AOL'S MOTION FOR SUMMARY JUDGMENT

A. The Internet

As one court has noted:

> The Internet has no territorial boundaries. To paraphrase Gertrude Stein, as far as the Internet is concerned, not only is there perhaps "no there there," the "there" is everywhere where there is Internet access. When business is

transacted over a computer network via a Web-site accessed by a computer in Massachusetts, it takes place as much in Massachusetts, literally or figuratively, as it does anywhere.

Digital Equipment Corp. v. AltaVista Technology, Inc., 960 F. Supp. 456, 462 (D. Mass. 1997)

The near instantaneous possibilities for the dissemination of information by millions of different information providers around the world . . . have created ever-increasing opportunities for the exchange of information and ideas in "cyberspace." This information revolution has also presented unprecedented challenges relating to rights of privacy and reputational rights of individuals, to the control of obscene and pornographic materials, and to competition among journalists and news organizations for instant news, rumors and other information that is communicated so quickly that it is too often unchecked and unverified. Needless to say, the legal rules that will govern this new medium are just beginning to take shape.

B. Communications Decency Act of 1996, Section 230

In February of 1996, Congress made an effort to deal with some of these challenges in enacting the Communications Decency Act of 1996. Whether wisely or not, it made the legislative judgment to effectively immunize providers of interactive computer services from civil liability in tort with respect to material disseminated by them but created by others. In recognition of the speed with which information may be disseminated and the near impossibility of regulating information content, Congress decided not to treat providers of interactive computer services like other information providers such as newspapers, magazines or television and radio stations, all of which may be held liable for publishing or distributing obscene or defamatory material written or prepared by others. While Congress could have made a different policy choice, it opted not to hold interactive computer services liable for their failure to edit, withhold or restrict access to offensive material disseminated through their medium.

Plaintiffs concede that AOL is a "provider . . . of an interactive computer service" for purposes of Section 230. . . . They also concede that Drudge is an "information content provider" because he wrote the alleged defamatory material about the Blumenthals contained in the Drudge Report.

AOL acknowledges both that Section 230(c)(1) would not immunize AOL with respect to any information AOL developed or created entirely by itself and that there are situations in which there may be two or more information content providers responsible for material disseminated on the Internet—joint authors, a lyricist and a composer, for example. While Section 230 does not preclude joint liability for the joint development of content, AOL maintains that there simply is no evidence here that AOL had any role in creating or developing any of the information in the Drudge Report. The Court agrees. It is undisputed that the Blumenthal story was written by Drudge without any substantive or editorial involvement by AOL. AOL was nothing more than a provider of an interactive computer service on which the Drudge Report was carried, and Congress has said quite clearly that such a provider shall not be treated as a "publisher or speaker" and therefore may not be held liable in tort. 47 U.S.C. § 230(c)(1).

Plaintiffs [argue] that Section 230 of the Communications Decency Act does not provide immunity to AOL in this case because Drudge was not just an anonymous person who sent a message over the Internet through AOL. He is a person with whom AOL contracted, whom AOL paid $3,000 a month— $36,000 a year, Drudge's sole, consistent source of income—and whom AOL promoted to its subscribers and potential subscribers as a reason to subscribe to AOL. Furthermore, the license agreement between AOL and Drudge by its terms contemplates more than a passive role for AOL; in it, AOL reserves the "right to remove, or direct [Drudge] to remove, any content which, as reasonably determined by AOL... violates AOL's then-standard Terms of Service...." By the terms of the agreement, AOL also is "entitled to require reasonable changes to... content, to the extent such content will, in AOL's good faith judgment, adversely affect operations of the AOL network."

In addition, shortly after it entered into the licensing agreement with Drudge, AOL issued a press release making clear the kind of material Drudge would provide to AOL subscribers—gossip and rumor—and urged potential subscribers to sign onto AOL in order to get the benefit of the Drudge Report. The press release was captioned: "AOL Hires Runaway Gossip Success Matt Drudge." It noted that "[m]averick gossip columnist Matt Drudge has teamed up with America Online," and stated: "Giving the Drudge Report a home on America Online (keyword: Drudge) opens up the floodgates to an audience ripe for Drudge's brand of reporting.... AOL has made Matt Drudge instantly accessible to members who crave instant gossip and news breaks." *Id.* Why is this different, the Blumenthals suggest, from AOL advertising and promoting a new purveyor of child pornography or other offensive material? Why should AOL be permitted to tout someone as a gossip columnist or rumor monger who will make such rumors and gossip "instantly accessible" to AOL subscribers, and then claim immunity when that person, as might be anticipated, defames another?

If it were writing on a clean slate, this Court would agree with plaintiffs. AOL has certain editorial rights with respect to the content provided by Drudge and disseminated by AOL, including the right to require changes in content and to remove it; and it has affirmatively promoted Drudge as a new source of unverified instant gossip on AOL. Yet it takes no responsibility for any damage he may cause. AOL is not a passive conduit like the telephone company, a common carrier with no control and therefore no responsibility for what is said over the telephone wires. Because it has the right to exercise editorial control over those with whom it contracts and whose words it disseminates, it would seem only fair to hold AOL to the liability standards applied to a publisher or, at least, like a book store owner or library, to the liability standards applied to a distributor. But Congress has made a different policy choice by providing immunity even where the interactive service provider has an active, even aggressive role in making available content prepared by others. In some sort of tacit quid pro quo arrangement with the service provider community, Congress has conferred immunity from tort liability as an incentive to Internet service providers to self-police the Internet for obscenity and other offensive material, even where the self-policing is unsuccessful or not even attempted.

Any attempt to distinguish between "publisher" liability and notice-based "distributor" liability and to argue that Section 230 was only intended to immunize the former would be unavailing. Congress made no distinction between publishers and distributors in providing immunity from liability. *Zeran.* While it appears to this Court that AOL in this case has taken advantage of all the benefits conferred by Congress in the Communications Decency Act, and then some, without accepting any of the burdens that Congress intended, the statutory language is clear: AOL is immune from suit, and the Court therefore must grant its motion for summary judgment.

NOTES & QUESTIONS

1. *Technological power.* Before the internet, could Matthew Drudge, sitting in an apartment in Los Angeles, otherwise unemployed, have defamed a powerful White House aide in front of hundreds of thousands of people?

2. *Accountability.* Why did the Blumenthals bother suing AOL? It was not as if Matthew Drudge was anonymous, as was the poster in the *Zeran* case. After all, he was listed as a defendant. Why not hold Drudge alone accountable?

3. *The specific players.* As in previous cases, make sure you understand in detail the contractual and supervisory relationships between America Online and Drudge.

4. *Blumenthals' best argument.* If you are counsel for the Blumenthals, you would try to characterize the relationship between America Online and Drudge as one of employment or at least agency. Does the court buy this argument? Go

back to the facts of *Cubby* and *Stratton Oakmont*, in which "vicarious liability" through agency was argued (and summarized at the end of each opinion in footnotes). How does the agency analysis compare in this case?

5. *Quid pro quo redux.* The Court very clearly recognizes that AOL has its cake and is eating it too. It notes that "even where the interactive service provider has an active, even aggressive role in making available content prepared by others," there is complete immunity. Does this make sense? Go back and re-read § 230 above. According to the plain language of the statute, is this what Congress actually intended?

6. *Section 230 triumphant.* The immunity provided by § 230 has been stunning in its scope and strength.

a. *Broad readings of "provider … of interactive computer service".* You might assume that a provider of an interactive computer service is just a clumsy way to say Internet Service Provider. But that term has been read much more broadly, to include commercial web sites including matchmaking sites,[*] auction sites (e.g., eBay),[†] on-line bookstores (e.g., Amazon),[‡] and chat rooms.[§] Also, physical locations such as libraries[**] and copy shops[††] that offer internet access have also been deemed providers of interactive computer services.

b. *Not only providers but also "users."* The statute specifically states that no "provider or *user*" of an interactive computer service shall be deemed a publisher. So, someone who merely *uses* an interactive computer service, for example, by selecting, editing (e.g., cutting text), then forwarding along a defamatory email authored by another, has also received protections.[‡‡]

c. *Not only defamation.* Although we have focused on defamation, § 230 immunity has been applied to suits regarding negligent sale of child pornography,[§§] federal civil rights,[***] state consumer protection statutes, and state business torts.[†††] By its own terms, the 230 immunity does not apply,

---

[*] *See, e.g.,* Carafano v. Metrosplash.Com, Inc, 339 F.3d 1119 (9th Cir. 2003).

[†] *See, e.g.,* Gentry v. eBay, Inc., 121 Cal. Rptr. 2d 703 & n.7 (2002) ("eBay").

[‡] *See, e.g.,* Schneider v. Amazon.com, Inc., 31 P.3d 37, 40-41 (Wash Ct. App. 2001) ("Amazon").

[§] *See, e.g.,* Green v. America Online, Inc., 318 F.3d 465 (3d Cir. 2003) (chatroom).

[**] *See, e.g.,* Kathleen R. v. City of Livermore, 87 Cal. App. 4th 684 (2001).

[††] *See, e.g.,* Patentwizard, Inc. v. Kinko's, Inc., 163 F. Supp. 2d 1069 (D.S.D. 2001) (Kinko's).

[‡‡] *See, e.g.,* Batzel v. Smith, 333 F.3d 1018, 1030-31 (9th Cir. 2003) (listserv and website archive of emails).

[§§] *See, e.g.,* Doe v. AOL, 783 So.2d 1010 (Fla. 2001) (child pornography exchanged through AOL chat rooms).

[***] *See* Noah v. AOL Time Warner Inc., 261 F. Supp. 2d 532, 538 (E.D. Va. 2003) (Title II public accommodations).

[†††] *See, e.g.,* Corbis Corp. v. Amazon.com, Inc., 351 F.Supp.2d 1090 (W.D. Wash. 2004) (applying § 230 to Washington consumer protection act and tortious interference of business relations).

however, to intellectual property claims,[*] criminal prosecutions,[†] and claims under the Electronic Communications Privacy Act.[‡]

2. CONTRACTION

The clear majority of courts addressing the issue have followed the reasoning in *Zeran*.[§] But in 2004, two California state appellate courts flatly rejected the *Zeran* elimination of distributor liability for defamation law. In *Barrett v. Rosenthal*,[**] plaintiffs sued a person for forwarding a defamatory e-mail to a newsgroup. After a thorough examination, the court rejected *Zeran* and held that § 230 did not destroy the distributor standard of liability. In *Grace v. eBay*,[††] a plaintiff sued eBay for defamatory comments made by a seller, whom Grace had earlier criticized. The court similarly concluded that § 230 "provides no immunity against liability for a distributor of information who knew or had reason to know that the information was defamatory."[‡‡] By 2006, however, the California Supreme Court had reasserted the *Zeran* interpretation of § 230, by reversing *Barrett* and dismissing the review of *Grace*, which already had been depublished.

Although the California state courts' reconsideration of the *Zeran* perspective was short-lived, the U.S. Court of Appeals for the Seventh Circuit has since shaken things up, courtesy of then-Chief Judge Frank Easterbrook. So has the Ninth Circuit, in an *en banc* opinion authored by then-Chief Judge Alex Kozinski. These cases must therefore be taken seriously. Interestingly, they both concern fair housing, not defamation.

---

[*] *See* § 230(e)(2) ("No effect on intellectual property law. Nothing in this section shall be construed to limit or expand any law pertaining to intellectual property."). There is confusion on whether "intellectual property" applies only to federal IP or also to state IP claims, which could include invasion of privacy and right of publicity claims. *Compare* Perfect 10, Inc. v. CCBill LLC, 488 F.3d 1102, 1118-19 (9th Cir. 2007) (interpreting "intellectual property" to mean only federal intellectual property) *with* Doe v. Friendfinder Network, Inc., 540 F.Supp. 2d 288, 299-302 (D. N.H. 2008) (interpreting phrase to include state intellectual property claims, thereby decreasing the scope of § 230 immunity).

[†] *See* § 230(e)(1) (no effect on any federal criminal statute).

[‡] *See* § 230(e)(4) (including ECPA and "any similar State law").

[§] *See, e.g.,* Ben Ezra, Weinstein & Co. v. America Online, Inc., 206 F.3d 980 (10th Cir. 2000); Green v. America Online, Inc., 318 F.3d 465 (3d Cir. 2003); Batzel v. Smith, 333 F.3d 1018 (9th Cir. 2003).

[**] 114 Cal. App. 4th 1379 (Cal. App. 1st Dist. 2004).

[††] 120 Cal. App. 4th 984 (2004).

[‡‡] *Id.* at 989.

CHICAGO LAWYERS' COMMITTEE
FOR CIVIL RIGHTS V. CRAIGSLIST, INC.
519 F.3d 666 (7th Cir. 2008).

EASTERBROOK, Chief Judge.

Section 804(a) of the Fair Housing Act forbids discrimination on account of race, religion, sex, or family status when selling or renting housing. 42 U.S.C. § 3604(a). This prohibition is accompanied by a ban on ads that state a preference with respect to any of the protected classes. It is illegal

> [t]o make, print, or publish, or cause to be made, printed, or published any notice, statement, or advertisement, with respect to the sale or rental of a dwelling that indicates any preference, limitation, or discrimination based on race, color, religion, sex, handicap, familial status, or national origin, or an intention to make any such preference, limitation, or discrimination.

42 U.S.C. § 3604(c). The Chicago Lawyers' Committee for Civil Rights Under Law [contends] that craigslist, which provides an electronic meeting place for those who want to buy, sell, or rent housing (and many other goods and services), is violating this statute.

Some notices on craigslist proclaim "NO MINORITIES" and "No children", along with multiple variations, bald or subtle. . . .

Online services are in some respects like the classified pages of newspapers, but in others they operate like common carriers such as telephone services, which are unaffected by § 3604(c) because they neither make nor publish any discriminatory advertisement, text message, or conversation that may pass over their networks. Ditto courier services such as FedEx and UPS, which do not read the documents inside packages and do not make or publish any of the customers' material. Web sites are not common carriers, but screening, though lawful, is hard. Simple filters along the lines of "postings may not contain the words 'white'" can't work. Statements such as "red brick house with white trim" do not violate any law, and prospective buyers and renters would be worse off if craigslist blocked descriptive statements.

An online service could hire a staff to vet the postings, but that would be expensive and may well be futile: if postings had to be reviewed before being put online, long delay could make the service much less useful, and if the vetting came only after the material was online the buyers and sellers might already have made their deals. Every month more than 30 million notices are posted to the craigslist system. Fewer than 30 people, all based in California, operate the system, which offers classifieds and forums for 450 cities. It would be necessary to increase that staff (and the expense that users must bear) substantially to conduct the sort of editorial review that the Lawyers' Committee demands-and even then errors would be frequent.

One of the ads to which the Lawyers' Committee objects contains the phrase "Catholic Church and beautiful Buddhist Temple within one block". The Committee sees this as a signal of religious preference; craigslist sees it as a description of the neighborhood, helping people zero in on properties most attractive to their preferences and no more implying exclusion than "elementary school within five minutes' walk" implies that the landlord won't rent to childless couples. Automated filters and human reviewers may be equally poor at sifting good from bad postings unless the discrimination is blatant; both false positives and false negatives are inevitable.

According to craigslist, the effort is unnecessary. It relies on 47 U.S.C. § 230(c), a part of the Communications Decency Act of 1996.

As craigslist understands this statute, § 230(c)(1) provides "broad immunity from liability for unlawful third-party content." That view has support in other circuits. See Zeran v. America Online (4th Cir.1997); Ben Ezra, Weinstein & Co. v. America Online (10th Cir.2000); Green v. America Online (3d Cir.2003); Batzel v. Smith (9th Cir.2003); Universal Communication Systems, Inc. v. Lycos, Inc. (1st Cir.2007). We have questioned whether § 230(c)(1) creates any form of "immunity," see Doe v. GTE Corp. (7th Cir.2003), and the Lawyers' Committee takes *Doe* as its cue. The caption of subsection (c) as a whole refers to "blocking and screening"; the Lawyers' Committee insists that unless an information content provider uses some form of filtering (a brief way to refer to "blocking and screening"), all of § 230(c) is irrelevant.

Neither side's argument finds much support in the statutory text. Subsection (c)(1) does not mention "immunity" or any synonym. Our opinion in *Doe* explains why § 230(c) as a whole cannot be understood as a general prohibition of civil liability for web-site operators and other online content hosts:

> Section 230(c)(2) tackles this problem [of potential liability for hosting pornographic pictures] not with a sword but with a safety net. A web host that *does* filter out offensive material is not liable to the censored customer. Removing the risk of civil liability may induce web hosts and other informational intermediaries to take more care to protect the privacy and sensibilities of third parties. The district court held that subsection (c)(1), though phrased as a definition rather than as an immunity, also blocks civil liability when web hosts and other Internet service providers (ISPs) *refrain* from filtering or censoring the information on their sites....
>
> If this reading is sound, then § 230(c) as a whole makes ISPs indifferent to the content of information they host or transmit: whether they do (subsection (c)(2)) or do not (subsection (c)(1)) take precautions, there is no liability under

either state or federal law. As precautions are costly, not only in direct outlay but also in lost revenue from the filtered customers, ISPs may be expected to take the do-nothing option and enjoy immunity under § 230(c)(1). Yet § 230(c)—which is, recall, part of the "Communications Decency Act"— bears the title "Protection for 'Good Samaritan' blocking and screening of offensive material", hardly an apt description if its principal effect is to induce ISPs to do nothing about the distribution of indecent and offensive materials via their services. Why should a law designed to eliminate ISPs' liability to the creators of offensive material end up defeating claims by the victims of tortious or criminal conduct?

True, a statute's caption must yield to its text when the two conflict, but whether there is a conflict is the question on the table. Why not read § 230(c)(1) as a definitional clause rather than as an immunity from liability, and thus harmonize the text with the caption? On this reading, an entity would remain a "provider or user"—and thus be eligible for the immunity under § 230(c)(2)— as long as the information came from someone else; but it would become a "publisher or speaker" and lose the benefit of § 230(c)(2) if it created the objectionable information. The difference between this reading and the district court's is that § 230(c)(2) never requires ISPs to filter offensive content, and thus § 230(e)(3) would not preempt state laws or common-law doctrines that induce or require ISPs to protect the interests of third parties, ... for such laws would not be "inconsistent with" this understanding of § 230(c)(1). There is yet another possibility: perhaps § 230(c)(1) forecloses any liability that depends on deeming the ISP a "publisher"—defamation law would be a good example of such liability—while permitting the states to regulate ISPs in their capacity as intermediaries.

To appreciate the limited role of § 230(c)(1), remember that "information content providers" may be liable for contributory infringement if their system is designed to help people steal music or other material in copyright. *See* Metro-Goldwyn-Mayer Studios Inc. v. Grokster, Ltd., (2005). *Grokster* is incompatible with treating § 230(c)(1) as a grant of comprehensive immunity from civil liability for content provided by a third party.

While craigslist wants to expand § 230(c)(1) beyond its language, the Lawyers' Committee proposes to limit its scope to screening under subsection (c)(2). Yet subsection (c)(2) does not deal with the liability of speakers and publishers, the subject of subsection (c)(1). We read each to do exactly what it says. So did the district court. A natural reading of § 230(c)(1) in conjunction with § 3604(c) led that court to grant summary judgment for craigslist.

What § 230(c)(1) says is that an online information system must not "be treated as the publisher or speaker of any information provided by" someone else. Yet only in a capacity as publisher could craigslist be liable under § 3604(c).

It is not the author of the ads and could not be treated as the "speaker" of the posters' words, given § 230(c)(1). The Lawyers' Committee responds that "nothing in § 230's text or history suggests that Congress meant to immunize an ISP from liability under the Fair Housing Act. In fact, Congress did not even remotely contemplate discriminatory housing advertisements when it passed § 230." That's true enough, but the reason a legislature writes a general statute is to avoid any need to traipse through the United States Code and consider all potential sources of liability, one at a time.

Section 230(c)(1) is general. Although the impetus for the enactment of § 230(c) as a whole was a court's opinion holding an information content provider liable, as a publisher, because it had exercised some selectivity with respect to the sexually oriented material it would host for customers, a law's scope often differs from its genesis. Once the legislative process gets rolling, interest groups seek (and often obtain) other provisions.

Congress could have written something like: "No provider or user of an interactive computer service shall be treated as the publisher or speaker of any *sexually oriented material* provided by another information content provider." That is not, however, what it enacted. Where the phrase "sexually oriented material" appears in our rephrasing, the actual statute has the word "information." That covers ads for housing, auctions of paintings that may have been stolen by Nazis, biting comments about steroids in baseball, efforts to verify the truth of politicians' promises, and everything else that third parties may post on a web site; "information" is the stock in trade of online service providers.

Almost in passing, the Lawyers' Committee insists that craigslist can be liable as one who "cause[d] to be made, printed, or published any [discriminatory] notice, statement, or advertisement". Doubtless craigslist plays a causal role in the sense that no one could post a discriminatory ad if craigslist did not offer a forum. That is not, however, a useful definition of cause. One might as well say that people who save money "cause" bank robbery, because if there were no banks there could be no bank robberies. An interactive computer service "causes" postings only in the sense of providing a place where people can post. Causation in a statute such as § 3604(c) must refer to causing a particular statement to be made, or perhaps the discriminatory content of a statement. That's the sense in which a non-publisher can cause a discriminatory ad, while one who causes the forbidden content may not be a publisher. Nothing in the service craigslist offers induces anyone to post any particular listing or express a preference for discrimination; for example, craigslist does not offer a lower price to people who include discriminatory statements in their postings. If craigslist "causes" the discriminatory notices, then so do phone companies and courier services (and, for that matter, the firms that make the computers and software that owners use to post their notices online), yet no one could think that Microsoft and Dell are liable for "causing" discriminatory advertisements.

Using the remarkably candid postings on craigslist, the Lawyers' Committee can identify many targets to investigate. It can dispatch testers and collect damages from any landlord or owner who engages in discrimination. It can assemble a list of names to send to the Attorney General for prosecution. But given § 230(c)(1) it cannot sue the messenger just because the message reveals a third party's plan to engage in unlawful discrimination.

NOTES & QUESTIONS

1. *Too much.* craigslist believes that a straightforward application of § 230(c)(1), as interpreted by *Zeran*, immunizes it from this lawsuit. The *Zeran* interpretation stakes out what might be called a *maximalist* position. As craigslist argued in its brief, § 230(c)(1) "broadly immunizes online providers such as craigslist from liability for dissemination of unlawful content that is created by others."[*] On this view, explain why craigslist would benefit from the immunity.

2. *Too little.* The Chicago Lawyer's Committee (CLC) stakes out the opposite end of the spectrum—a *minimalist* position. Drawing on *dicta* that Judge Easterbrook himself had written in a prior case, *Doe v. GTE* (7th Cir. 2003), the CLC argued that § 230(c)(1) wasn't even an immunity provision. Instead, it was merely definitional, and the only immunity was in § 230(c)(2), which immunized the screening of offensive content. On this view, explain why craigslist would *not* enjoy any immunity.

3. *Just right.* The Seventh Circuit disagrees with both extremes.

    a. *Rejecting the maximum.* Explain why the court rejects the maximalist approach. Do you agree with its behavioral predictions of what interactive computer service providers would do, under this reading of the statute? Is this a sufficient reason to prefer this interpretation when nearly all other courts have gone the other way?

    b. *Rejecting the minimum.* Explain why the court rejects the minimalist approach.

    c. *Embracing "just right."* What precisely is the "just right" view of immunity? Under this approach, §§ 230(c)(1) and (c)(2) do independent "immunity" work. And as the court breezily explains, "We read each to do

---

[*] Brief of Defendant-Appellee craigslist, Inc., at 9.

exactly what it says. So did the district court." Here's what the district court thought it was doing:

> Limiting the immunity afforded under Section 230 to those claims that *require "publishing" as an essential element*—as opposed to any cause of action— gives effect to the different language in Sections 230(c)(1) and (c)(2). Moreover, the Court's reading does not clash with the statutory captions. Indeed, as the Seventh Circuit has observed, it seems rather unlikely that, in enacting the CDA and in trying to protect Good Samaritans from filtering offensive conduct, Congress would have intended a broad grant of immunity for ICSs [Interactive Computer Services] that do not screen any third-party content whatsoever. [*Doe v.*] *GTE*. And because it is *something less than an absolute grant of immunity*, state legislatures may be able to enact, consistent with Section 230, initiatives that induce or require online service providers to protect the interests of third parties (under *Zeran*'s holding, states cannot enact such initiatives because they would be inconsistent with the statute and thus preempted under Section 230(e)(3)). For all these reasons, the Court here holds that, at a minimum, Section 230(c)(1) bars claims, like the CLC's claim, that requires *publishing as a critical element*.[*]

4. *Application to the Fair Housing Act claim.* Try to apply the "just right" immunity to the facts of this case. Is § 230(c)(2) relevant? What about (c)(1)? What is it about 42 U.S.C. § 3604(a) that makes craigslist immune?

5. *Right result?* Is this the right result? Why should the Chicago Tribune be liable for allowing a racially discriminatory advertisement to run in its newspaper, but be immune for allowing the same ad to be posted (in exchange for money) on the classified section of chicagotribune.com?

6. Grokster *reference.* Judge Easterbrook refers to the Supreme Court's *Grokster* case, which addressed contributory liability for violating copyright law. Somehow this is supposed to encourage a particular reading of § 230. But § 230(e)(2) explicitly states: "Nothing in this section shall be construed to limit or expand any law pertaining to intellectual property."

7. *Back to* Zeran. How would the "just right" immunity view apply to the *Zeran* facts? On the one hand, "publishing" seems to be an essential or critical element of a defamation tort. That said, (c)(1) doesn't even use the word "publishing"; it uses the word "publisher." So even if America Online cannot be called a "publisher," why can't it still be called a "distributor"? Or is a distributor a species of publisher for the purposes of § 230? Are we back to square zero?

---

[*] CLC v. craigslist, Inc., 461 F. Supp. 681, 697-98 (N.D.Il. 2006) (emphasis added).

8. *Artful pleading.* If the "just right" immunity applies only to causes of action that require publishing as an essential element, can't smart plaintiffs simply plead around this obstacle? Recall that Zeran's claim against AOL was "negligence" in allowing the falsely attributed messages to remain and reappear. The court concluded: "Although Zeran attempts to artfully plead his claims as ones of negligence, they are indistinguishable from a garden variety defamation action."[*]

9. Barnes v. Yahoo (9th Cir. 2009): *artful pleading and promises.*

a. *Distinguishing "artful" from "genuine".* How can we tell whether it's artful pleading of a publication tort versus a genuinely different tort? Here's some guidance from the Ninth Circuit in *Barnes v. Yahoo*:

> Thus, what matters is not the name of the cause of action—defamation versus negligence versus intentional infliction of emotional distress—what matters is whether the cause of action inherently requires the court to treat the defendant as the "publisher or speaker" of content provided by another. To put it another way, courts must ask whether the duty that the plaintiff alleges the defendant violated derives from the defendant's status or conduct as a "publisher or speaker." If it does, section 230(c)(1) precludes liability.

> * * *

> And what is the undertaking that Barnes alleges Yahoo failed to perform with due care? The removal of the indecent profiles that her former boyfriend posted on Yahoo's website. But removing content is something publishers do, and to impose liability on the basis of such conduct necessarily involves treating the liable party as a publisher of the content it failed to remove. *See* Craigslist. In other words, the duty that Barnes claims Yahoo violated derives from Yahoo's conduct as a publisher—the steps it allegedly took, but later supposedly abandoned, to de-publish the offensive profiles. It is because such conduct is *publishing conduct* that we have insisted that section 230 protects from liability "any activity that can be boiled down to deciding whether to exclude material that third parties seek to post online." *Roommates.*[†]

b. *The promise of promissory estoppel.* In *Barnes v. Yahoo!*, the court seemed to shut down creative reframing of causes of action to get around § 230 immunity. But it did allow a claim based on promissory estoppel to get past the motion to dismiss. Yahoo's Director of Communications had telephoned the

---

[*] Zeran v. AOL, 129 F.3d 327, 332 (4th Cir. 1997). *See also* Doe v. MySpace, 528 F.3d 413, 420 (5th Cir. 2008) (holding that negligence allegations regarding a sexual assault of a minor facilitated through MySpace "are merely another way of claiming that MySpace was liable for publishing the communications"); UCS v. Lycos, 478 F.3d 413, 418 (1st Cir. 2007) (rejecting "artful pleading" to try to fall into statutory exceptions of § 230 immunity).

[†] 530 F.3d 1096, 1101-02, 1103 (9th Cir. 2009).

plaintiff and told her that "she would 'personally walk the statements over to the division responsible for stopping unauthorized profiles and they would take care of it.'"[*] Under relevant state law, this could state a claim under promissory estoppel, which the court distinguished from the plaintiff's negligence claims:

> Contract liability here would come not from Yahoo's publishing conduct, but from Yahoo's manifest intention to be legally obligated to do something, which happens to be removal of material from publication. Contract law treats the outwardly manifested intention to create an expectation on the part of another as a legally significant event. That event generates a legal duty distinct from the conduct at hand, be it the conduct of a publisher, of a doctor, or of an overzealous uncle.[†]

If you were general counsel of Yahoo!, what policy changes would you immediately adopt for all help desk and public relations employees at your firm?

10. *Being an accomplice.* The penultimate paragraph of the *craigslist* opinion addresses whether craigslist can be held responsible simply by assisting the discriminatory publication. This possibility is created by the specific language of the Federal Housing Act ("*causes* to be ... published"). Interestingly, a conceptually similar question can arise with respect to § 230 because even if one enjoys immunity from the content posted by another, the editing assistance could produce a sort of joint authorship such that the offending materials can no longer be deemed content by "*another* information content provider." In *Carafano v. Metrosplash.Com, Inc.*, the Ninth Circuit set a very high bar: "[S]o long as a third party willingly provides the essential published content, the interactive service provider receives full immunity regardless of the specific editing or selection process."[‡] How much of this holding survives the case we read next?

---

[*] Id. at 1099.

[†] *Id.* at 1107.

[‡] 339 F.3d 1119, 1123 (9th Cir. 2003). For example, AOL's e-mailing a third party content provider to correct stock data and AOL's deleting of incorrect data were not enough to transform AOL into an "information content provider." *See* Ben Ezra, Weinstein, & Co. v. America Online, Inc., 206 F.3d 980, 986 (10th Cir. 2000). *See also* Batzel v. Smith, 333 F.3d at 1031 (selecting emails, and making minor edits before forwarding to list is insufficient). *But see* MCW, Inc. v. BADBUSINESSBUREAU.COM, L.L.C., 2004 WL 833595 (N.D. Tex. 2004) (finding that web site operator actively instructed third-party to take pictures and collect more content for posting, which made the web-site operator the "information content provider" for some of the defamatory material).

FAIR HOUSING COUNCIL OF
SAN FERNANDO VALLEY V. ROOMMATES.COM
521 F.3d 1157 (9th Cir. 2008) (en banc)

KOZINSKI, Chief Judge:

FACTS

Defendant Roommate.com, LLC ("Roommate") operates a website designed to match people renting out spare rooms with people looking for a place to live. . . .

Before subscribers can search listings or post housing opportunities on Roommate's website, they must create profiles . . . . In addition to requesting basic information—such as name, location and email address—Roommate requires each subscriber to disclose his sex, sexual orientation and whether he would bring children to a household. Each subscriber must also describe his preferences in roommates with respect to the same three criteria: sex, sexual orientation and whether they will bring children to the household. The site also encourages subscribers to provide "Additional Comments" describing themselves and their desired roommate in an open-ended essay. After a new subscriber completes the application, Roommate assembles his answers into a "profile page." The profile page displays the subscriber's pseudonym, his description and his preferences, as divulged through answers to Roommate's questions.

The Fair Housing Councils of the San Fernando Valley and San Diego ("Councils") sued Roommate in federal court, alleging that Roommate's business violates the federal Fair Housing Act ("FHA"), 42 U.S.C. § 3601 et seq., and California housing discrimination laws. Councils claim that Roommate is effectively a housing broker doing online what it may not lawfully do off-line. The district court held that Roommate is immune under section 230 of the CDA, 47 U.S.C. § 230(c) . . . .

ANALYSIS

Section 230 . . . immunity applies only if the interactive computer service provider is not also an "information content provider," which is defined as someone who is "responsible, in whole or in part, for the creation or development of" the offending content. § 230(f)(3).

A website operator can be both a service provider and a content provider: If it passively displays content that is created entirely by third parties, then it is only a service provider with respect to that content. But as to content that it creates itself, or is "responsible, in whole or in part" for creating or developing, the website is also a content provider.

In passing section 230, Congress sought to spare interactive computer services [the] grim choice [posed by *Stratton Oakmont*] by allowing them to perform some editing on user-generated content without thereby becoming liable for all defamatory or otherwise unlawful messages that they didn't edit or delete. In other words, Congress sought to immunize the *removal* of user-generated content, not the *creation* of content.... Indeed, the section is titled "Protection for 'good samaritan' blocking and screening of offensive material".....

With this backdrop in mind, we examine three specific functions performed by Roommate that are alleged to violate the Fair Housing Act and California law.

1. Councils first argue that the questions Roommate poses to prospective subscribers during the registration process violate the Fair Housing Act and the analogous California law.

Here, we ... need not decide whether any of Roommate's questions actually violate the Fair Housing Act or California law ... However, we note that asking questions certainly *can* violate the Fair Housing Act and analogous laws in the physical world. For example, a real estate broker may not inquire as to the race of a prospective buyer, and an employer may not inquire as to the religion of a prospective employee. If such questions are unlawful when posed face-to-face or by telephone, they don't magically become lawful when asked electronically online. The Communications Decency Act was not meant to create a lawless no-man's-land on the Internet.[15]

Roommate's own acts—posting the questionnaire and requiring answers to it—are entirely its doing and thus section 230 of the CDA does not apply to them. Roommate is entitled to no immunity.

2. Councils also charge that Roommate's development and display of subscribers' discriminatory preferences is unlawful. Roommate publishes a "profile page" for each subscriber on its website.

Here, the part of the profile that is alleged to offend the Fair Housing Act and state housing discrimination laws—the information about sex, family status

---

[15] The dissent stresses the importance of the Internet to modern life and commerce, and we, of course, agree: The Internet is no longer a fragile new means of communication that could easily be smothered in the cradle by overzealous enforcement of laws and regulations applicable to brick-and-mortar businesses. Rather, it has become a dominant-perhaps the preeminent-means through which commerce is conducted. And its vast reach into the lives of millions is exactly why we must be careful not to exceed the scope of the immunity provided by Congress and thus give online businesses an unfair advantage over their real-world counterparts, which must comply with laws of general applicability.

and sexual orientation—is provided by subscribers in response to Roommate's questions, which they cannot refuse to answer if they want to use defendant's services. By requiring subscribers to provide the information as a condition of accessing its service, and by providing a limited set of pre-populated answers, Roommate becomes much more than a passive transmitter of information provided by others; it becomes the developer, at least in part, of that information. And section 230 provides immunity only if the interactive computer service does not "creat[e] or develop[ ]" the information "in whole or in part." *See* 47 U.S.C. § 230(f)(3).

Our dissenting colleague ... concludes that Roommate does not develop the information because "[a]ll Roommate does is to provide a form with options for standardized answers." But Roommate does much more than provide options. To begin with, it asks discriminatory questions .... Unlawful questions solicit (a.k.a. "develop") unlawful answers. Not only does Roommate ask these questions, Roommate makes answering the discriminatory questions a condition of doing business. This is no different from a real estate broker in real life saying, "Tell me whether you're Jewish or you can find yourself another broker." When a business enterprise extracts such information from potential customers as a condition of accepting them as clients, it is no stretch to say that the enterprise is responsible, at least in part, for developing that information.

Similarly, Roommate is not entitled to CDA immunity for the operation of its search system, which filters listings, or of its email notification system, which directs emails to subscribers according to discriminatory criteria. Roommate designed its search system so it would steer users based on the preferences and personal characteristics that Roommate itself forces subscribers to disclose. If Roommate has no immunity for asking the discriminatory questions ... it can certainly have no immunity for using the answers to the unlawful questions to limit who has access to housing.

For example, a subscriber who self-identifies as a "Gay male" will not receive email notifications of new housing opportunities supplied by owners who limit the universe of acceptable tenants to "Straight male(s)," "Straight female(s)" and "Lesbian(s)." ... It is, Councils allege, no different from a real estate broker saying to a client: "Sorry, sir, but I can't show you any listings on this block because you are [gay/female/black/a parent]." If such screening is prohibited when practiced in person or by telephone, we see no reason why Congress would have wanted to make it lawful to profit from it online.

Roommate's search function is similarly designed to steer users based on discriminatory criteria. Roommate's search engine thus differs materially from generic search engines such as Google, Yahoo! and MSN Live Search, in that

Roommate designed its system to use allegedly unlawful criteria so as to limit the results of each search, and to force users to participate in its discriminatory process. In other words, Councils allege that Roommate's search is designed to make it more difficult or impossible for individuals with certain protected characteristics to find housing—something the law prohibits. By contrast, ordinary search engines do not use unlawful criteria to limit the scope of searches conducted on them, nor are they designed to achieve illegal ends—as Roommate's search function is alleged to do here. Therefore, such search engines play no part in the "development" of any unlawful searches.

It's true that the broadest sense of the term "develop" could include the functions of an ordinary search engine . . . . But to read the term so broadly would defeat the purposes of section 230 by swallowing up every bit of the immunity that the section otherwise provides. At the same time, reading the exception for co-developers as applying only to content that originates entirely with the website—as the dissent would seem to suggest—ignores the words "development ... in part" in the statutory passage "creation *or development* in whole *or in part.*" 47 U.S.C. § 230(f)(3) (emphasis added). We believe that both the immunity for passive conduits and the exception for co-developers must be given their proper scope and, to that end, we interpret the term "development" as referring not merely to augmenting the content generally, but to materially contributing to its alleged unlawfulness. In other words, a website helps to develop unlawful content, and thus falls within the exception to section 230, if it contributes materially to the alleged illegality of the conduct.

In an abundance of caution, and to avoid the kind of misunderstanding the dissent seems to encourage, we offer a few examples to elucidate what does and does not amount to "development" ... If an individual uses an ordinary search engine to query for a "white roommate," the search engine has not contributed to any alleged unlawfulness in the individual's conduct; providing neutral tools to carry out what may be unlawful or illicit searches does not amount to "development" for purposes of the immunity exception. A dating website that requires users to enter their sex, race, religion and marital status through drop-down menus, and that provides means for users to search along the same lines, retains its CDA immunity insofar as it does not contribute to any alleged illegality;[23] this immunity is retained even if the website is sued for libel based on these characteristics because the website would not have contributed materially to any alleged defamation. Similarly, a housing website that allows users to specify whether they will or will not receive emails by means of user-defined

---

[23] It is perfectly legal to discriminate along those lines in dating, and thus there can be no claim based solely on the content of these questions.

criteria might help some users exclude email from other users of a particular race or sex. However, that website would be immune, so long as it does not require the use of discriminatory criteria. A website operator who edits user-created content—such as by correcting spelling, removing obscenity or trimming for length—retains his immunity for any illegality in the user-created content, provided that the edits are unrelated to the illegality. However, a website operator who edits in a manner that contributes to the alleged illegality—such as by removing the word "not" from a user's message reading "[Name] did *not* steal the artwork" in order to transform an innocent message into a libelous one—is directly involved in the alleged illegality and thus not immune.[24]

Here, Roommate's connection to the discriminatory filtering process is direct and palpable: Roommate designed its search and email systems to limit the listings available to subscribers based on sex, sexual orientation and presence of children. Roommate selected the criteria used to hide listings, and Councils allege that the act of hiding certain listings is itself unlawful under the Fair Housing Act, which prohibits brokers from steering clients in accordance with discriminatory preferences.[26]

Roommate's situation stands in stark contrast to *Stratton Oakmont....* There, defendant Prodigy was held liable for a user's unsolicited message because it attempted to *remove* some problematic content from its website, but didn't remove enough. Here, Roommate is not being sued for removing some harmful messages . . . instead, it is being sued for the predictable consequences of creating a website designed to solicit and enforce housing preferences that are alleged to be illegal.

We take this opportunity to clarify two of our previous rulings . . . . [In *Batzel v. Smith*, 333 F.3d 1018 (9th Cir. 2003),] the editor of an email newsletter received a tip about some artwork, which the tipster falsely alleged to be stolen. The newsletter editor incorporated the tipster's email into the next issue of his

---

[24] Requiring website owners to refrain from taking affirmative acts that are unlawful does not strike us as an undue burden. These are, after all, businesses that are being held responsible only for their own conduct; there is no vicarious liability for the misconduct of their customers. Compliance with laws of general applicability seems like an entirely justified burden for all businesses, whether they operate online or through quaint brick-and-mortar facilities. Insofar, however, as a plaintiff would bring a claim under state or federal law based on a website operator's passive acquiescence in the misconduct of its users, the website operator would likely be entitled to CDA immunity. This is true even if the users committed their misconduct using electronic tools of general applicability provided by the website operator.

[26] The dissent argues that Roommate is not liable because the decision to discriminate on these grounds does not originate with Roommate; instead, "users have chosen to select characteristics that they find desirable." But, it is Roommate that forces users to express a preference and Roommate that forces users to disclose the information that can form the basis of discrimination by others. Thus, Roommate makes discrimination both possible and respectable.

newsletter and added a short headnote, which he then emailed to his subscribers. The art owner sued for libel and a split panel held the newsletter editor to be immune under section 230 of the CDA.[28]

Our opinion is entirely consistent with that part of *Batzel* which holds that an editor's minor changes to the spelling, grammar and length of third-party content do not strip him of section 230 immunity. None of those changes contributed to the libelousness of the message, so they do not add up to "development" as we interpret the term. *Batzel* went on to hold that the editor could be liable for selecting the tipster's email for inclusion in the newsletter, depending on whether or not the tipster had tendered the piece to the editor for posting online, and remanded for a determination of that issue.

The distinction drawn by *Batzel* anticipated the approach we take today. As *Batzel* explained, if the tipster tendered the material for posting online, then the editor's job was, essentially, to determine whether or not to prevent its posting—precisely the kind of activity for which section 230 was meant to provide immunity.... But if the editor publishes material that he does not believe was tendered to him for posting online, then he is the one making the affirmative decision to publish, and so he contributes materially to its allegedly unlawful dissemination. He is thus properly deemed a developer and not entitled to CDA immunity.[30]

We must also clarify the reasoning undergirding our holding in *Carafano v. Metrosplash.com, Inc.*, 339 F.3d 1119 (9th Cir. 2003), as we used language there that was unduly broad. In *Carafano*, an unknown prankster impersonating actress Christianne Carafano created a profile for her on an online dating site. The profile included Carafano's home address and suggested that she was looking for an unconventional liaison. When Carafano received threatening phone calls, she sued the dating site for publishing the unauthorized profile. The

---

[28] As an initial matter, the *Batzel* panel held that the defendant newsletter editor was a "user" of an interactive computer service within the definition provided by section 230. While we have our doubts, we express no view on this issue because it is not presented to us. Thus, we assume that the editor fell within the scope of section 230's coverage without endorsing Batzel's analysis on this point.

[30] The dissent scores a debater's point by noting that the same activity might amount to "development" or not, depending on whether it contributes materially to the illegality of the content. But we are not defining "development" for all purposes; we are defining the term only for purposes of determining whether the defendant is entitled to immunity for a particular act. This definition does not depend on finding substantive liability, but merely requires analyzing the context in which a claim is brought. A finding that a defendant is not immune is quite distinct from finding liability: On remand, Roommate may still assert other defenses to liability under the Fair Housing Act, or argue that its actions do not violate the Fair Housing Act at all. Our holding is limited to a determination that the CDA provides no immunity to Roommate's actions in soliciting and developing the content of its website; whether that content is in fact illegal is a question we leave to the district court.

site asserted immunity under section 230. We correctly held that the website was immune, but incorrectly suggested that it could never be liable because "no [dating] profile has any content until a user actively creates it." As we explain above, even if the data are supplied by third parties, a website operator may still contribute to the content's illegality and thus be liable as a developer.[31]

We believe a more plausible rationale for the unquestionably correct result in *Carafano* is this: The allegedly libelous content there—the false implication that Carafano was unchaste—was created and developed entirely by the malevolent user, without prompting or help from the website operator. To be sure, the website provided neutral tools, which the anonymous dastard used to publish the libel, but the website did absolutely nothing to encourage the posting of defamatory content—indeed, the defamatory posting was contrary to the website's express policies. The claim against the website was, in effect, that it failed to review each user—created profile to ensure that it wasn't defamatory. That is precisely the kind of activity for which Congress intended to grant absolution with the passage of section 230. With respect to the defamatory content, the website operator was merely a passive conduit and thus could not be held liable for failing to detect and remove it.

By contrast, Roommate both elicits the allegedly illegal content and makes aggressive use of it in conducting its business. . . .

Our ruling today also dovetails with another facet of *Carafano*: The mere fact that an interactive computer service "classifies user characteristics ... does not transform [it] into a 'developer' of the 'underlying misinformation.'" *Carafano*.

The salient fact in *Carafano* was that the website's classifications of user characteristics did absolutely nothing to enhance the defamatory sting of the message, to encourage defamation or to make defamation easier: The site provided neutral tools specifically designed to match romantic partners depending on their voluntary inputs. By sharp contrast, Roommate's website is designed to force subscribers to divulge protected characteristics and discriminatory preferences, and to match those who have rooms with those who are looking for rooms based on criteria that appear to be prohibited by the FHA.[33]

---

[31] We disavow any suggestion that *Carafano* holds an information content provider automatically immune so long as the content originated with another information content provider.

[33] The dissent coyly suggests that our opinion "sets us apart from" other circuits, carefully avoiding the phrase "intercircuit conflict." And with good reason: No other circuit has considered a case like ours and none has a case that even arguably conflicts with our holding today. No case cited by the dissent involves active participation by the defendant in the creation or development of the allegedly unlawful content; in each, the interactive computer service provider passively relayed content generated by third parties, just as in *Stratton Oakmont*, and did not design its system around the dissemination of unlawful content.

In *Chicago Lawyers' Committee for Civil Rights Under Law, Inc. v. craigslist*, Inc., 519 F.3d 666 (7th

3. Councils finally argue that Roommate should be held liable for the discriminatory statements displayed in the "Additional Comments" section of profile pages. At the end of the registration process, on a separate page from the other registration steps, Roommate prompts subscribers to "tak[e] a moment to personalize your profile by writing a paragraph or two describing yourself and what you are looking for in a roommate."

Subscribers provide a variety of provocative, and often very revealing, answers. The contents range from subscribers who "[p]ref[er] white Male roommates" or require that "[t]he person applying for the room MUST be a BLACK GAY MALE" to those who are "NOT looking for black muslims." Some common themes are a desire to live without "drugs, kids or animals" or "smokers, kids or druggies," while a few subscribers express more particular preferences, such as preferring to live in a home free of "psychos or anyone on

---

Cir. 2008), the Seventh Circuit held the online classified website craigslist immune from liability for discriminatory housing advertisements submitted by users. Craigslist's service works very much like the "Additional Comments" section of Roommate's website, in that users are given an open text prompt in which to enter any description of the rental property without any structure imposed on their content or any requirement to enter discriminatory information: "Nothing in the service craigslist offers induces anyone to post any particular listing or express a preference for discrimination...." We similarly hold the "Additional Comments" section of Roommate's site immune. Consistent with our opinion, the Seventh Circuit explained the limited scope of section 230(c) immunity. More directly, the Seventh Circuit noted in dicta that "causing a *particular* statement to be made, or perhaps [causing] the *discriminatory content of a statement*" might be sufficient to create liability for a website. (emphasis added). Despite the dissent's attempt to imply the contrary, the Seventh Circuit's opinion is actually in line with our own.

In *Universal Communication Systems v. Lycos, Inc.*, the First Circuit held a message board owner immune under the CDA for defamatory comments posted on a message board. 478 F.3d 413 (1st Cir. 2007). The allegedly defamatory comments were made without any prompting or encouragement by defendant: "[T]here is not even a colorable argument that any misinformation was prompted by Lycos's registration process or its link structure."

Green v. America Online, 318 F.3d 465 (3d Cir. 2003), falls yet farther from the mark. There, AOL was held immune for derogatory comments and malicious software transmitted by other defendants through AOL's "Romance over 30" "chat room." There was no allegation that AOL solicited the content, encouraged users to post harmful content or otherwise had any involvement whatsoever with the harmful content, other than through providing "chat rooms" for general use.

In *Ben Ezra, Weinstein, and Co. v. America Online Inc.*, 206 F.3d 980 (10th Cir. 2000), the Tenth Circuit held AOL immune for relaying inaccurate stock price information it received from other vendors. While AOL undoubtedly participated in the decision to make stock quotations available to members, it did not cause the errors in the stock data, nor did it encourage or solicit others to provide inaccurate data. AOL was immune because "Plaintiff could not identify any evidence indicating Defendant [AOL] developed or created the stock quotation information."

And, finally, in *Zeran v. America Online, Inc.*, 129 F.3d 327 (4th Cir. 1997), the Fourth Circuit held AOL immune for yet another set of defamatory and harassing message board postings. Again, AOL did not solicit the harassing content, did not encourage others to post it, and had nothing to do with its creation other than through AOL's role as the provider of a generic message board for general discussions.

mental medication." Some subscribers are just looking for someone who will get along with their significant other[34] or with their most significant Other.[35]

Roommate publishes these comments as written. It does not provide any specific guidance as to what the essay should contain, nor does it urge subscribers to input discriminatory preferences. Roommate is not responsible, in whole or in part, for the development of this content, which comes entirely from subscribers and is passively displayed by Roommate. Without reviewing every essay, Roommate would have no way to distinguish unlawful discriminatory preferences from perfectly legitimate statements.... This is precisely the kind of situation for which section 230 was designed to provide immunity.

The fact that Roommate encourages subscribers to provide something in response to the prompt is not enough to make it a "develop[er]" of the information.... Its simple, generic prompt does not make it a developer of the information posted.[37]

Councils argue that—given the context of the discriminatory questions presented earlier in the registration process—the "Additional Comments" prompt impliedly suggests that subscribers should make statements expressing a desire to discriminate on the basis of protected classifications.... But the encouragement that bleeds over from one part of the registration process to another is extremely weak, if it exists at all. Such weak encouragement cannot strip a website of its section 230 immunity, lest that immunity be rendered meaningless as a practical matter.

We must keep firmly in mind that this is an immunity statute we are expounding, a provision enacted to protect websites against the evil of liability for failure to remove offensive content.... [T]here will always be close cases where a clever lawyer could argue that something the website operator did encouraged the illegality. Such close cases, we believe, must be resolved in favor of immunity, lest we cut the heart out of section 230....

The dissent prophesies doom and gloom for countless Internet services, but fails to recognize that we hold part of Roommate's service entirely immune from liability. The search engines the dissent worries about closely resemble the

---

[34] "The female we are looking for hopefully wont [sic] mind having a little sexual incounter [sic] with my boyfriend and I [very sic]."

[35] "We are 3 Christian females who Love our Lord Jesus Christ.... We have weekly bible studies and bi-weekly times of fellowship."

[37] Nor would Roommate be the developer of discriminatory content if it provided a free-text search that enabled users to find keywords in the "Additional Comments" of others, even if users utilized it to search for discriminatory keywords. Providing neutral tools for navigating websites is fully protected by CDA immunity, absent substantial affirmative conduct on the part of the website creator promoting the use of such tools for unlawful purposes.

"Additional Comments" section of Roommate's website. Both involve a generic text prompt with no direct encouragement to perform illegal searches or to publish illegal content. We hold Roommate immune and there is no reason to believe that future courts will have any difficulty applying this principle.[39] The message to website operators is clear: If you don't encourage illegal content, or design your website to require users to input illegal content, you will be immune.

* * *

In light of our determination that the CDA does not provide immunity to Roommate for all of the content of its website and email newsletters, we remand for the district court to determine in the first instance whether the alleged actions for which Roommate is not immune violate the Fair Housing Act, 42 U.S.C. § 3604(c).

REVERSED in part, VACATED in part, AFFIRMED in part and REMANDED.

MCKEOWN, Circuit Judge, with whom RYMER and BEA, Circuit Judges, join, concurring in part and dissenting in part:

The majority repeatedly harps that if something is prohibited in the physical world, Congress could not have intended it to be legal in cyberspace. Yet that is precisely the path Congress took with the CDA: the anomaly that a webhost may be immunized for conducting activities in cyberspace that would traditionally be cause for liability is exactly what Congress intended by enacting the CDA.

APPLICATION OF § 230(C)(1) TO ROOMMATE'S WEBSITE

The critical question is whether Roommate is itself an "information content provider," such that it cannot claim that the information at issue was "provided by another information content provider." A close reading of the statute leads to the conclusion that Roommate is not an information content provider for two reasons: (1) providing a drop-down menu does not constitute "creating" or

---

[39] The dissent also accuses us of creating uncertainty that will chill the continued growth of commerce on the Internet. Even looking beyond the fact that the Internet has outgrown its swaddling clothes and no longer needs to be so gently coddled, some degree of uncertainty is inevitable at the edge of any rule of law. Any immunity provision, including section 230, has its limits and there will always be close cases. Our opinion extensively clarifies where that edge lies, and gives far more guidance than our previous cases. While the dissent disagrees about the scope of the immunity, there can be little doubt that website operators today know more about how to conform their conduct to the law than they did yesterday.

However, a larger point remains about the scope of immunity provisions. It's no surprise that defendants want to extend immunity as broadly as possible. We have long . . . observed many defendants argue that the risk of getting a close case wrong is a justification for broader immunity. Accepting such an argument would inevitably lead to an endless broadening of immunity, as every new holding creates its own borderline cases.

"developing" information; and (2) the structure and text of the statute make plain that Congress intended to immunize Roommate's sorting, displaying, and transmitting of third-party information.

Roommate neither "creates" nor "develops" the information that is challenged by the Councils .... All Roommate does is to provide a form with options for standardized answers.

Displaying the prompt "Gender" and offering the list of choices, "Straight male; Gay male; Straight female; Gay female" does not develop the information, "I am a Gay male." The user has identified himself as such and provided that information to Roommate to publish. Thus, the user is the sole creator of that information; no "development" has occurred.

The thrust of the majority's proclamation that Roommate is "developing" the information that it publishes, sorts, and transmits is as follows: "[W]e interpret the term 'development' as referring not merely to augmenting the content generally, but to materially contributing to its unlawfulness." This definition is original to say the least and springs forth untethered to anything in the statute.

The majority's definition of "development" epitomizes its consistent collapse of substantive liability with the issue of immunity. Where in the statute does Congress say anything about unlawfulness? Whether Roommate is entitled to immunity for publishing and sorting profiles is wholly distinct from whether Roommate may be liable for violations of the FHA. Immunity has meaning only when there is something to be immune from, whether a disease or the violation of a law. It would be nonsense to claim to be immune only from the innocuous. But the majority's immunity analysis is built on substantive liability: to the majority, CDA immunity depends on whether a webhost materially contributed to the unlawfulness of the information. Whether the information at issue is unlawful and whether the webhost has contributed to its unlawfulness are issues analytically independent of the determination of immunity. Grasping at straws to distinguish Roommate from other interactive websites such as Google and Yahoo!, the majority repeatedly gestures to Roommate's potential substantive liability as sufficient reason to disturb its immunity. But our task is to determine whether the question of substantive liability may be reached in the first place.

Keep in mind that "unlawfulness" would include not only purported statutory violations but also potential defamatory statements. The irony is that the majority would have us determine "guilt" or liability in order to decide whether immunity is available. This upside-down approach would knock out even the narrowest immunity offered under § 230(c)—immunity for defamation as a publisher or speaker.

Another flaw in the majority's approach is that it fails to account for all of the other information allegedly developed by the webhost. For purposes of determining whether Roommate is an information content provider vis-a-vis the profiles, the inquiry about geography and the inquiry about gender should stand on the same footing. Both are single word prompts followed by a drop-down menu of options. If a prompt about gender constitutes development, then so too does the prompt about geography. And therein lies the rub.

Millions of websites use prompts and drop-down menus. Inquiries range from what credit card you want to use and consumer satisfaction surveys asking about age, sex and household income, to dating sites, e.g., match.com, sites lambasting corporate practices, e.g., ripoffreports.com, and sites that allow truckers to link up with available loads, e.g., getloaded.com. Some of these sites are innocuous while others may not be. Some may solicit illegal information; others may not. But that is not the point. The majority's definition of "development" would transform every interactive site into an information content provider and the result would render illusory any immunity under § 230(c). Virtually every site could be responsible in part for developing content.

For example, the majority purports to carve out a place for Google and other search engines. But the modern Google is more than a match engine: it ranks search results, provides prompts beyond what the user enters, and answers questions. In contrast, Roommate is a straight match service that searches information and criteria provided by the user, not Roommate. It should be afforded no less protection than Google, Yahoo!, or other search engines.

The majority then argues that "providing neutral tools to carry out what may be unlawful or illicit searches does not amount to 'development.'" But this effort to distinguish Google, Yahoo!, and other search engines from Roommate is unavailing. Under the majority's definition of "development," these search engines are equivalent to Roommate. Google "encourages" or "contributes" (the majority's catch phrases) to the unlawfulness by offering search tools that allow the user to perform an allegedly unlawful match. If a user types into Google's search box, "looking for a single, Christian, female roommate," and Google displays responsive listings, Google is surely "materially contributing to the alleged unlawfulness" of information created by third parties, by publishing their intention to discriminate on the basis of protected characteristics. In the defamation arena, a webhost's publication of a defamatory statement "materially contributes" to its unlawfulness, as publication to third parties is an element of the offense. At bottom, the majority's definition of "development" can be tucked in, let out, or hemmed up to fit almost any search engine, creating tremendous uncertainty in an area where Congress expected predictability.

"Development" is not without meaning.

Because the statute does not define "development," we should give the term its ordinary meaning. "Development" is defined in Webster's Dictionary as a "gradual advance or growth through progressive changes." . . . Defining "development" in this way keeps intact the settled rule that the CDA immunizes a webhost who exercises a publisher's "traditional editorial functions-such as deciding whether to publish, withdraw, post-pone, or alter content." *Batzel.*

Applying the plain meaning of "development" to Roommate's sorting and transmitting of third-party information demonstrates that it was not transformed into an "information content provider." In searching, sorting, and transmitting information, Roommate made no changes to the information provided to it by users. Even having notice that users may be using its site to make discriminatory statements is not sufficient to invade Roommate's immunity.

Even if Roommate's prompts and drop-down menus could be construed to seek out, or encourage, information from users, the CDA does not withhold immunity for the encouragement or solicitation of information. The CDA does not countenance an exception for the solicitation or encouragement of information provided by users.

A number of district courts have recently encountered the claim that an interactive website's solicitation of information, by requiring user selection of content from drop-down menus, transformed it into an information content provider. Unsurprisingly, these courts reached the same commonsense solution that I reach here: § 230(c)(1) immunizes the interactive service provider. *See Whitney Info. Network, Inc. v. Xcentric Ventures* (M.D. Fla. Feb. 15, 2008) (stating that the "mere fact that Xcentric provides categories from which a poster must make a selection in order to submit a report on the [ ] website is not sufficient to treat Defendants as information content providers of the reports"); *Global Royalties, Ltd. v. Xcentric Ventures* (D. Ariz. Oct. 10, 2007). Simply supplying a list of options from which a user must select options "is minor and passive participation" that does not defeat CDA immunity.

Carafano presented circumstances virtually indistinguishable from those before us, yet the majority comes to the exact opposite conclusion here in denying immunity for sorting and matching third-party information provided in response to webhost prompts.

RAMIFICATIONS OF THE MAJORITY OPINION

The consequences of the majority's interpretation are far-reaching. Its position will chill speech on the Internet . . . . To the extent the majority strips immunity because of sorting, channeling, and categorizing functions, it guts the heart of § 230(c)(1) immunity. Countless websites operate just like Roommate: they organize information provided by their users into a standardized format, and provide structured searches to help users find information. These sites, and their attendant display, search, and inquiry tools, are an indispensable part of the Internet tool box. Putting a lid on the sorting and searching functions of interactive websites stifles the core of their services.

To the extent the majority strips immunity because the information or query may be illegal under some statute or federal law, this circumstance puts the webhost in the role of a policeman for the laws of the fifty states and the federal system. There are not enough Net Nannies in cyberspace to implement this restriction, and the burden of filtering content would be unfathomable.

To the extent the majority strips immunity because a site solicits or actively encourages content, the result is a direct restriction on the free exchange of ideas and information on the Internet.

To the extent the majority strips immunity because a website "materially contributed" to the content or output of a website by "specialization" of content, this approach would essentially swallow the immunity provision. The combination of solicitation, sorting, and potential for liability would put virtually every interactive website in this category. Having a website directed to Christians, Muslims, gays, disabled veterans, or childless couples could land the website provider in hot water.[14]

Because the statute itself is cumbersome to interpret in light of today's Internet architecture, and because the decision today will ripple through the billions of web pages already online, and the countless pages to come in the future, I would take a cautious, careful, and precise approach to the restriction of immunity, not the broad swath cut by the majority. I respectfully dissent . . . .

NOTES & QUESTIONS

1. *The magic words.* The entire case turns on interpreting key terms within § 230. Which terms are at issue?

2. *The easy case of "questions asked": no immunity.* Roomate.com asks specific questions on its website. Those questions themselves may violate housing laws. Explain why § 230 provides no immunity for asking these questions. (Both the majority and dissent agree on this.)

---

[14] It is no surprise that there are countless specialized roommate sites. See, e.g., http://islam.tc/housing/index.php, http://christian-roommates.com, and http://prideroommates.com.

3. *The other easy case of "Additional Comments": yes immunity.* Roomate.com allows subscribers to type whatever they'd like into an "Additional Comments" field. This material is published as written. Explain why § 230 provides immunity for publishing this material. (Again, both the majority and dissent agree.)

4. *The hard case of profile tags.* Now consider the fact that Roomate.com requires its users to complete various fields of information, with drop-down options to choose from. Further, these fields of information ("tags" in Web 2.0-speak) about oneself and one's preferences are used for searching, sorting, and disseminating information. Is such information provided exclusively by the subscriber? Or is Roommate.com "responsible, in whole or in part, for [its] development," § 230(f)(3)?

5. *"Development".* What is the majority's definition of "development"? What is the dissent's complaint about that definition? Who is more persuasive?

6. *Relevant factors?* If we unpack the various arguments, it appears that the following factors may be relevant to deciding whether an Interactive Computer Service's (ICS) use of tags amounts to "development":

- mandatory / optional: can a subscriber choose not to fill out some field of information?[*]

- multiple-choice / essay: can a subscriber simply click on one of the pre-populated options, or must she type in some answer into a form box? (In forms that feature auto-complete, typing a few characters might prompt commonly or previously used tags.)

- illegal / legal: is the information that the ICS requested and processed somehow related to the alleged illegality?

- material / de minimis: does the information that the ICS requested and processed materially contribute to the alleged illegality?

- neutral (or generic) / specific: is the ICS processing information through some neutral or generic tool, such as a search engine, or is it doing so in a targeted manner presumably connected to the alleged illegality?

- ill-intentioned / innocent: was the ICS designed for (alleged) illegality, or was it innocently crafted (even if a subscriber could use it for illegal purposes)?

---

[*] *See, e.g.,* Doe IX v. MySpace, 629 F.Supp.2d 663, 665 (E.D. Tex. 2009) (distinguishing Roommates.com on the grounds that "users of MySpace.com are not required to provide any additional information to their profiles").

Does this list describe accurately the factors raised in the opinions? Is any variable missing? Finally, does any of this make sense?

7. *The search engine problem.* Imagine you are a summer associate in-house at Google. Your boss wants to know whether the company should be worried because of this opinion. Sketch out the key points of your memo.

8. *The Blog problem.* Suppose your professor is an active blogger and often allows anonymous comments to be appended to blog entries. Sometimes she edits, sometimes she doesn't. Sometimes she redacts, sometimes she doesn't. Sometimes she deletes, sometimes she doesn't. Does she have anything to worry about after this opinion?

9. *The racymatch.com hypo.* Imagine a dating site with a "naughty" brand. Individuals tag themselves and look for other individuals that are compatible based on their self-tags. One required field of information includes "Number of Sexual Partners You've Had". The answer options are: "0-10"; "10-20"; "20-50"; "50-100"; and "100+". Some miscreant signs up as you at racymatch.com, includes your name and email address, and checks "100+". In other words, you've just been tagged as sexually dissolute. You think you've been defamed. Is racymatch.com immune under § 230? Would your answer be different if there was a "I'm not telling" answer choice, or if this question were entirely optional?

10. *The GossipGirl problem.* Imagine a site that actively solicits gossip. It proudly states on its home page:

> Tell us the worst dirt you have on anyone you despise. Include names, pictures, details. We love the spicy details!!! Here's the blank form to type into. Here's the link to upload files of whatever sort (we love those unauthorized videos!!!).
>
> You stay anonymous because we erase our server logs immediately. We stay liability-free because of our favorite statute, § 230. So gossip away!!!!!
>
> [But respect criminal law, copyright law, and the Electronic Communications Privacy Act—cuz that's not covered. Total bummer. ☹]

Immunity? What would the majority say? What about the minority?

11. *Direct solicitation of illegal information.* Accusearch.* On its website, Accusearch advertised access to personal telephone records. It acted as a middleman between end-consumers and relayed them to third party "researchers", who broke federal laws to acquire the calling records. The FTC claimed that this was an "unfair practice" in violation of the Federal Trade Commission Act, 15 U.S.C. § 45(a). Accusearch claimed immunity under § 230, but the court held that the information was not provided by "another

---

* FTC v. Accusearch Inc., 570 F.3d 1187 (10th Cir. 2009).

information content provider". In other words, Accusearch would be deemed "responsible, in whole or in part, for the . . . development of [the illegally obtained] information."* In its analysis, the court parsed what the words "development" and "responsible" meant in the statutory definition of "information content provider". The U.S. Court of Appeals for the Tenth Circuit concluded that "a service provider is 'responsible' for the development of offensive content only if it in some way specifically encourages development of what is offensive about the content."† Applying this standard, the court concluded that the third party researchers who illegally obtained the telephone records were not "another" information content provider.

> By paying its researchers to acquire telephone records, knowing that the confidentiality of the records was protected by law, it contributed mightily to the unlawful conduct of its researchers. Indeed, Accusearch's responsibility is more pronounced than that of Roommates.com. Roommates.com may have encouraged users to post offending content; but the offensive postings were Accusearch's *raison d'etre* and it affirmatively solicited them.‡

12. *Any other theory?* Even if a web-site operator is not originally the information content provider, can it subsequently become one if it steadfastly refuses to remove the material, even after overwhelming knowledge of its defamatory or otherwise tortious character?§

Consider a district court decision in a defamation case brought against Ripoff Report, a website with the tagline "By Consumers, for consumers" that states on its homepage "Complaints Reviews Scams Lawsuits Frauds Reported, File your review. Consumers educating consumers."** The court found that the plaintiff's allegations—including the fact that Ripoff Report "encourages

---

* *Id.* at1197.

† *Id.* at 1199

‡ *Id.* at 1200. There are many cases in which the provider of interactive computer service is deemed to be separate from the "information content provider" when the provider does not specifically induce or encourage illegal content. *See, e.g.,* Jonhsnon v. Arden, 614 F.3d 785, 792 (8th Cir. 2010) (holding that a website hosting company did not induce defamatory comments posted on one of its hosted websites); Nemet Chevrolet, Ltd. v. Consumeraffairs.com, Inc., 591 F.3d 250, 257 (4th Cir. 2007) (distinguishing Roommates.com on the grounds that no illegal information had to be inputted into Consumeraffairs.com, a website collecting information for possible class actions).

§ *See* Restatement (Second) of Torts § 577(2) ("One who intentionally and unreasonably fails to remove defamatory matter that he knows to be exhibited on land or chattels in his possession or under his control is subject to liability for its continued publication."); Tacket v. General Motors Corp., 836 F.2d 1042, 1046-47 (7th Cir. 1987) (finding a triable issue on whether GM had adopted a defamation posted by some third-party by refusing to remove a small but visible sign on GM's property for over seven months) (Easterbrook, J.)

** Order Denying Motion to Alter Judgment, Vision Security LLC v. Xcentric Ventures LLC, No. 13-926 (D. Utah, Aug. 27, 2015), *available at* http://digitalcommons.law.scu.edu/cgi/viewcontent.cgi?article=2036&context=historical.

negative content" and offers a "corporate advocacy program" to companies who have suffered negative postings—supported a "reasonable inference that [Ripoff Report] was not a neutral publisher" and that it "refused to remove offensive content to promote its own corporate advocacy program." The court relied, in particular, on the Tenth Circuit's decision in *Accusearch.*

What if the website fails to take some affirmative action to protect its own users from abuse caused by their own postings? Can it be held liable for negligence? That was the question at issue before the Ninth Circuit in *Doe v. Internet Brands*, a case brought by an "aspiring model who posted information about herself on the website" Model Mayhem and alleged that the site failed to warn her of a known risk—that she would be targeted by rapists. The district court had dismissed the claim on § 230 grounds, but the Ninth Circuit reversed. The court found that a negligence claim based on a "duty to warn a potential victim of third-party harm when a person has a 'special relationship to either the person or whose conduct needs to be controlled or . . . to the foreseeable victim of that conduct" was not barred by § 230. Specifically, the court held that because the plaintiff "does not seek to hold [the website] liable as a 'publisher or speaker' of content," the immunity does not apply.

A similar argument was made in a case brought by an individual whose name and likeness were used by a former boyfriend to create fake profiles on the gay dating site Grindr.[*] The plaintiff alleged that these fake Grindr profiles caused harassment and abuse because the communications with other men on the platform included his home and work addresses and represented that he was interested in rape fantasies and role play. The plaintiff alleged that he repeatedly notified Grindr of the harassment and fake accounts, and that the platform did nothing in response. A state trial court in New York initially ordered Grindr to take down the profiles, but Grindr removed the case to federal court and a judge in the U.S. District Court for the Southern District of New York held that Grindr was immune from suit under § 230. That decision was upheld by the U.S. Court of Appeals for the Second Circuit.[†]

NOTE: CONGRESSIONAL ATTENTION ON 230 IMMUNITY

After a long period of expansion and some contraction of the scope of § 230, Congress has in recent years begun to introduce legislation that would modify 230 immunity in various contexts. There have been many different legislative

---

[*] Herrick v. Grindr, LLC et al., 306 F. Supp. 3d 579 (S.D.N.Y. 2018).

[†] Herrick v. Grindr, LLC et al., 765 F. App'x 586 (2d Cir. 2019).

proposals introduced, but so far only one has passed. In 2018 Congress enacted a bill to address a somewhat narrow issue (but with broad implications): the use of online platforms to facilitate sex trafficking and prostitution. The statute was enacted with nearly unanimous[*] bipartisan support in both the House and Senate, and on April 11, 2018, the President signed it into law. The "Allow States and Victims to Fight Online Sex Trafficking Act of 2017," amended § 230 by adding an additional exception to section (e) as follows:

> (e) Effect on other laws
>
> (1) No effect on criminal law
>
> > Nothing in this section shall be construed to impair the enforcement of section 223 or 231 of this title, chapter 71 (relating to obscenity) or 110 (relating to sexual exploitation of children) of title 18, or any other Federal criminal statute.
>
> (2) No effect on intellectual property law
>
> > Nothing in this section shall be construed to limit or expand any law pertaining to intellectual property.
>
> (3) State law
>
> > Nothing in this section shall be construed to prevent any State from enforcing any State law that is consistent with this section. No cause of action may be brought and no liability may be imposed under any State or local law that is inconsistent with this section.
>
> (4) No effect on communications privacy law
>
> > Nothing in this section shall be construed to limit the application of the Electronic Communications Privacy Act of 1986 or any of the amendments made by such Act, or any similar State law.
>
> (5) No effect on sex trafficking law
>
> > Nothing in this section (other than subsection (c)(2)(A)) shall be construed to impair or limit-
> >
> > > (A) any claim in a civil action brought under section 1595 of title 18, if the conduct underlying the claim constitutes a violation of section 1591 of that title;
> > >
> > > (B) any charge in a criminal prosecution brought under State law if the conduct underlying the charge would constitute a violation of section 1591 of title 18; or
> > >
> > > (C) any charge in a criminal prosecution brought under State law if the conduct underlying the charge would constitute a violation of section 2421A of title 18, and promotion or facilitation of prostitution is illegal in the jurisdiction where the defendant's promotion or facilitation of prostitution was targeted.

The law also created a new criminal penalty for "Promotion or facilitation of prostitution and reckless disregard of sex trafficking"[†] and expanded civil liability for "knowingly assisting, supporting, or facilitating a violation" of the broad criminal prohibitions related to participation in child sex trafficking.[‡]

---

[*] Only 25 members of the House voted against and only 2 members of the Senate voted against.

[†] 18 U.S.C. § 2421A.

[‡] 18 U.S.C. § 1591.

The law, which is commonly referred to by the acronyms used in the House and Senate bill versions—"FOSTA" (Fight Online Sex Trafficking Act) and "SESTA" (Stop Enabling Sex Traffic Servers Act)—has faced harsh criticism for its damaging impacts on certain at-risk communities. Specifically, the most immediate impact of FOSTA was the shuttering of online platforms that were used by sex workers to communicate with and vet clients remotely.[*] Since the law's passage, some cities have seen the unintended consequence of increased street-based crimes against sex workers. Critics also warned that the new liability risk created by the law would lead platforms to shut down any forums that could potentially be used by sex workers, while driving criminal sex trafficking forums into the dark web where they are harder to track.

But Members of Congress have not stopped with FOSTA. Many members have become interested in modifying Section 230 to address a broad range of issues, from distribution of child sex abuse material to perceived "political bias" of internet platforms, to the encouragement of reasonable content moderation policies. As you may recall from CHAPTER 4: ACCESS, prior to the mid-1980s the FCC had sought to promote fair access to the broadcast airwaves through a series of complicated and controversial rules known as the "Fairness Doctrine." The theory behind the doctrine was, as the Supreme Court articulated in *Red Lion*, that spectrum scarcity and public ownership of the airwaves justified statutory protections for equal access. Many of the recent criticisms of Section 230 by Members of Congress sound surprisingly similar to the justifications for the Fairness Doctrine.

One such example is the bill introduced in 2019 by Senator Josh Hawley (R-MO) called the "Ending Support for Internet Censorship Act."[†] The stated purpose of this act is to ensure that internet platforms "provide content moderation that is politically neutral." It would require larger service providers to seek a "certification" from the Federal Trade Commission. Specifically, the bill would add the following new subsection at the end of Section 230:

> (3) REQUIREMENT OF POLITICALLY UNBIASED CONTENT MODERATION BY COVERED COMPANIES.—
>> (A) IN GENERAL.—Paragraphs (1) and (2) shall not apply in the case of a covered company unless the company has in effect an immunity certification from the Federal Trade Commission (referred to in this paragraph as the 'Commission') under subparagraph (B) that the company does not moderate

---

[*] *See generally* Daisy Soderberg-Rivkin, *The Lessons of FOSTA-SESTA from a Former Content Moderator*, R St. Inst. (Apr. 8, 2020), https://www.rstreet.org/2020/04/08/the-lessons-of-fosta-sesta-from-a-former-content-moderator/.

[†] S. 1914, 116th Cong. (2019).

> information provided by other information content providers in a manner that is
> biased against a political party, political candidate, or political viewpoint.

The bill also included a definition of biased moderation:

> (ii) POLITICALLY BIASED MODERATION.—The moderation practices of a provider
> of an interactive computer service are politically biased if—
>> (I) the provider moderates information provided by other information content
>> providers in a manner that—
>>> (aa) is designed to negatively affect a political party, political candidate, or
>>> political viewpoint; or
>>> (bb) disproportionately restricts or promotes access to, or the availability of,
>>> information from a political party, political candidate, or political viewpoint;
>>> or
>> (II) an officer or employee of the provider makes a decision about moderating
>> information provided by other information content providers that is motivated by
>> an intent to negatively affect a political party, political candidate, or political
>> viewpoint.

Senator Hawley's bill was not cosponsored by any of his colleagues in Congress and appears dead in the water, but the claim that internet platforms are "biased" against conservative viewpoints is frequently raised as a point of criticism by GOP Members of Congress.

And those Members are not alone. President Trump has also taken the opportunity to take a swing at content moderation practices by issuing an Executive Order on "Preventing Online Censorship."[*] The President followed up his Executive Order with a Petition filed with the FCC by the Department of Commerce, National Telecommunications and Information Administration (NTIA), requesting that the FCC "initiate a rulemaking to clarify the provisions of section 230" in line with the President's views.[†] That may sound like a confusing and improper way to change the law that Congress passed in 1996. One of the Republican Commissioners at the FCC, Michael O'Rielly, felt the same way, as he explained in public remarks a few days after the NTIA petition was filed, noting that "I shudder to think of a day in which the Fairness Doctrine could be reincarnated fot the Internet, especially at the ironic behest of so-called free speech 'defenders.'"[‡] A few days after that speech, President Trump withdrew Commissioner O'Rielly's then-pending renomination to the FCC.

Meanwhile, several other bills targeting Section 230 have been supported by bipartisan leaders of key Committees in the Senate. The leaders of the Senate Judiciary Committee, Senators Graham (R-SC) and Blumenthal (D-CT)

---

[*] Exec. Order 13,925, 85 Fed. Reg. 34,079 (June 2, 2020).

[†] https://www.ntia.gov/files/ntia/publications/ntia_petition_for_rulemaking_7.27.20.pdf.

[‡] Remarks of FCC Commissioner Michael O'Rielly Before The Media Institute's Luncheon Series July 29, 2020, https://docs.fcc.gov/public/attachments/DOC-365814A1.pdf.

recently introduced the "Eliminating Abusive and Rampant Neglect of Interactive Technologies Act of 2020" (EARN IT Act), part of which would amend Section 230 to remove immunity for certain crimes related to distribution of child sex abuse material.* The bill would amend Section 230(c) by adding two new subsections:

> (6) NO EFFECT ON CHILD SEXUAL EXPLOITATION LAW.—Nothing in this section (other than subsection (c)(2)(A)) shall be construed to impair or limit—
>
>> (A) any claim in a civil action brought against a provider of an interactive computer service under section 2255 of title 18, United States Code, if the conduct underlying the claim constitutes a violation of section 2252 or section 2252A of that title;
>>
>> (B) any charge in a criminal prosecution brought against a provider of an interactive computer service under State law regarding the advertisement, promotion, presentation, distribution, or solicitation of child sexual abuse material, as defined in section 2256(8) of title 18, United States Code; or
>>
>> (C) any claim in a civil action brought against a provider of an interactive computer service under State law regarding the advertisement, promotion, presentation, distribution, or solicitation of child sexual abuse material, as defined in section 2256(8) of title 18, United States Code.
>
> (7) CYBERSECURITY PROTECTIONS DO NOT GIVE RISE TO LIABILITY.— Notwithstanding paragraph (6), a provider of an interactive computer service shall not be deemed to be in violation of section 2252 or 2252A of title 18, United States Code, for the purposes of subparagraph (A) of such paragraph (6), and shall not otherwise be subject to any charge in a criminal prosecution under State law under subparagraph (B) of such paragraph (6), or any claim in a civil action under State law under subparagraph (C) of such paragraph (6), because the provider—
>
>> (A) utilizes full end-to-end encrypted messaging services, device encryption, or other encryption services;
>>
>> (B) does not possess the information necessary to decrypt a communication; or
>>
>> (C) fails to take an action that would otherwise undermine the ability of the provider to offer full end-to-end encrypted messaging services, device encryption, or other encryption services.".

The first new subsection would remove immunity against civil claims for activities that would violate two specific federal criminal laws (prohibiting distribution of child sex abuse material) as well as a much broader and amorphous category of state criminal laws. The second new subsection was added to defray criticisms that the EARN IT Act was intended, in part, to punish platforms that offered encrypted messaging services.

Another bipartisan bill introduced by Senator Thune (R-SD) and Senator Schatz (D-HI) includes a broader framework for addressing some of the common criticisms of the Section 230 framework. The "Platform Accountability and Consumer Transparency Act" (PACT Act) would impose certain transparency and process requirements on platforms regarding their

---

* S. 3398, 116th Cong. (2020).

content moderation policies.[*] The bill would also remove Section 230 immunity for claims regarding a platform's refusal to take down content that a court has found to be unlawful.

> (3) INTERMEDIARY LIABILITY STANDARD.—
>
>> (A) IN GENERAL.—The protection under paragraph (1) shall not apply to a provider of an interactive computer service, with respect to illegal content shared or illegal activity occurring on the interactive computer service, if the provider—
>>
>>> (i) has knowledge of the illegal content or illegal activity; and
>>>
>>> (ii) subject to subparagraph (C), does not remove the illegal content or stop the illegal activity within 24 hours of acquiring that knowledge, subject to reasonable exceptions based on concerns about the legitimacy of the notice.

The key terms are defined as:

> (5) ILLEGAL ACTIVITY.—The term 'illegal activity' means activity conducted by an information content provider that has been determined by a Federal or State court to violate Federal criminal or civil law.
>
> (6) ILLEGAL CONTENT.—The term 'illegal content' means information provided by an information content provider that has been determined by a Federal or State court to violate Federal criminal or civil law or State defamation law.

And the bill also includes specific rules and exceptions for these unlawful content "notice and takedown" processes.

There have been many other bills proposed and hearings held concerning possible amendments to (or the outright elimination of) Section 230. On the one hand, there is a strong possibility that one of the proposals introduced above could be enacted into law in the next few years. On the other hand, it's hard to predict which one.

NOTES & QUESTIONS

1. *Expected impacts and unintended consequences of liability.* The key legal instrument at issue in all debates about reforming or modifying Section 230 is the liability protection provided in 47 U.S.C. § 230(c). As you have learned in this chapter, most of the focus in legal cases is on § 230(c)(1), which makes clear that online platforms will not be "treated as the publisher or speaker of any information provided by" a user. Congress added an exception to that rule in FOSTA for sex trafficking laws, and there are already several other exceptions (see below). What do you expect to happen because of these exceptions to the liability shield? Can you think of any unintended consequences?

> (e) Effect on other laws
> (1) No effect on criminal law

---

[*] S. 4066, 116th Cong. (2020).

Nothing in this section shall be construed to impair the enforcement of section 223 or 231 of this title, chapter 71 (relating to obscenity) or 110 (relating to sexual exploitation of children) of title 18, or any other Federal criminal statute.

(2) No effect on intellectual property law

Nothing in this section shall be construed to limit or expand any law pertaining to intellectual property.

(3) State law

Nothing in this section shall be construed to prevent any State from enforcing any State law that is consistent with this section. No cause of action may be brought and no liability may be imposed under any State or local law that is inconsistent with this section.

(4) No effect on communications privacy law

Nothing in this section shall be construed to limit the application of the Electronic Communications Privacy Act of 1986 or any of the amendments made by such Act, or any similar State law.

(5) No effect on sex trafficking law

Nothing in this section (other than subsection (c)(2)(A)) shall be construed to impair or limit—

(A) any claim in a civil action brought under section 1595 of title 18, if the conduct underlying the claim constitutes a violation of section 1591 of that title;

(B) any charge in a criminal prosecution brought under State law if the conduct underlying the charge would constitute a violation of section 1591 of title 18; or

(C) any charge in a criminal prosecution brought under State law if the conduct underlying the charge would constitute a violation of section 2421A of title 18, and promotion or facilitation of prostitution is illegal in the jurisdiction where the defendant's promotion or facilitation of prostitution was targeted.

2. *Return to First Principles.* At times the debate over Section 230 can feel very disconnected from both its text and its roots. Recall that the law was passed in the wake of the *Stratton Oakmont, Inc. v. Prodigy* decision, which many feared would imperil platforms that chose to moderate their forums and other content. Congress explicitly referenced these "Good Samaritans" in Section 230. Given the cases that you have read so far, how well do you think Section 230 has served that purpose? If you wanted to encourage providers to engage in more active content moderation, what might you change? *See, e.g.,* Danielle Keats Citron & Benjamin Wittes, *The Internet Will Not Break: Denying Bad Samaritans Section 230 Immunity,* 2017-22 UNIV. OF MD. LEG. STUD. RES. PAPER 1 (2017).

3. *The First Amendment and online forums.* The history leading up to FOSTA goes back more than five years to a series of actions brought against Backpage.com. *See, e.g., Doe ex rel. Roe v. Backpage.com, LLC,* 104 F. Supp. 3d 149 (D. Mass. 2015), *aff'd sub nom. Doe No. 1 v. Backpage.com, LLC,* 817 F.3d 12 (1st Cir. 2016). In 2000, Congress had created a civil remedy for victims

of sex trafficking in the Trafficking Victims Protection Act, 18 U.S.C. § 1591, but the courts found that Backpage was immune from such claims under Section 230. Congress subsequently passed FOSTA largely to target Backpage, but the impact of the law has been much broader than that. Meanwhile, a group of human rights organizations advocating for and providing information to sex workers around the world have sued the Government to challenge the constitutionality of FOSTA on First Amendment, Fifth Amendment, and Ex Post Facto Clause grounds. *See Woodhull Freedom Found. v. United States,* 948 F.3d 363 (D.C. Cir. 2020) (finding that the plaintiffs had standing to pursue these claims). One of the plaintiffs noted specifically that his business had relied on advertisements posted on the Craigslist Therapeutic Services section, which was shuttered after Congress passed FOSTA. The potential for increased civil liability led Craigslist and other online platforms to shut down certain forums, which then gave rise to these constitutional challenges. Do you think these challenges will succeed under the First Amendment?

4. *Speaking of the First Amendment...* What legal claims would you expect to be brought against the Federal Trade Commission if Senator Hawley's political neutrality certification requirement were enacted into law? What about claims against the FCC if they adopt President Trump and the NTIA's proposed rulemaking changes to Section 230? What cases would you look to if you were researching these issues for the FTC or FCC General Counsel's Office?

5. *Is this all about money?* Most of the focus of the cases interpreting Section 230 and bills modifying Section 230 has been on civil liability, but the law has also had a broad impact by shielding companies from injunctive actions. The California Supreme Court recently ruled in *Hassell v. Bird,* 5 Cal. 5th 522 (Cal. S. Ct. 2018), that Yelp could not be ordered to remove customer reviews even though the plaintiffs had a court judgment that the reviews were defamatory. The court held that ordering Yelp to remove the defamatory material would be akin to treating Yelp as the "publisher or speaker" of that content. Do you think this is consistent with what Congress intended to do in enacting Section 230? If not, why not? Explain how the PACT Act would change this rule.

In this chapter, we have examined the final concept essential to understanding communications law and policy: *intermediary liability.* To be sure, the question of how to respond to harmful content predates modern communications systems. But, modern communications systems have greatly expanded the number and types of intermediaries that facilitate the distribution of content. The internet also makes it much easier make content available broadly and anonymously. In many cases, the flow of content that intermediaries facilitate leads to real and alleged violations of law, including privacy, intellectual property, defamation, and indecency laws. Society must decide when and how these intermediaries are to be held responsible, if at all, for their role.

CPSIA information can be obtained
at www.ICGtesting.com
Printed in the USA
LVHW060832040123
736228LV00012B/228